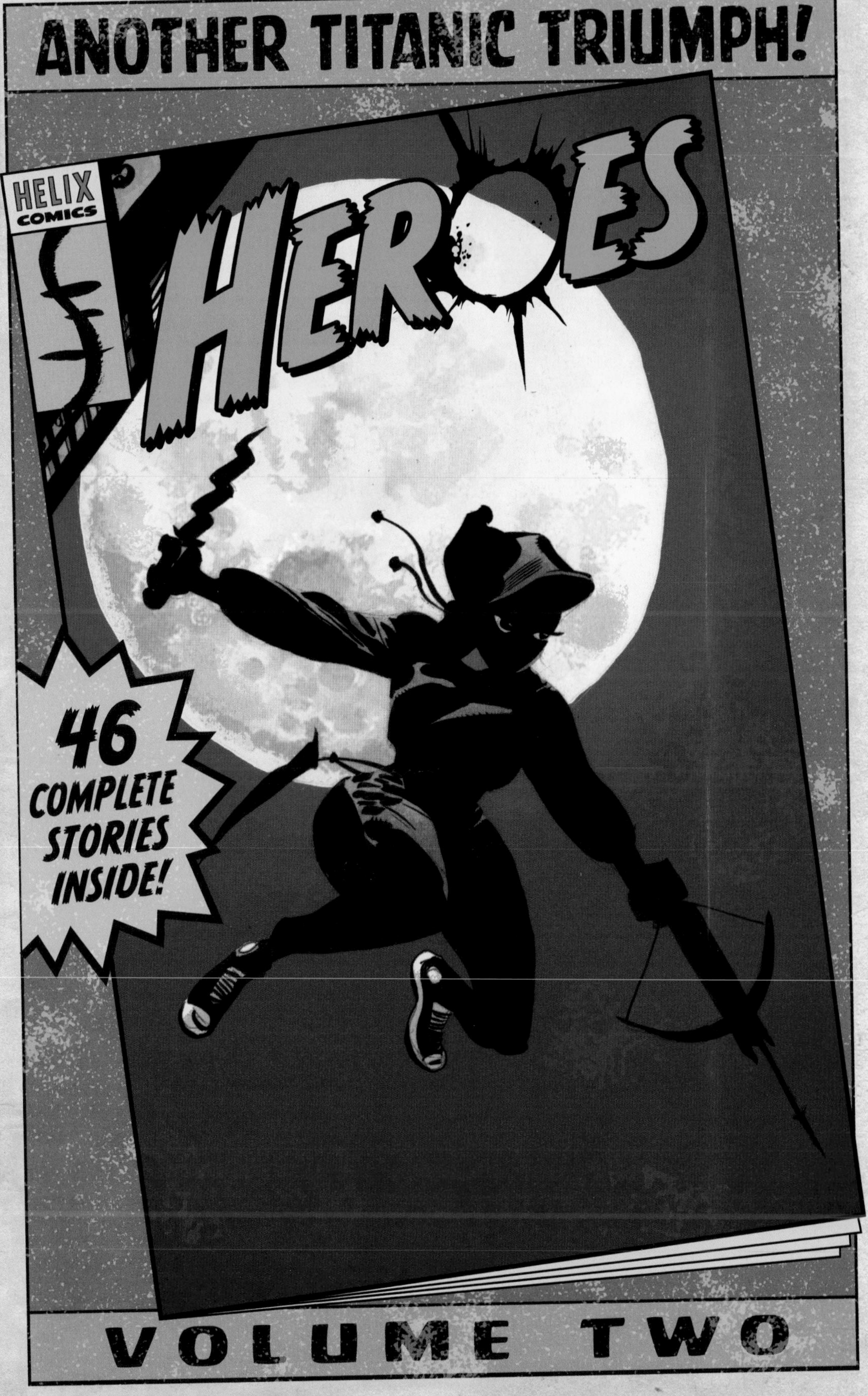
ANOTHER TITANIC TRIUMPH!
HELIX COMICS
HEROES
46 COMPLETE STORIES INSIDE!
VOLUME TWO

# Uncle Burk's Fine Comics

CALL TOLL FREE
1-888-266-4226



**ORDER QUANTITIES AND SAVE!**

Lettering and design by JG ROSHELL OF COMICRAFT

Collected Edition Dustjacket A by TIM SALE & JG ROSHELL

Collected Edition Dustjacket B by GENE HA

Paintings by TIM SALE and DAVE STEWART

**SUPER SALE!**
**ALL COMICS ONLY**
**50¢ EACH**
**20/$9.00**
**100/$40.00**
**Your Choice**



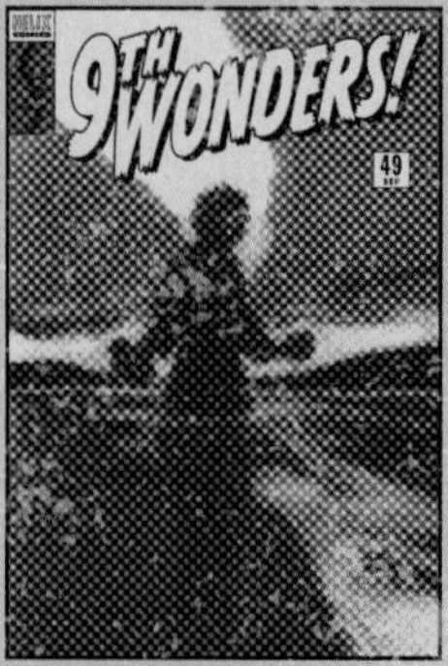
9TH WONDERS!
49



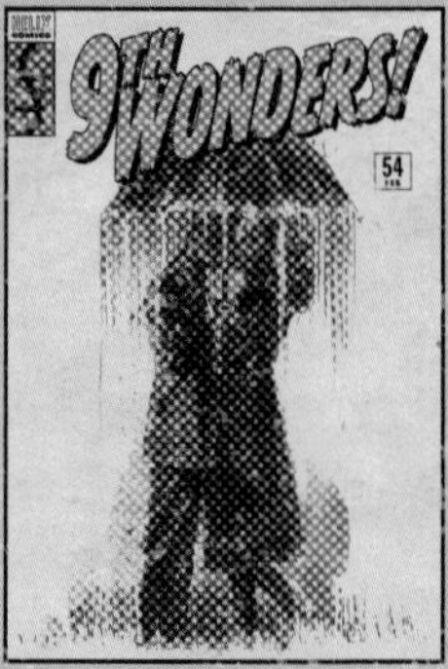
9TH WONDERS!
54

# Uncle Burk's Fine Comics

CALL TOLL FREE
1-888-COMIC-BOOK

**SUPER SALE!**
**ALL COMICS ONLY**
**50¢ EACH**
**20/$9.00**
**100/$40.00**
**Your Choice**



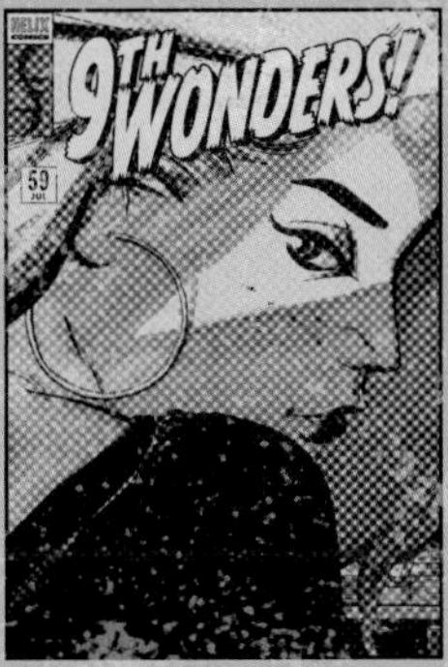

9TH WONDERS!
59




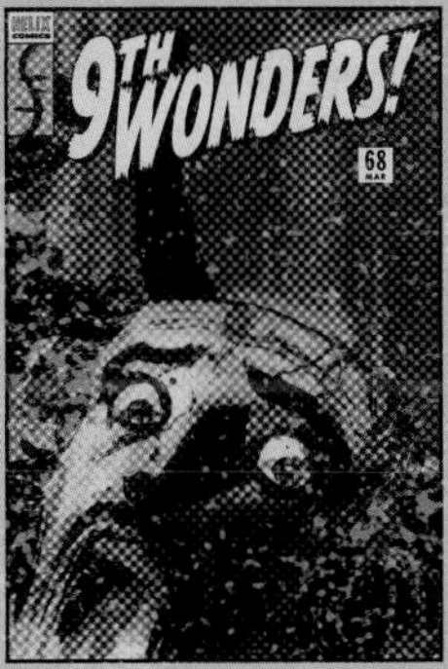

9TH WONDERS!
68
MAR




**LOOKING FOR LOWER PRICES?**


Special Thanks to
FRANK MASTROMAURO and NANCI QUESADA
and the folks from Helix Comics:
ARON ELI COLEITE
JOE POKASKI
JESSE ALEXANDER
JEPH LOEB
CHUCK KIM
MARK WARSHAW

## HEROES Volume 2

published by WildStorm Productions
888 Prospect St. #240, La Jolla, CA 92037

WildStorm and logo are trademarks of DC Comics. The stories,
characters, and incidents mentioned in this magazine are entirely
fictional. Printed on recyclable paper. WildStorm does not read
or accept unsolicited submissions of ideas, stories or artwork.
Printed in the United States.

❑ Hardcover ISBN (Standard): 978-1-4012-1925-3
❑ Hardcover: ISBN (Ha Variant): 978-1-4012-2353-3
❑ Softcover ISBN: 978-1-4012-2229-1

### MAIL THIS COUPON TODAY!

DC Comics, a Warner Bros. Entertainment Company

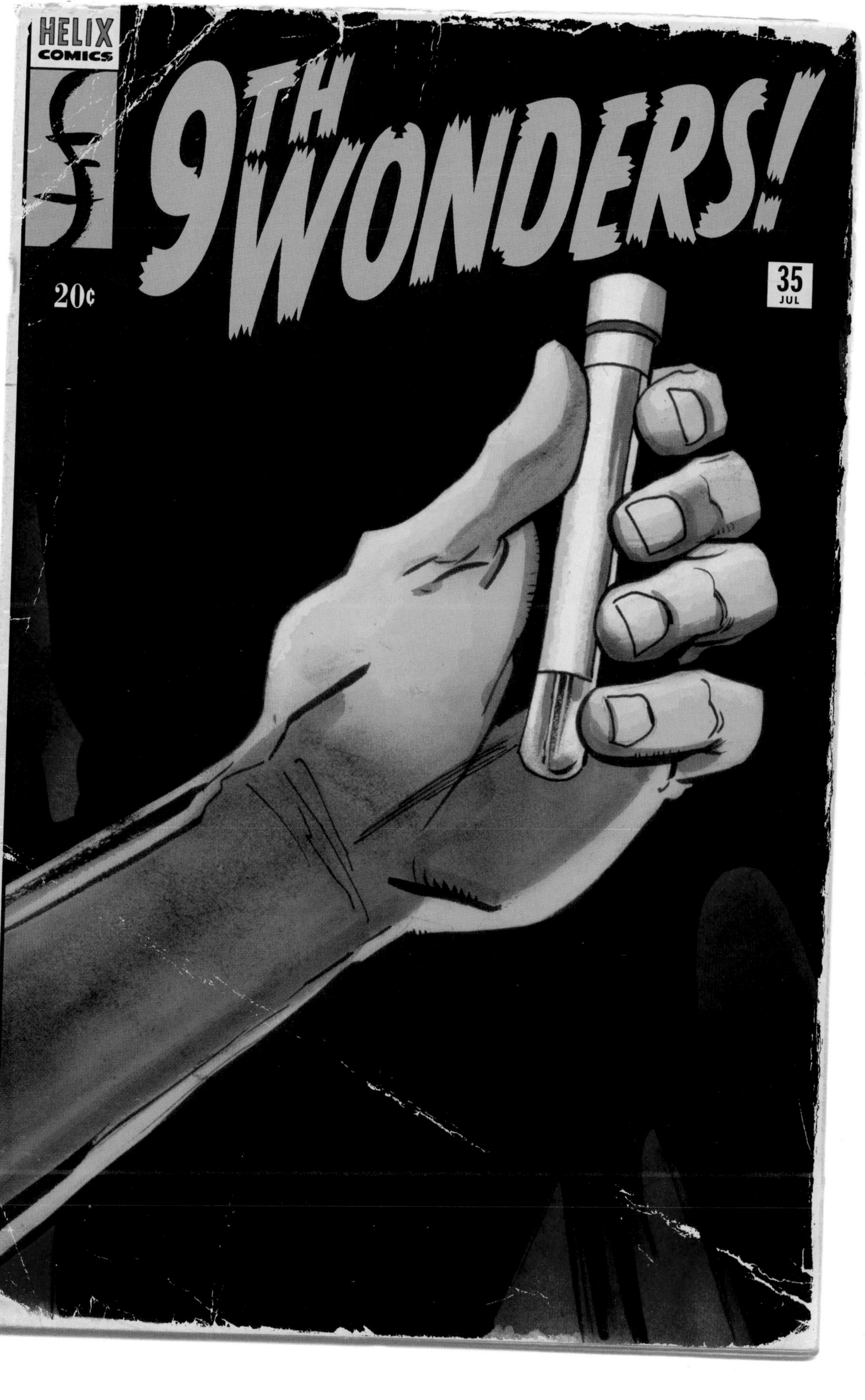
HELIX
COMICS
9TH WONDERS!
20¢
35
JUL

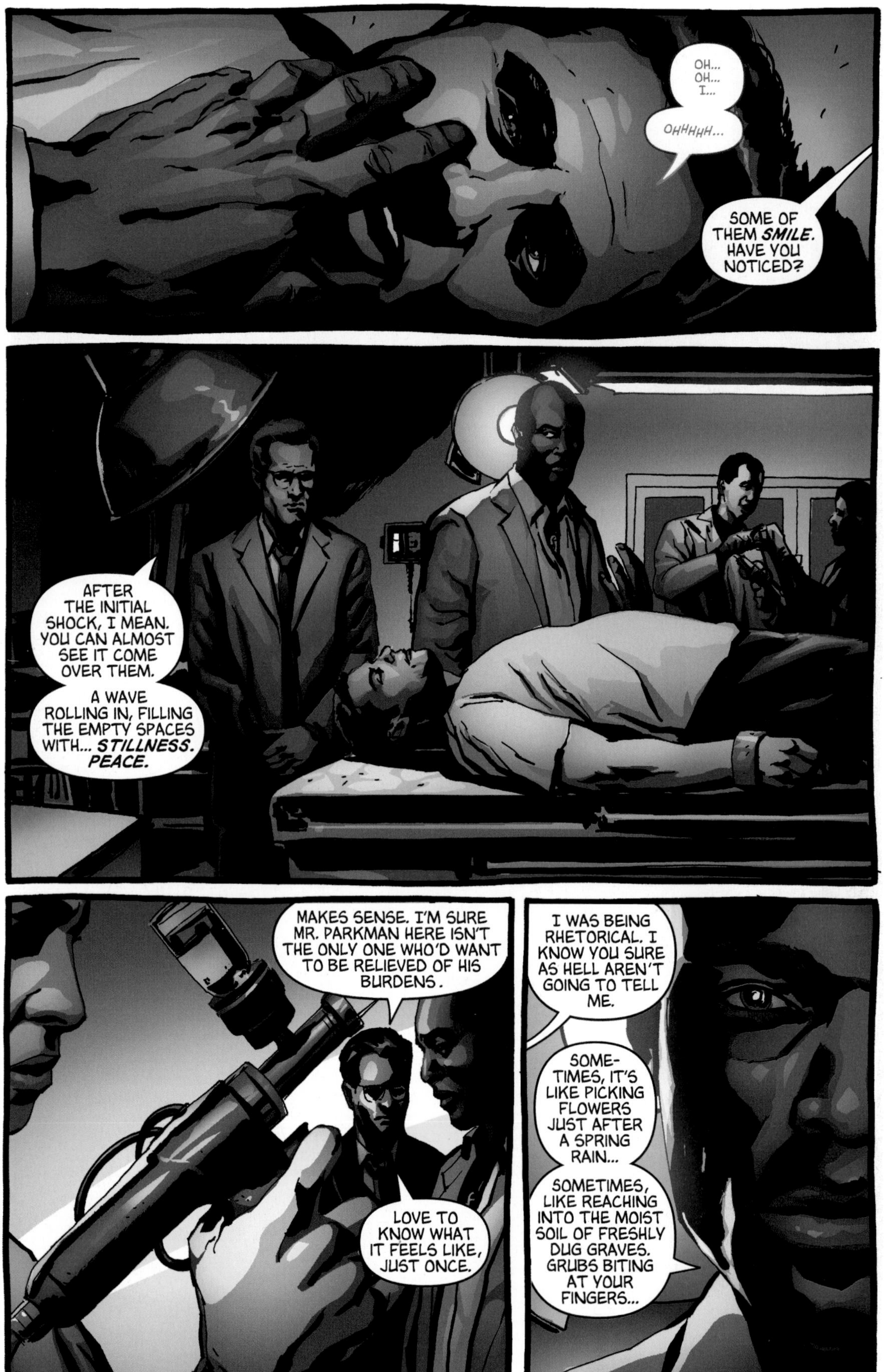

OH... OH... I...
OHHHHH...
SOME OF THEM *SMILE.* HAVE YOU NOTICED?
AFTER THE INITIAL SHOCK, I MEAN. YOU CAN ALMOST SEE IT COME OVER THEM.
A WAVE ROLLING IN, FILLING THE EMPTY SPACES WITH... ***STILLNESS. PEACE.***
MAKES SENSE. I'M SURE MR. PARKMAN HERE ISN'T THE ONLY ONE WHO'D WANT TO BE RELIEVED OF HIS BURDENS.
LOVE TO KNOW WHAT IT FEELS LIKE, JUST ONCE.
I WAS BEING RHETORICAL. I KNOW YOU SURE AS HELL AREN'T GOING TO TELL ME.
SOME-TIMES, IT'S LIKE PICKING FLOWERS JUST AFTER A SPRING RAIN...
SOMETIMES, LIKE REACHING INTO THE MOIST SOIL OF FRESHLY DUG GRAVES. GRUBS BITING AT YOUR FINGERS...

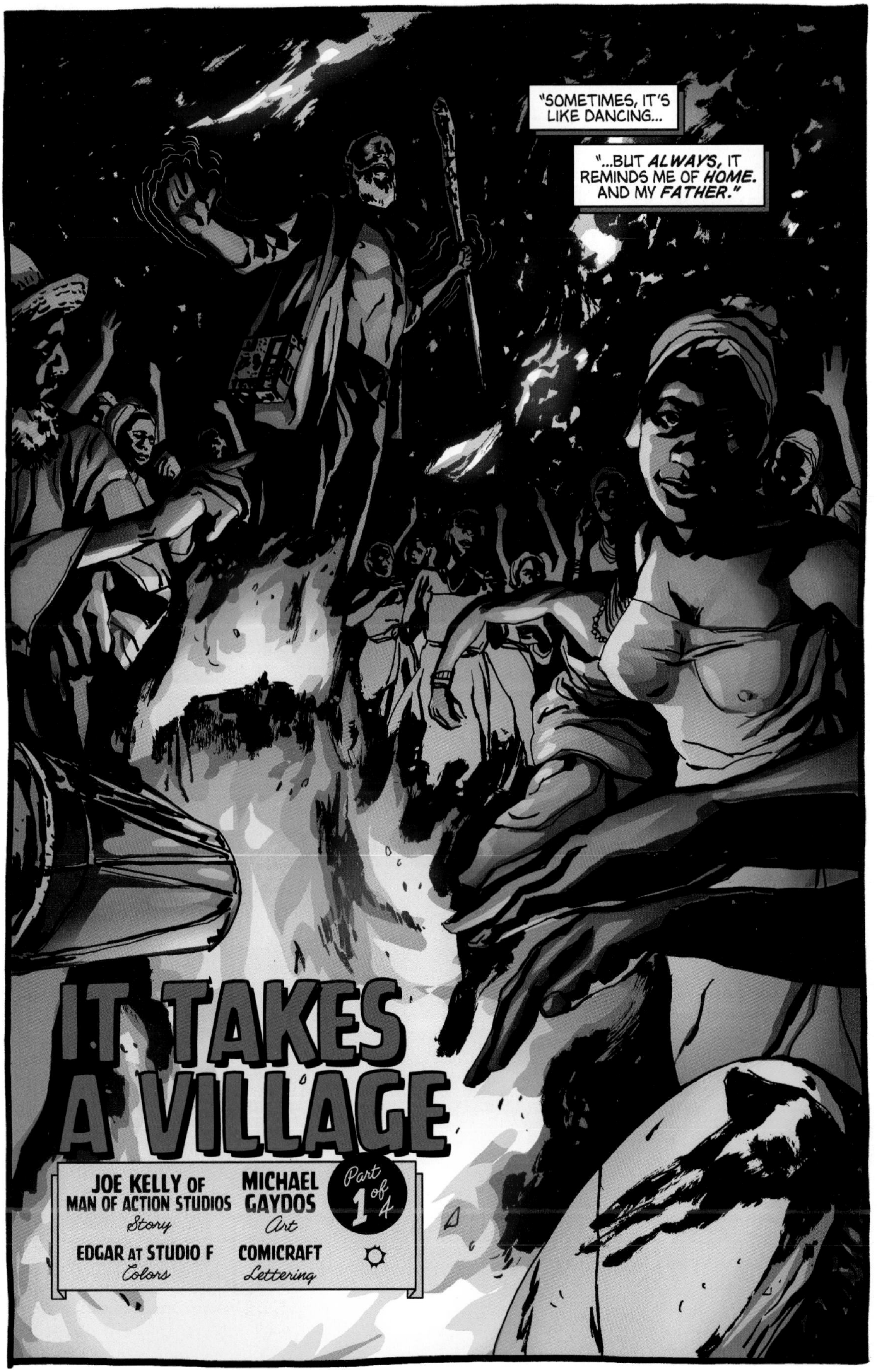
"SOMETIMES, IT'S LIKE DANCING...
"...BUT *ALWAYS*, IT REMINDS ME OF *HOME*. AND MY *FATHER*."
IT TAKES A VILLAGE
JOE KELLY OF MAN OF ACTION STUDIOS Story
MICHAEL GAYDOS Art
EDGAR AT STUDIO F Colors
COMICRAFT Lettering
Part 1 of 4

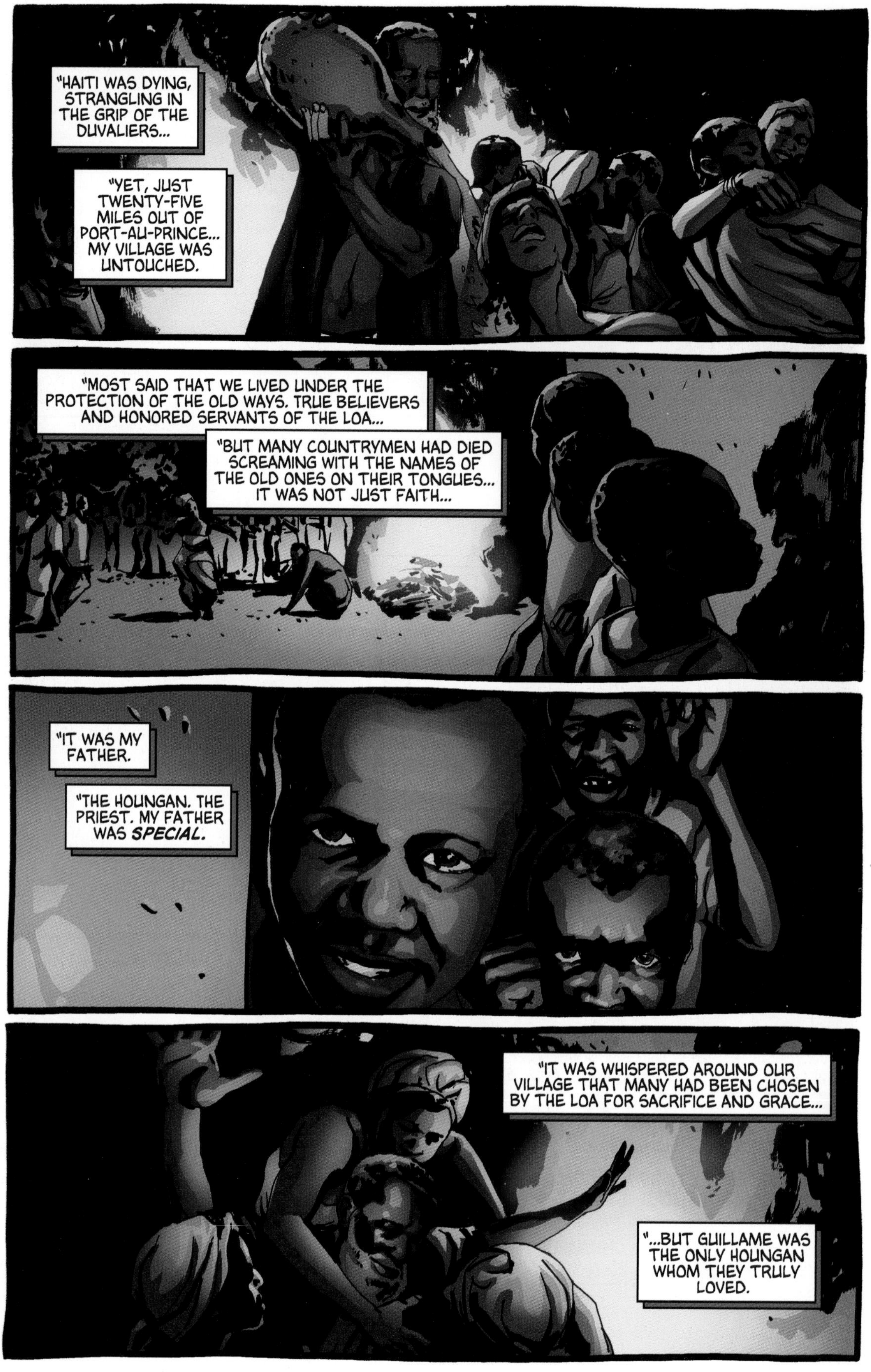
"HAITI WAS DYING, STRANGLING IN THE GRIP OF THE DUVALIERS...
"YET, JUST TWENTY-FIVE MILES OUT OF PORT-AU-PRINCE... MY VILLAGE WAS UNTOUCHED.
"MOST SAID THAT WE LIVED UNDER THE PROTECTION OF THE OLD WAYS. TRUE BELIEVERS AND HONORED SERVANTS OF THE LOA...
"BUT MANY COUNTRYMEN HAD DIED SCREAMING WITH THE NAMES OF THE OLD ONES ON THEIR TONGUES... IT WAS NOT JUST FAITH...
"IT WAS MY FATHER.
"THE HOUNGAN. THE PRIEST. MY FATHER WAS *SPECIAL.*
"IT WAS WHISPERED AROUND OUR VILLAGE THAT MANY HAD BEEN CHOSEN BY THE LOA FOR SACRIFICE AND GRACE...
"...BUT GUILLAME WAS THE ONLY HOUNGAN WHOM THEY TRULY LOVED.

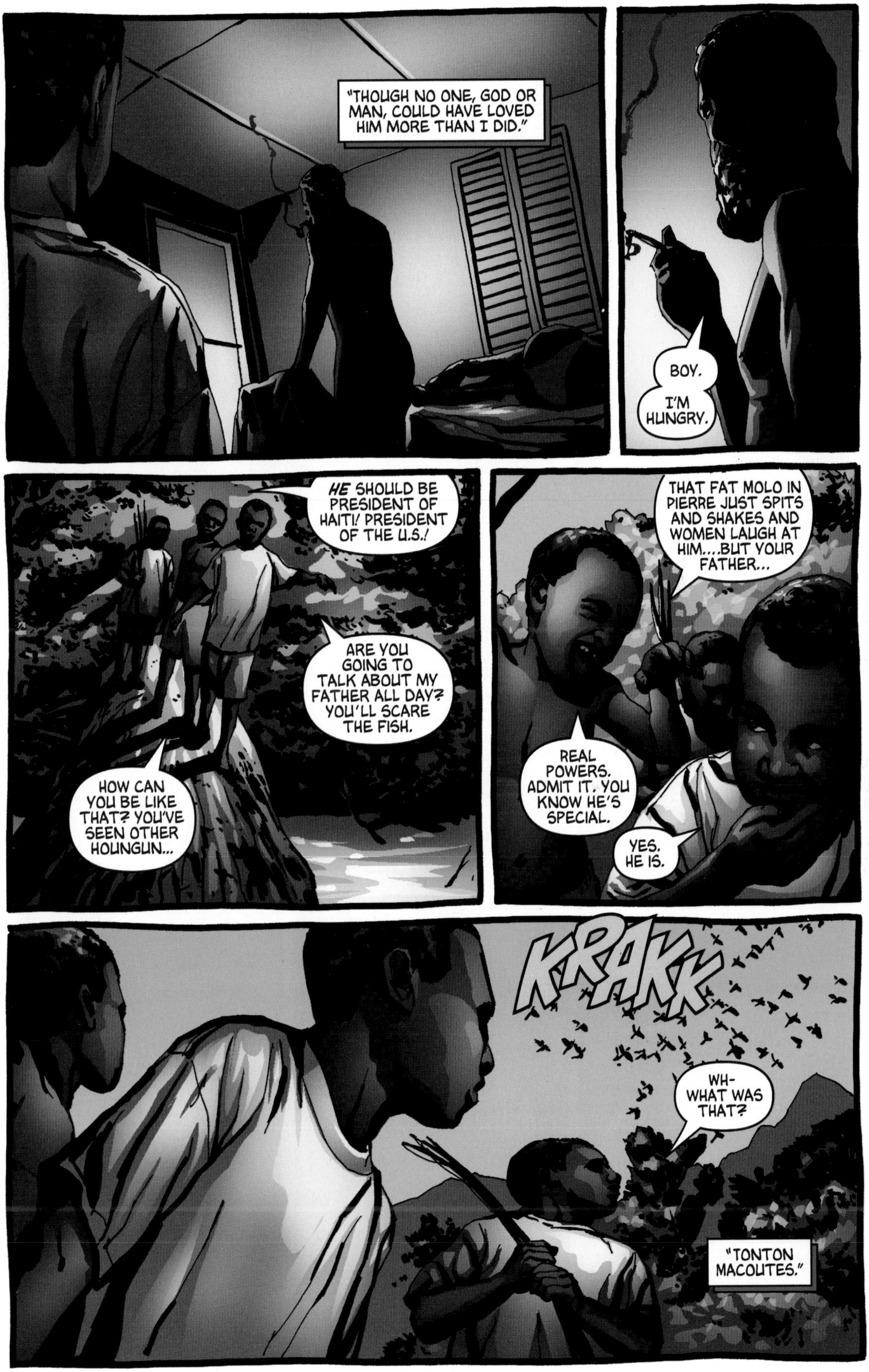
"THOUGH NO ONE, GOD OR MAN, COULD HAVE LOVED HIM MORE THAN I DID."
BOY.
I'M HUNGRY.
HE SHOULD BE PRESIDENT OF HAITI! PRESIDENT OF THE U.S.!
ARE YOU GOING TO TALK ABOUT MY FATHER ALL DAY? YOU'LL SCARE THE FISH.
HOW CAN YOU BE LIKE THAT? YOU'VE SEEN OTHER HOUNGUN...
THAT FAT MOLO IN PIERRE JUST SPITS AND SHAKES AND WOMEN LAUGH AT HIM....BUT YOUR FATHER...
REAL POWERS. ADMIT IT. YOU KNOW HE'S SPECIAL.
YES. HE IS.
KRAKK
WH- WHAT WAS THAT?
"TONTON MACOUTES."

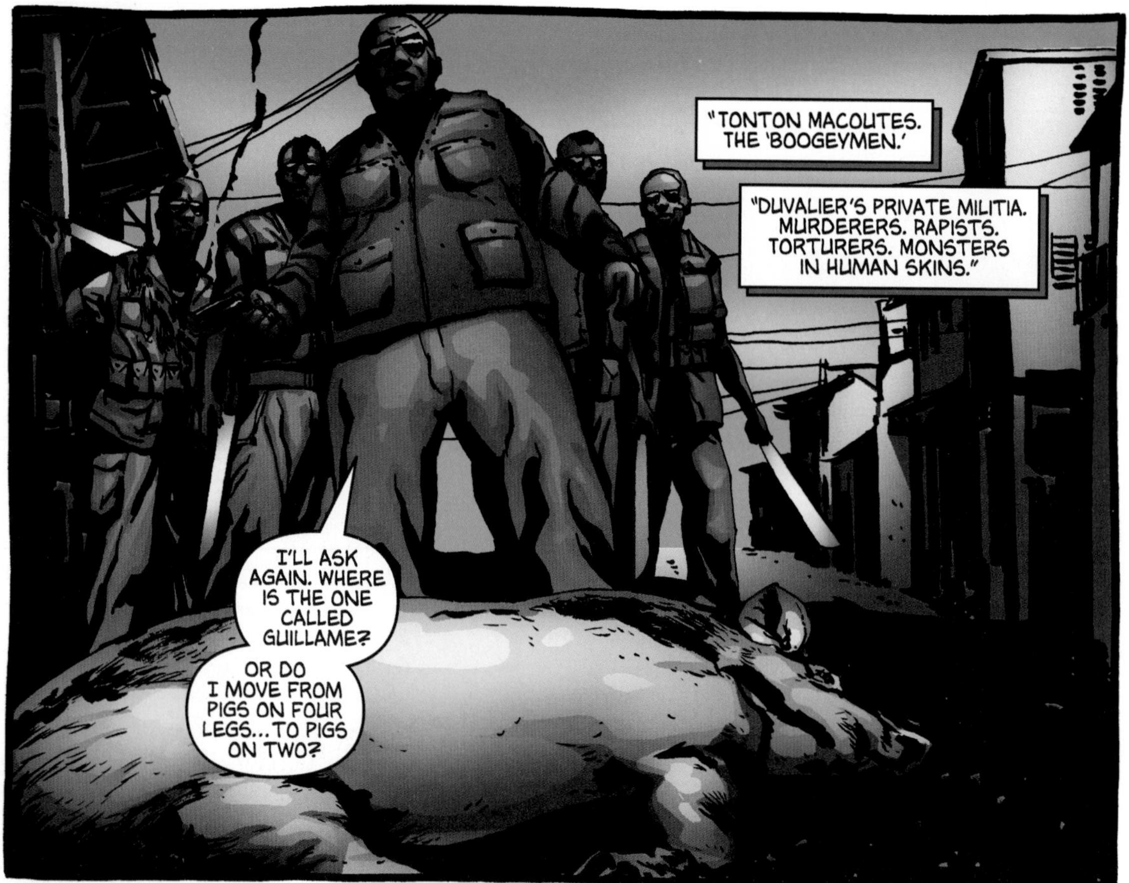
"TONTON MACOUTES. THE 'BOOGEYMEN.'
"DUVALIER'S PRIVATE MILITIA. MURDERERS. RAPISTS. TORTURERS. MONSTERS IN HUMAN SKINS."
I'LL ASK AGAIN. WHERE IS THE ONE CALLED GUILLAME?
OR DO I MOVE FROM PIGS ON FOUR LEGS...TO PIGS ON TWO?

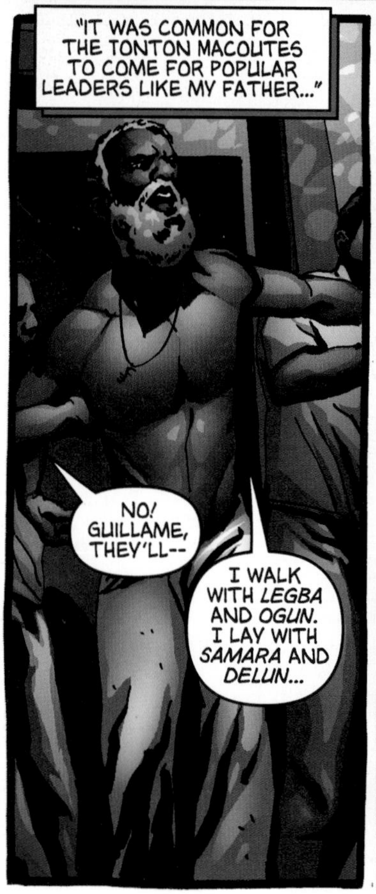
"IT WAS COMMON FOR THE TONTON MACOUTES TO COME FOR POPULAR LEADERS LIKE MY FATHER..."
NO! GUILLAME, THEY'LL--
I WALK WITH *LEGBA* AND *OGUN*. I LAY WITH *SAMARA* AND *DELUN*...

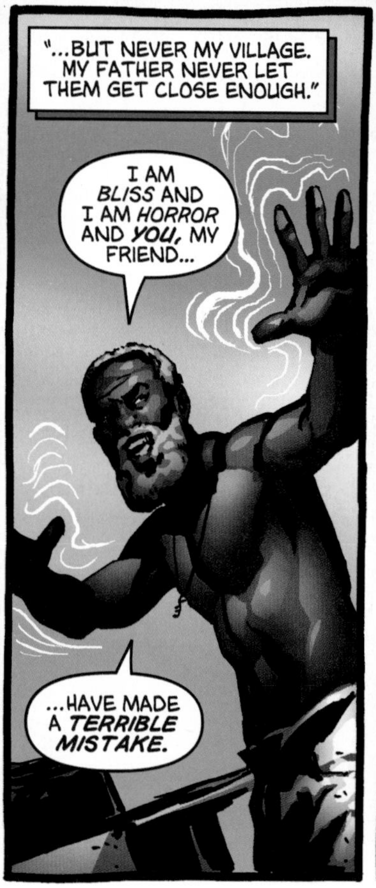
"...BUT NEVER MY VILLAGE. MY FATHER NEVER LET THEM GET CLOSE ENOUGH."
I AM *BLISS* AND I AM *HORROR* AND ***YOU***, MY FRIEND...
...HAVE MADE A ***TERRIBLE MISTAKE.***

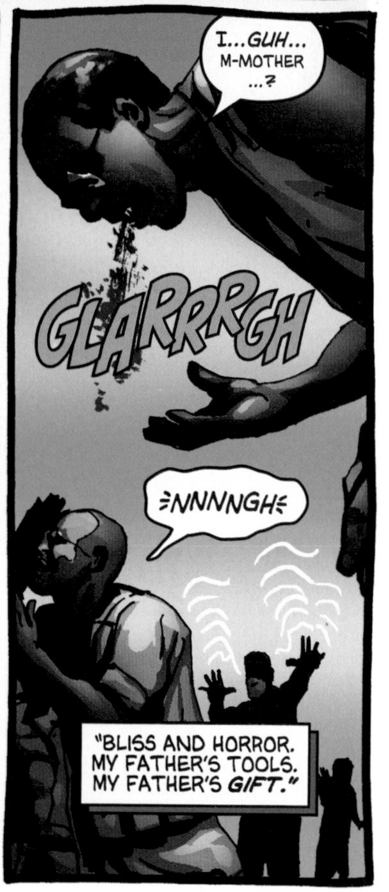
I...*GUH*... M-MOTHER ...?
GLARRRGH
NNNNGH
"BLISS AND HORROR. MY FATHER'S TOOLS. MY FATHER'S *GIFT*."

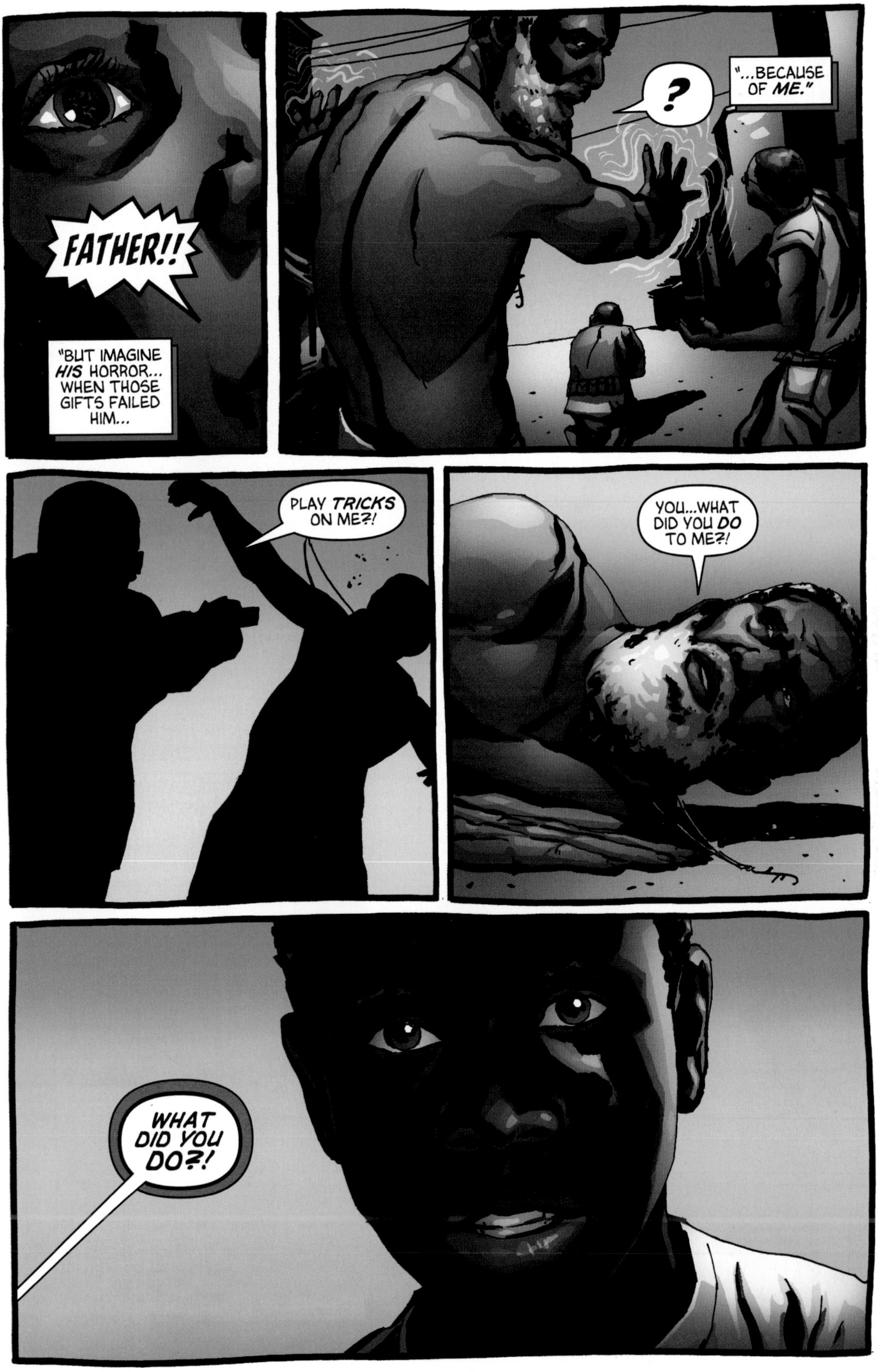
FATHER!!
"BUT IMAGINE HIS HORROR... WHEN THOSE GIFTS FAILED HIM...
?
"...BECAUSE OF ME."
PLAY TRICKS ON ME?!
YOU...WHAT DID YOU DO TO ME?!
WHAT DID YOU DO?!

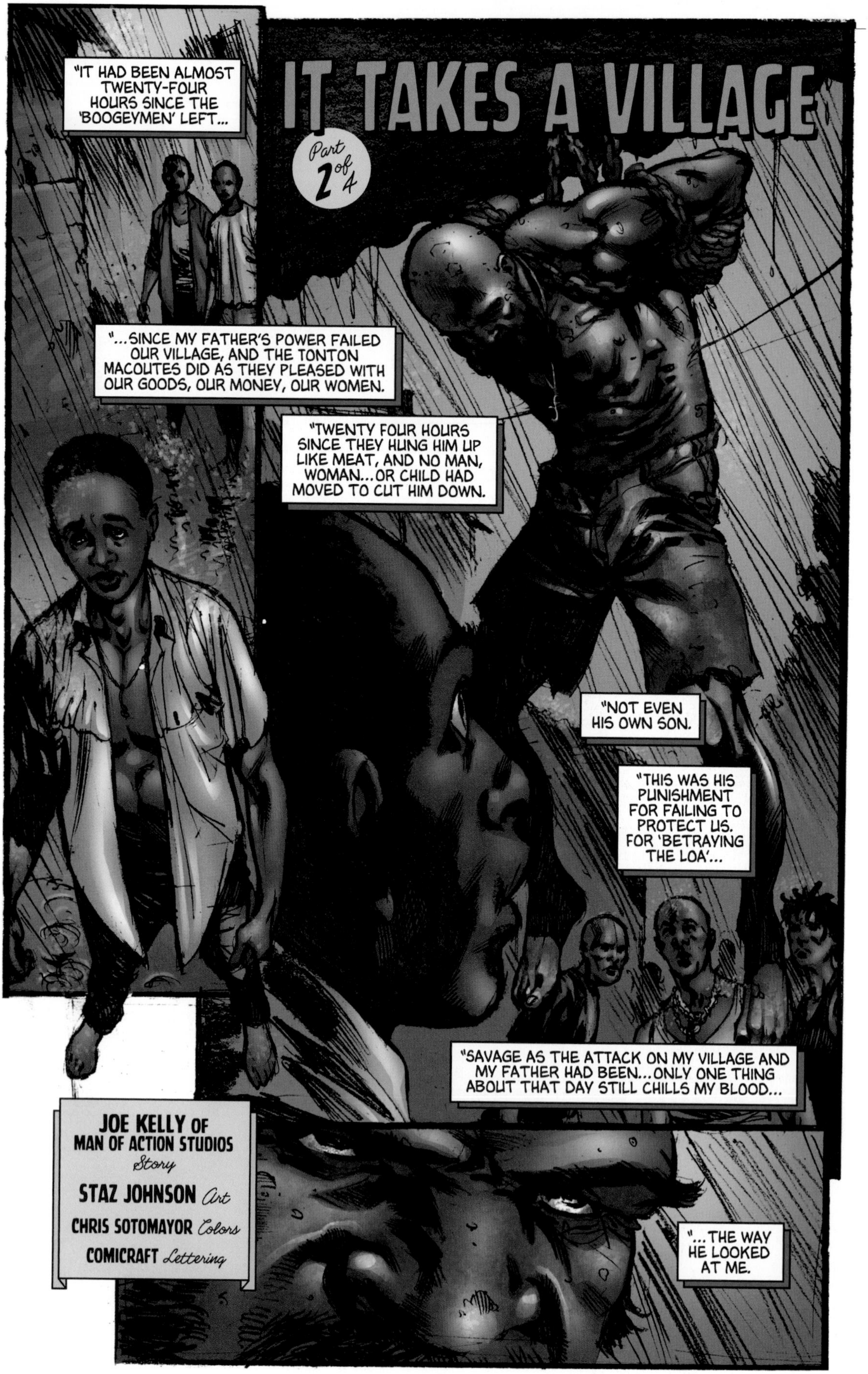
"IT HAD BEEN ALMOST TWENTY-FOUR HOURS SINCE THE 'BOOGEYMEN' LEFT...
IT TAKES A VILLAGE
Part 2 of 4
"...SINCE MY FATHER'S POWER FAILED OUR VILLAGE, AND THE TONTON MACOUTES DID AS THEY PLEASED WITH OUR GOODS, OUR MONEY, OUR WOMEN.
"TWENTY FOUR HOURS SINCE THEY HUNG HIM UP LIKE MEAT, AND NO MAN, WOMAN...OR CHILD HAD MOVED TO CUT HIM DOWN.
"NOT EVEN HIS OWN SON.
"THIS WAS HIS PUNISHMENT FOR FAILING TO PROTECT US. FOR 'BETRAYING THE LOA'...
"SAVAGE AS THE ATTACK ON MY VILLAGE AND MY FATHER HAD BEEN...ONLY ONE THING ABOUT THAT DAY STILL CHILLS MY BLOOD...
JOE KELLY OF MAN OF ACTION STUDIOS Story
STAZ JOHNSON Art
CHRIS SOTOMAYOR Colors
COMICRAFT Lettering
"...THE WAY HE LOOKED AT ME.

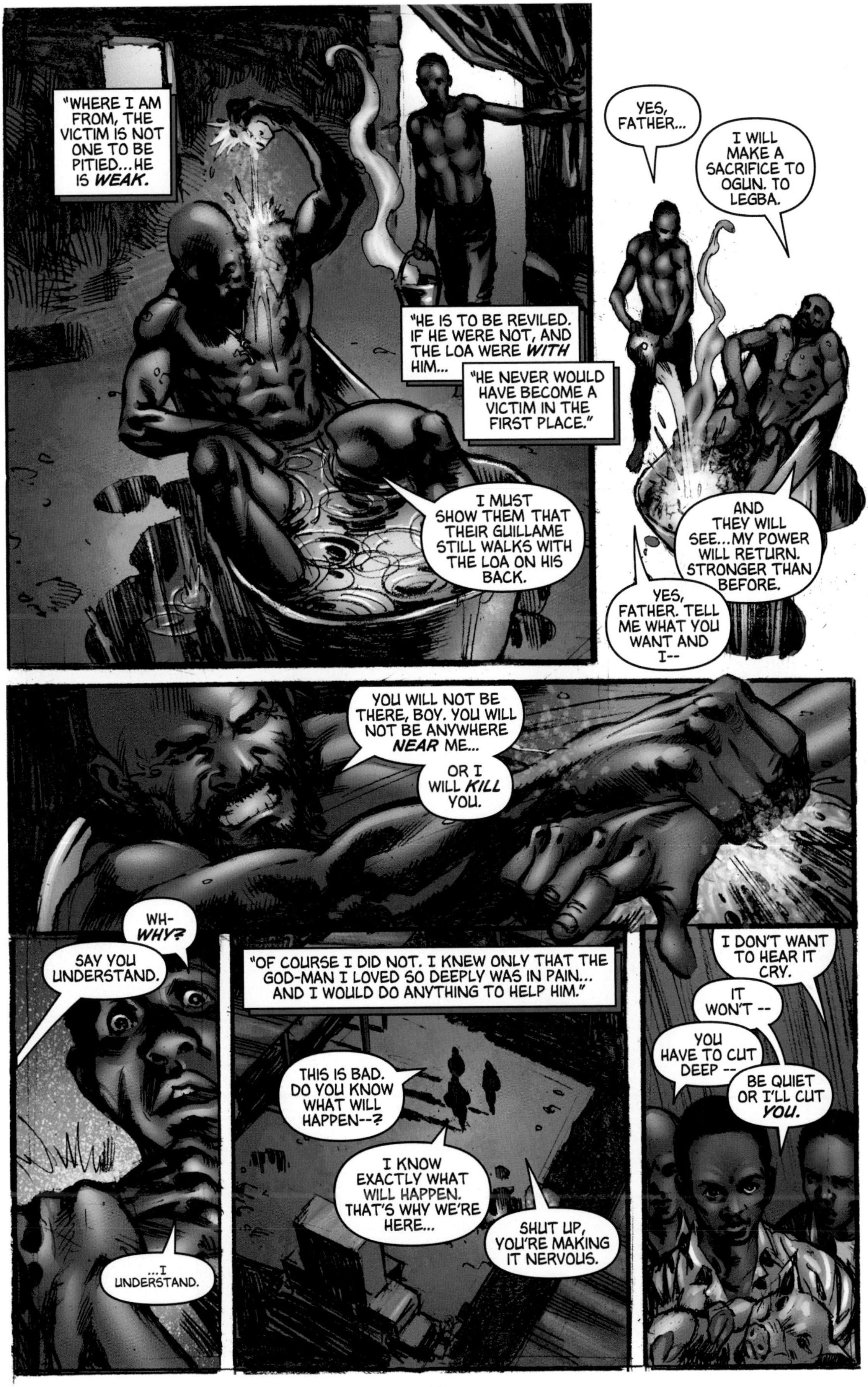
"WHERE I AM FROM, THE VICTIM IS NOT ONE TO BE PITIED... HE IS *WEAK.*
"HE IS TO BE REVILED. IF HE WERE NOT, AND THE LOA WERE *WITH* HIM...
"HE NEVER WOULD HAVE BECOME A VICTIM IN THE FIRST PLACE."
I MUST SHOW THEM THAT THEIR GUILLAME STILL WALKS WITH THE LOA ON HIS BACK.
YES, FATHER...
I WILL MAKE A SACRIFICE TO OGUN. TO LEGBA.
AND THEY WILL SEE... MY POWER WILL RETURN. STRONGER THAN BEFORE.
YES, FATHER. TELL ME WHAT YOU WANT AND I--
YOU WILL NOT BE THERE, BOY. YOU WILL NOT BE ANYWHERE *NEAR* ME...
OR I WILL *KILL* YOU.
WH- *WHY?*
SAY YOU UNDERSTAND.
...I UNDERSTAND.
"OF COURSE I DID NOT. I KNEW ONLY THAT THE GOD-MAN I LOVED SO DEEPLY WAS IN PAIN... AND I WOULD DO ANYTHING TO HELP HIM."
THIS IS BAD. DO YOU KNOW WHAT WILL HAPPEN--?
I KNOW EXACTLY WHAT WILL HAPPEN. THAT'S WHY WE'RE HERE...
SHUT UP, YOU'RE MAKING IT NERVOUS.
I DON'T WANT TO HEAR IT CRY.
IT WON'T --
YOU HAVE TO CUT DEEP --
BE QUIET OR I'LL CUT *YOU.*

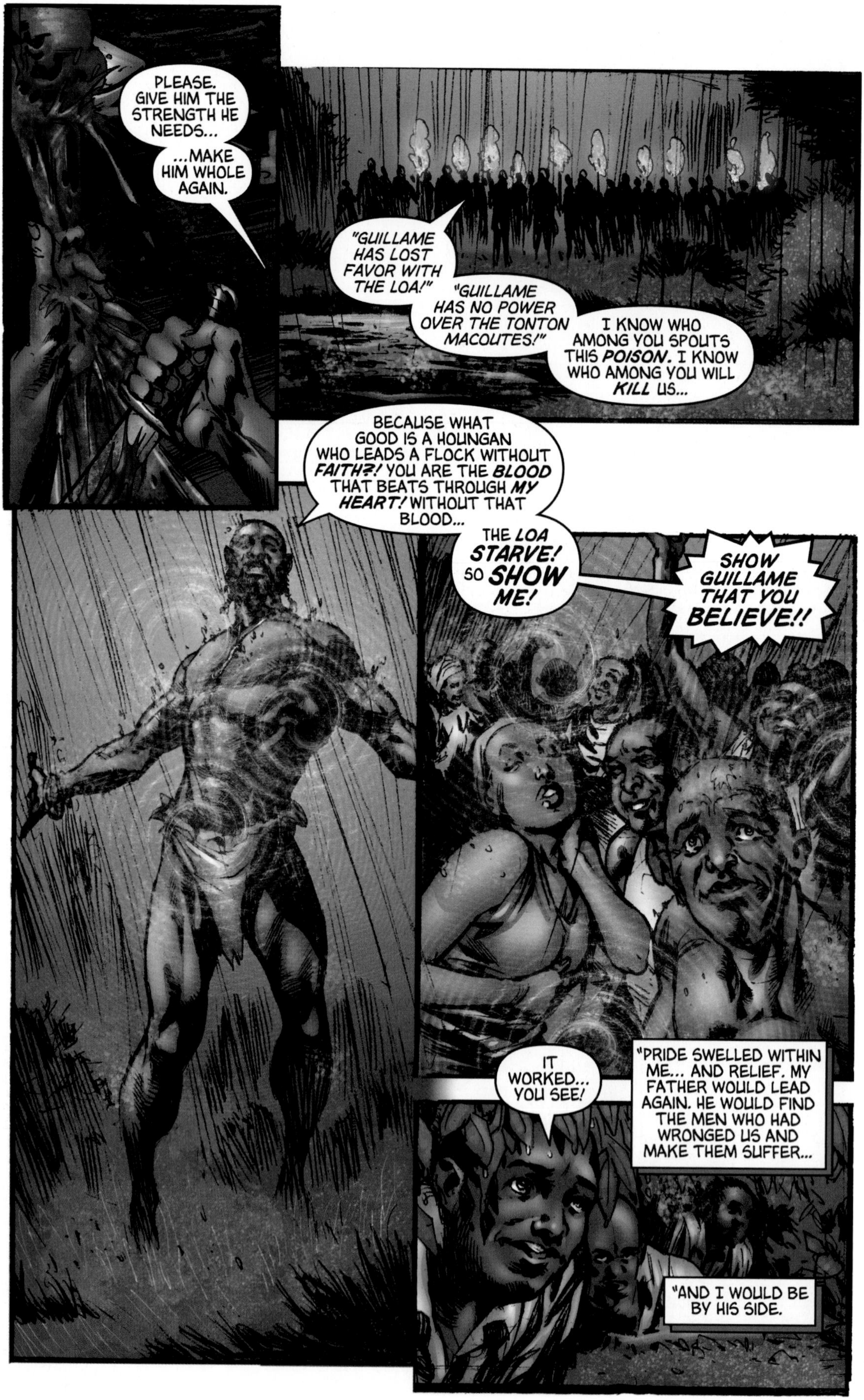
PLEASE. GIVE HIM THE STRENGTH HE NEEDS...
...MAKE HIM WHOLE AGAIN.
"GUILLAME HAS LOST FAVOR WITH THE LOA!"
"GUILLAME HAS NO POWER OVER THE TONTON MACOUTES!"
I KNOW WHO AMONG YOU SPOUTS THIS POISON. I KNOW WHO AMONG YOU WILL KILL US...
BECAUSE WHAT GOOD IS A HOUNGAN WHO LEADS A FLOCK WITHOUT FAITH?! YOU ARE THE BLOOD THAT BEATS THROUGH MY HEART! WITHOUT THAT BLOOD...
THE LOA STARVE! SO SHOW ME!
SHOW GUILLAME THAT YOU BELIEVE!!
IT WORKED... YOU SEE!
"PRIDE SWELLED WITHIN ME... AND RELIEF. MY FATHER WOULD LEAD AGAIN. HE WOULD FIND THE MEN WHO HAD WRONGED US AND MAKE THEM SUFFER...
"AND I WOULD BE BY HIS SIDE.

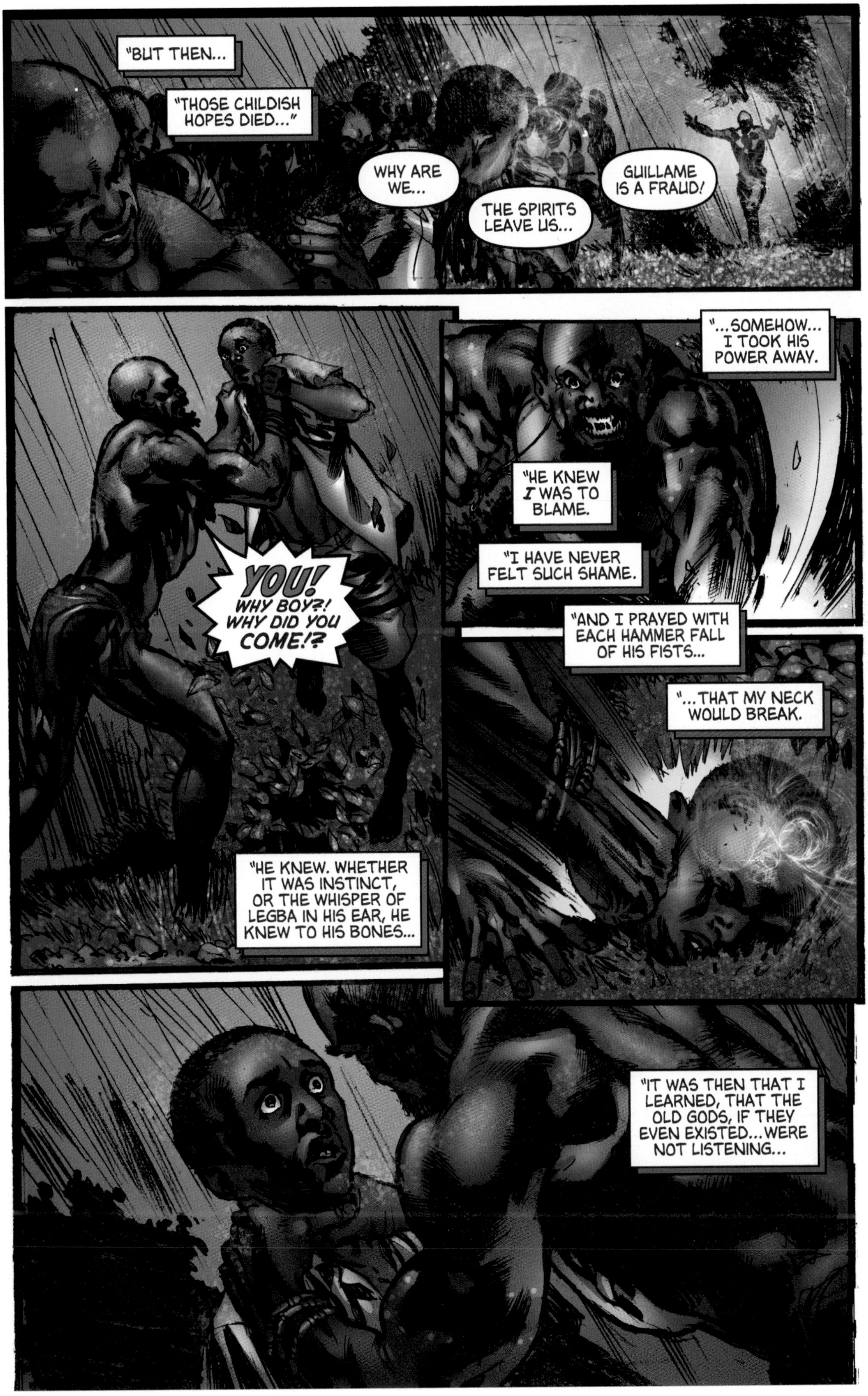
"BUT THEN...
"THOSE CHILDISH HOPES DIED..."
WHY ARE WE...
THE SPIRITS LEAVE US...
GUILLAME IS A FRAUD!
YOU! WHY BOY?! WHY DID YOU COME!?
"HE KNEW. WHETHER IT WAS INSTINCT, OR THE WHISPER OF LEGBA IN HIS EAR, HE KNEW TO HIS BONES...
"...SOMEHOW... I TOOK HIS POWER AWAY.
"HE KNEW I WAS TO BLAME.
"I HAVE NEVER FELT SUCH SHAME.
"AND I PRAYED WITH EACH HAMMER FALL OF HIS FISTS...
"...THAT MY NECK WOULD BREAK.
"IT WAS THEN THAT I LEARNED, THAT THE OLD GODS, IF THEY EVEN EXISTED...WERE NOT LISTENING...

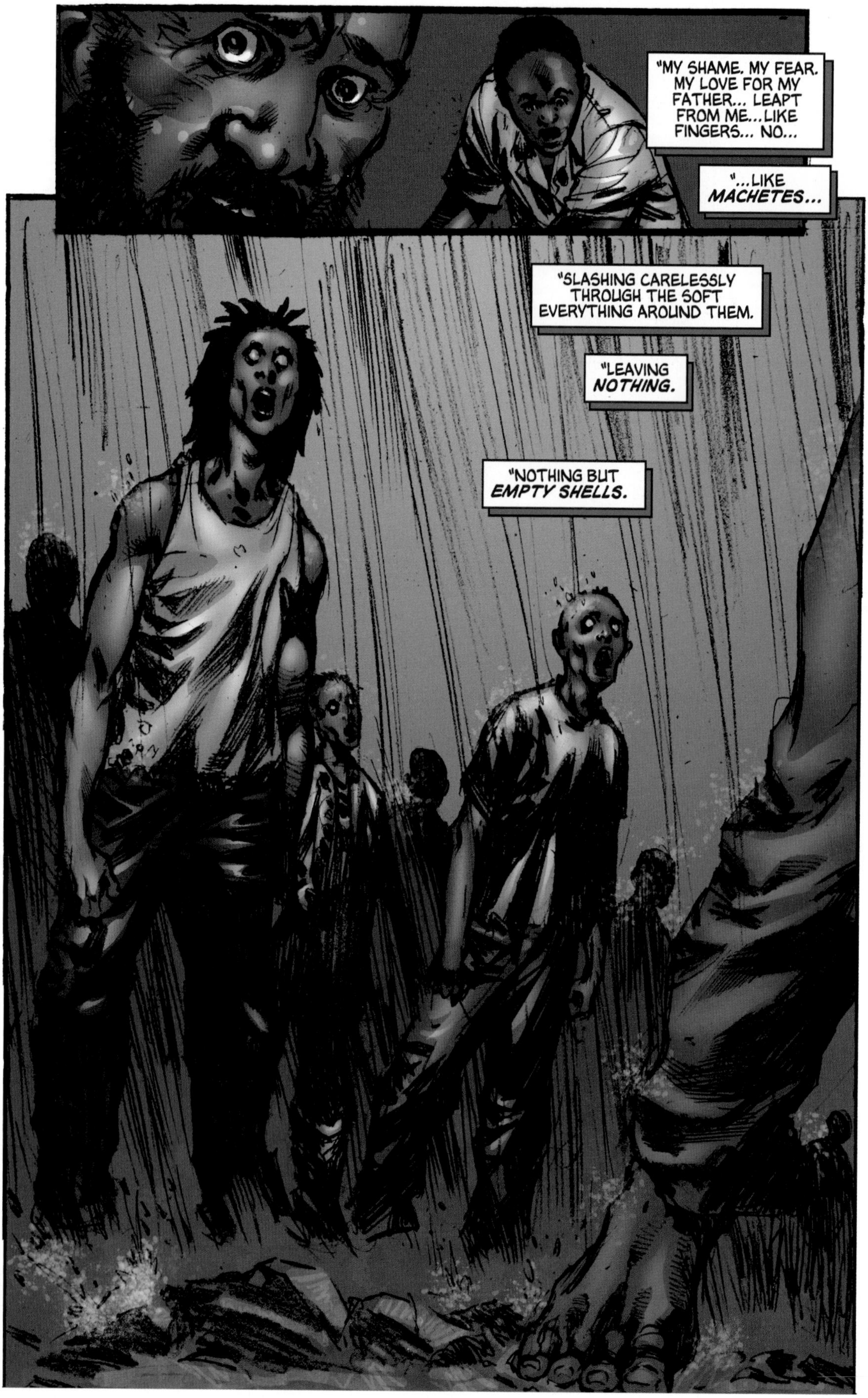
"MY SHAME. MY FEAR. MY LOVE FOR MY FATHER... LEAPT FROM ME...LIKE FINGERS... NO...
"...LIKE *MACHETES...*
"SLASHING CARELESSLY THROUGH THE SOFT EVERYTHING AROUND THEM.
"LEAVING *NOTHING.*
"NOTHING BUT *EMPTY SHELLS.*

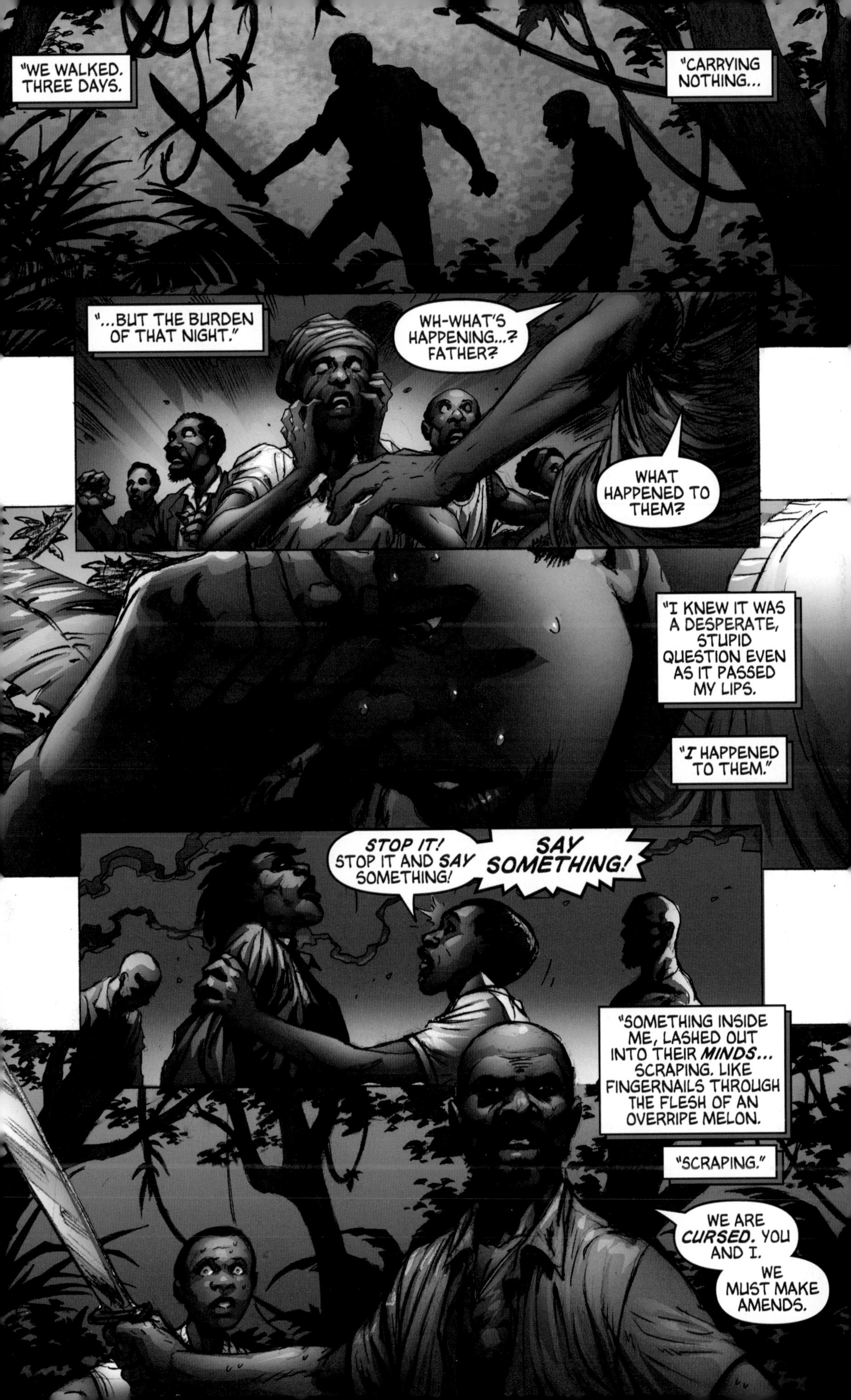
"WE WALKED. THREE DAYS.
"CARRYING NOTHING...
"...BUT THE BURDEN OF THAT NIGHT."
WH-WHAT'S HAPPENING...? FATHER?
WHAT HAPPENED TO THEM?
"I KNEW IT WAS A DESPERATE, STUPID QUESTION EVEN AS IT PASSED MY LIPS.
"*I* HAPPENED TO THEM."
*STOP IT!* STOP IT AND *SAY* SOMETHING!
SAY SOMETHING!
"SOMETHING INSIDE ME, LASHED OUT INTO THEIR *MINDS*... SCRAPING. LIKE FINGERNAILS THROUGH THE FLESH OF AN OVERRIPE MELON.
"SCRAPING."
WE ARE *CURSED*. YOU AND I.
WE MUST MAKE AMENDS.

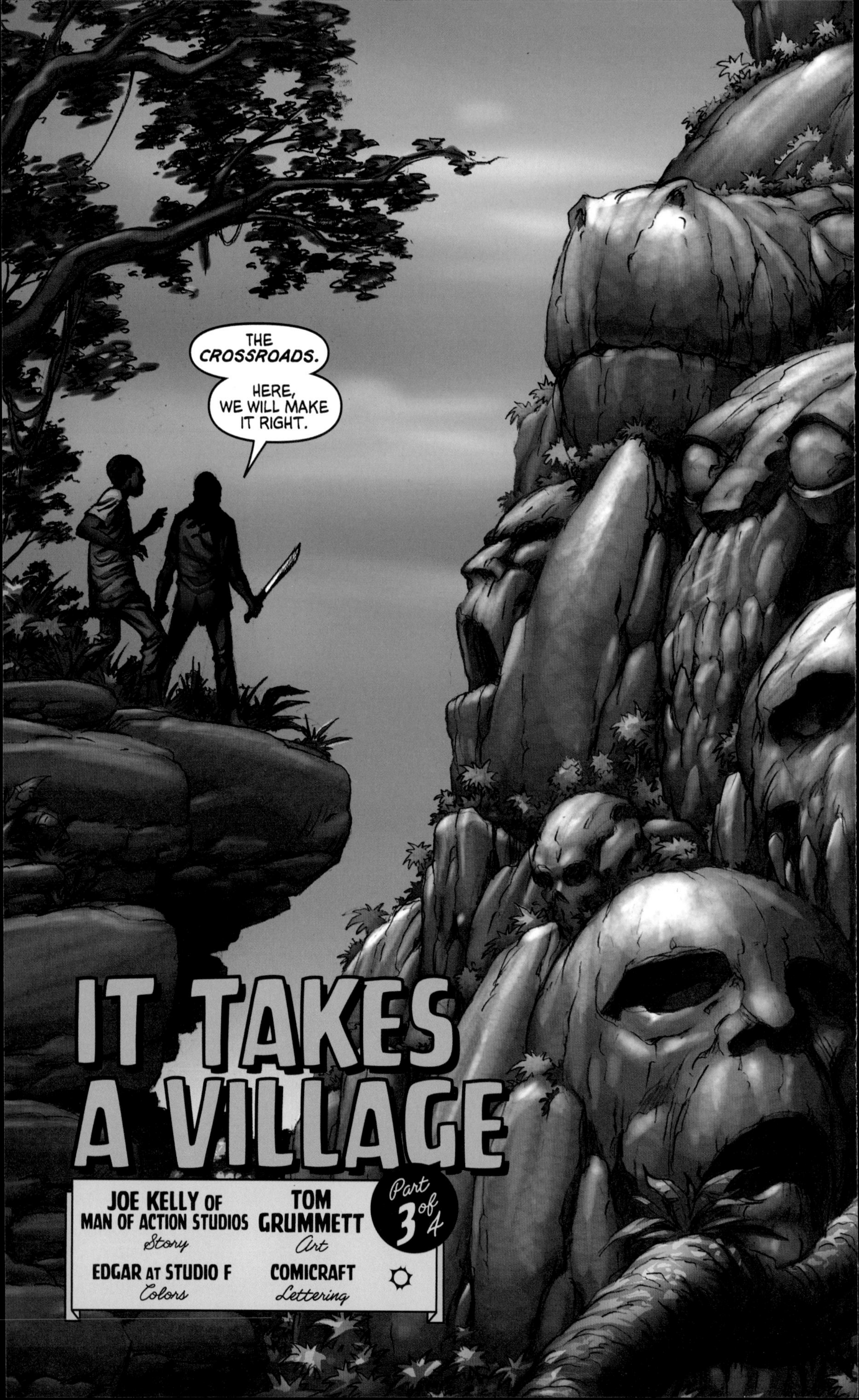
THE CROSSROADS.
HERE, WE WILL MAKE IT RIGHT.
IT TAKES A VILLAGE
Part 3 of 4
JOE KELLY OF MAN OF ACTION STUDIOS
Story
TOM GRUMMETT
Art
EDGAR AT STUDIO F
Colors
COMICRAFT
Lettering

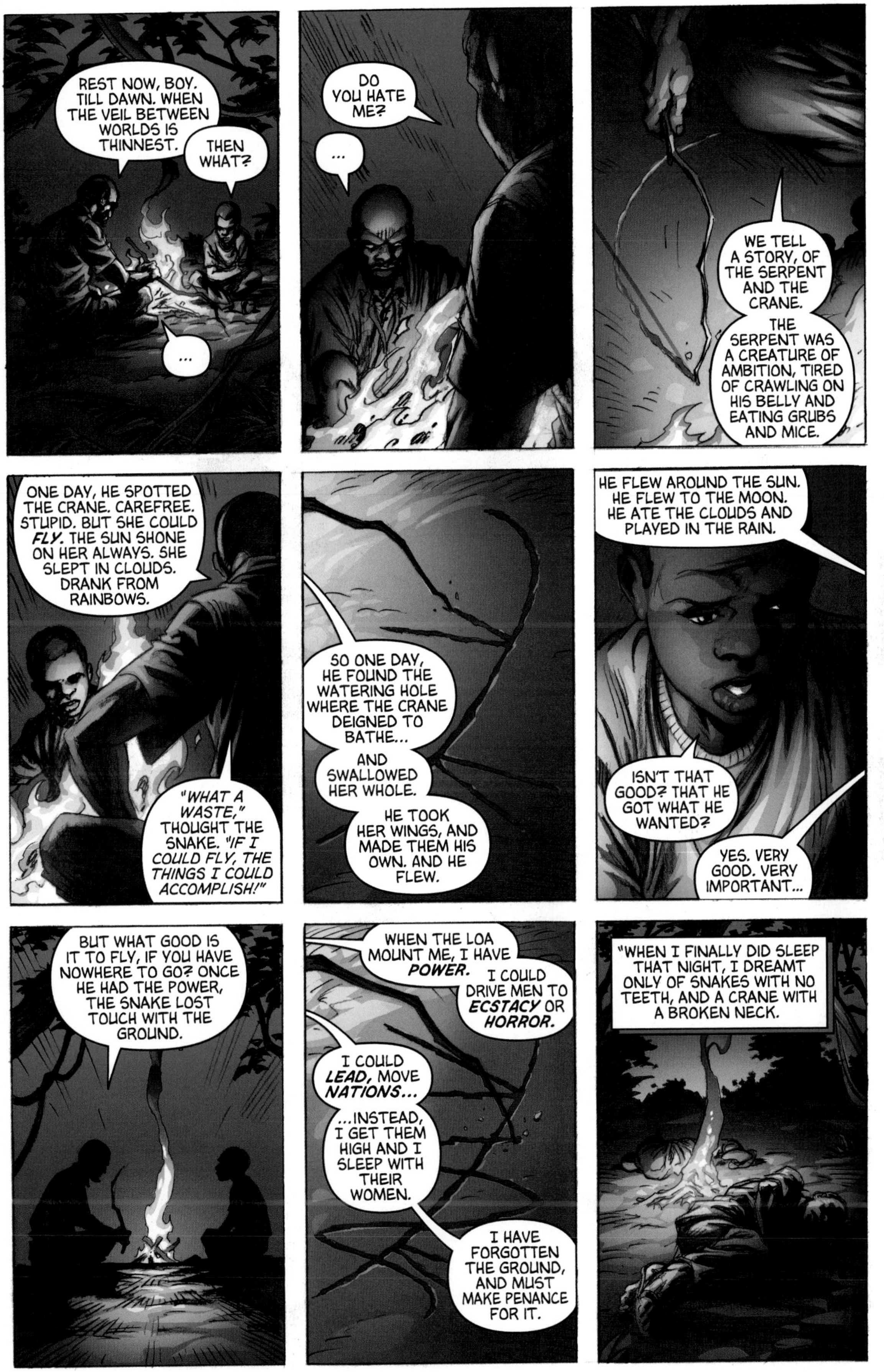
REST NOW, BOY. TILL DAWN. WHEN THE VEIL BETWEEN WORLDS IS THINNEST.
THEN WHAT?
...
DO YOU HATE ME?
...
WE TELL A STORY, OF THE SERPENT AND THE CRANE.
THE SERPENT WAS A CREATURE OF AMBITION, TIRED OF CRAWLING ON HIS BELLY AND EATING GRUBS AND MICE.
ONE DAY, HE SPOTTED THE CRANE. CAREFREE. STUPID. BUT SHE COULD *FLY*. THE SUN SHONE ON HER ALWAYS. SHE SLEPT IN CLOUDS. DRANK FROM RAINBOWS.
*"WHAT A WASTE,"* THOUGHT THE SNAKE. *"IF I COULD FLY, THE THINGS I COULD ACCOMPLISH!"*
SO ONE DAY, HE FOUND THE WATERING HOLE WHERE THE CRANE DEIGNED TO BATHE...
AND SWALLOWED HER WHOLE.
HE TOOK HER WINGS, AND MADE THEM HIS OWN. AND HE FLEW.
HE FLEW AROUND THE SUN. HE FLEW TO THE MOON. HE ATE THE CLOUDS AND PLAYED IN THE RAIN.
ISN'T THAT GOOD? THAT HE GOT WHAT HE WANTED?
YES. VERY GOOD. VERY IMPORTANT...
BUT WHAT GOOD IS IT TO FLY, IF YOU HAVE NOWHERE TO GO? ONCE HE HAD THE POWER, THE SNAKE LOST TOUCH WITH THE GROUND.
WHEN THE LOA MOUNT ME, I HAVE **POWER.**
I COULD DRIVE MEN TO ***ECSTACY*** OR ***HORROR.***
I COULD ***LEAD,*** MOVE ***NATIONS...***
...INSTEAD, I GET THEM HIGH AND I SLEEP WITH THEIR WOMEN.
I HAVE FORGOTTEN THE GROUND, AND MUST MAKE PENANCE FOR IT.
"WHEN I FINALLY DID SLEEP THAT NIGHT, I DREAMT ONLY OF SNAKES WITH NO TEETH, AND A CRANE WITH A BROKEN NECK.

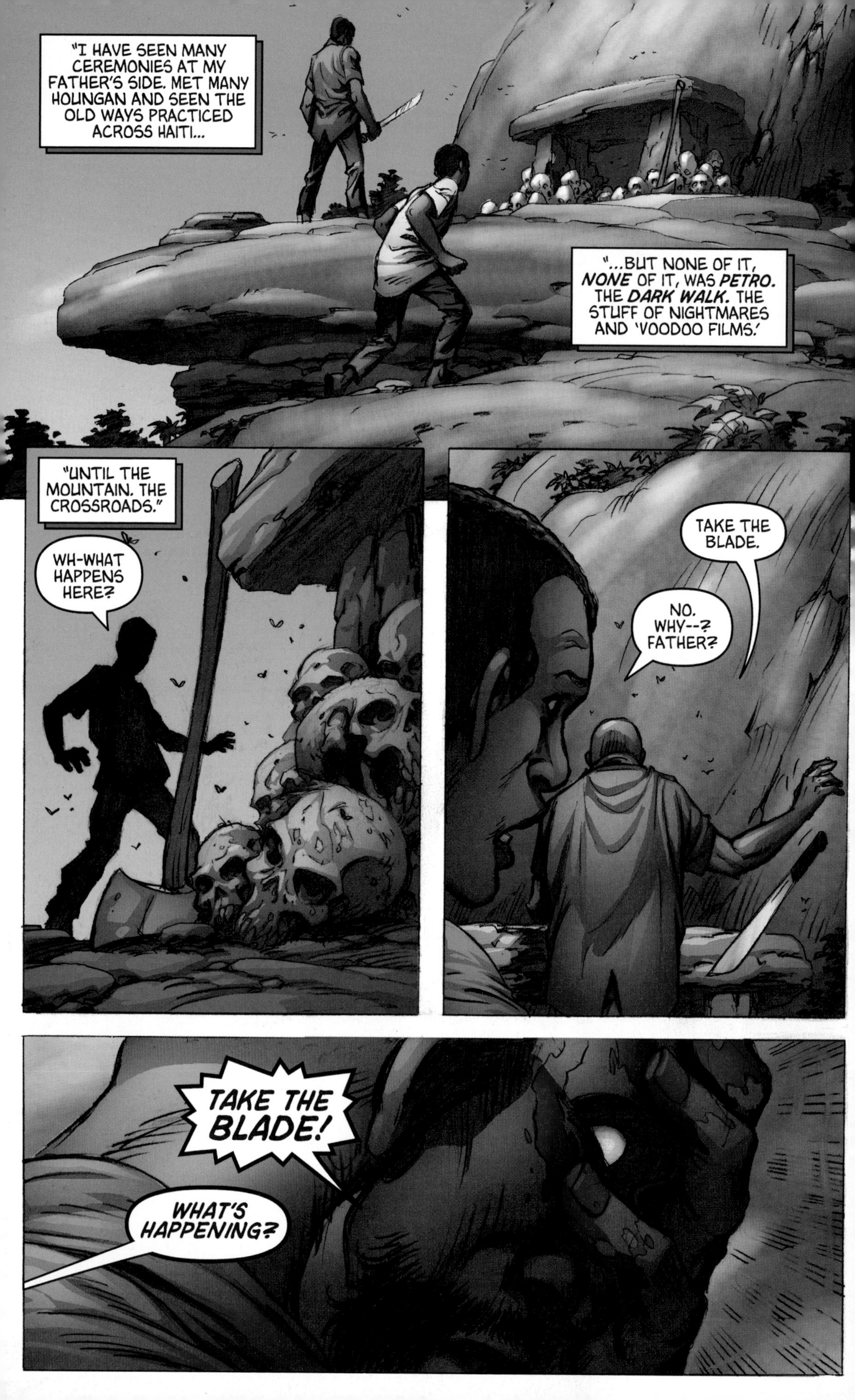

"I HAVE SEEN MANY CEREMONIES AT MY FATHER'S SIDE. MET MANY HOUNGAN AND SEEN THE OLD WAYS PRACTICED ACROSS HAITI...
"...BUT NONE OF IT, NONE OF IT, WAS PETRO. THE DARK WALK. THE STUFF OF NIGHTMARES AND 'VOODOO FILMS.'
"UNTIL THE MOUNTAIN. THE CROSSROADS."
WH-WHAT HAPPENS HERE?
TAKE THE BLADE.
NO. WHY--? FATHER?
TAKE THE BLADE!
WHAT'S HAPPENING?

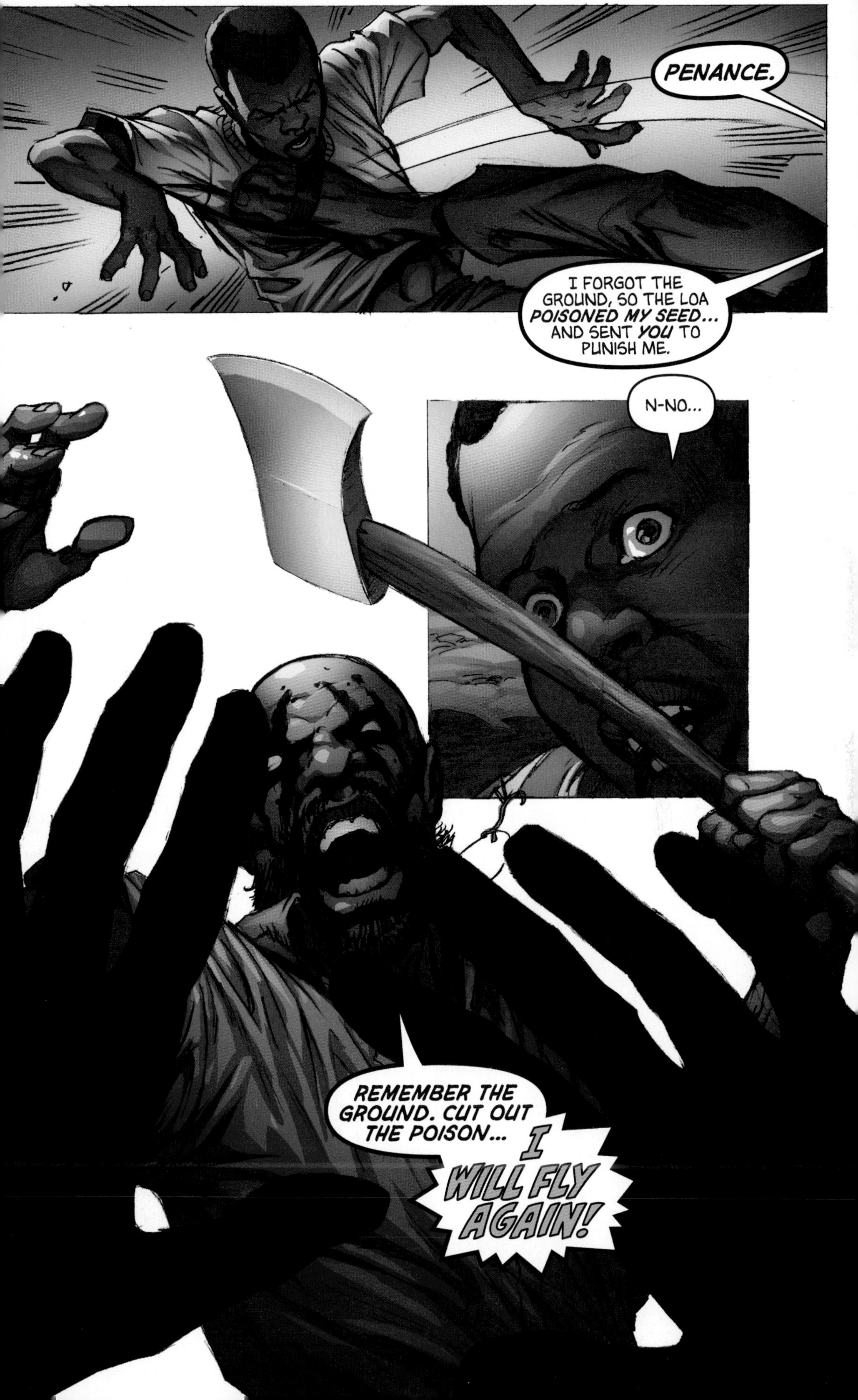
PENANCE.
I FORGOT THE GROUND, SO THE LOA POISONED MY SEED... AND SENT YOU TO PUNISH ME.
N-NO...
REMEMBER THE GROUND. CUT OUT THE POISON...
I WILL FLY AGAIN!

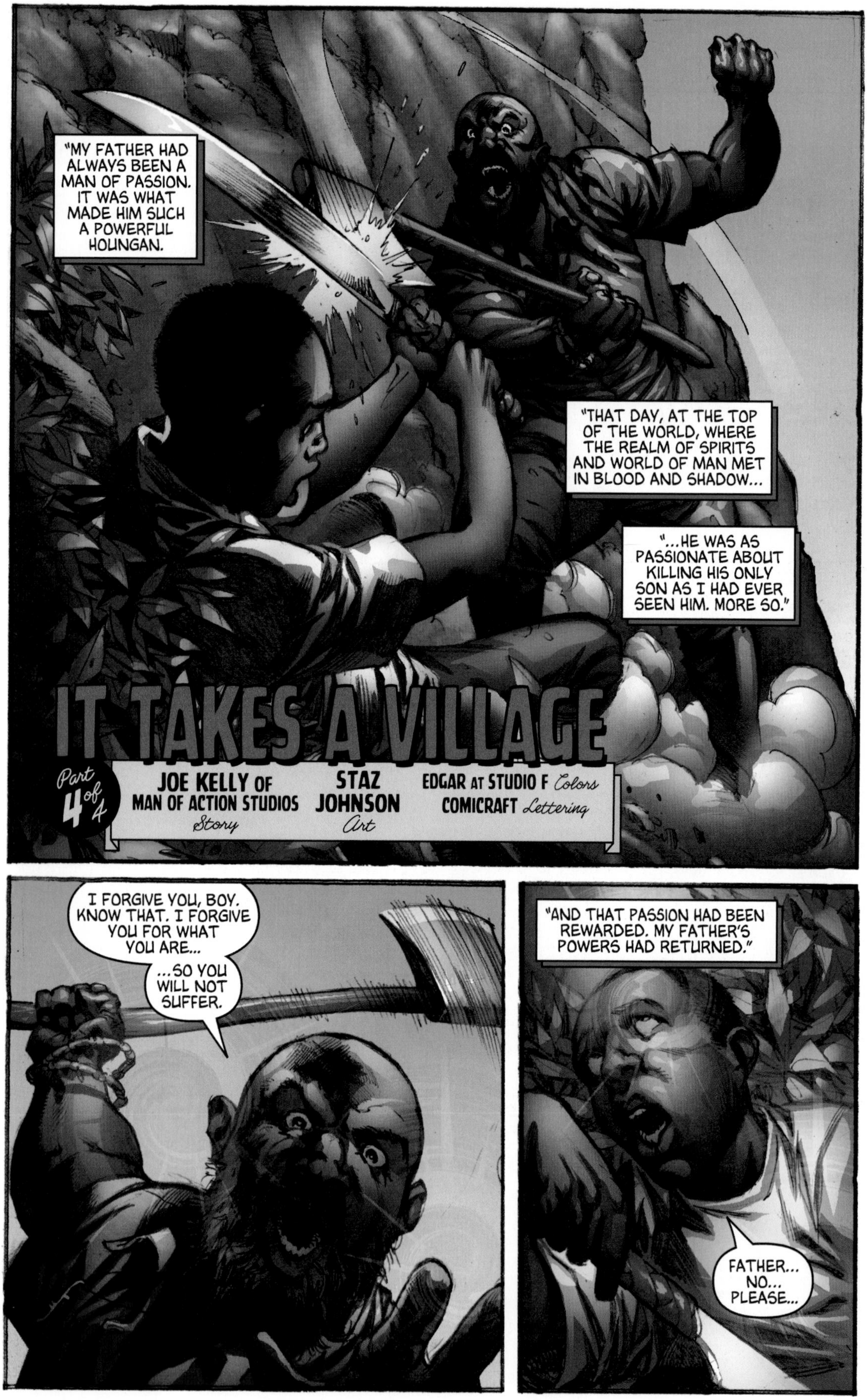
"MY FATHER HAD ALWAYS BEEN A MAN OF PASSION. IT WAS WHAT MADE HIM SUCH A POWERFUL HOUNGAN.
"THAT DAY, AT THE TOP OF THE WORLD, WHERE THE REALM OF SPIRITS AND WORLD OF MAN MET IN BLOOD AND SHADOW...
"...HE WAS AS PASSIONATE ABOUT KILLING HIS ONLY SON AS I HAD EVER SEEN HIM. MORE SO."
IT TAKES A VILLAGE
Part 4 of 4
JOE KELLY OF MAN OF ACTION STUDIOS Story
STAZ JOHNSON Art
EDGAR AT STUDIO F Colors
COMICRAFT Lettering
I FORGIVE YOU, BOY. KNOW THAT. I FORGIVE YOU FOR WHAT YOU ARE...
...SO YOU WILL NOT SUFFER.
"AND THAT PASSION HAD BEEN REWARDED. MY FATHER'S POWERS HAD RETURNED."
FATHER... NO... PLEASE...

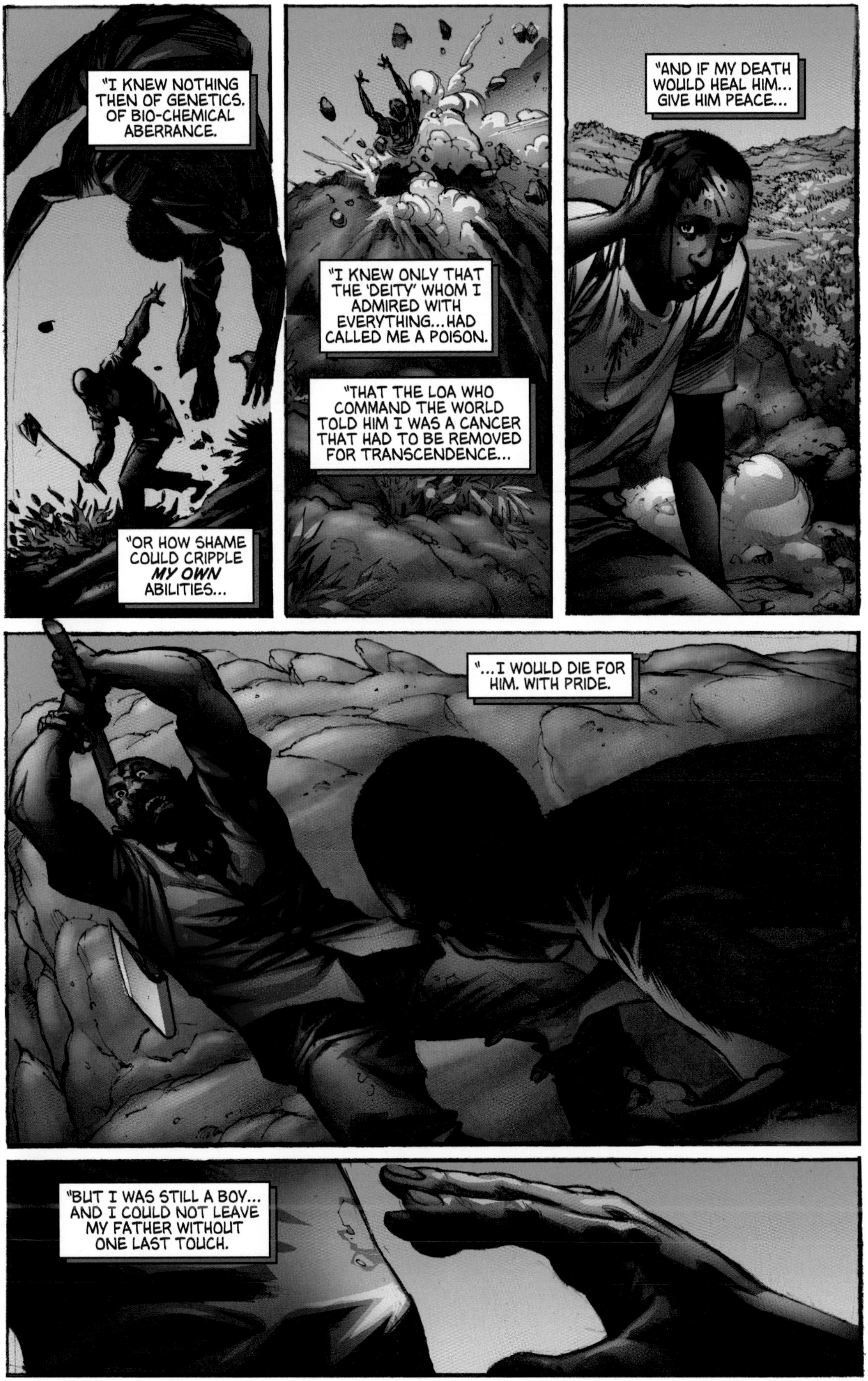
"I KNEW NOTHING THEN OF GENETICS. OF BIO-CHEMICAL ABERRANCE.
"OR HOW SHAME COULD CRIPPLE *MY OWN* ABILITIES...
"I KNEW ONLY THAT THE 'DEITY' WHOM I ADMIRED WITH EVERYTHING...HAD CALLED ME A POISON.
"THAT THE LOA WHO COMMAND THE WORLD TOLD HIM I WAS A CANCER THAT HAD TO BE REMOVED FOR TRANSCENDENCE...
"AND IF MY DEATH WOULD HEAL HIM... GIVE HIM PEACE...
"...I WOULD DIE FOR HIM. WITH PRIDE.
"BUT I WAS STILL A BOY... AND I COULD NOT LEAVE MY FATHER WITHOUT ONE LAST TOUCH.

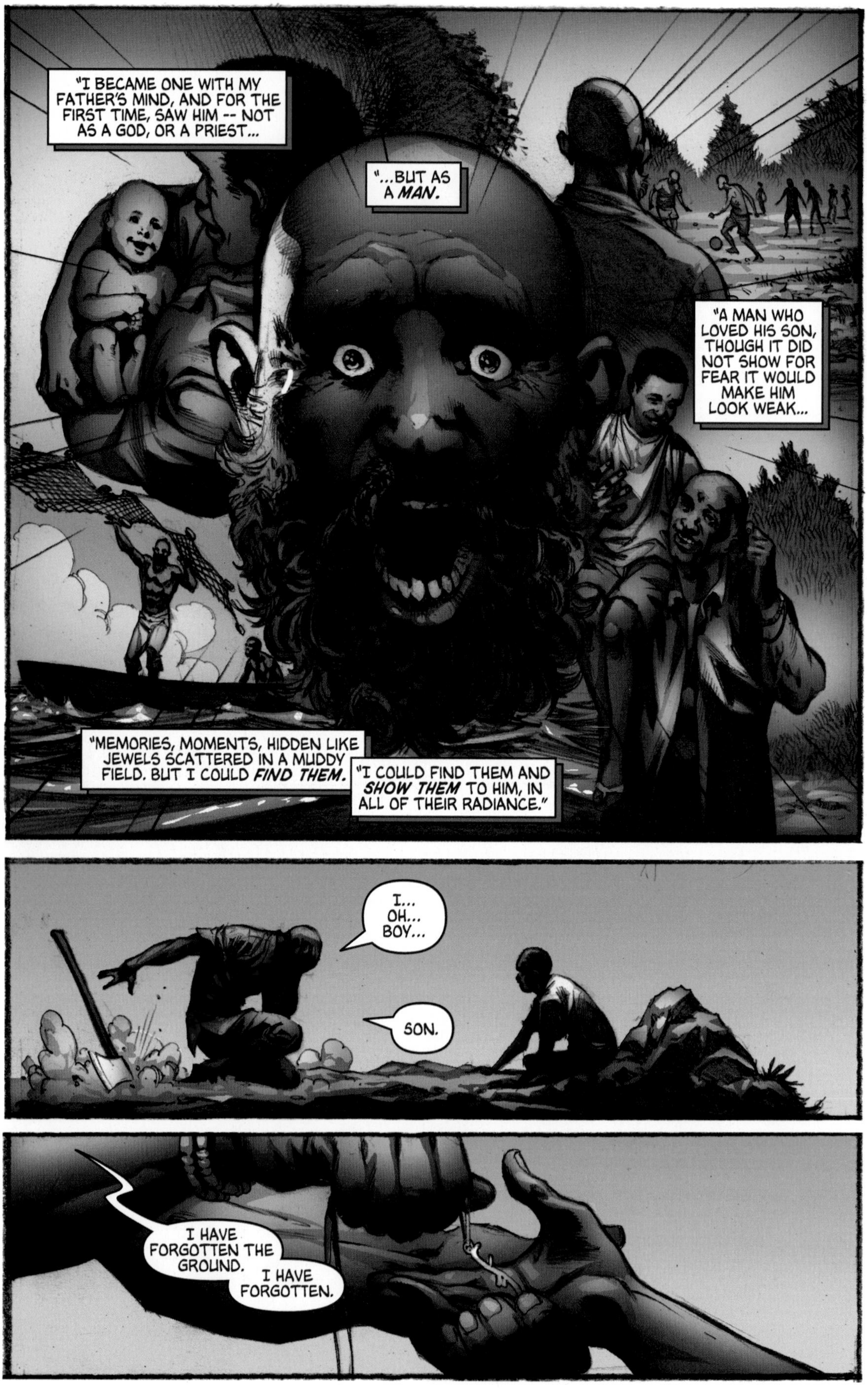
"I BECAME ONE WITH MY FATHER'S MIND, AND FOR THE FIRST TIME, SAW HIM -- NOT AS A GOD, OR A PRIEST...
"...BUT AS A MAN.
"A MAN WHO LOVED HIS SON, THOUGH IT DID NOT SHOW FOR FEAR IT WOULD MAKE HIM LOOK WEAK...
"MEMORIES, MOMENTS, HIDDEN LIKE JEWELS SCATTERED IN A MUDDY FIELD. BUT I COULD FIND THEM.
"I COULD FIND THEM AND SHOW THEM TO HIM, IN ALL OF THEIR RADIANCE."
I... OH... BOY...
SON.
I HAVE FORGOTTEN THE GROUND.
I HAVE FORGOTTEN.

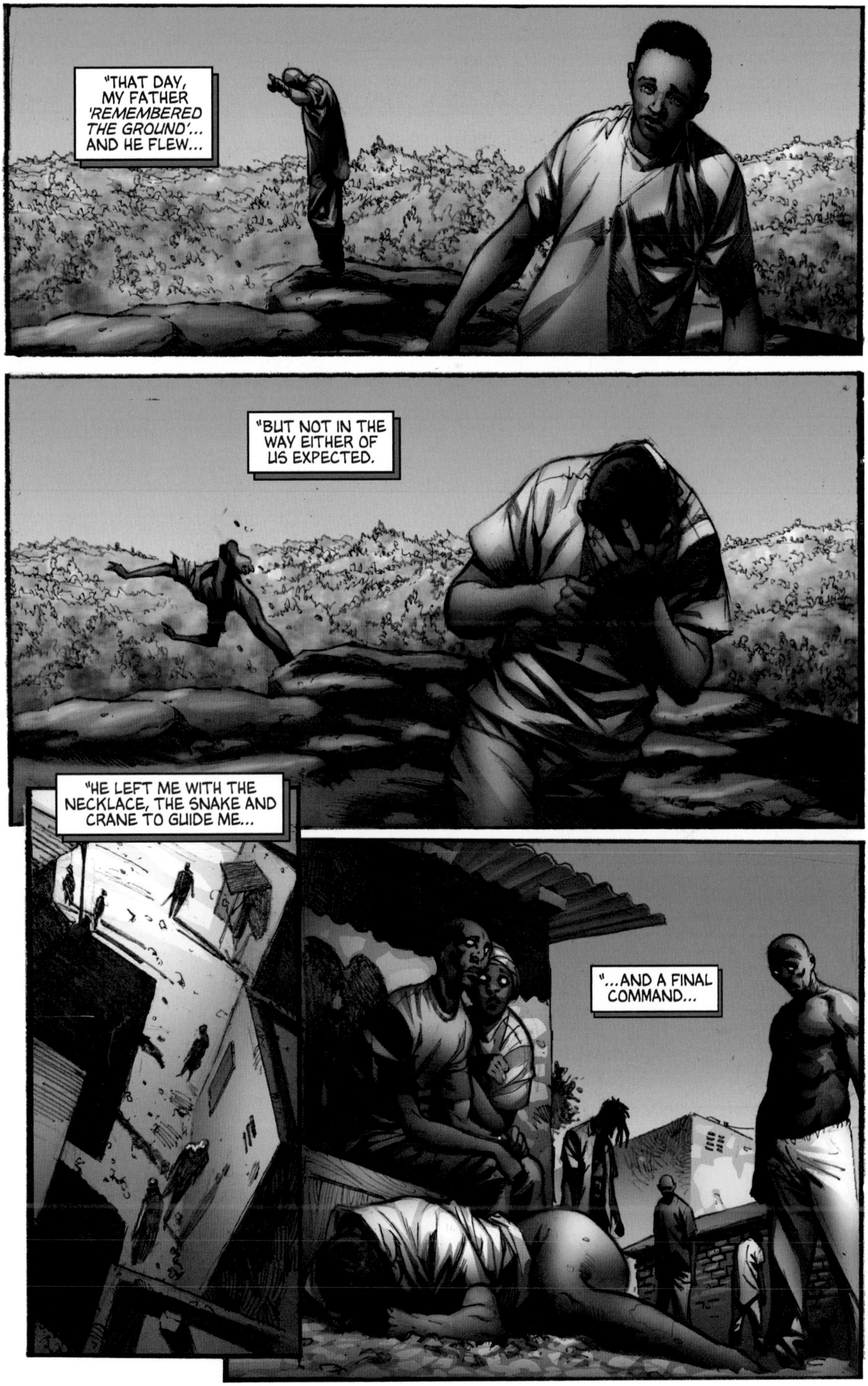
"THAT DAY, MY FATHER 'REMEMBERED THE GROUND'... AND HE FLEW...
"BUT NOT IN THE WAY EITHER OF US EXPECTED.
"HE LEFT ME WITH THE NECKLACE, THE SNAKE AND CRANE TO GUIDE ME...
"...AND A FINAL COMMAND...

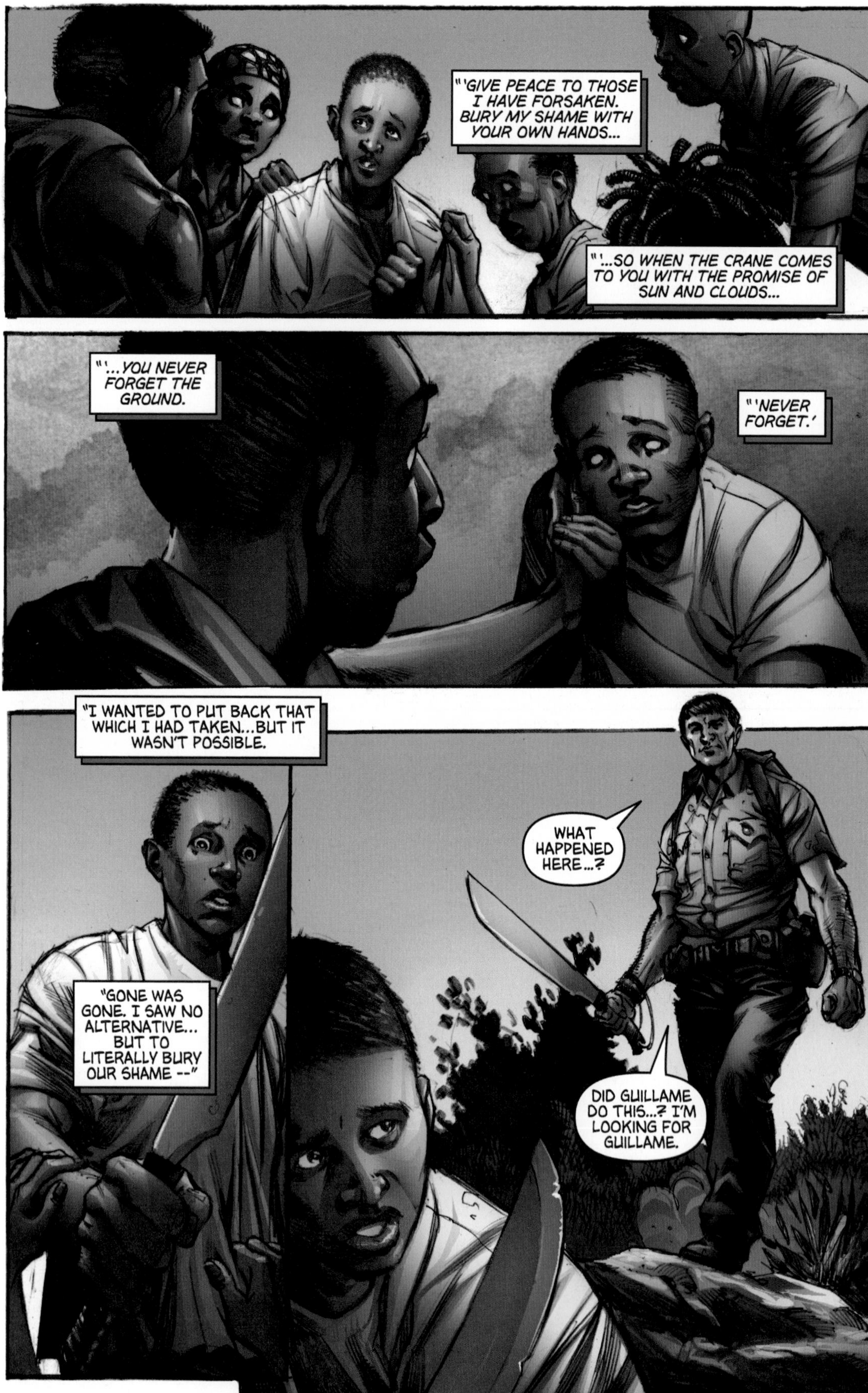
"'GIVE PEACE TO THOSE I HAVE FORSAKEN. BURY MY SHAME WITH YOUR OWN HANDS...
"'...SO WHEN THE CRANE COMES TO YOU WITH THE PROMISE OF SUN AND CLOUDS...
"'...YOU NEVER FORGET THE GROUND.
"'NEVER FORGET.'
"I WANTED TO PUT BACK THAT WHICH I HAD TAKEN...BUT IT WASN'T POSSIBLE.
WHAT HAPPENED HERE...?
"GONE WAS GONE. I SAW NO ALTERNATIVE... BUT TO LITERALLY BURY OUR SHAME --"
DID GUILLAME DO THIS...? I'M LOOKING FOR GUILLAME.

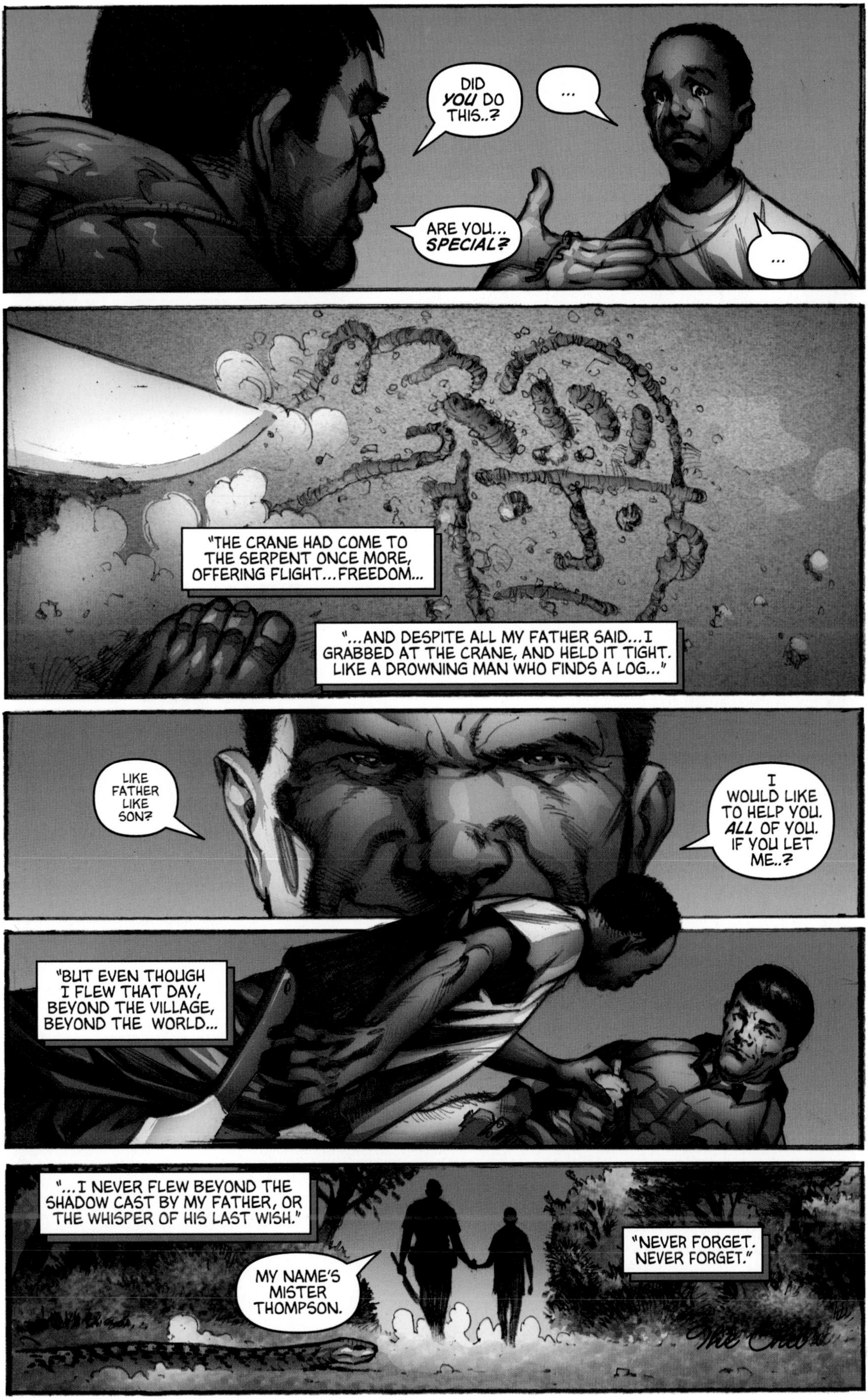
DID YOU DO THIS..?
...
ARE YOU... SPECIAL?
...
"THE CRANE HAD COME TO THE SERPENT ONCE MORE, OFFERING FLIGHT...FREEDOM...
"...AND DESPITE ALL MY FATHER SAID...I GRABBED AT THE CRANE, AND HELD IT TIGHT. LIKE A DROWNING MAN WHO FINDS A LOG..."
LIKE FATHER LIKE SON?
I WOULD LIKE TO HELP YOU. ALL OF YOU. IF YOU LET ME..?
"BUT EVEN THOUGH I FLEW THAT DAY, BEYOND THE VILLAGE, BEYOND THE WORLD...
"...I NEVER FLEW BEYOND THE SHADOW CAST BY MY FATHER, OR THE WHISPER OF HIS LAST WISH."
MY NAME'S MISTER THOMPSON.
"NEVER FORGET. NEVER FORGET."

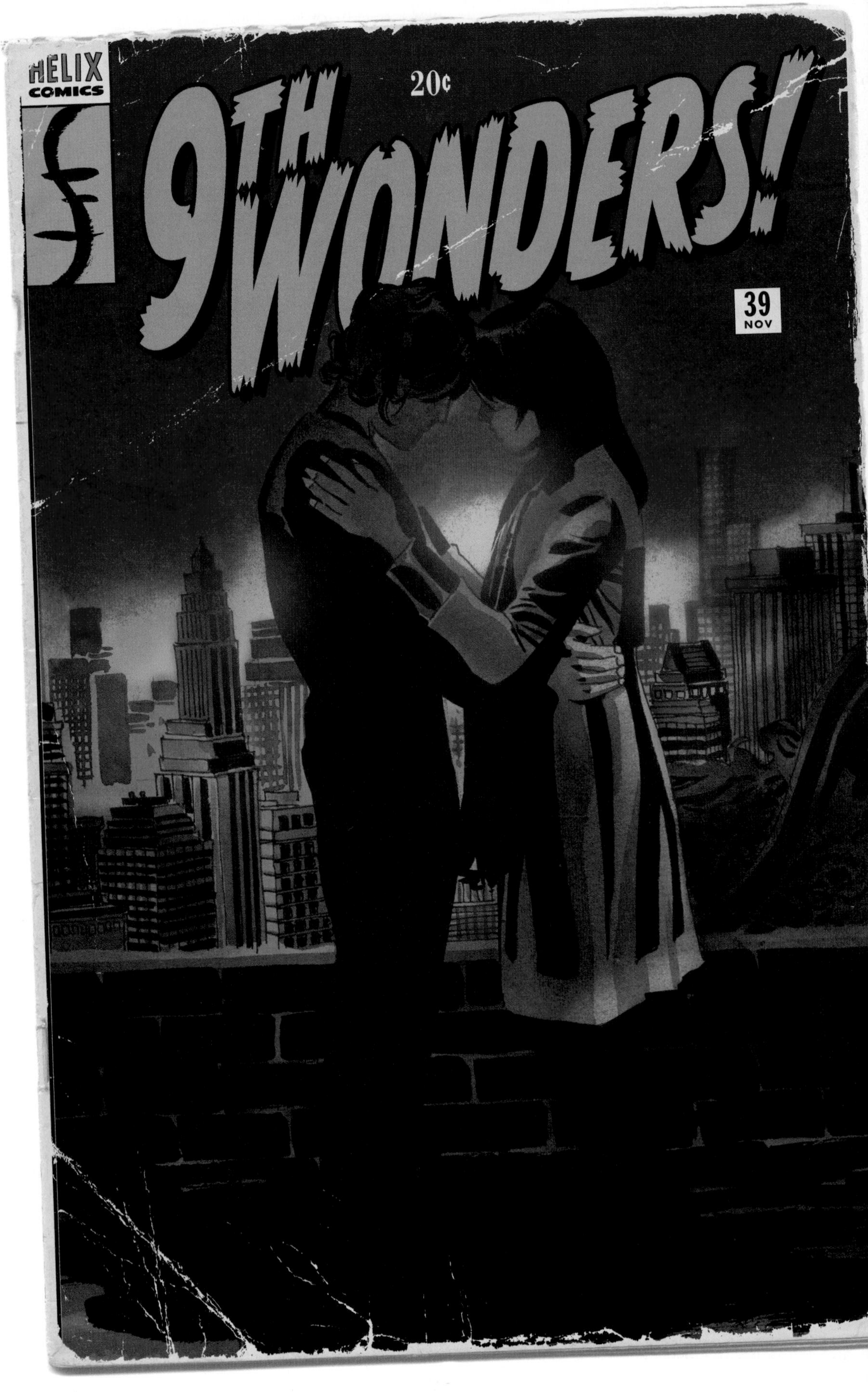
HELIX
COMICS
20¢
9TH WONDERS!
39
NOV

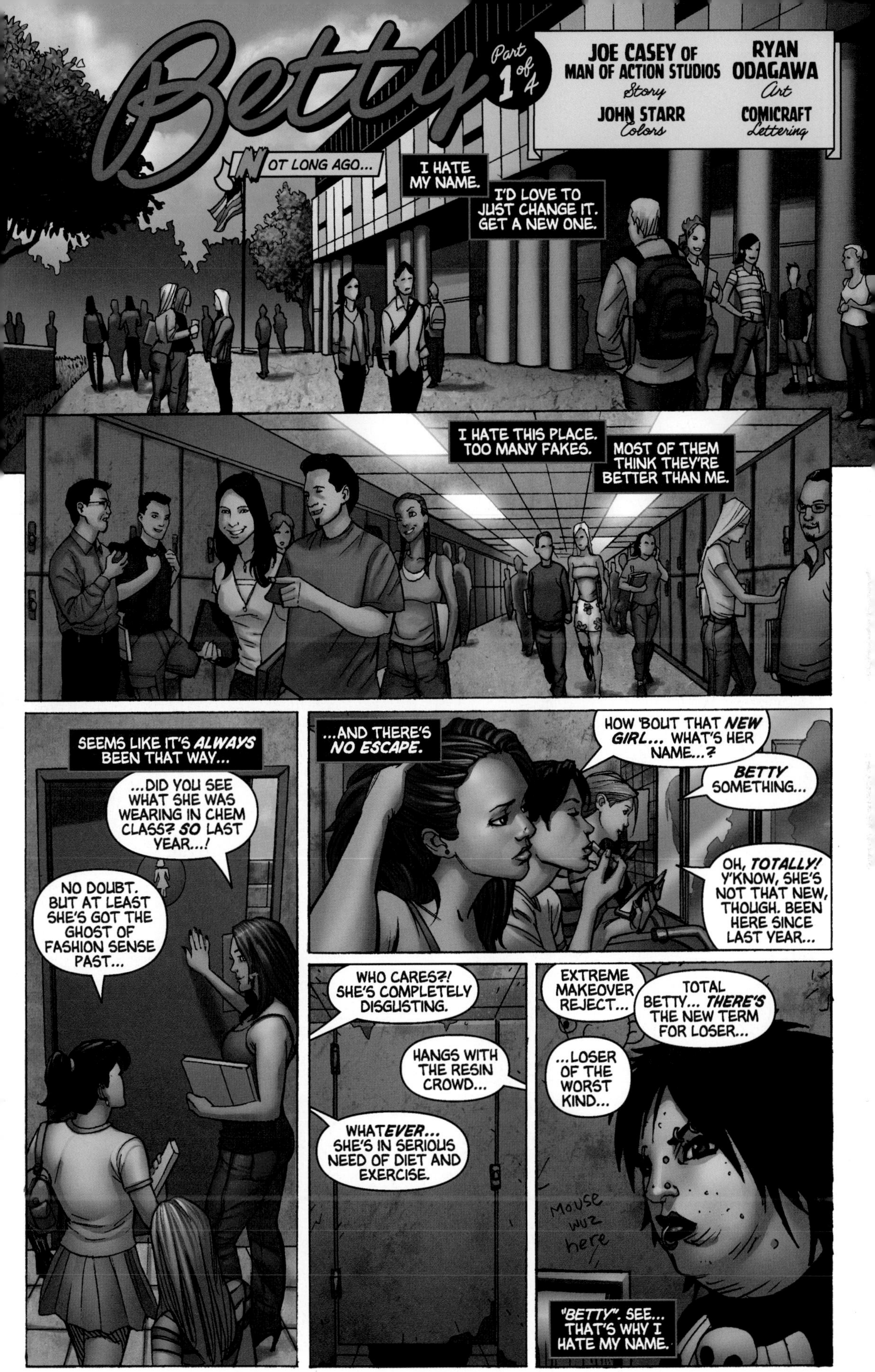
Betty
Part 1 of 4
JOE CASEY OF MAN OF ACTION STUDIOS Story
RYAN ODAGAWA Art
JOHN STARR Colors
COMICRAFT Lettering
NOT LONG AGO...
I HATE MY NAME.
I'D LOVE TO JUST CHANGE IT. GET A NEW ONE.
I HATE THIS PLACE. TOO MANY FAKES.
MOST OF THEM THINK THEY'RE BETTER THAN ME.
SEEMS LIKE IT'S ALWAYS BEEN THAT WAY...
...DID YOU SEE WHAT SHE WAS WEARING IN CHEM CLASS? SO LAST YEAR...!
NO DOUBT. BUT AT LEAST SHE'S GOT THE GHOST OF FASHION SENSE PAST...
...AND THERE'S NO ESCAPE.
HOW 'BOUT THAT NEW GIRL... WHAT'S HER NAME...?
BETTY SOMETHING...
OH, TOTALLY! Y'KNOW, SHE'S NOT THAT NEW, THOUGH. BEEN HERE SINCE LAST YEAR...
WHO CARES?! SHE'S COMPLETELY DISGUSTING.
HANGS WITH THE RESIN CROWD...
WHATEVER... SHE'S IN SERIOUS NEED OF DIET AND EXERCISE.
EXTREME MAKEOVER REJECT...
TOTAL BETTY... THERE'S THE NEW TERM FOR LOSER...
...LOSER OF THE WORST KIND...
MOUSE WUZ HERE
"BETTY". SEE... THAT'S WHY I HATE MY NAME.

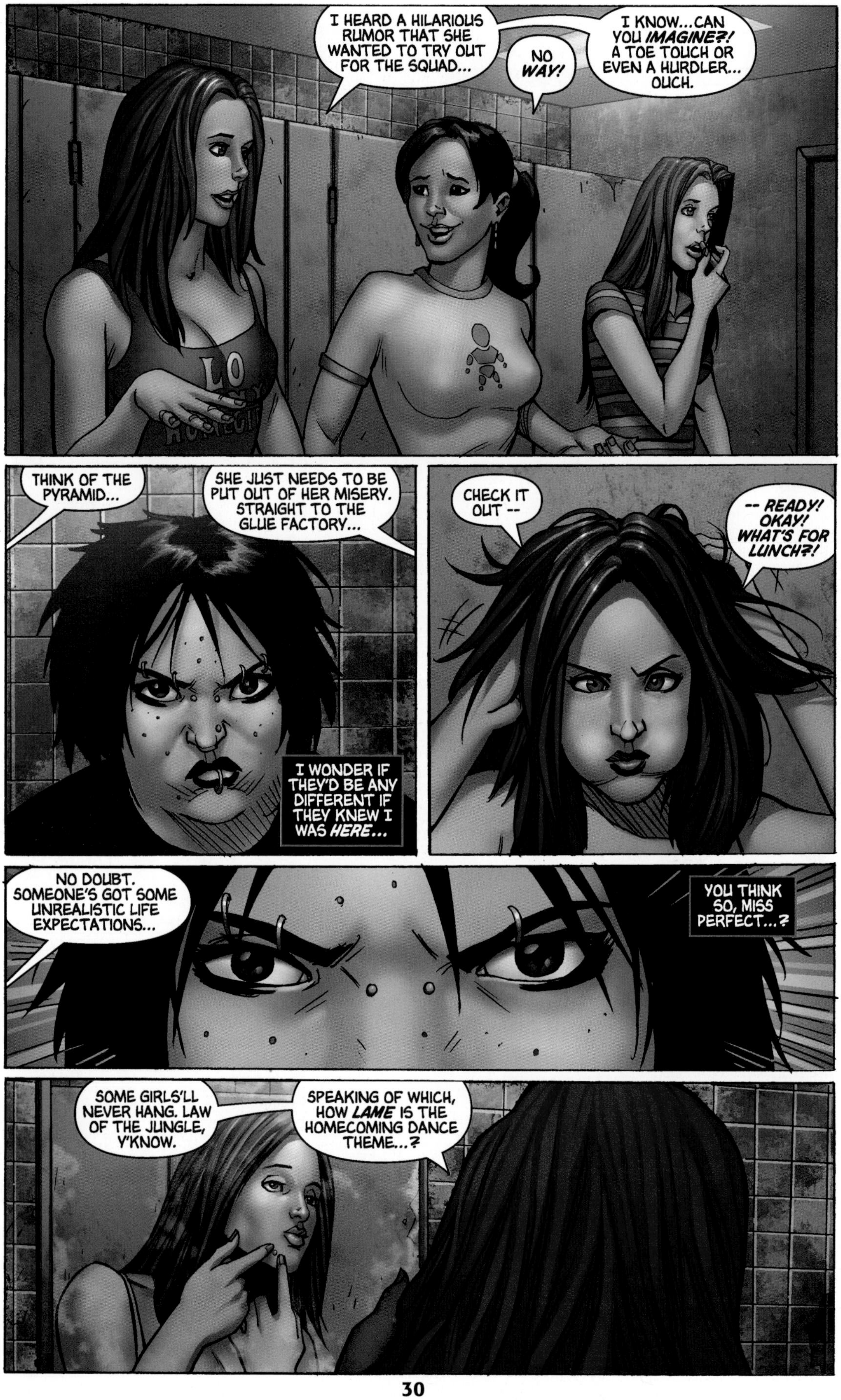
I HEARD A HILARIOUS RUMOR THAT SHE WANTED TO TRY OUT FOR THE SQUAD...
NO WAY!
I KNOW...CAN YOU IMAGINE?! A TOE TOUCH OR EVEN A HURDLER... OUCH.
THINK OF THE PYRAMID...
SHE JUST NEEDS TO BE PUT OUT OF HER MISERY. STRAIGHT TO THE GLUE FACTORY...
I WONDER IF THEY'D BE ANY DIFFERENT IF THEY KNEW I WAS HERE...
CHECK IT OUT --
-- READY! OKAY! WHAT'S FOR LUNCH?!
NO DOUBT. SOMEONE'S GOT SOME UNREALISTIC LIFE EXPECTATIONS...
YOU THINK SO, MISS PERFECT...?
SOME GIRLS'LL NEVER HANG. LAW OF THE JUNGLE, Y'KNOW.
SPEAKING OF WHICH, HOW LAME IS THE HOMECOMING DANCE THEME...?

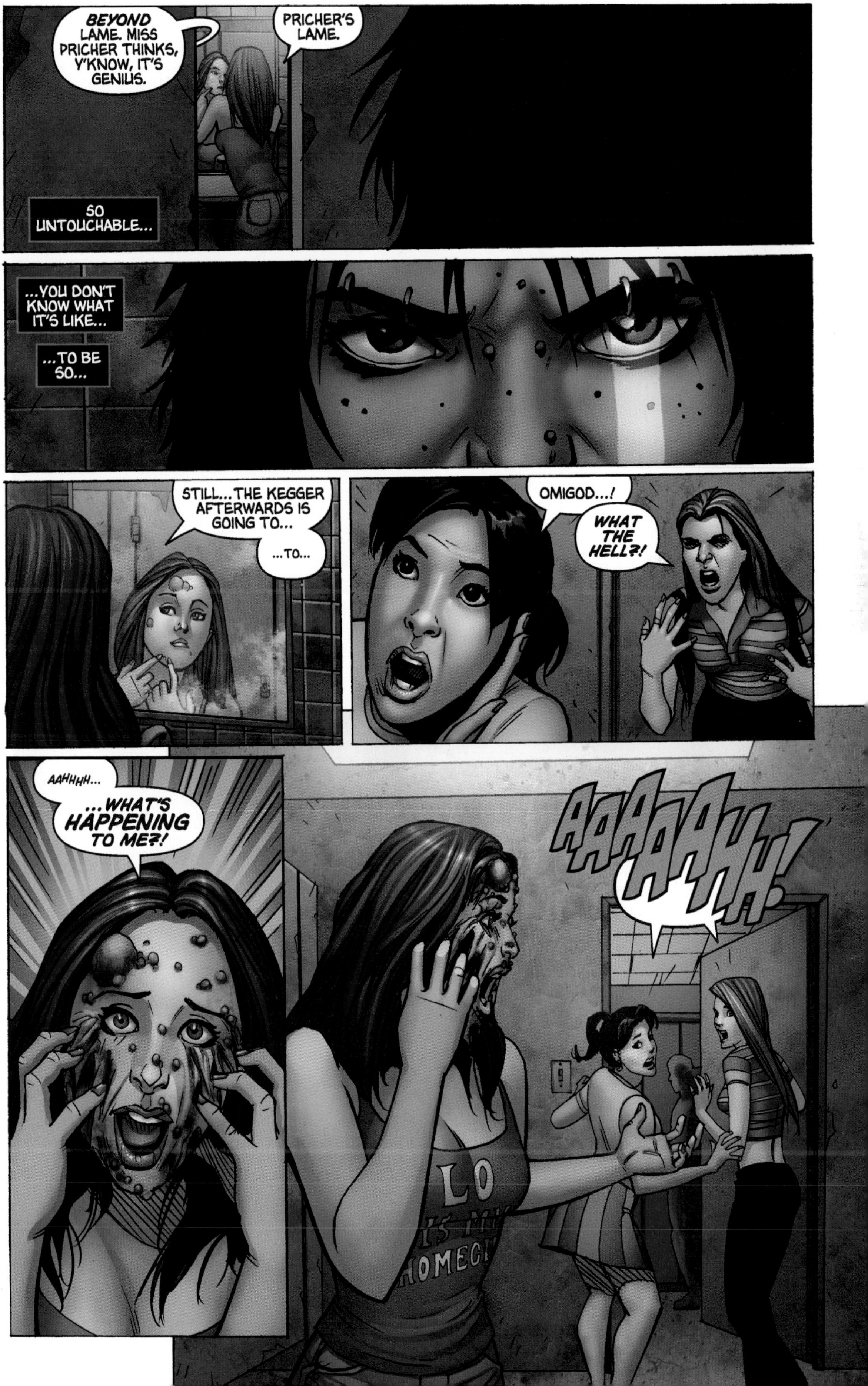
BEYOND LAME. MISS PRICHER THINKS, Y'KNOW, IT'S GENIUS.
PRICHER'S LAME.
SO UNTOUCHABLE...
...YOU DON'T KNOW WHAT IT'S LIKE...
...TO BE SO...
STILL...THE KEGGER AFTERWARDS IS GOING TO...
...TO...
OMIGOD...!
WHAT THE HELL?!
AAHHHH...
...WHAT'S HAPPENING TO ME?!
AAAAAHH!
LO

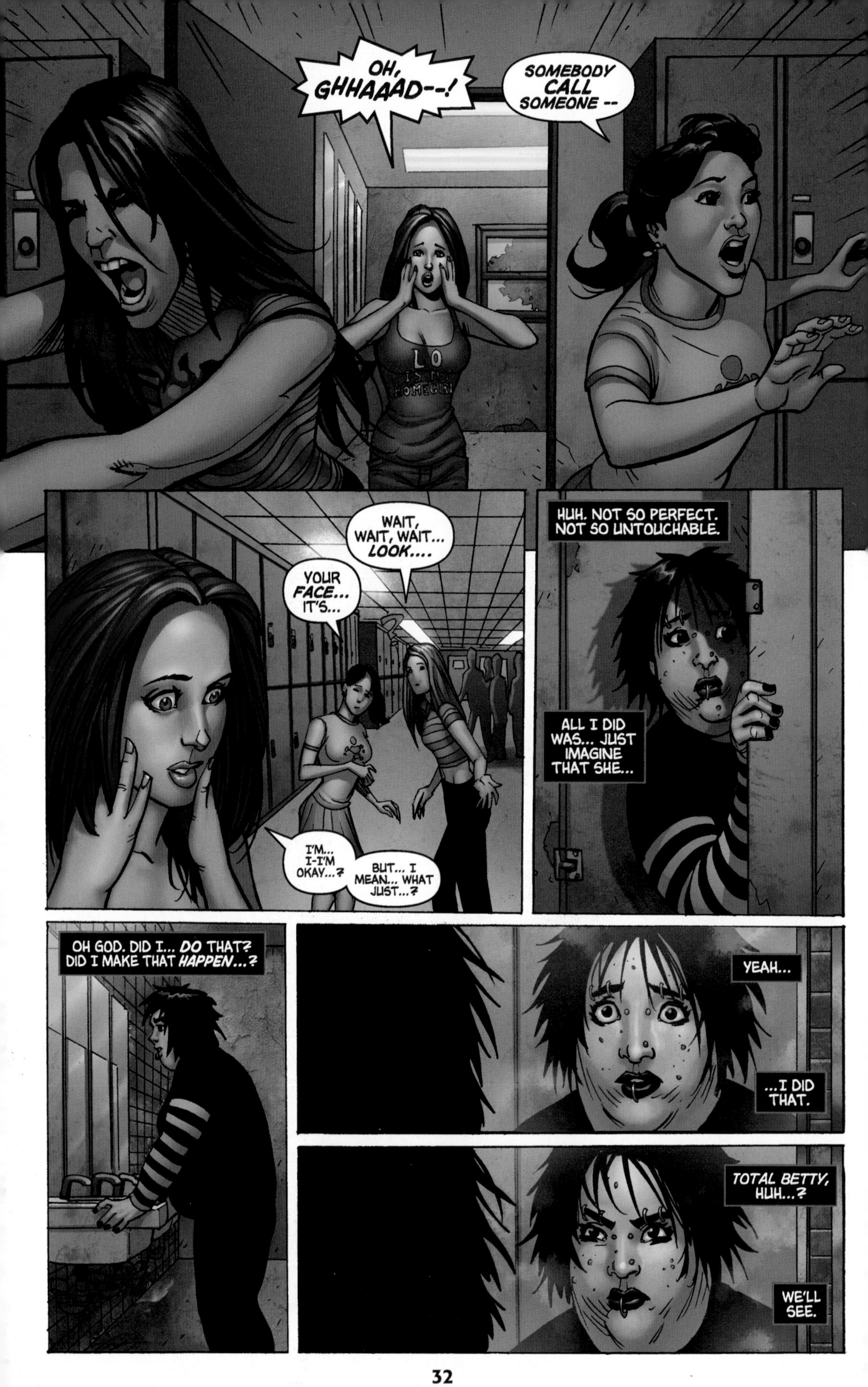
OH, GHHAAAD--!
SOMEBODY CALL SOMEONE --
WAIT, WAIT, WAIT... LOOK....
YOUR FACE... IT'S...
I'M... I-I'M OKAY...?
BUT... I MEAN... WHAT JUST...?
HUH. NOT SO PERFECT. NOT SO UNTOUCHABLE.
ALL I DID WAS... JUST IMAGINE THAT SHE...
OH GOD. DID I... DO THAT? DID I MAKE THAT HAPPEN...?
YEAH...
...I DID THAT.
TOTAL BETTY, HUH...?
WE'LL SEE.

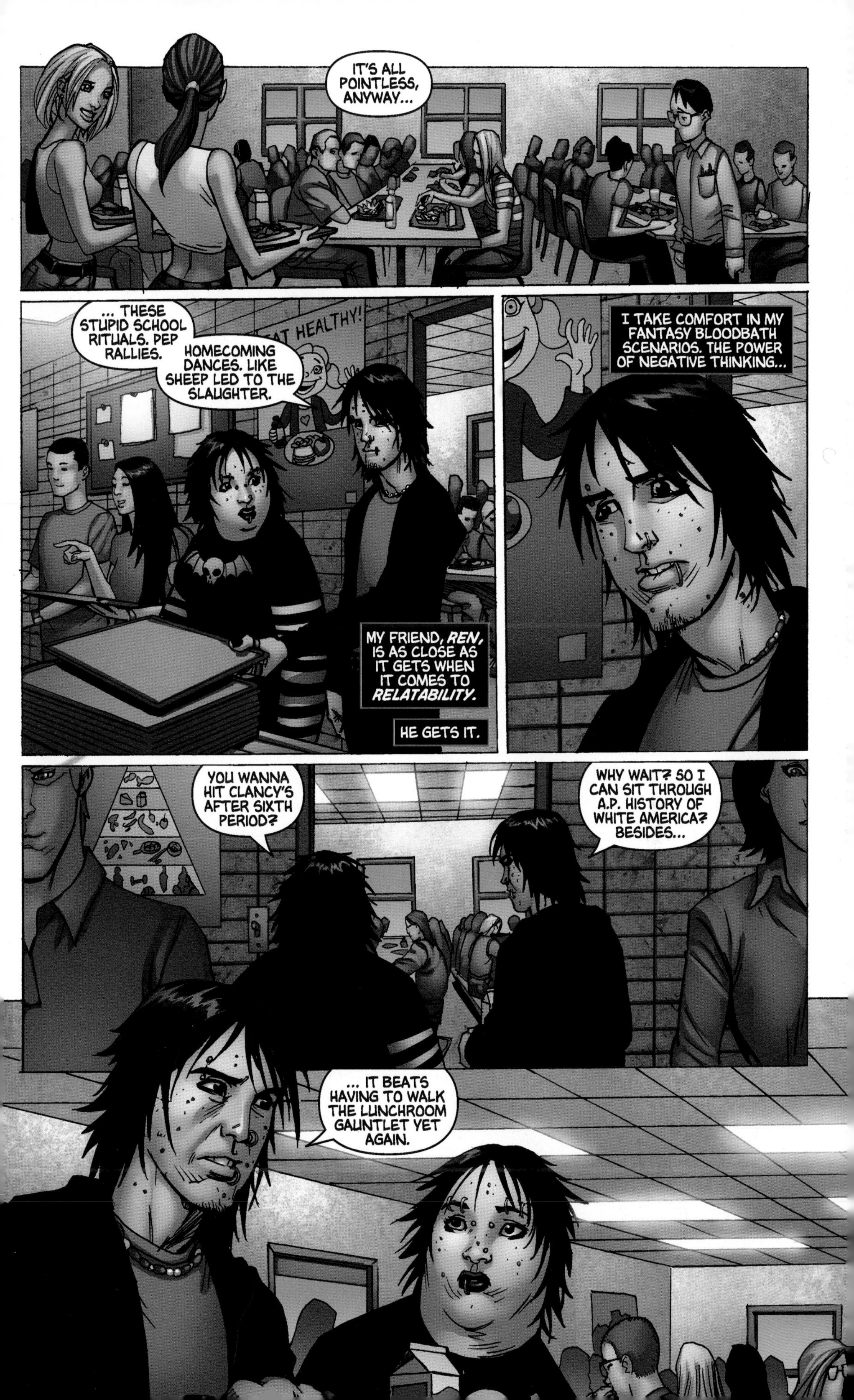
IT'S ALL POINTLESS, ANYWAY...
... THESE STUPID SCHOOL RITUALS. PEP RALLIES.
HOMECOMING DANCES. LIKE SHEEP LED TO THE SLAUGHTER.
EAT HEALTHY!
MY FRIEND, REN, IS AS CLOSE AS IT GETS WHEN IT COMES TO RELATABILITY.
HE GETS IT.
I TAKE COMFORT IN MY FANTASY BLOODBATH SCENARIOS. THE POWER OF NEGATIVE THINKING...
YOU WANNA HIT CLANCY'S AFTER SIXTH PERIOD?
WHY WAIT? SO I CAN SIT THROUGH A.P. HISTORY OF WHITE AMERICA? BESIDES...
... IT BEATS HAVING TO WALK THE LUNCHROOM GAUNTLET YET AGAIN.

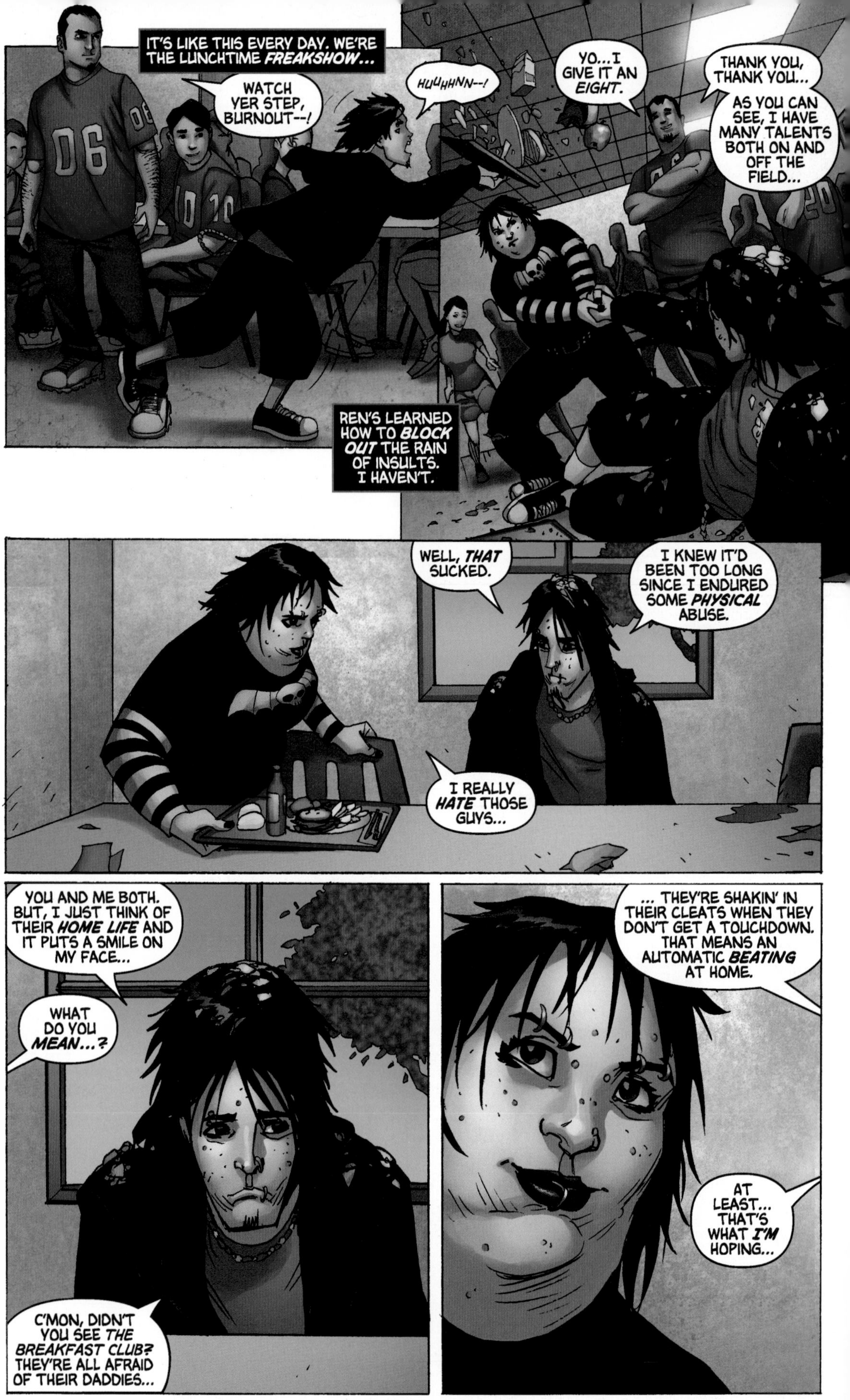
IT'S LIKE THIS EVERY DAY. WE'RE THE LUNCHTIME FREAKSHOW...
WATCH YER STEP, BURNOUT--!
HUUHHNN--!
YO...I GIVE IT AN EIGHT.
THANK YOU, THANK YOU...
AS YOU CAN SEE, I HAVE MANY TALENTS BOTH ON AND OFF THE FIELD...
REN'S LEARNED HOW TO BLOCK OUT THE RAIN OF INSULTS. I HAVEN'T.
WELL, THAT SUCKED.
I KNEW IT'D BEEN TOO LONG SINCE I ENDURED SOME PHYSICAL ABUSE.
I REALLY HATE THOSE GUYS...
YOU AND ME BOTH. BUT, I JUST THINK OF THEIR HOME LIFE AND IT PUTS A SMILE ON MY FACE...
WHAT DO YOU MEAN...?
C'MON, DIDN'T YOU SEE THE BREAKFAST CLUB? THEY'RE ALL AFRAID OF THEIR DADDIES...
... THEY'RE SHAKIN' IN THEIR CLEATS WHEN THEY DON'T GET A TOUCHDOWN. THAT MEANS AN AUTOMATIC BEATING AT HOME.
AT LEAST... THAT'S WHAT I'M HOPING...

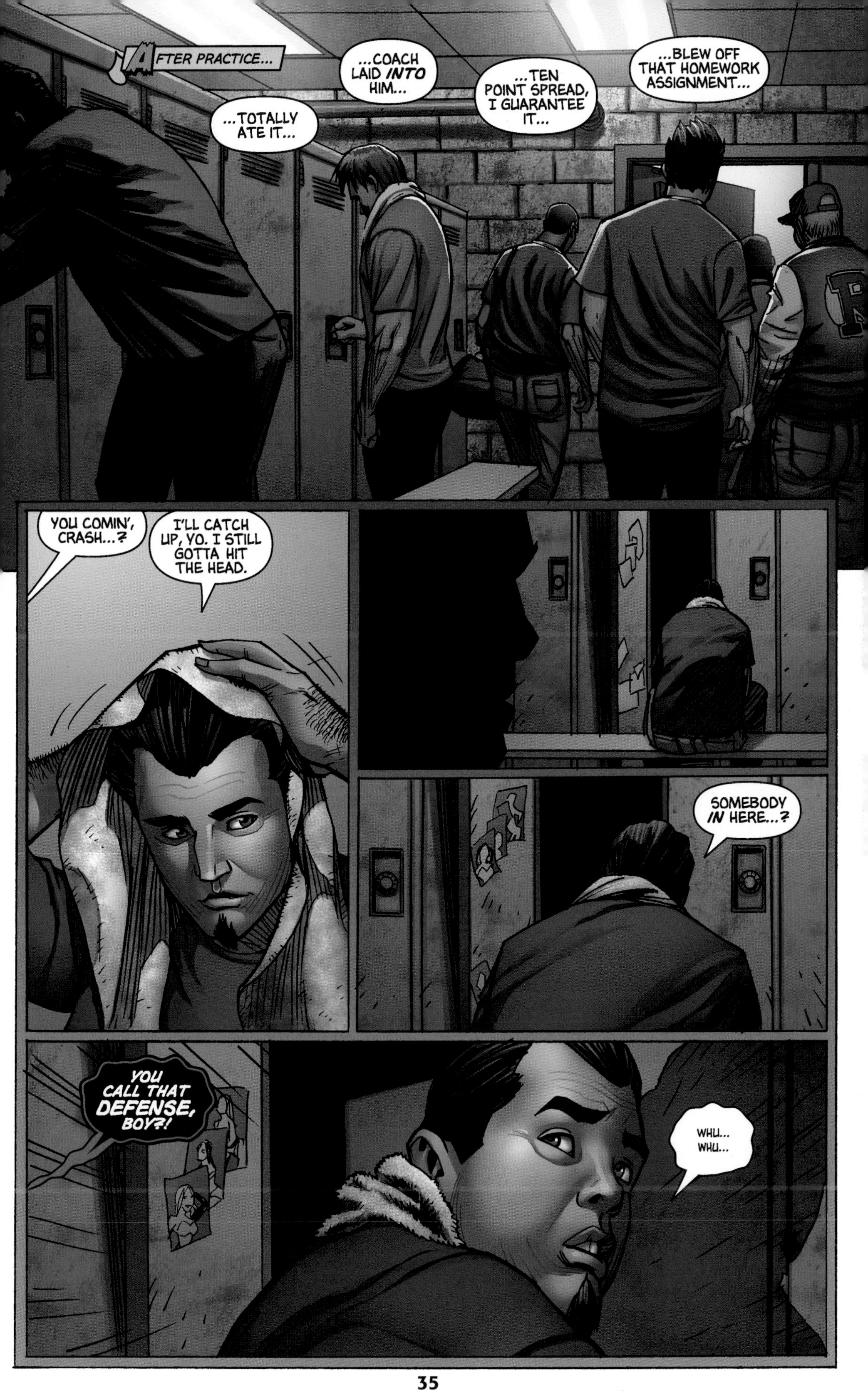
AFTER PRACTICE...
...TOTALLY ATE IT...
...COACH LAID *INTO* HIM...
...TEN POINT SPREAD, I GUARANTEE IT...
...BLEW OFF THAT HOMEWORK ASSIGNMENT...
YOU COMIN', CRASH...?
I'LL CATCH UP, YO. I STILL GOTTA HIT THE HEAD.
SOMEBODY *IN* HERE...?
YOU CALL THAT DEFENSE, BOY?!
WHU... WHU...

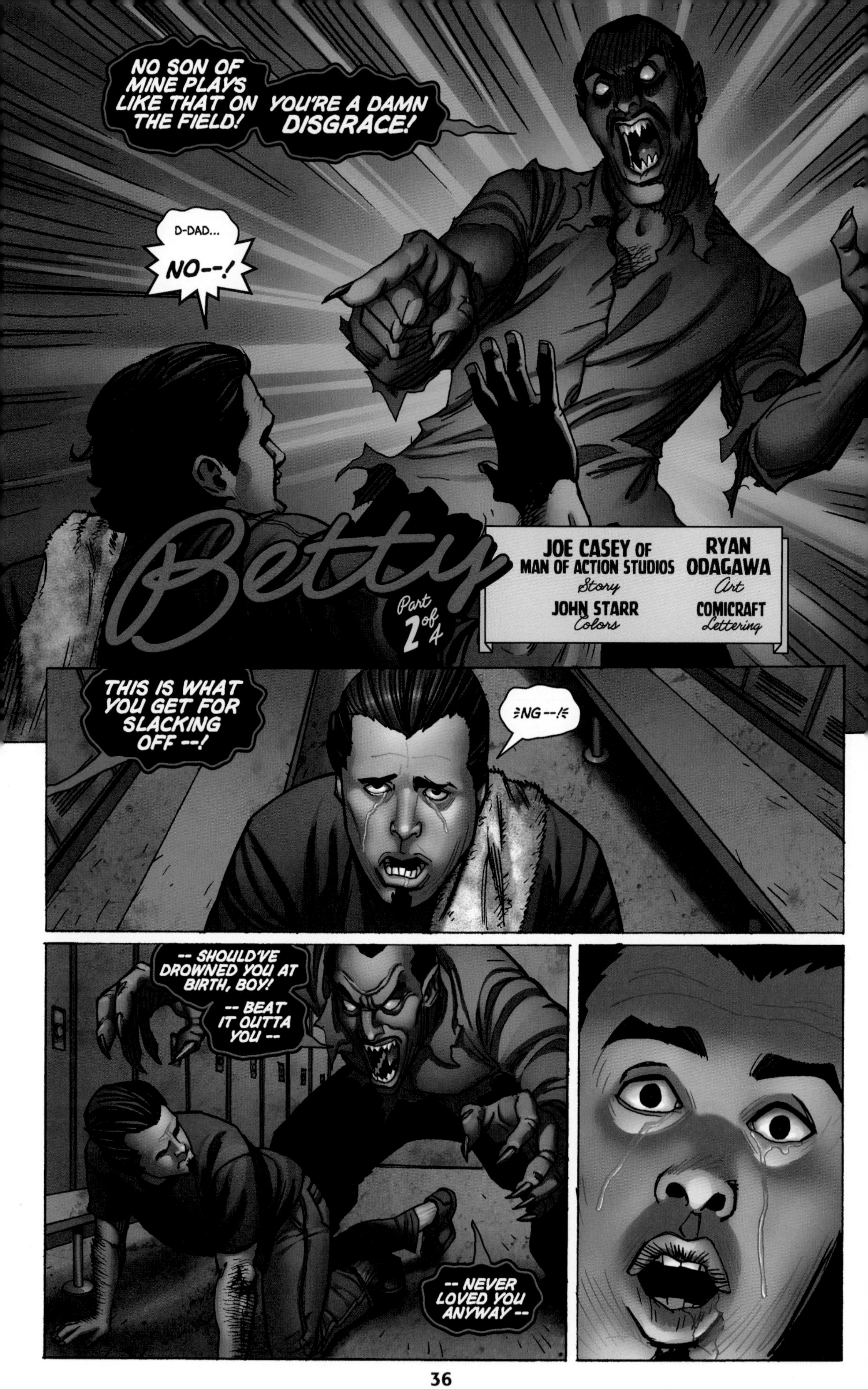

NO SON OF MINE PLAYS LIKE THAT ON THE FIELD!
YOU'RE A DAMN DISGRACE!
D-DAD... NO--!
Betty
Part 2 of 4
JOE CASEY OF MAN OF ACTION STUDIOS Story
RYAN ODAGAWA Art
JOHN STARR Colors
COMICRAFT Lettering
THIS IS WHAT YOU GET FOR SLACKING OFF --!
NG--!
-- SHOULD'VE DROWNED YOU AT BIRTH, BOY!
-- BEAT IT OUTTA YOU --
-- NEVER LOVED YOU ANYWAY --

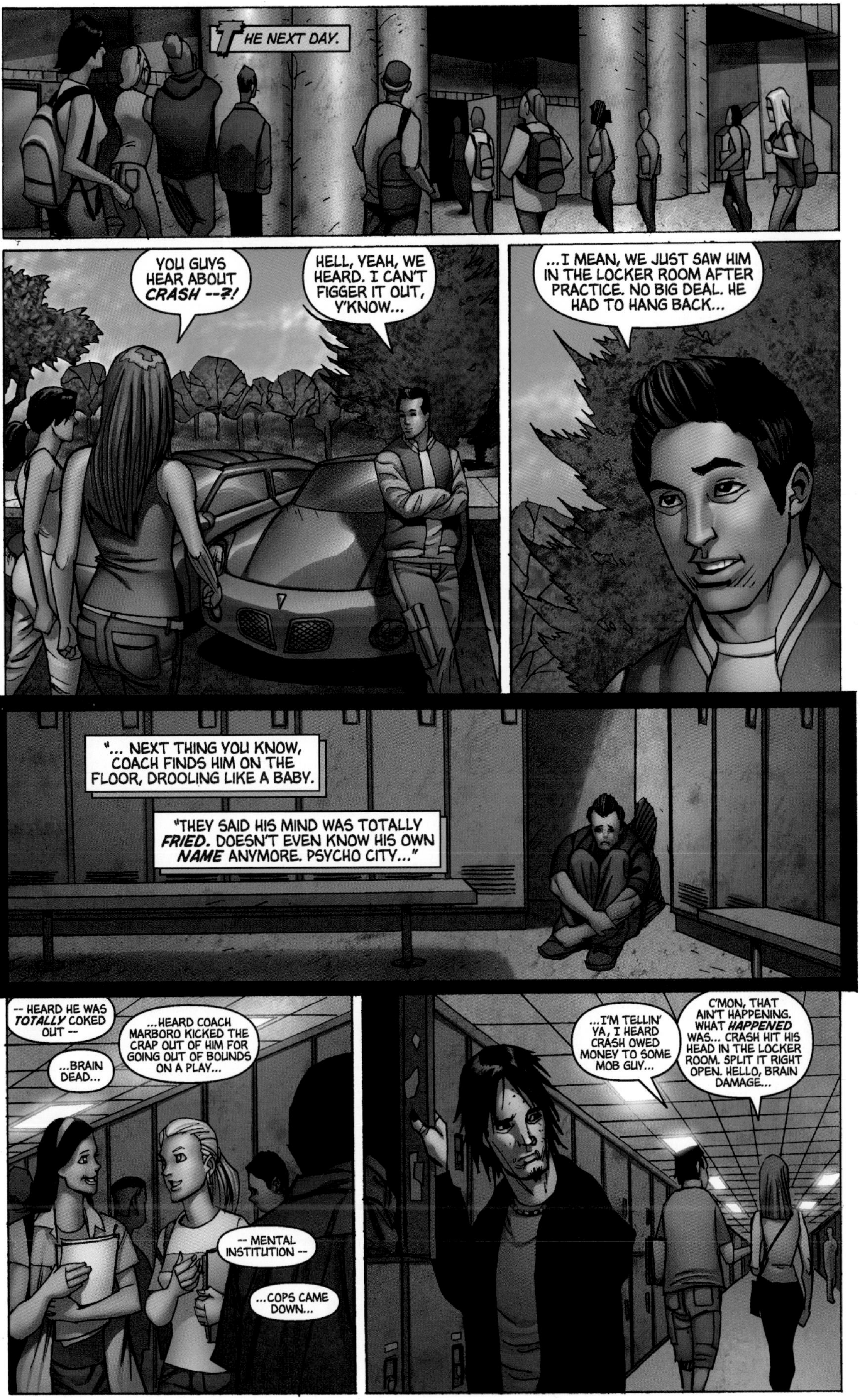
THE NEXT DAY.
YOU GUYS HEAR ABOUT CRASH --?!
HELL, YEAH, WE HEARD. I CAN'T FIGGER IT OUT, Y'KNOW...
...I MEAN, WE JUST SAW HIM IN THE LOCKER ROOM AFTER PRACTICE. NO BIG DEAL. HE HAD TO HANG BACK...
"... NEXT THING YOU KNOW, COACH FINDS HIM ON THE FLOOR, DROOLING LIKE A BABY.
"THEY SAID HIS MIND WAS TOTALLY FRIED. DOESN'T EVEN KNOW HIS OWN NAME ANYMORE. PSYCHO CITY..."
-- HEARD HE WAS TOTALLY COKED OUT --
...BRAIN DEAD...
...HEARD COACH MARBORO KICKED THE CRAP OUT OF HIM FOR GOING OUT OF BOUNDS ON A PLAY...
-- MENTAL INSTITUTION --
...COPS CAME DOWN...
...I'M TELLIN' YA, I HEARD CRASH OWED MONEY TO SOME MOB GUY...
C'MON, THAT AIN'T HAPPENING. WHAT HAPPENED WAS... CRASH HIT HIS HEAD IN THE LOCKER ROOM. SPLIT IT RIGHT OPEN. HELLO, BRAIN DAMAGE...

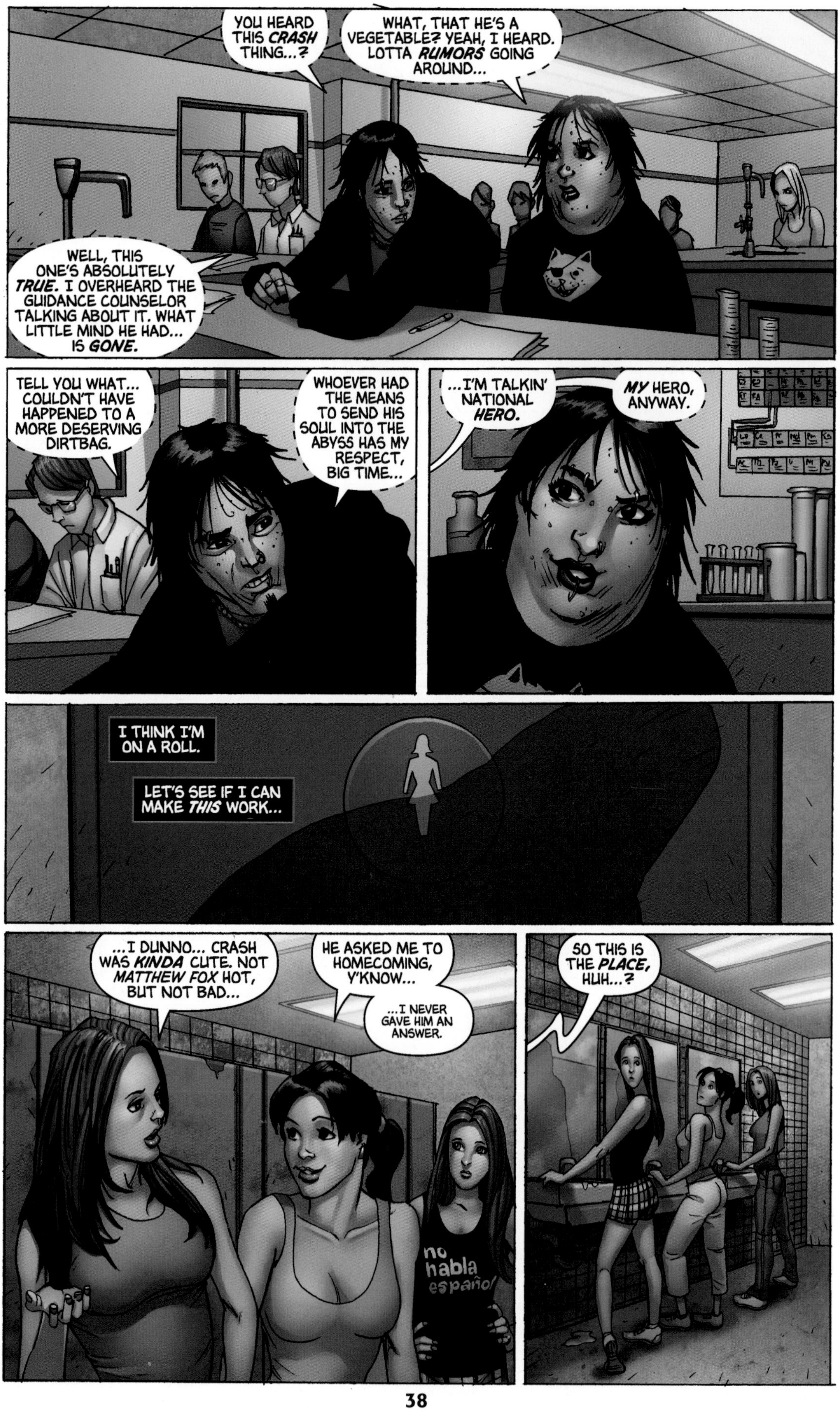
YOU HEARD THIS CRASH THING...?
WHAT, THAT HE'S A VEGETABLE? YEAH, I HEARD. LOTTA RUMORS GOING AROUND...
WELL, THIS ONE'S ABSOLUTELY TRUE. I OVERHEARD THE GUIDANCE COUNSELOR TALKING ABOUT IT. WHAT LITTLE MIND HE HAD... IS GONE.
TELL YOU WHAT... COULDN'T HAVE HAPPENED TO A MORE DESERVING DIRTBAG.
WHOEVER HAD THE MEANS TO SEND HIS SOUL INTO THE ABYSS HAS MY RESPECT, BIG TIME...
...I'M TALKIN' NATIONAL HERO.
MY HERO, ANYWAY.
I THINK I'M ON A ROLL.
LET'S SEE IF I CAN MAKE THIS WORK...
...I DUNNO... CRASH WAS KINDA CUTE. NOT MATTHEW FOX HOT, BUT NOT BAD...
HE ASKED ME TO HOMECOMING, Y'KNOW...
...I NEVER GAVE HIM AN ANSWER.
no habla español
SO THIS IS THE PLACE, HUH...?

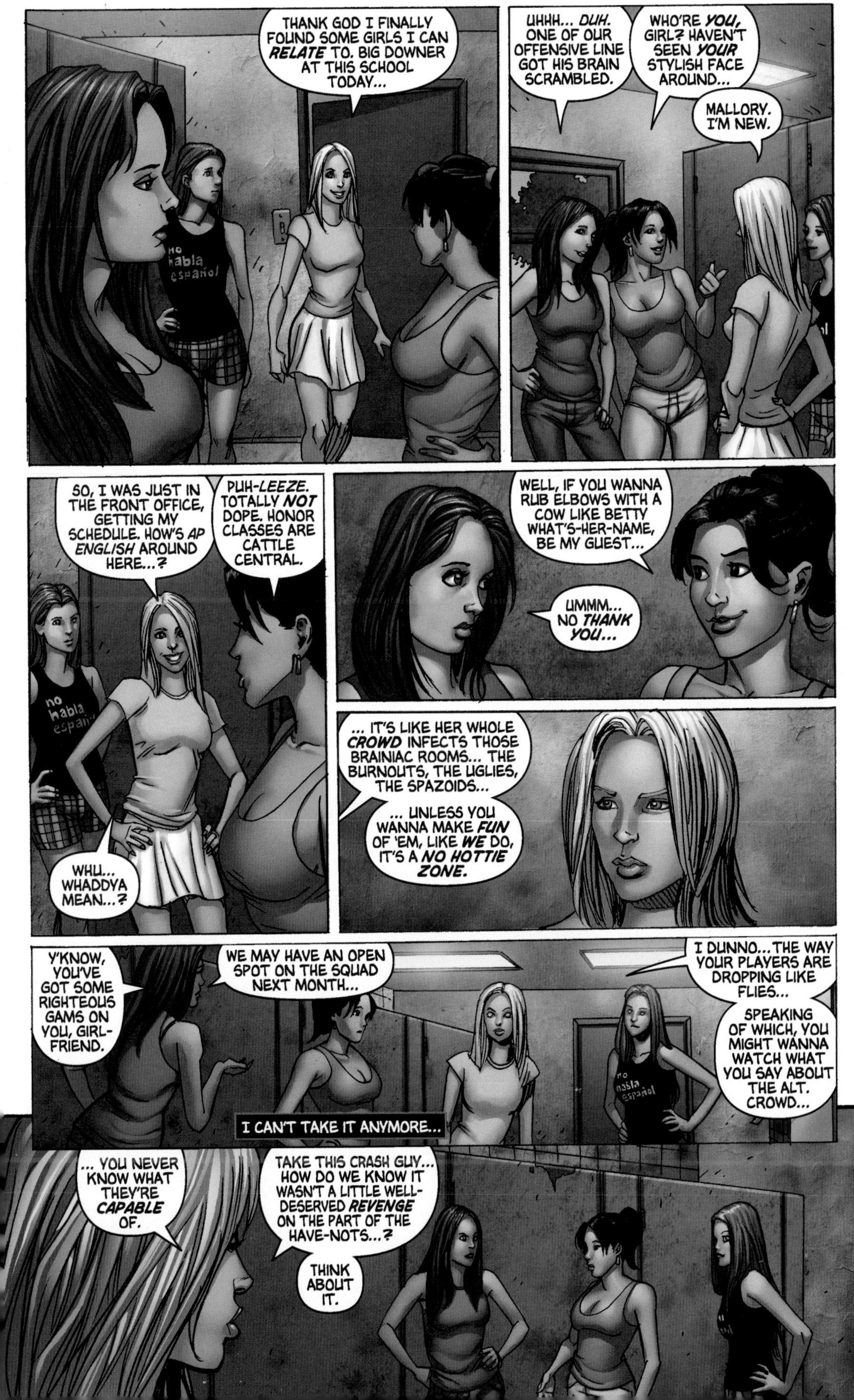
THANK GOD I FINALLY FOUND SOME GIRLS I CAN RELATE TO. BIG DOWNER AT THIS SCHOOL TODAY...
no habla español
UHHH... DUH. ONE OF OUR OFFENSIVE LINE GOT HIS BRAIN SCRAMBLED.
WHO'RE YOU, GIRL? HAVEN'T SEEN YOUR STYLISH FACE AROUND...
MALLORY. I'M NEW.
SO, I WAS JUST IN THE FRONT OFFICE, GETTING MY SCHEDULE. HOW'S AP ENGLISH AROUND HERE...?
PUH-LEEZE. TOTALLY NOT DOPE. HONOR CLASSES ARE CATTLE CENTRAL.
WHU... WHADDYA MEAN...?
WELL, IF YOU WANNA RUB ELBOWS WITH A COW LIKE BETTY WHAT'S-HER-NAME, BE MY GUEST...
UMMM... NO THANK YOU...
... IT'S LIKE HER WHOLE CROWD INFECTS THOSE BRAINIAC ROOMS... THE BURNOUTS, THE UGLIES, THE SPAZOIDS...
... UNLESS YOU WANNA MAKE FUN OF 'EM, LIKE WE DO, IT'S A NO HOTTIE ZONE.
Y'KNOW, YOU'VE GOT SOME RIGHTEOUS GAMS ON YOU, GIRL-FRIEND.
WE MAY HAVE AN OPEN SPOT ON THE SQUAD NEXT MONTH...
I DUNNO... THE WAY YOUR PLAYERS ARE DROPPING LIKE FLIES...
SPEAKING OF WHICH, YOU MIGHT WANNA WATCH WHAT YOU SAY ABOUT THE ALT. CROWD...
I CAN'T TAKE IT ANYMORE...
... YOU NEVER KNOW WHAT THEY'RE CAPABLE OF.
TAKE THIS CRASH GUY... HOW DO WE KNOW IT WASN'T A LITTLE WELL-DESERVED REVENGE ON THE PART OF THE HAVE-NOTS...?
THINK ABOUT IT.

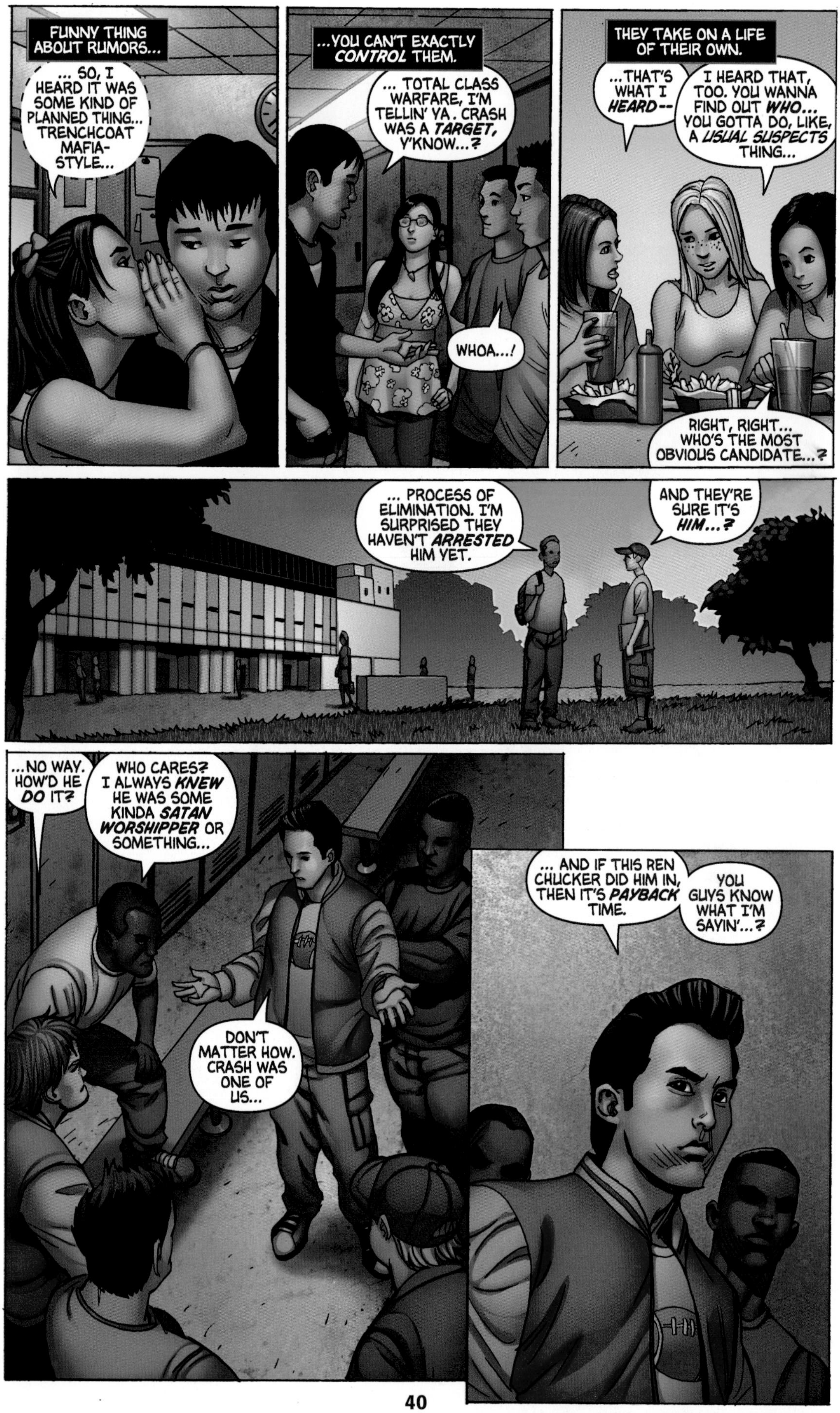
FUNNY THING ABOUT RUMORS...
... SO, I HEARD IT WAS SOME KIND OF PLANNED THING... TRENCHCOAT MAFIA-STYLE...
...YOU CAN'T EXACTLY CONTROL THEM.
... TOTAL CLASS WARFARE, I'M TELLIN' YA. CRASH WAS A TARGET, Y'KNOW...?
WHOA...!
THEY TAKE ON A LIFE OF THEIR OWN.
...THAT'S WHAT I HEARD--
I HEARD THAT, TOO. YOU WANNA FIND OUT WHO... YOU GOTTA DO, LIKE, A USUAL SUSPECTS THING...
RIGHT, RIGHT... WHO'S THE MOST OBVIOUS CANDIDATE...?
... PROCESS OF ELIMINATION. I'M SURPRISED THEY HAVEN'T ARRESTED HIM YET.
AND THEY'RE SURE IT'S HIM...?
...NO WAY. HOW'D HE DO IT?
WHO CARES? I ALWAYS KNEW HE WAS SOME KINDA SATAN WORSHIPPER OR SOMETHING...
DON'T MATTER HOW. CRASH WAS ONE OF US...
... AND IF THIS REN CHUCKER DID HIM IN, THEN IT'S PAYBACK TIME.
YOU GUYS KNOW WHAT I'M SAYIN'...?

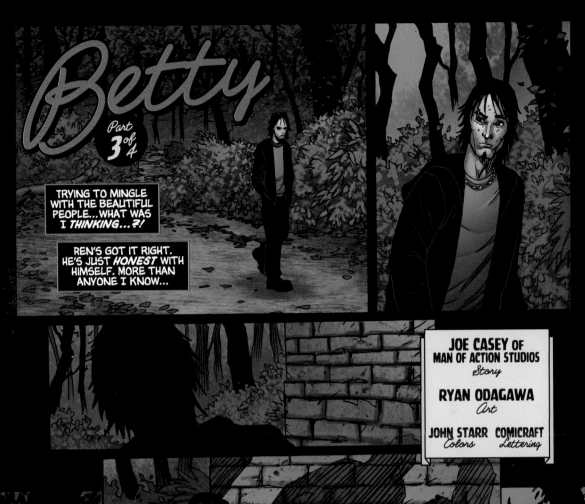

# Betty

TRYING TO MINGLE WITH THE BEAUTIFUL PEOPLE...WHAT WAS I *THINKING...?!*

REN'S GOT IT RIGHT. HE'S JUST *HONEST* WITH HIMSELF. MORE THAN ANYONE I KNOW...

**JOE CASEY** OF
**MAN OF ACTION STUDIOS**
*Story*

**RYAN ODAGAWA**
*Art*

**JOHN STARR**      **COMICRAFT**
*Colors*         *Lettering*

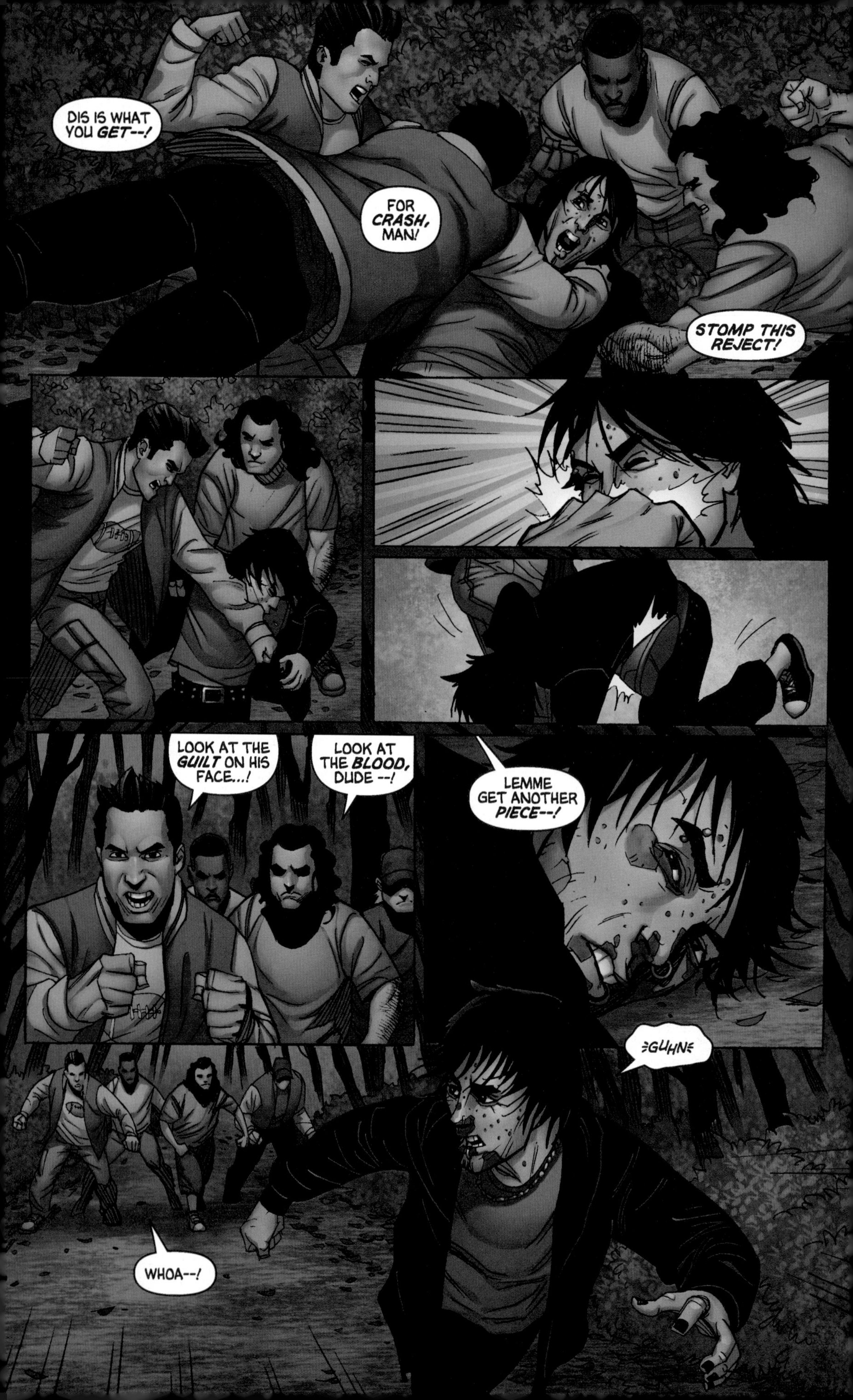
DIS IS WHAT YOU GET--!
FOR CRASH, MAN!
STOMP THIS REJECT!
LOOK AT THE GUILT ON HIS FACE...!
LOOK AT THE BLOOD, DUDE --!
LEMME GET ANOTHER PIECE--!
GUHN
WHOA--!

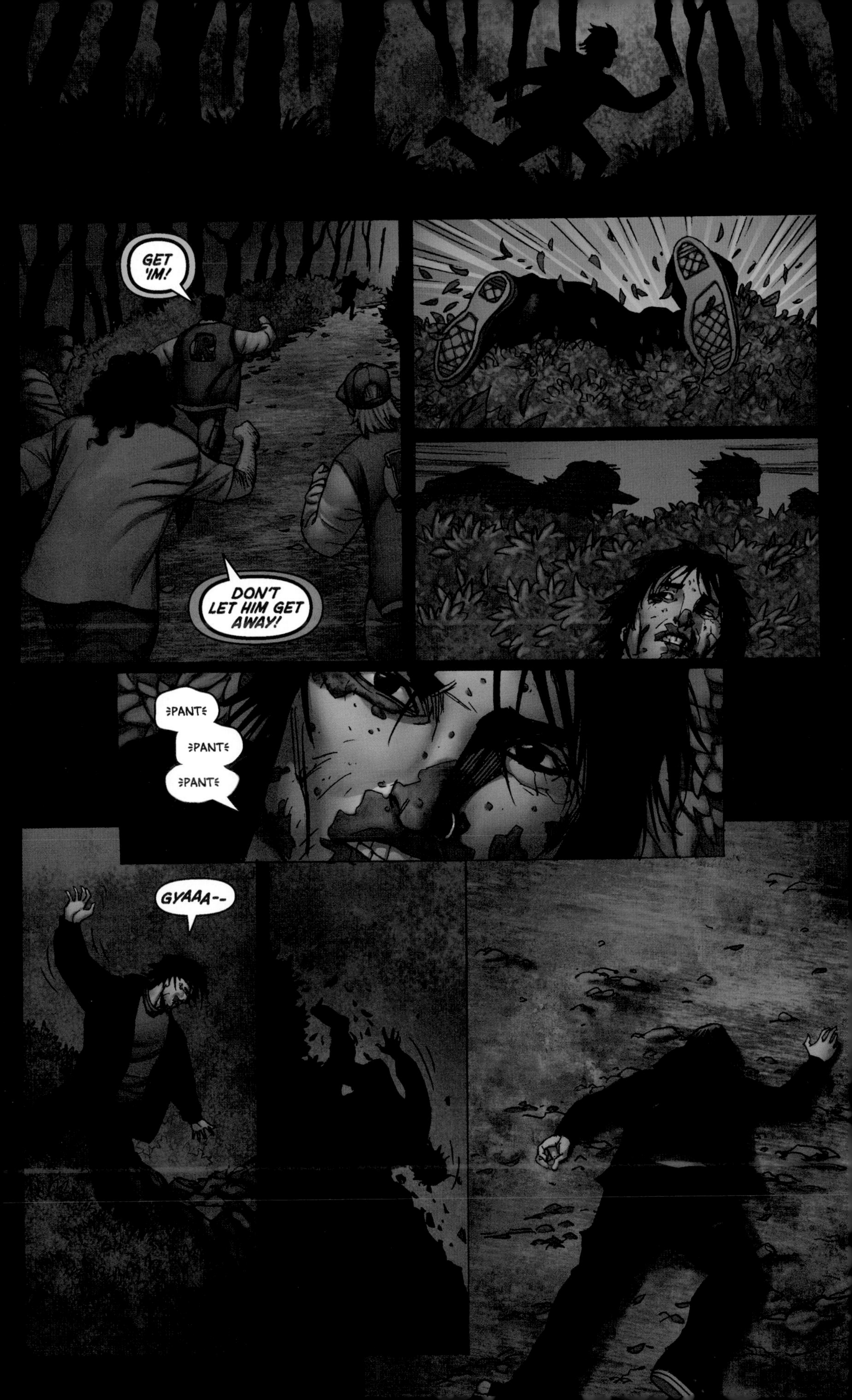
GET 'IM!
DON'T LET HIM GET AWAY!
PANT
PANT
PANT
GYAAA--

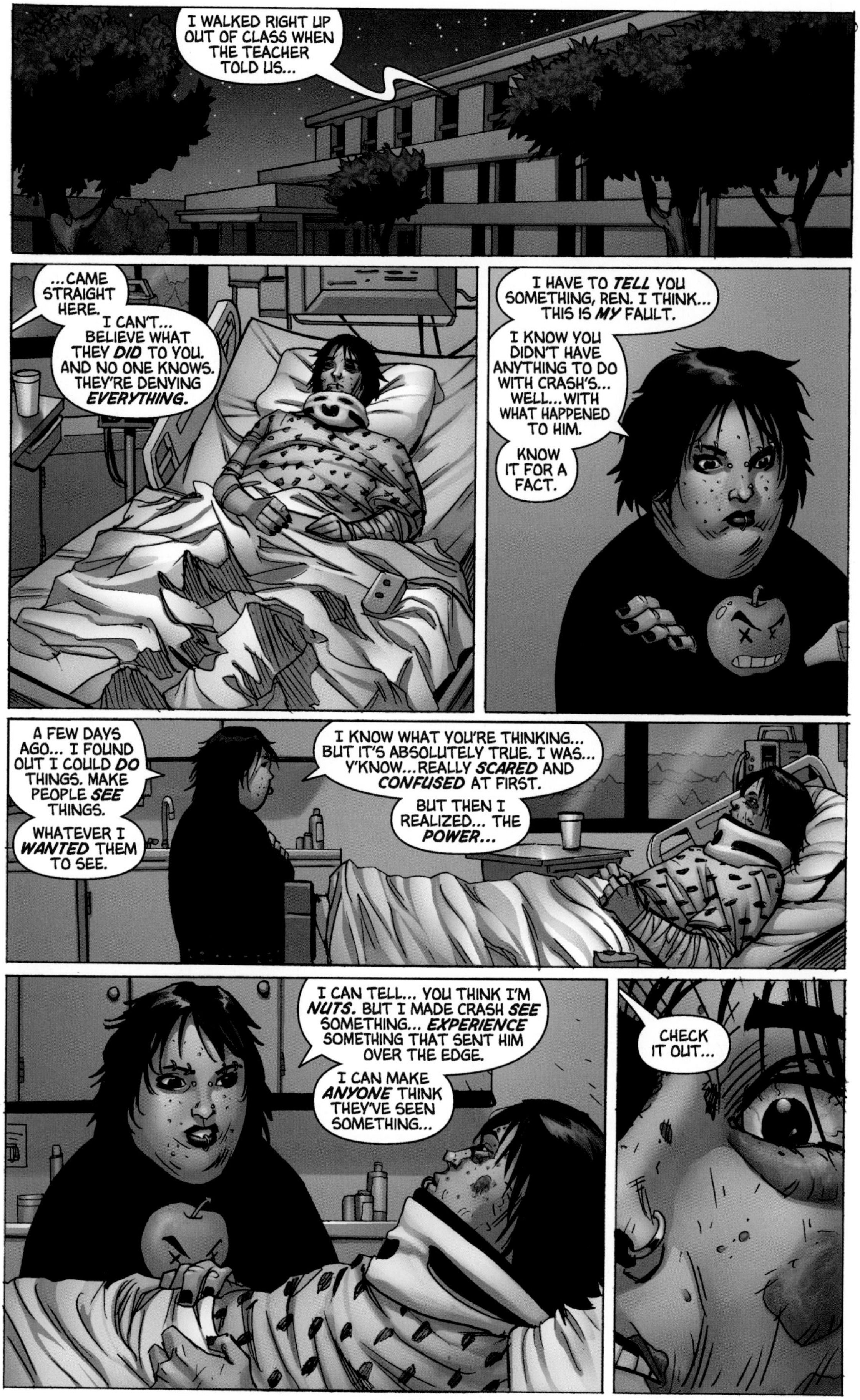
I WALKED RIGHT UP OUT OF CLASS WHEN THE TEACHER TOLD US...
...CAME STRAIGHT HERE. I CAN'T... BELIEVE WHAT THEY *DID* TO YOU. AND NO ONE KNOWS. THEY'RE DENYING ***EVERYTHING.***
I HAVE TO ***TELL*** YOU SOMETHING, REN. I THINK... THIS IS ***MY*** FAULT.
I KNOW YOU DIDN'T HAVE ANYTHING TO DO WITH CRASH'S... WELL...WITH WHAT HAPPENED TO HIM.
KNOW IT FOR A FACT.
A FEW DAYS AGO... I FOUND OUT I COULD ***DO*** THINGS. MAKE PEOPLE ***SEE*** THINGS.
WHATEVER I ***WANTED*** THEM TO SEE.
I KNOW WHAT YOU'RE THINKING... BUT IT'S ABSOLUTELY TRUE. I WAS... Y'KNOW...REALLY ***SCARED*** AND ***CONFUSED*** AT FIRST.
BUT THEN I REALIZED... THE ***POWER...***
I CAN TELL... YOU THINK I'M ***NUTS.*** BUT I MADE CRASH ***SEE*** SOMETHING... ***EXPERIENCE*** SOMETHING THAT SENT HIM OVER THE EDGE.
I CAN MAKE ***ANYONE*** THINK THEY'VE SEEN SOMETHING...
CHECK IT OUT...

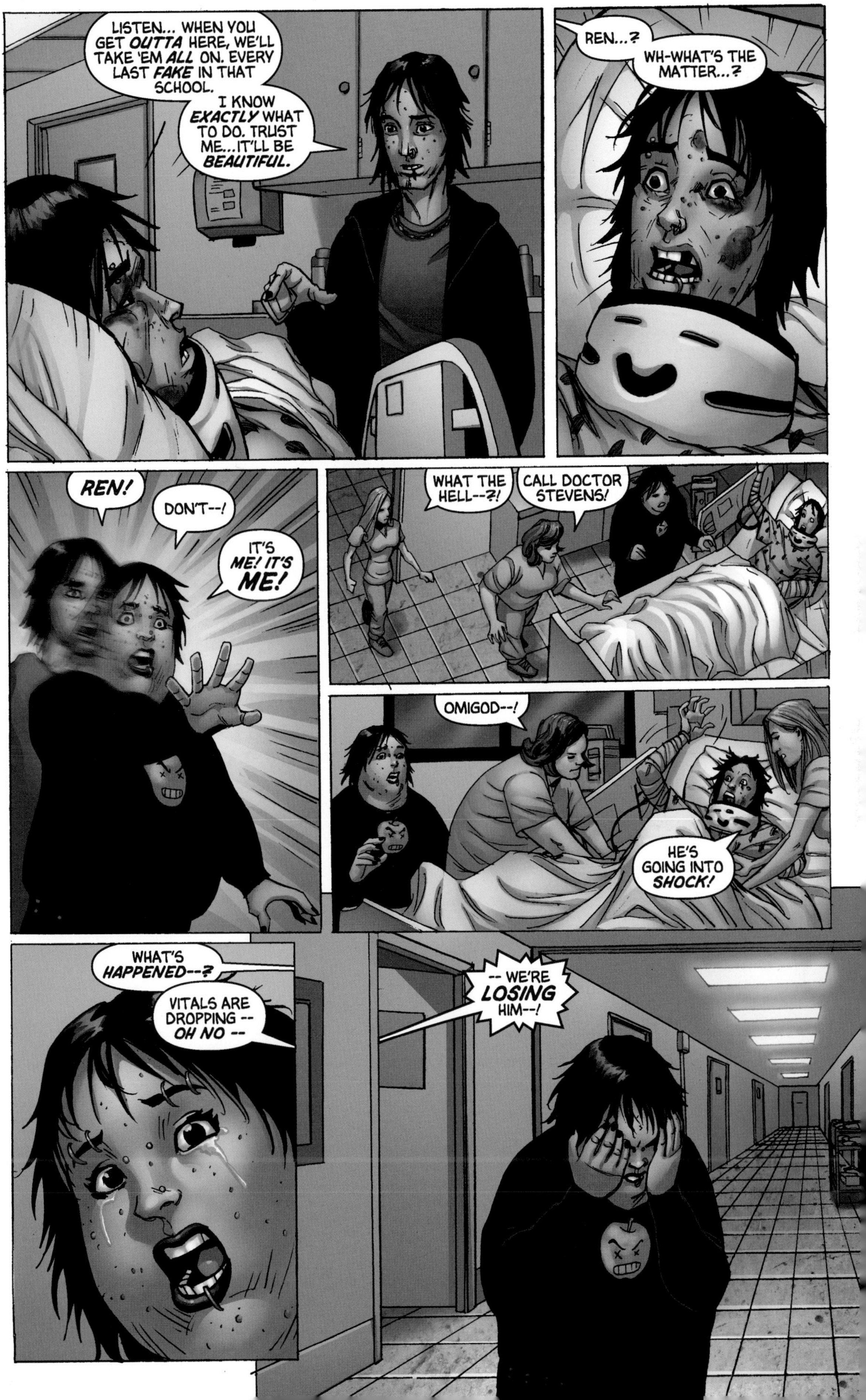
LISTEN... WHEN YOU GET OUTTA HERE, WE'LL TAKE 'EM ALL ON. EVERY LAST FAKE IN THAT SCHOOL.
I KNOW EXACTLY WHAT TO DO. TRUST ME...IT'LL BE BEAUTIFUL.
REN...?
WH-WHAT'S THE MATTER...?
REN!
DON'T--!
IT'S ME! IT'S ME!
WHAT THE HELL--?!
CALL DOCTOR STEVENS!
OMIGOD--!
HE'S GOING INTO SHOCK!
WHAT'S HAPPENED--?
VITALS ARE DROPPING -- OH NO --
-- WE'RE LOSING HIM--!

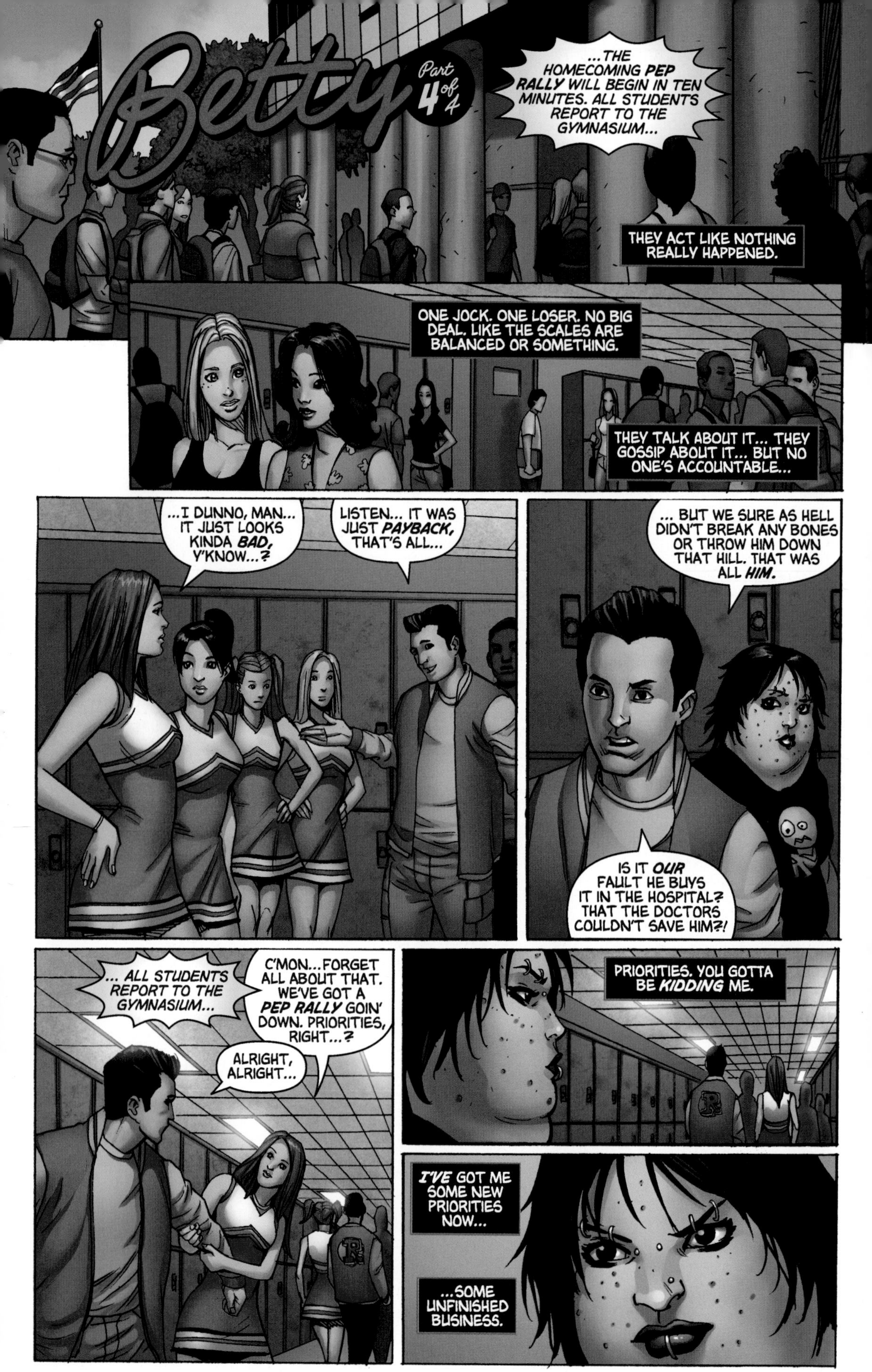
Betty Part 4 of 4
...THE HOMECOMING PEP RALLY WILL BEGIN IN TEN MINUTES. ALL STUDENTS REPORT TO THE GYMNASIUM...
THEY ACT LIKE NOTHING REALLY HAPPENED.
ONE JOCK. ONE LOSER. NO BIG DEAL. LIKE THE SCALES ARE BALANCED OR SOMETHING.
THEY TALK ABOUT IT... THEY GOSSIP ABOUT IT... BUT NO ONE'S ACCOUNTABLE...
...I DUNNO, MAN... IT JUST LOOKS KINDA BAD, Y'KNOW...?
LISTEN... IT WAS JUST PAYBACK, THAT'S ALL...
... BUT WE SURE AS HELL DIDN'T BREAK ANY BONES OR THROW HIM DOWN THAT HILL. THAT WAS ALL HIM.
IS IT OUR FAULT HE BUYS IT IN THE HOSPITAL? THAT THE DOCTORS COULDN'T SAVE HIM?!
... ALL STUDENTS REPORT TO THE GYMNASIUM...
C'MON...FORGET ALL ABOUT THAT. WE'VE GOT A PEP RALLY GOIN' DOWN. PRIORITIES, RIGHT...?
ALRIGHT, ALRIGHT...
PRIORITIES. YOU GOTTA BE KIDDING ME.
I'VE GOT ME SOME NEW PRIORITIES NOW...
...SOME UNFINISHED BUSINESS.

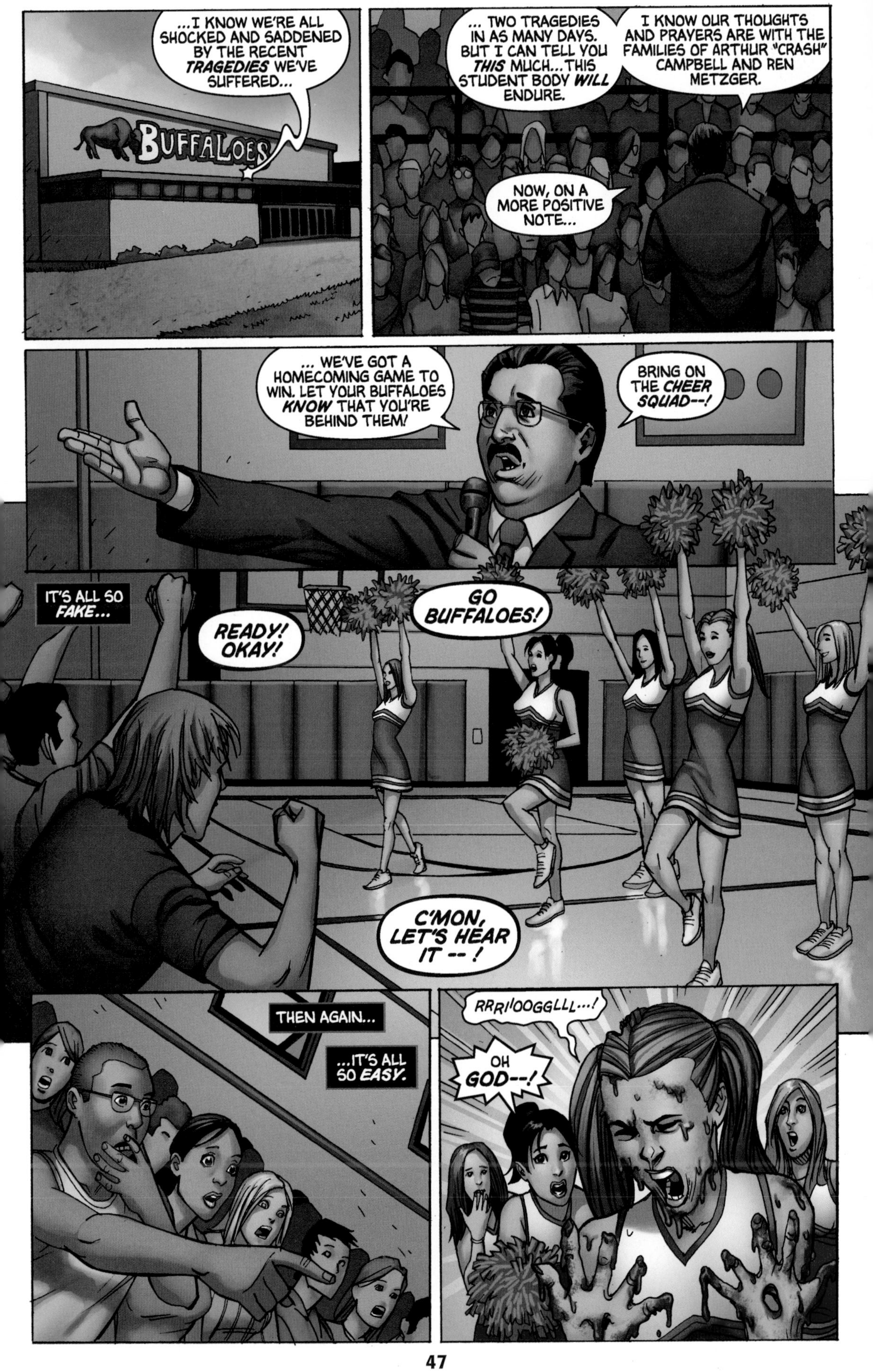

...I KNOW WE'RE ALL SHOCKED AND SADDENED BY THE RECENT TRAGEDIES WE'VE SUFFERED...
BUFFALOES
... TWO TRAGEDIES IN AS MANY DAYS. BUT I CAN TELL YOU THIS MUCH...THIS STUDENT BODY WILL ENDURE.
I KNOW OUR THOUGHTS AND PRAYERS ARE WITH THE FAMILIES OF ARTHUR "CRASH" CAMPBELL AND REN METZGER.
NOW, ON A MORE POSITIVE NOTE...
... WE'VE GOT A HOMECOMING GAME TO WIN. LET YOUR BUFFALOES KNOW THAT YOU'RE BEHIND THEM!
BRING ON THE CHEER SQUAD--!
IT'S ALL SO FAKE...
READY! OKAY!
GO BUFFALOES!
C'MON, LET'S HEAR IT -- !
THEN AGAIN...
...IT'S ALL SO EASY.
RRRI!OOGGLLL...!
OH GOD--!

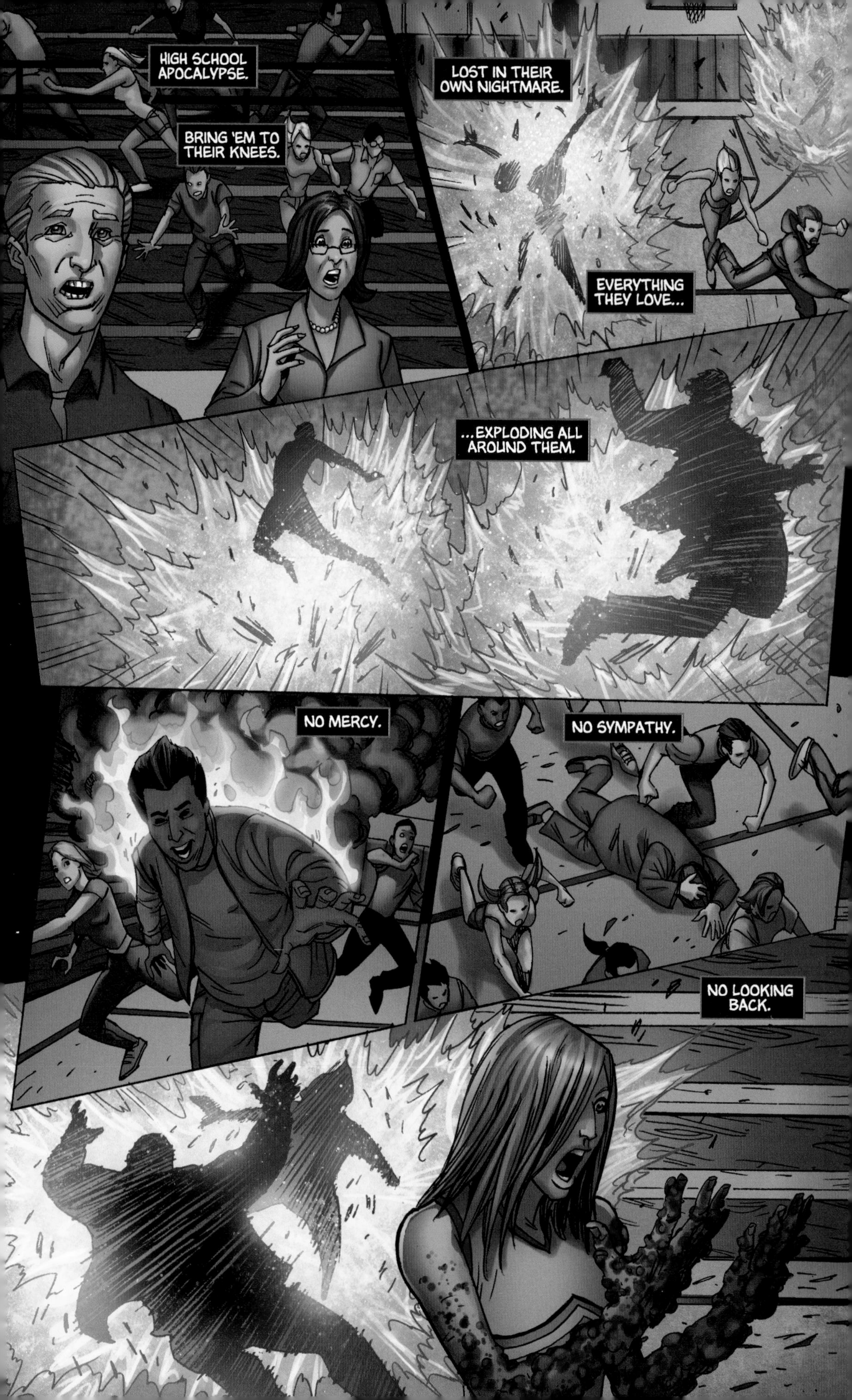
HIGH SCHOOL APOCALYPSE.
BRING 'EM TO THEIR KNEES.
LOST IN THEIR OWN NIGHTMARE.
EVERYTHING THEY LOVE...
...EXPLODING ALL AROUND THEM.
NO MERCY.
NO SYMPATHY.
NO LOOKING BACK.

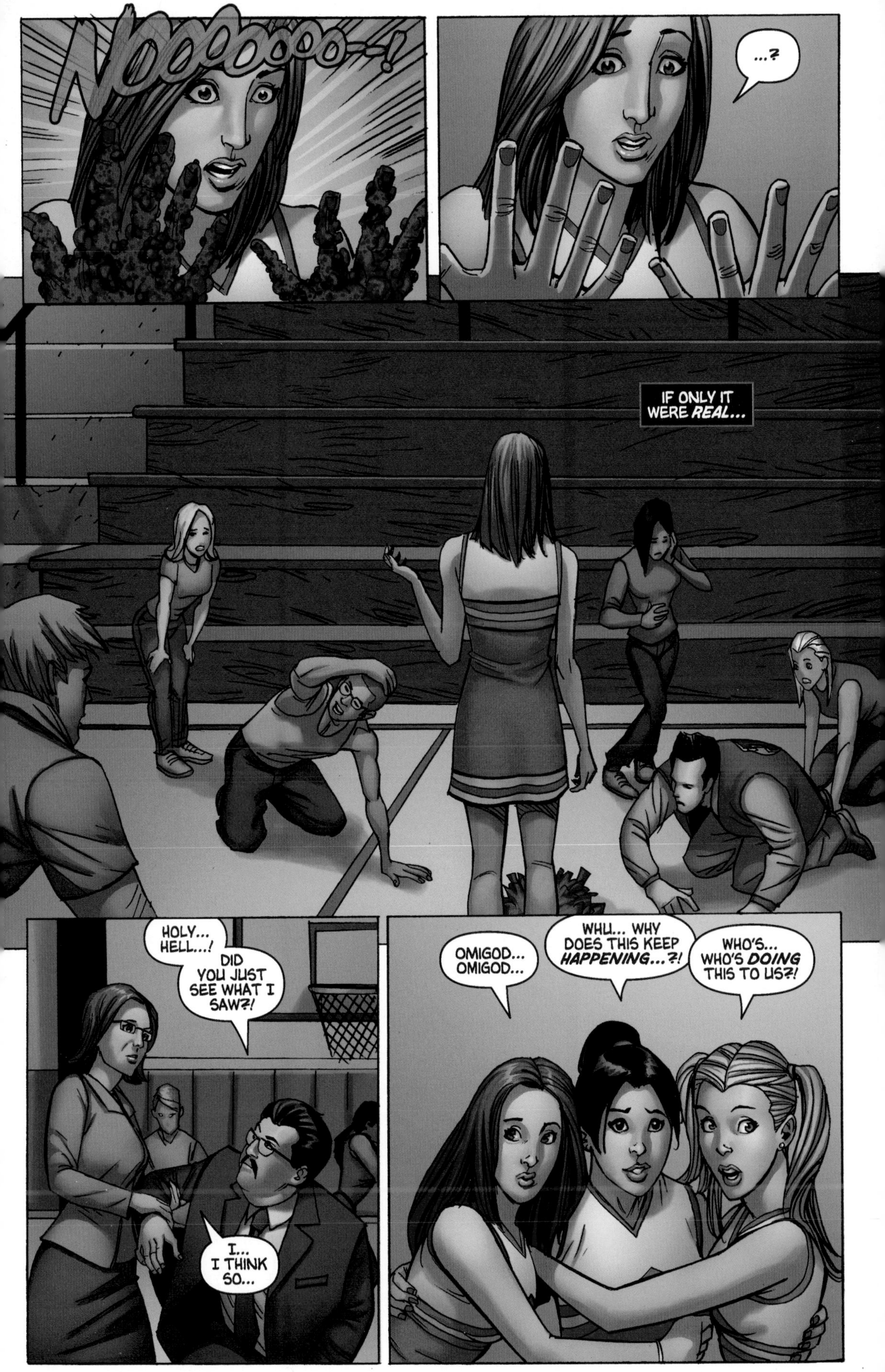
NOOOOOOO--!
...?
IF ONLY IT WERE REAL...
HOLY... HELL...!
DID YOU JUST SEE WHAT I SAW?!
I... I THINK SO...
OMIGOD... OMIGOD...
WHU... WHY DOES THIS KEEP HAPPENING...?!
WHO'S... WHO'S DOING THIS TO US?!

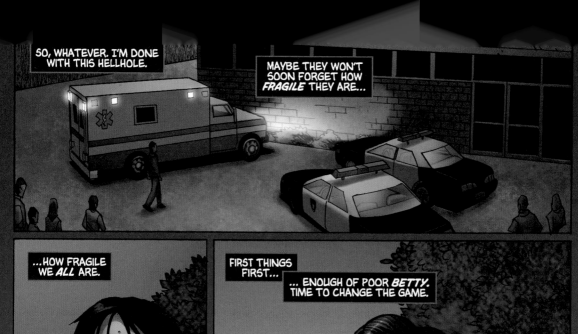

SO, WHATEVER. I'M DONE WITH THIS HELLHOLE.

MAYBE THEY WON'T SOON FORGET HOW *FRAGILE* THEY ARE...

...HOW FRAGILE WE *ALL* ARE.

AND NOW THAT I KNOW EXACTLY WHAT I'M *CAPABLE* OF, I SHOULD PUT IT TO SOME *USE*, RIGHT?

FIRST THINGS FIRST...

... ENOUGH OF POOR *BETTY*. TIME TO CHANGE THE GAME.

FROM NOW ON... THEY'LL ALL SEE WHAT I *WANT* THEM TO SEE...

SOMETIMES YOU JUST NEED THE RIGHT *NAME*... SOMETHING THAT SETS A TONE... SOMETHING THAT GOES WITH MY NEW *LOOK*...

CANDICE.

THAT'S A GOOD NAME.

JOE CASEY OF
MAN OF ACTION STUDIOS
*Story*

RYAN ODAGAWA
*Art*

JOHN STARR    COMICRAFT
*Colors*        *Lettering*

*End*

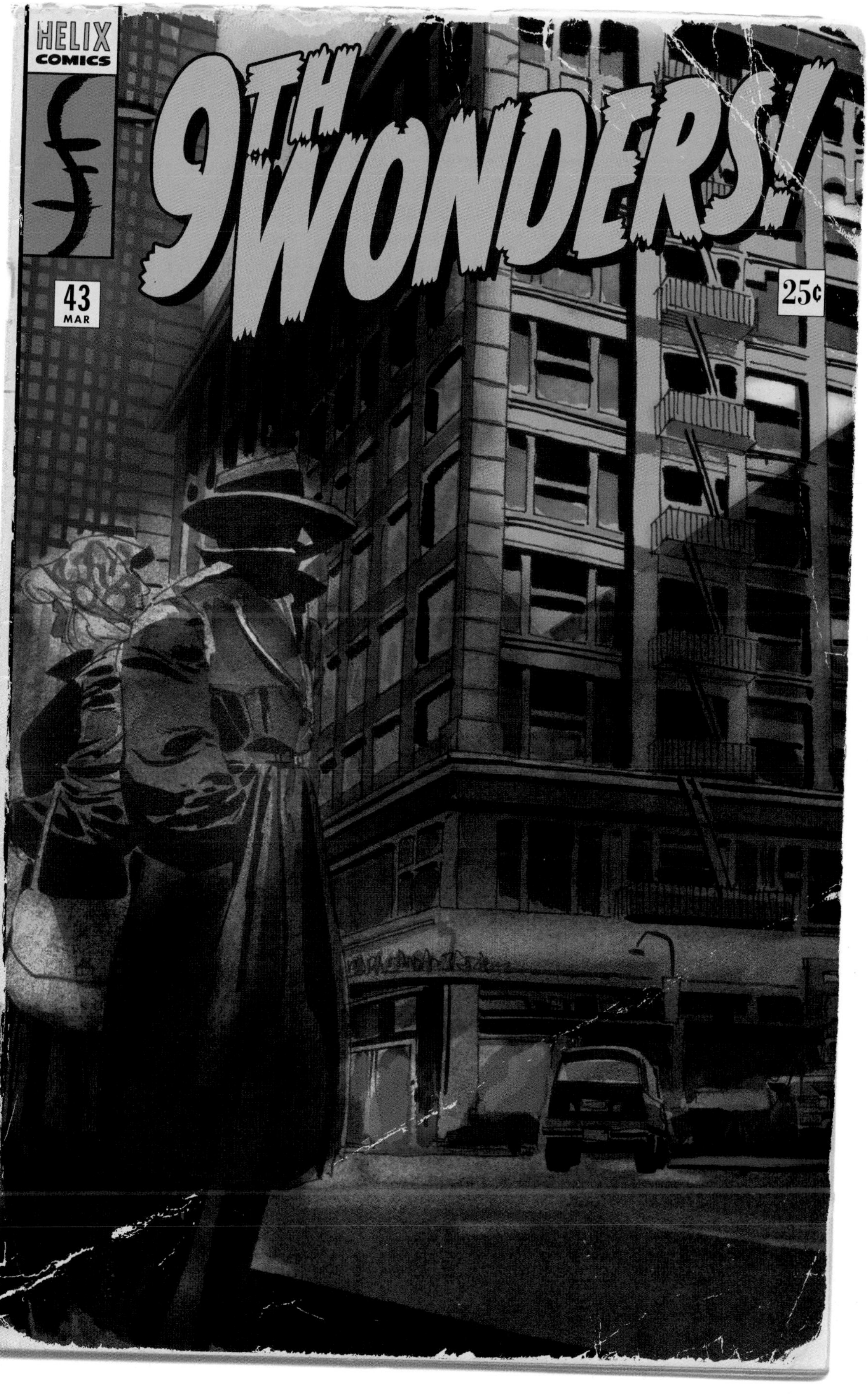
HELIX
COMICS
9TH WONDERS!
43
MAR
25¢

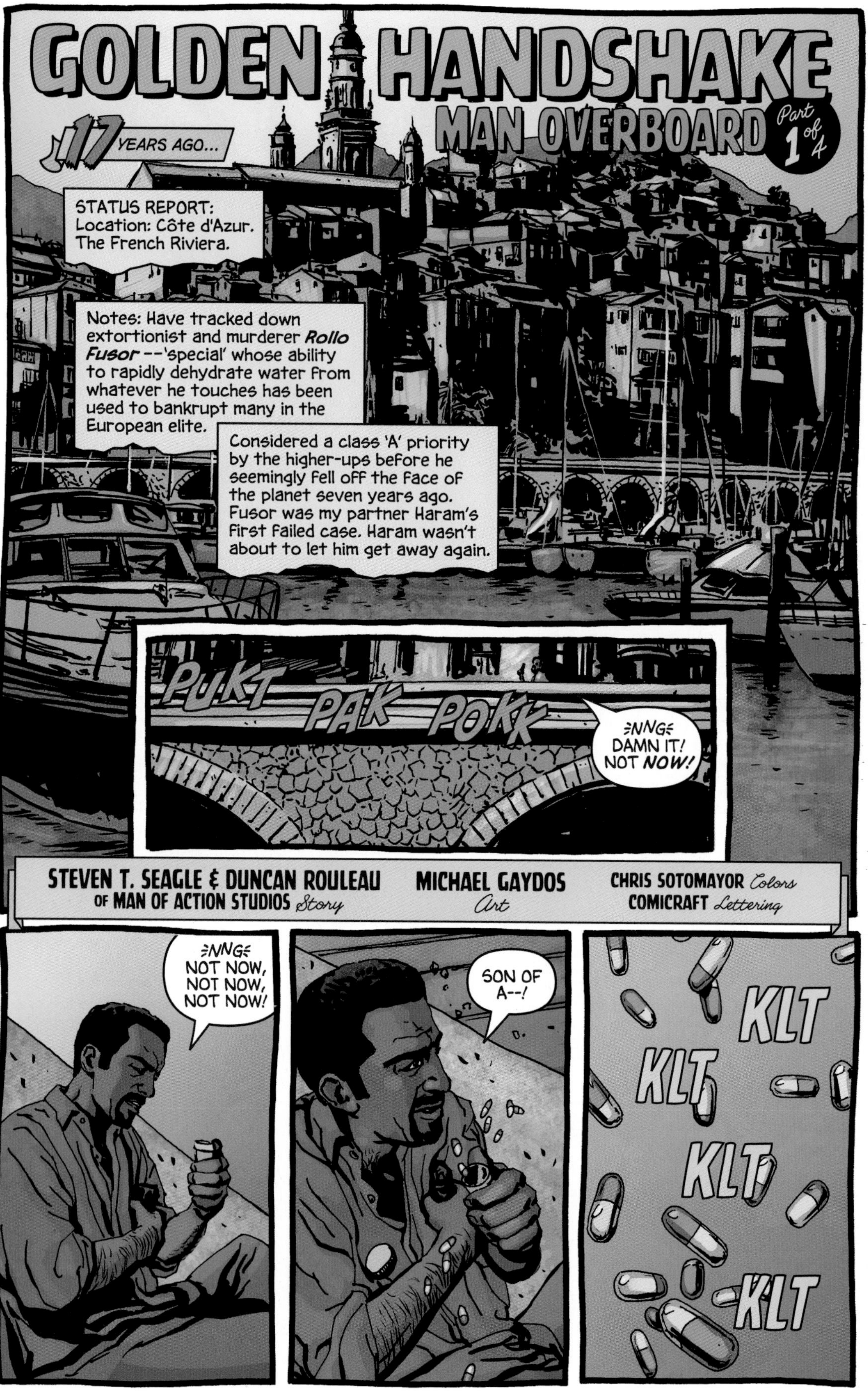
GOLDEN HANDSHAKE
MAN OVERBOARD
Part 1 of 4
17 YEARS AGO...
STATUS REPORT:
Location: Côte d'Azur.
The French Riviera.
Notes: Have tracked down extortionist and murderer *Rollo Fusor* --'special' whose ability to rapidly dehydrate water from whatever he touches has been used to bankrupt many in the European elite.
Considered a class 'A' priority by the higher-ups before he seemingly fell off the face of the planet seven years ago. Fusor was my partner Haram's first failed case. Haram wasn't about to let him get away again.
PUKT PAK POKK
NNG DAMN IT! NOT *NOW!*
STEVEN T. SEAGLE & DUNCAN ROULEAU OF MAN OF ACTION STUDIOS Story
MICHAEL GAYDOS Art
CHRIS SOTOMAYOR Colors
COMICRAFT Lettering
NNG NOT NOW, NOT NOW, NOT NOW!
SON OF A--!
KLT
KLT
KLT
KLT

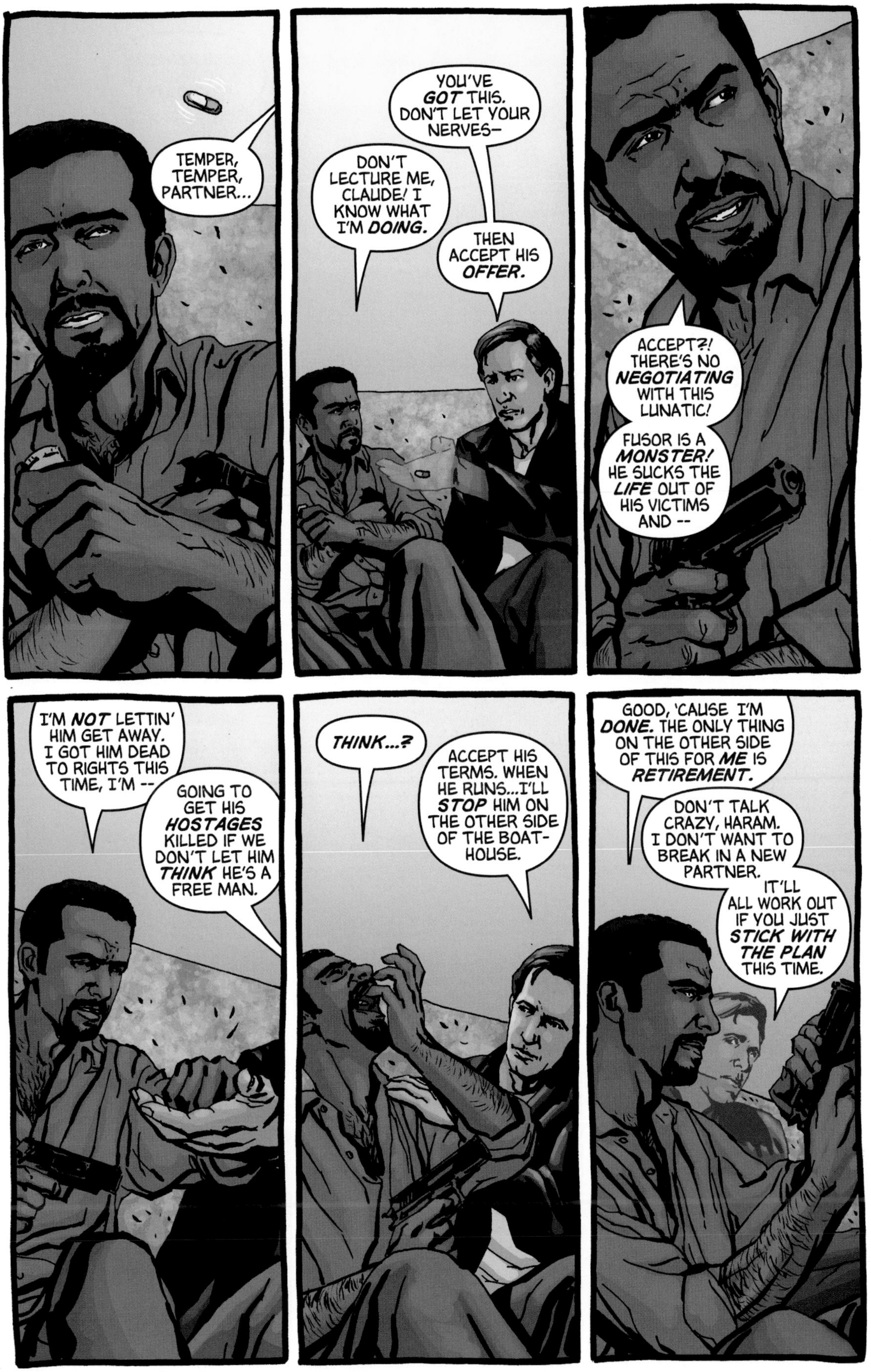
TEMPER, TEMPER, PARTNER...
YOU'VE *GOT* THIS. DON'T LET YOUR NERVES–
DON'T LECTURE ME, CLAUDE! I KNOW WHAT I'M *DOING*.
THEN ACCEPT HIS *OFFER*.
ACCEPT?! THERE'S NO *NEGOTIATING* WITH THIS LUNATIC!
FUSOR IS A *MONSTER!* HE SUCKS THE *LIFE* OUT OF HIS VICTIMS AND --
I'M *NOT* LETTIN' HIM GET AWAY. I GOT HIM DEAD TO RIGHTS THIS TIME, I'M --
GOING TO GET HIS *HOSTAGES* KILLED IF WE DON'T LET HIM *THINK* HE'S A FREE MAN.
*THINK...?*
ACCEPT HIS TERMS. WHEN HE RUNS...I'LL *STOP* HIM ON THE OTHER SIDE OF THE BOAT-HOUSE.
GOOD, 'CAUSE I'M *DONE.* THE ONLY THING ON THE OTHER SIDE OF THIS FOR *ME* IS *RETIREMENT*.
DON'T TALK CRAZY, HARAM. I DON'T WANT TO BREAK IN A NEW PARTNER.
IT'LL ALL WORK OUT IF YOU JUST *STICK WITH THE PLAN* THIS TIME.

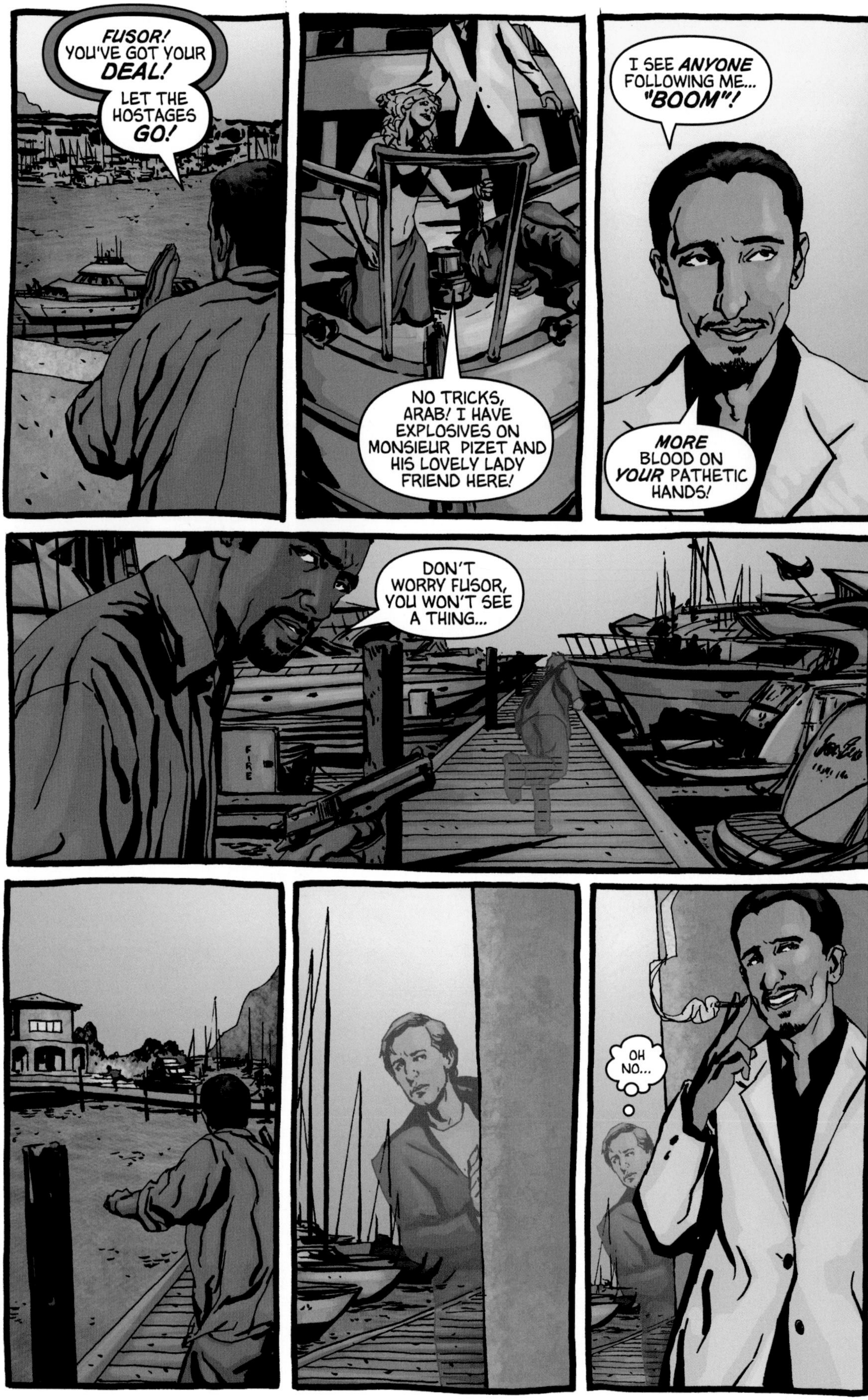
FUSOR! YOU'VE GOT YOUR DEAL!
LET THE HOSTAGES GO!
NO TRICKS, ARAB! I HAVE EXPLOSIVES ON MONSIEUR PIZET AND HIS LOVELY LADY FRIEND HERE!
I SEE ANYONE FOLLOWING ME... "BOOM"!
MORE BLOOD ON YOUR PATHETIC HANDS!
DON'T WORRY FUSOR, YOU WON'T SEE A THING...
FIRE
OH NO...

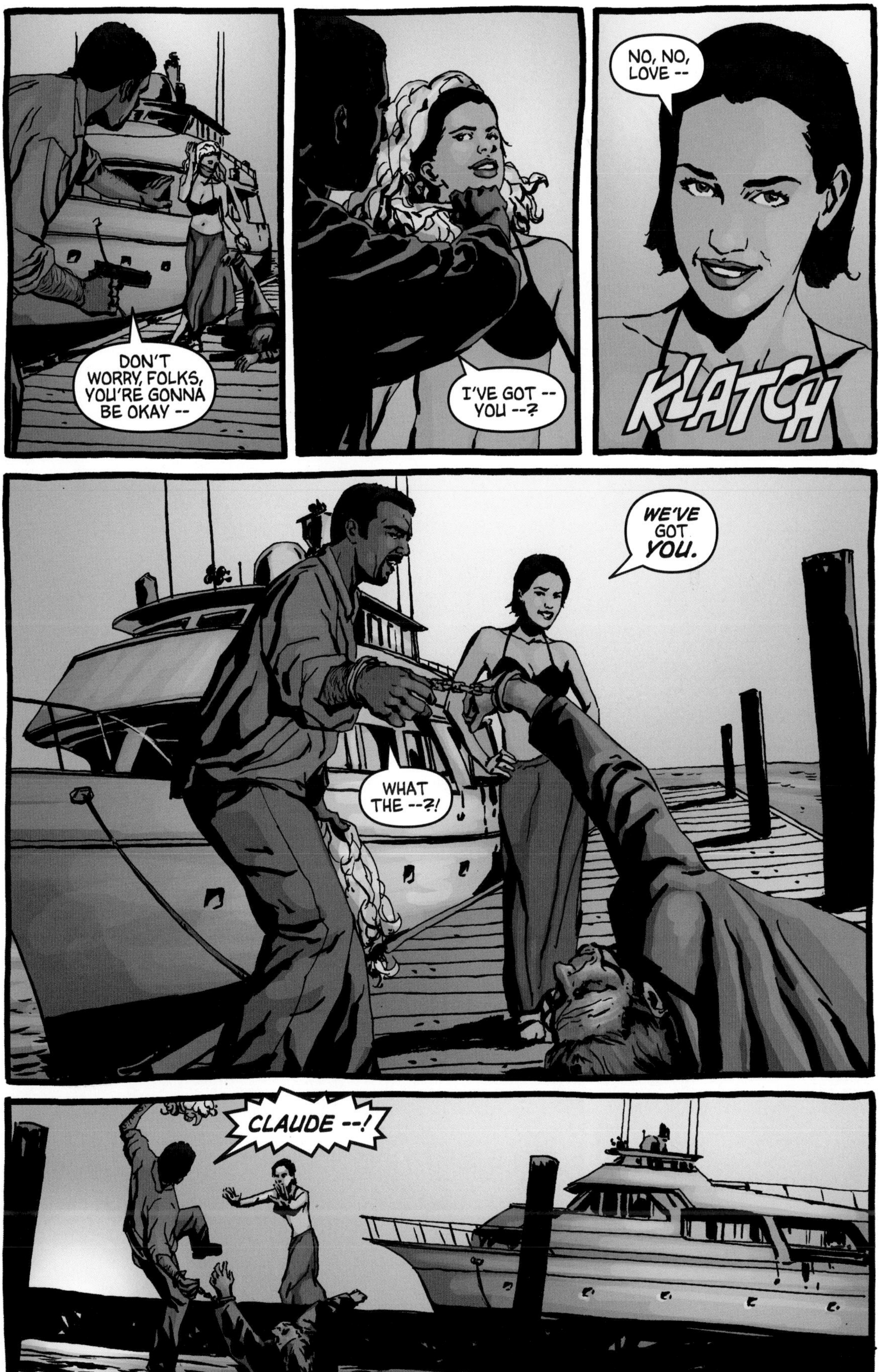
DON'T WORRY, FOLKS, YOU'RE GONNA BE OKAY --
I'VE GOT -- YOU --?
NO, NO, LOVE --
KLATCH
WE'VE GOT YOU.
WHAT THE --?!
CLAUDE --!

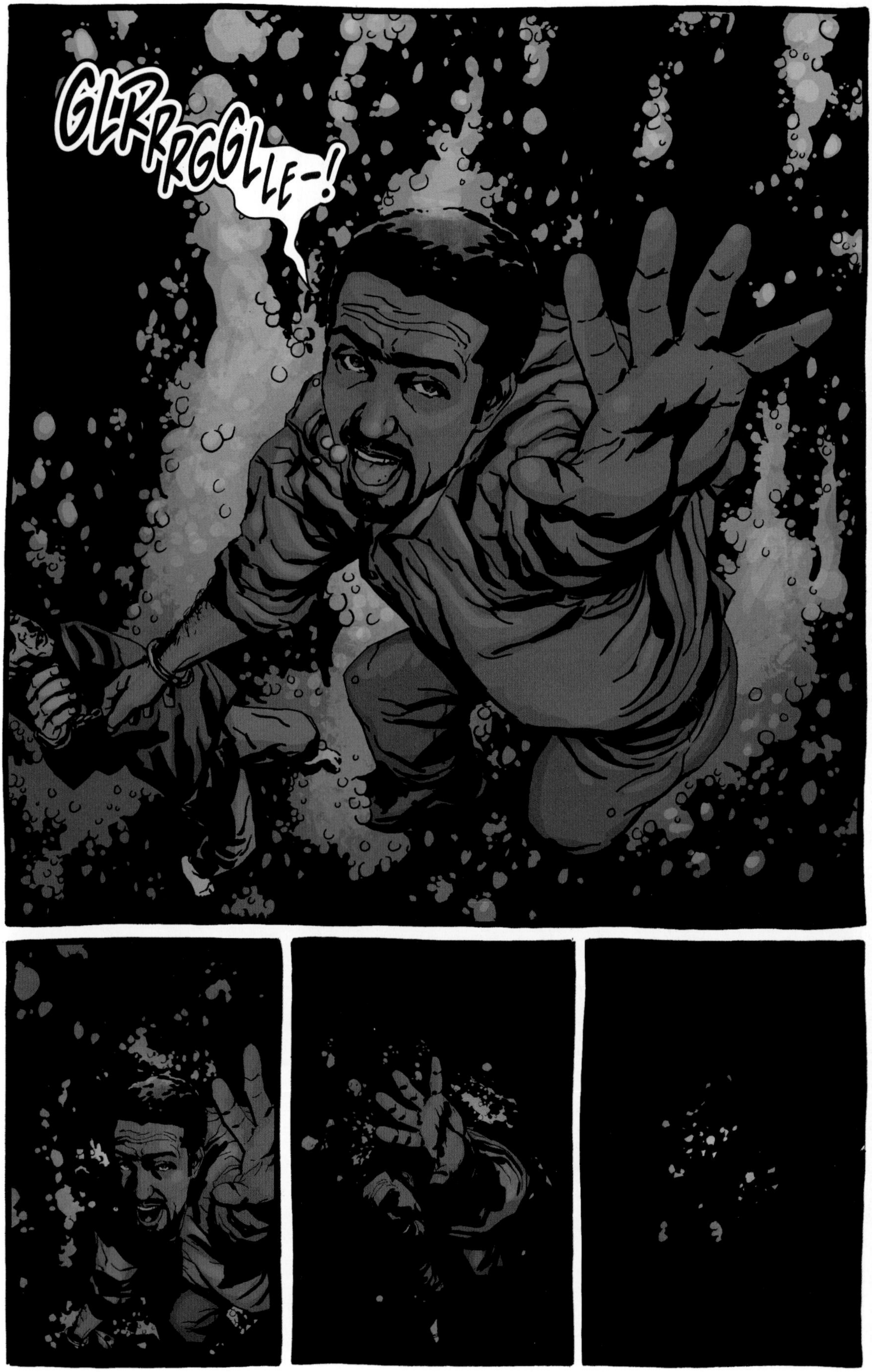
GLRRRGGLLE-!

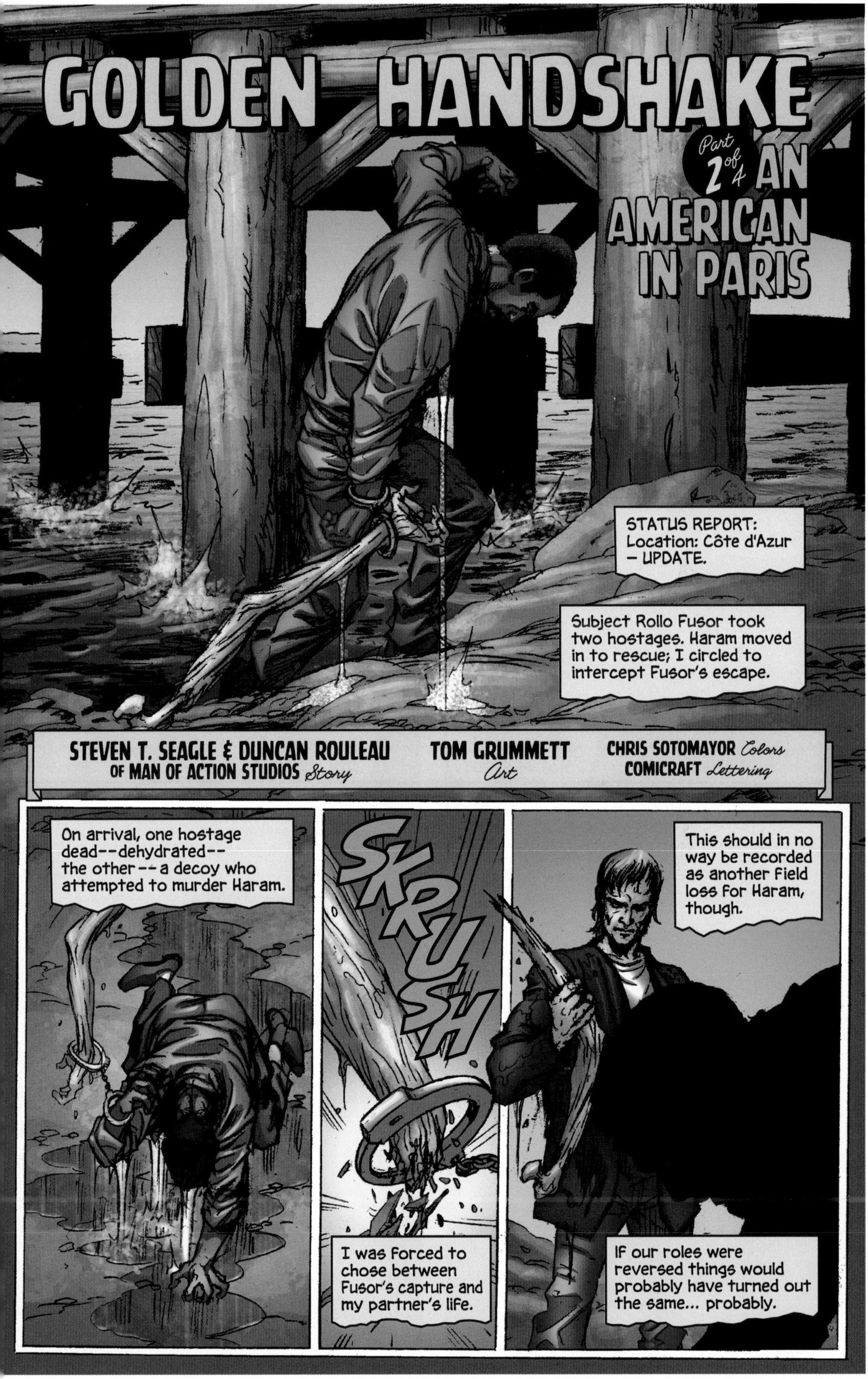
GOLDEN HANDSHAKE
Part 2 of 4
AN AMERICAN IN PARIS
STATUS REPORT:
Location: Côte d'Azur
– UPDATE.
Subject Rollo Fusor took two hostages. Haram moved in to rescue; I circled to intercept Fusor's escape.
STEVEN T. SEAGLE & DUNCAN ROULEAU OF MAN OF ACTION STUDIOS Story
TOM GRUMMETT Art
CHRIS SOTOMAYOR Colors
COMICRAFT Lettering
On arrival, one hostage dead--dehydrated-- the other--a decoy who attempted to murder Haram.
SKRUSH
I was forced to chose between Fusor's capture and my partner's life.
This should in no way be recorded as another field loss for Haram, though.
If our roles were reversed things would probably have turned out the same... probably.

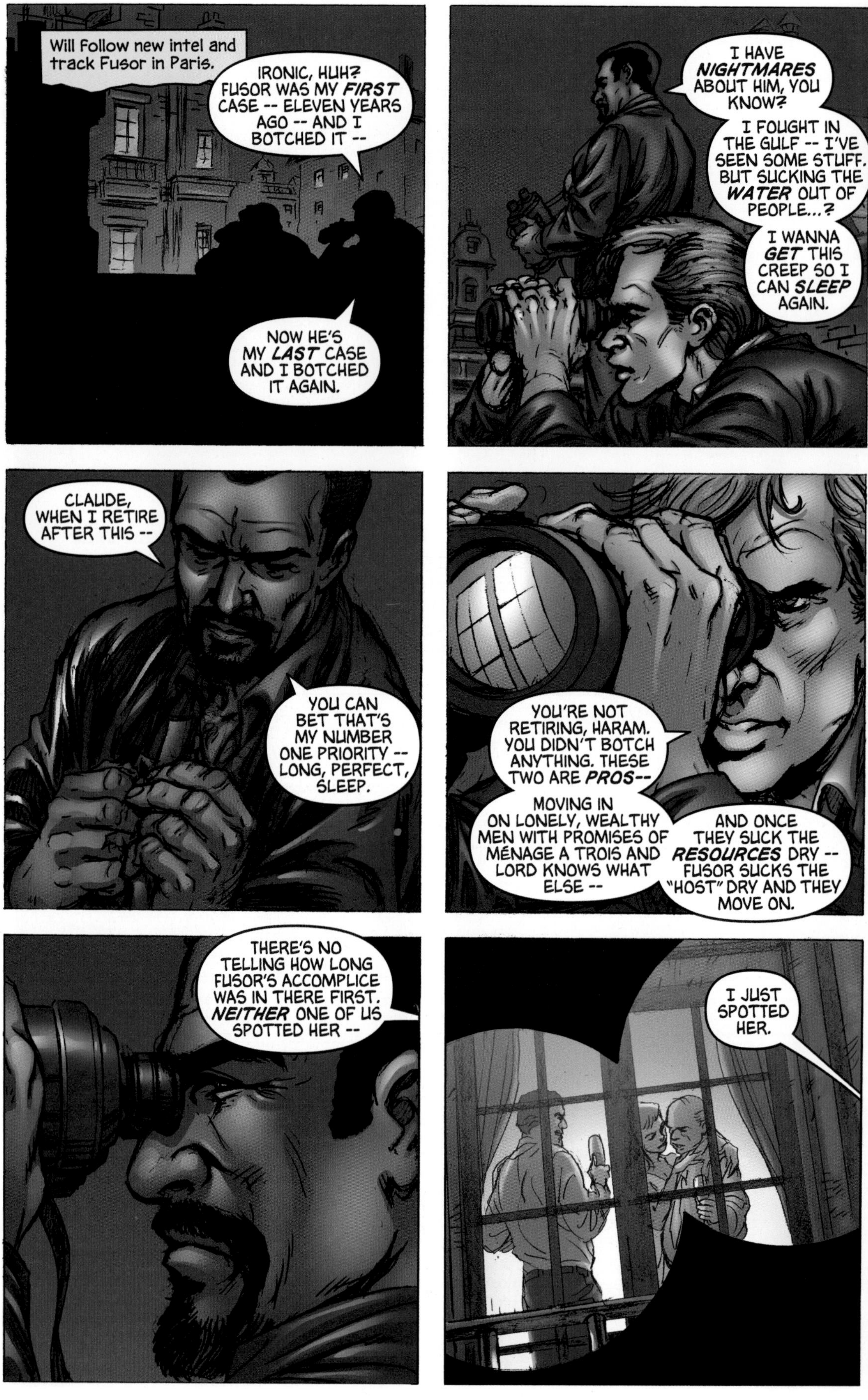
Will Follow new intel and track Fusor in Paris.
IRONIC, HUH? FUSOR WAS MY FIRST CASE -- ELEVEN YEARS AGO -- AND I BOTCHED IT --
NOW HE'S MY LAST CASE AND I BOTCHED IT AGAIN.
I HAVE NIGHTMARES ABOUT HIM, YOU KNOW?
I FOUGHT IN THE GULF -- I'VE SEEN SOME STUFF. BUT SUCKING THE WATER OUT OF PEOPLE...?
I WANNA GET THIS CREEP SO I CAN SLEEP AGAIN.
CLAUDE, WHEN I RETIRE AFTER THIS --
YOU CAN BET THAT'S MY NUMBER ONE PRIORITY -- LONG, PERFECT, SLEEP.
YOU'RE NOT RETIRING, HARAM. YOU DIDN'T BOTCH ANYTHING. THESE TWO ARE PROS--
MOVING IN ON LONELY, WEALTHY MEN WITH PROMISES OF MÉNAGE A TROIS AND LORD KNOWS WHAT ELSE --
AND ONCE THEY SUCK THE RESOURCES DRY -- FUSOR SUCKS THE "HOST" DRY AND THEY MOVE ON.
THERE'S NO TELLING HOW LONG FUSOR'S ACCOMPLICE WAS IN THERE FIRST. NEITHER ONE OF US SPOTTED HER --
I JUST SPOTTED HER.

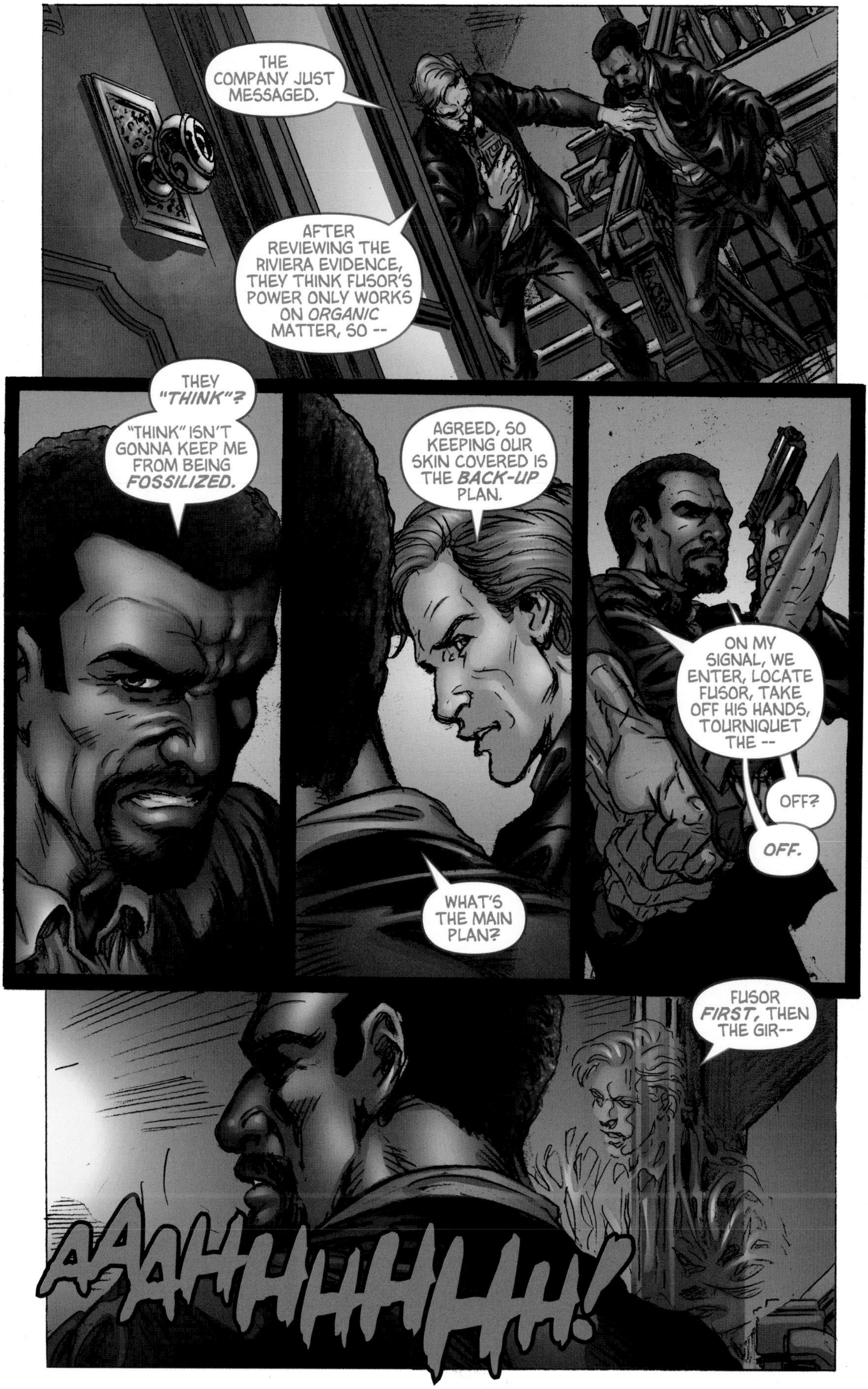
THE COMPANY JUST MESSAGED.
AFTER REVIEWING THE RIVIERA EVIDENCE, THEY THINK FUSOR'S POWER ONLY WORKS ON ORGANIC MATTER, SO --
THEY "THINK"?
"THINK" ISN'T GONNA KEEP ME FROM BEING FOSSILIZED.
AGREED, SO KEEPING OUR SKIN COVERED IS THE BACK-UP PLAN.
WHAT'S THE MAIN PLAN?
ON MY SIGNAL, WE ENTER, LOCATE FUSOR, TAKE OFF HIS HANDS, TOURNIQUET THE --
OFF?
OFF.
FUSOR FIRST, THEN THE GIR--
AAAHHHHHHH!

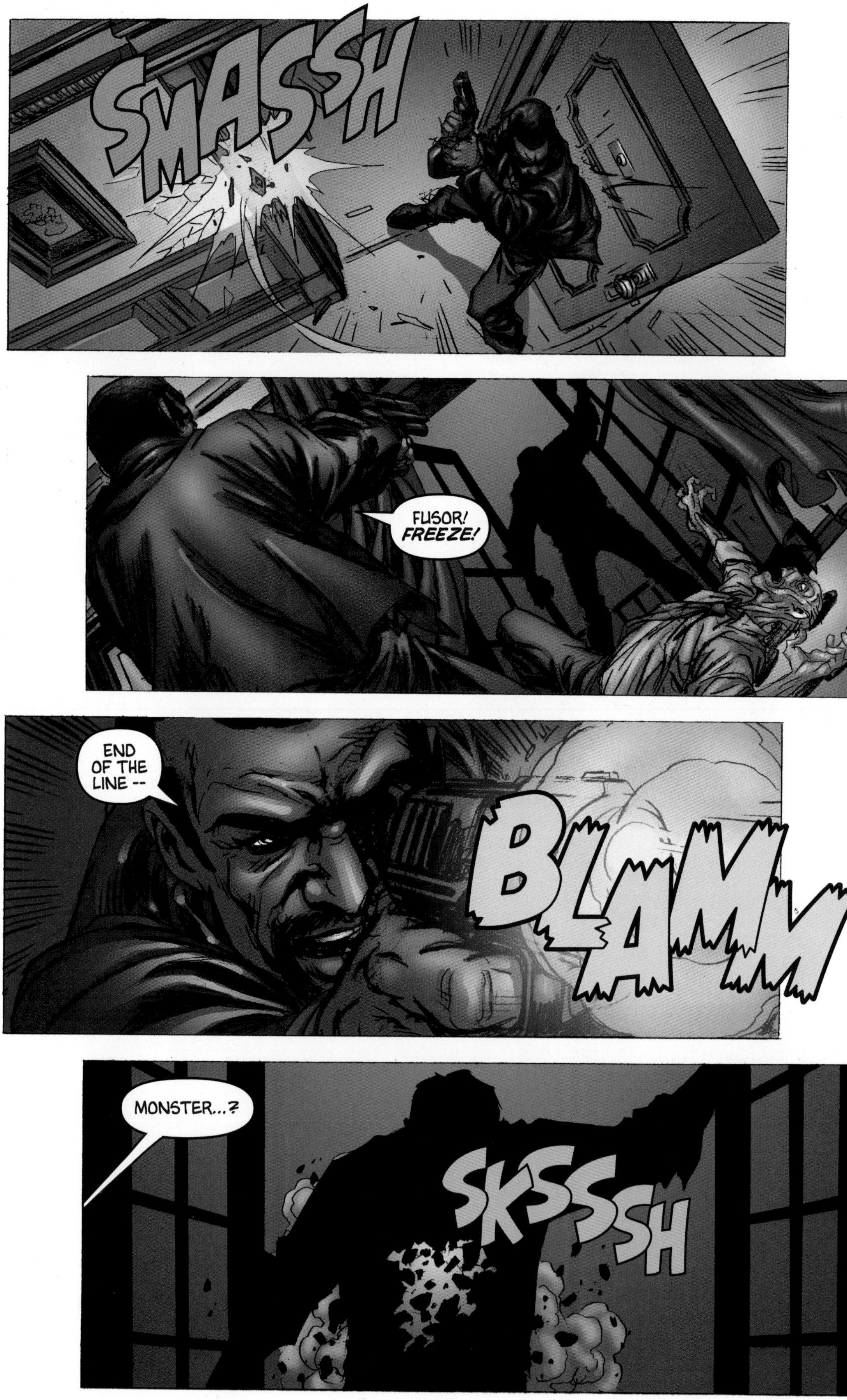
SMASSH
FUSOR! FREEZE!
END OF THE LINE --
BLAMM
MONSTER...?
SKSSSH

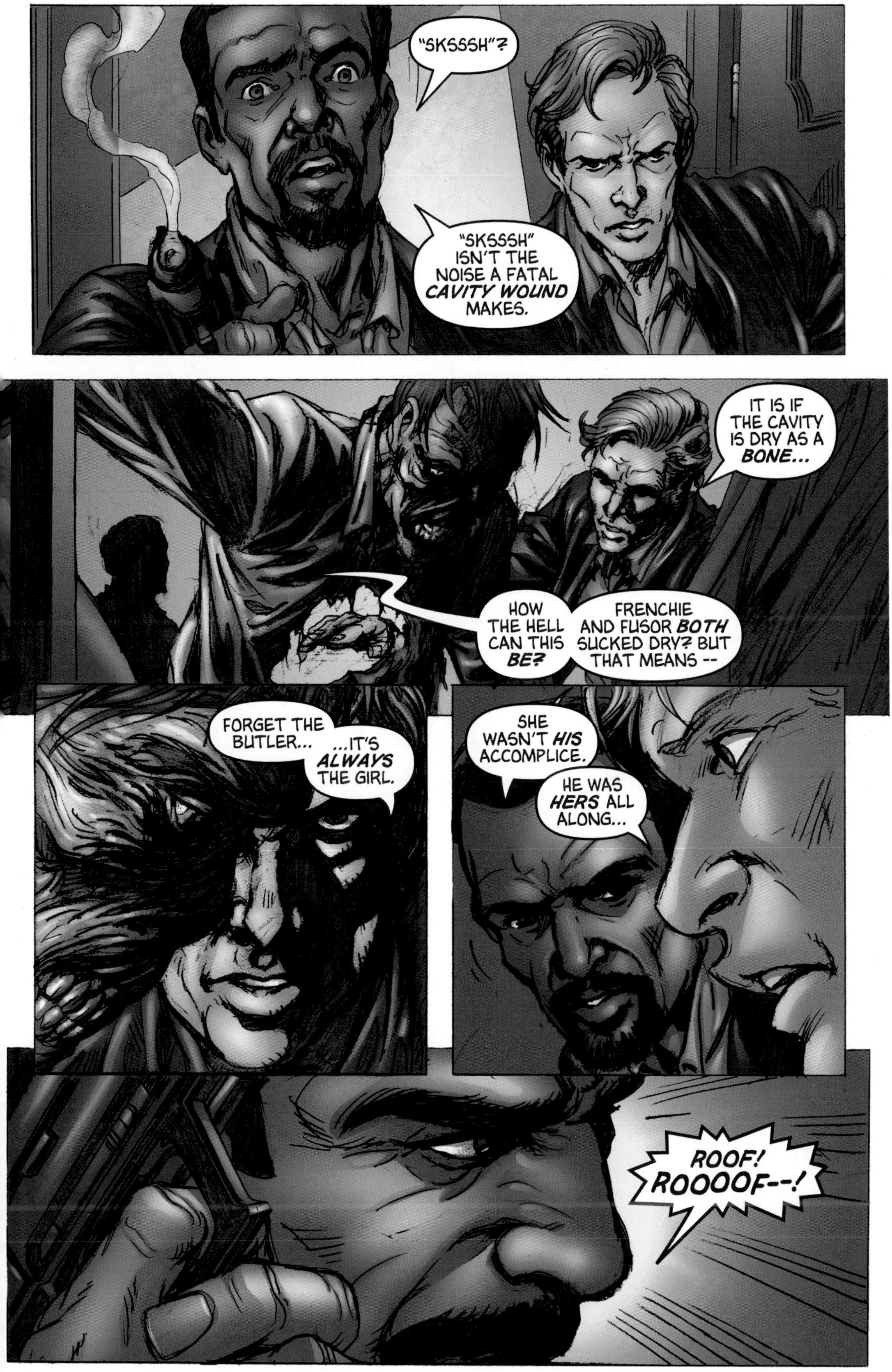
"SKSSSH"?
"SKSSSH" ISN'T THE NOISE A FATAL CAVITY WOUND MAKES.
IT IS IF THE CAVITY IS DRY AS A BONE...
HOW THE HELL CAN THIS BE?
FRENCHIE AND FUSOR BOTH SUCKED DRY? BUT THAT MEANS --
FORGET THE BUTLER...
...IT'S ALWAYS THE GIRL.
SHE WASN'T HIS ACCOMPLICE.
HE WAS HERS ALL ALONG...
ROOF! ROOOOF--!

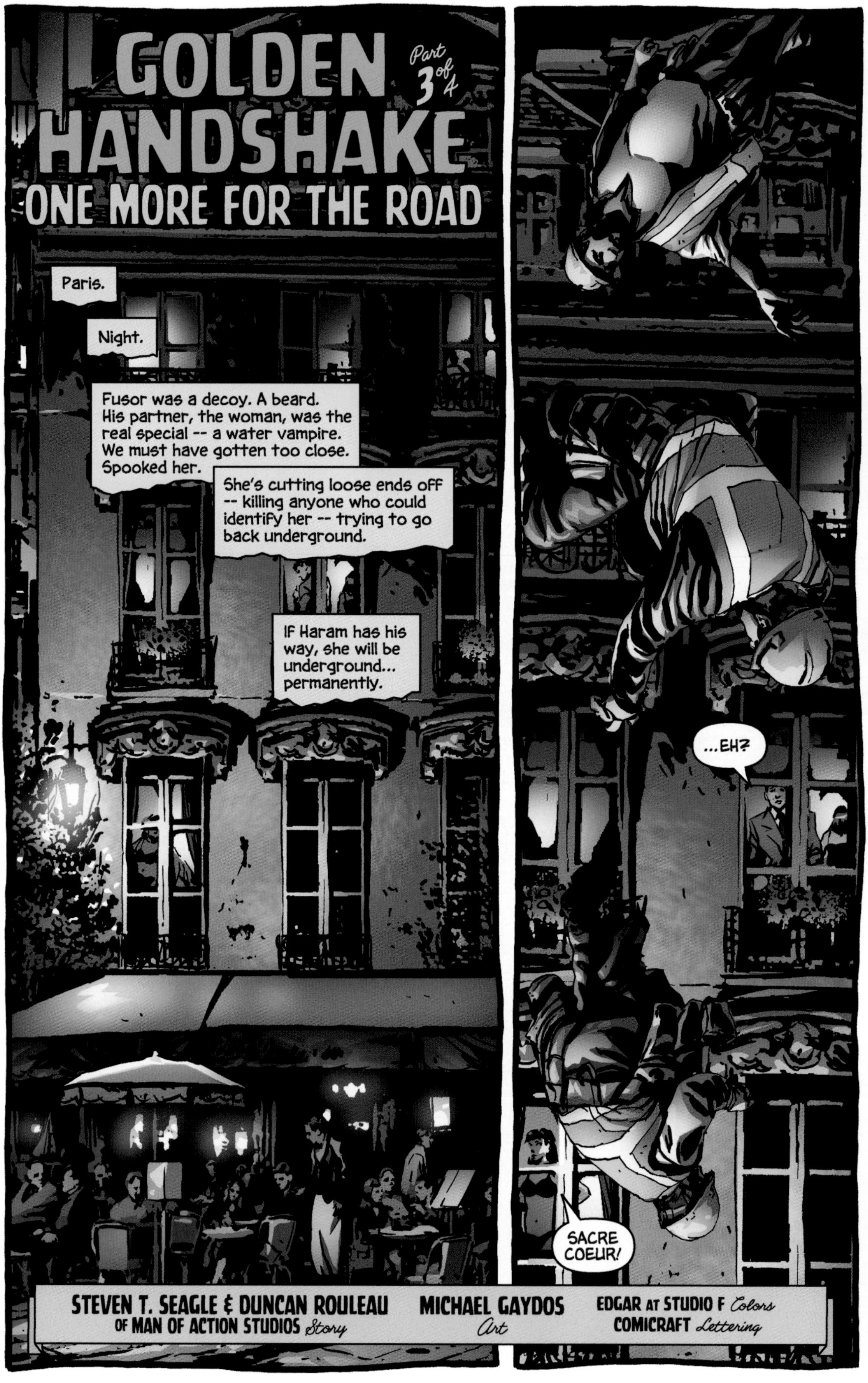
GOLDEN HANDSHAKE Part 3 of 4
ONE MORE FOR THE ROAD
Paris.
Night.
Fusor was a decoy. A beard. His partner, the woman, was the real special -- a water vampire. We must have gotten too close. Spooked her.
She's cutting loose ends off -- killing anyone who could identify her -- trying to go back underground.
If Haram has his way, she will be underground... permanently.
...EH?
SACRE COEUR!
STEVEN T. SEAGLE & DUNCAN ROULEAU OF MAN OF ACTION STUDIOS Story
MICHAEL GAYDOS Art
EDGAR AT STUDIO F Colors
COMICRAFT Lettering

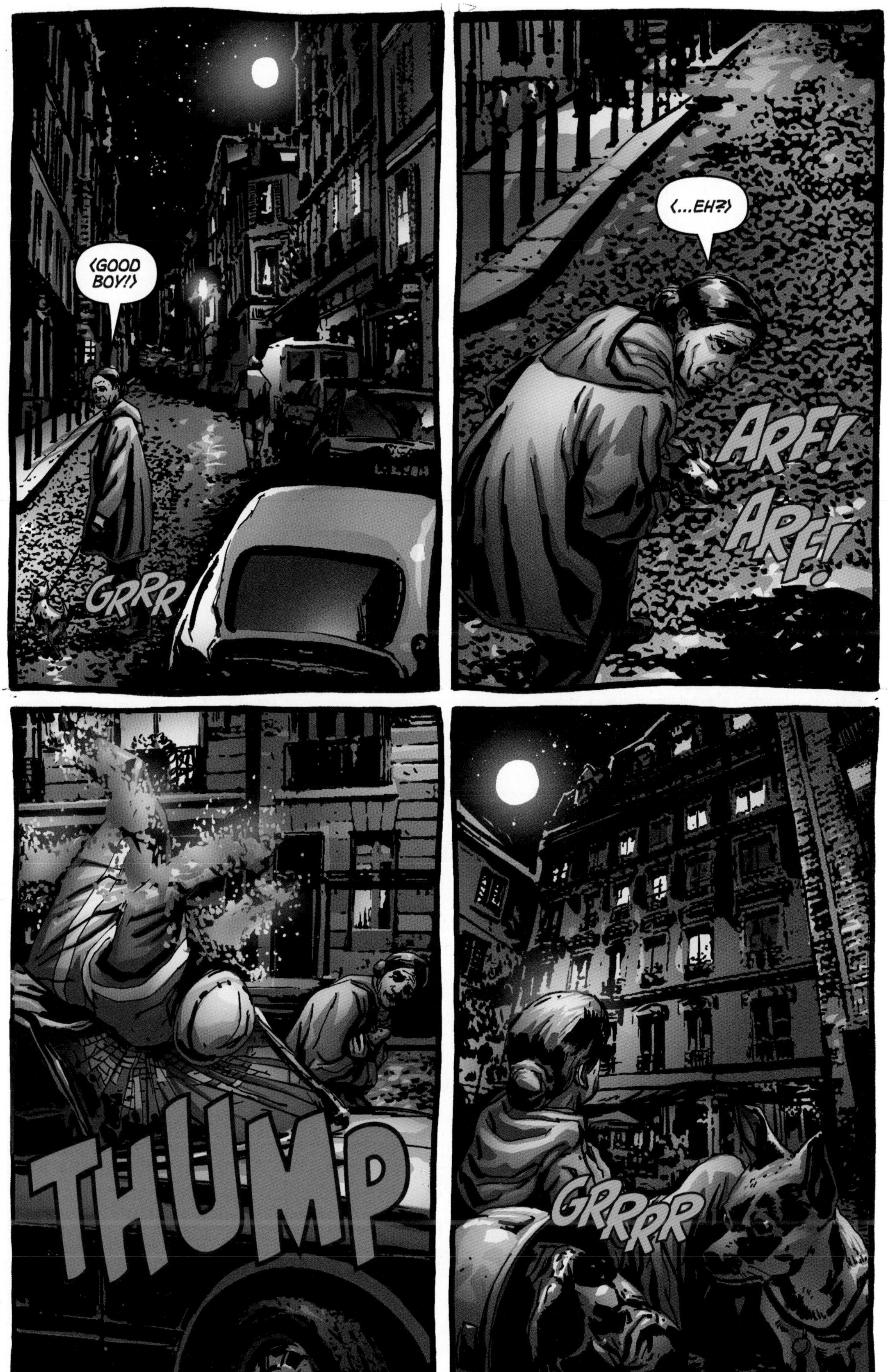
‹GOOD BOY!›
GRRR
‹...EH?›
ARF!
ARF!
THUMP
GRRRR

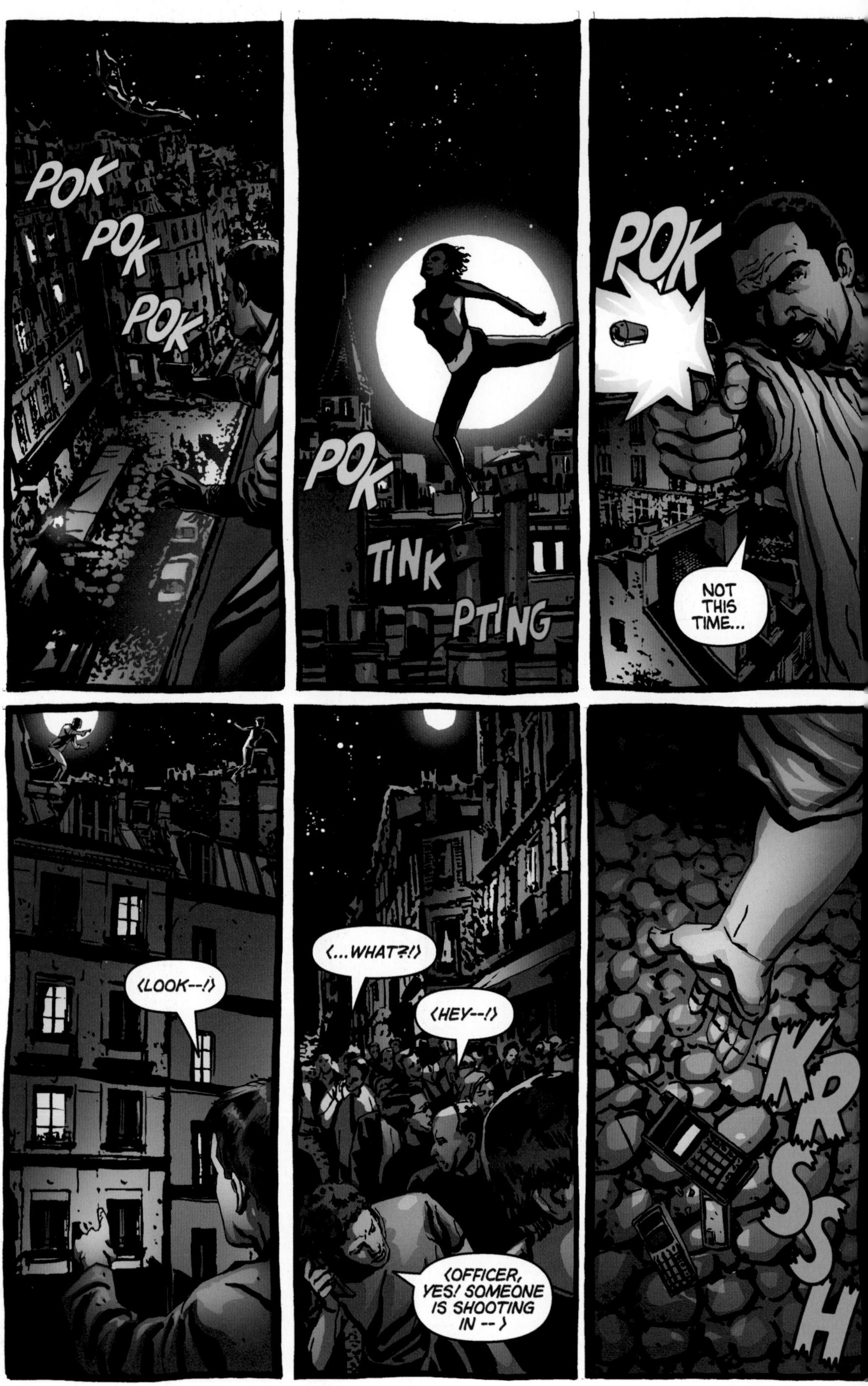
POK
POK
POK
POK
TINK
PTING
POK
NOT THIS TIME...
‹LOOK--!›
‹...WHAT?!›
‹HEY--!›
‹OFFICER, YES! SOMEONE IS SHOOTING IN --›
KRSSH

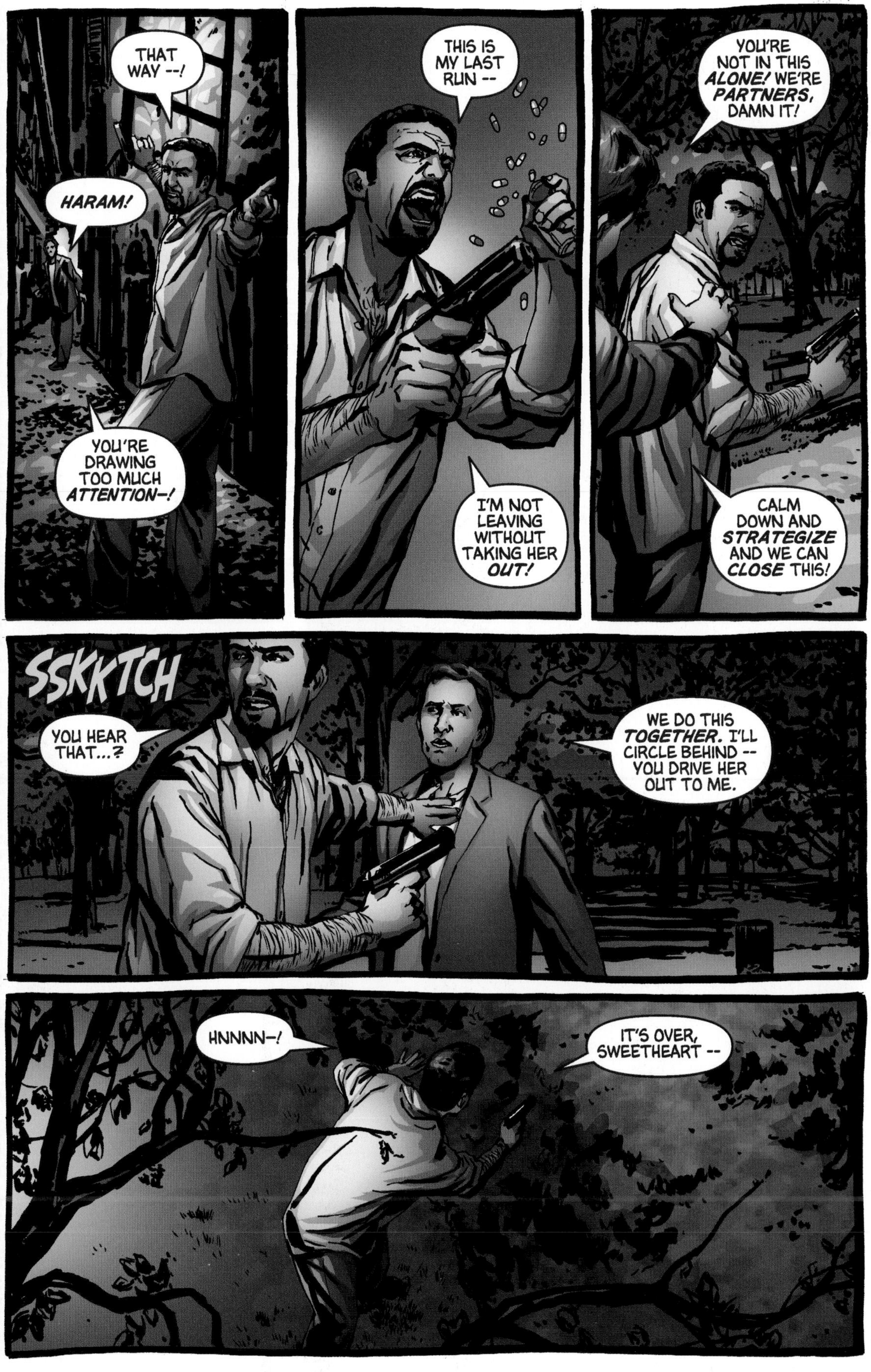
THAT WAY --!
HARAM!
YOU'RE DRAWING TOO MUCH ATTENTION--!
THIS IS MY LAST RUN --
I'M NOT LEAVING WITHOUT TAKING HER OUT!
YOU'RE NOT IN THIS ALONE! WE'RE PARTNERS, DAMN IT!
CALM DOWN AND STRATEGIZE AND WE CAN CLOSE THIS!
SSKKTCH
YOU HEAR THAT...?
WE DO THIS TOGETHER. I'LL CIRCLE BEHIND -- YOU DRIVE HER OUT TO ME.
HNNNN-!
IT'S OVER, SWEETHEART --

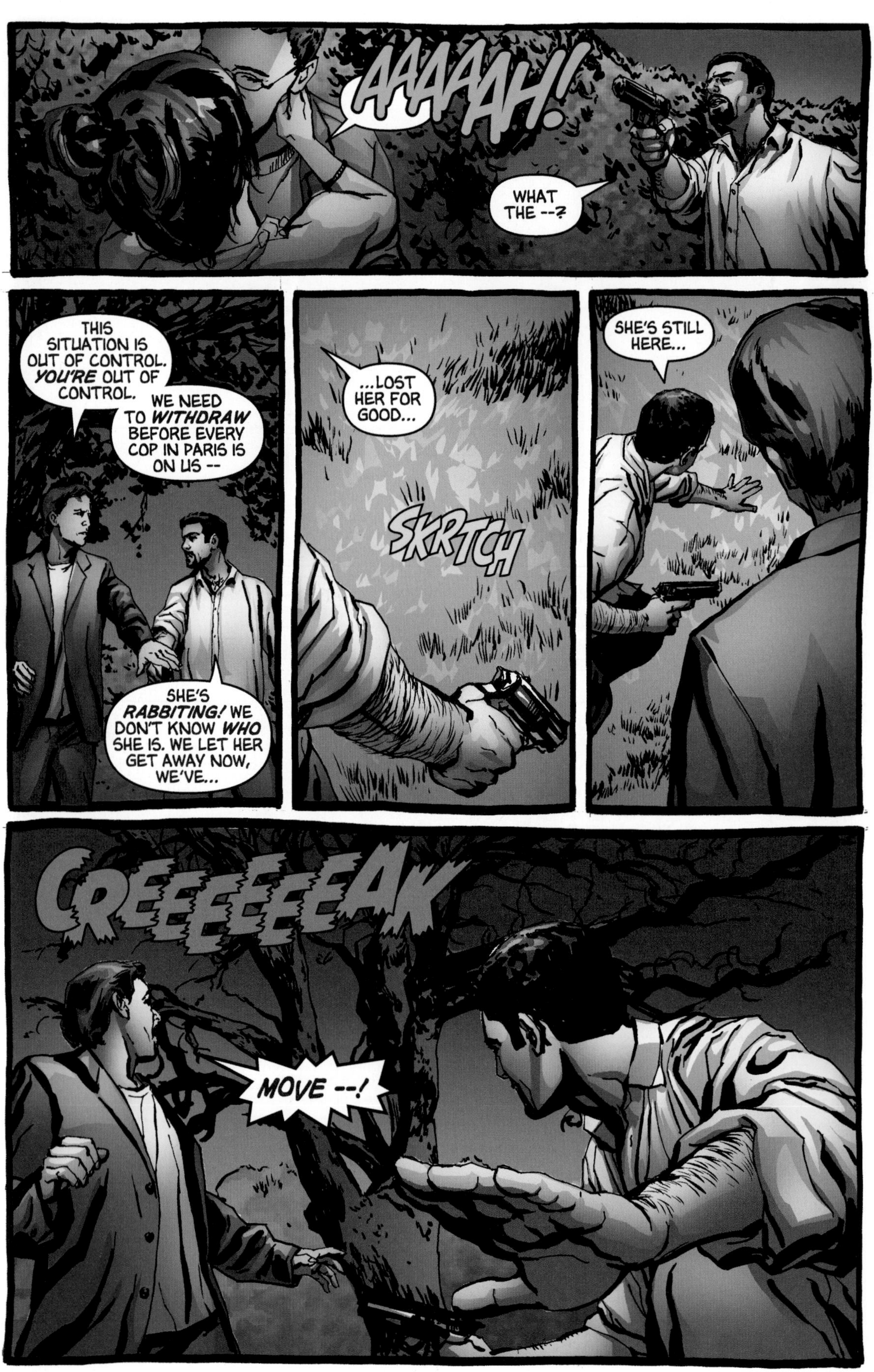
AAAAAH!
WHAT THE --?
THIS SITUATION IS OUT OF CONTROL. YOU'RE OUT OF CONTROL.
WE NEED TO WITHDRAW BEFORE EVERY COP IN PARIS IS ON US --
SHE'S RABBITING! WE DON'T KNOW WHO SHE IS. WE LET HER GET AWAY NOW, WE'VE...
...LOST HER FOR GOOD...
SKRTCH
SHE'S STILL HERE...
CREEEEEEAK
MOVE --!

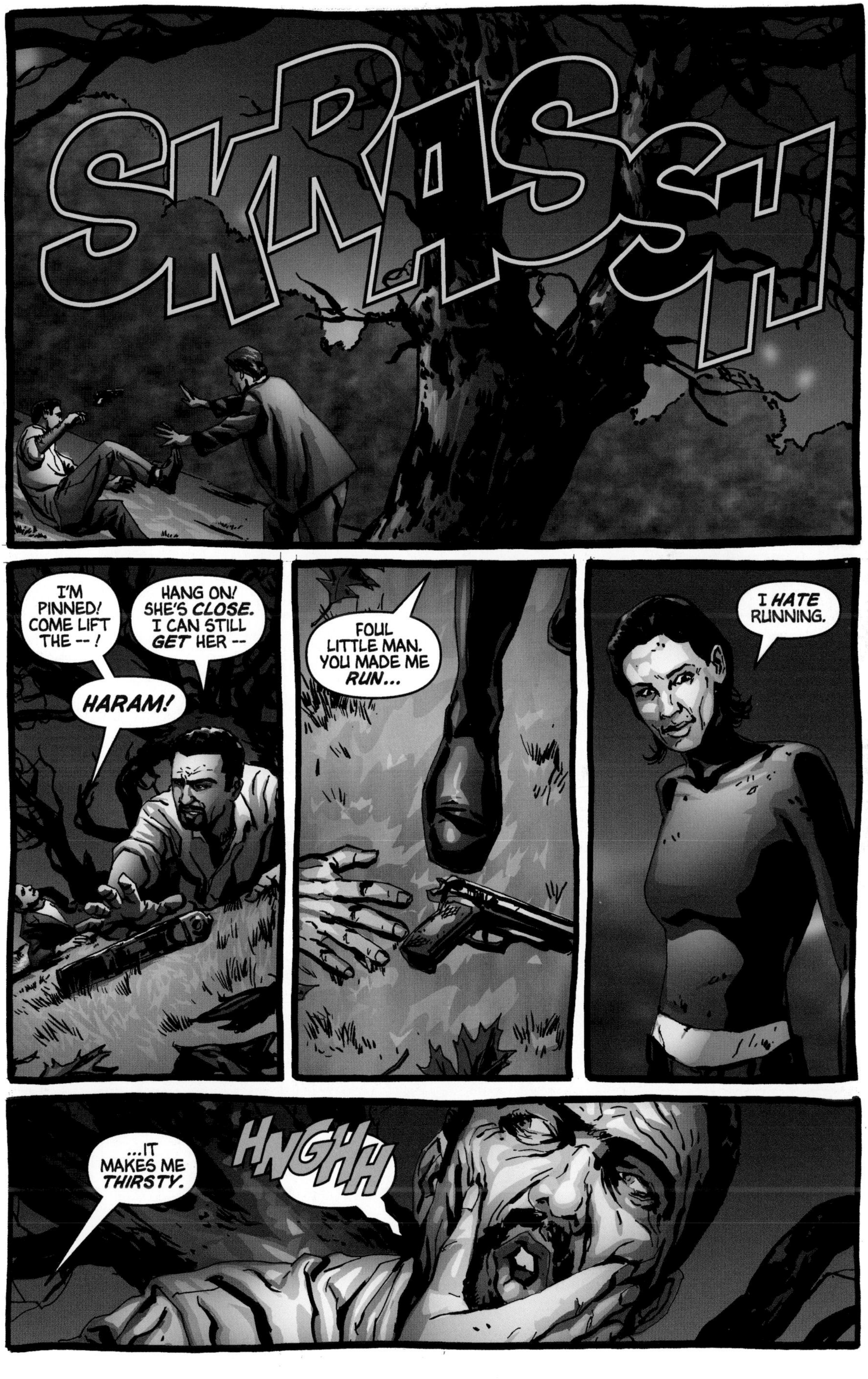
SKRASSH
I'M PINNED! COME LIFT THE -- !
HARAM!
HANG ON! SHE'S CLOSE. I CAN STILL GET HER --
FOUL LITTLE MAN. YOU MADE ME RUN...
I HATE RUNNING.
...IT MAKES ME THIRSTY.
HNGHH

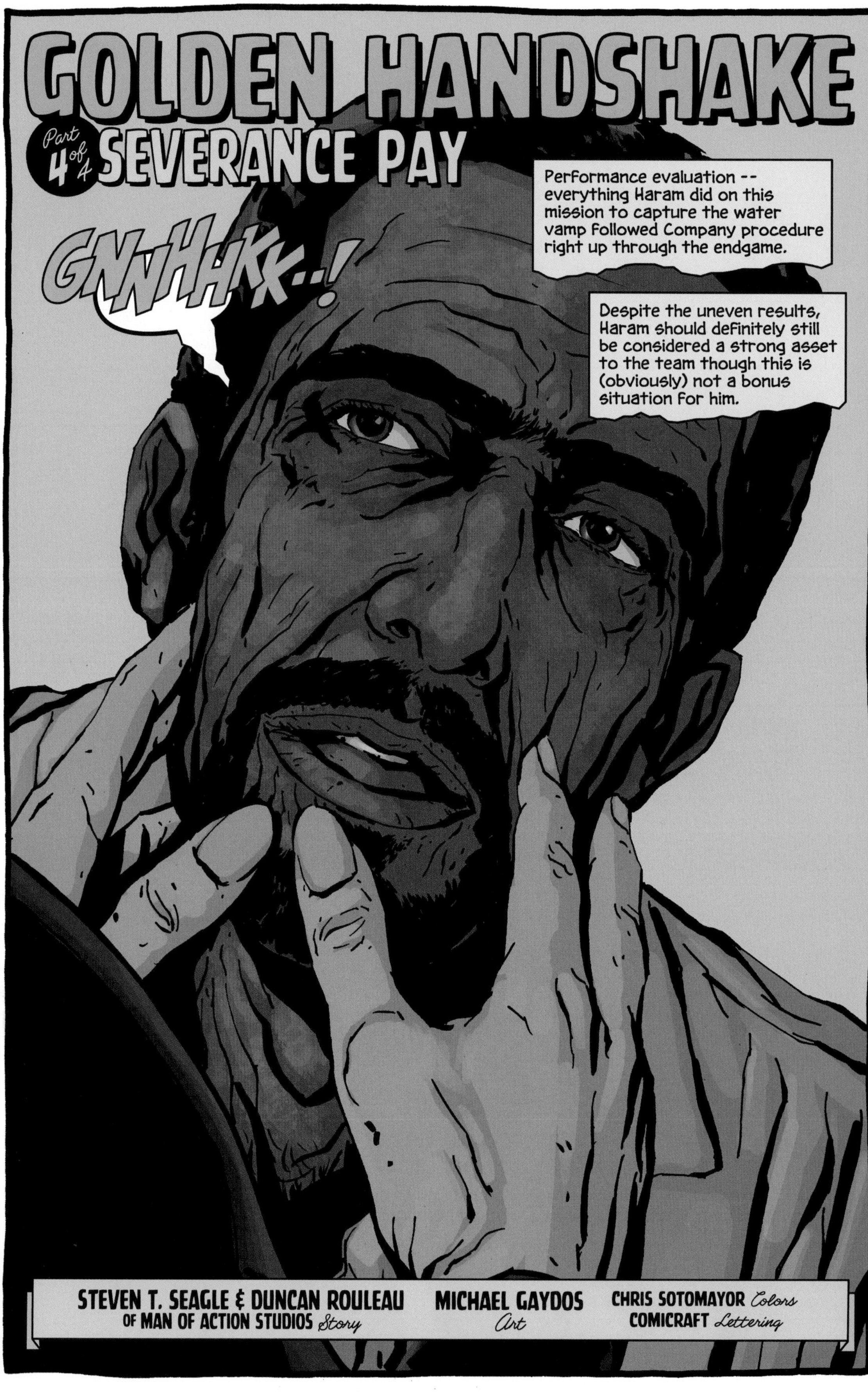
GOLDEN HANDSHAKE
Part 4 of 4 SEVERANCE PAY
GNNHHKK..!
Performance evaluation -- everything Haram did on this mission to capture the water vamp followed Company procedure right up through the endgame.
Despite the uneven results, Haram should definitely still be considered a strong asset to the team though this is (obviously) not a bonus situation for him.
STEVEN T. SEAGLE & DUNCAN ROULEAU OF MAN OF ACTION STUDIOS Story
MICHAEL GAYDOS Art
CHRIS SOTOMAYOR Colors
COMICRAFT Lettering

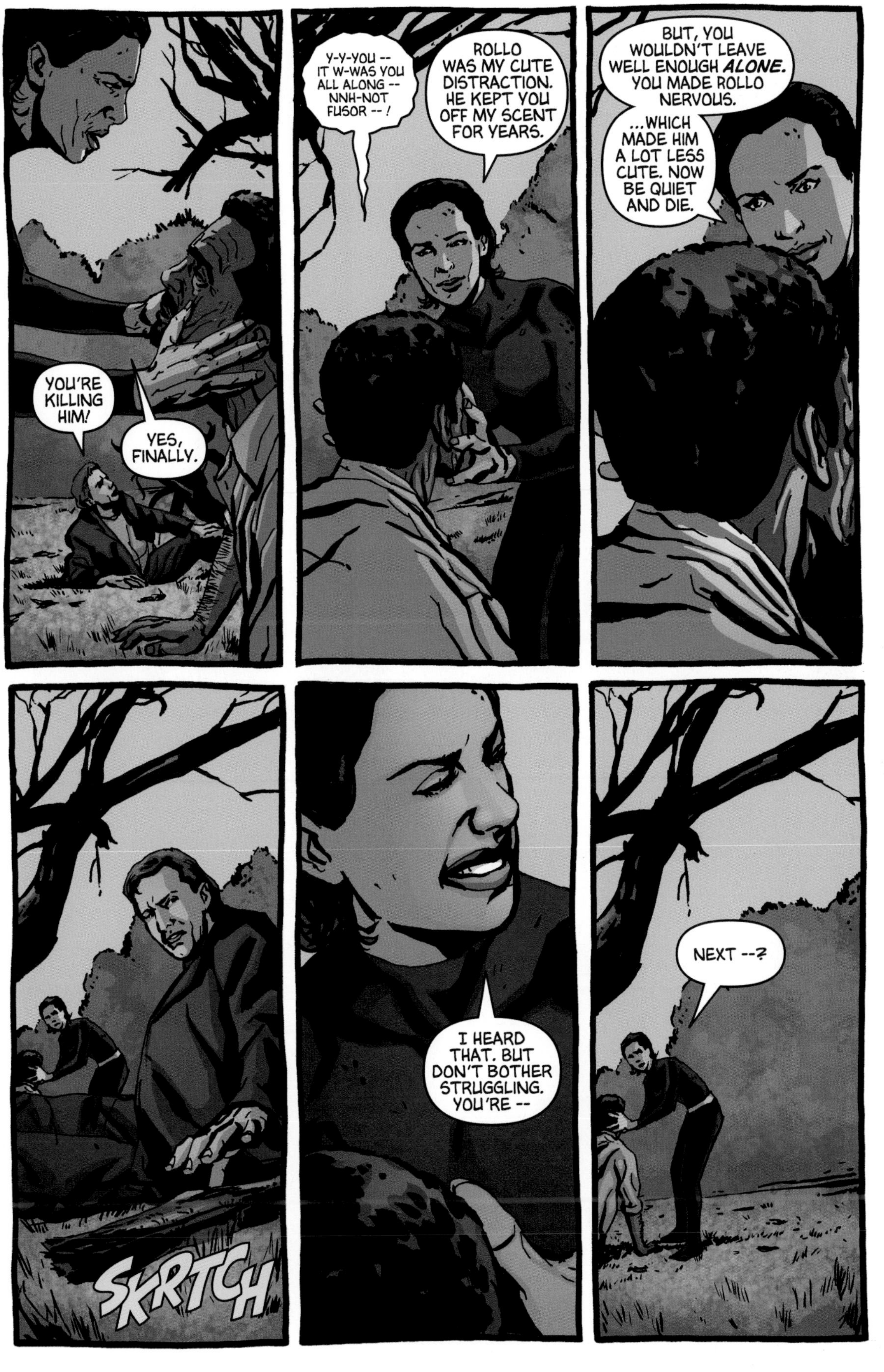
YOU'RE KILLING HIM!
YES, FINALLY.
Y-Y-YOU -- IT W-WAS YOU ALL ALONG -- NNH-NOT FUSOR -- !
ROLLO WAS MY CUTE DISTRACTION. HE KEPT YOU OFF MY SCENT FOR YEARS.
BUT, YOU WOULDN'T LEAVE WELL ENOUGH ALONE. YOU MADE ROLLO NERVOUS.
...WHICH MADE HIM A LOT LESS CUTE. NOW BE QUIET AND DIE.
SKRTCH
I HEARD THAT. BUT DON'T BOTHER STRUGGLING. YOU'RE --
NEXT --?

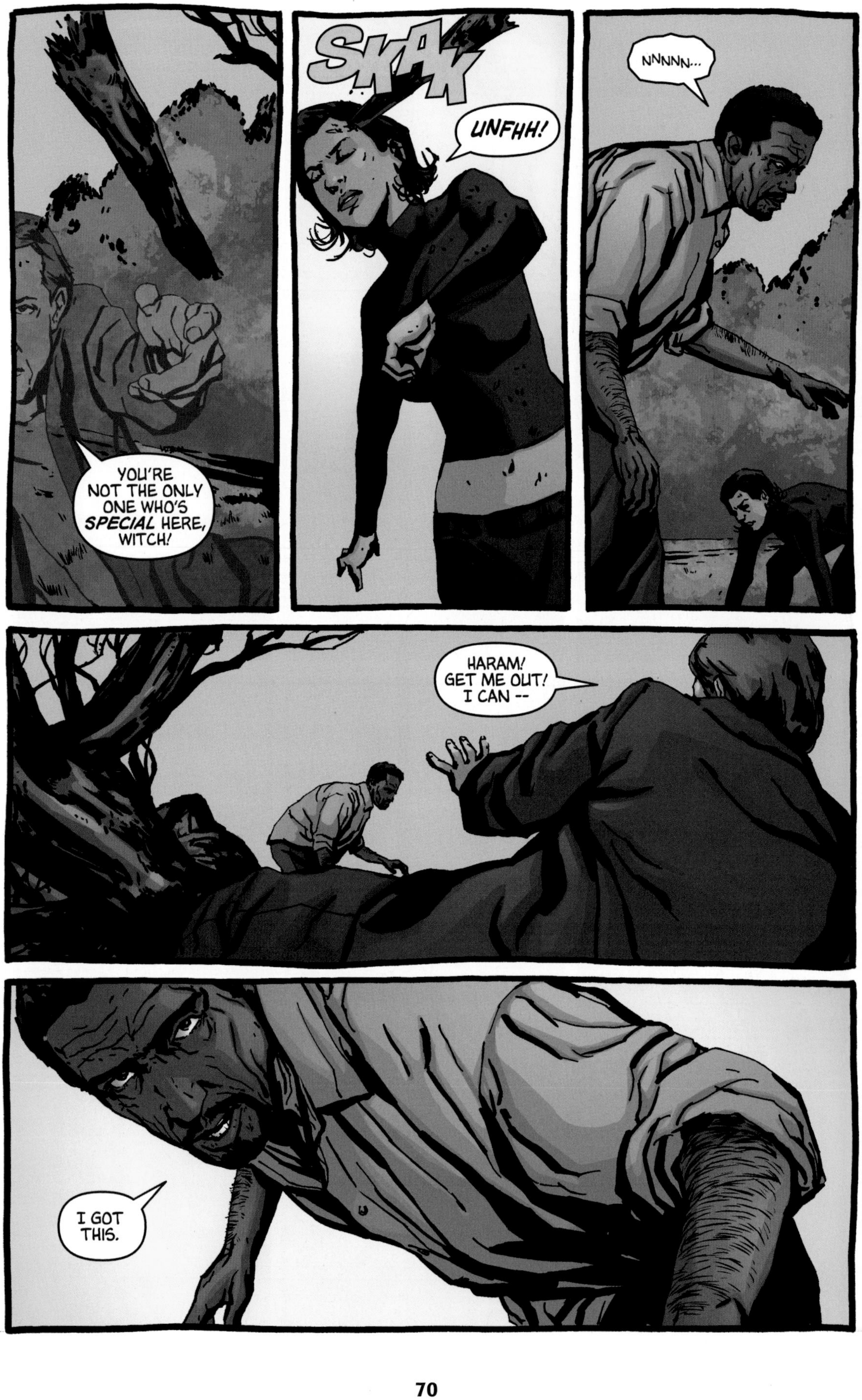
YOU'RE NOT THE ONLY ONE WHO'S *SPECIAL* HERE, WITCH!
SKAK
*UNFHH!*
NNNNN...
HARAM! GET ME OUT! I CAN --
I GOT THIS.

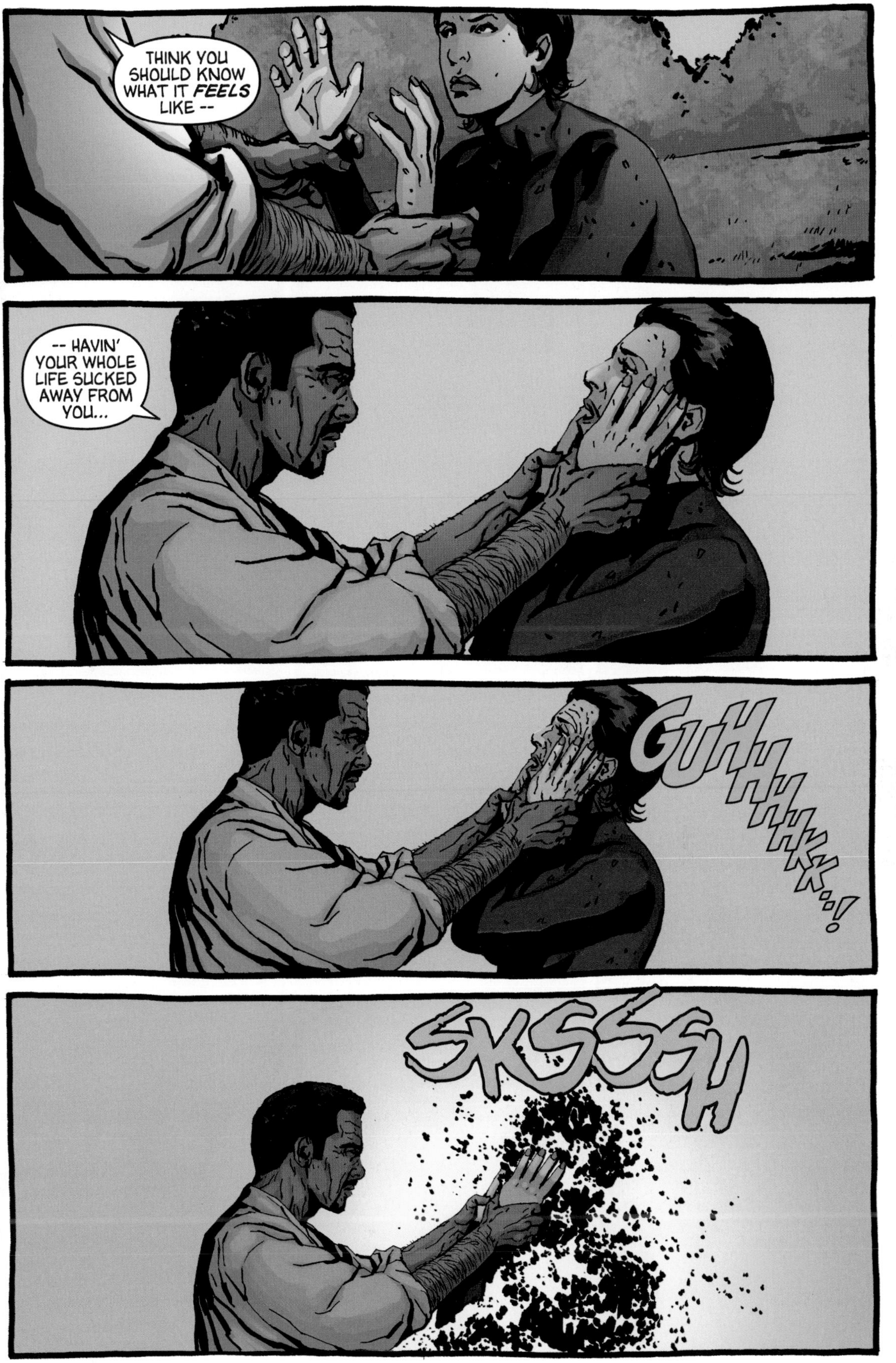
THINK YOU SHOULD KNOW WHAT IT *FEELS* LIKE --
-- HAVIN' YOUR WHOLE LIFE SUCKED AWAY FROM YOU...
GUHHHHKK..!
SKSSSH

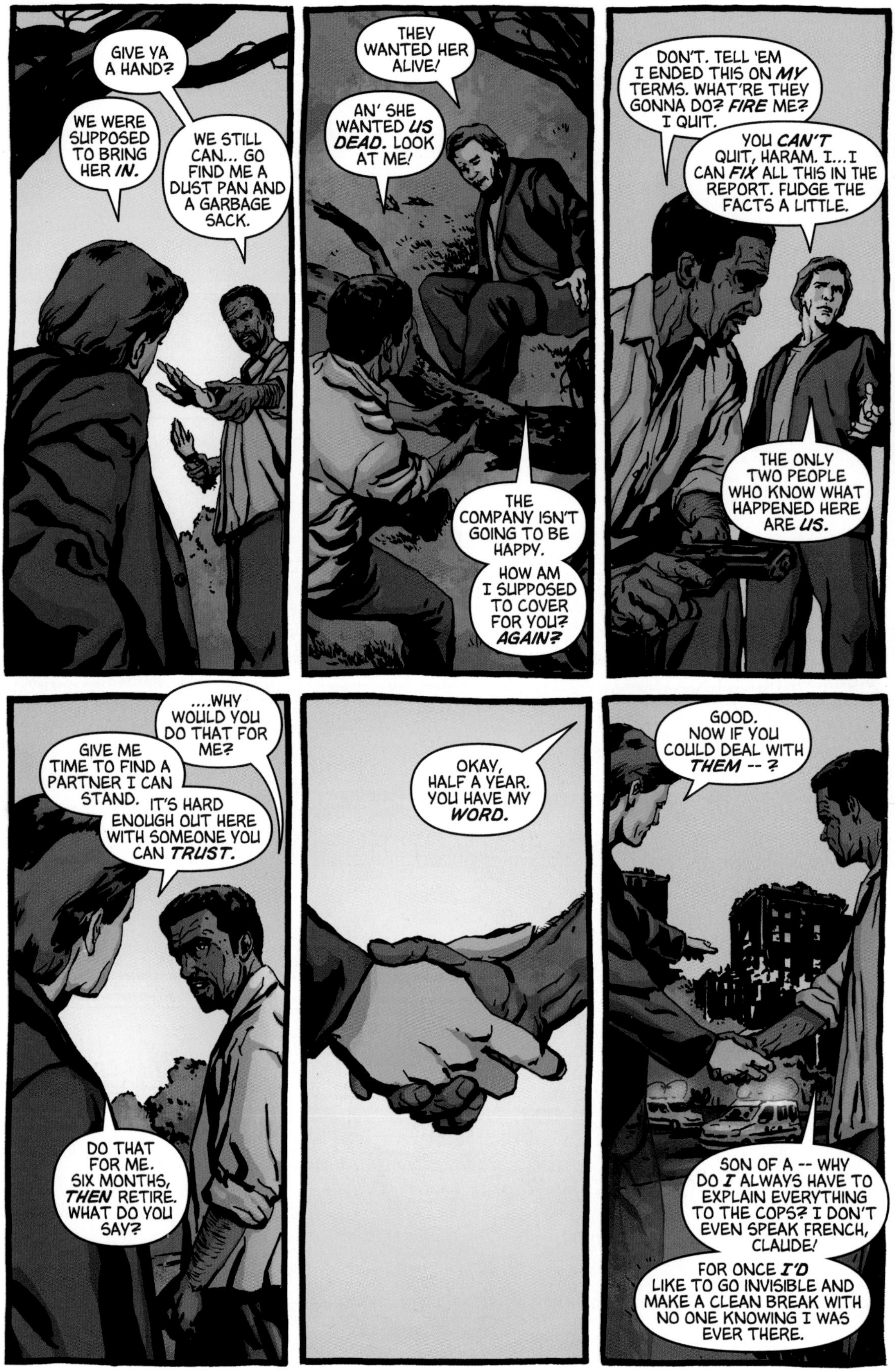
GIVE YA A HAND?
WE WERE SUPPOSED TO BRING HER *IN.*
WE STILL CAN... GO FIND ME A DUST PAN AND A GARBAGE SACK.
THEY WANTED HER ALIVE!
AN' SHE WANTED *US DEAD.* LOOK AT ME!
THE COMPANY ISN'T GOING TO BE HAPPY.
HOW AM I SUPPOSED TO COVER FOR YOU? *AGAIN?*
DON'T. TELL 'EM I ENDED THIS ON *MY* TERMS. WHAT'RE THEY GONNA DO? *FIRE* ME? I QUIT.
YOU *CAN'T* QUIT, HARAM. I...I CAN *FIX* ALL THIS IN THE REPORT. FUDGE THE FACTS A LITTLE.
THE ONLY TWO PEOPLE WHO KNOW WHAT HAPPENED HERE ARE *US.*
....WHY WOULD YOU DO THAT FOR ME?
GIVE ME TIME TO FIND A PARTNER I CAN STAND. IT'S HARD ENOUGH OUT HERE WITH SOMEONE YOU CAN *TRUST.*
DO THAT FOR ME. SIX MONTHS, *THEN* RETIRE. WHAT DO YOU SAY?
OKAY, HALF A YEAR. YOU HAVE MY *WORD.*
GOOD. NOW IF YOU COULD DEAL WITH *THEM* -- ?
SON OF A -- WHY DO *I* ALWAYS HAVE TO EXPLAIN EVERYTHING TO THE COPS? I DON'T EVEN SPEAK FRENCH, CLAUDE!
FOR ONCE *I'D* LIKE TO GO INVISIBLE AND MAKE A CLEAN BREAK WITH NO ONE KNOWING I WAS EVER THERE.

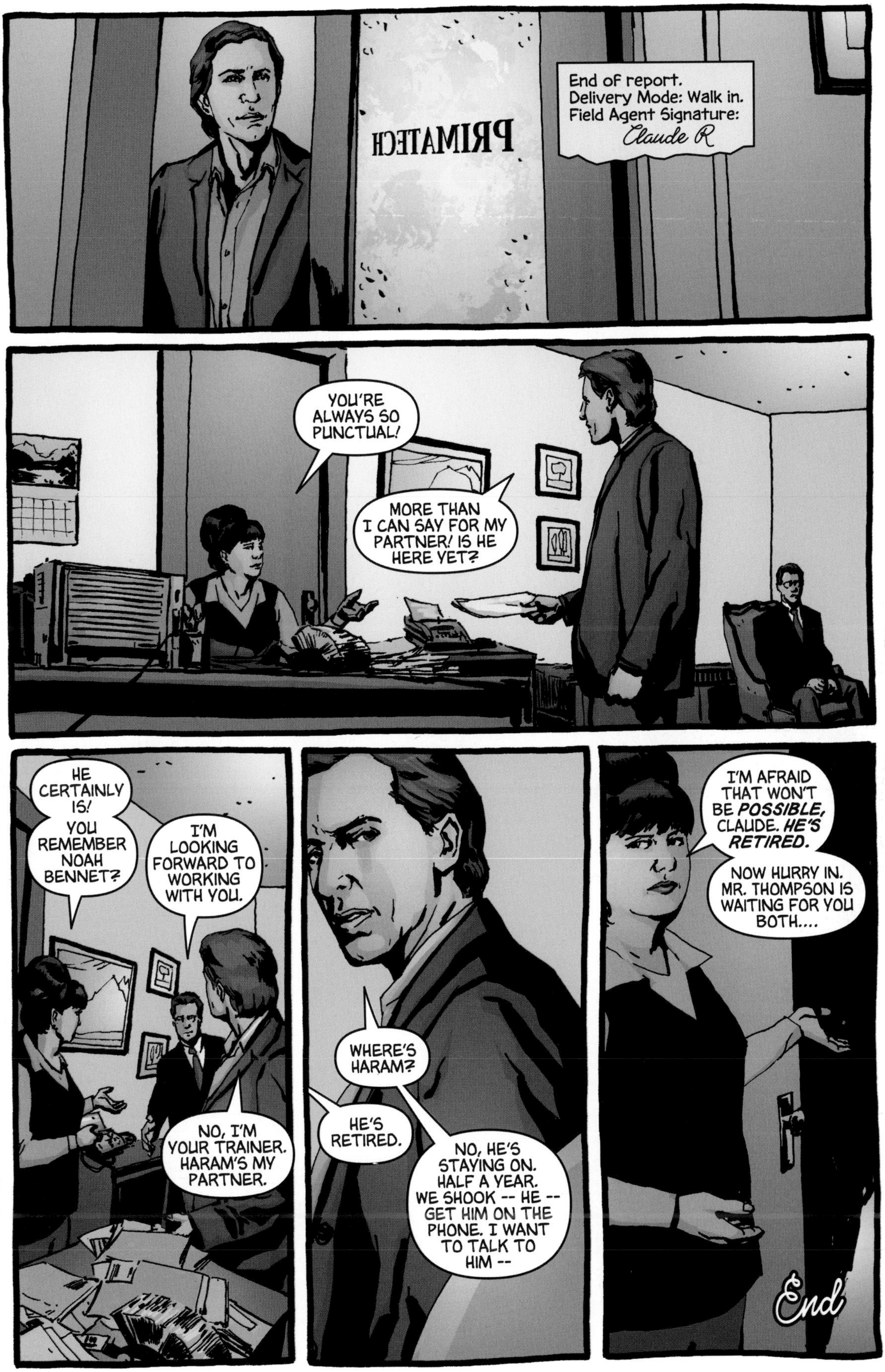
End of report.
Delivery Mode: Walk in.
Field Agent Signature:
Claude R
PRIMATECH
YOU'RE ALWAYS SO PUNCTUAL!
MORE THAN I CAN SAY FOR MY PARTNER! IS HE HERE YET?
HE CERTAINLY IS!
YOU REMEMBER NOAH BENNET?
I'M LOOKING FORWARD TO WORKING WITH YOU.
NO, I'M YOUR TRAINER. HARAM'S MY PARTNER.
WHERE'S HARAM?
HE'S RETIRED.
NO, HE'S STAYING ON. HALF A YEAR. WE SHOOK -- HE -- GET HIM ON THE PHONE. I WANT TO TALK TO HIM --
I'M AFRAID THAT WON'T BE *POSSIBLE,* CLAUDE. *HE'S RETIRED.*
NOW HURRY IN. MR. THOMPSON IS WAITING FOR YOU BOTH....
End

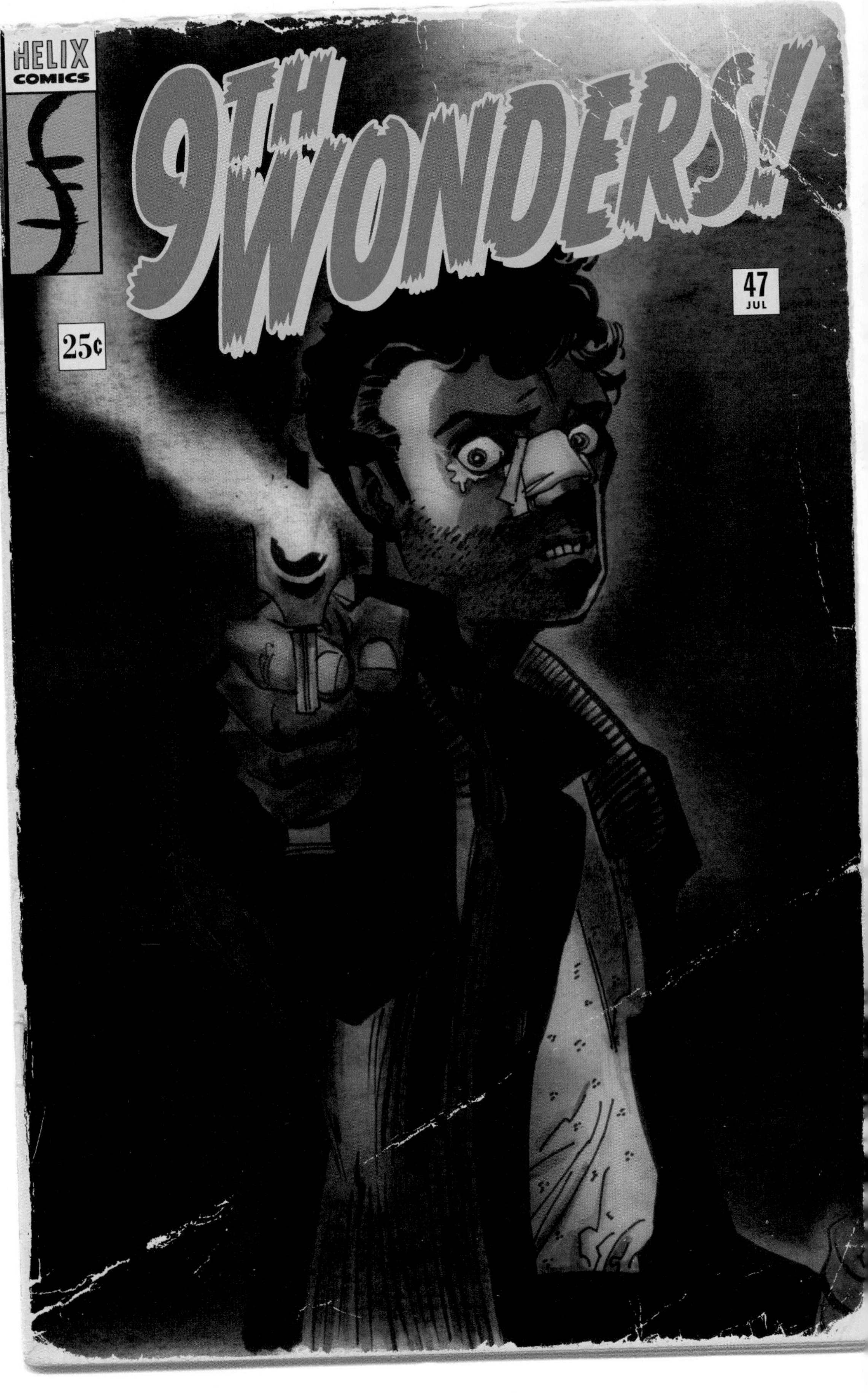

HELIX
COMICS
9TH WONDERS!
47
JUL
25¢

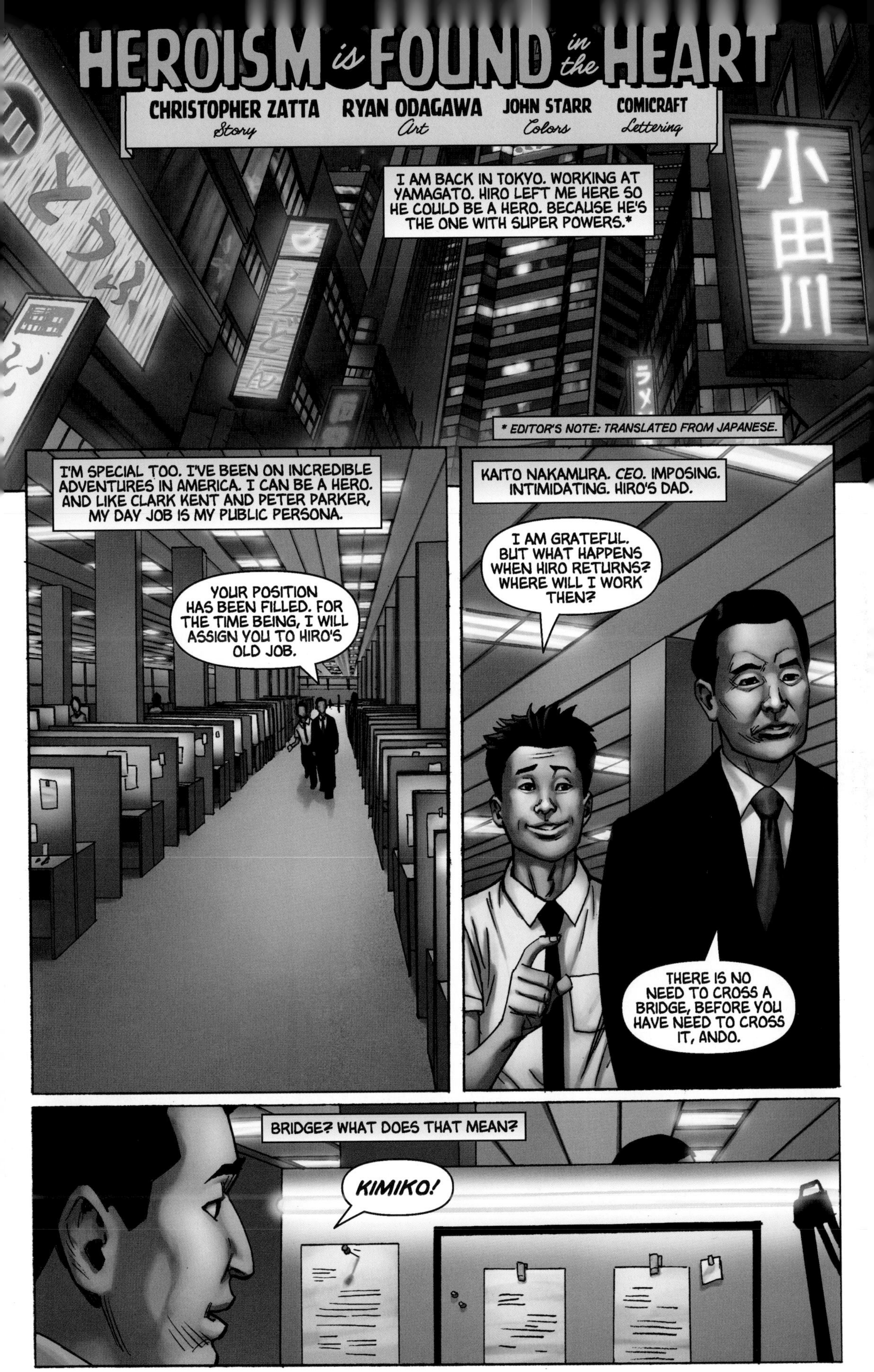
HEROISM is FOUND in the HEART
CHRISTOPHER ZATTA Story
RYAN ODAGAWA Art
JOHN STARR Colors
COMICRAFT Lettering
I AM BACK IN TOKYO. WORKING AT YAMAGATO. HIRO LEFT ME HERE SO HE COULD BE A HERO. BECAUSE HE'S THE ONE WITH SUPER POWERS.*
小田川
うどん
* EDITOR'S NOTE: TRANSLATED FROM JAPANESE.
I'M SPECIAL TOO. I'VE BEEN ON INCREDIBLE ADVENTURES IN AMERICA. I CAN BE A HERO. AND LIKE CLARK KENT AND PETER PARKER, MY DAY JOB IS MY PUBLIC PERSONA.
YOUR POSITION HAS BEEN FILLED. FOR THE TIME BEING, I WILL ASSIGN YOU TO HIRO'S OLD JOB.
KAITO NAKAMURA. CEO. IMPOSING. INTIMIDATING. HIRO'S DAD.
I AM GRATEFUL. BUT WHAT HAPPENS WHEN HIRO RETURNS? WHERE WILL I WORK THEN?
THERE IS NO NEED TO CROSS A BRIDGE, BEFORE YOU HAVE NEED TO CROSS IT, ANDO.
BRIDGE? WHAT DOES THAT MEAN?
KIMIKO!

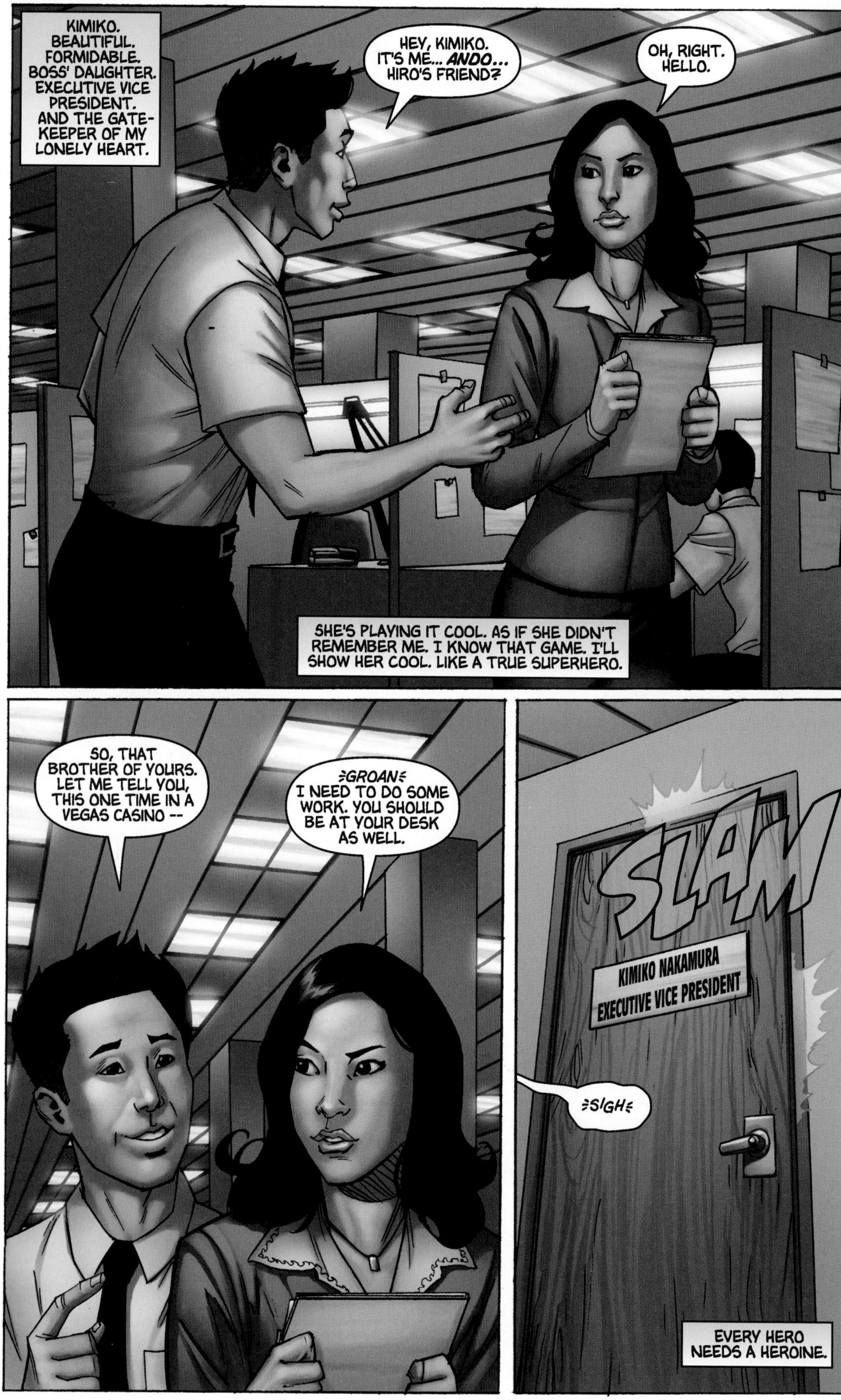
KIMIKO. BEAUTIFUL. FORMIDABLE. BOSS' DAUGHTER. EXECUTIVE VICE PRESIDENT. AND THE GATE-KEEPER OF MY LONELY HEART.
HEY, KIMIKO. IT'S ME... ANDO... HIRO'S FRIEND?
OH, RIGHT. HELLO.
SHE'S PLAYING IT COOL. AS IF SHE DIDN'T REMEMBER ME. I KNOW THAT GAME. I'LL SHOW HER COOL. LIKE A TRUE SUPERHERO.
SO, THAT BROTHER OF YOURS. LET ME TELL YOU, THIS ONE TIME IN A VEGAS CASINO --
GROAN
I NEED TO DO SOME WORK. YOU SHOULD BE AT YOUR DESK AS WELL.
SLAM
KIMIKO NAKAMURA
EXECUTIVE VICE PRESIDENT
SIGH
EVERY HERO NEEDS A HEROINE.

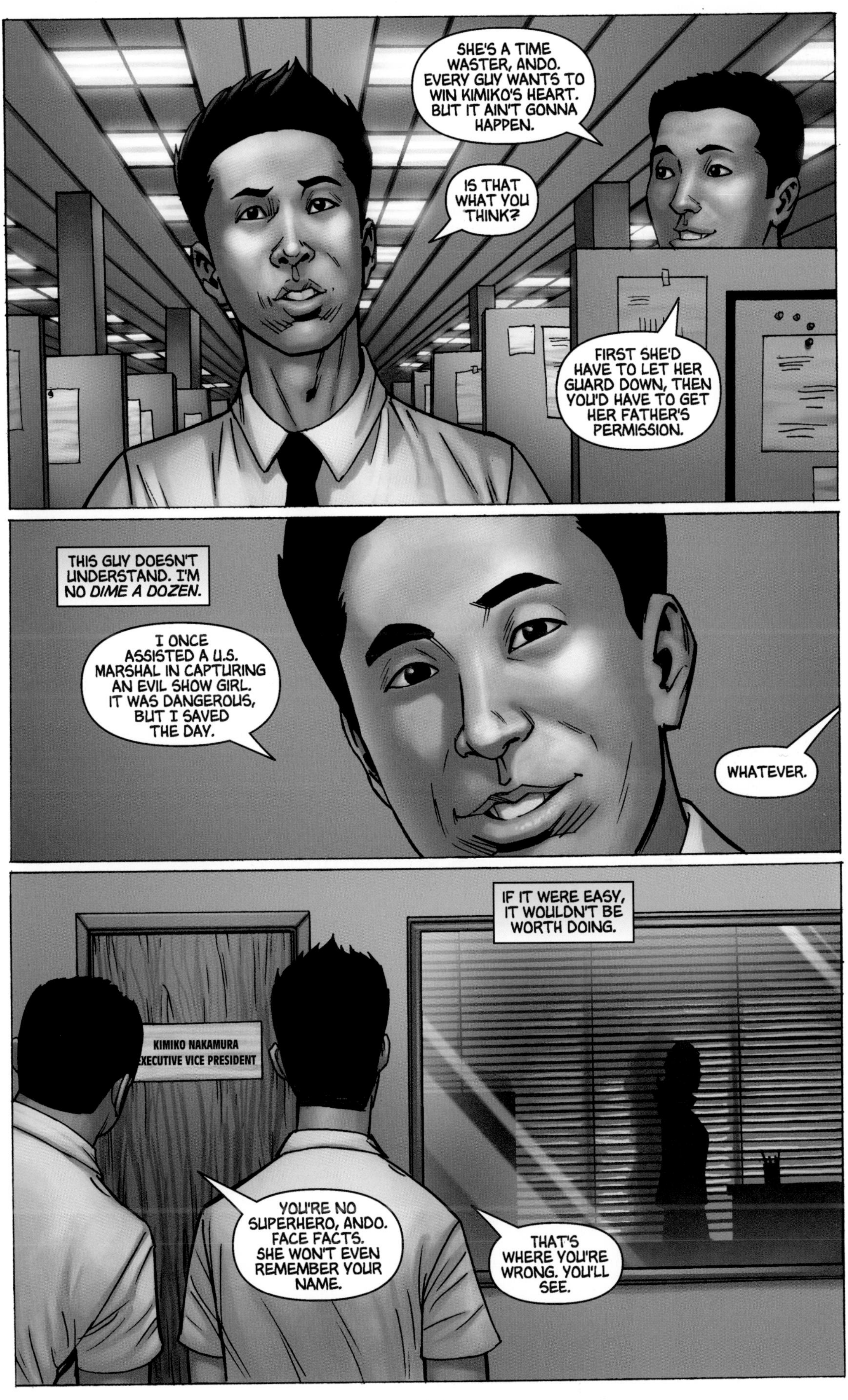
SHE'S A TIME WASTER, ANDO. EVERY GUY WANTS TO WIN KIMIKO'S HEART. BUT IT AIN'T GONNA HAPPEN.
IS THAT WHAT YOU THINK?
FIRST SHE'D HAVE TO LET HER GUARD DOWN, THEN YOU'D HAVE TO GET HER FATHER'S PERMISSION.
THIS GUY DOESN'T UNDERSTAND. I'M NO *DIME A DOZEN*.
I ONCE ASSISTED A U.S. MARSHAL IN CAPTURING AN EVIL SHOW GIRL. IT WAS DANGEROUS, BUT I SAVED THE DAY.
WHATEVER.
IF IT WERE EASY, IT WOULDN'T BE WORTH DOING.
KIMIKO NAKAMURA
EXECUTIVE VICE PRESIDENT
YOU'RE NO SUPERHERO, ANDO. FACE FACTS. SHE WON'T EVEN REMEMBER YOUR NAME.
THAT'S WHERE YOU'RE WRONG. YOU'LL SEE.

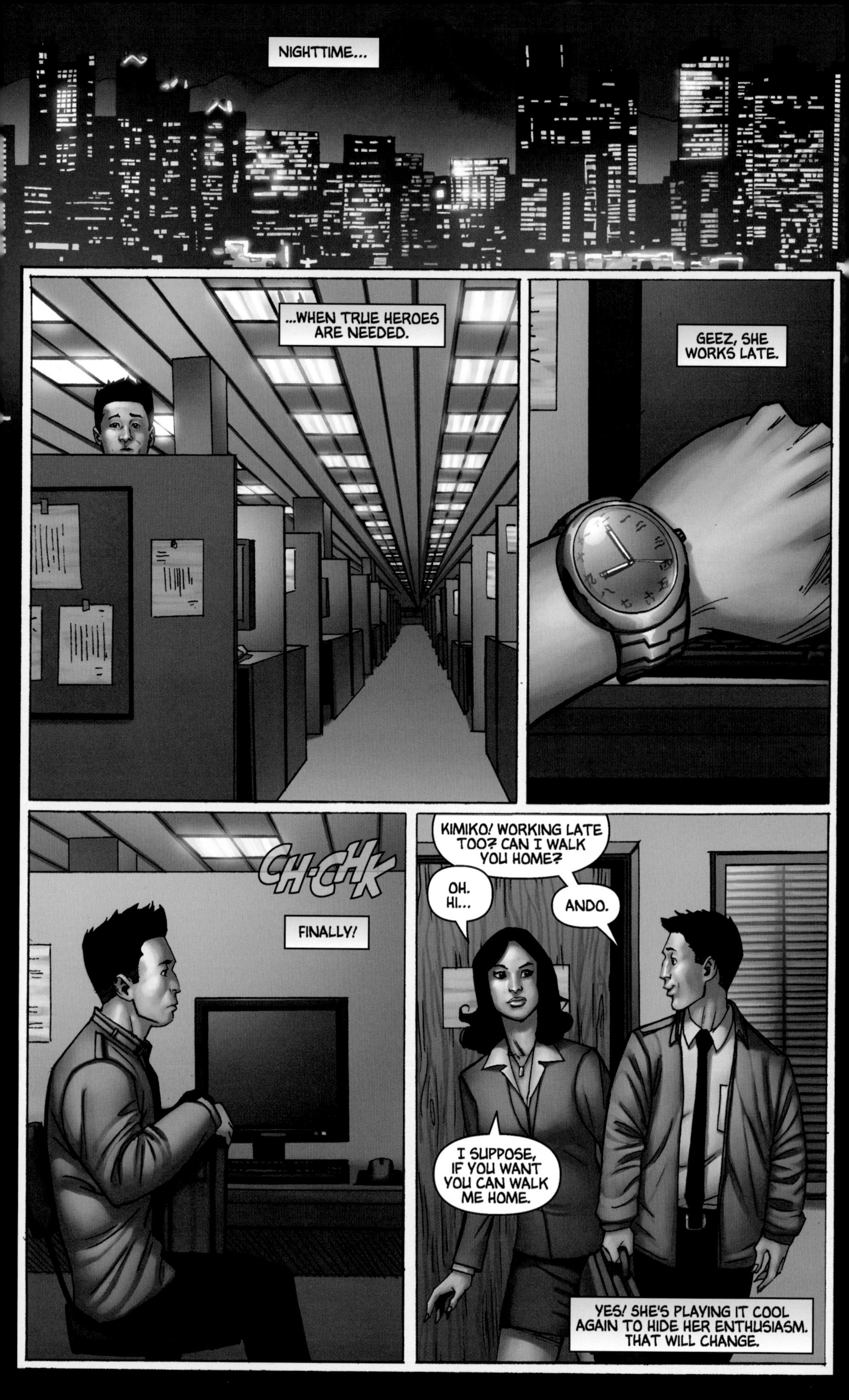
NIGHTTIME...
...WHEN TRUE HEROES ARE NEEDED.
GEEZ, SHE WORKS LATE.
CH-CHK
FINALLY!
KIMIKO! WORKING LATE TOO? CAN I WALK YOU HOME?
OH. HI...
ANDO.
I SUPPOSE, IF YOU WANT YOU CAN WALK ME HOME.
YES! SHE'S PLAYING IT COOL AGAIN TO HIDE HER ENTHUSIASM. THAT WILL CHANGE.

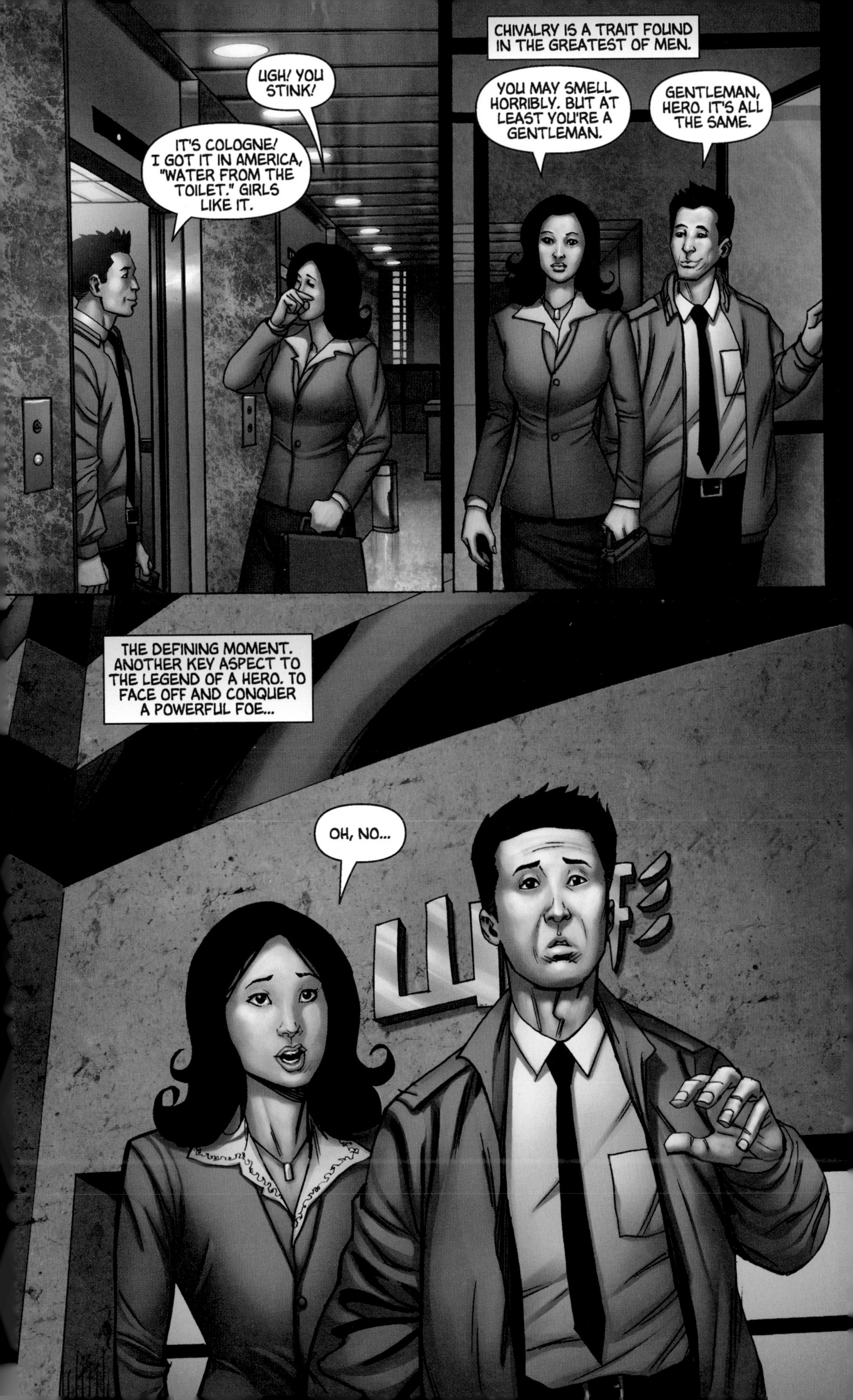
UGH! YOU STINK!
IT'S COLOGNE! I GOT IT IN AMERICA, "WATER FROM THE TOILET." GIRLS LIKE IT.
CHIVALRY IS A TRAIT FOUND IN THE GREATEST OF MEN.
YOU MAY SMELL HORRIBLY. BUT AT LEAST YOU'RE A GENTLEMAN.
GENTLEMAN, HERO. IT'S ALL THE SAME.
THE DEFINING MOMENT. ANOTHER KEY ASPECT TO THE LEGEND OF A HERO. TO FACE OFF AND CONQUER A POWERFUL FOE...
OH, NO...

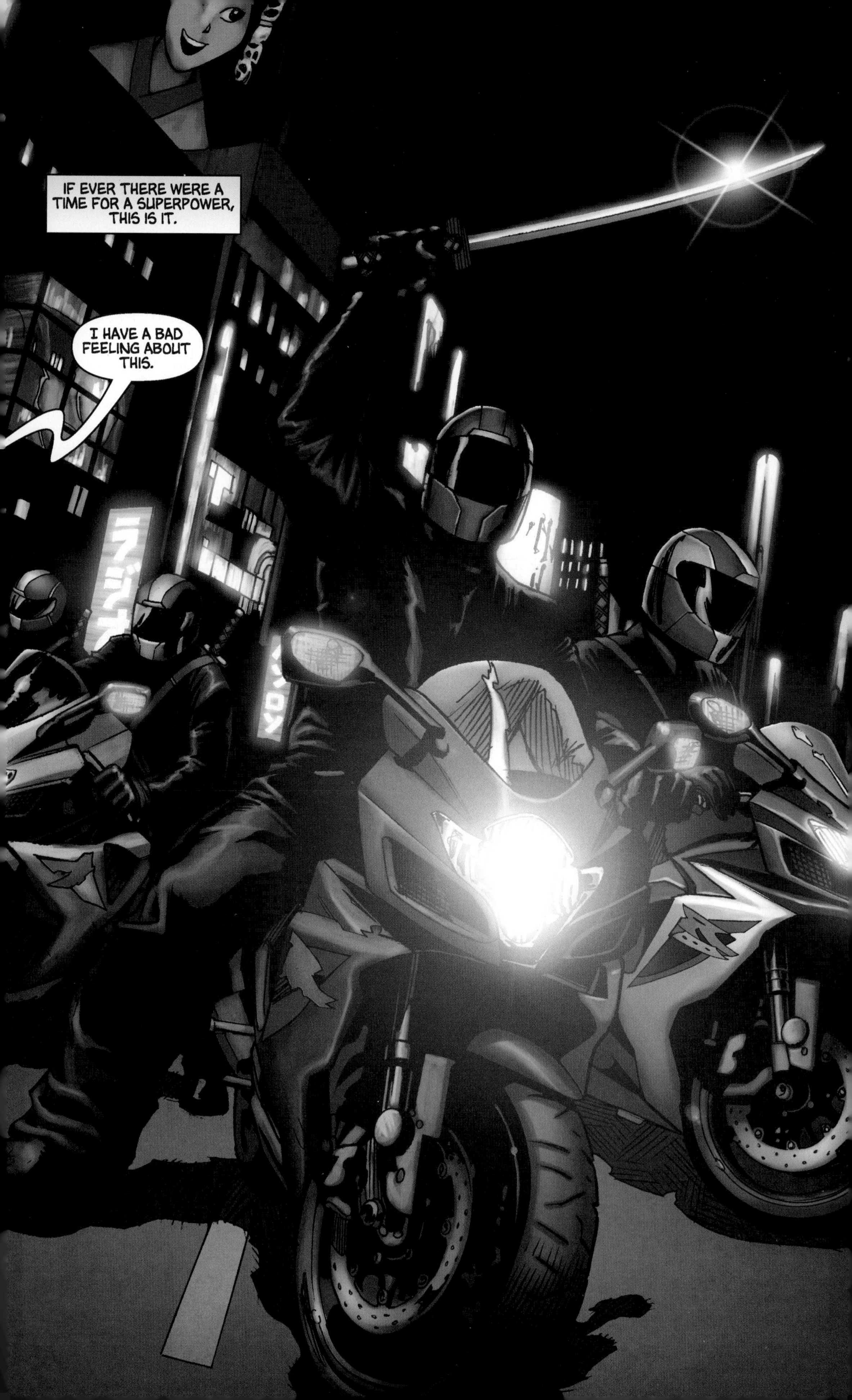

IF EVER THERE WERE A TIME FOR A SUPERPOWER, THIS IS IT.
I HAVE A BAD FEELING ABOUT THIS.

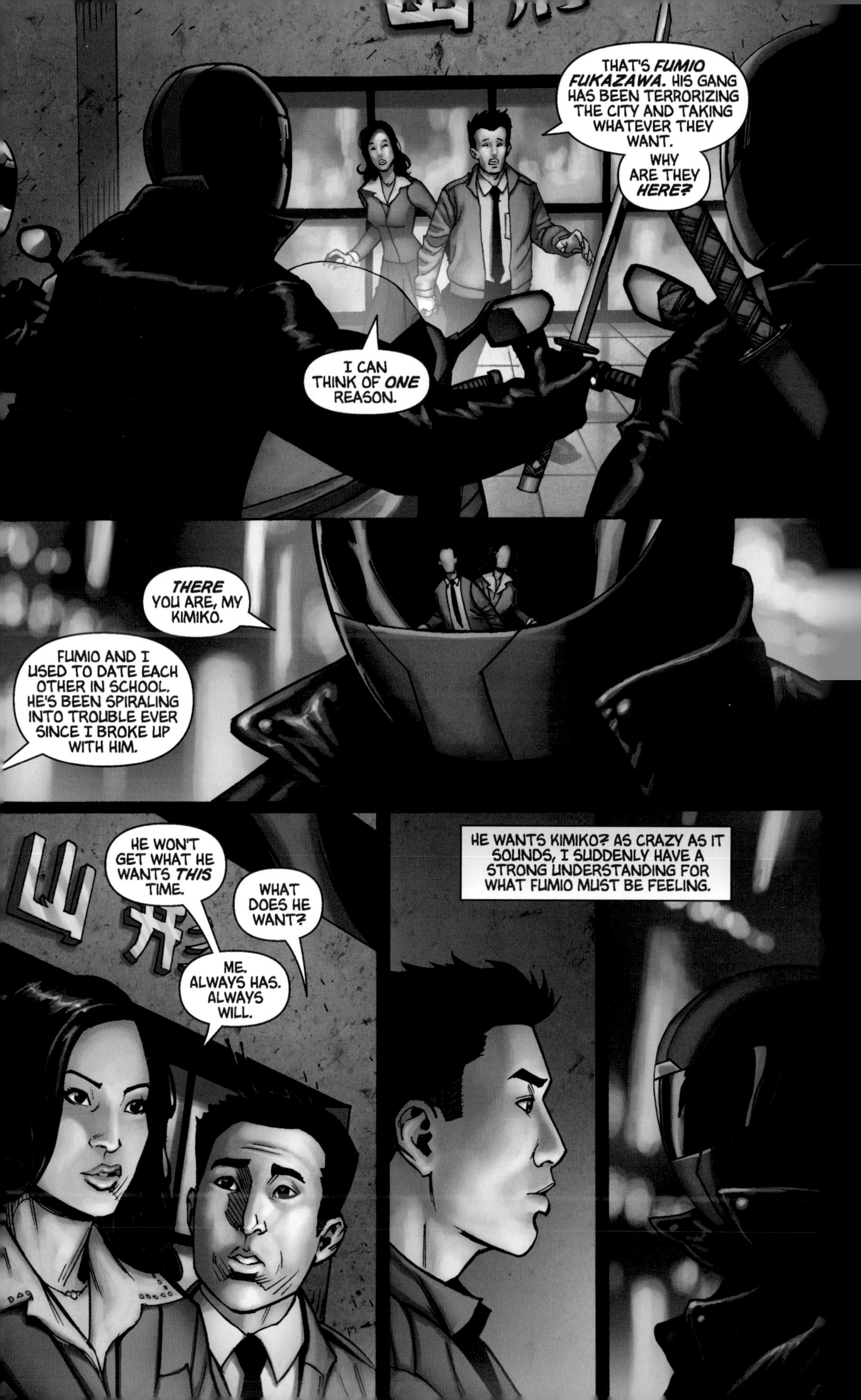
THAT'S FUMIO FUKAZAWA. HIS GANG HAS BEEN TERRORIZING THE CITY AND TAKING WHATEVER THEY WANT.
WHY ARE THEY HERE?
I CAN THINK OF ONE REASON.
THERE YOU ARE, MY KIMIKO.
FUMIO AND I USED TO DATE EACH OTHER IN SCHOOL. HE'S BEEN SPIRALING INTO TROUBLE EVER SINCE I BROKE UP WITH HIM.
HE WON'T GET WHAT HE WANTS THIS TIME.
WHAT DOES HE WANT?
ME. ALWAYS HAS. ALWAYS WILL.
HE WANTS KIMIKO? AS CRAZY AS IT SOUNDS, I SUDDENLY HAVE A STRONG UNDERSTANDING FOR WHAT FUMIO MUST BE FEELING.

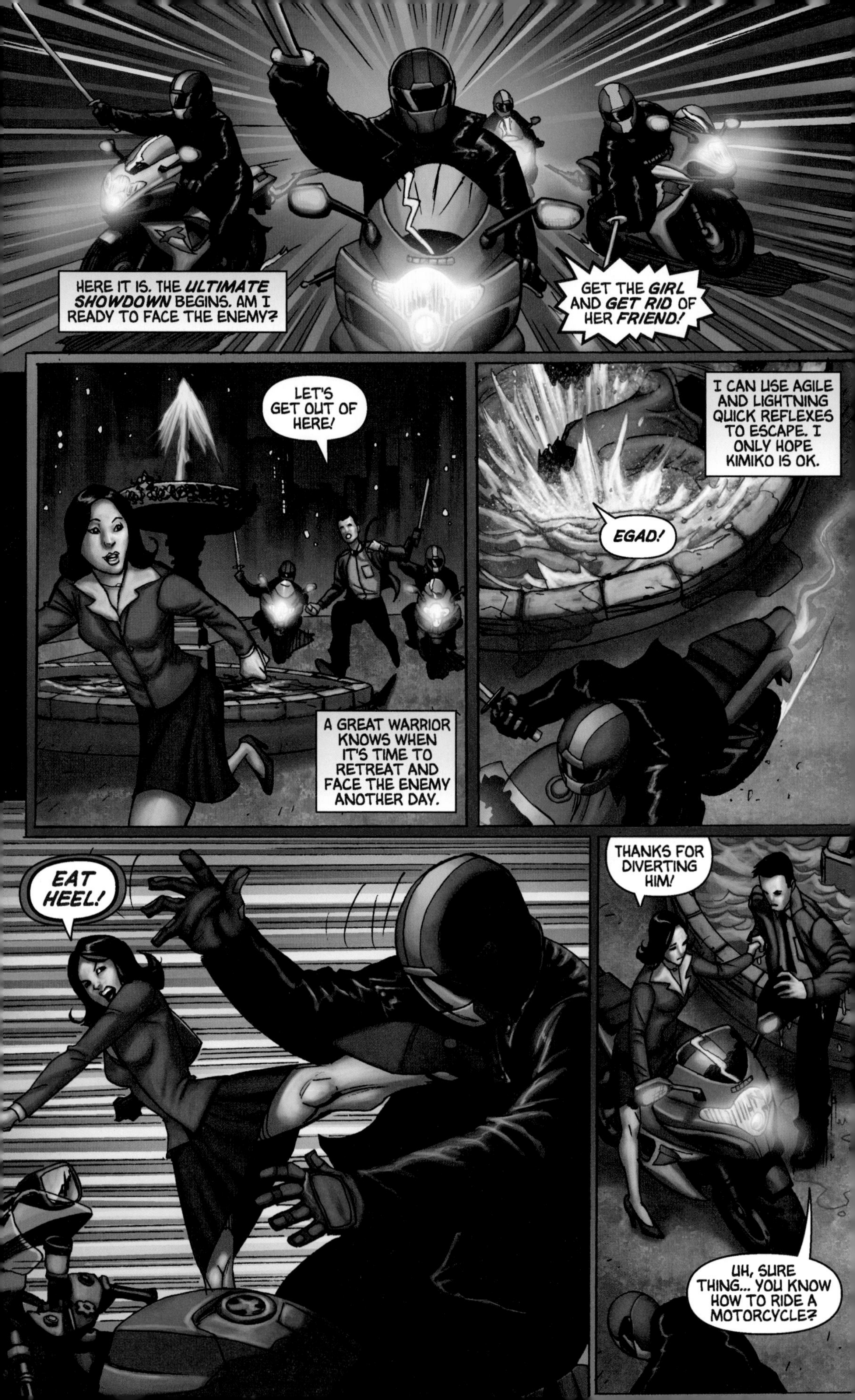
HERE IT IS. THE ULTIMATE SHOWDOWN BEGINS. AM I READY TO FACE THE ENEMY?
GET THE GIRL AND GET RID OF HER FRIEND!
LET'S GET OUT OF HERE!
A GREAT WARRIOR KNOWS WHEN IT'S TIME TO RETREAT AND FACE THE ENEMY ANOTHER DAY.
I CAN USE AGILE AND LIGHTNING QUICK REFLEXES TO ESCAPE. I ONLY HOPE KIMIKO IS OK.
EGAD!
EAT HEEL!
THANKS FOR DIVERTING HIM!
UH, SURE THING... YOU KNOW HOW TO RIDE A MOTORCYCLE?

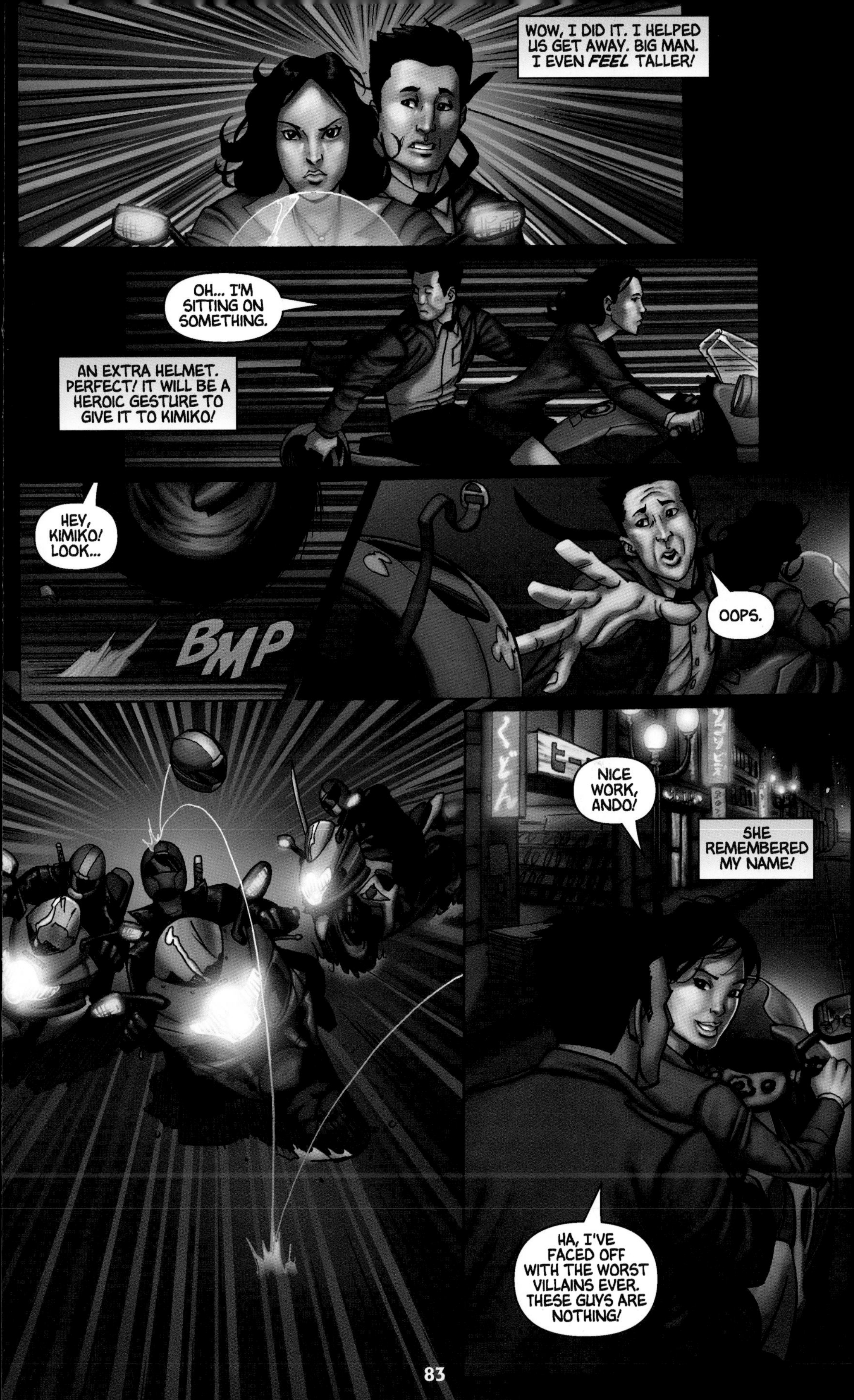
WOW, I DID IT. I HELPED US GET AWAY. BIG MAN. I EVEN *FEEL* TALLER!
OH... I'M SITTING ON SOMETHING.
AN EXTRA HELMET. PERFECT! IT WILL BE A HEROIC GESTURE TO GIVE IT TO KIMIKO!
HEY, KIMIKO! LOOK...
BMP
OOPS.
NICE WORK, ANDO!
SHE REMEMBERED MY NAME!
HA, I'VE FACED OFF WITH THE WORST VILLAINS EVER. THESE GUYS ARE NOTHING!

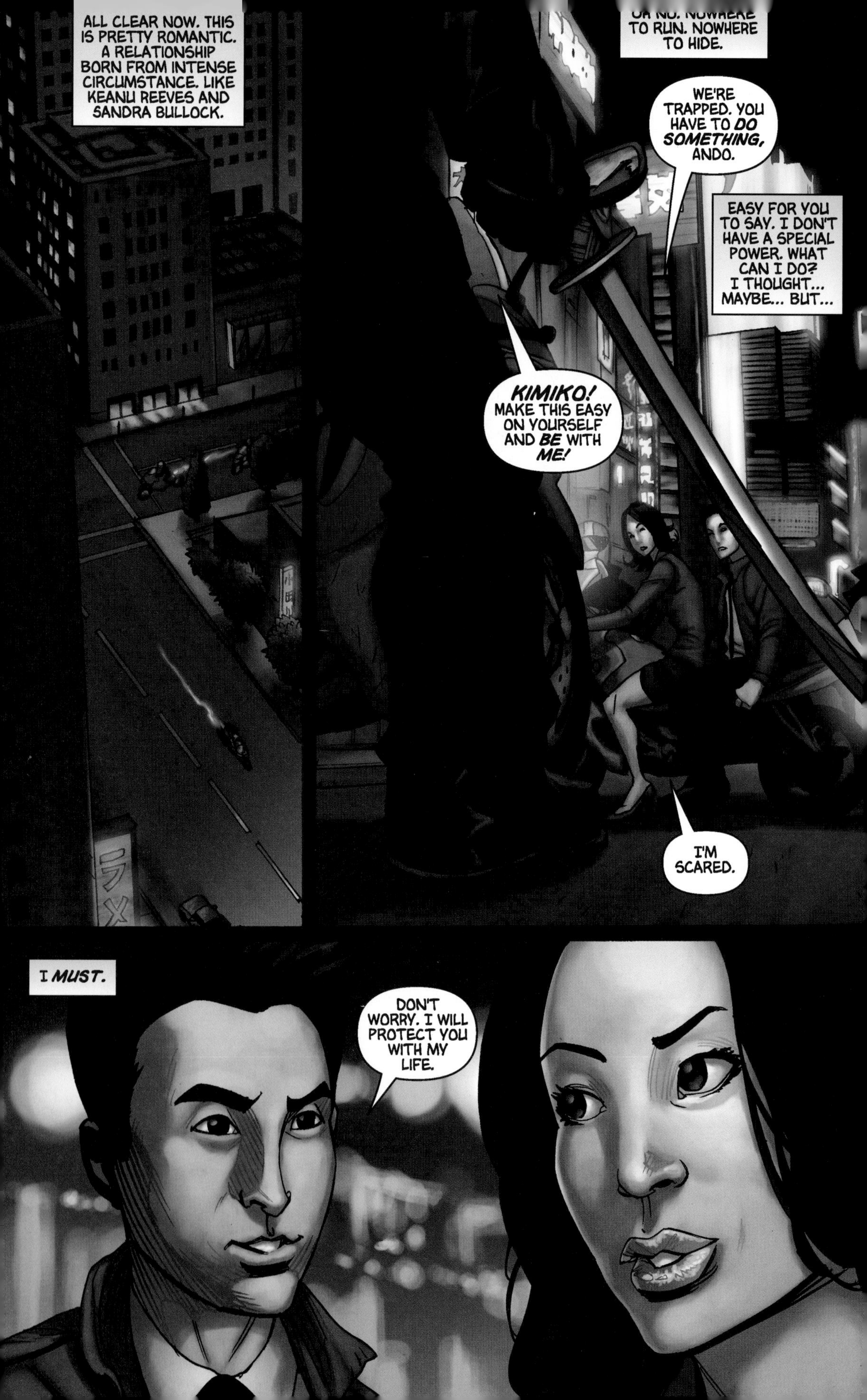
ALL CLEAR NOW. THIS IS PRETTY ROMANTIC. A RELATIONSHIP BORN FROM INTENSE CIRCUMSTANCE. LIKE KEANU REEVES AND SANDRA BULLOCK.
TO RUN. NOWHERE TO HIDE.
WE'RE TRAPPED. YOU HAVE TO *DO SOMETHING,* ANDO.
EASY FOR YOU TO SAY. I DON'T HAVE A SPECIAL POWER. WHAT CAN I DO? I THOUGHT... MAYBE... BUT...
*KIMIKO!* MAKE THIS EASY ON YOURSELF AND *BE* WITH *ME!*
I'M SCARED.
I *MUST.*
DON'T WORRY. I WILL PROTECT YOU WITH MY LIFE.

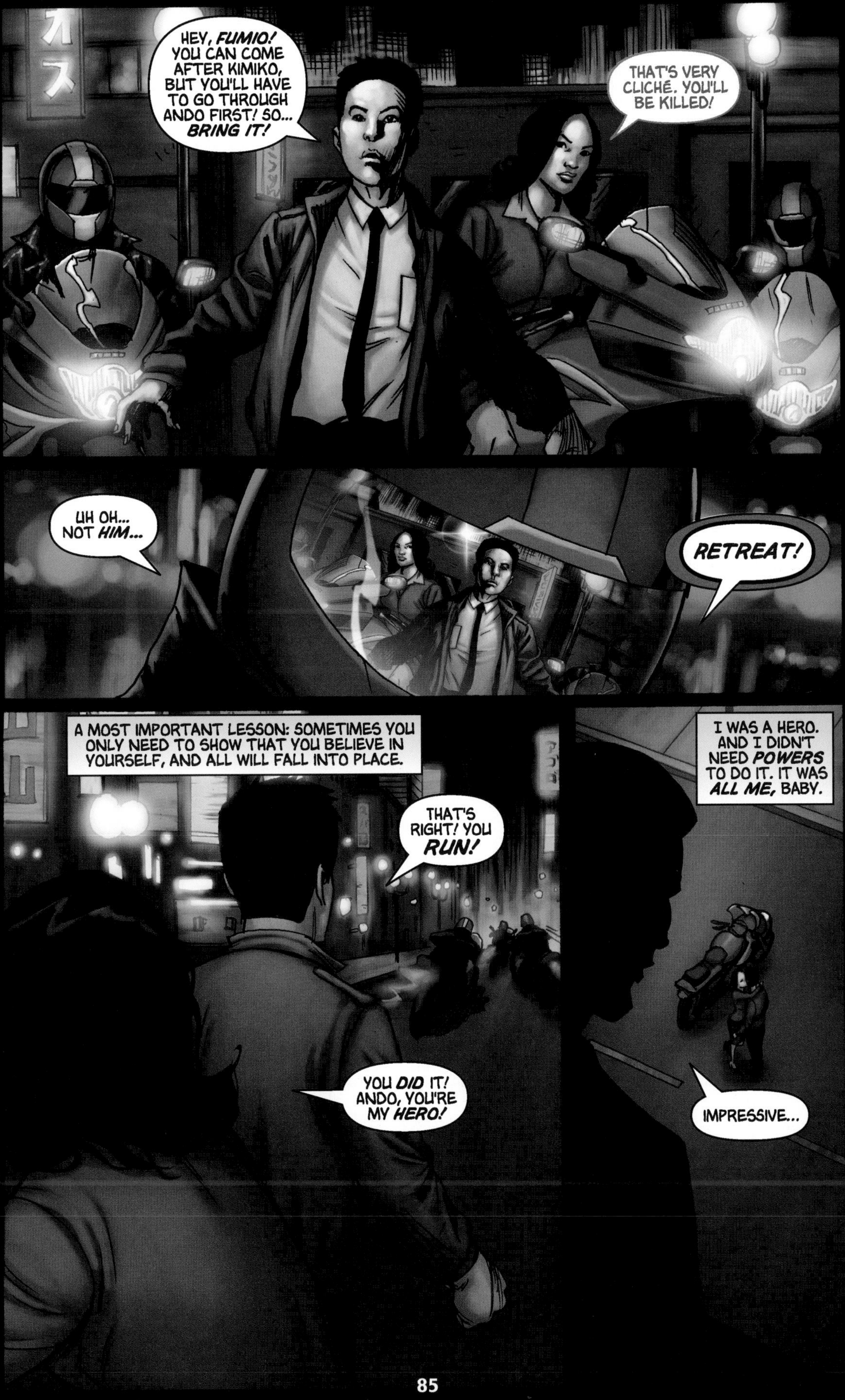

HEY, FUMIO! YOU CAN COME AFTER KIMIKO, BUT YOU'LL HAVE TO GO THROUGH ANDO FIRST! SO... BRING IT!
THAT'S VERY CLICHÉ. YOU'LL BE KILLED!
UH OH... NOT HIM...
RETREAT!
A MOST IMPORTANT LESSON: SOMETIMES YOU ONLY NEED TO SHOW THAT YOU BELIEVE IN YOURSELF, AND ALL WILL FALL INTO PLACE.
THAT'S RIGHT! YOU RUN!
YOU DID IT! ANDO, YOU'RE MY HERO!
I WAS A HERO. AND I DIDN'T NEED POWERS TO DO IT. IT WAS ALL ME, BABY.
IMPRESSIVE...

YOU'VE PROTECTED MY DAUGHTER AND PROVEN YOUR WORTH, ANDO.
ENJOY YOUR MOMENT IN THE SUN. WE ALL NEED THEM.
HEROISM is FOUND in the HEART
Part 2
CHRISTOPHER ZATTA Story
RYAN ODAGAWA Art
JOHN STARR Colors
COMICRAFT Lettering

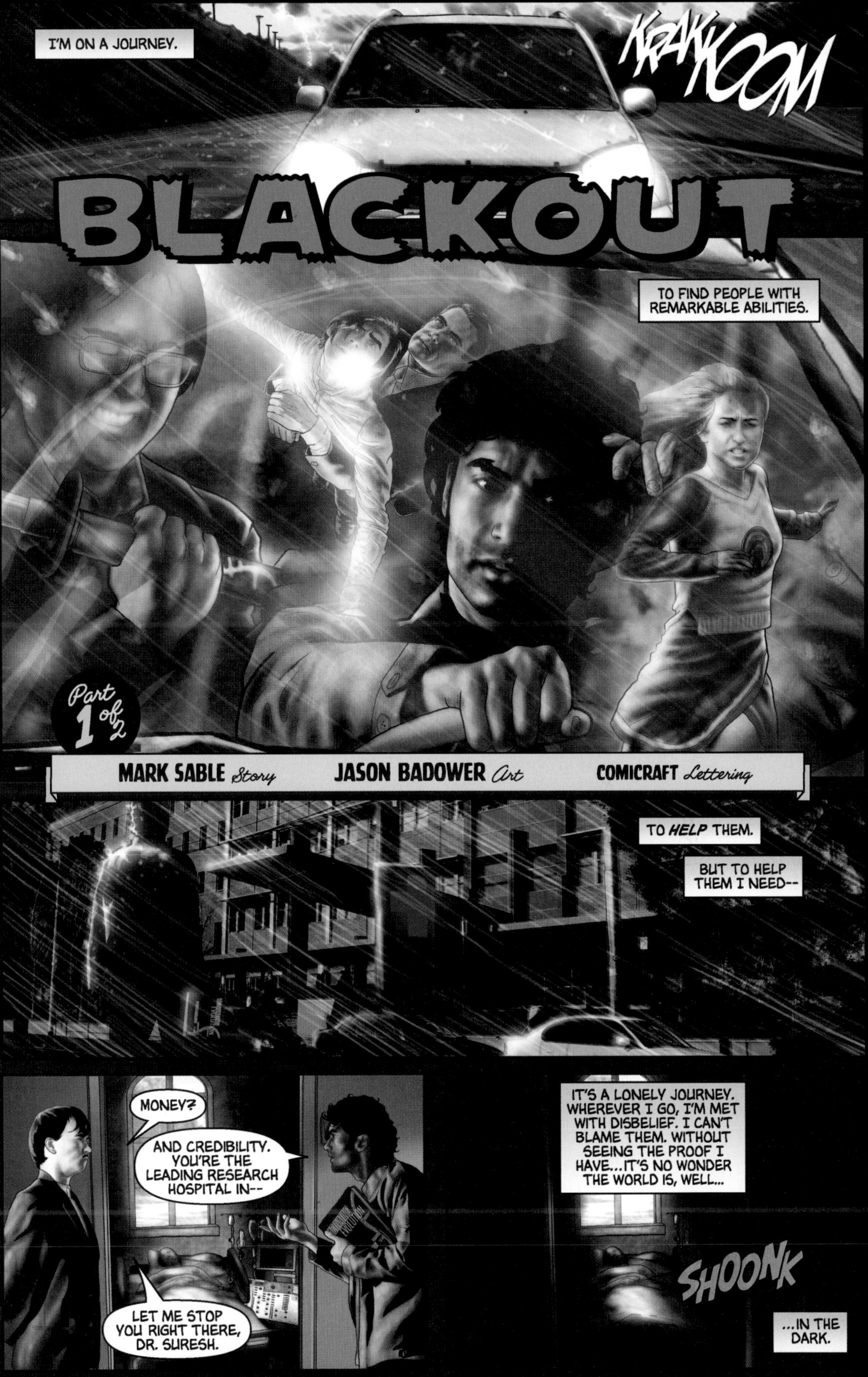
I'M ON A JOURNEY.
KRAKKOOM
BLACKOUT
TO FIND PEOPLE WITH REMARKABLE ABILITIES.
Part 1 of 2
MARK SABLE Story JASON BADOWER Art COMICRAFT Lettering
TO HELP THEM.
BUT TO HELP THEM I NEED--
MONEY?
AND CREDIBILITY. YOU'RE THE LEADING RESEARCH HOSPITAL IN--
LET ME STOP YOU RIGHT THERE, DR. SURESH.
IT'S A LONELY JOURNEY. WHEREVER I GO, I'M MET WITH DISBELIEF. I CAN'T BLAME THEM. WITHOUT SEEING THE PROOF I HAVE...IT'S NO WONDER THE WORLD IS, WELL...
SHOONK
...IN THE DARK.

BZZZZZZZZ

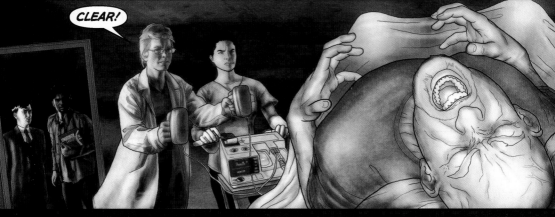

CLEAR!

DEFIBRILLATOR'S DEAD!

NOT AGAIN...

GET SOME ADRENALINE.

SHOONK

WELCOME BACK TO THE LAND OF THE LIVING.

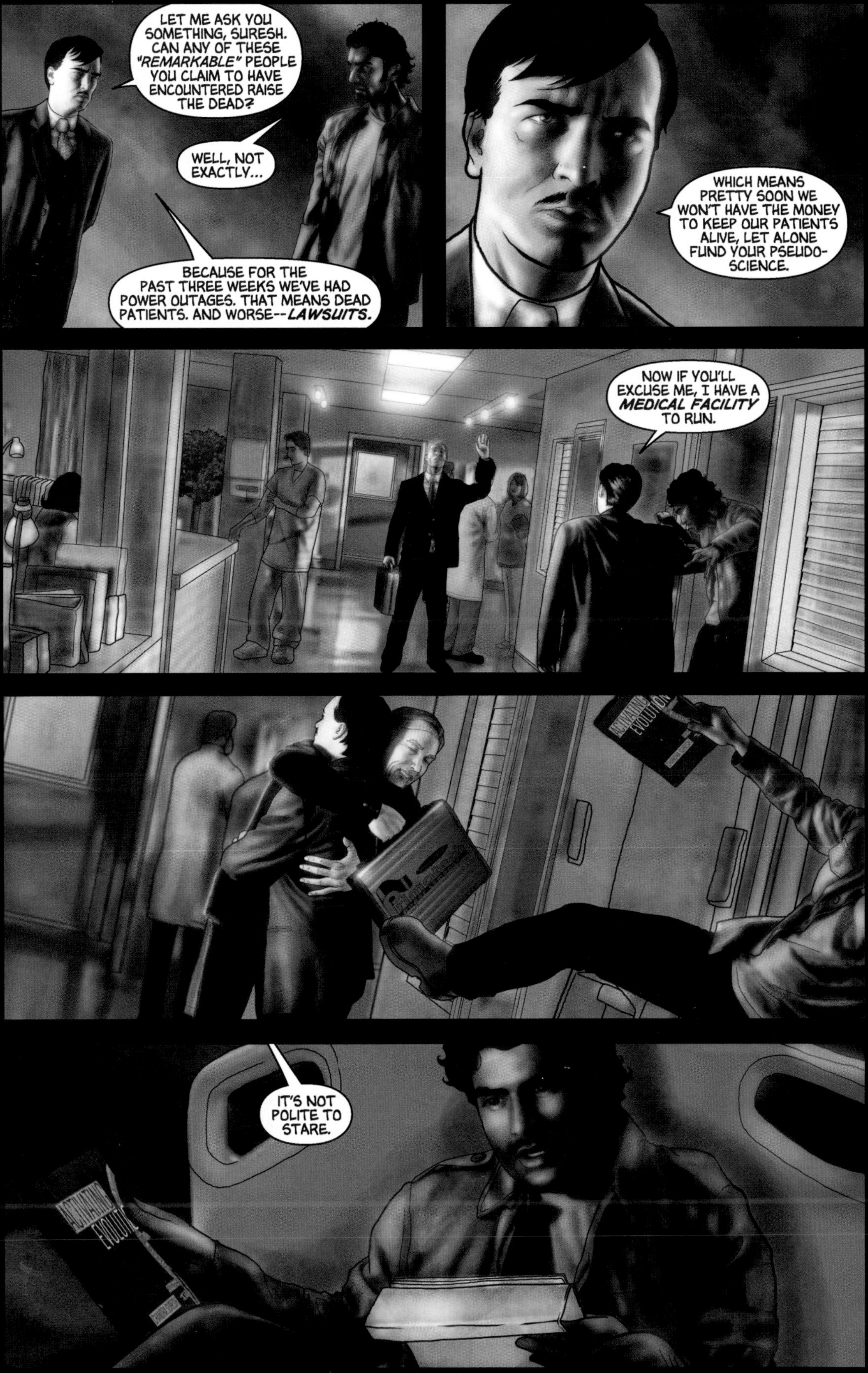
LET ME ASK YOU SOMETHING, SURESH. CAN ANY OF THESE "REMARKABLE" PEOPLE YOU CLAIM TO HAVE ENCOUNTERED RAISE THE DEAD?
WELL, NOT EXACTLY...
BECAUSE FOR THE PAST THREE WEEKS WE'VE HAD POWER OUTAGES. THAT MEANS DEAD PATIENTS. AND WORSE--LAWSUITS.
WHICH MEANS PRETTY SOON WE WON'T HAVE THE MONEY TO KEEP OUR PATIENTS ALIVE, LET ALONE FUND YOUR PSEUDO-SCIENCE.
NOW IF YOU'LL EXCUSE ME, I HAVE A MEDICAL FACILITY TO RUN.
ACTIVATING EVOLUTION
IT'S NOT POLITE TO STARE.
ACTIVATING EVOLUTI

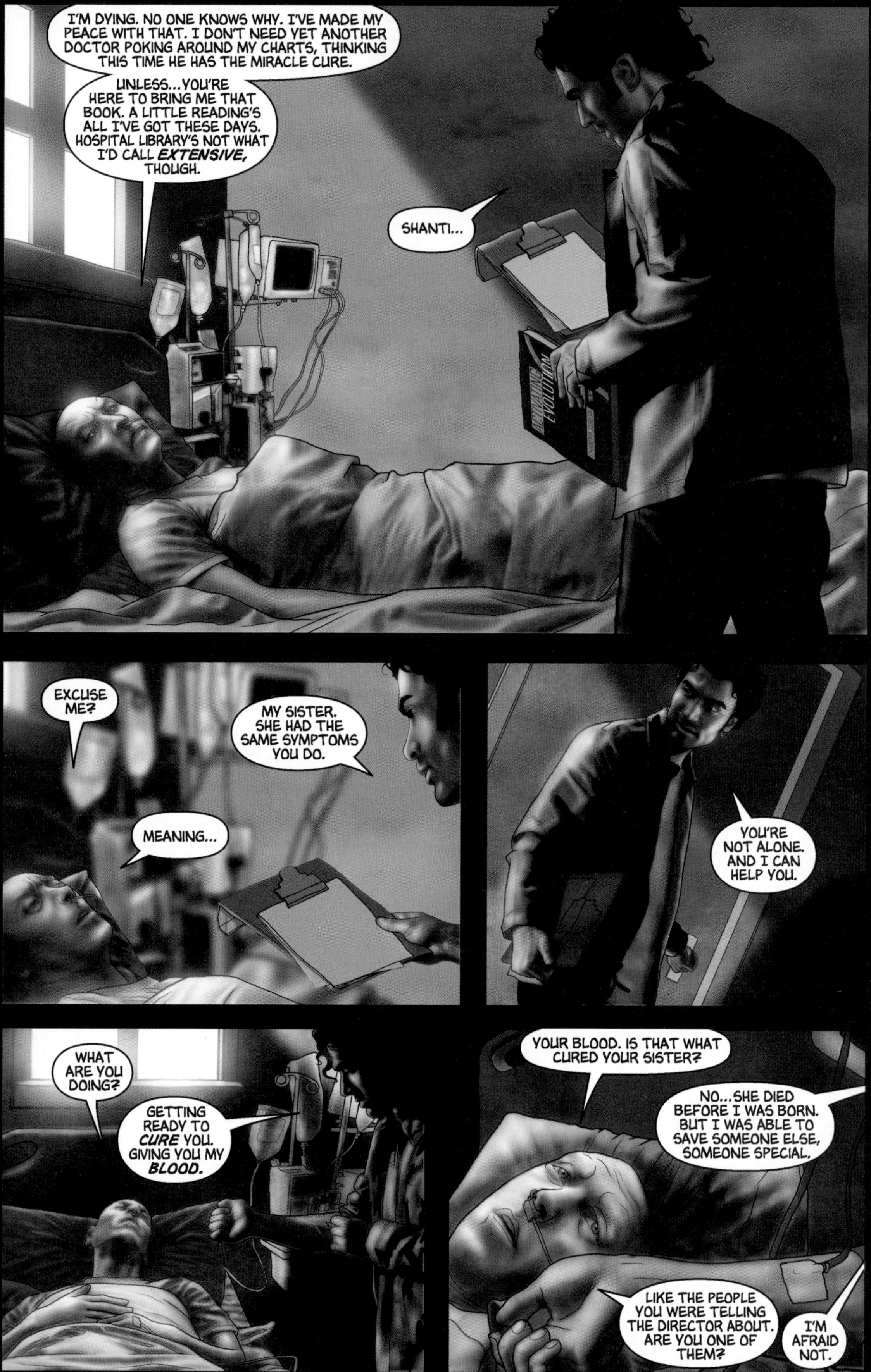
I'M DYING. NO ONE KNOWS WHY. I'VE MADE MY PEACE WITH THAT. I DON'T NEED YET ANOTHER DOCTOR POKING AROUND MY CHARTS, THINKING THIS TIME HE HAS THE MIRACLE CURE.
UNLESS...YOU'RE HERE TO BRING ME THAT BOOK. A LITTLE READING'S ALL I'VE GOT THESE DAYS. HOSPITAL LIBRARY'S NOT WHAT I'D CALL *EXTENSIVE,* THOUGH.
SHANTI...
EVOLUTION
EXCUSE ME?
MY SISTER. SHE HAD THE SAME SYMPTOMS YOU DO.
MEANING...
YOU'RE NOT ALONE. AND I CAN HELP YOU.
WHAT ARE YOU DOING?
GETTING READY TO *CURE* YOU. GIVING YOU MY *BLOOD.*
YOUR BLOOD. IS THAT WHAT CURED YOUR SISTER?
NO...SHE DIED BEFORE I WAS BORN. BUT I WAS ABLE TO SAVE SOMEONE ELSE, SOMEONE SPECIAL.
LIKE THE PEOPLE YOU WERE TELLING THE DIRECTOR ABOUT. ARE YOU ONE OF THEM?
I'M AFRAID NOT.

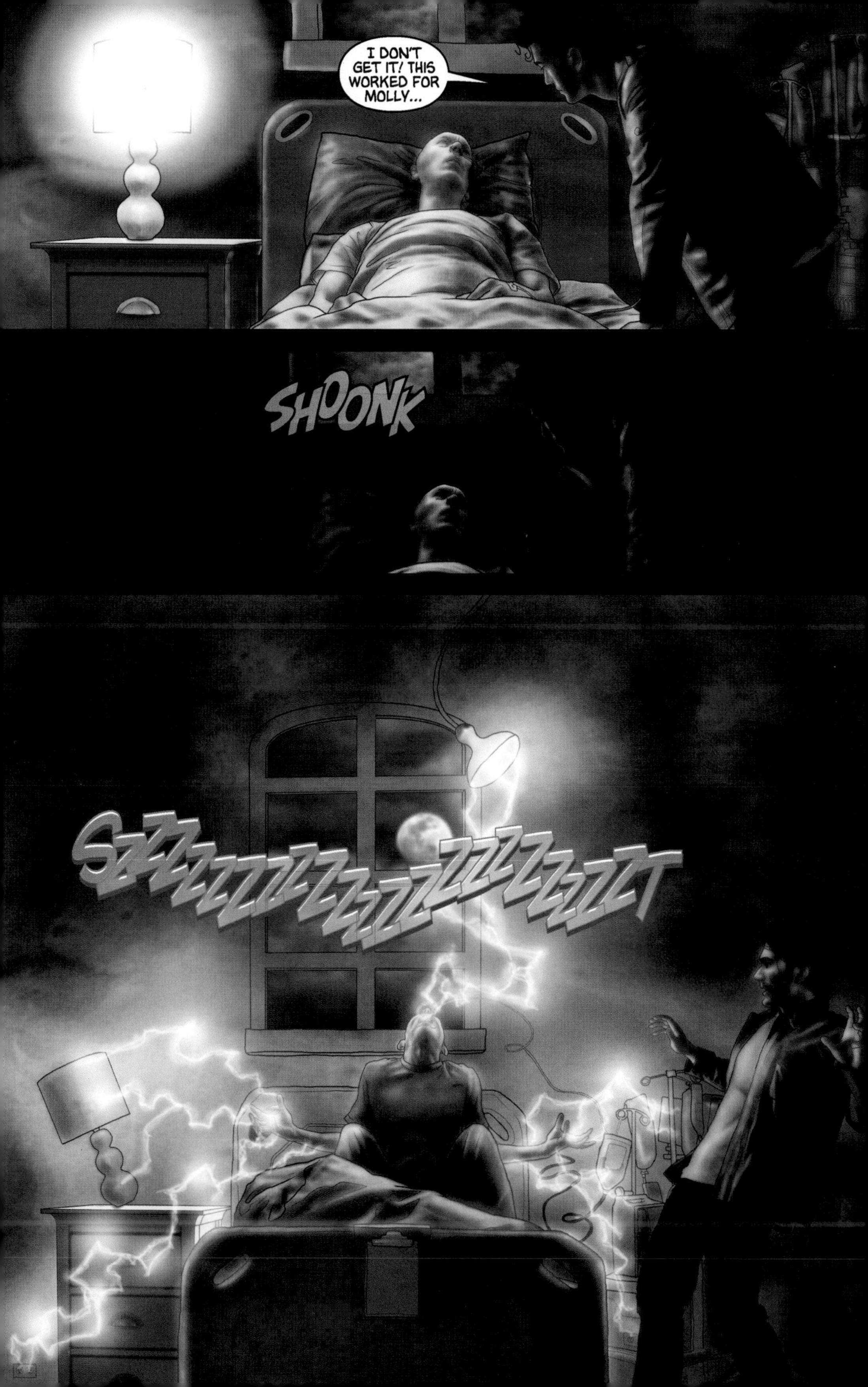

I DON'T GET IT! THIS WORKED FOR MOLLY...
SHOONK
SZZZZZZZZZZZZZZZZZZZZZZZZZT

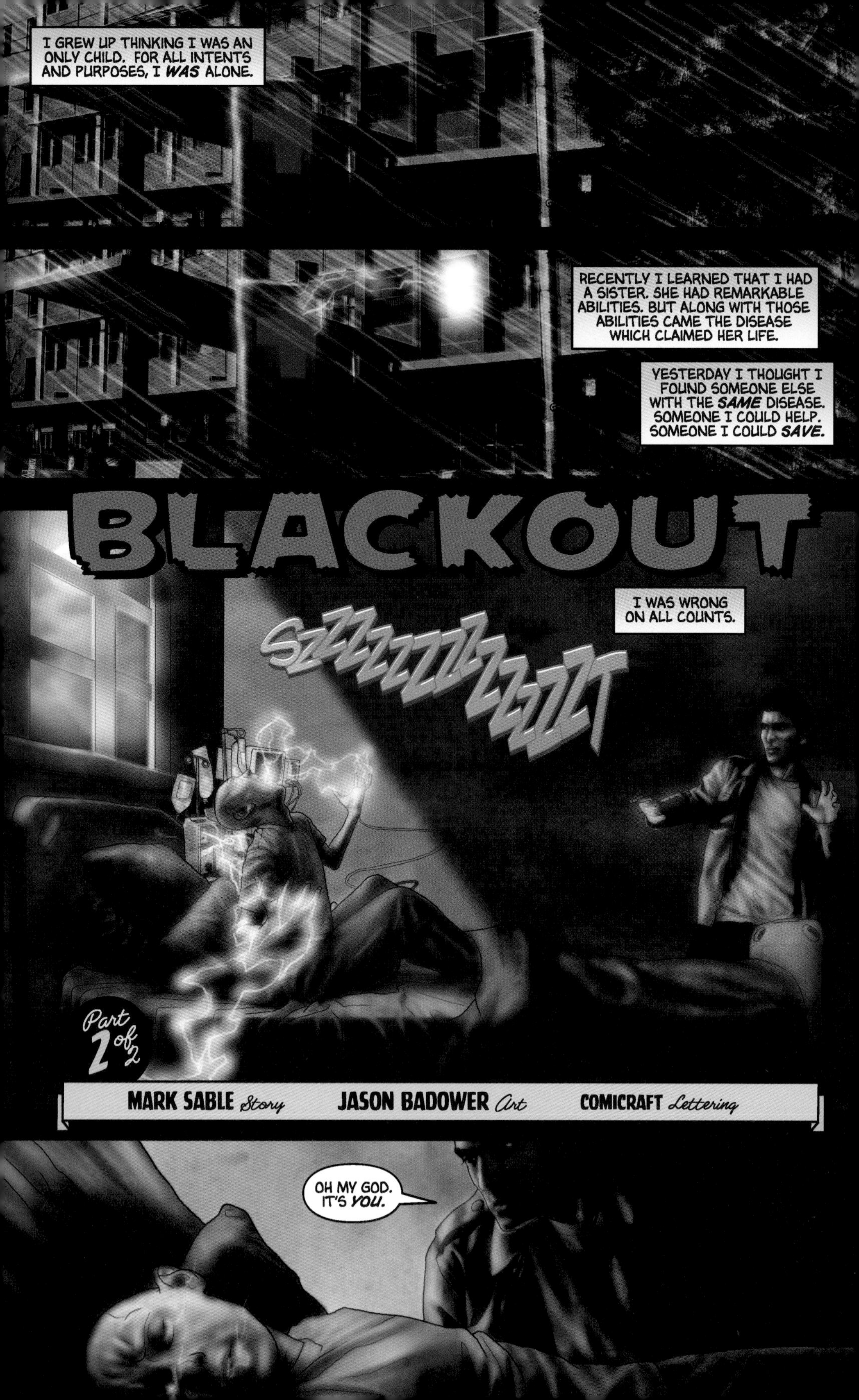
I GREW UP THINKING I WAS AN ONLY CHILD. FOR ALL INTENTS AND PURPOSES, I *WAS* ALONE.
RECENTLY I LEARNED THAT I HAD A SISTER. SHE HAD REMARKABLE ABILITIES. BUT ALONG WITH THOSE ABILITIES CAME THE DISEASE WHICH CLAIMED HER LIFE.
YESTERDAY I THOUGHT I FOUND SOMEONE ELSE WITH THE *SAME* DISEASE. SOMEONE I COULD HELP. SOMEONE I COULD *SAVE*.
BLACKOUT
I WAS WRONG ON ALL COUNTS.
SZZZZZZZZZZZZZT
Part 2 of 2
MARK SABLE Story JASON BADOWER Art COMICRAFT Lettering
OH MY GOD. IT'S *YOU*.

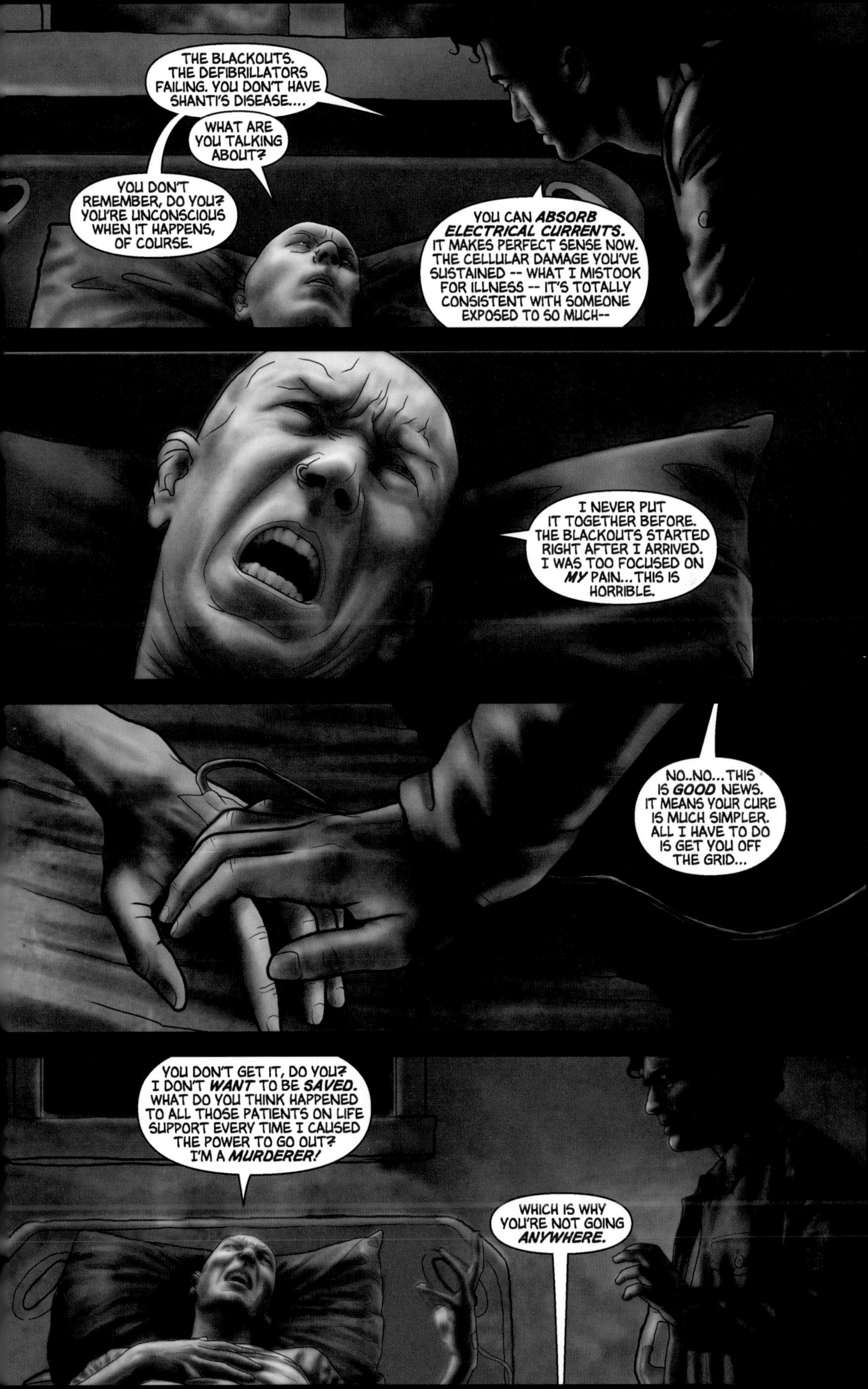
THE BLACKOUTS. THE DEFIBRILLATORS FAILING. YOU DON'T HAVE SHANTI'S DISEASE....
WHAT ARE YOU TALKING ABOUT?
YOU DON'T REMEMBER, DO YOU? YOU'RE UNCONSCIOUS WHEN IT HAPPENS, OF COURSE.
YOU CAN ABSORB ELECTRICAL CURRENTS. IT MAKES PERFECT SENSE NOW. THE CELLULAR DAMAGE YOU'VE SUSTAINED -- WHAT I MISTOOK FOR ILLNESS -- IT'S TOTALLY CONSISTENT WITH SOMEONE EXPOSED TO SO MUCH--
I NEVER PUT IT TOGETHER BEFORE. THE BLACKOUTS STARTED RIGHT AFTER I ARRIVED. I WAS TOO FOCUSED ON MY PAIN...THIS IS HORRIBLE.
NO..NO...THIS IS GOOD NEWS. IT MEANS YOUR CURE IS MUCH SIMPLER. ALL I HAVE TO DO IS GET YOU OFF THE GRID...
YOU DON'T GET IT, DO YOU? I DON'T WANT TO BE SAVED. WHAT DO YOU THINK HAPPENED TO ALL THOSE PATIENTS ON LIFE SUPPORT EVERY TIME I CAUSED THE POWER TO GO OUT? I'M A MURDERER!
WHICH IS WHY YOU'RE NOT GOING ANYWHERE.

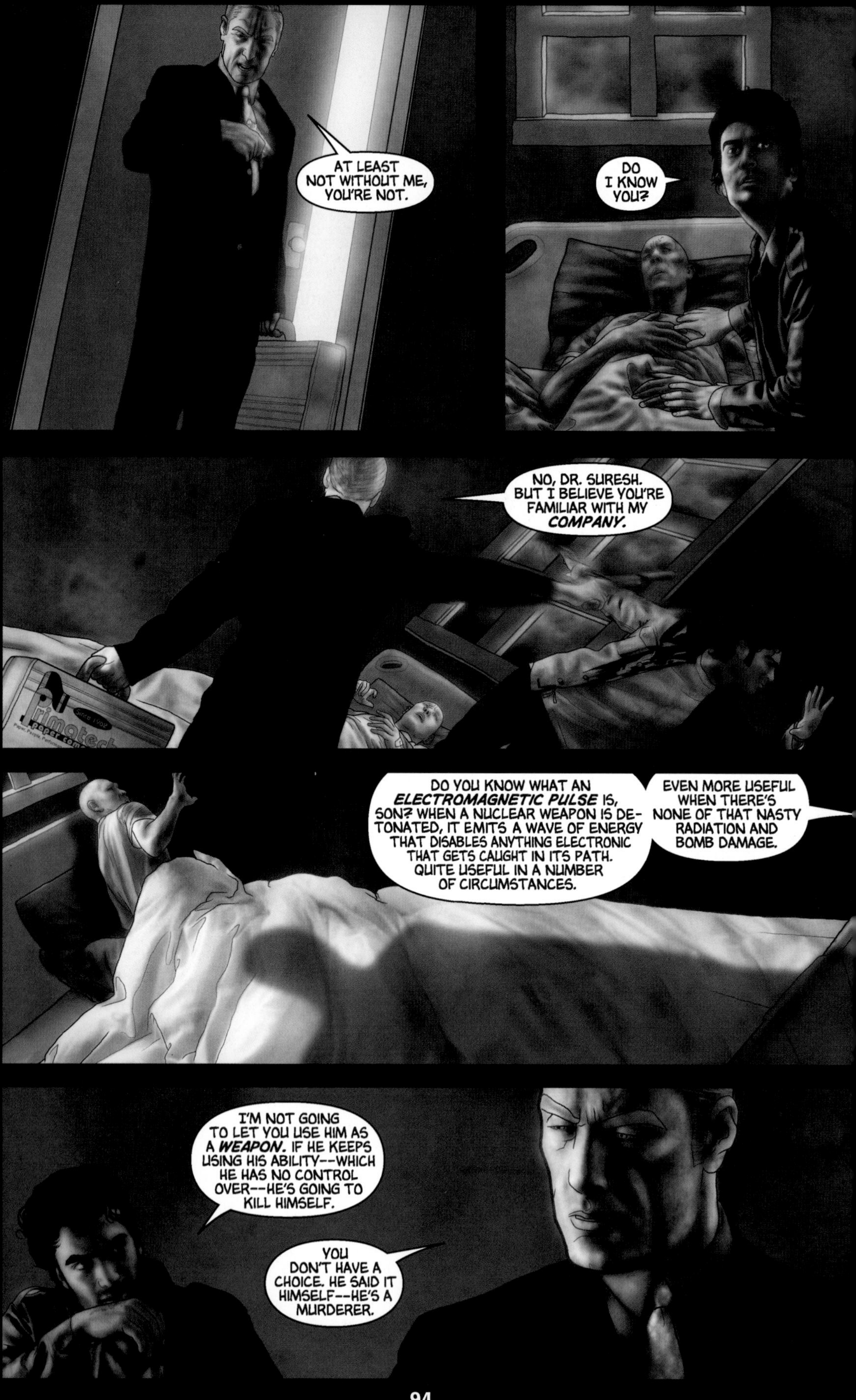
AT LEAST NOT WITHOUT ME, YOU'RE NOT.
DO I KNOW YOU?
NO, DR. SURESH. BUT I BELIEVE YOU'RE FAMILIAR WITH MY *COMPANY.*
DO YOU KNOW WHAT AN *ELECTROMAGNETIC PULSE* IS, SON? WHEN A NUCLEAR WEAPON IS DETONATED, IT EMITS A WAVE OF ENERGY THAT DISABLES ANYTHING ELECTRONIC THAT GETS CAUGHT IN ITS PATH. QUITE USEFUL IN A NUMBER OF CIRCUMSTANCES.
EVEN MORE USEFUL WHEN THERE'S NONE OF THAT NASTY RADIATION AND BOMB DAMAGE.
I'M NOT GOING TO LET YOU USE HIM AS A *WEAPON.* IF HE KEEPS USING HIS ABILITY--WHICH HE HAS NO CONTROL OVER--HE'S GOING TO KILL HIMSELF.
YOU DON'T HAVE A CHOICE. HE SAID IT HIMSELF--HE'S A MURDERER.

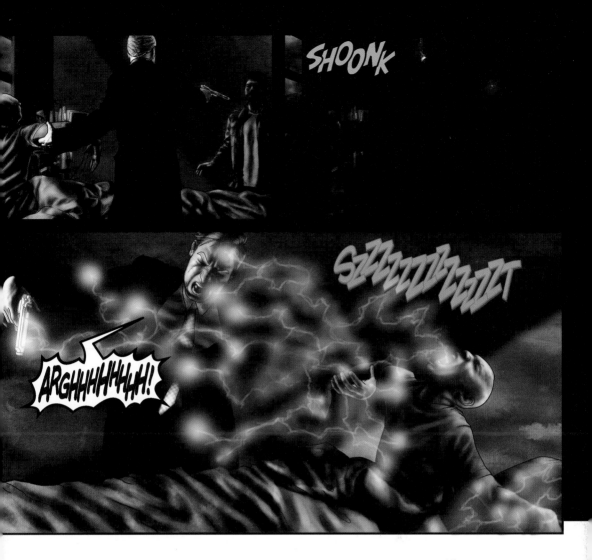

SHOONK

SZZZZZZZOOZZT

ARGHHHHH'HHH!

DID I...

NO...HE'LL LIVE. BUT HE, AND THE PEOPLE HE WORKS FOR, THEY'LL KEEP COMING FOR YOU. WHICH IS WHY I HAVE TO GET YOU TO--

SCREEEEEEECH

SZZZT

THUD

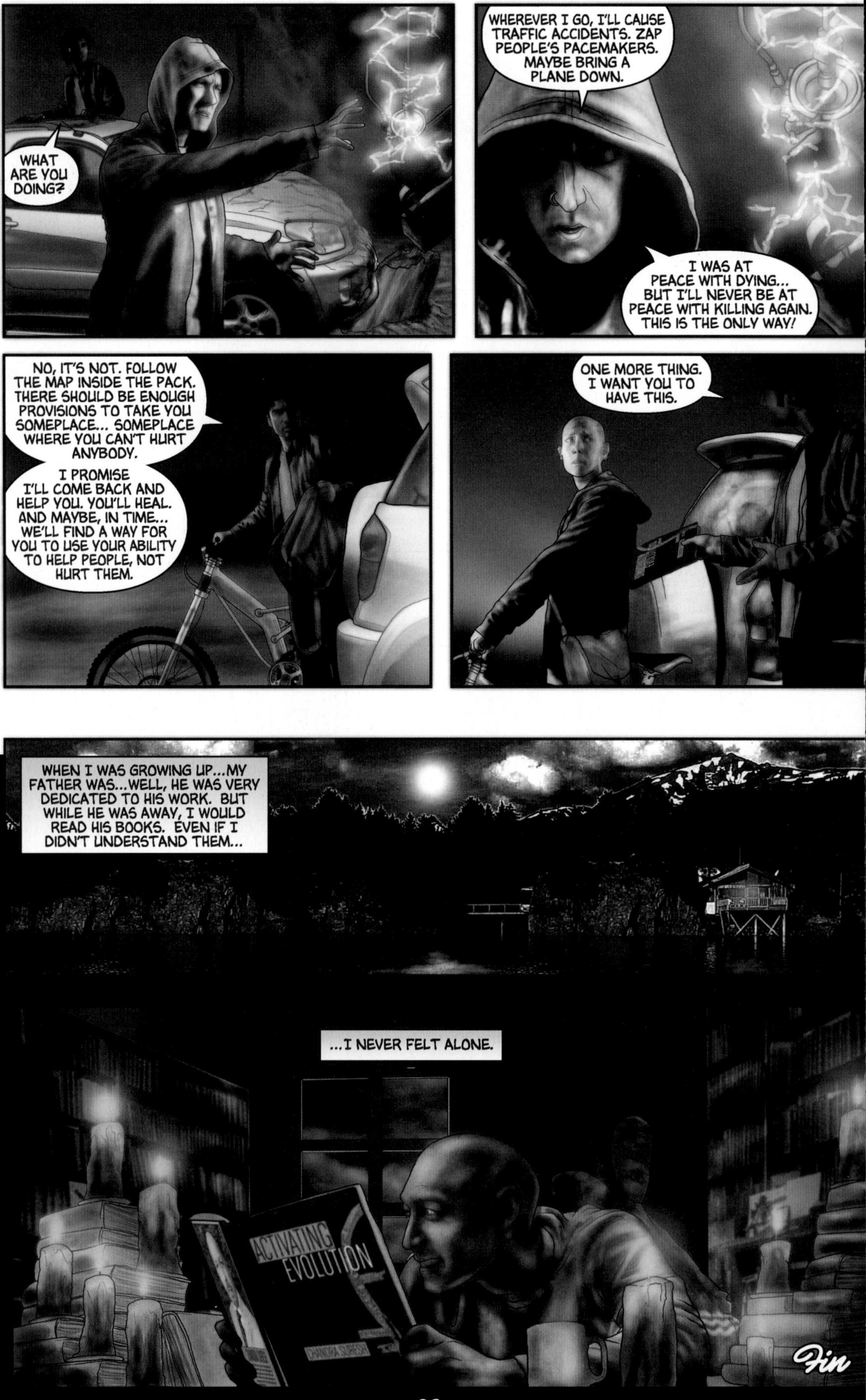
WHAT ARE YOU DOING?
WHEREVER I GO, I'LL CAUSE TRAFFIC ACCIDENTS. ZAP PEOPLE'S PACEMAKERS. MAYBE BRING A PLANE DOWN.
I WAS AT PEACE WITH DYING... BUT I'LL NEVER BE AT PEACE WITH KILLING AGAIN. THIS IS THE ONLY WAY!
NO, IT'S NOT. FOLLOW THE MAP INSIDE THE PACK. THERE SHOULD BE ENOUGH PROVISIONS TO TAKE YOU SOMEPLACE... SOMEPLACE WHERE YOU CAN'T HURT ANYBODY.
I PROMISE I'LL COME BACK AND HELP YOU. YOU'LL HEAL. AND MAYBE, IN TIME... WE'LL FIND A WAY FOR YOU TO USE YOUR ABILITY TO HELP PEOPLE, NOT HURT THEM.
ONE MORE THING. I WANT YOU TO HAVE THIS.
WHEN I WAS GROWING UP...MY FATHER WAS...WELL, HE WAS VERY DEDICATED TO HIS WORK. BUT WHILE HE WAS AWAY, I WOULD READ HIS BOOKS. EVEN IF I DIDN'T UNDERSTAND THEM...
...I NEVER FELT ALONE.
ACTIVATING EVOLUTION
Fin

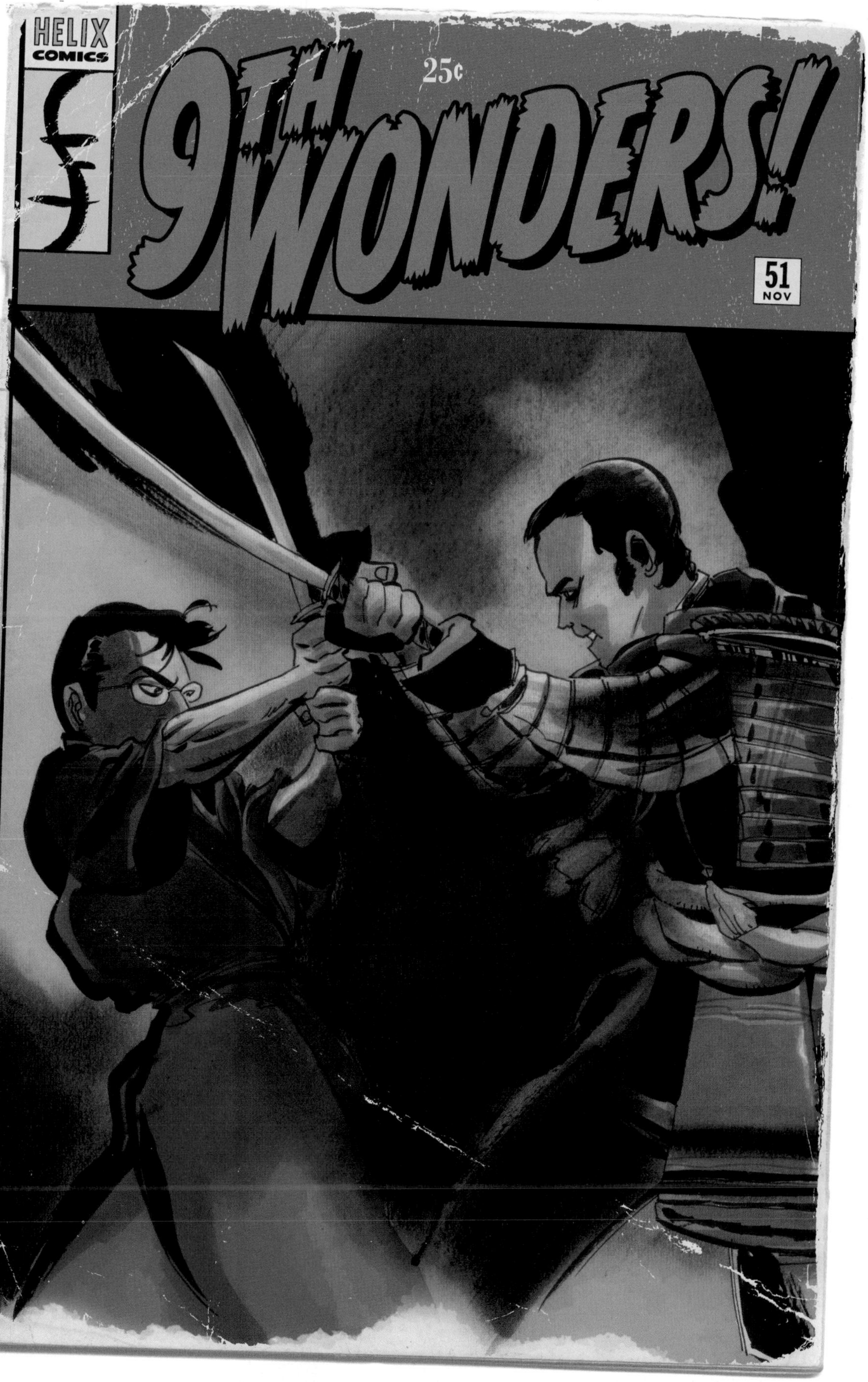
HELIX
COMICS
25¢
9TH WONDERS!
51
NOV

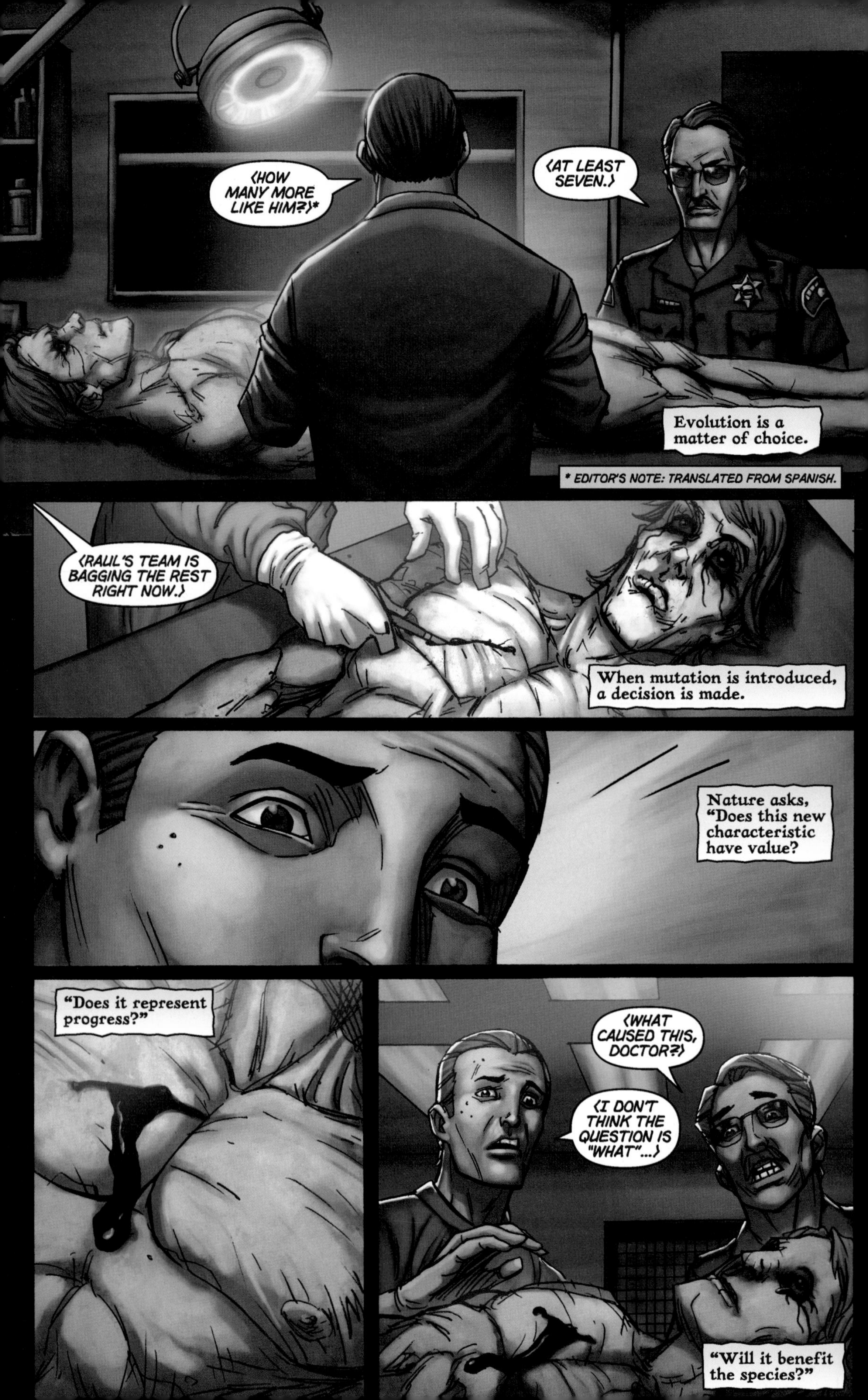

‹HOW MANY MORE LIKE HIM?›*
‹AT LEAST SEVEN.›
Evolution is a matter of choice.
* EDITOR'S NOTE: TRANSLATED FROM SPANISH.
‹RAUL'S TEAM IS BAGGING THE REST RIGHT NOW.›
When mutation is introduced, a decision is made.
Nature asks, "Does this new characteristic have value?
"Does it represent progress?"
‹WHAT CAUSED THIS, DOCTOR?›
‹I DON'T THINK THE QUESTION IS "WHAT"...›
"Will it benefit the species?"

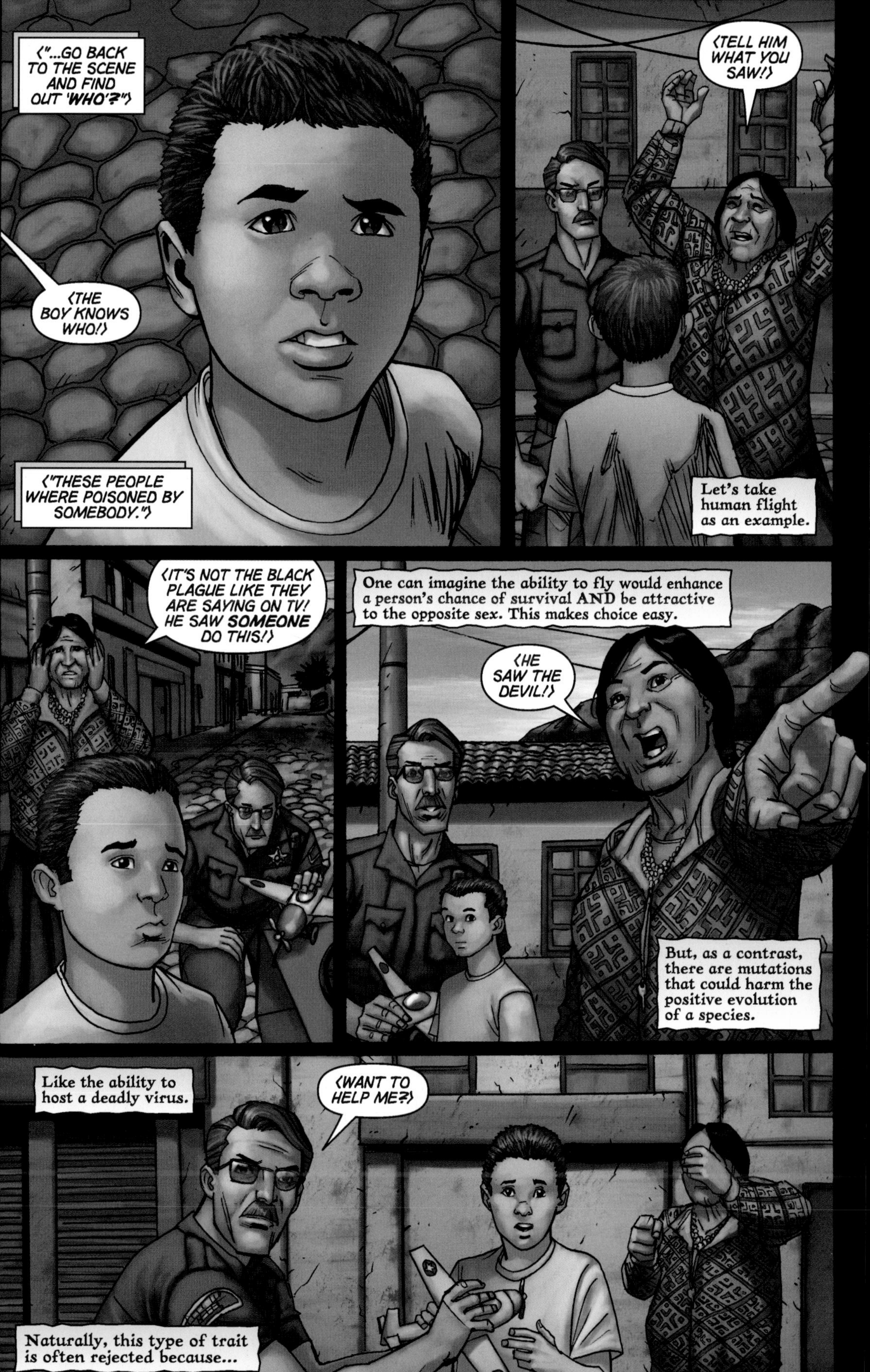
⟨"...GO BACK TO THE SCENE AND FIND OUT 'WHO'?"⟩
⟨THE BOY KNOWS WHO!⟩
⟨"THESE PEOPLE WHERE POISONED BY SOMEBODY."⟩
⟨TELL HIM WHAT YOU SAW!⟩
Let's take human flight as an example.
⟨IT'S NOT THE BLACK PLAGUE LIKE THEY ARE SAYING ON TV! HE SAW SOMEONE DO THIS!⟩
One can imagine the ability to fly would enhance a person's chance of survival AND be attractive to the opposite sex. This makes choice easy.
⟨HE SAW THE DEVIL!⟩
But, as a contrast, there are mutations that could harm the positive evolution of a species.
Like the ability to host a deadly virus.
⟨WANT TO HELP ME?⟩
Naturally, this type of trait is often rejected because...

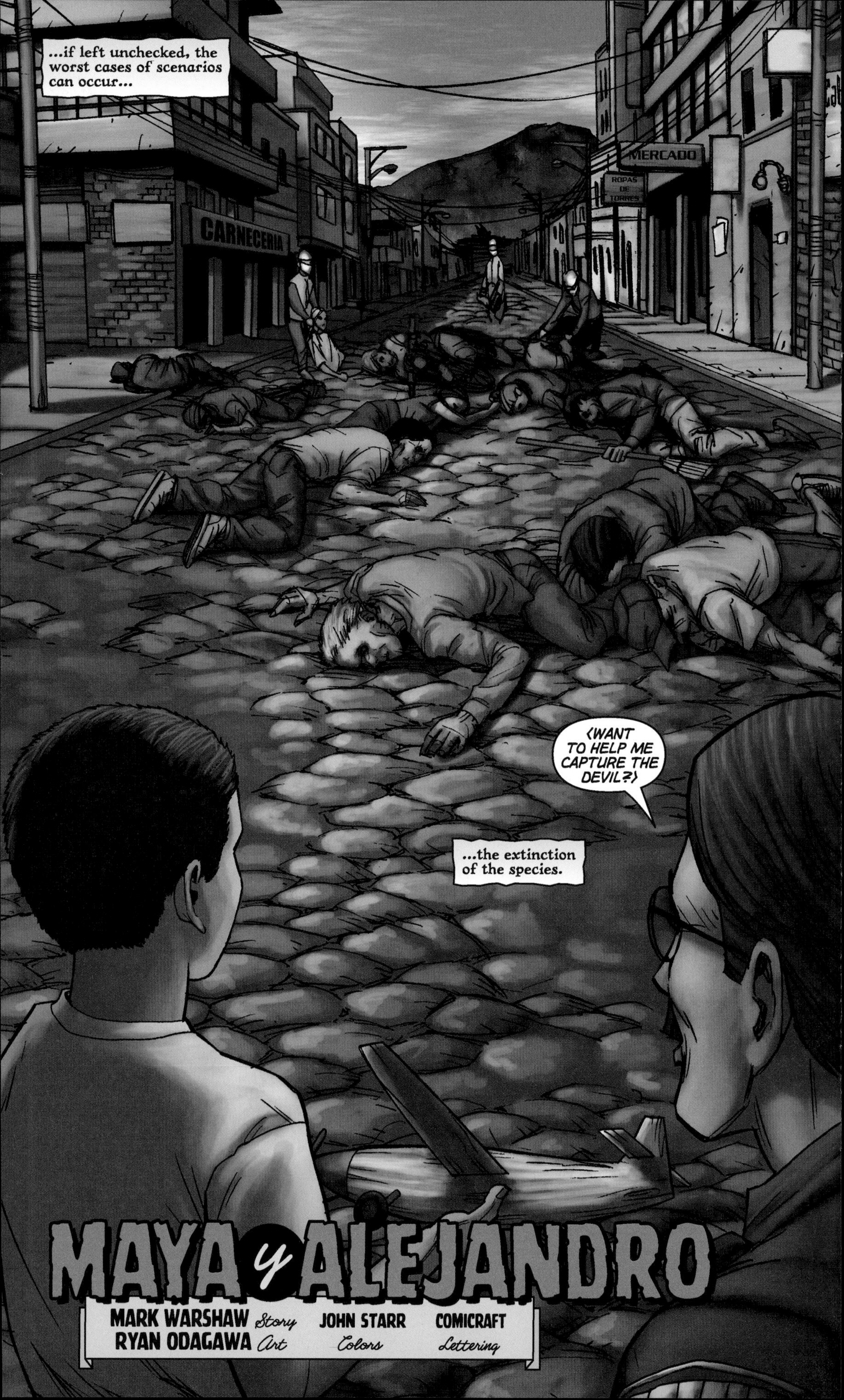
...if left unchecked, the worst cases of scenarios can occur...
CARNECERIA
MERCADO
ROPAS DE TORRES
‹WANT TO HELP ME CAPTURE THE DEVIL?›
...the extinction of the species.
MAYA y ALEJANDRO
MARK WARSHAW Story
RYAN ODAGAWA Art
JOHN STARR Colors
COMICRAFT Lettering

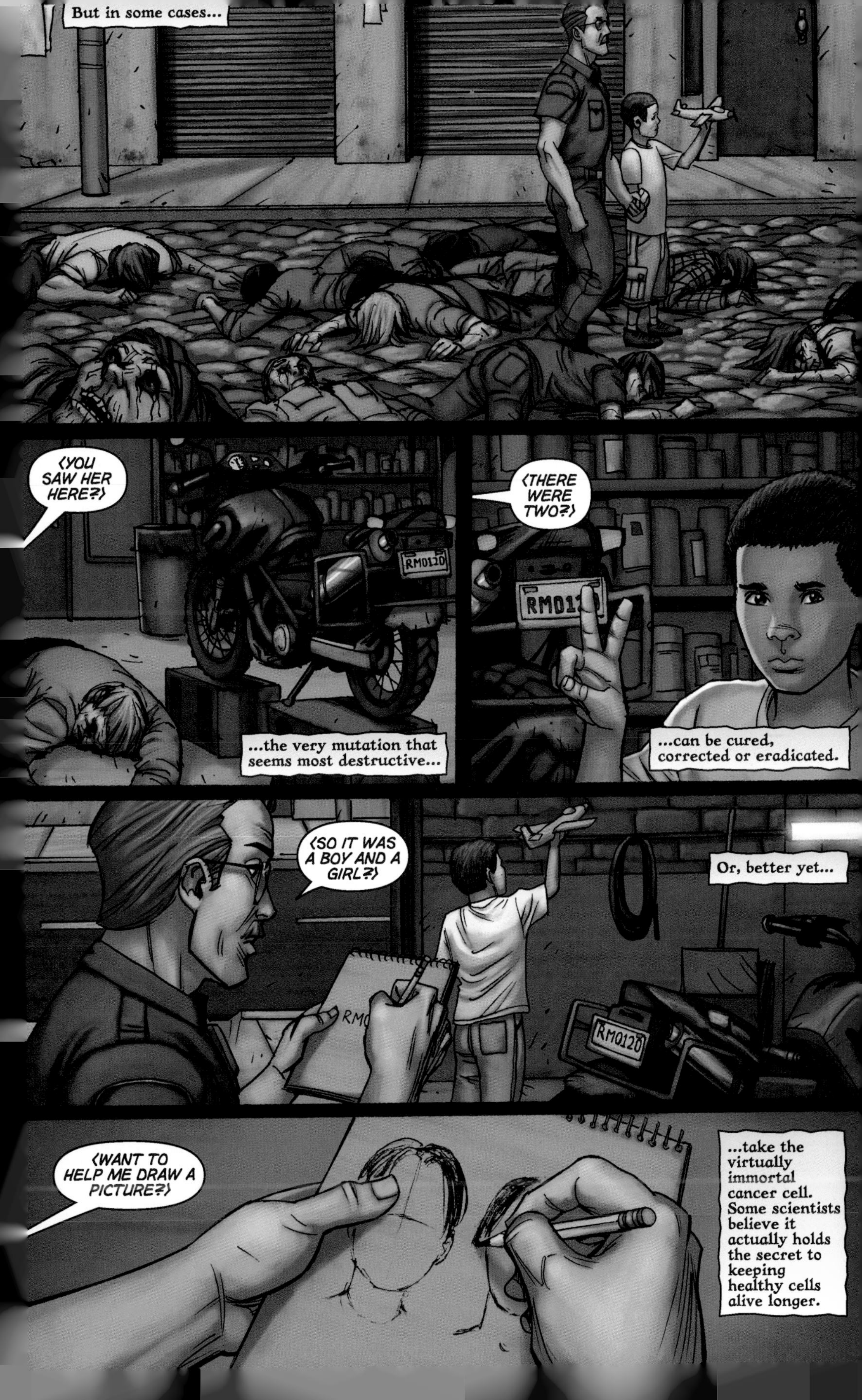
But in some cases...
‹YOU SAW HER HERE?›
...the very mutation that seems most destructive...
‹THERE WERE TWO?›
RM0120
...can be cured, corrected or eradicated.
‹SO IT WAS A BOY AND A GIRL?›
Or, better yet...
RM0120
‹WANT TO HELP ME DRAW A PICTURE?›
...take the virtually immortal cancer cell. Some scientists believe it actually holds the secret to keeping healthy cells alive longer.

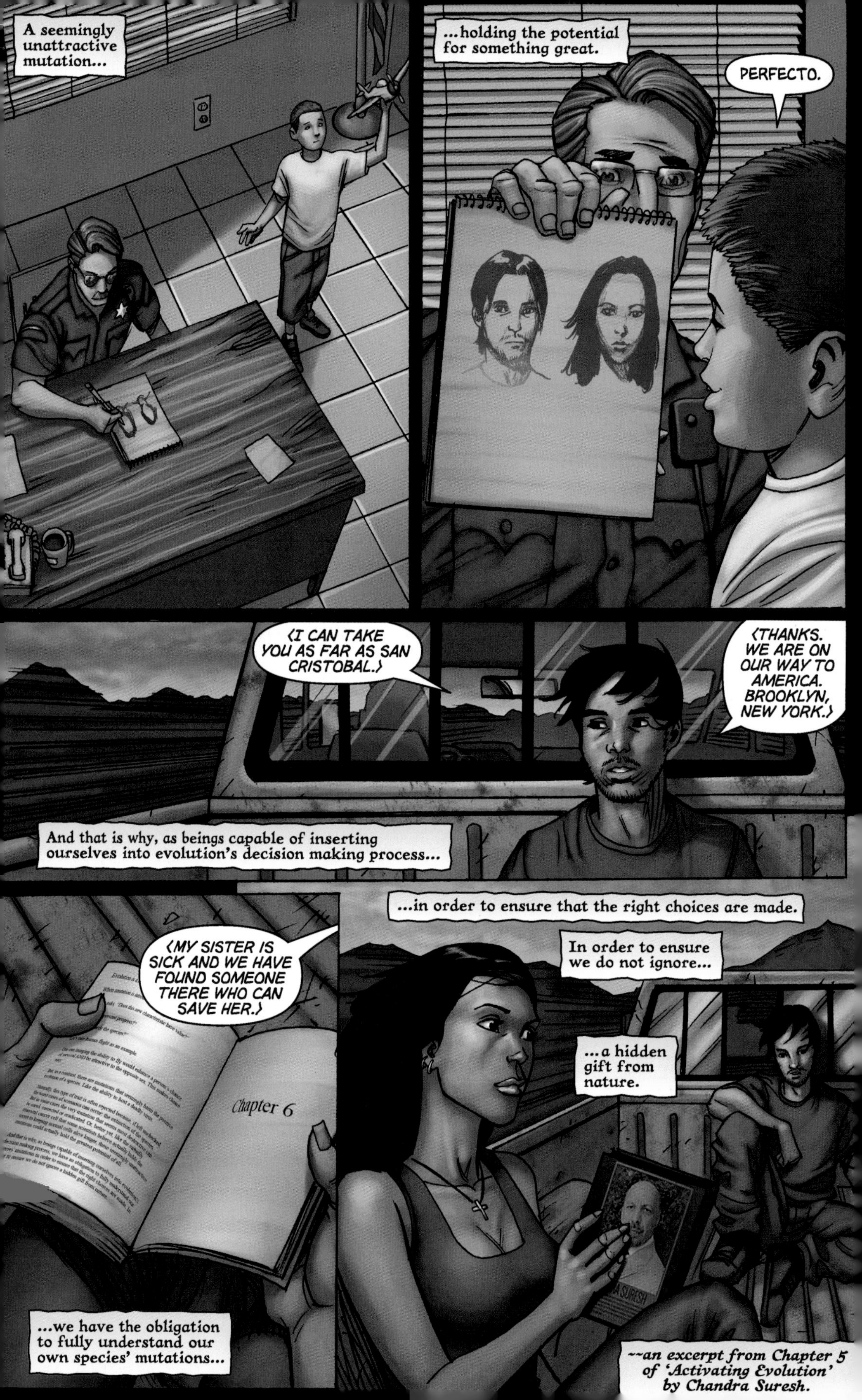

A seemingly unattractive mutation...
...holding the potential for something great.
PERFECTO.
‹I CAN TAKE YOU AS FAR AS SAN CRISTOBAL.›
‹THANKS. WE ARE ON OUR WAY TO AMERICA. BROOKLYN, NEW YORK.›
And that is why, as beings capable of inserting ourselves into evolution's decision making process...
‹MY SISTER IS SICK AND WE HAVE FOUND SOMEONE THERE WHO CAN SAVE HER.›
Chapter 6
...we have the obligation to fully understand our own species' mutations...
...in order to ensure that the right choices are made.
In order to ensure we do not ignore...
...a hidden gift from nature.
--an excerpt from Chapter 5 of 'Activating Evolution' by Chandra Suresh.

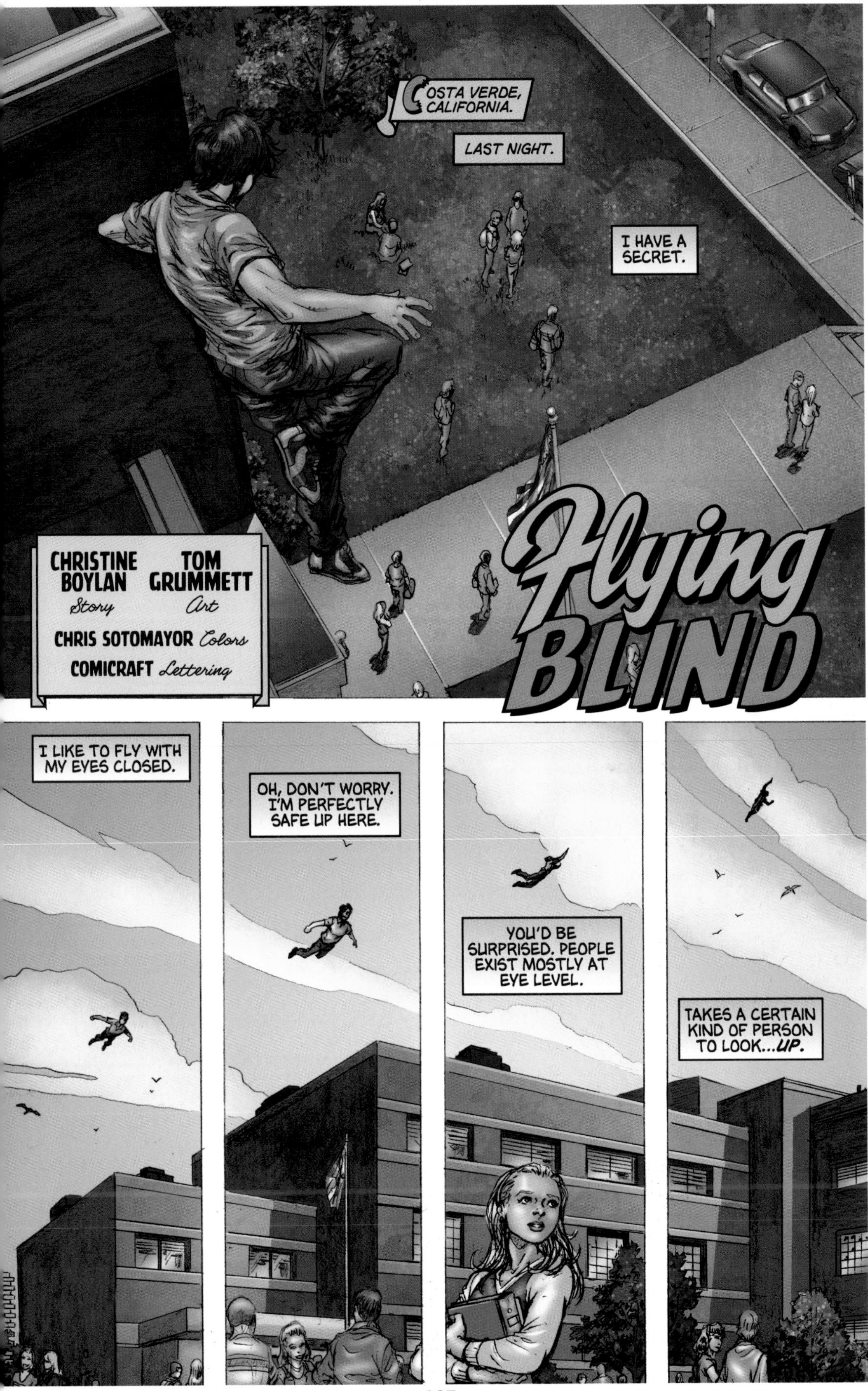
COSTA VERDE, CALIFORNIA.
LAST NIGHT.
I HAVE A SECRET.
Flying BLIND
CHRISTINE BOYLAN Story
TOM GRUMMETT Art
CHRIS SOTOMAYOR Colors
COMICRAFT Lettering
I LIKE TO FLY WITH MY EYES CLOSED.
OH, DON'T WORRY. I'M PERFECTLY SAFE UP HERE.
YOU'D BE SURPRISED. PEOPLE EXIST MOSTLY AT EYE LEVEL.
TAKES A CERTAIN KIND OF PERSON TO LOOK...*UP.*

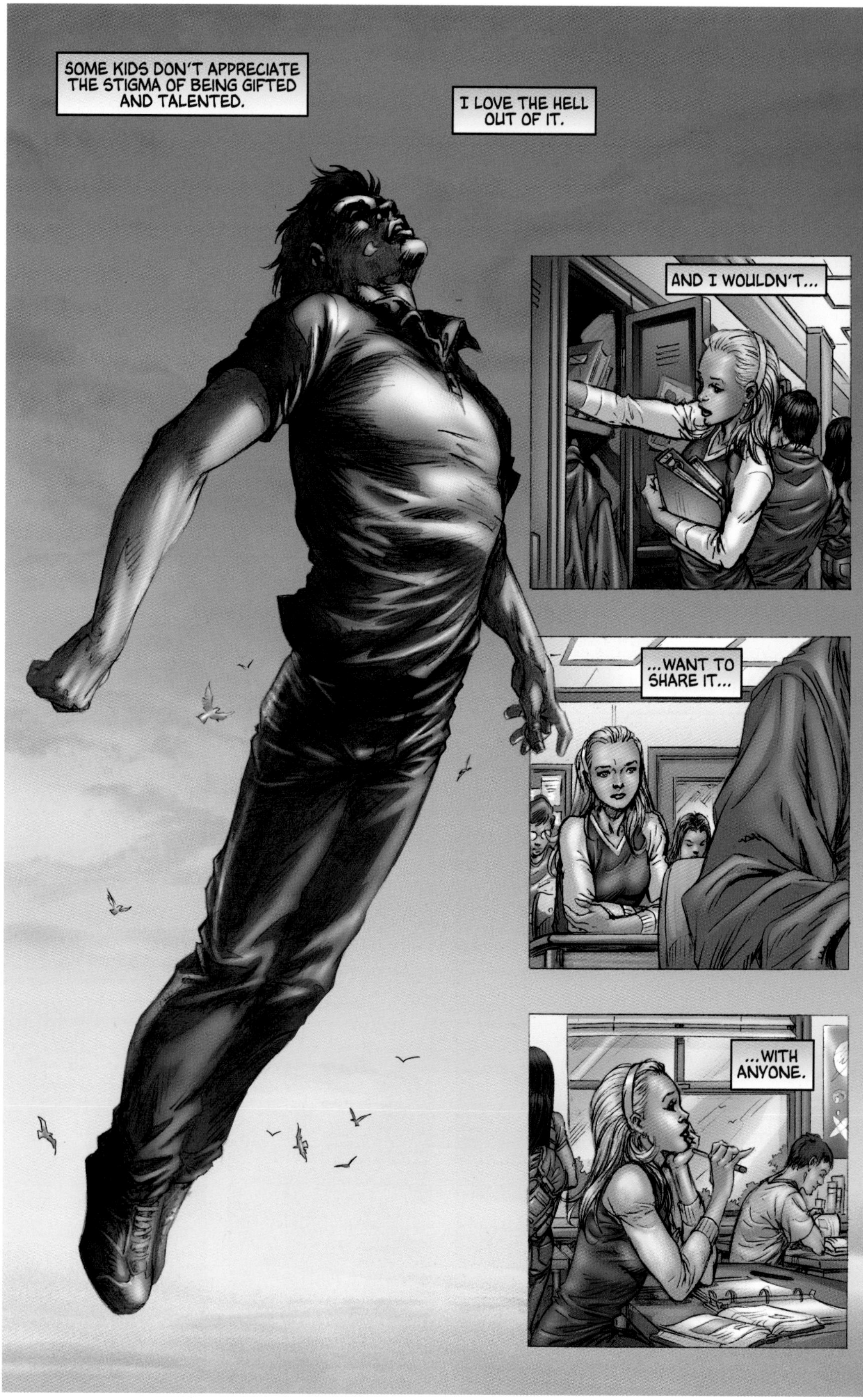
SOME KIDS DON'T APPRECIATE THE STIGMA OF BEING GIFTED AND TALENTED.
I LOVE THE HELL OUT OF IT.
AND I WOULDN'T...
...WANT TO SHARE IT...
...WITH ANYONE.

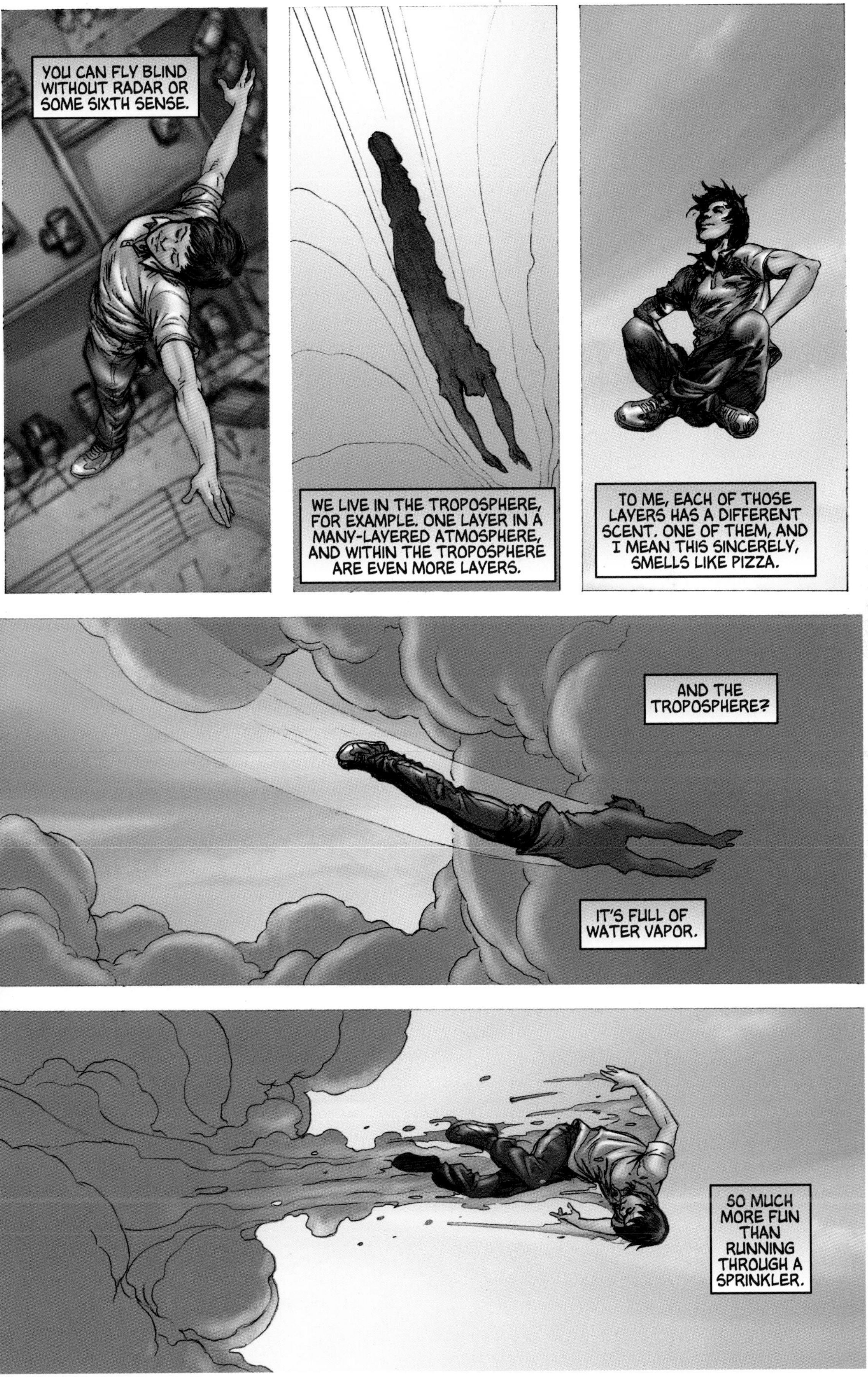
YOU CAN FLY BLIND WITHOUT RADAR OR SOME SIXTH SENSE.
WE LIVE IN THE TROPOSPHERE, FOR EXAMPLE. ONE LAYER IN A MANY-LAYERED ATMOSPHERE, AND WITHIN THE TROPOSPHERE ARE EVEN MORE LAYERS.
TO ME, EACH OF THOSE LAYERS HAS A DIFFERENT SCENT. ONE OF THEM, AND I MEAN THIS SINCERELY, SMELLS LIKE PIZZA.
AND THE TROPOSPHERE?
IT'S FULL OF WATER VAPOR.
SO MUCH MORE FUN THAN RUNNING THROUGH A SPRINKLER.

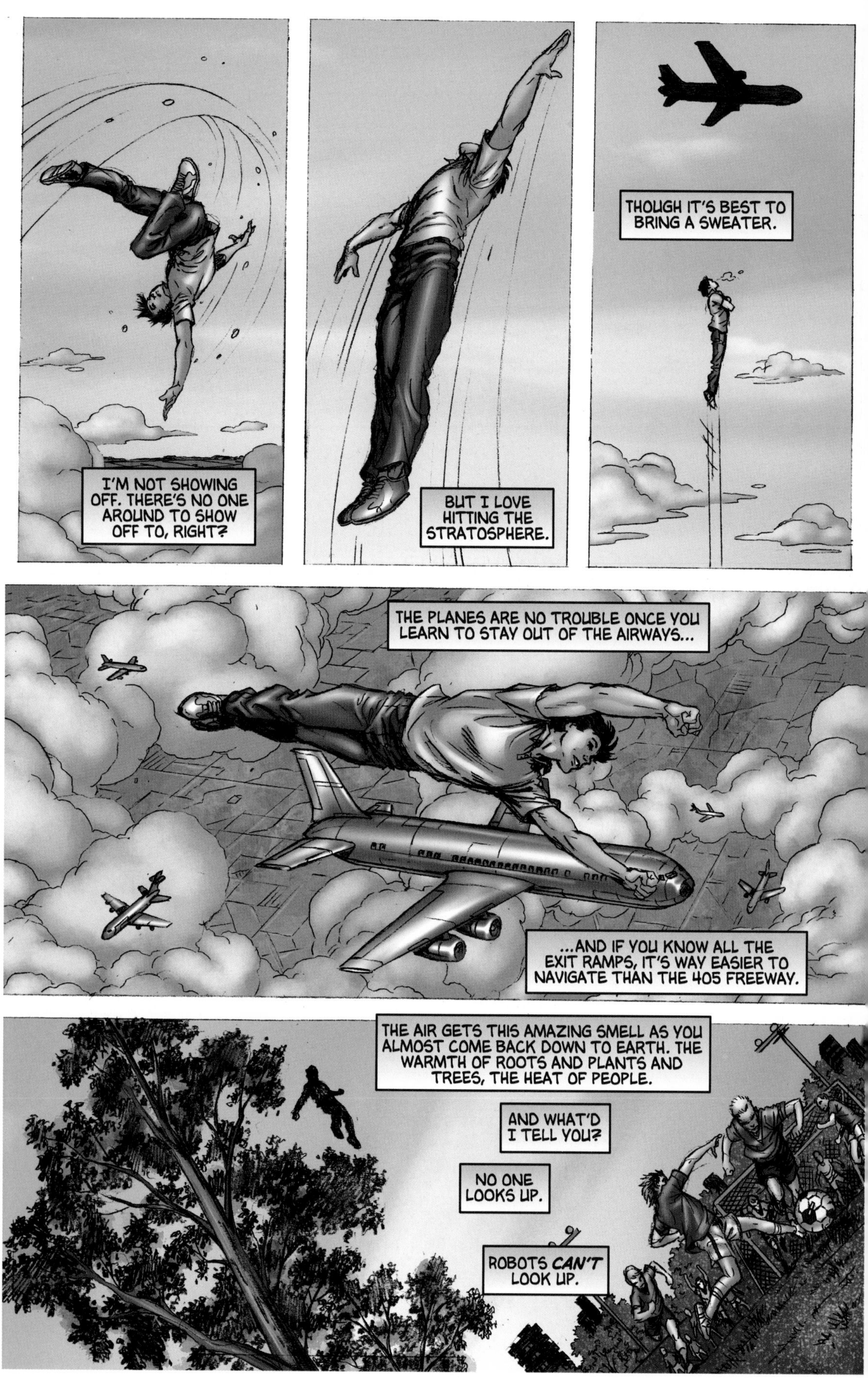
I'M NOT SHOWING OFF. THERE'S NO ONE AROUND TO SHOW OFF TO, RIGHT?
BUT I LOVE HITTING THE STRATOSPHERE.
THOUGH IT'S BEST TO BRING A SWEATER.
THE PLANES ARE NO TROUBLE ONCE YOU LEARN TO STAY OUT OF THE AIRWAYS...
...AND IF YOU KNOW ALL THE EXIT RAMPS, IT'S WAY EASIER TO NAVIGATE THAN THE 405 FREEWAY.
THE AIR GETS THIS AMAZING SMELL AS YOU ALMOST COME BACK DOWN TO EARTH. THE WARMTH OF ROOTS AND PLANTS AND TREES, THE HEAT OF PEOPLE.
AND WHAT'D I TELL YOU?
NO ONE LOOKS UP.
ROBOTS *CAN'T* LOOK UP.

COSTA VERDE, CALIFORNIA.

THIS MORNING.

SEE, I HAVE THIS THEORY.

WHETHER IT'S FATE OR CHOICE...

...PEOPLE BREAK DOWN INTO ONLY TWO CATEGORIES.

YOU'RE EITHER A *ROBOT* OR AN *ALIEN*.

MY DEBATE TEACHER WOULD CALL THAT REDUCTIVE.

I CALL IT A NEAT EXPRESSION OF A LARGER TRUTH.

ROBOTS OPERATE OUT OF PROGRAMS...

...*CONVENTIONAL* LOGIC.

THEY FOLLOW THE RULES.

ROBOTS SCAN THE WORLD FROM SIDE TO SIDE.

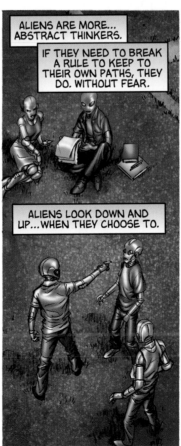

ALIENS ARE MORE... ABSTRACT THINKERS.

IF THEY NEED TO BREAK A RULE TO KEEP TO THEIR OWN PATHS, THEY DO. WITHOUT FEAR.

ALIENS LOOK DOWN AND UP...WHEN THEY CHOOSE TO.

I'M NOT CONDEMNING ONE OR THE OTHER, BUT...

...I'D RATHER BE ALONE THAN BE SURROUNDED BY ROBOTS.

AND ROBOTS COULD NEVER EVEN SEE SOMEONE LIKE ME.

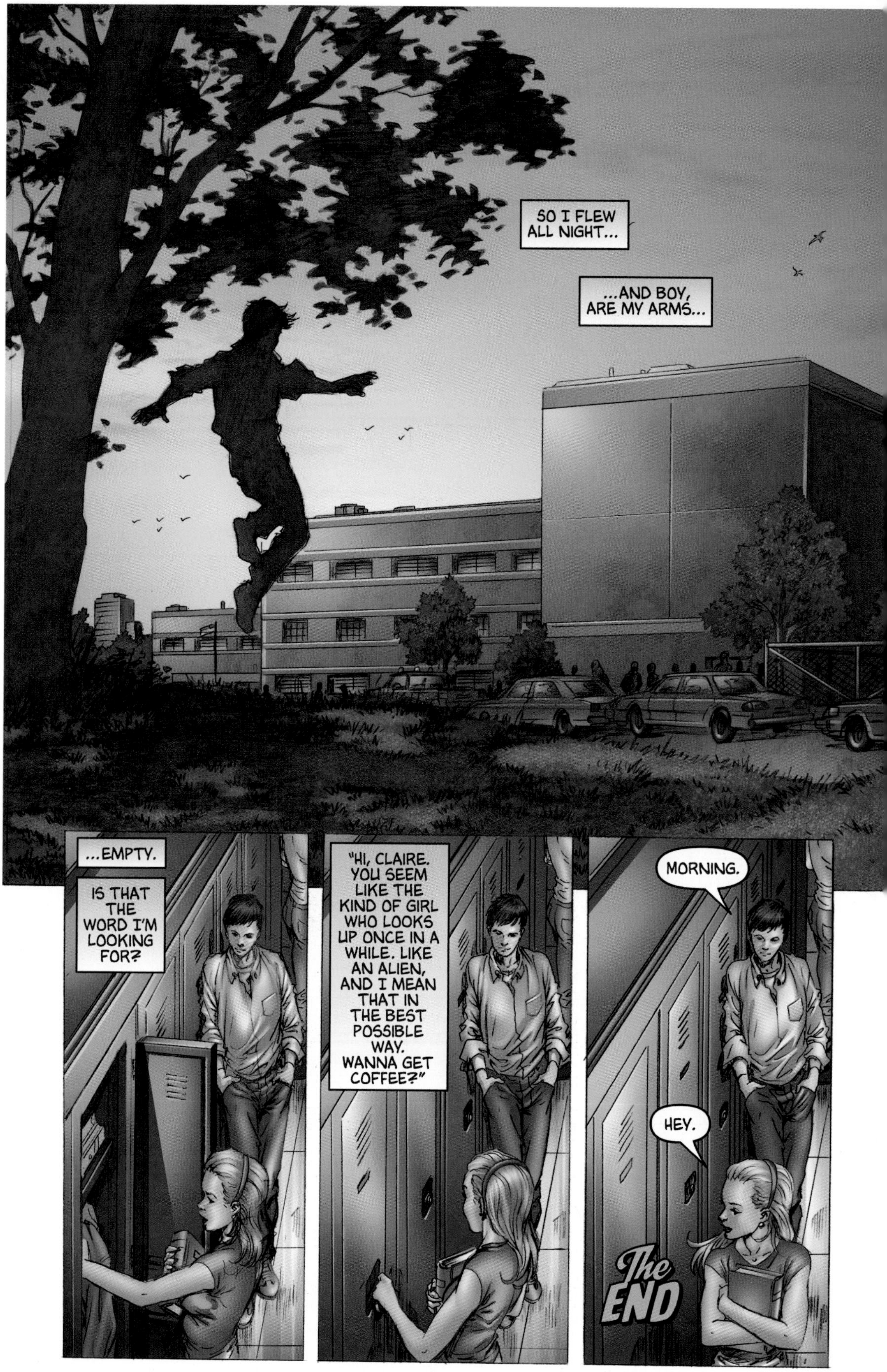

SO I FLEW ALL NIGHT...
...AND BOY, ARE MY ARMS...
...EMPTY.
IS THAT THE WORD I'M LOOKING FOR?
"HI, CLAIRE. YOU SEEM LIKE THE KIND OF GIRL WHO LOOKS UP ONCE IN A WHILE. LIKE AN ALIEN, AND I MEAN THAT IN THE BEST POSSIBLE WAY. WANNA GET COFFEE?"
MORNING.
HEY.
The END

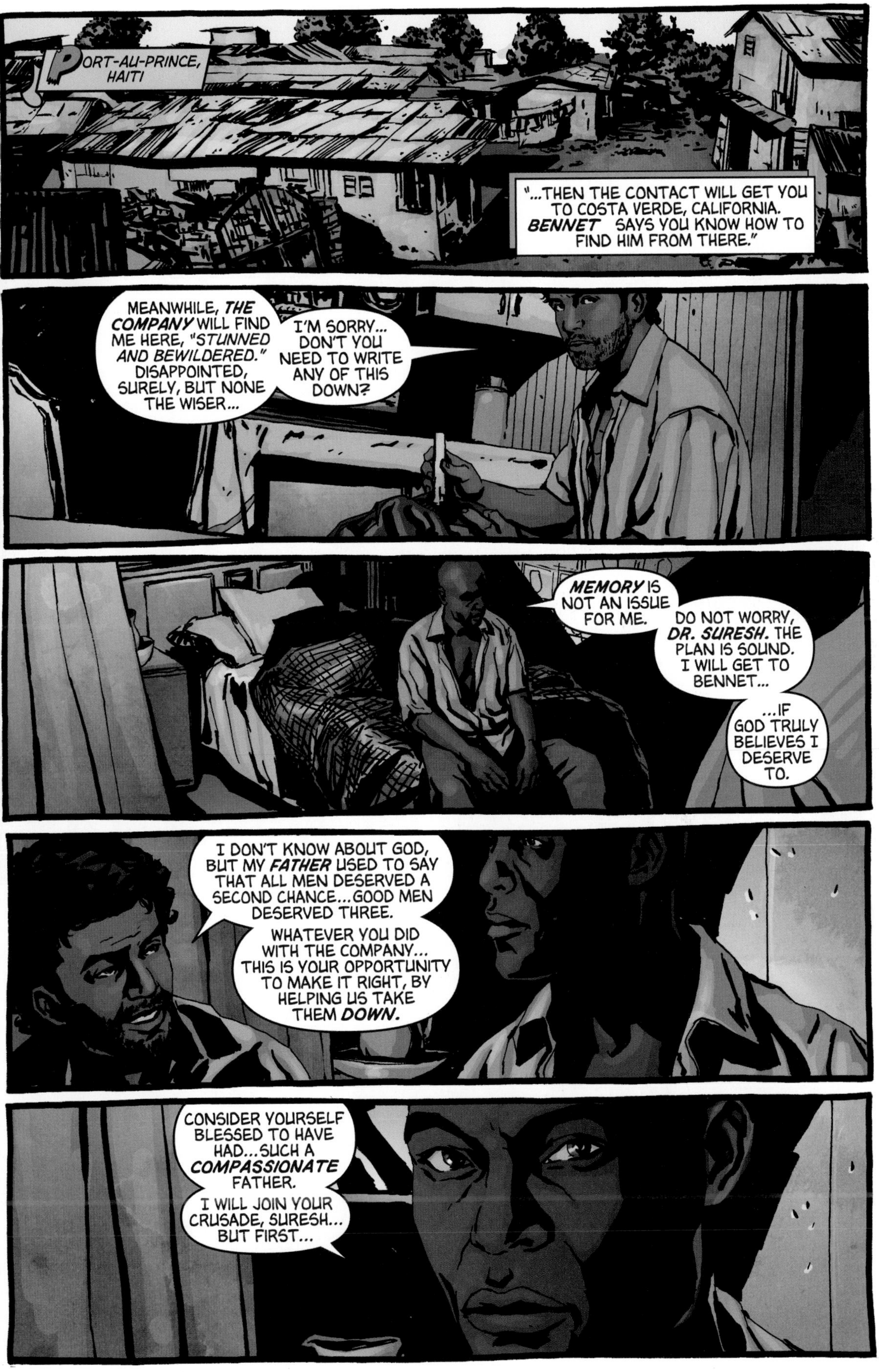
PORT-AU-PRINCE, HAITI
"...THEN THE CONTACT WILL GET YOU TO COSTA VERDE, CALIFORNIA. BENNET SAYS YOU KNOW HOW TO FIND HIM FROM THERE."
MEANWHILE, THE COMPANY WILL FIND ME HERE, "STUNNED AND BEWILDERED." DISAPPOINTED, SURELY, BUT NONE THE WISER...
I'M SORRY... DON'T YOU NEED TO WRITE ANY OF THIS DOWN?
MEMORY IS NOT AN ISSUE FOR ME.
DO NOT WORRY, DR. SURESH. THE PLAN IS SOUND. I WILL GET TO BENNET...
...IF GOD TRULY BELIEVES I DESERVE TO.
I DON'T KNOW ABOUT GOD, BUT MY FATHER USED TO SAY THAT ALL MEN DESERVED A SECOND CHANCE...GOOD MEN DESERVED THREE.
WHATEVER YOU DID WITH THE COMPANY... THIS IS YOUR OPPORTUNITY TO MAKE IT RIGHT, BY HELPING US TAKE THEM DOWN.
CONSIDER YOURSELF BLESSED TO HAVE HAD...SUCH A COMPASSIONATE FATHER.
I WILL JOIN YOUR CRUSADE, SURESH... BUT FIRST...

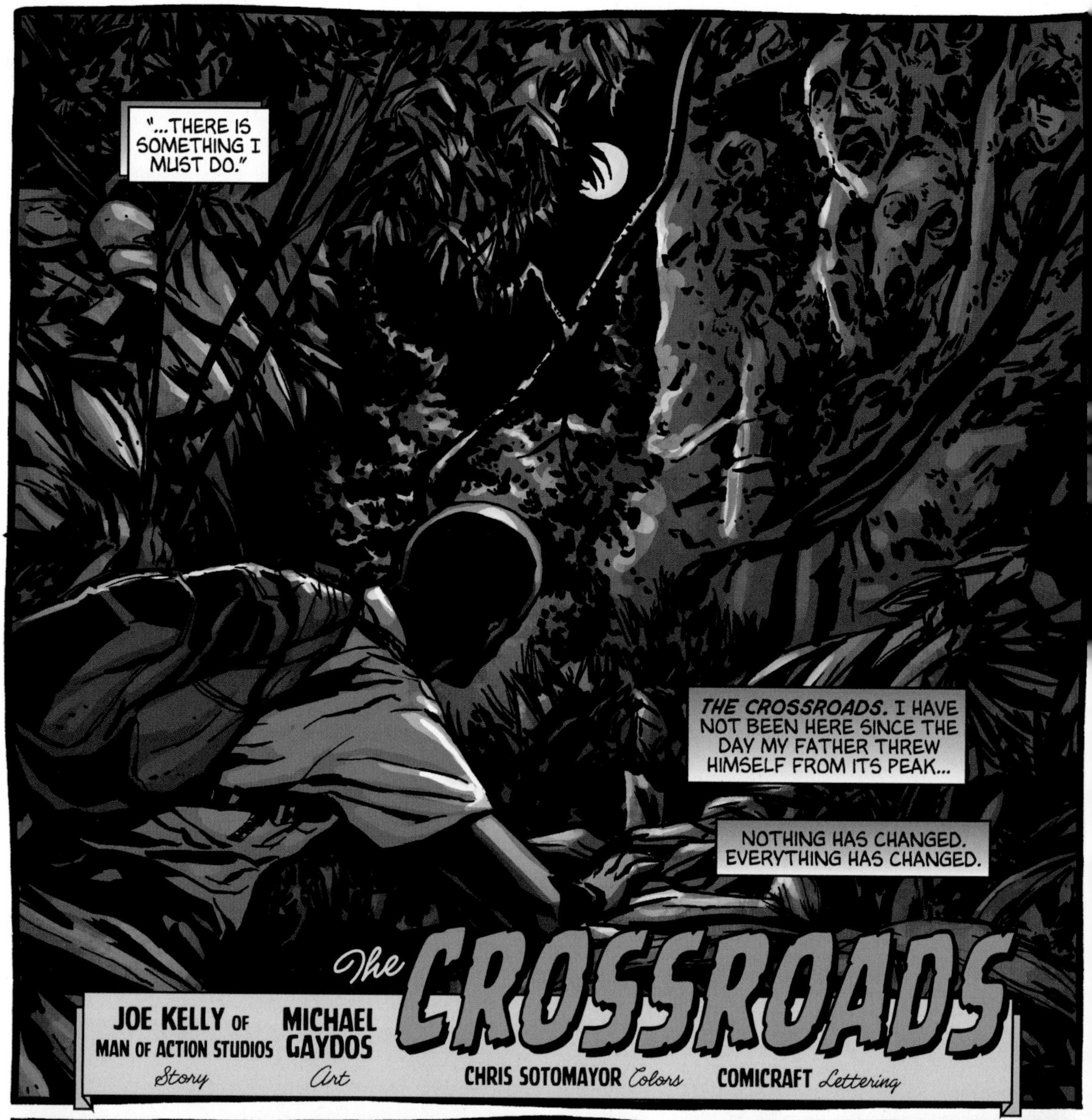
"...THERE IS SOMETHING I MUST DO."
THE CROSSROADS. I HAVE NOT BEEN HERE SINCE THE DAY MY FATHER THREW HIMSELF FROM ITS PEAK...
NOTHING HAS CHANGED. EVERYTHING HAS CHANGED.
The CROSSROADS
JOE KELLY OF MAN OF ACTION STUDIOS Story
MICHAEL GAYDOS Art
CHRIS SOTOMAYOR Colors
COMICRAFT Lettering

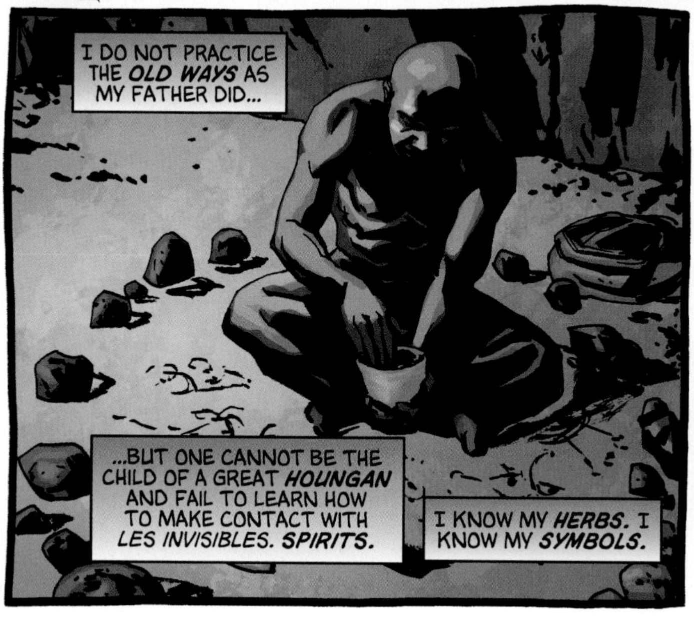
I DO NOT PRACTICE THE OLD WAYS AS MY FATHER DID...
...BUT ONE CANNOT BE THE CHILD OF A GREAT HOUNGAN AND FAIL TO LEARN HOW TO MAKE CONTACT WITH LES INVISIBLES. SPIRITS.
I KNOW MY HERBS. I KNOW MY SYMBOLS.

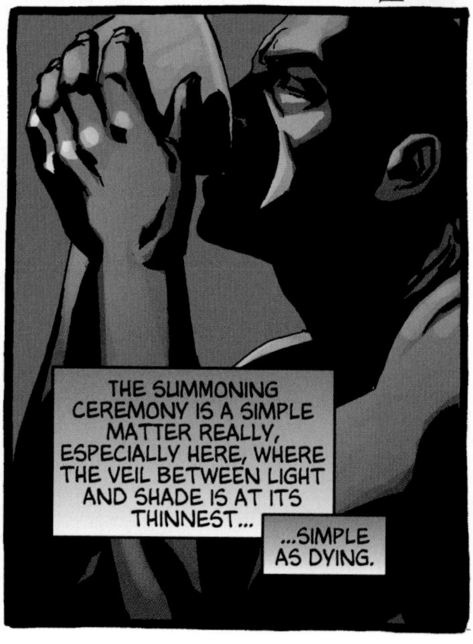
THE SUMMONING CEREMONY IS A SIMPLE MATTER REALLY, ESPECIALLY HERE, WHERE THE VEIL BETWEEN LIGHT AND SHADE IS AT ITS THINNEST...
...SIMPLE AS DYING.

I KNEW *THEY* WOULD APPEAR TO ME FIRST...BUT I DID NOT ANTICIPATE HOW MUCH IT WOULD *HURT.*

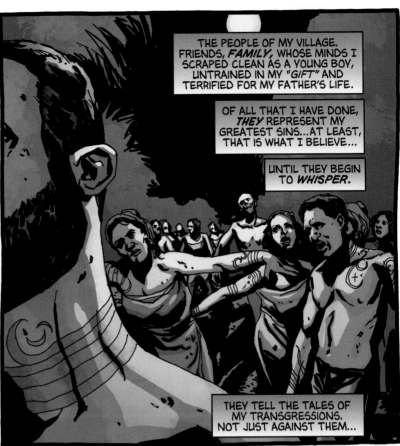

THE PEOPLE OF MY VILLAGE. FRIENDS, *FAMILY,* WHOSE MINDS I SCRAPED CLEAN AS A YOUNG BOY, UNTRAINED IN MY *"GIFT"* AND TERRIFIED FOR MY FATHER'S LIFE.

OF ALL THAT I HAVE DONE, *THEY* REPRESENT MY GREATEST SINS...AT LEAST, THAT IS WHAT I BELIEVE...

UNTIL THEY BEGIN TO *WHISPER.*

THEY TELL THE TALES OF MY TRANSGRESSIONS. NOT JUST AGAINST THEM...

...BUT AGAINST EVERY PERSON I'VE EVER *"BAGGED AND TAGGED"* IN THE NAME OF *"THE COMPANY." EVERY ONE.*

IT TAKES HALF THE NIGHT.

I WANT TO BEG FOR *FORGIVENESS,* BUT I MUST NOT.

PENITENCE IS *WEAKNESS* ACCORDING TO THE *OLD WAYS.* TO SURVIVE, I MUST *ACCEPT* WHAT THE SPIRITS GIVE ME AND *ENDURE* WHO I HAVE BEEN...

...IF I AM EVER TO *BECOME* SOMETHING ELSE.

111

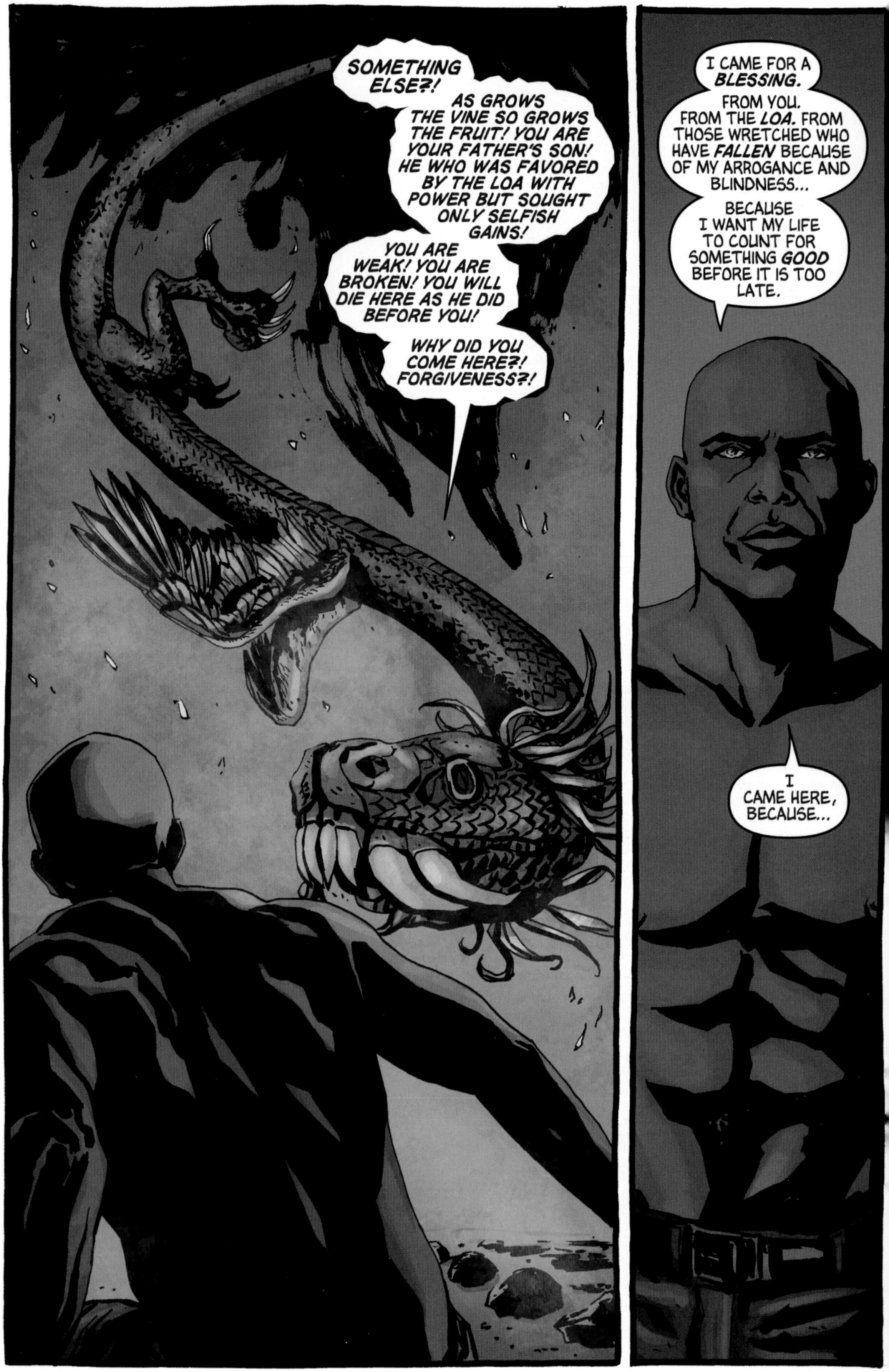
SOMETHING ELSE?!
AS GROWS THE VINE SO GROWS THE FRUIT! YOU ARE YOUR FATHER'S SON! HE WHO WAS FAVORED BY THE LOA WITH POWER BUT SOUGHT ONLY SELFISH GAINS!
YOU ARE WEAK! YOU ARE BROKEN! YOU WILL DIE HERE AS HE DID BEFORE YOU!
WHY DID YOU COME HERE?! FORGIVENESS?!
I CAME HERE, BECAUSE...
I CAME FOR A BLESSING.
FROM YOU. FROM THE LOA. FROM THOSE WRETCHED WHO HAVE FALLEN BECAUSE OF MY ARROGANCE AND BLINDNESS...
BECAUSE I WANT MY LIFE TO COUNT FOR SOMETHING GOOD BEFORE IT IS TOO LATE.

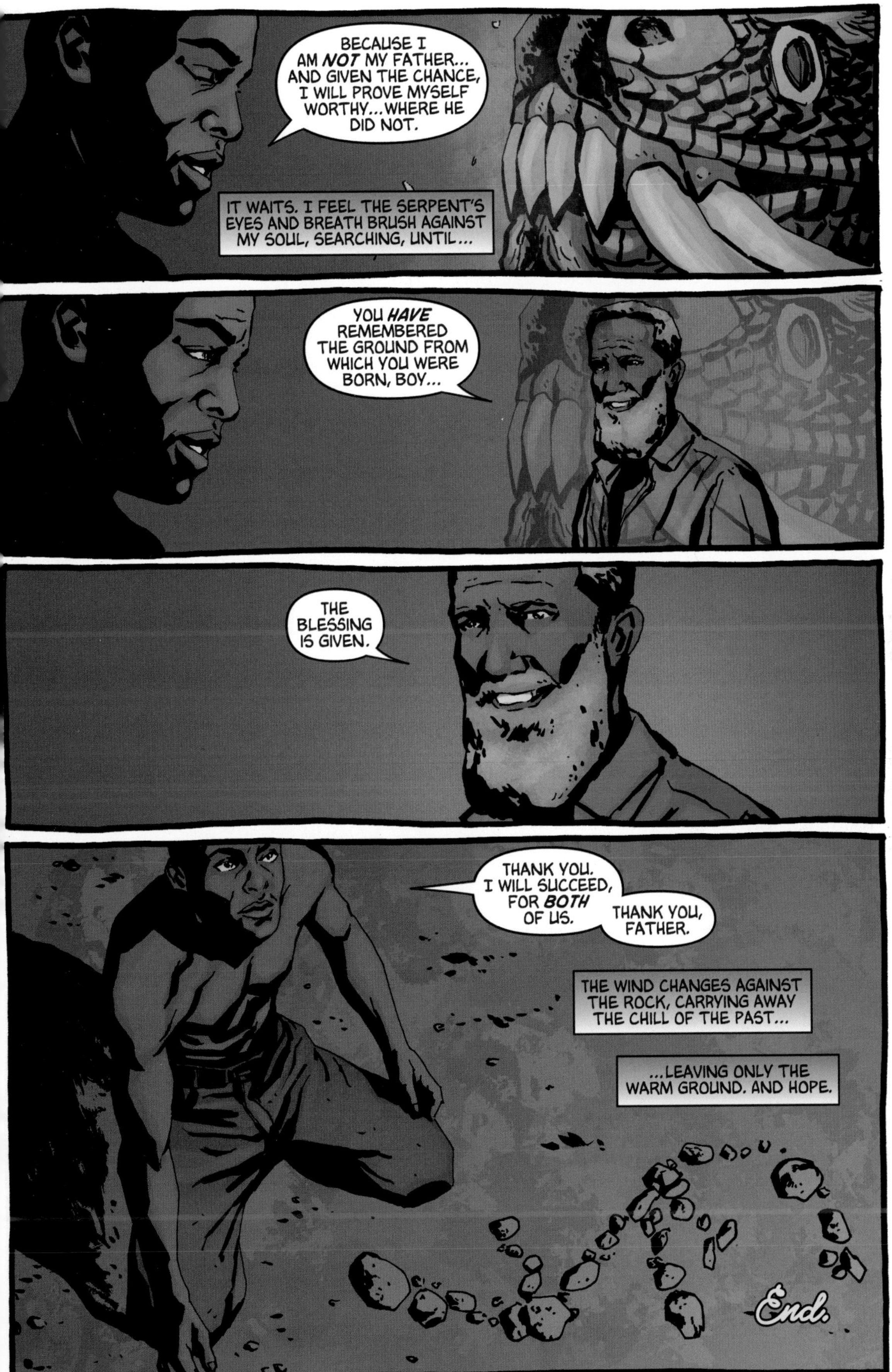
BECAUSE I AM NOT MY FATHER... AND GIVEN THE CHANCE, I WILL PROVE MYSELF WORTHY...WHERE HE DID NOT.
IT WAITS. I FEEL THE SERPENT'S EYES AND BREATH BRUSH AGAINST MY SOUL, SEARCHING, UNTIL...
YOU HAVE REMEMBERED THE GROUND FROM WHICH YOU WERE BORN, BOY...
THE BLESSING IS GIVEN.
THANK YOU. I WILL SUCCEED, FOR BOTH OF US.
THANK YOU, FATHER.
THE WIND CHANGES AGAINST THE ROCK, CARRYING AWAY THE CHILL OF THE PAST...
...LEAVING ONLY THE WARM GROUND. AND HOPE.
End.

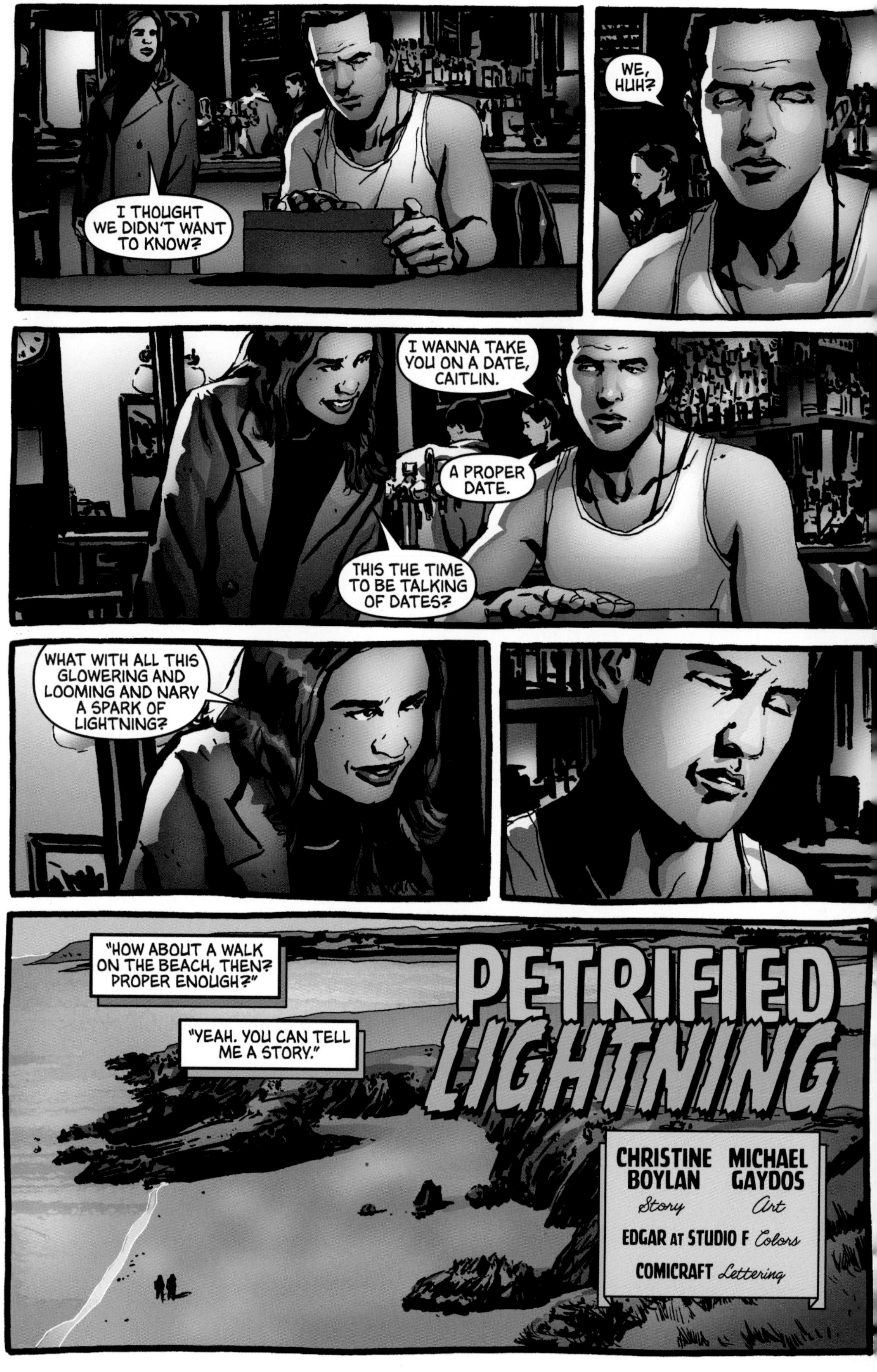
I THOUGHT WE DIDN'T WANT TO KNOW?
WE, HUH?
I WANNA TAKE YOU ON A DATE, CAITLIN.
A PROPER DATE.
THIS THE TIME TO BE TALKING OF DATES?
WHAT WITH ALL THIS GLOWERING AND LOOMING AND NARY A SPARK OF LIGHTNING?
"HOW ABOUT A WALK ON THE BEACH, THEN? PROPER ENOUGH?"
"YEAH. YOU CAN TELL ME A STORY."
PETRIFIED LIGHTNING
CHRISTINE BOYLAN Story
MICHAEL GAYDOS Art
EDGAR AT STUDIO F Colors
COMICRAFT Lettering

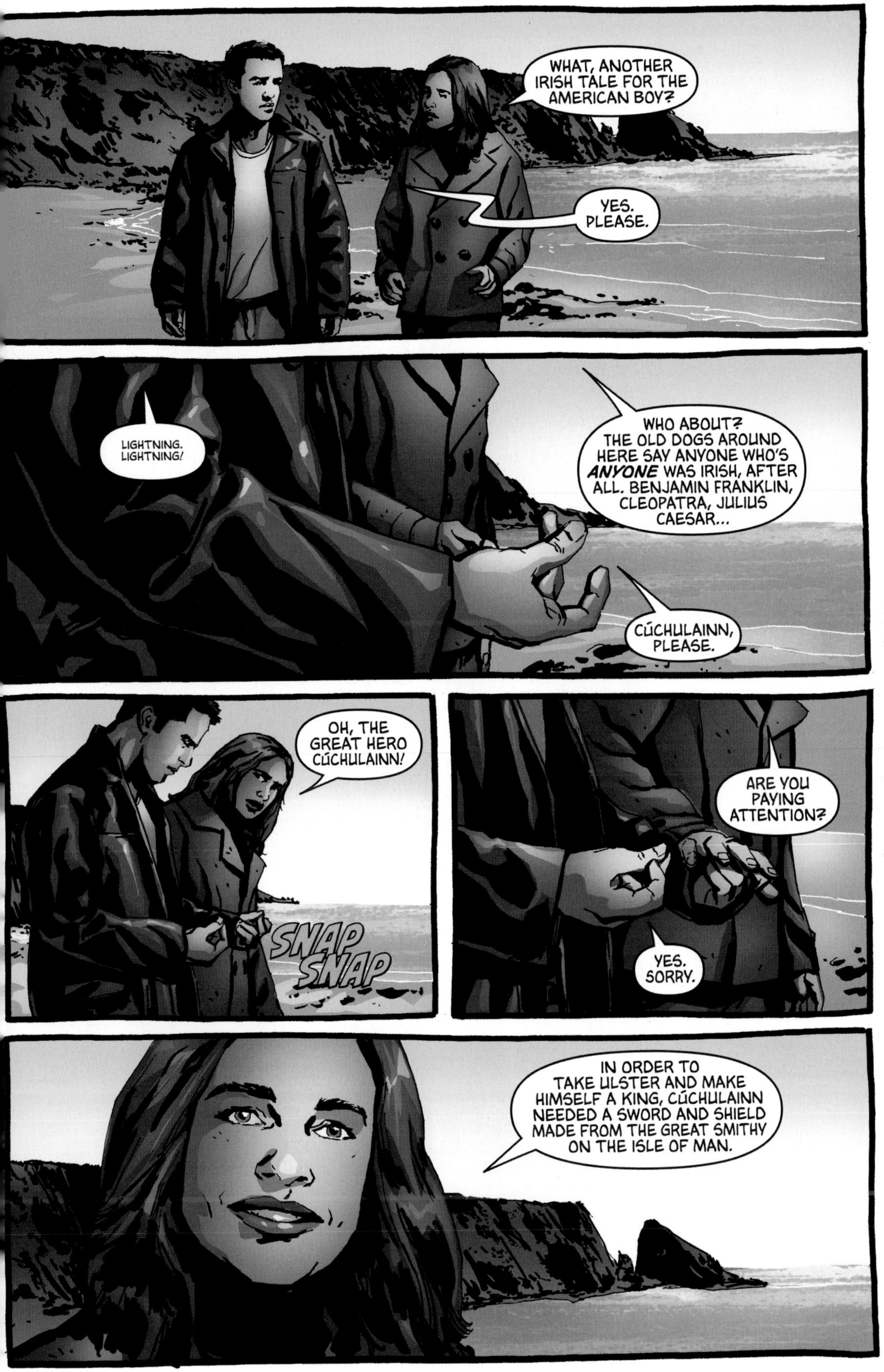
WHAT, ANOTHER IRISH TALE FOR THE AMERICAN BOY?
YES. PLEASE.
LIGHTNING. LIGHTNING!
WHO ABOUT? THE OLD DOGS AROUND HERE SAY ANYONE WHO'S *ANYONE* WAS IRISH, AFTER ALL. BENJAMIN FRANKLIN, CLEOPATRA, JULIUS CAESAR...
CÚCHULAINN, PLEASE.
OH, THE GREAT HERO CÚCHULAINN!
SNAP SNAP
ARE YOU PAYING ATTENTION?
YES. SORRY.
IN ORDER TO TAKE ULSTER AND MAKE HIMSELF A KING, CÚCHULAINN NEEDED A SWORD AND SHIELD MADE FROM THE GREAT SMITHY ON THE ISLE OF MAN.

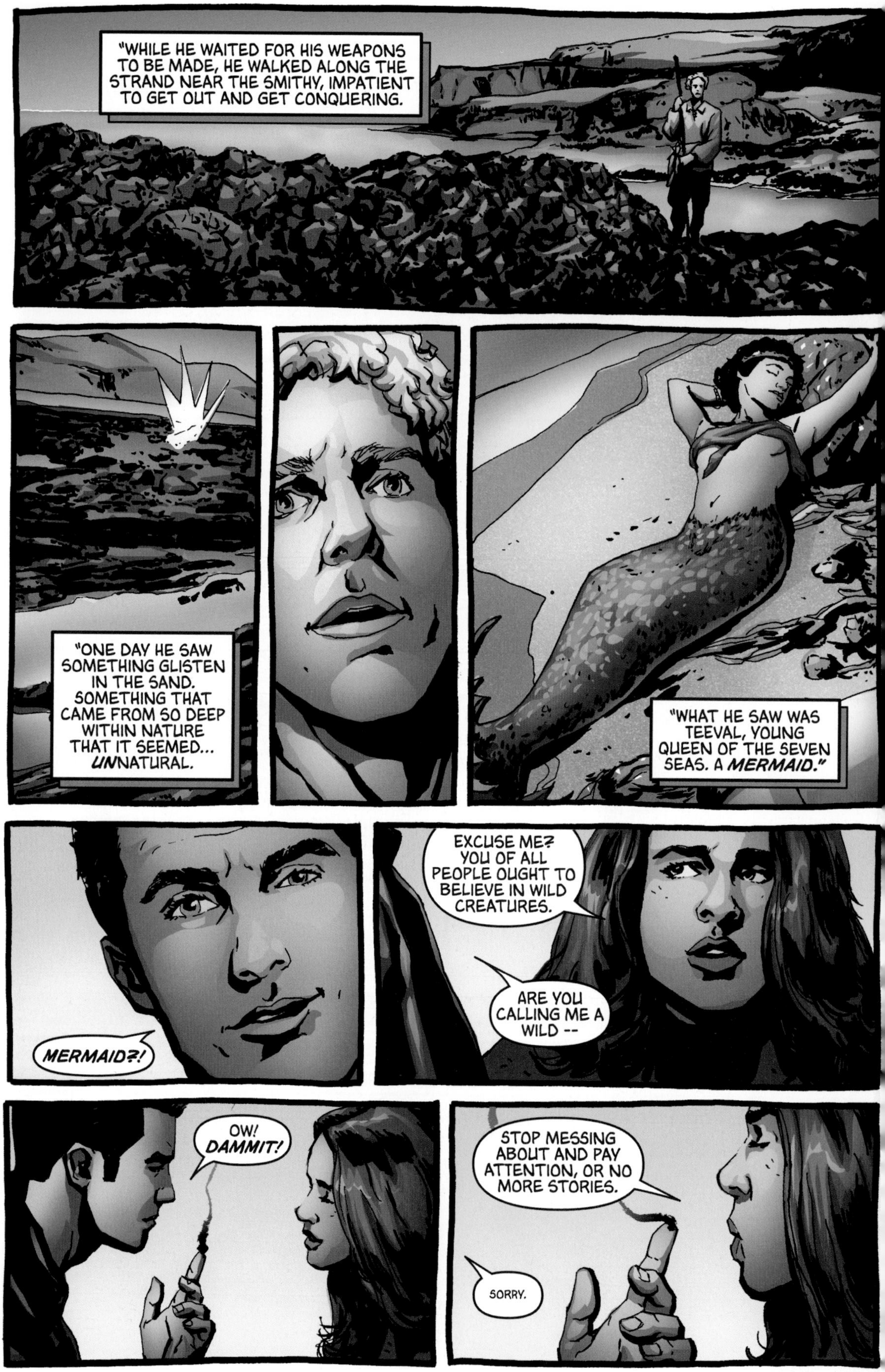
"WHILE HE WAITED FOR HIS WEAPONS TO BE MADE, HE WALKED ALONG THE STRAND NEAR THE SMITHY, IMPATIENT TO GET OUT AND GET CONQUERING.
"ONE DAY HE SAW SOMETHING GLISTEN IN THE SAND. SOMETHING THAT CAME FROM SO DEEP WITHIN NATURE THAT IT SEEMED... *UN*NATURAL.
"WHAT HE SAW WAS TEEVAL, YOUNG QUEEN OF THE SEVEN SEAS. A *MERMAID*."
*MERMAID?!*
EXCUSE ME? YOU OF ALL PEOPLE OUGHT TO BELIEVE IN WILD CREATURES.
ARE YOU CALLING ME A WILD --
OW! *DAMMIT!*
STOP MESSING ABOUT AND PAY ATTENTION, OR NO MORE STORIES.
SORRY.

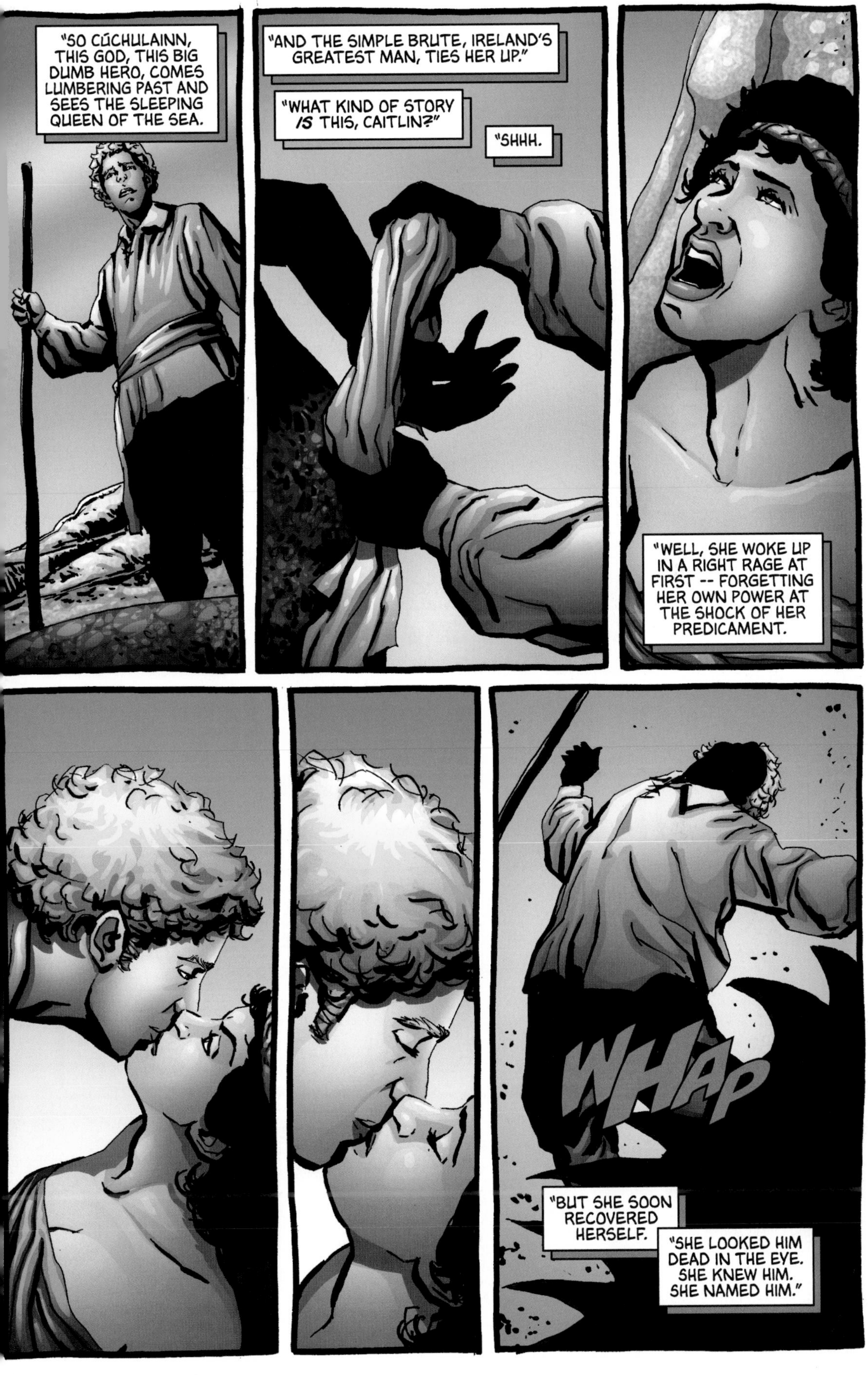
"SO CÚCHULAINN, THIS GOD, THIS BIG DUMB HERO, COMES LUMBERING PAST AND SEES THE SLEEPING QUEEN OF THE SEA.
"AND THE SIMPLE BRUTE, IRELAND'S GREATEST MAN, TIES HER UP."
"WHAT KIND OF STORY *IS* THIS, CAITLIN?"
"SHHH.
"WELL, SHE WOKE UP IN A RIGHT RAGE AT FIRST -- FORGETTING HER OWN POWER AT THE SHOCK OF HER PREDICAMENT.
WHAP
"BUT SHE SOON RECOVERED HERSELF.
"SHE LOOKED HIM DEAD IN THE EYE. SHE KNEW HIM. SHE NAMED HIM."

LET ME GO, MORTAL.

NO. I CAN'T. I'LL LOSE YOU.

"AND SHE MADE HIM AN OFFER."

UNBIND ME, AND I WILL GIVE YOU SOMETHING MORE USEFUL THAN MYSELF.

BUT I...I LOVE YOU.

DON'T BE FOOLISH. DO YOU WANT TO CONQUER THE LAND OR DROWN WITH ME IN THE SEA?

GO TO THE SMITHY. TELL THE ARTISAN TO CARVE MY NAME AND IMAGE ON THE INSIDE OF YOUR SHIELD, JUST AS YOU SEE ME NOW.

IN BATTLE, LOOK YOU ON THE SHIELD AND CALL MY NAME, AND YOUR STRENGTH WILL BE MULTIPLIED EVEN AS YOUR ENEMIES WEAKEN AND FALL.

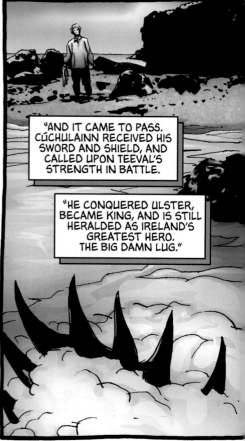

"AND IT CAME TO PASS. CÚCHULAINN RECEIVED HIS SWORD AND SHIELD, AND CALLED UPON TEEVAL'S STRENGTH IN BATTLE.

"HE CONQUERED ULSTER, BECAME KING, AND IS STILL HERALDED AS IRELAND'S GREATEST HERO. THE BIG DAMN LUG."

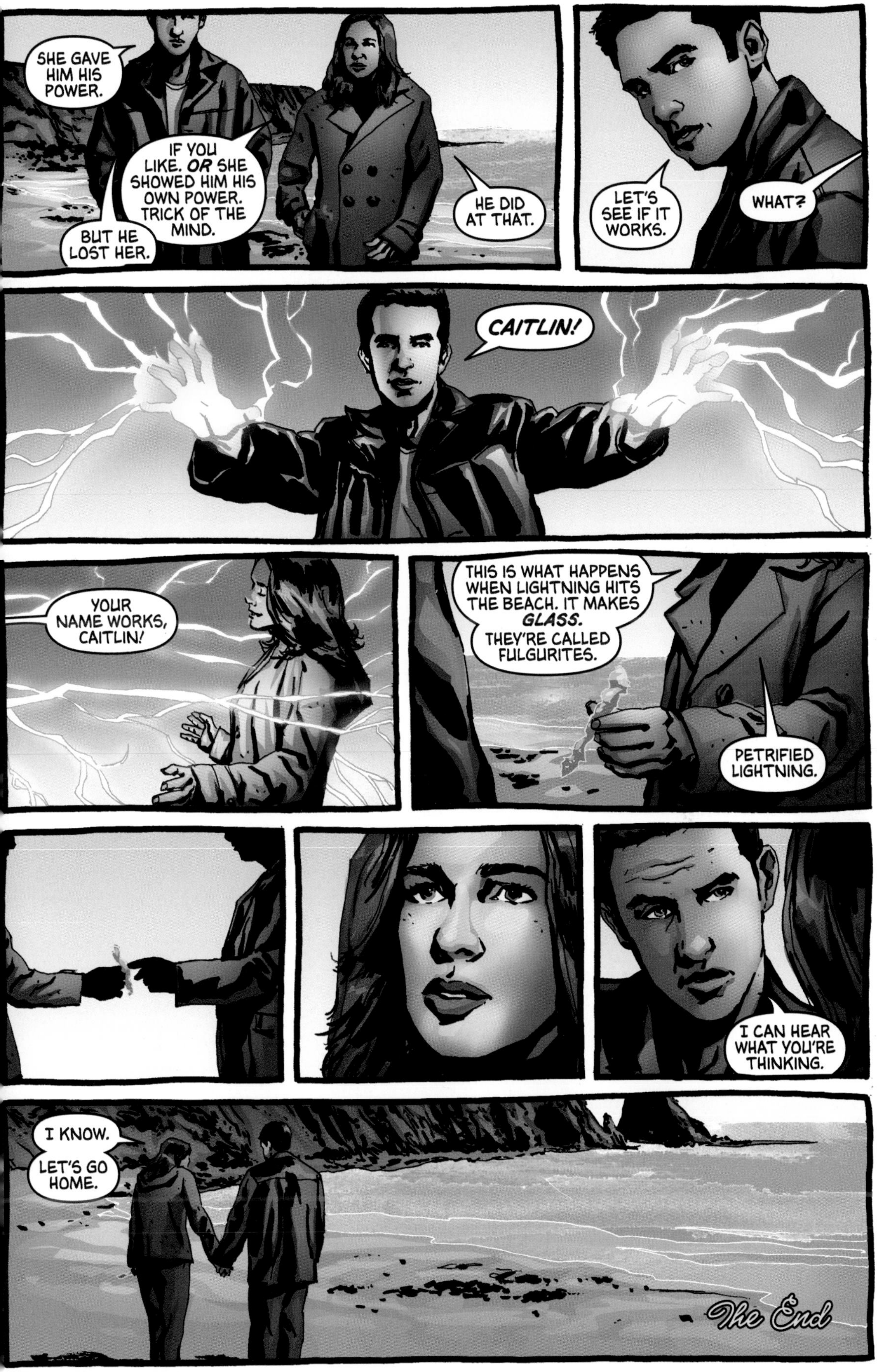
SHE GAVE HIM HIS POWER.
IF YOU LIKE. OR SHE SHOWED HIM HIS OWN POWER. TRICK OF THE MIND.
BUT HE LOST HER.
HE DID AT THAT.
LET'S SEE IF IT WORKS.
WHAT?
CAITLIN!
YOUR NAME WORKS, CAITLIN!
THIS IS WHAT HAPPENS WHEN LIGHTNING HITS THE BEACH. IT MAKES GLASS.
THEY'RE CALLED FULGURITES.
PETRIFIED LIGHTNING.
I CAN HEAR WHAT YOU'RE THINKING.
I KNOW.
LET'S GO HOME.
The End

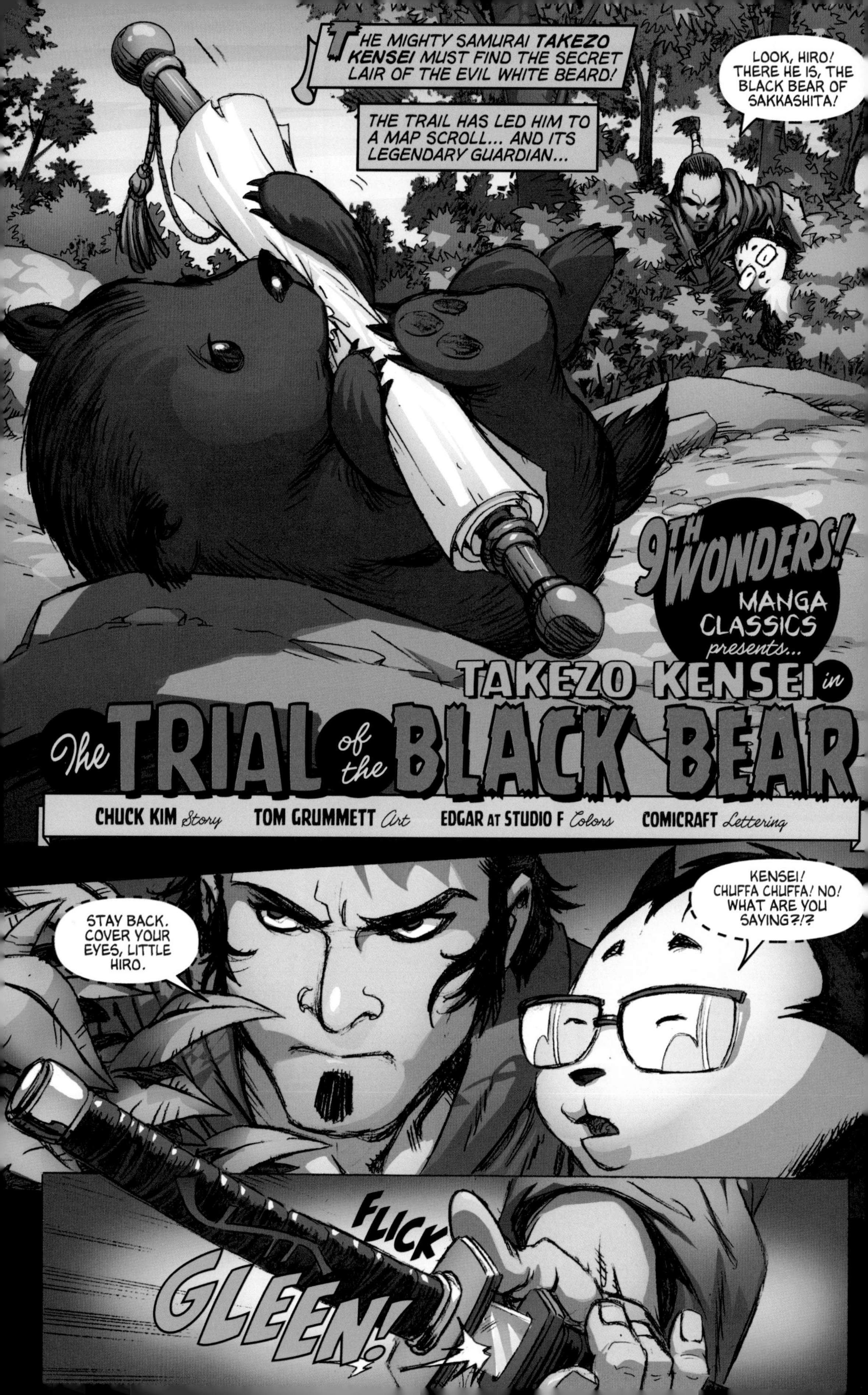
THE MIGHTY SAMURAI TAKEZO KENSEI MUST FIND THE SECRET LAIR OF THE EVIL WHITE BEARD!
THE TRAIL HAS LED HIM TO A MAP SCROLL... AND ITS LEGENDARY GUARDIAN...
LOOK, HIRO! THERE HE IS, THE BLACK BEAR OF SAKKASHITA!
9TH WONDERS! MANGA CLASSICS presents...
TAKEZO KENSEI in
The TRIAL of the BLACK BEAR
CHUCK KIM Story TOM GRUMMETT Art EDGAR AT STUDIO F Colors COMICRAFT Lettering
STAY BACK. COVER YOUR EYES, LITTLE HIRO.
KENSEI! CHUFFA CHUFFA! NO! WHAT ARE YOU SAYING?!?
FLICK
GLEEN!

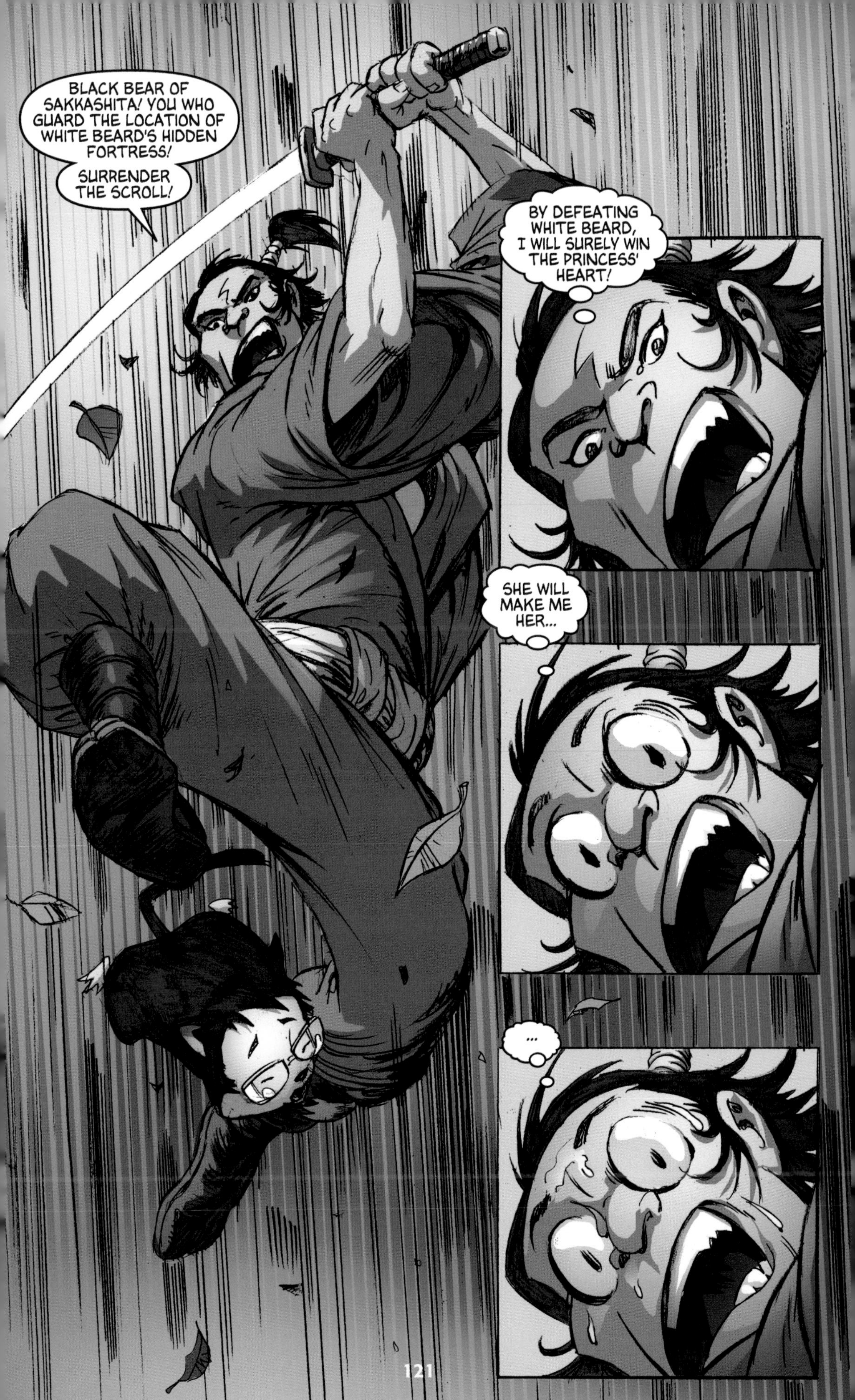
BLACK BEAR OF SAKKASHITA! YOU WHO GUARD THE LOCATION OF WHITE BEARD'S HIDDEN FORTRESS!
SURRENDER THE SCROLL!
BY DEFEATING WHITE BEARD, I WILL SURELY WIN THE PRINCESS' HEART!
SHE WILL MAKE ME HER...
...

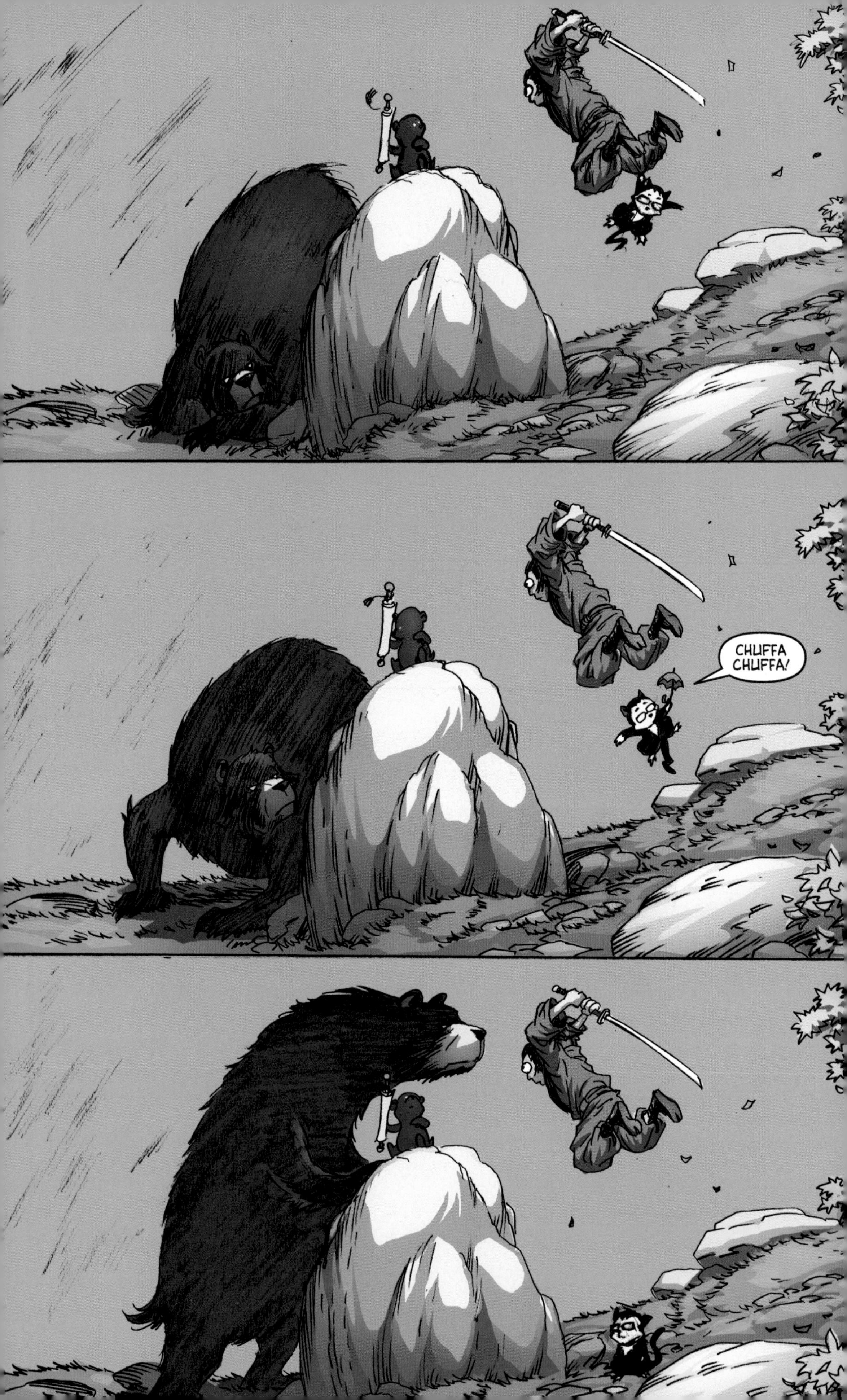
CHUFFA CHUFFA!

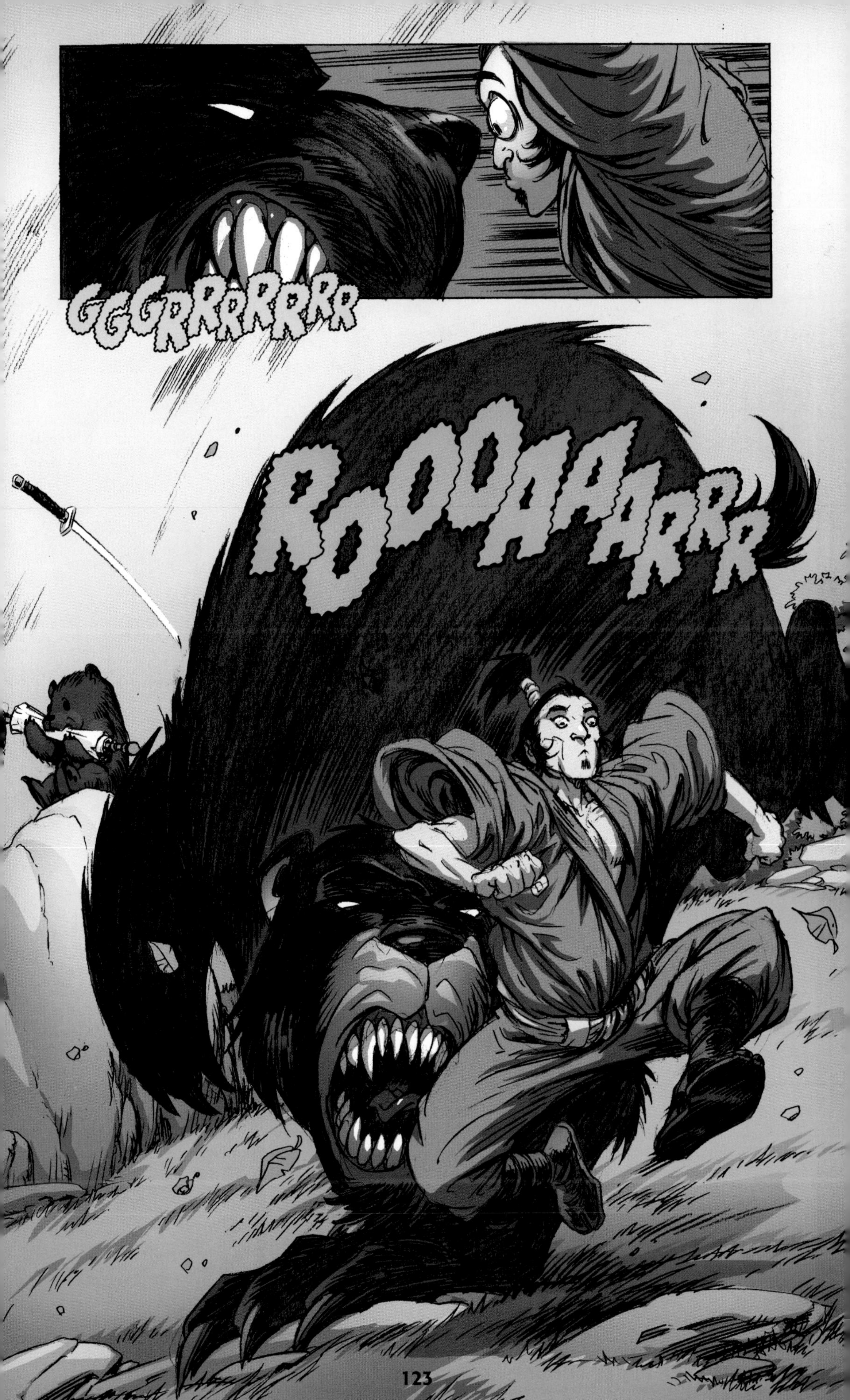
GGGRRRRRRRR
ROOOAAARRR

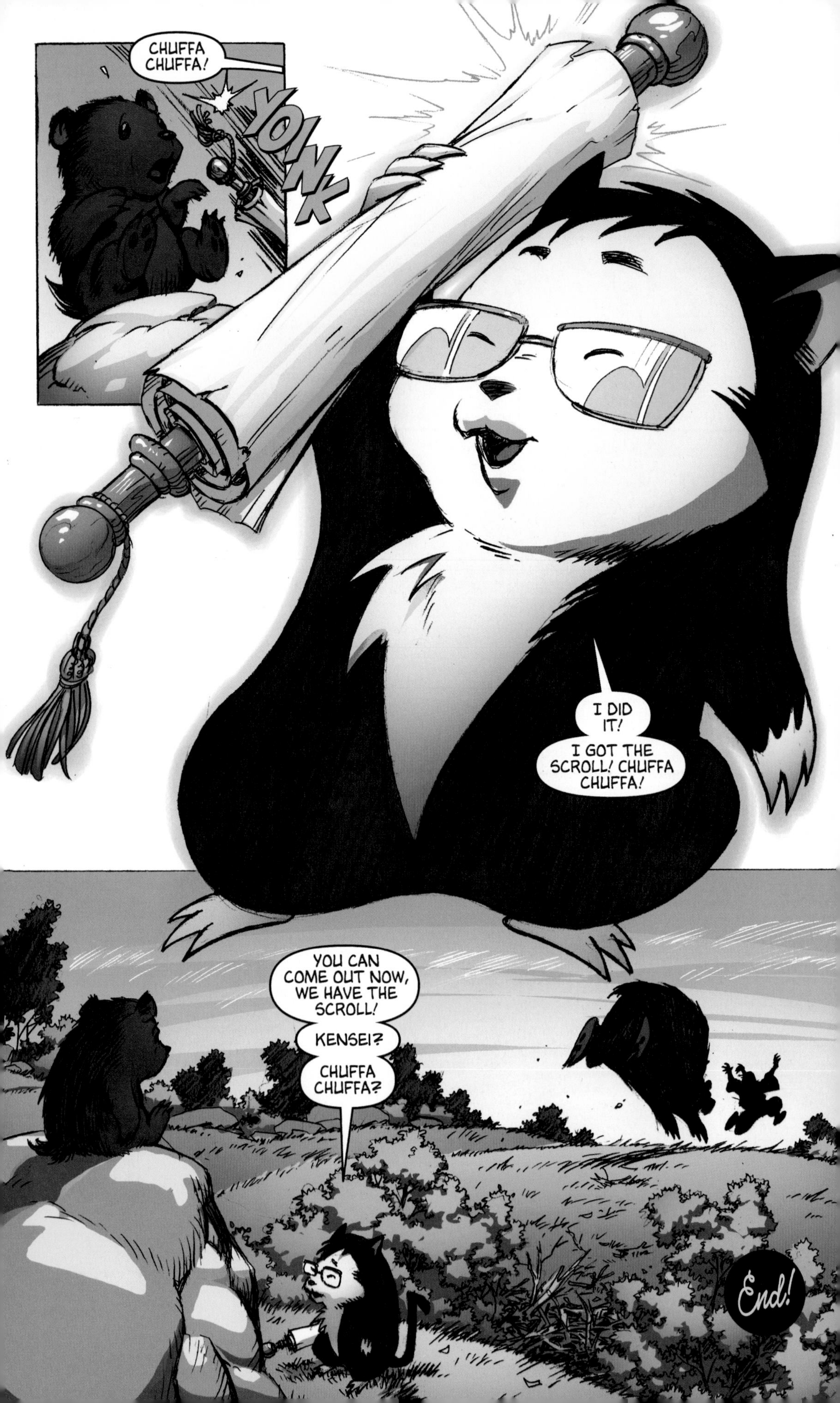
CHUFFA CHUFFA!
YOINK
I DID IT!
I GOT THE SCROLL! CHUFFA CHUFFA!
YOU CAN COME OUT NOW, WE HAVE THE SCROLL!
KENSEI?
CHUFFA CHUFFA?
End!

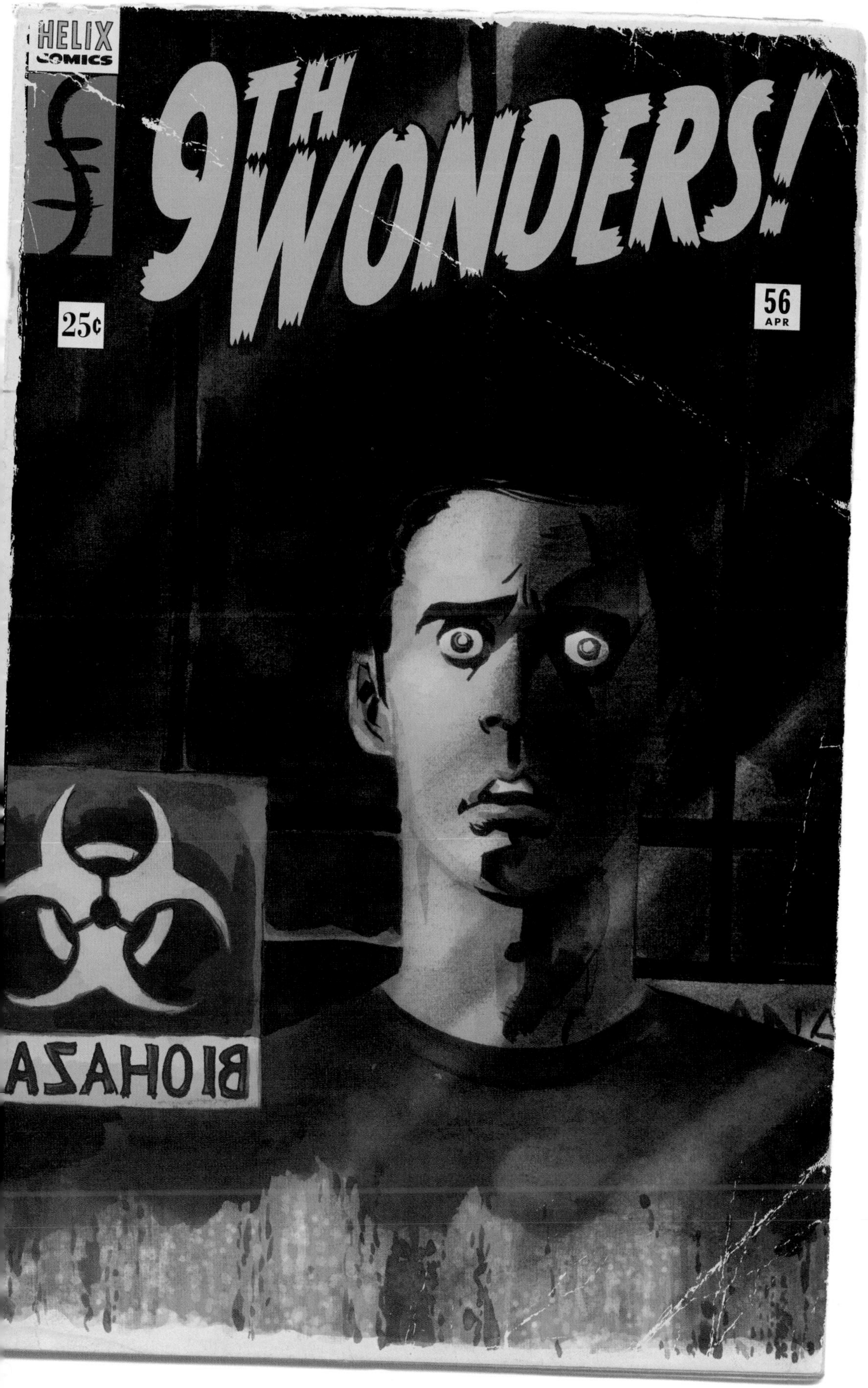
HELIX COMICS
9TH WONDERS!
25¢
56 APR
BIOHAZA

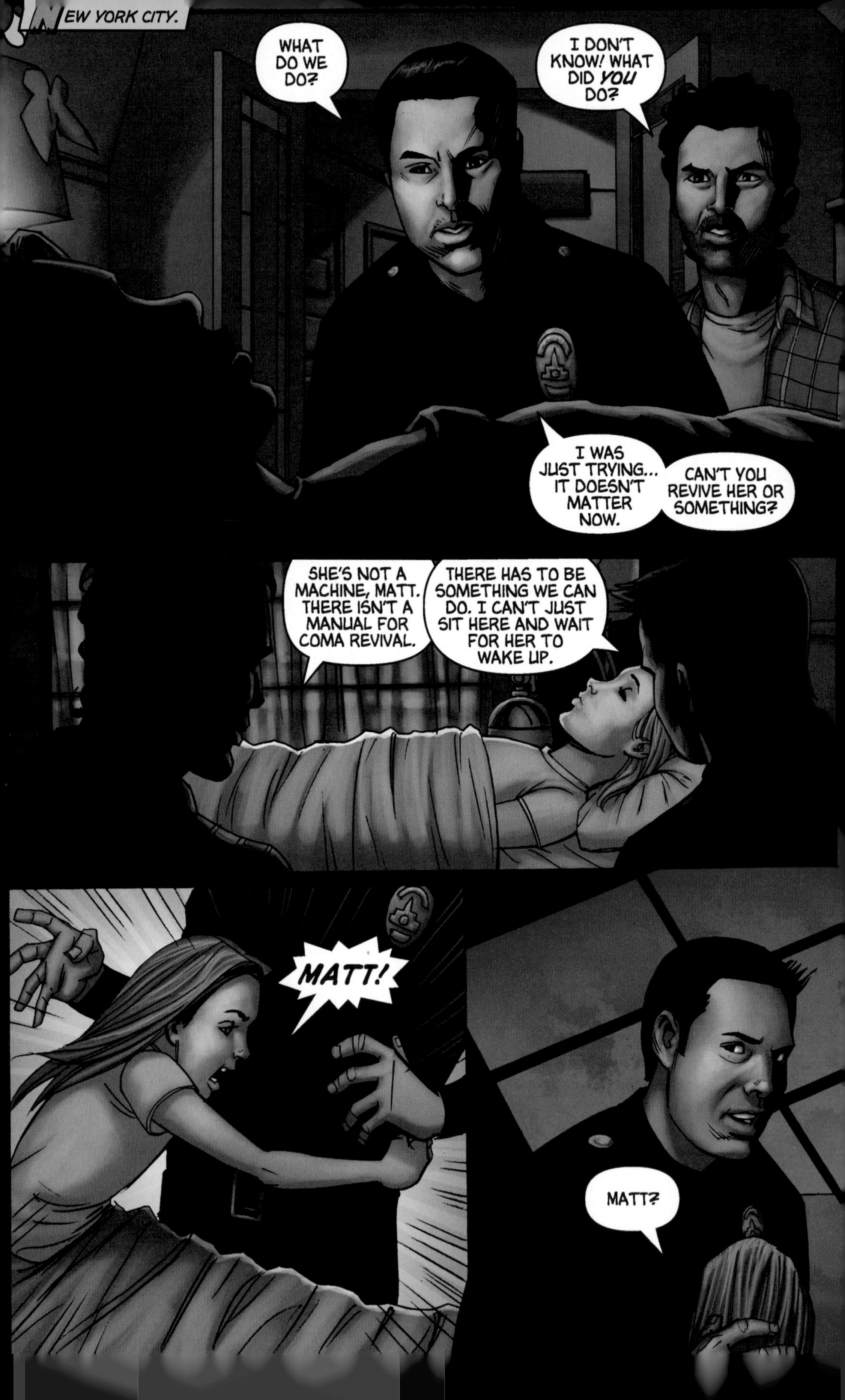
NEW YORK CITY.
WHAT DO WE DO?
I DON'T KNOW! WHAT DID YOU DO?
I WAS JUST TRYING... IT DOESN'T MATTER NOW.
CAN'T YOU REVIVE HER OR SOMETHING?
SHE'S NOT A MACHINE, MATT. THERE ISN'T A MANUAL FOR COMA REVIVAL.
THERE HAS TO BE SOMETHING WE CAN DO. I CAN'T JUST SIT HERE AND WAIT FOR HER TO WAKE UP.
MATT!
MATT?

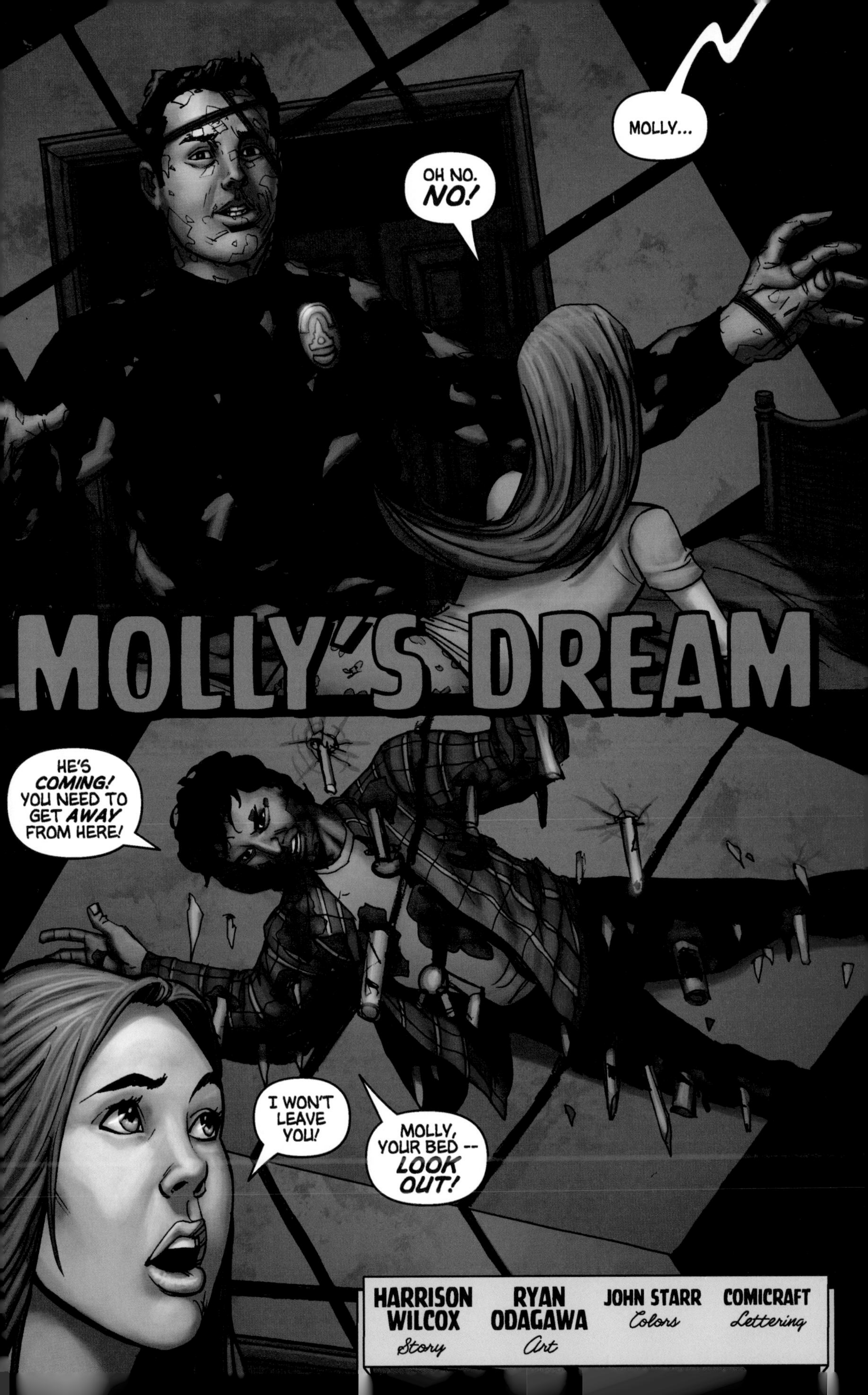
MOLLY...
OH NO. NO!
MOLLY'S DREAM
HE'S COMING! YOU NEED TO GET AWAY FROM HERE!
I WON'T LEAVE YOU!
MOLLY, YOUR BED -- LOOK OUT!
HARRISON WILCOX Story
RYAN ODAGAWA Art
JOHN STARR Colors
COMICRAFT Lettering

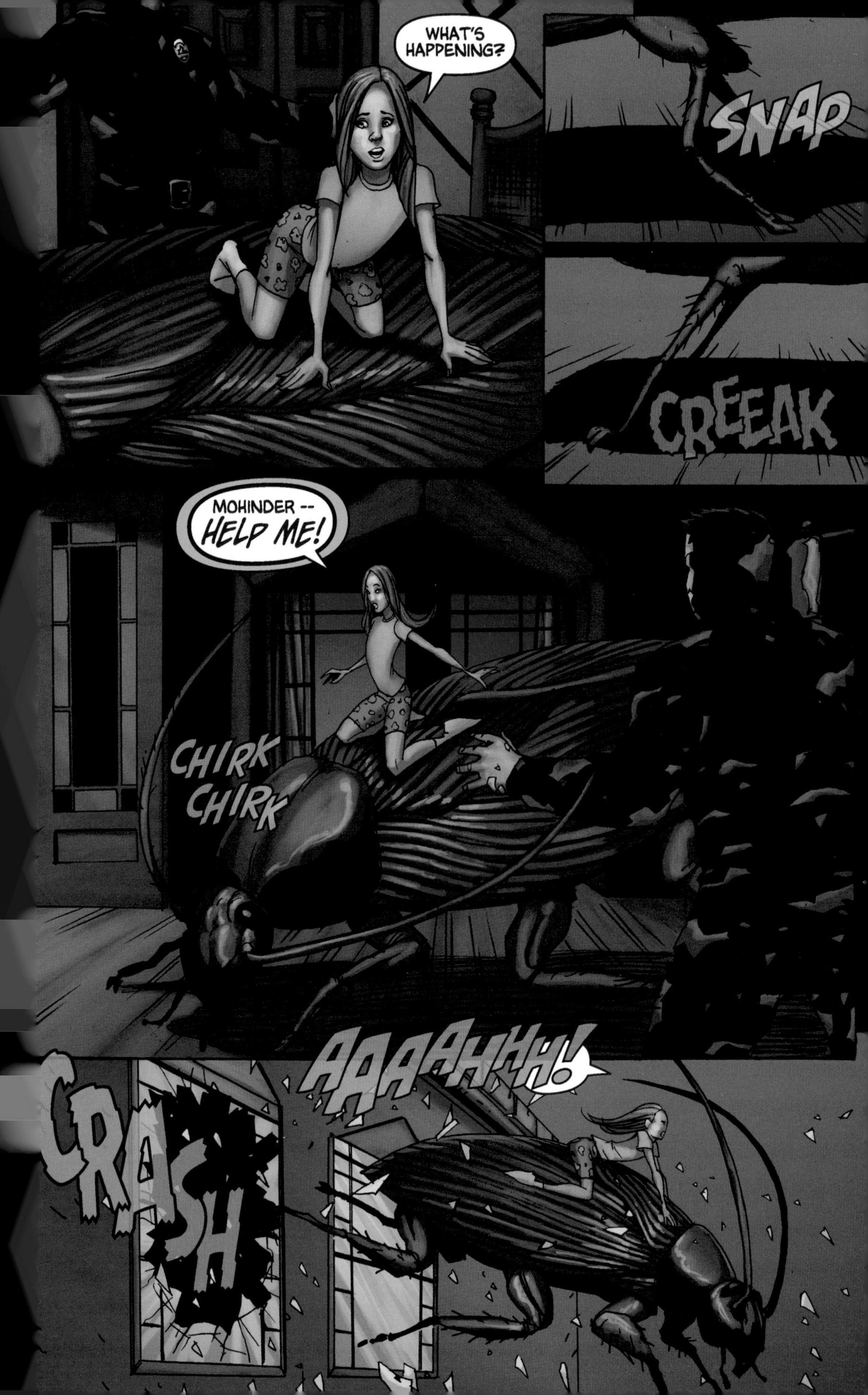
WHAT'S HAPPENING?
SNAP
CREEAK
MOHINDER -- HELP ME!
CHIRK CHIRK
AAAAHHH!
CRASH

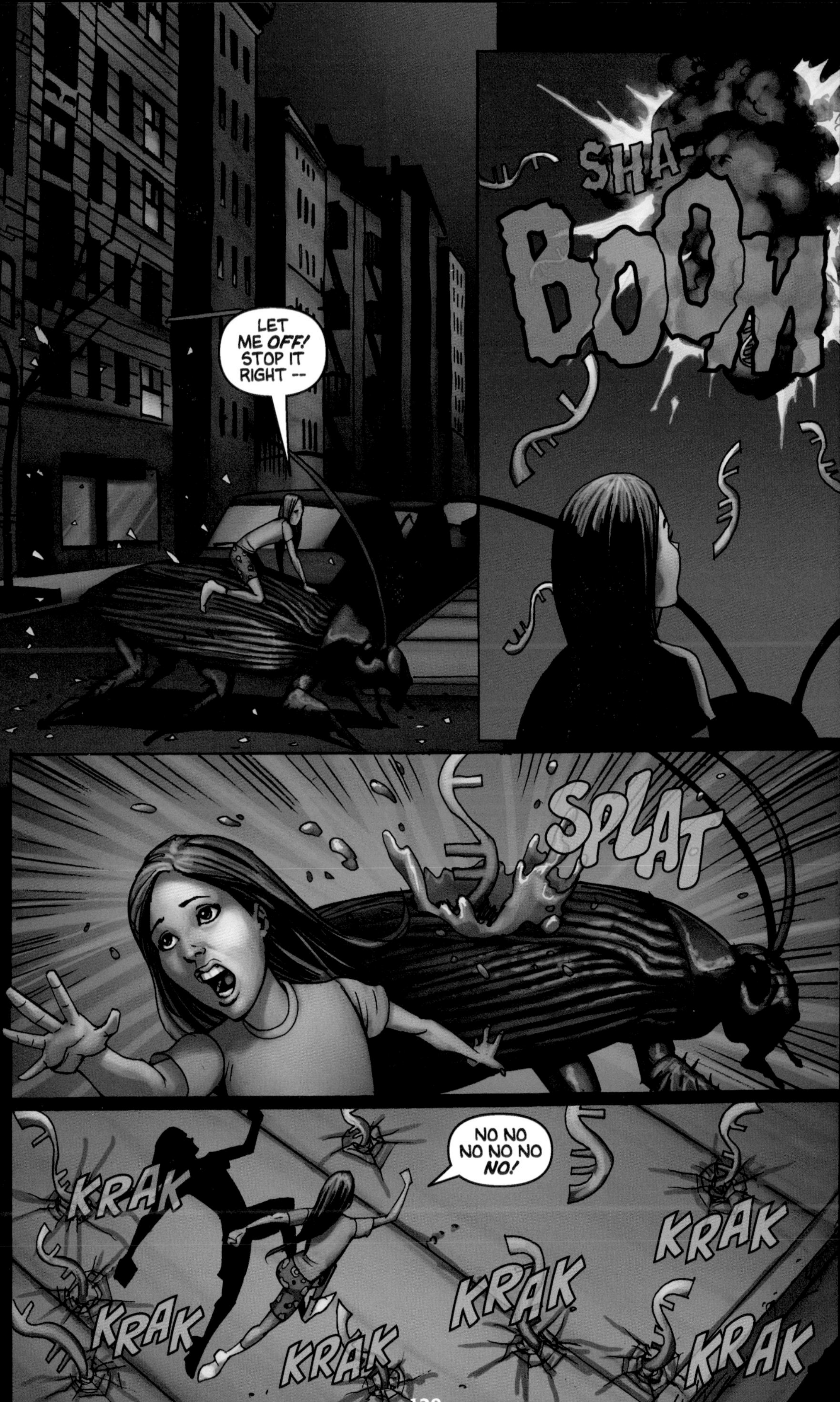
LET ME *OFF!* STOP IT RIGHT --
SHA-BOOM
SPLAT
NO NO NO NO NO *NO!*
KRAK
KRAK
KRAK
KRAK
KRAK
KRAK

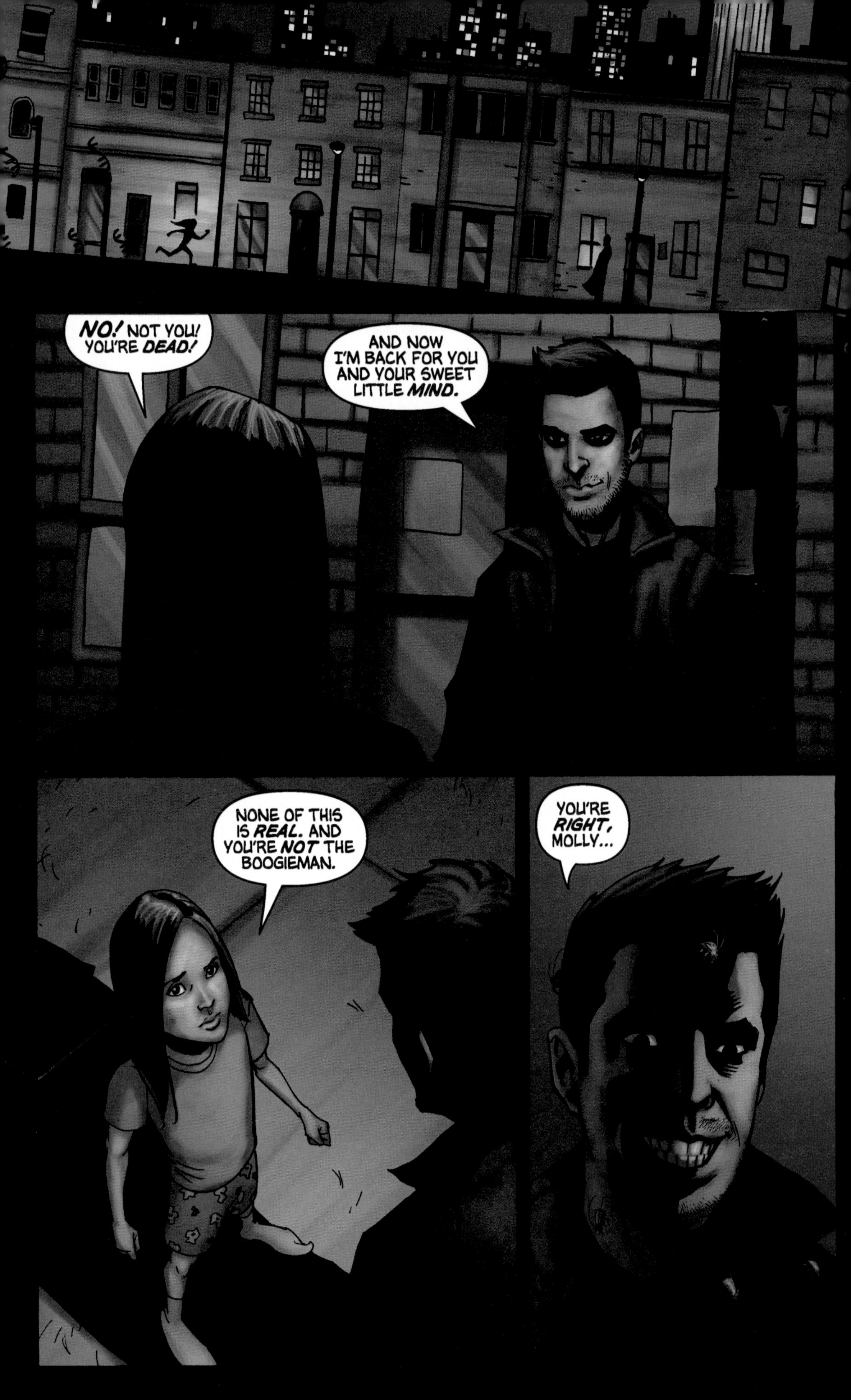
NO! NOT YOU! YOU'RE DEAD!
AND NOW I'M BACK FOR YOU AND YOUR SWEET LITTLE MIND.
NONE OF THIS IS REAL. AND YOU'RE NOT THE BOOGIEMAN.
YOU'RE RIGHT, MOLLY...

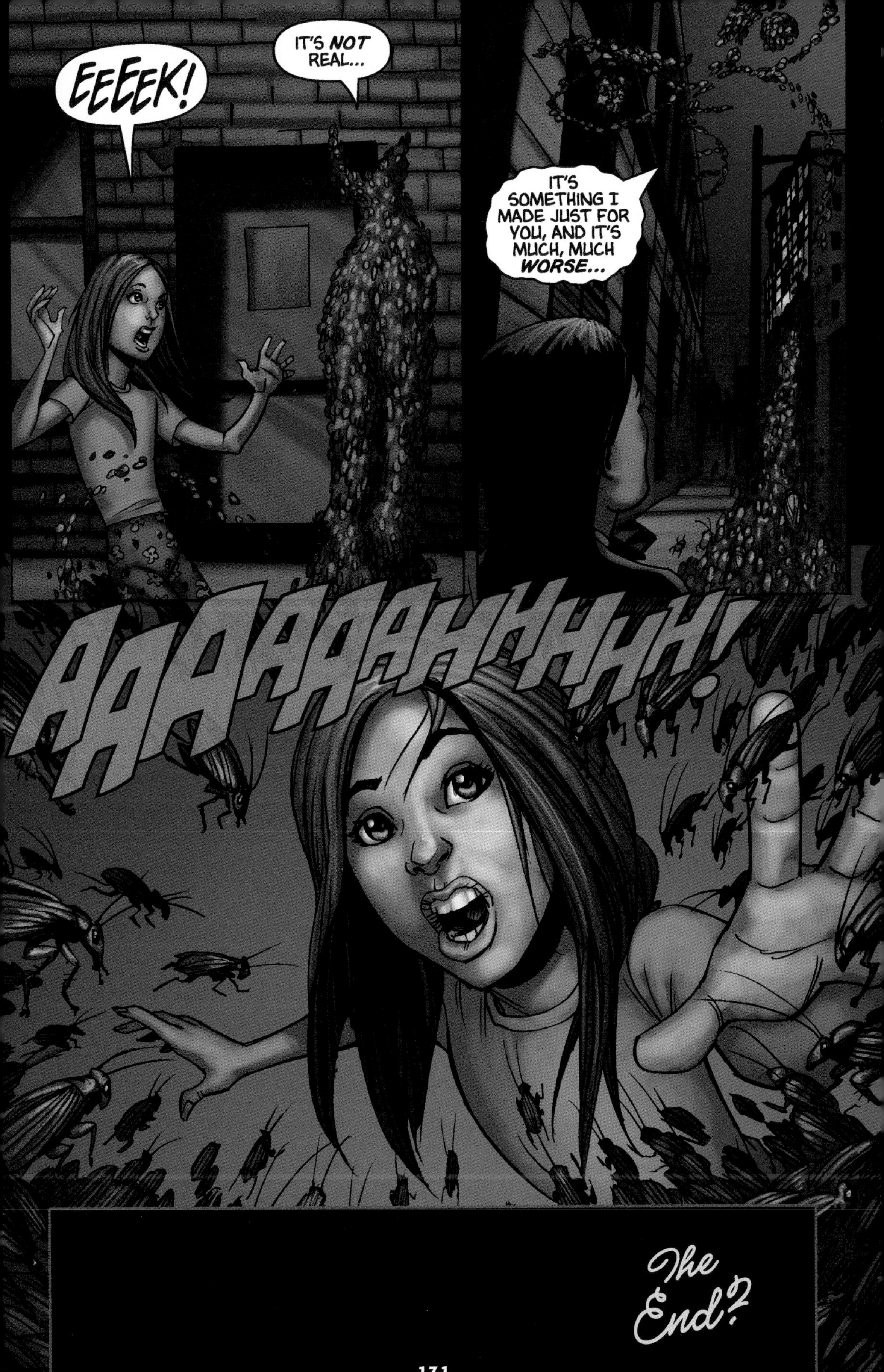
EEEEK!
IT'S NOT REAL...
IT'S SOMETHING I MADE JUST FOR YOU, AND IT'S MUCH, MUCH WORSE...
AAAAAHHHHH!
The End?

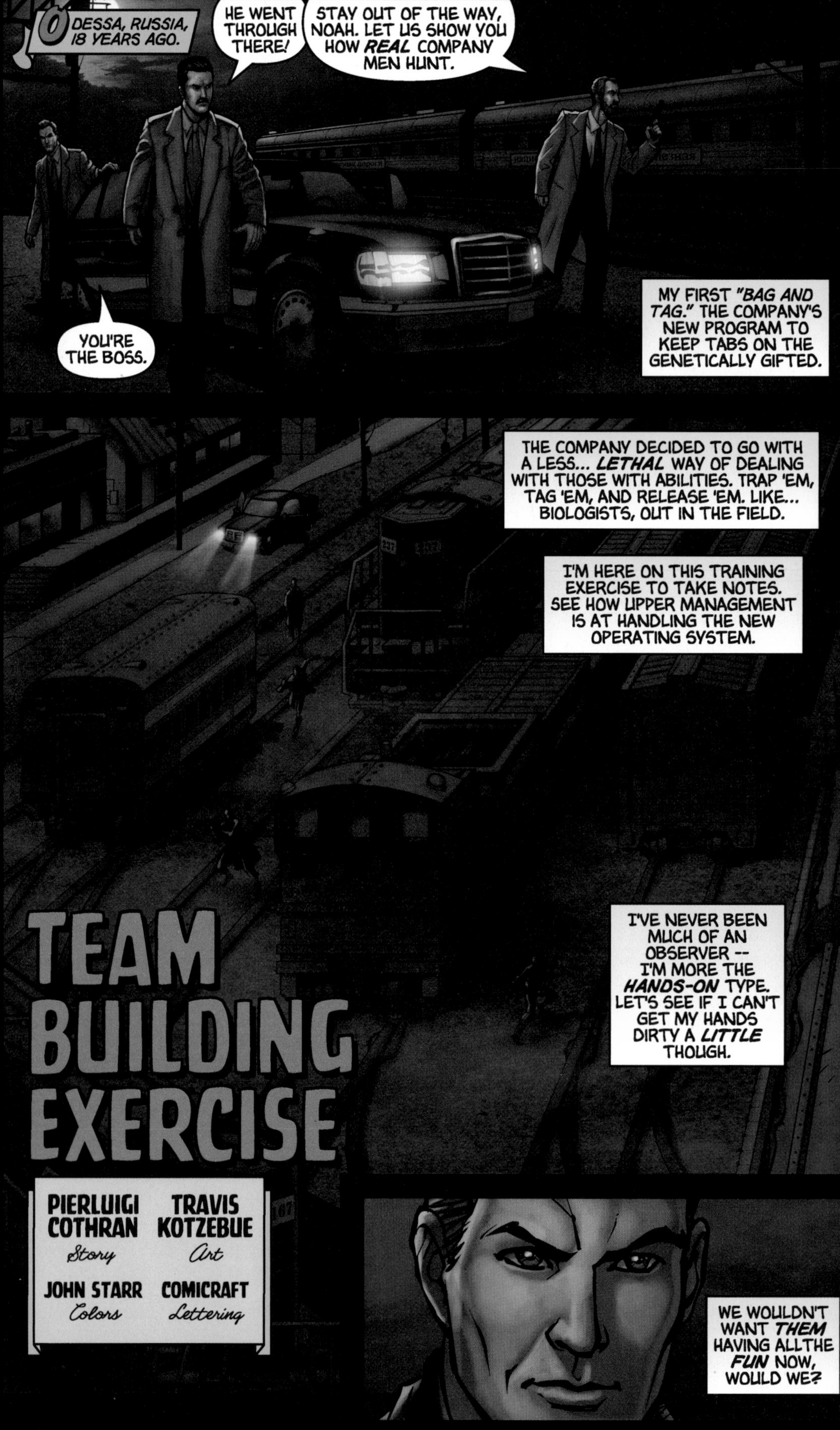
ODESSA, RUSSIA, 18 YEARS AGO.
HE WENT THROUGH THERE!
STAY OUT OF THE WAY, NOAH. LET US SHOW YOU HOW REAL COMPANY MEN HUNT.
YOU'RE THE BOSS.
MY FIRST "BAG AND TAG." THE COMPANY'S NEW PROGRAM TO KEEP TABS ON THE GENETICALLY GIFTED.
THE COMPANY DECIDED TO GO WITH A LESS... LETHAL WAY OF DEALING WITH THOSE WITH ABILITIES. TRAP 'EM, TAG 'EM, AND RELEASE 'EM. LIKE... BIOLOGISTS, OUT IN THE FIELD.
I'M HERE ON THIS TRAINING EXERCISE TO TAKE NOTES. SEE HOW UPPER MANAGEMENT IS AT HANDLING THE NEW OPERATING SYSTEM.
I'VE NEVER BEEN MUCH OF AN OBSERVER -- I'M MORE THE HANDS-ON TYPE. LET'S SEE IF I CAN'T GET MY HANDS DIRTY A LITTLE THOUGH.
TEAM BUILDING EXERCISE
PIERLUIGI COTHRAN Story
TRAVIS KOTZEBUE Art
JOHN STARR Colors
COMICRAFT Lettering
WE WOULDN'T WANT THEM HAVING ALLTHE FUN NOW, WOULD WE?

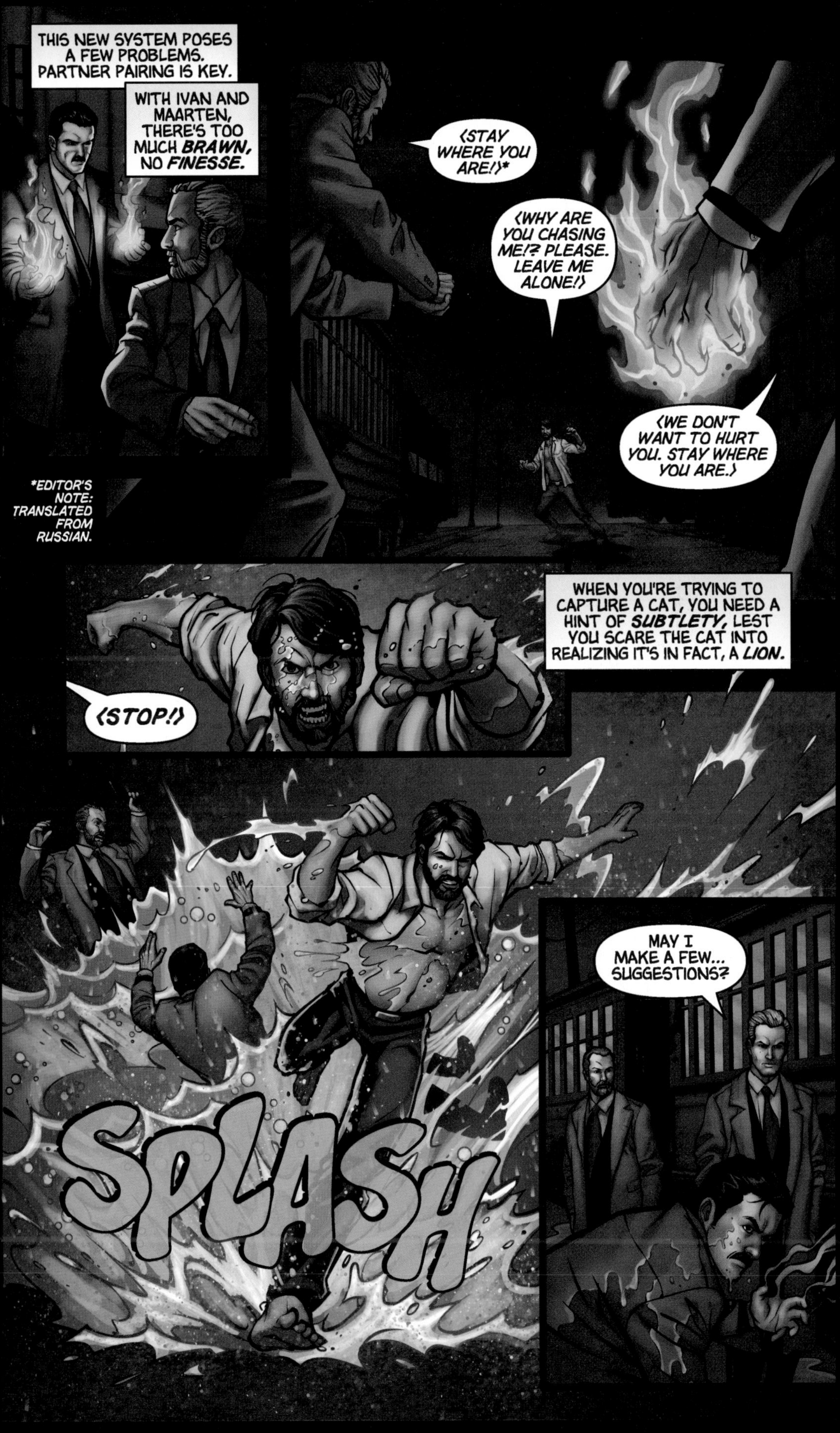

THIS NEW SYSTEM POSES A FEW PROBLEMS. PARTNER PAIRING IS KEY.
WITH IVAN AND MAARTEN, THERE'S TOO MUCH BRAWN, NO FINESSE.
‹STAY WHERE YOU ARE!›*
‹WHY ARE YOU CHASING ME!? PLEASE. LEAVE ME ALONE!›
‹WE DON'T WANT TO HURT YOU. STAY WHERE YOU ARE.›
*EDITOR'S NOTE: TRANSLATED FROM RUSSIAN.
WHEN YOU'RE TRYING TO CAPTURE A CAT, YOU NEED A HINT OF SUBTLETY, LEST YOU SCARE THE CAT INTO REALIZING IT'S IN FACT, A LION.
‹STOP!›
SPLASH
MAY I MAKE A FEW... SUGGESTIONS?

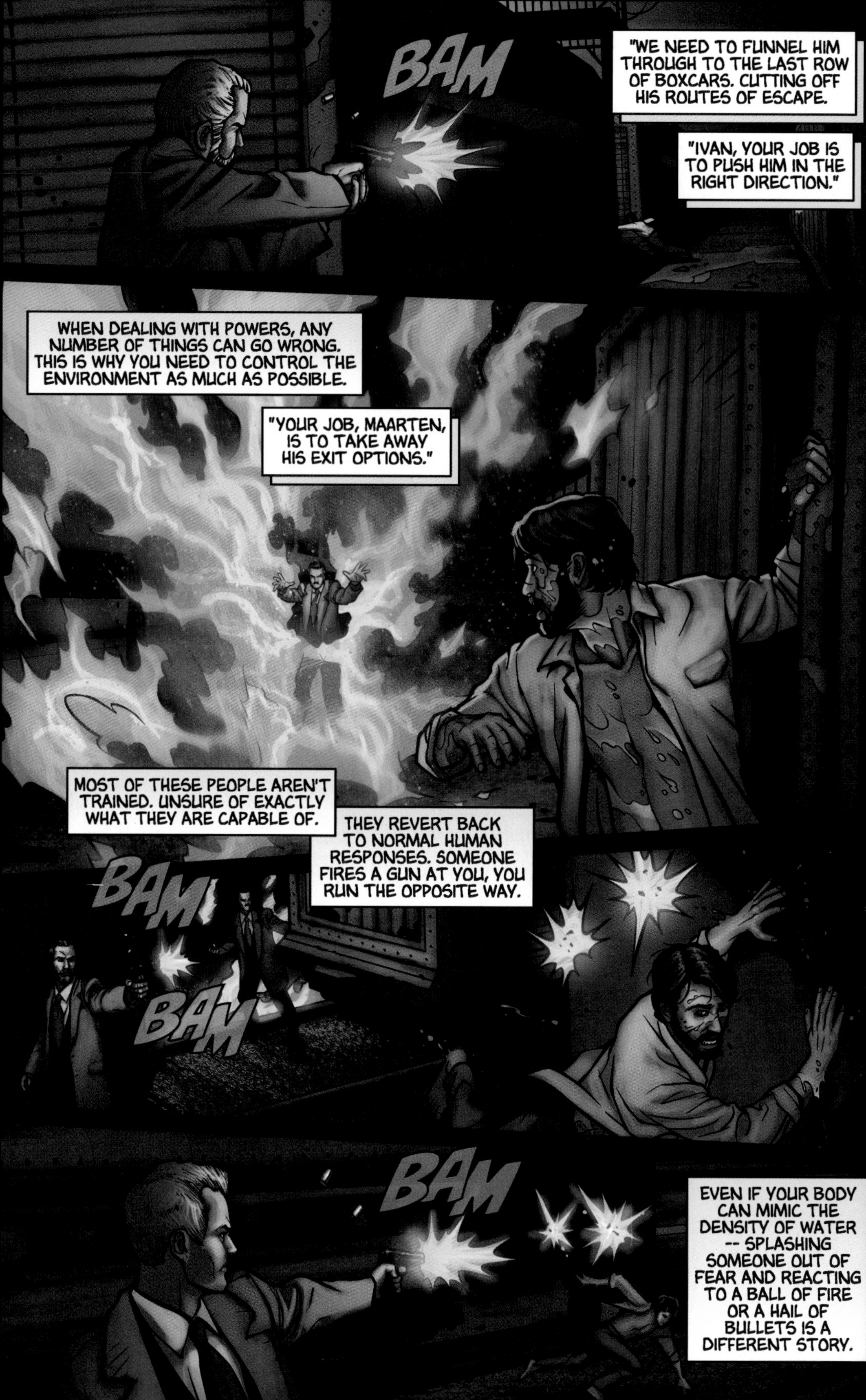
BAM
"WE NEED TO FUNNEL HIM THROUGH TO THE LAST ROW OF BOXCARS. CUTTING OFF HIS ROUTES OF ESCAPE.
"IVAN, YOUR JOB IS TO PUSH HIM IN THE RIGHT DIRECTION."
WHEN DEALING WITH POWERS, ANY NUMBER OF THINGS CAN GO WRONG. THIS IS WHY YOU NEED TO CONTROL THE ENVIRONMENT AS MUCH AS POSSIBLE.
"YOUR JOB, MAARTEN, IS TO TAKE AWAY HIS EXIT OPTIONS."
MOST OF THESE PEOPLE AREN'T TRAINED. UNSURE OF EXACTLY WHAT THEY ARE CAPABLE OF.
THEY REVERT BACK TO NORMAL HUMAN RESPONSES. SOMEONE FIRES A GUN AT YOU, YOU RUN THE OPPOSITE WAY.
BAM
BAM
BAM
EVEN IF YOUR BODY CAN MIMIC THE DENSITY OF WATER -- SPLASHING SOMEONE OUT OF FEAR AND REACTING TO A BALL OF FIRE OR A HAIL OF BULLETS IS A DIFFERENT STORY.

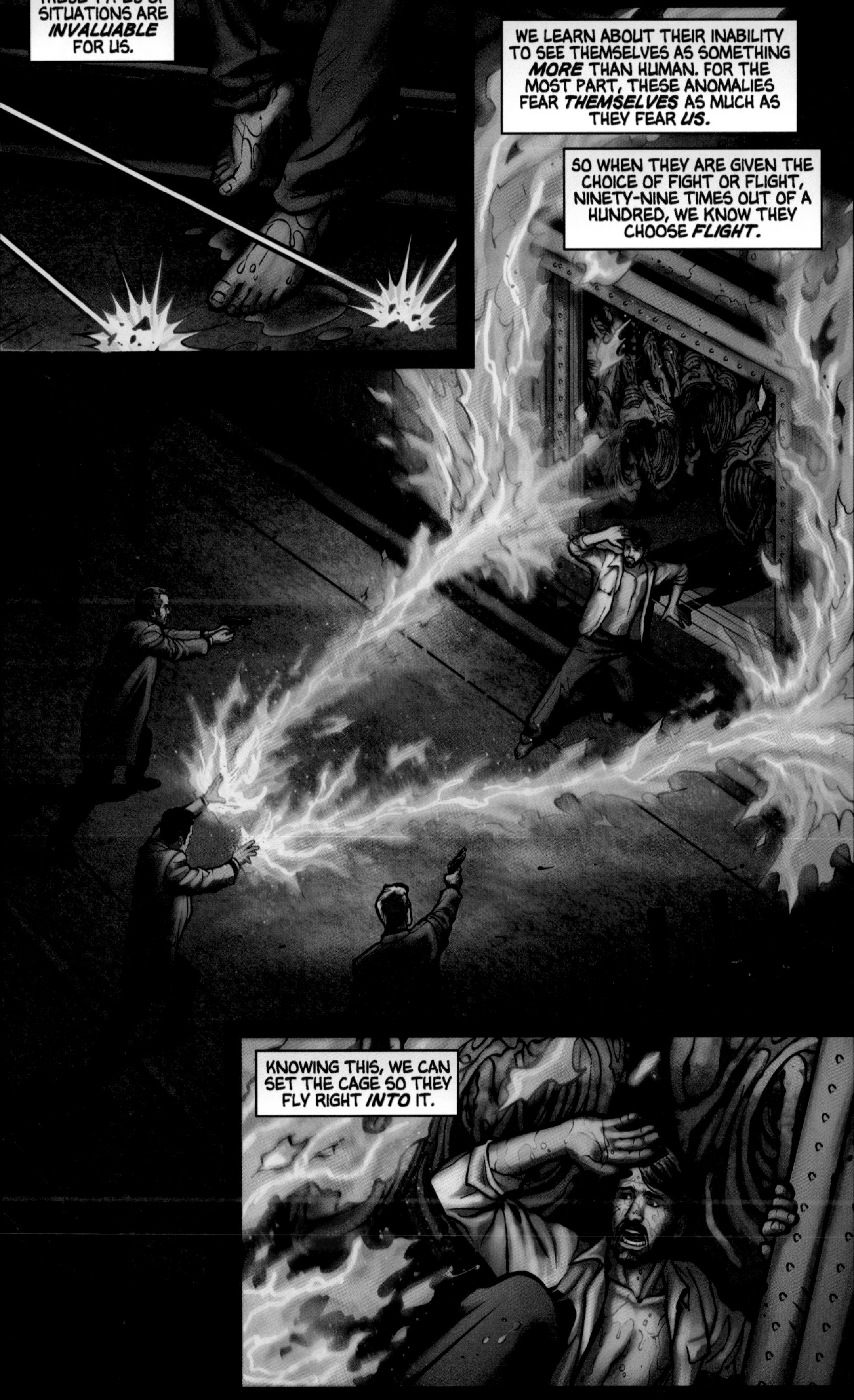
SITUATIONS ARE *INVALUABLE* FOR US.
WE LEARN ABOUT THEIR INABILITY TO SEE THEMSELVES AS SOMETHING *MORE* THAN HUMAN. FOR THE MOST PART, THESE ANOMALIES FEAR *THEMSELVES* AS MUCH AS THEY FEAR *US.*
SO WHEN THEY ARE GIVEN THE CHOICE OF FIGHT OR FLIGHT, NINETY-NINE TIMES OUT OF A HUNDRED, WE KNOW THEY CHOOSE *FLIGHT.*
KNOWING THIS, WE CAN SET THE CAGE SO THEY FLY RIGHT *INTO* IT.

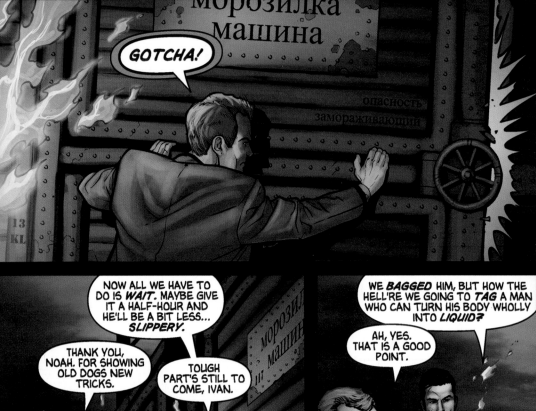

морозилка
машина
GOTCHA!
опасность
замораживающий
13
KL
NOW ALL WE HAVE TO DO IS WAIT. MAYBE GIVE IT A HALF-HOUR AND HE'LL BE A BIT LESS... SLIPPERY.
THANK YOU, NOAH. FOR SHOWING OLD DOGS NEW TRICKS.
TOUGH PART'S STILL TO COME, IVAN.
BEST NOT TO TAKE TOO MUCH CREDIT IN FRONT OF MY SUPERIORS. HUMBLENESS THROUGH GRITTED TEETH -- THAT'S MY MOTTO HERE AT THE COMPANY.
WE BAGGED HIM, BUT HOW THE HELL'RE WE GOING TO TAG A MAN WHO CAN TURN HIS BODY WHOLLY INTO LIQUID?
AH, YES. THAT IS A GOOD POINT.
MIGHT HAVE TO PUT OUR HEADS TOGETHER FOR THIS ONE, GENTLEMEN.
LUCKILY HE'S NOT GOING ANYWHERE FOR A WHILE.
WITH THE RIGHT COMBINATION OF PARTNERS, AND THE RIGHT AMOUNT OF PRACTICE AND FORETHOUGHT, THIS PROCESS WILL BECOME MUCH EASIER.
UNTIL THEN, WE'VE GOT TO SETTLE FOR IMPROVISATION...
The End

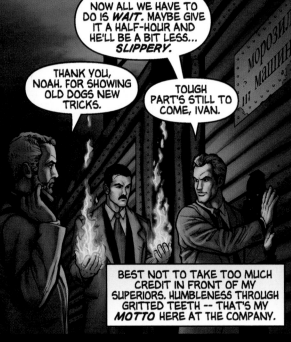

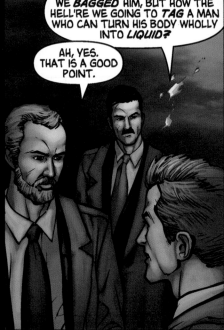

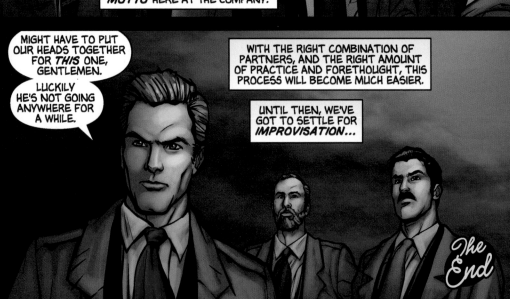

# QUARANTINE

**JIM MARTIN** *Story*  **MARCUS TO** *Penciler*  **MARK ROSLAN** *Digital Inks*  **BETH SOTELO** *Colors*  **COMICRAFT** *Lettering*

THE VIRUS WAS SPREADING TOO FAST TO STAY IN THE CITY... THE PARANOIA, THE IRRATIONALITY, THE FEAR...

IT'S TERRIFYING -- A VIRUS REDUCING AN AMERICAN CITY INTO A THIRD WORLD EPIDEMIC.

WE'D BEEN TRYING TO CONTAIN THE VIRUS FOR MOST OF THE MONTH...THIS WAS THE THIRD ATTEMPT WE'D MADE AT QUARANTINING A COMMUNITY --

IT WAS ALSO OUR LAST. TOO MANY PEOPLE WERE ALREADY SICK, DYING OR DEAD... IT'S A MIRACLE WE'RE ALIVE.

I HAD BEEN WORKING OUT OF THE CDC'S PITTSBURGH OFFICES TO HELP WITH THE OVERFLOW... THAT'S WHEN THEY DECLARED A NATIONAL EMERGENCY.

CLIK POP HSSS

DEPARTMENT OF AND SECURITY LEMAY, HOWARD

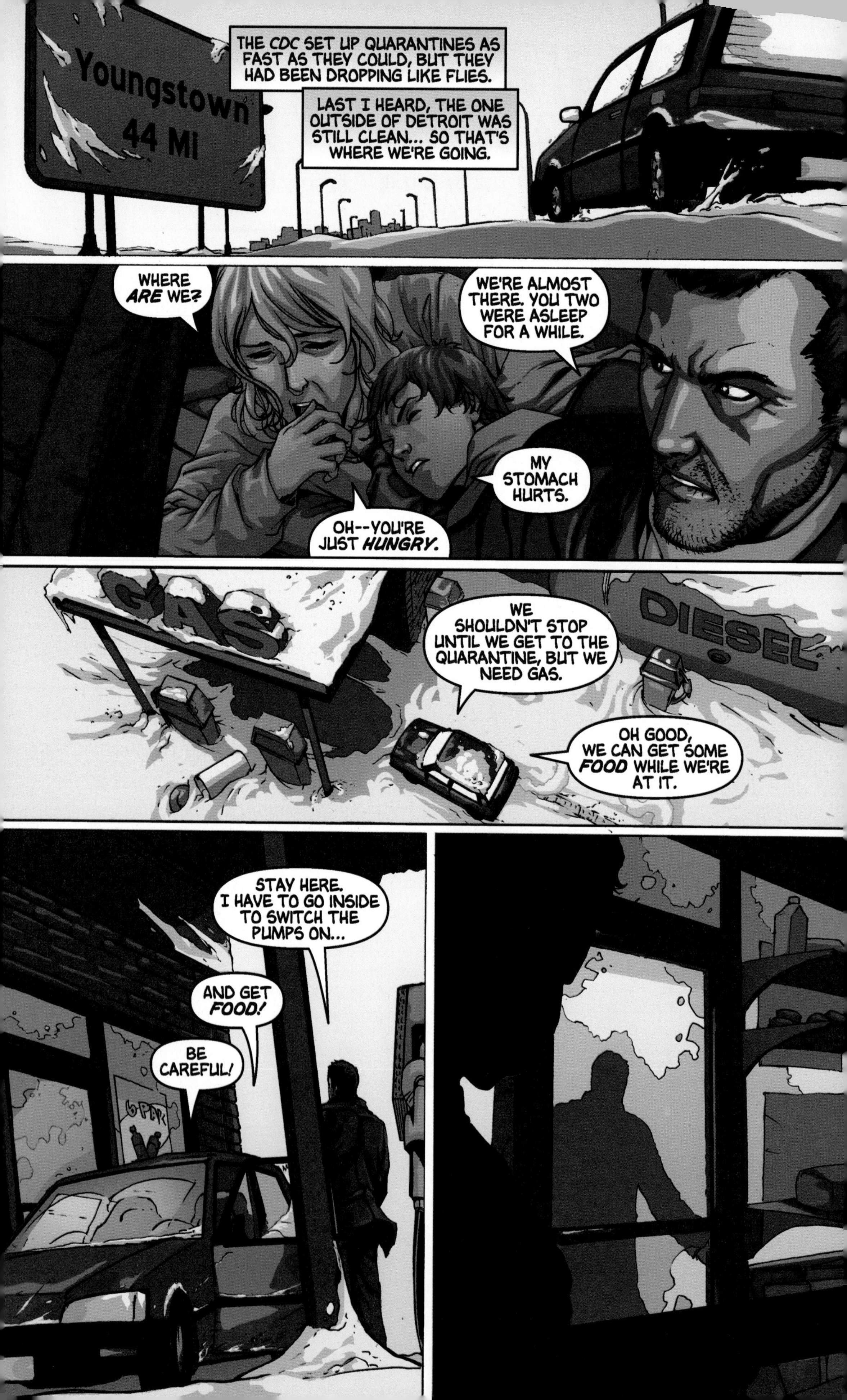
Youngstown
44 Mi
THE CDC SET UP QUARANTINES AS FAST AS THEY COULD, BUT THEY HAD BEEN DROPPING LIKE FLIES.
LAST I HEARD, THE ONE OUTSIDE OF DETROIT WAS STILL CLEAN... SO THAT'S WHERE WE'RE GOING.
WHERE ARE WE?
WE'RE ALMOST THERE. YOU TWO WERE ASLEEP FOR A WHILE.
MY STOMACH HURTS.
OH--YOU'RE JUST HUNGRY.
GAS
DIESEL
WE SHOULDN'T STOP UNTIL WE GET TO THE QUARANTINE, BUT WE NEED GAS.
OH GOOD, WE CAN GET SOME FOOD WHILE WE'RE AT IT.
STAY HERE. I HAVE TO GO INSIDE TO SWITCH THE PUMPS ON...
AND GET FOOD!
BE CAREFUL!

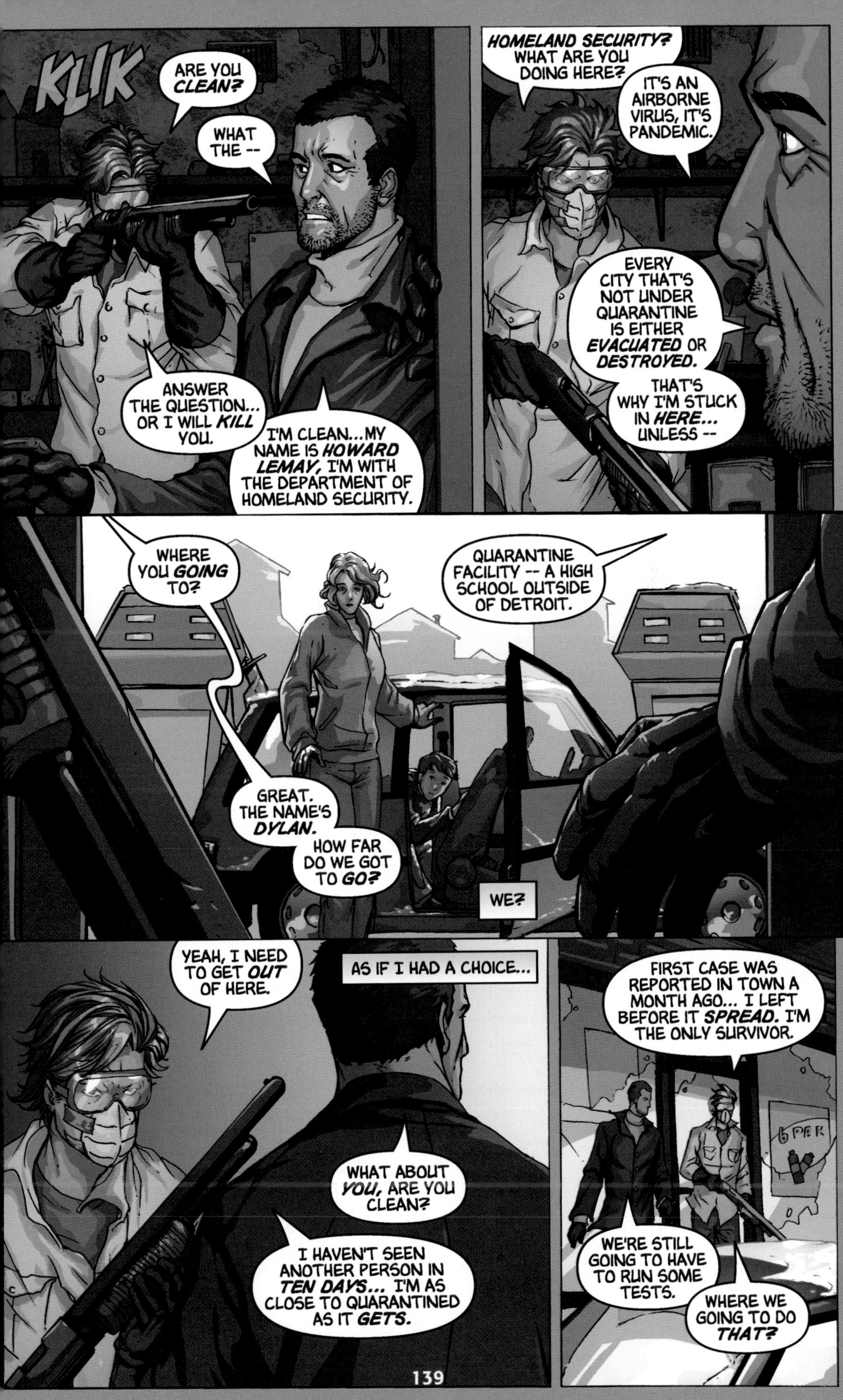
KLIK
ARE YOU CLEAN?
WHAT THE --
ANSWER THE QUESTION... OR I WILL KILL YOU.
I'M CLEAN...MY NAME IS HOWARD LEMAY, I'M WITH THE DEPARTMENT OF HOMELAND SECURITY.
HOMELAND SECURITY? WHAT ARE YOU DOING HERE?
IT'S AN AIRBORNE VIRUS, IT'S PANDEMIC.
EVERY CITY THAT'S NOT UNDER QUARANTINE IS EITHER EVACUATED OR DESTROYED.
THAT'S WHY I'M STUCK IN HERE... UNLESS --
WHERE YOU GOING TO?
QUARANTINE FACILITY -- A HIGH SCHOOL OUTSIDE OF DETROIT.
GREAT. THE NAME'S DYLAN.
HOW FAR DO WE GOT TO GO?
WE?
YEAH, I NEED TO GET OUT OF HERE.
AS IF I HAD A CHOICE...
WHAT ABOUT YOU, ARE YOU CLEAN?
I HAVEN'T SEEN ANOTHER PERSON IN TEN DAYS... I'M AS CLOSE TO QUARANTINED AS IT GETS.
FIRST CASE WAS REPORTED IN TOWN A MONTH AGO... I LEFT BEFORE IT SPREAD. I'M THE ONLY SURVIVOR.
WE'RE STILL GOING TO HAVE TO RUN SOME TESTS.
WHERE WE GOING TO DO THAT?

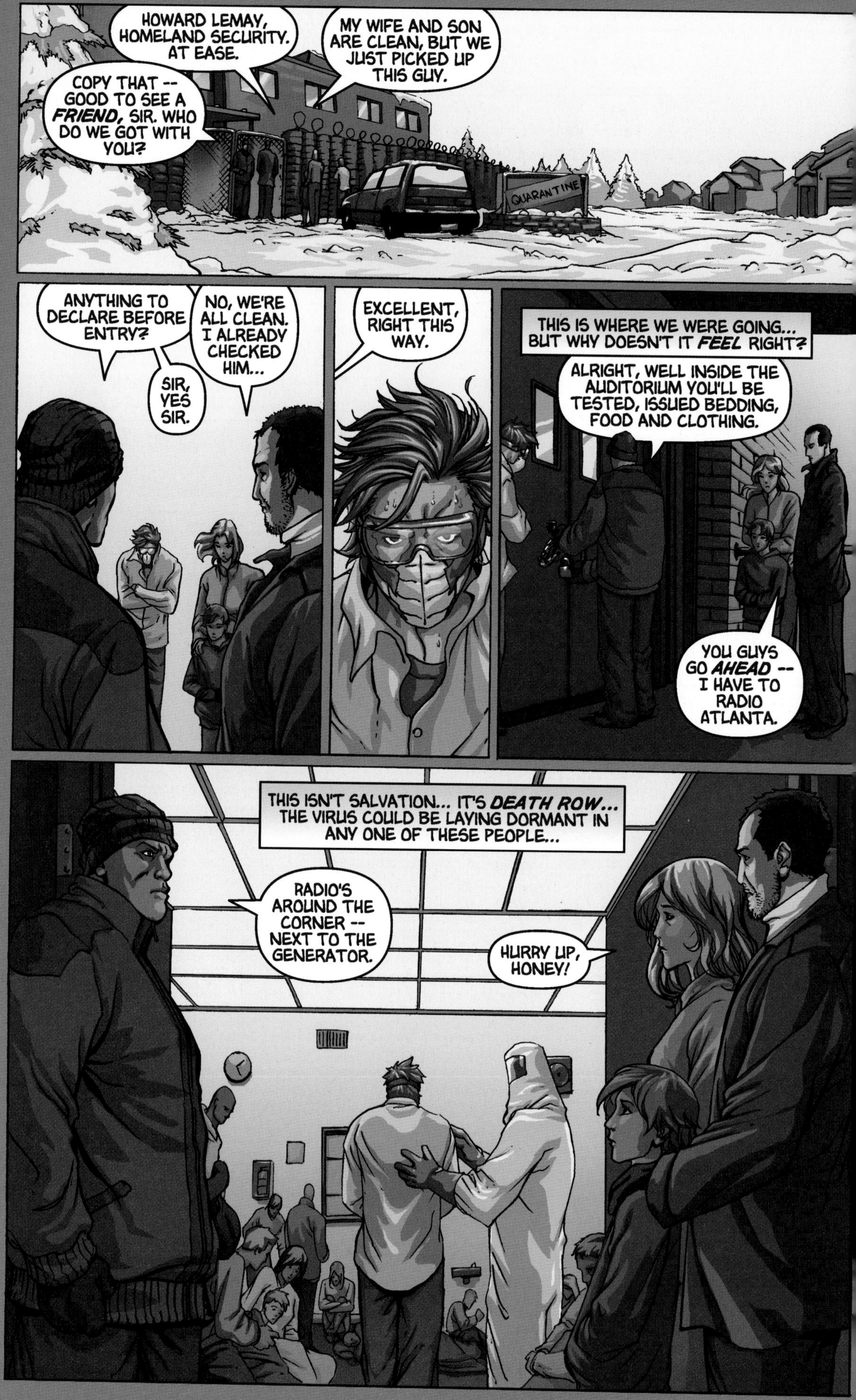

HOWARD LEMAY, HOMELAND SECURITY. AT EASE.
COPY THAT -- GOOD TO SEE A *FRIEND,* SIR. WHO DO WE GOT WITH YOU?
MY WIFE AND SON ARE CLEAN, BUT WE JUST PICKED UP THIS GUY.
QUARANTINE
ANYTHING TO DECLARE BEFORE ENTRY?
SIR, YES SIR.
NO, WE'RE ALL CLEAN. I ALREADY CHECKED HIM...
EXCELLENT, RIGHT THIS WAY.
THIS IS WHERE WE WERE GOING... BUT WHY DOESN'T IT *FEEL* RIGHT?
ALRIGHT, WELL INSIDE THE AUDITORIUM YOU'LL BE TESTED, ISSUED BEDDING, FOOD AND CLOTHING.
YOU GUYS GO *AHEAD* -- I HAVE TO RADIO ATLANTA.
THIS ISN'T SALVATION... IT'S *DEATH ROW...* THE VIRUS COULD BE LAYING DORMANT IN ANY ONE OF THESE PEOPLE...
RADIO'S AROUND THE CORNER -- NEXT TO THE GENERATOR.
HURRY UP, HONEY!

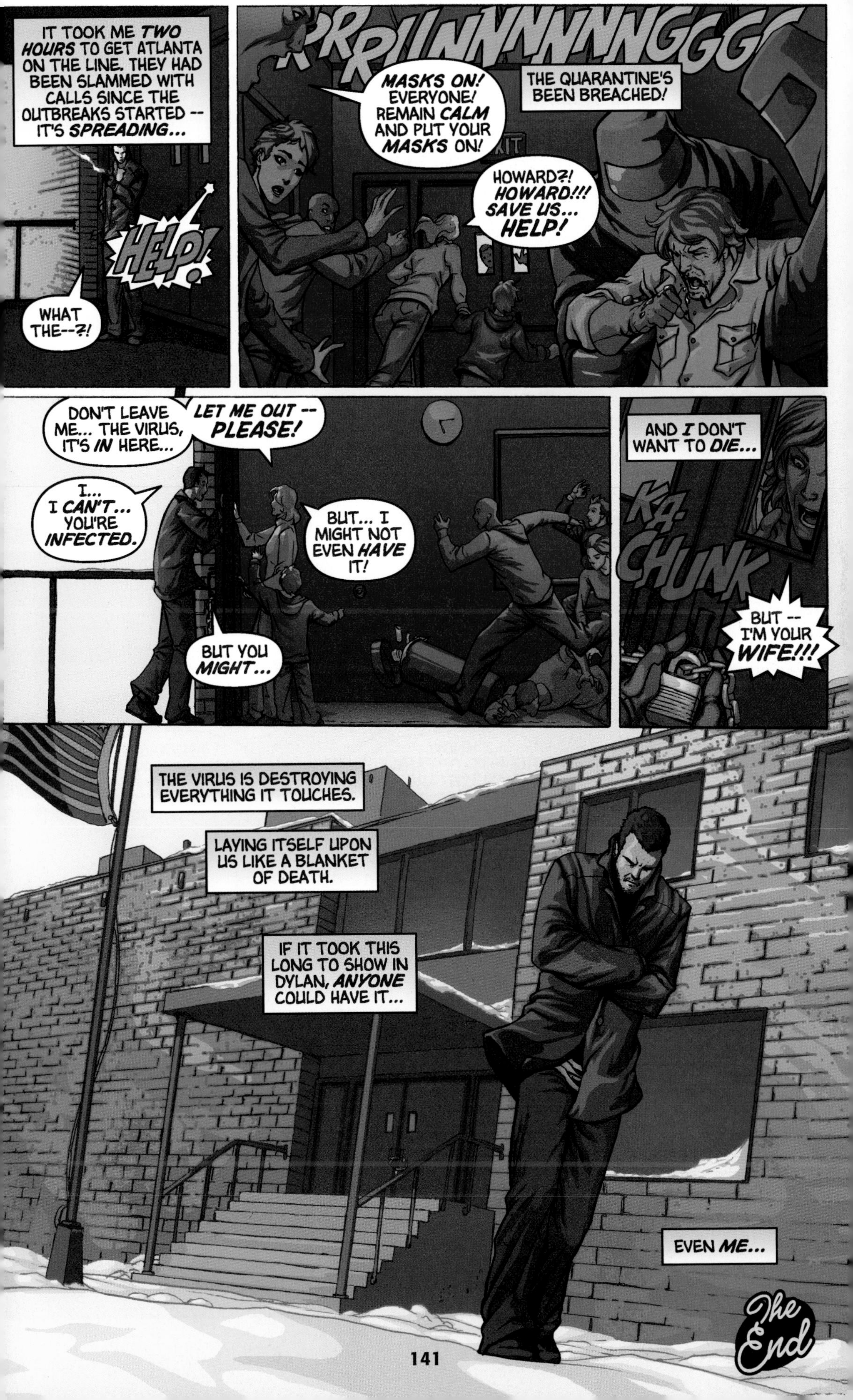
IT TOOK ME TWO HOURS TO GET ATLANTA ON THE LINE. THEY HAD BEEN SLAMMED WITH CALLS SINCE THE OUTBREAKS STARTED -- IT'S SPREADING...
HELP!
WHAT THE--?!
PRRIINNNNNNNGGGG
MASKS ON! EVERYONE! REMAIN CALM AND PUT YOUR MASKS ON!
THE QUARANTINE'S BEEN BREACHED!
HOWARD?! HOWARD!!! SAVE US... HELP!
DON'T LEAVE ME... THE VIRUS, IT'S IN HERE...
LET ME OUT -- PLEASE!
I... I CAN'T... YOU'RE INFECTED.
BUT... I MIGHT NOT EVEN HAVE IT!
BUT YOU MIGHT...
AND I DON'T WANT TO DIE...
KA-CHUNK
BUT -- I'M YOUR WIFE!!!
THE VIRUS IS DESTROYING EVERYTHING IT TOUCHES.
LAYING ITSELF UPON US LIKE A BLANKET OF DEATH.
IF IT TOOK THIS LONG TO SHOW IN DYLAN, ANYONE COULD HAVE IT...
EVEN ME...
The End

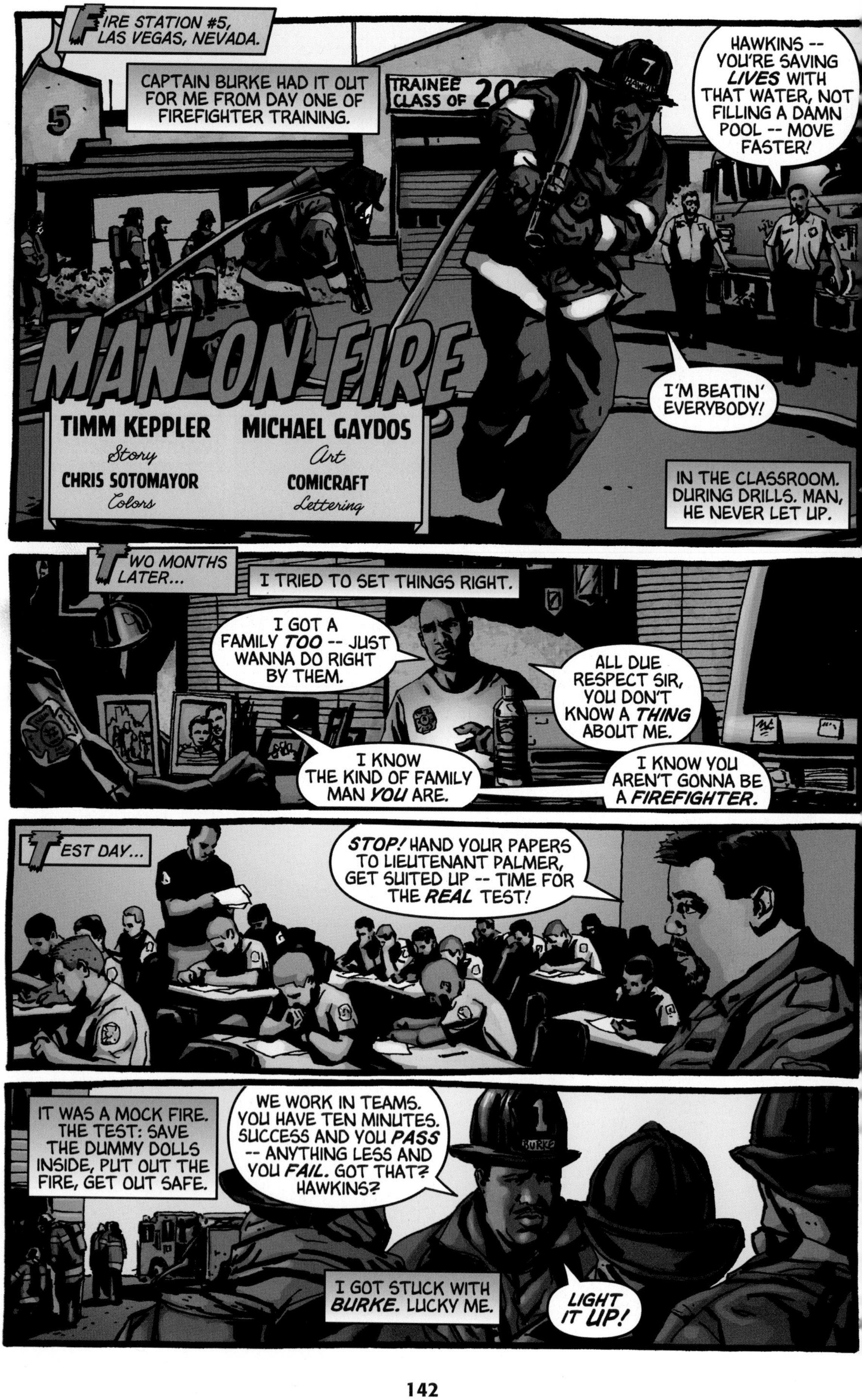
FIRE STATION #5, LAS VEGAS, NEVADA.
CAPTAIN BURKE HAD IT OUT FOR ME FROM DAY ONE OF FIREFIGHTER TRAINING.
TRAINEE CLASS OF 20
5
HAWKINS -- YOU'RE SAVING LIVES WITH THAT WATER, NOT FILLING A DAMN POOL -- MOVE FASTER!
MAN ON FIRE
TIMM KEPPLER Story
MICHAEL GAYDOS Art
CHRIS SOTOMAYOR Colors
COMICRAFT Lettering
I'M BEATIN' EVERYBODY!
IN THE CLASSROOM. DURING DRILLS. MAN, HE NEVER LET UP.
TWO MONTHS LATER...
I TRIED TO SET THINGS RIGHT.
I GOT A FAMILY TOO -- JUST WANNA DO RIGHT BY THEM.
ALL DUE RESPECT SIR, YOU DON'T KNOW A THING ABOUT ME.
I KNOW THE KIND OF FAMILY MAN YOU ARE.
I KNOW YOU AREN'T GONNA BE A FIREFIGHTER.
TEST DAY...
STOP! HAND YOUR PAPERS TO LIEUTENANT PALMER, GET SUITED UP -- TIME FOR THE REAL TEST!
IT WAS A MOCK FIRE. THE TEST: SAVE THE DUMMY DOLLS INSIDE, PUT OUT THE FIRE, GET OUT SAFE.
WE WORK IN TEAMS. YOU HAVE TEN MINUTES. SUCCESS AND YOU PASS -- ANYTHING LESS AND YOU FAIL. GOT THAT? HAWKINS?
I GOT STUCK WITH BURKE. LUCKY ME.
LIGHT IT UP!

REMEMBER: VENTILATE! PROTECT EXPOSURE! KEEP AN EYE ON EACH OTHER!

WE SHOULDA NOTICED THE FIRE WAS TOO HOT. TOO BIG. BUT *ADRENALINE* GOT IN THE WAY.

KRAKK

SECURE THE BEDROOM -- MEET IN THE KITCHEN!

*COPY THAT!*

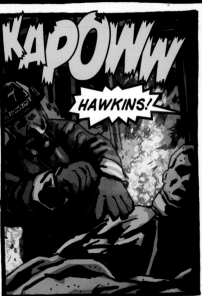

KAPOWW

HAWKINS!

IT'S *TOO HOT* -- I CAN'T *PASS!*

PALMER -- THE *GAS LINE* -- IT'S SET TOO *HIGH!* THE SHUT-OFF VALVE'S IN THE *BASEMENT!* SOUTHEAST CORNER!

CAN'T GET IN, CAPTAIN -- IT'S *COLLAPSED!*

GET *OUTTA HERE,* HAWKINS!

KRKSSH

I'M NOT *LEAVIN'* YOU!

GOT NO MORE THAN *30 SECONDS* 'FORE EVERYTHING *FALLS!*

HAWKINS! THERE'S NO TIME!

HAWKINS

7

I HAD TO SAVE EVERYONE. AND THE FASTEST WAY TO THE BASEMENT WAS *STRAIGHT DOWN.*

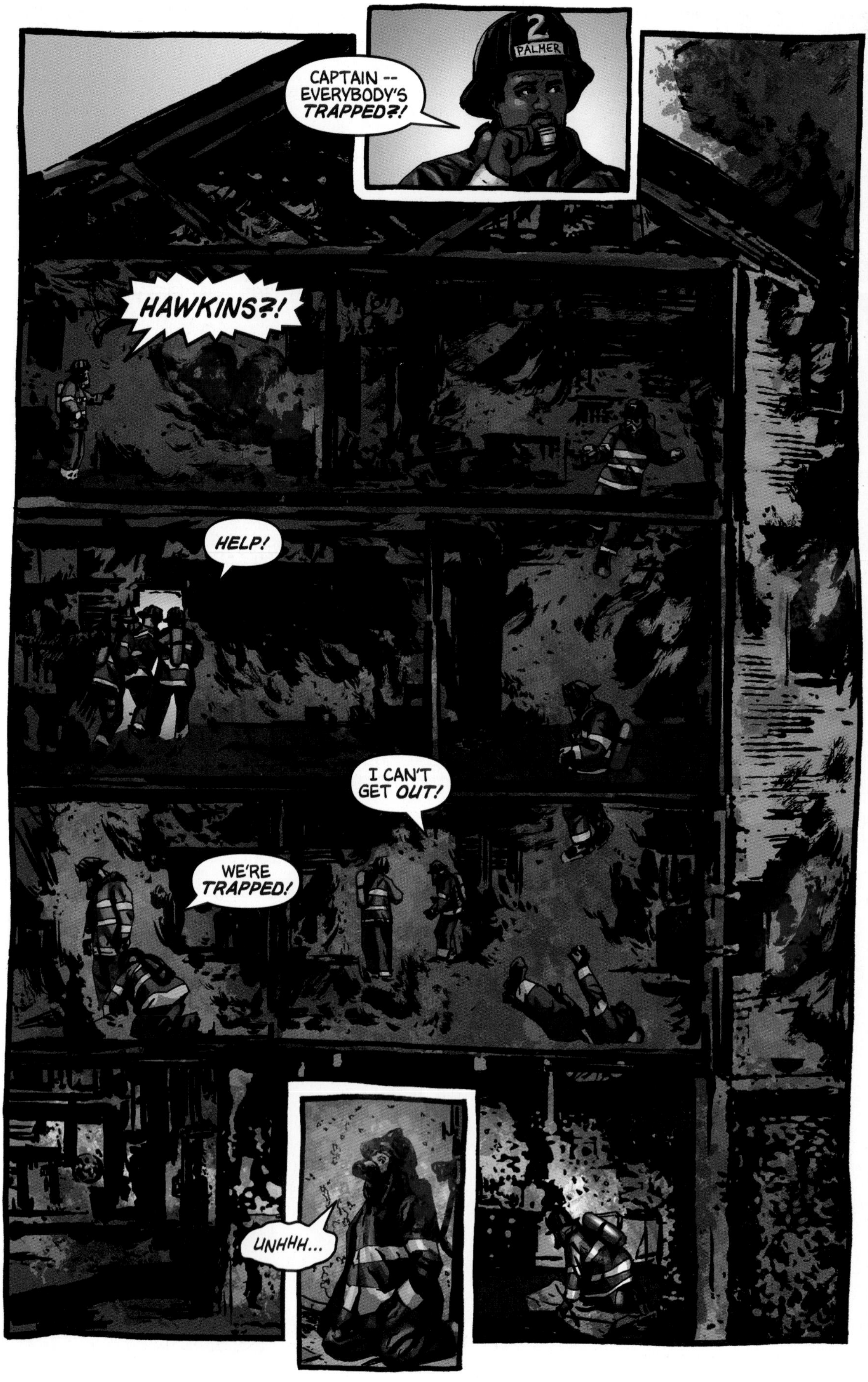

2
PALMER
CAPTAIN -- EVERYBODY'S *TRAPPED?!*
HAWKINS?!
HELP!
I CAN'T GET *OUT!*
WE'RE *TRAPPED!*
UNHHH...

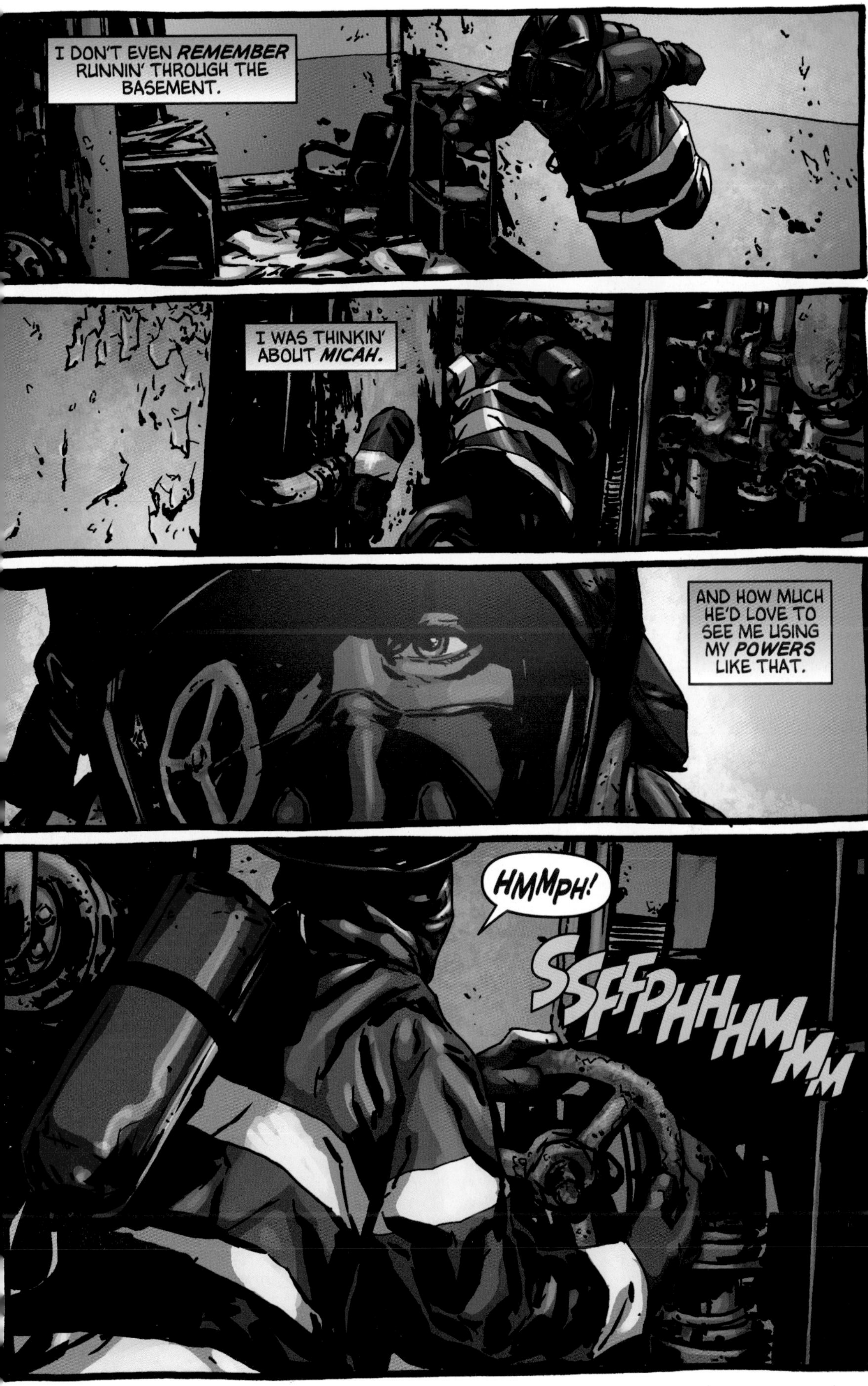
I DON'T EVEN REMEMBER RUNNIN' THROUGH THE BASEMENT.
I WAS THINKIN' ABOUT MICAH.
AND HOW MUCH HE'D LOVE TO SEE ME USING MY POWERS LIKE THAT.
HMMph!
SSFFPHHHMMMM

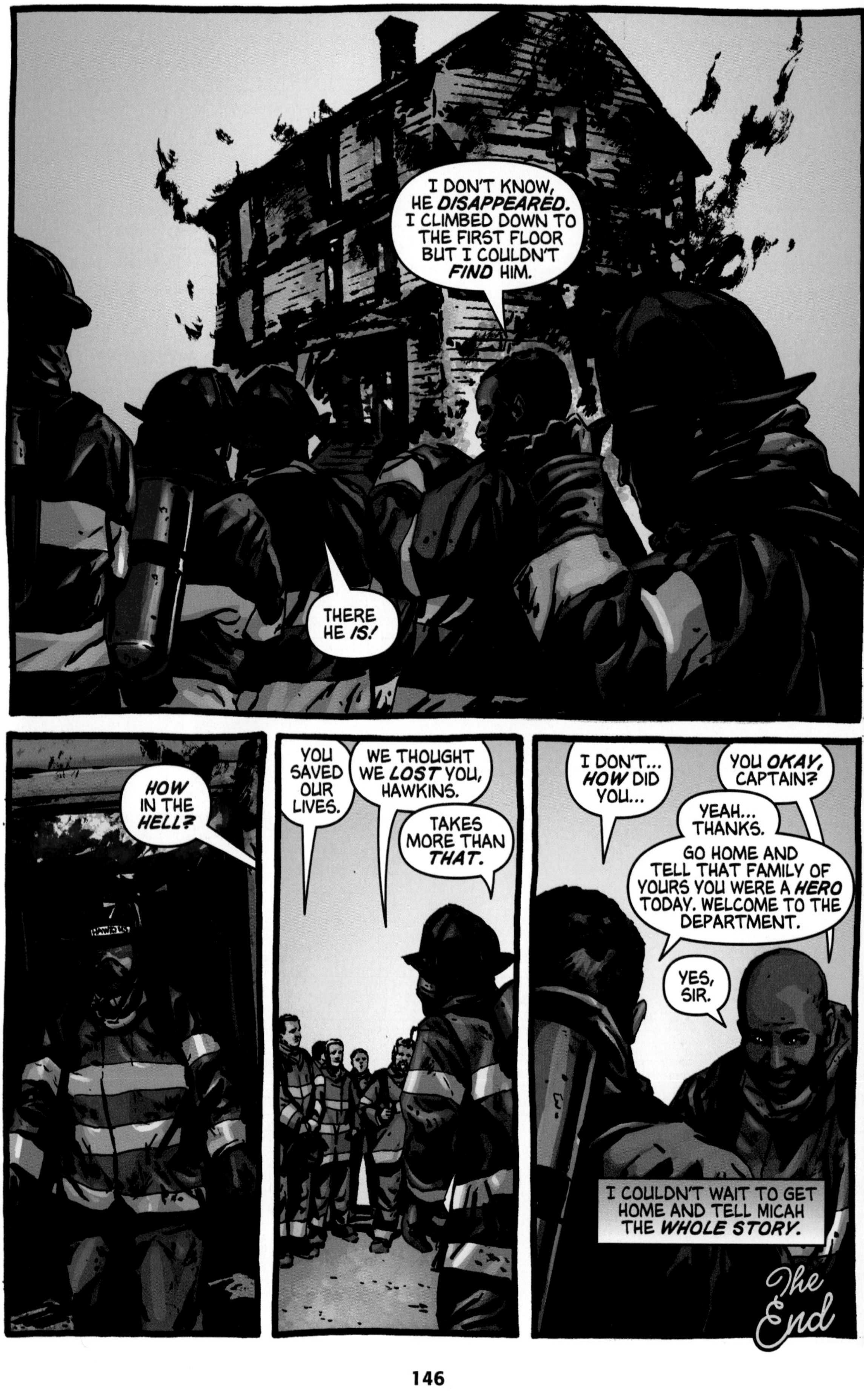
I DON'T KNOW, HE *DISAPPEARED*. I CLIMBED DOWN TO THE FIRST FLOOR BUT I COULDN'T *FIND* HIM.
THERE HE *IS!*
*HOW* IN THE *HELL?*
YOU SAVED OUR LIVES.
WE THOUGHT WE *LOST* YOU, HAWKINS.
TAKES MORE THAN *THAT*.
I DON'T... *HOW* DID YOU...
YOU *OKAY,* CAPTAIN?
YEAH... THANKS.
GO HOME AND TELL THAT FAMILY OF YOURS YOU WERE A *HERO* TODAY. WELCOME TO THE DEPARTMENT.
YES, SIR.
I COULDN'T WAIT TO GET HOME AND TELL MICAH THE *WHOLE STORY*.
The End

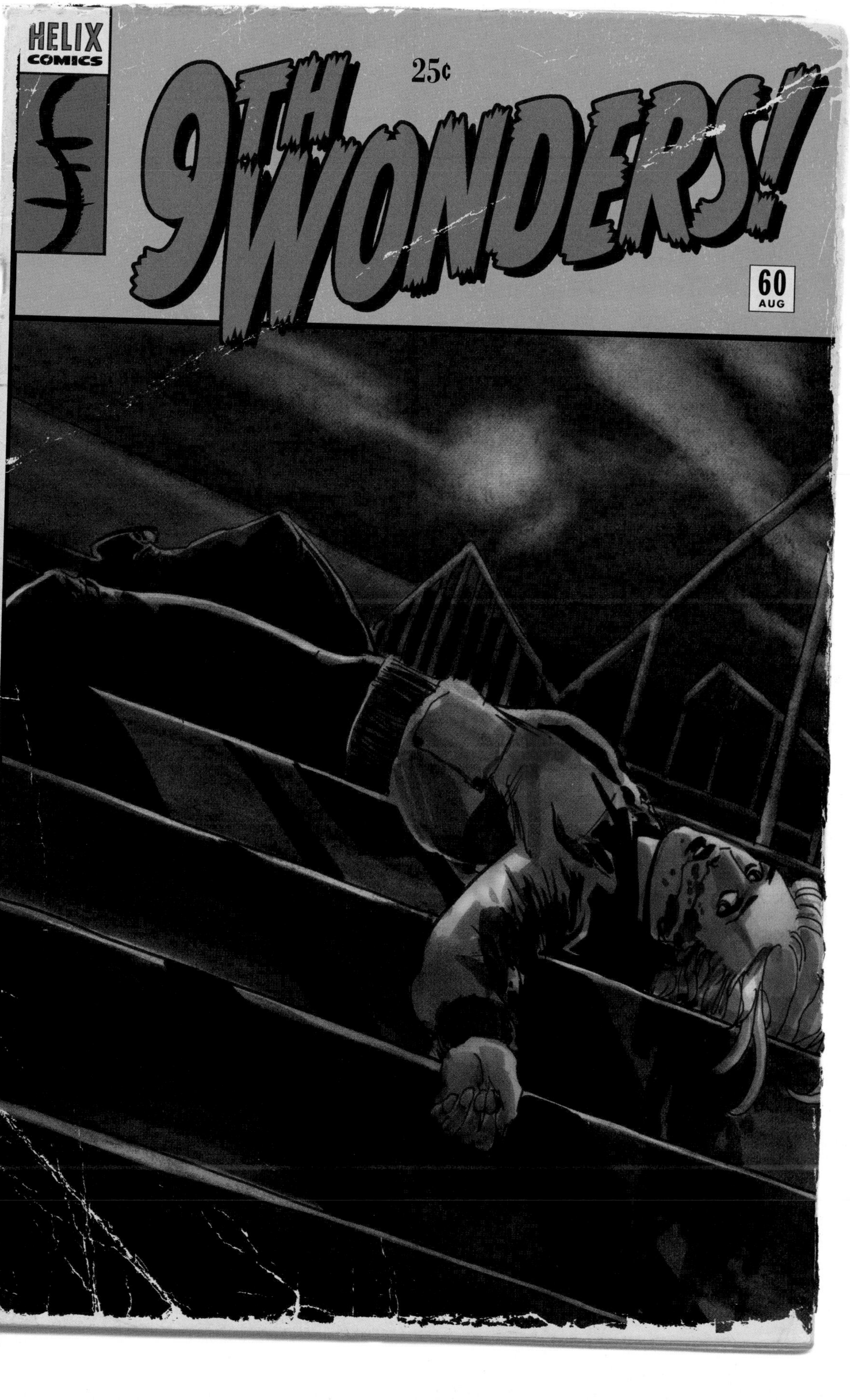
HELIX
COMICS
25¢
9TH WONDERS!
60
AUG

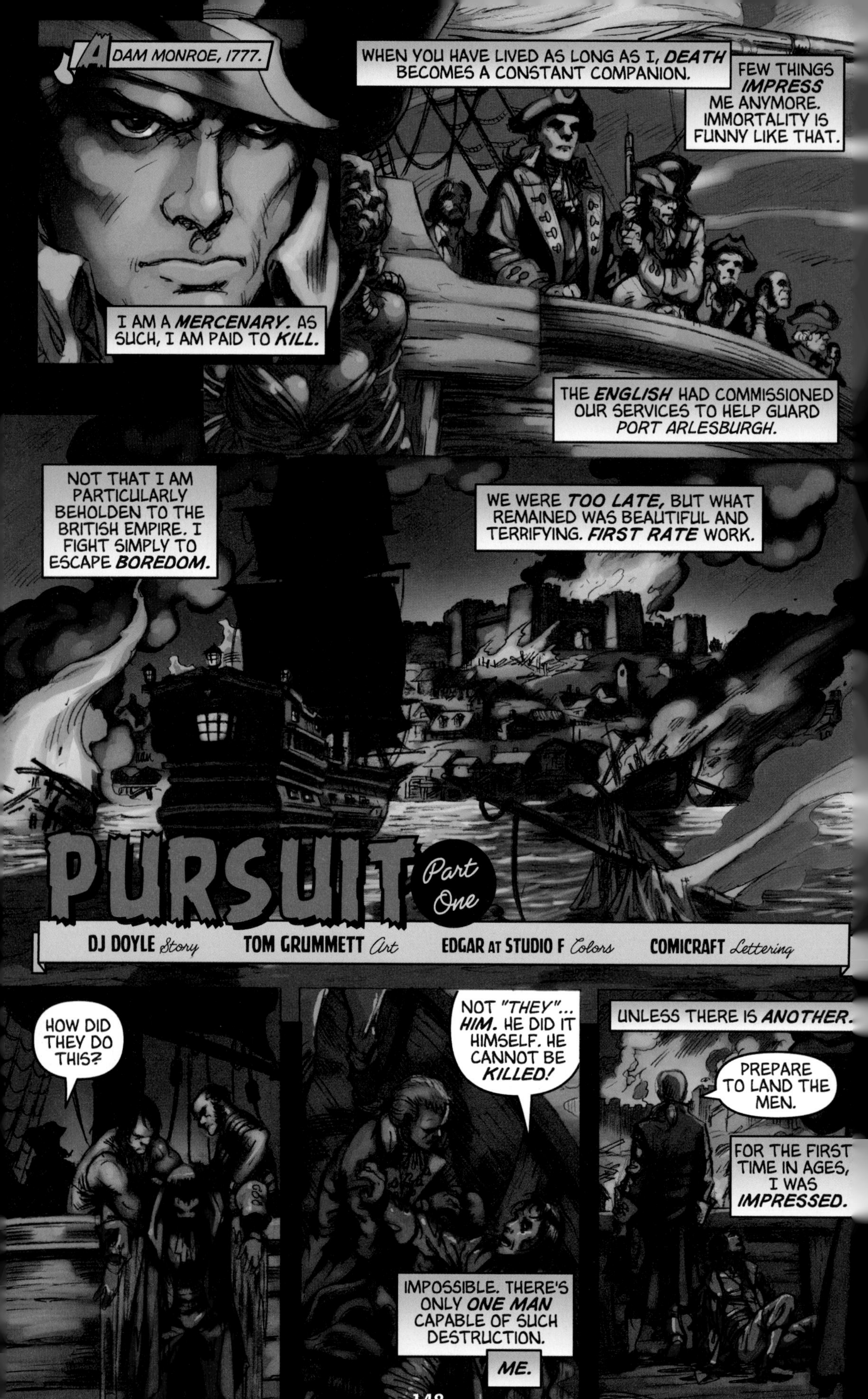

ADAM MONROE, 1777.
WHEN YOU HAVE LIVED AS LONG AS I, DEATH BECOMES A CONSTANT COMPANION.
FEW THINGS IMPRESS ME ANYMORE. IMMORTALITY IS FUNNY LIKE THAT.
I AM A MERCENARY. AS SUCH, I AM PAID TO KILL.
THE ENGLISH HAD COMMISSIONED OUR SERVICES TO HELP GUARD PORT ARLESBURGH.
NOT THAT I AM PARTICULARLY BEHOLDEN TO THE BRITISH EMPIRE. I FIGHT SIMPLY TO ESCAPE BOREDOM.
WE WERE TOO LATE, BUT WHAT REMAINED WAS BEAUTIFUL AND TERRIFYING. FIRST RATE WORK.
PURSUIT Part One
DJ DOYLE Story TOM GRUMMETT Art EDGAR AT STUDIO F Colors COMICRAFT Lettering
HOW DID THEY DO THIS?
NOT "THEY"... HIM. HE DID IT HIMSELF. HE CANNOT BE KILLED!
IMPOSSIBLE. THERE'S ONLY ONE MAN CAPABLE OF SUCH DESTRUCTION.
ME.
UNLESS THERE IS ANOTHER.
PREPARE TO LAND THE MEN.
FOR THE FIRST TIME IN AGES, I WAS IMPRESSED.

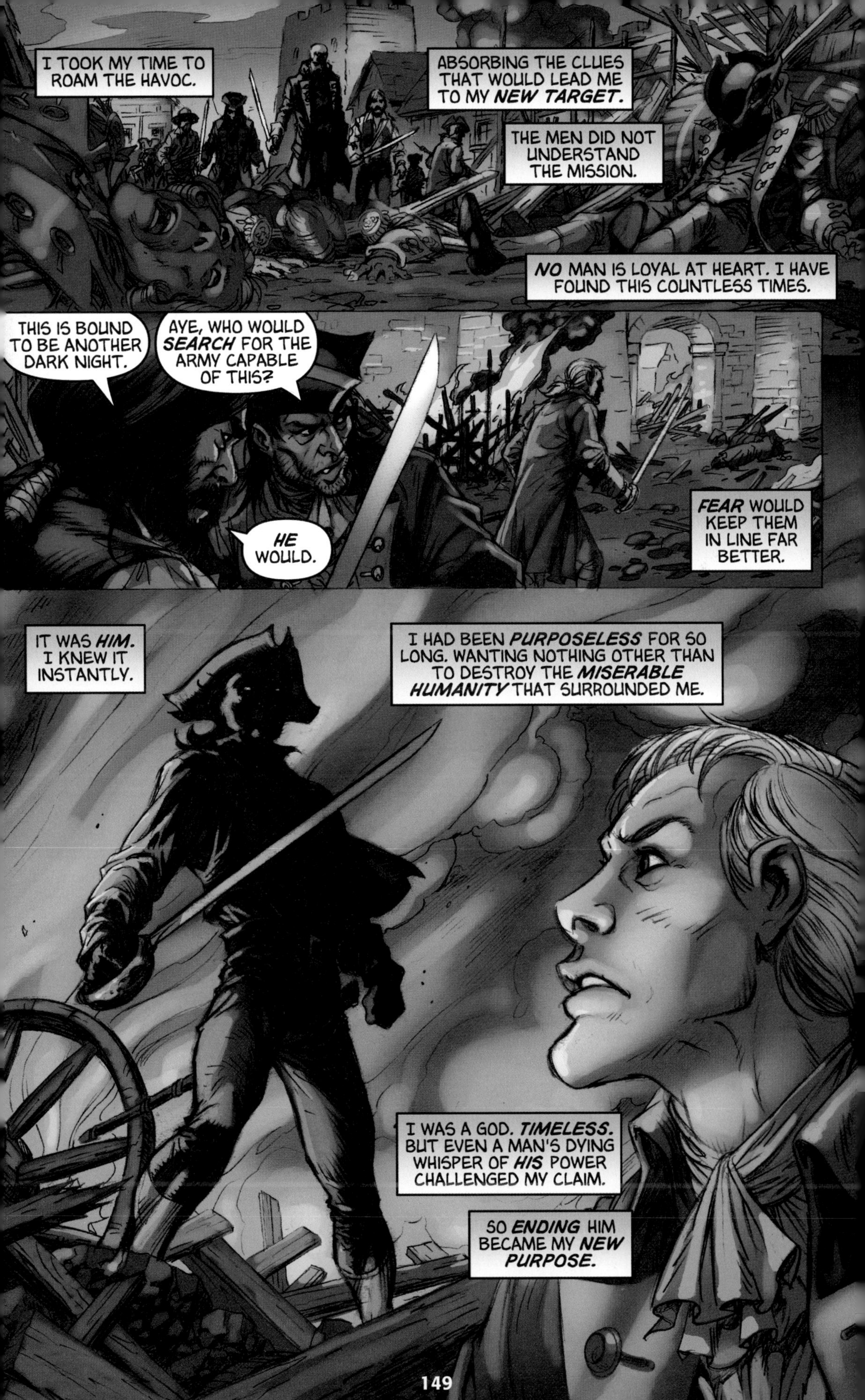
I TOOK MY TIME TO ROAM THE HAVOC.
ABSORBING THE CLUES THAT WOULD LEAD ME TO MY *NEW TARGET*.
THE MEN DID NOT UNDERSTAND THE MISSION.
*NO* MAN IS LOYAL AT HEART. I HAVE FOUND THIS COUNTLESS TIMES.
THIS IS BOUND TO BE ANOTHER DARK NIGHT.
AYE, WHO WOULD *SEARCH* FOR THE ARMY CAPABLE OF THIS?
*HE* WOULD.
*FEAR* WOULD KEEP THEM IN LINE FAR BETTER.
IT WAS *HIM*. I KNEW IT INSTANTLY.
I HAD BEEN *PURPOSELESS* FOR SO LONG. WANTING NOTHING OTHER THAN TO DESTROY THE *MISERABLE HUMANITY* THAT SURROUNDED ME.
I WAS A GOD. *TIMELESS.* BUT EVEN A MAN'S DYING WHISPER OF *HIS* POWER CHALLENGED MY CLAIM.
SO *ENDING* HIM BECAME MY *NEW PURPOSE.*

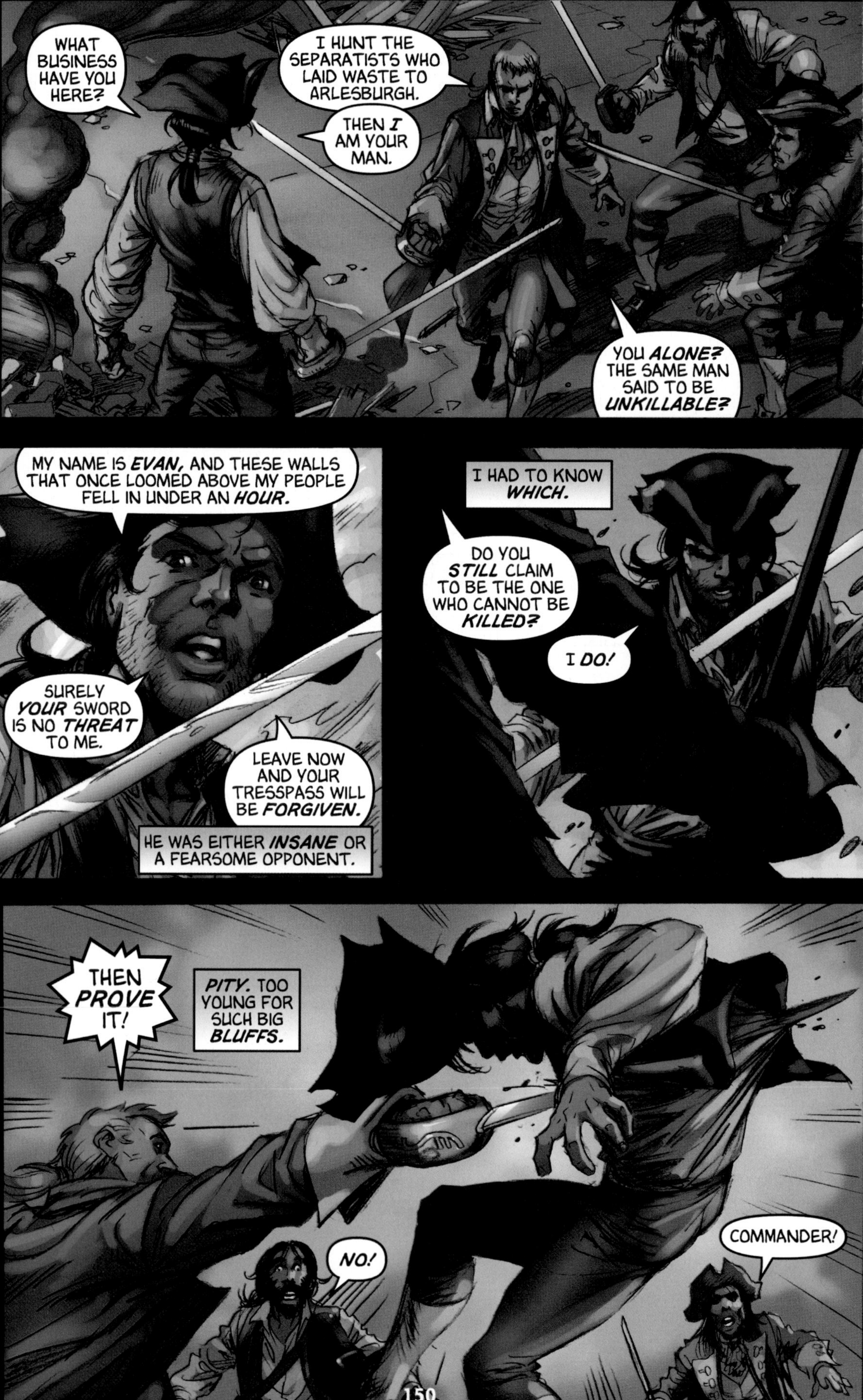
WHAT BUSINESS HAVE YOU HERE?
I HUNT THE SEPARATISTS WHO LAID WASTE TO ARLESBURGH.
THEN *I* AM YOUR MAN.
YOU *ALONE?* THE SAME MAN SAID TO BE *UNKILLABLE?*
MY NAME IS *EVAN,* AND THESE WALLS THAT ONCE LOOMED ABOVE MY PEOPLE FELL IN UNDER AN *HOUR.*
SURELY *YOUR* SWORD IS NO *THREAT* TO ME.
LEAVE NOW AND YOUR TRESSPASS WILL BE *FORGIVEN.*
HE WAS EITHER *INSANE* OR A FEARSOME OPPONENT.
I HAD TO KNOW *WHICH.*
DO YOU *STILL* CLAIM TO BE THE ONE WHO CANNOT BE *KILLED?*
I *DO!*
THEN *PROVE* IT!
*PITY.* TOO YOUNG FOR SUCH BIG *BLUFFS.*
*NO!*
COMMANDER!

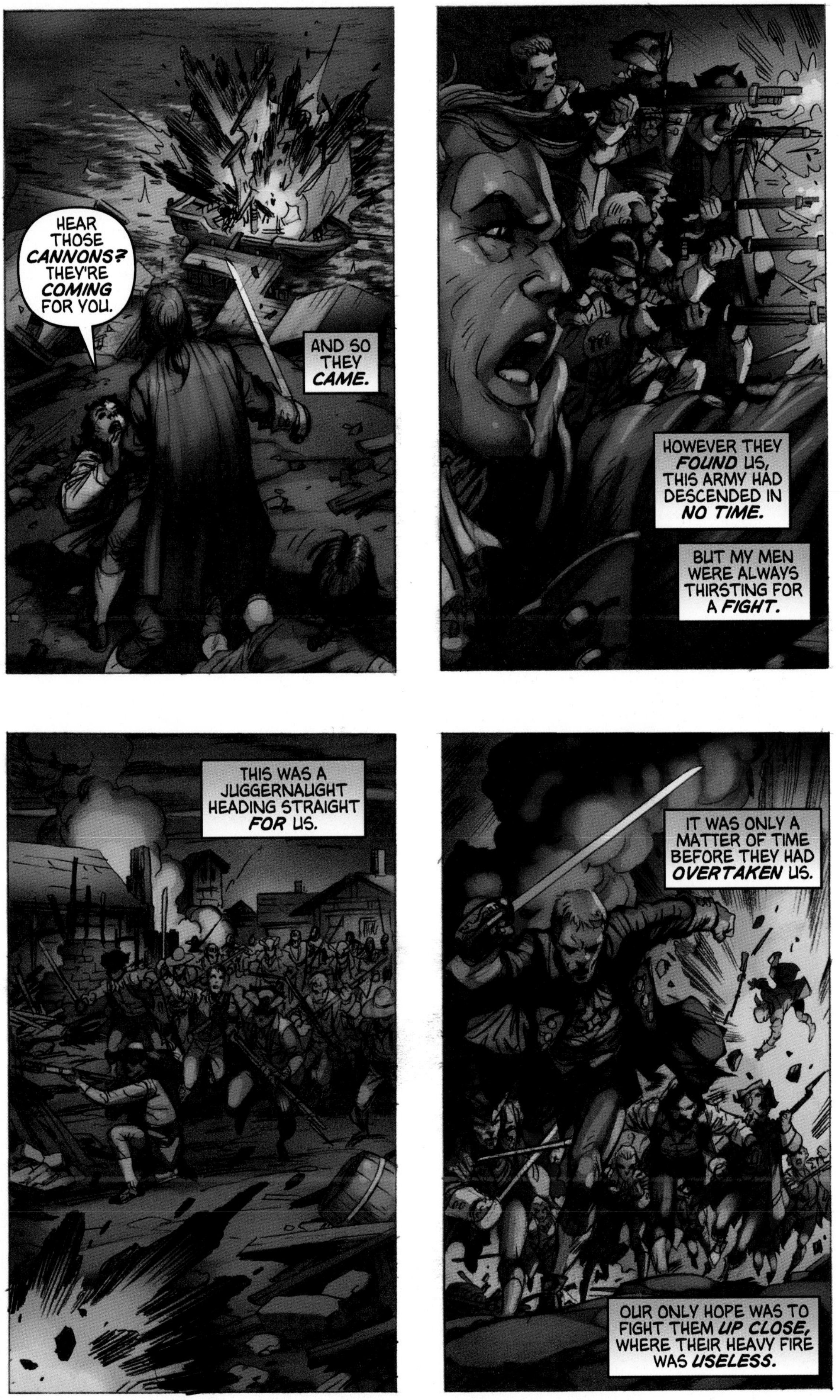
HEAR THOSE CANNONS? THEY'RE COMING FOR YOU.
AND SO THEY CAME.
HOWEVER THEY FOUND US, THIS ARMY HAD DESCENDED IN NO TIME.
BUT MY MEN WERE ALWAYS THIRSTING FOR A FIGHT.
THIS WAS A JUGGERNAUGHT HEADING STRAIGHT FOR US.
IT WAS ONLY A MATTER OF TIME BEFORE THEY HAD OVERTAKEN US.
OUR ONLY HOPE WAS TO FIGHT THEM UP CLOSE, WHERE THEIR HEAVY FIRE WAS USELESS.

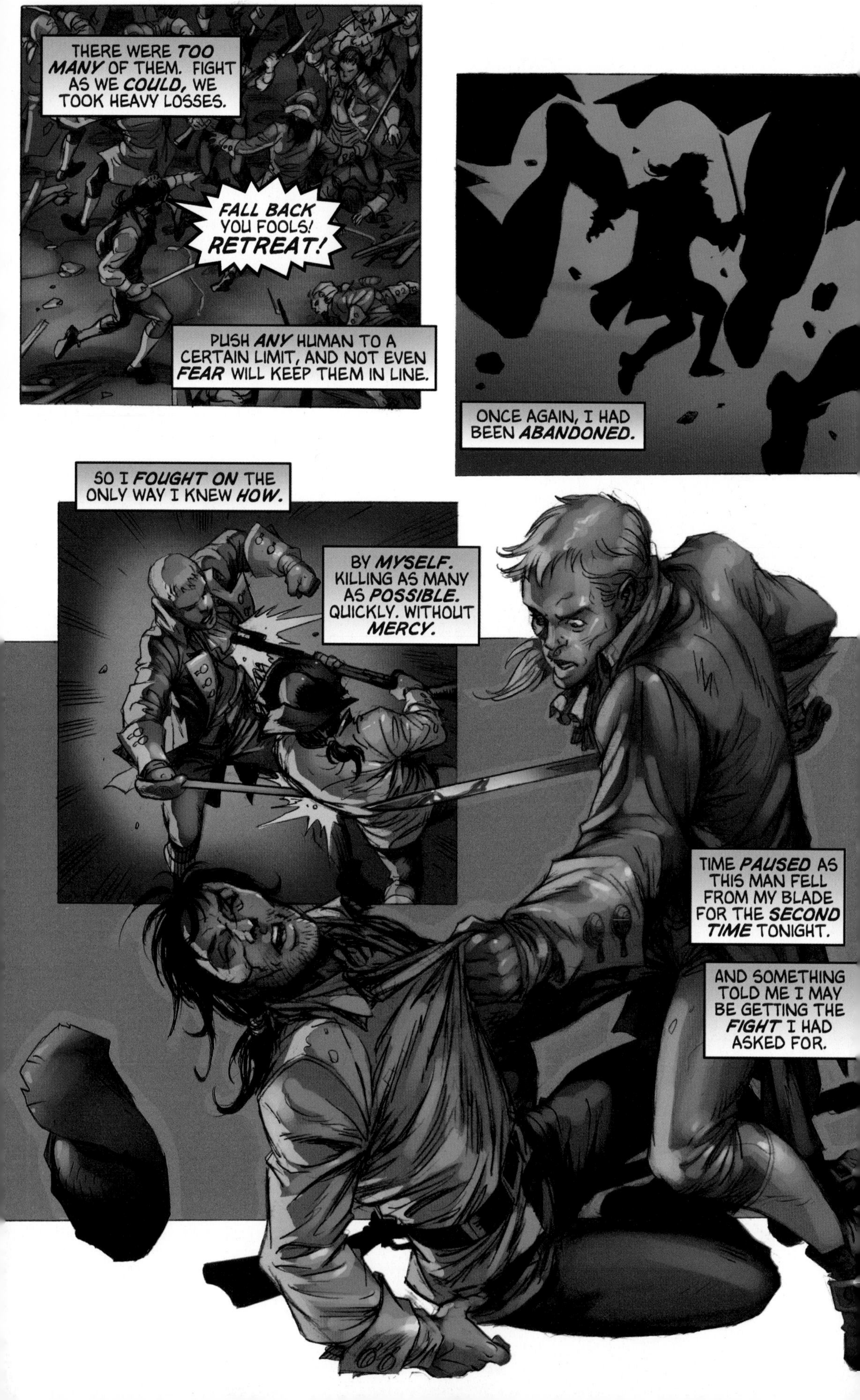
THERE WERE *TOO MANY* OF THEM. FIGHT AS WE *COULD,* WE TOOK HEAVY LOSSES.
*FALL BACK* YOU FOOLS! *RETREAT!*
PUSH *ANY* HUMAN TO A CERTAIN LIMIT, AND NOT EVEN *FEAR* WILL KEEP THEM IN LINE.
ONCE AGAIN, I HAD BEEN *ABANDONED.*
SO I *FOUGHT ON* THE ONLY WAY I KNEW *HOW.*
BY *MYSELF.* KILLING AS MANY AS *POSSIBLE.* QUICKLY. WITHOUT *MERCY.*
TIME *PAUSED* AS THIS MAN FELL FROM MY BLADE FOR THE *SECOND TIME* TONIGHT.
AND SOMETHING TOLD ME I MAY BE GETTING THE *FIGHT* I HAD ASKED FOR.

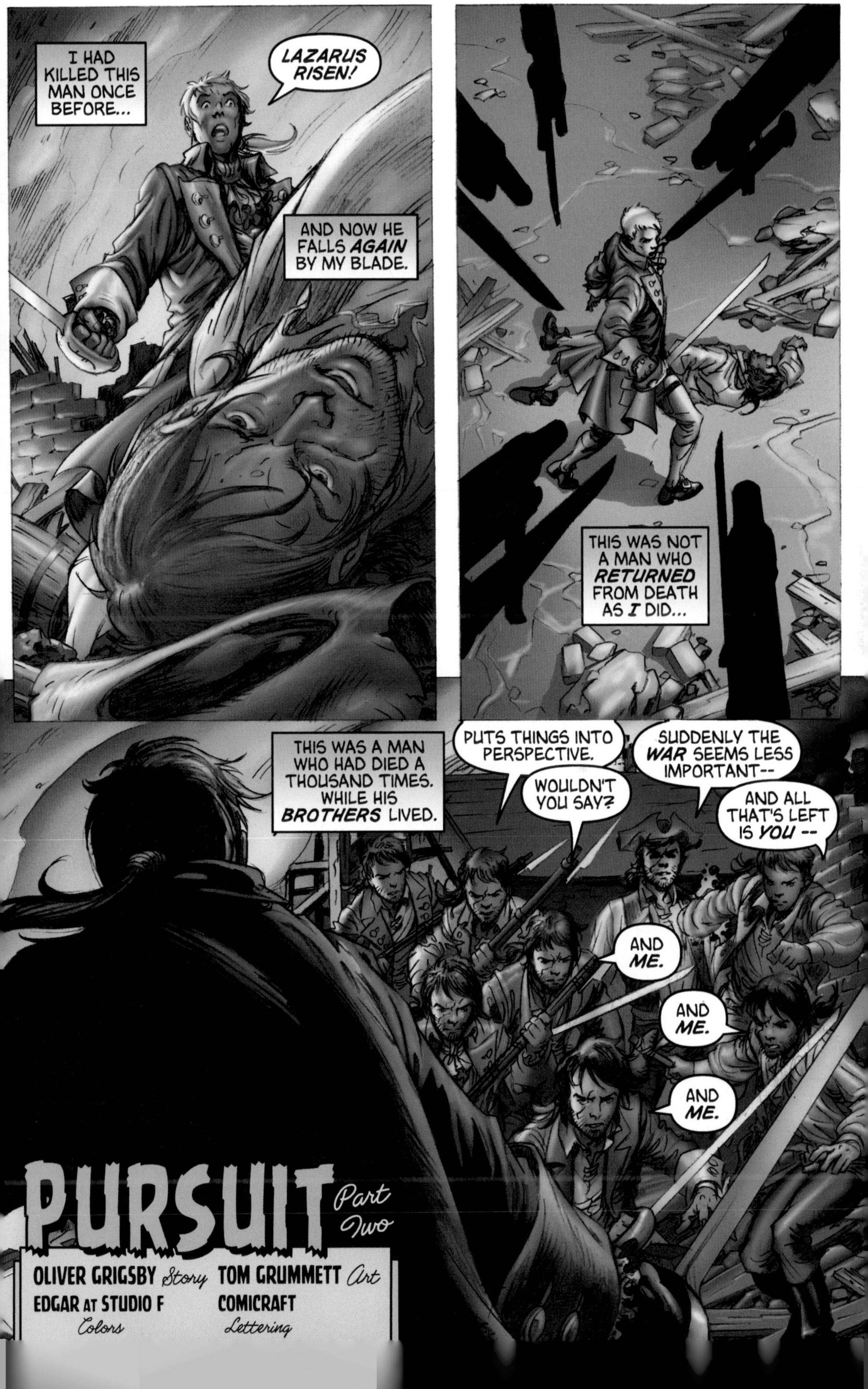
I HAD KILLED THIS MAN ONCE BEFORE...
LAZARUS RISEN!
AND NOW HE FALLS AGAIN BY MY BLADE.
THIS WAS NOT A MAN WHO RETURNED FROM DEATH AS I DID...
THIS WAS A MAN WHO HAD DIED A THOUSAND TIMES. WHILE HIS BROTHERS LIVED.
PUTS THINGS INTO PERSPECTIVE.
WOULDN'T YOU SAY?
SUDDENLY THE WAR SEEMS LESS IMPORTANT--
AND ALL THAT'S LEFT IS YOU --
AND ME.
AND ME.
AND ME.
PURSUIT Part Two
OLIVER GRIGSBY Story TOM GRUMMETT Art
EDGAR AT STUDIO F Colors
COMICRAFT Lettering

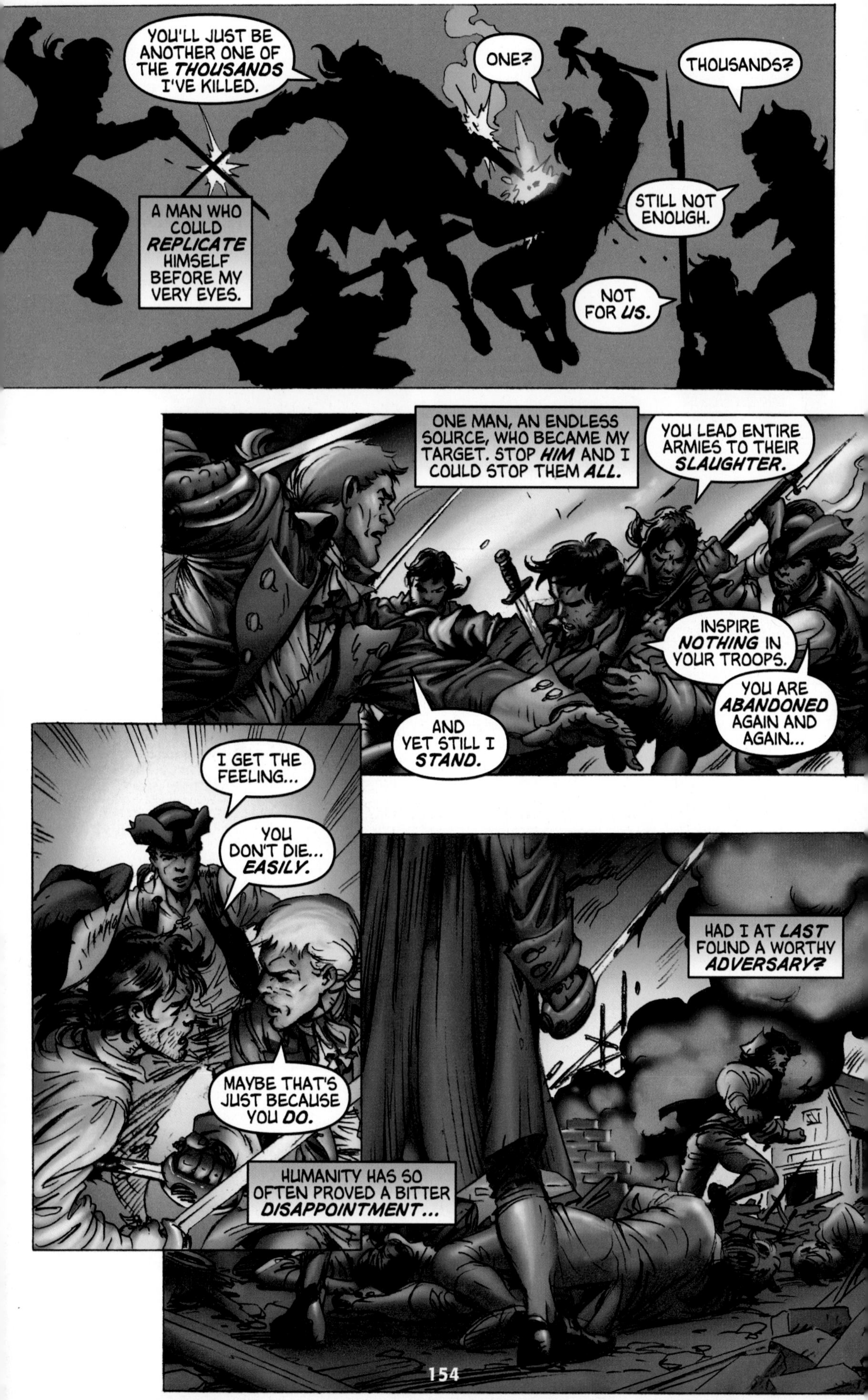
YOU'LL JUST BE ANOTHER ONE OF THE THOUSANDS I'VE KILLED.
A MAN WHO COULD REPLICATE HIMSELF BEFORE MY VERY EYES.
ONE?
THOUSANDS?
STILL NOT ENOUGH.
NOT FOR US.
ONE MAN, AN ENDLESS SOURCE, WHO BECAME MY TARGET. STOP HIM AND I COULD STOP THEM ALL.
YOU LEAD ENTIRE ARMIES TO THEIR SLAUGHTER.
INSPIRE NOTHING IN YOUR TROOPS.
YOU ARE ABANDONED AGAIN AND AGAIN...
AND YET STILL I STAND.
I GET THE FEELING...
YOU DON'T DIE... EASILY.
MAYBE THAT'S JUST BECAUSE YOU DO.
HUMANITY HAS SO OFTEN PROVED A BITTER DISAPPOINTMENT...
HAD I AT LAST FOUND A WORTHY ADVERSARY?

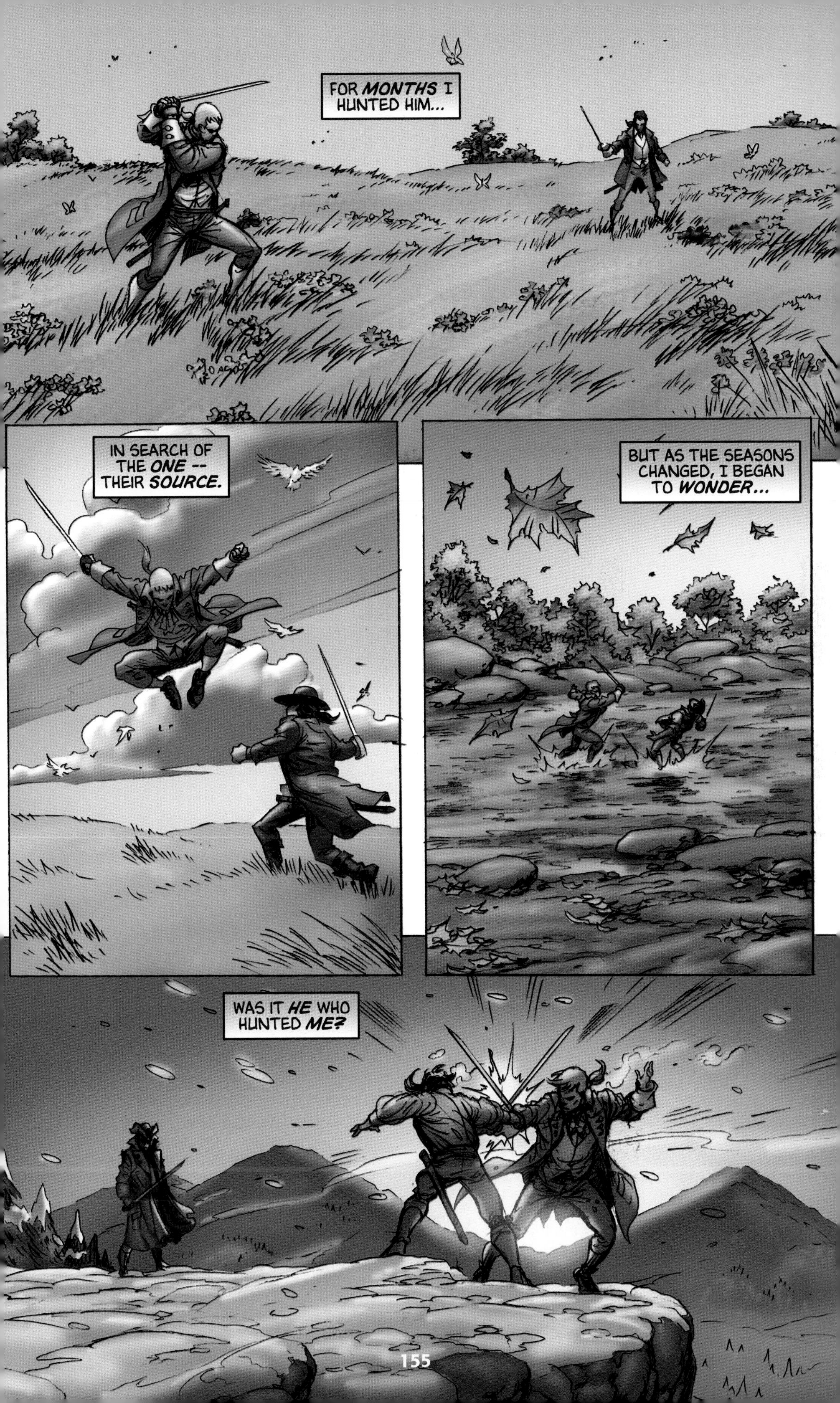
FOR MONTHS I HUNTED HIM...
IN SEARCH OF THE ONE -- THEIR SOURCE.
BUT AS THE SEASONS CHANGED, I BEGAN TO WONDER...
WAS IT HE WHO HUNTED ME?

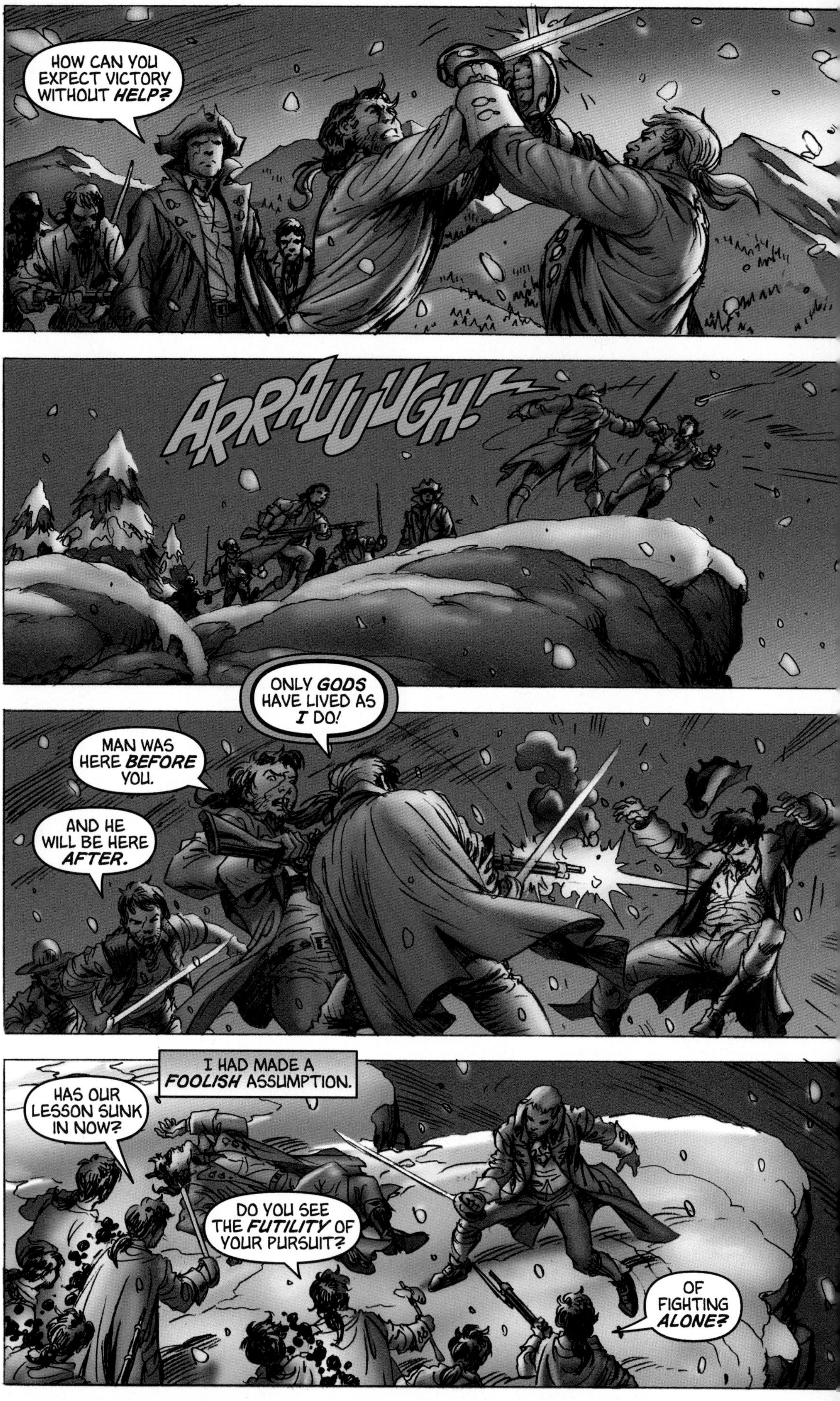
HOW CAN YOU EXPECT VICTORY WITHOUT HELP?
ARRAUUUGH!
ONLY GODS HAVE LIVED AS I DO!
MAN WAS HERE BEFORE YOU.
AND HE WILL BE HERE AFTER.
I HAD MADE A FOOLISH ASSUMPTION.
HAS OUR LESSON SUNK IN NOW?
DO YOU SEE THE FUTILITY OF YOUR PURSUIT?
OF FIGHTING ALONE?

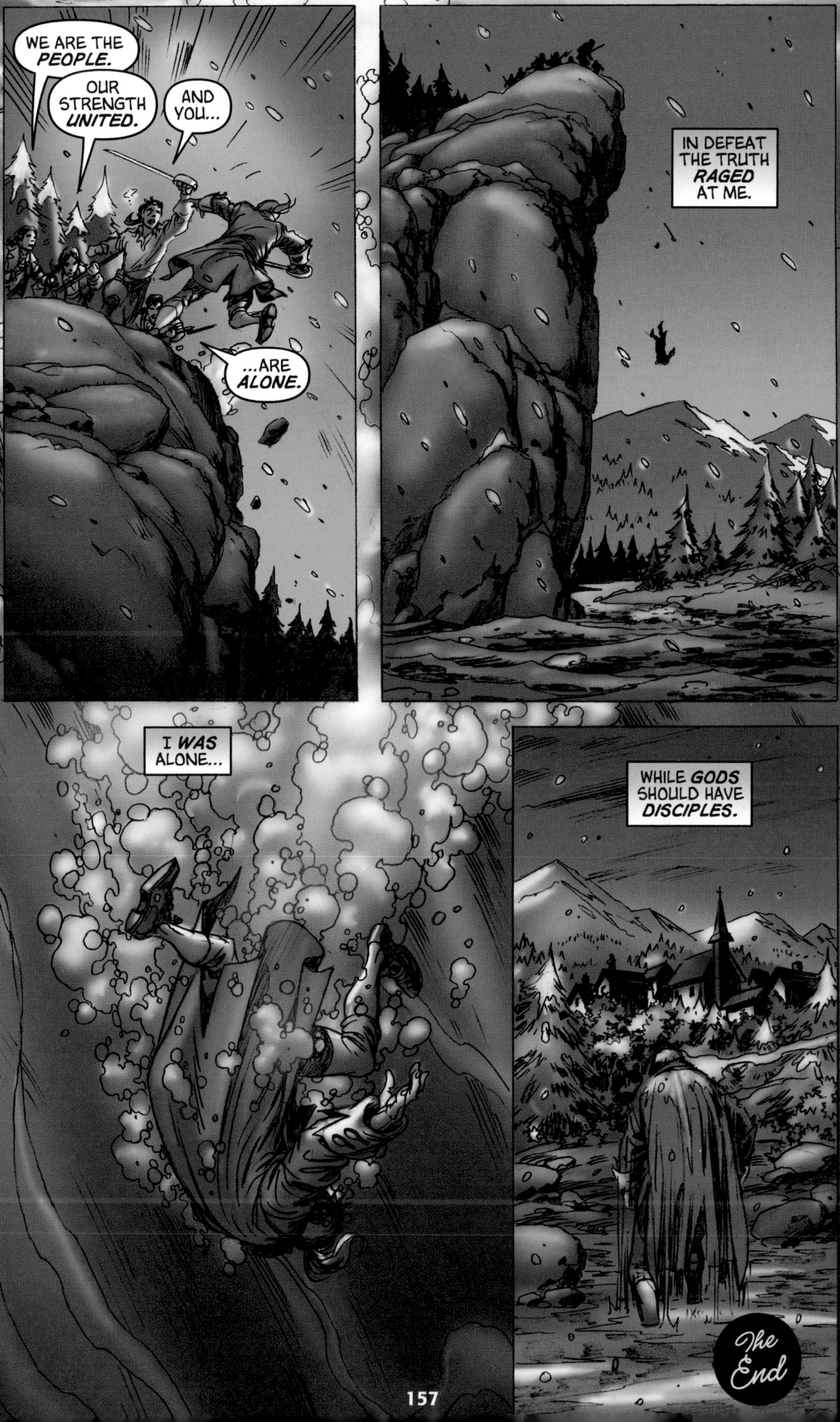
WE ARE THE PEOPLE.
OUR STRENGTH UNITED.
AND YOU...
...ARE ALONE.
IN DEFEAT THE TRUTH RAGED AT ME.
I WAS ALONE...
WHILE GODS SHOULD HAVE DISCIPLES.
The End

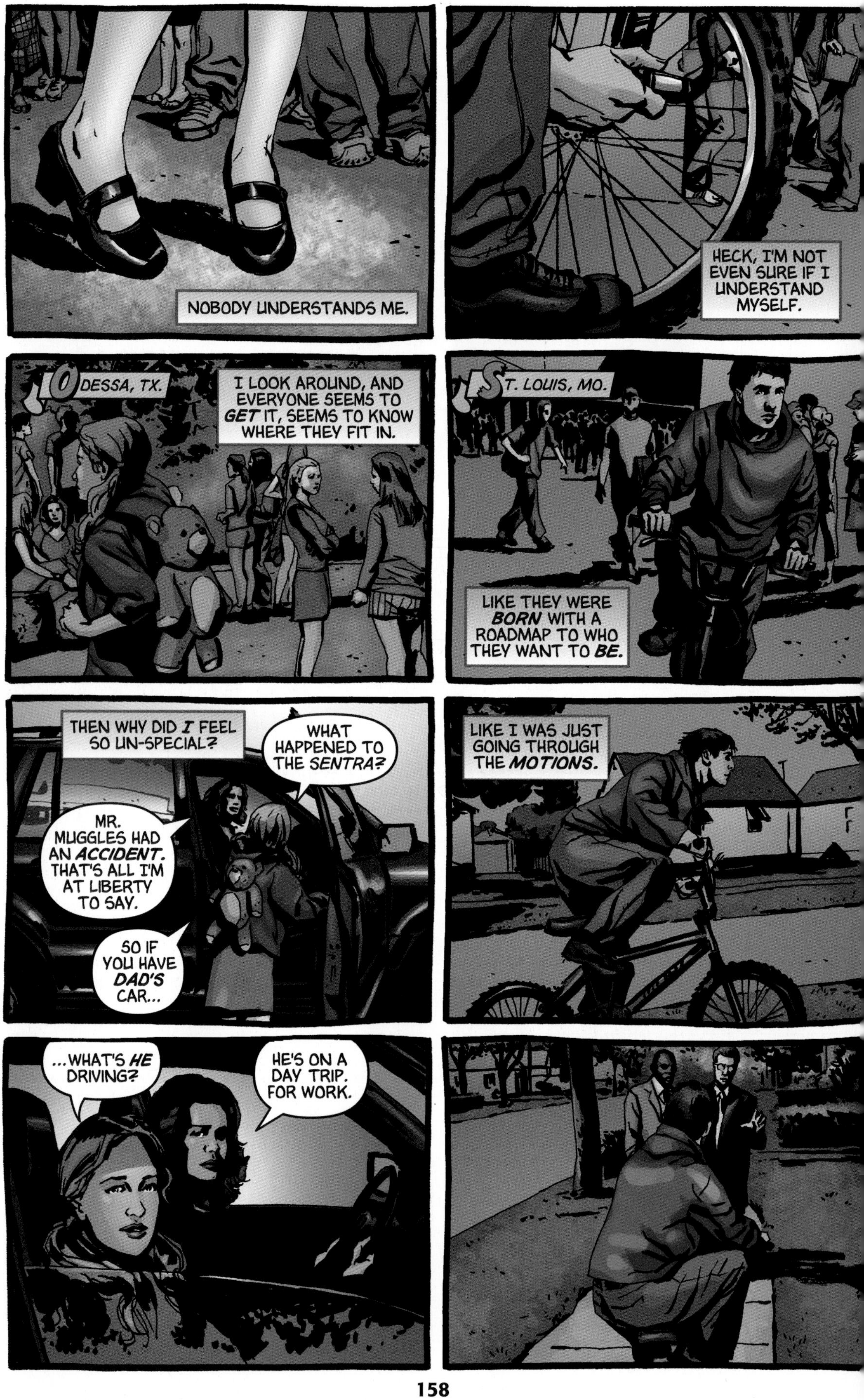
NOBODY UNDERSTANDS ME.
HECK, I'M NOT EVEN SURE IF I UNDERSTAND MYSELF.
ODESSA, TX.
I LOOK AROUND, AND EVERYONE SEEMS TO GET IT, SEEMS TO KNOW WHERE THEY FIT IN.
ST. LOUIS, MO.
LIKE THEY WERE BORN WITH A ROADMAP TO WHO THEY WANT TO BE.
THEN WHY DID I FEEL SO UN-SPECIAL?
WHAT HAPPENED TO THE SENTRA?
MR. MUGGLES HAD AN ACCIDENT. THAT'S ALL I'M AT LIBERTY TO SAY.
SO IF YOU HAVE DAD'S CAR...
LIKE I WAS JUST GOING THROUGH THE MOTIONS.
...WHAT'S HE DRIVING?
HE'S ON A DAY TRIP. FOR WORK.

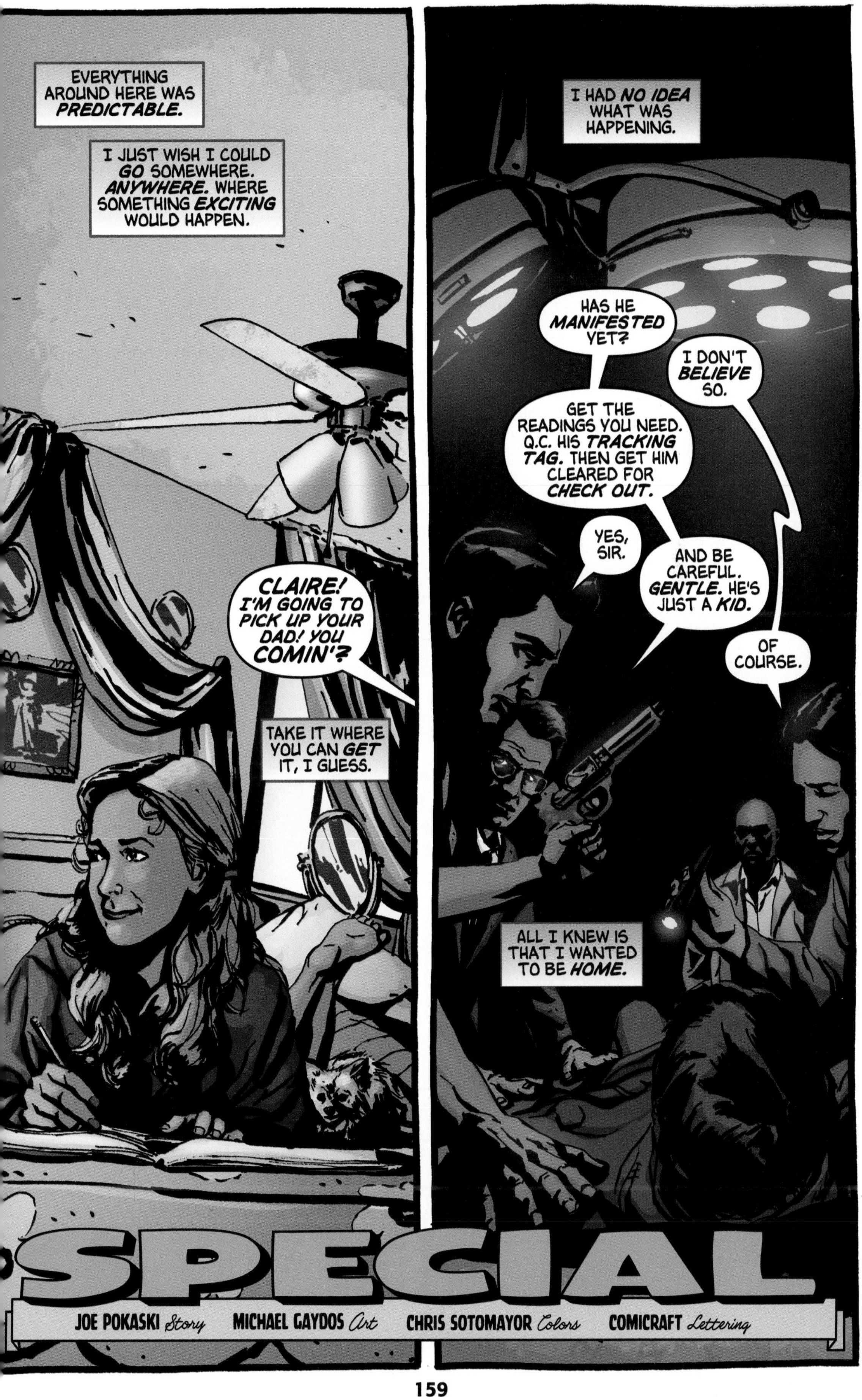
EVERYTHING AROUND HERE WAS PREDICTABLE.
I JUST WISH I COULD GO SOMEWHERE. ANYWHERE. WHERE SOMETHING EXCITING WOULD HAPPEN.
CLAIRE! I'M GOING TO PICK UP YOUR DAD! YOU COMIN'?
TAKE IT WHERE YOU CAN GET IT, I GUESS.
I HAD NO IDEA WHAT WAS HAPPENING.
HAS HE MANIFESTED YET?
I DON'T BELIEVE SO.
GET THE READINGS YOU NEED. Q.C. HIS TRACKING TAG. THEN GET HIM CLEARED FOR CHECK OUT.
YES, SIR.
AND BE CAREFUL. GENTLE. HE'S JUST A KID.
OF COURSE.
ALL I KNEW IS THAT I WANTED TO BE HOME.
SPECIAL
JOE POKASKI Story MICHAEL GAYDOS Art CHRIS SOTOMAYOR Colors COMICRAFT Lettering

CAN I GO IN AND *GET* HIM?

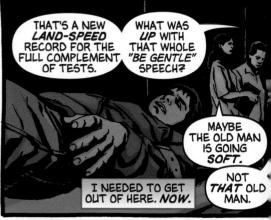

THAT'S A NEW *LAND-SPEED* RECORD FOR THE FULL COMPLEMENT OF TESTS.

WHAT WAS *UP* WITH THAT WHOLE *"BE GENTLE"* SPEECH?

MAYBE THE OLD MAN IS GOING *SOFT.*

I NEEDED TO GET OUT OF HERE. *NOW.*

NOT *THAT* OLD MAN.

THERE'S SOMETHING *ABOUT* DAD'S PAPER FACTORY.

SOMETHING'S *HAPPENING....*

I LIKED TO PRETEND THERE WERE *MYSTERIES* BEHIND HERE.

SOMETHING KIND OF *INSANE.*

WHAT THE HECK DID THEY *DO* TO ME?!

AND COULD I USE IT TO GET *OUT* OF HERE?

WHAT KIND OF MYSTERIES WOULD I FIND *TODAY?*

UP THERE. AN *EXIT.*

AT LEAST, I *HOPE.*

HOW AM I *DOING* THIS?

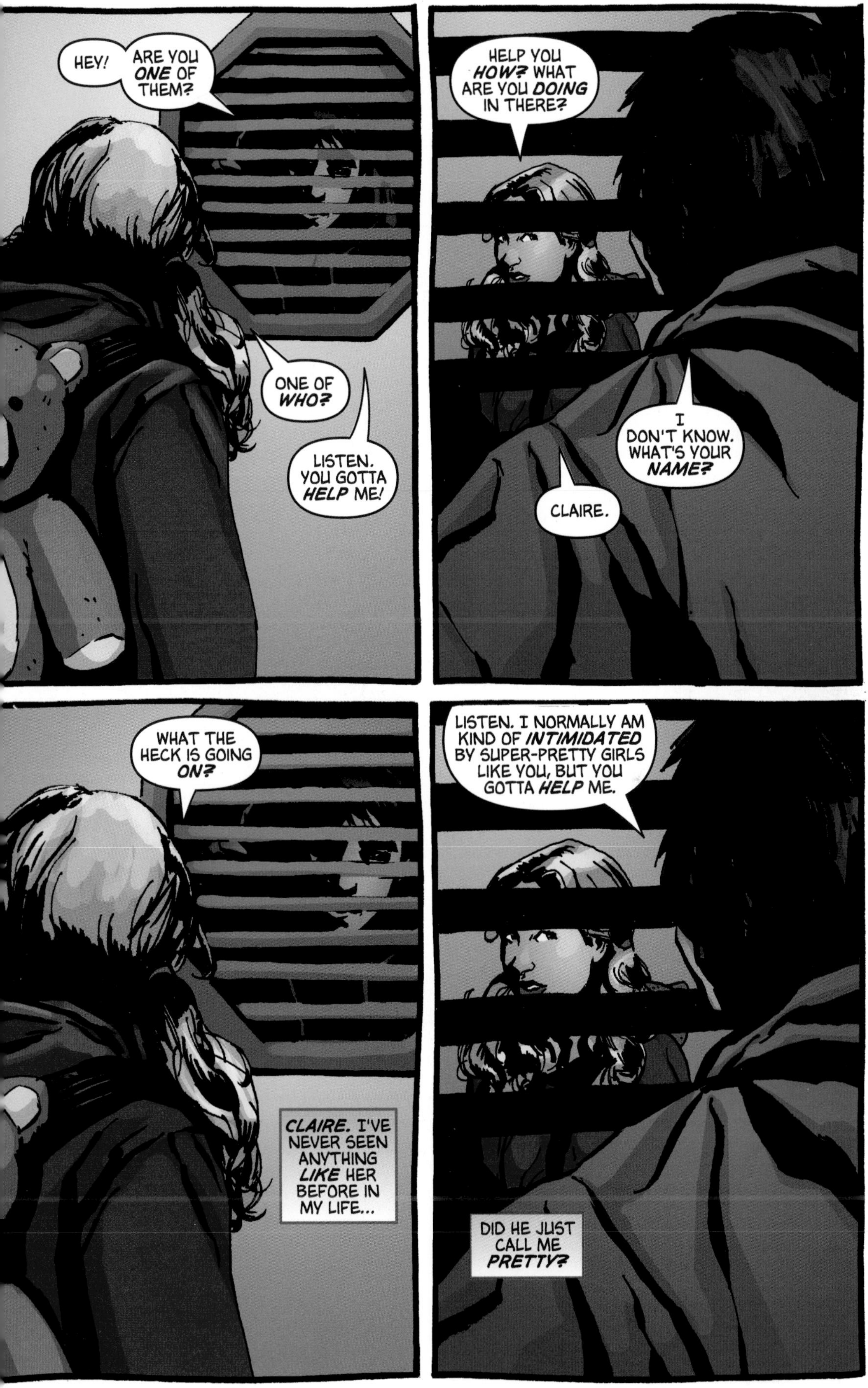
HEY!
ARE YOU ONE OF THEM?
ONE OF WHO?
LISTEN. YOU GOTTA HELP ME!
HELP YOU HOW? WHAT ARE YOU DOING IN THERE?
I DON'T KNOW. WHAT'S YOUR NAME?
CLAIRE.
WHAT THE HECK IS GOING ON?
CLAIRE. I'VE NEVER SEEN ANYTHING LIKE HER BEFORE IN MY LIFE...
LISTEN. I NORMALLY AM KIND OF INTIMIDATED BY SUPER-PRETTY GIRLS LIKE YOU, BUT YOU GOTTA HELP ME.
DID HE JUST CALL ME PRETTY?

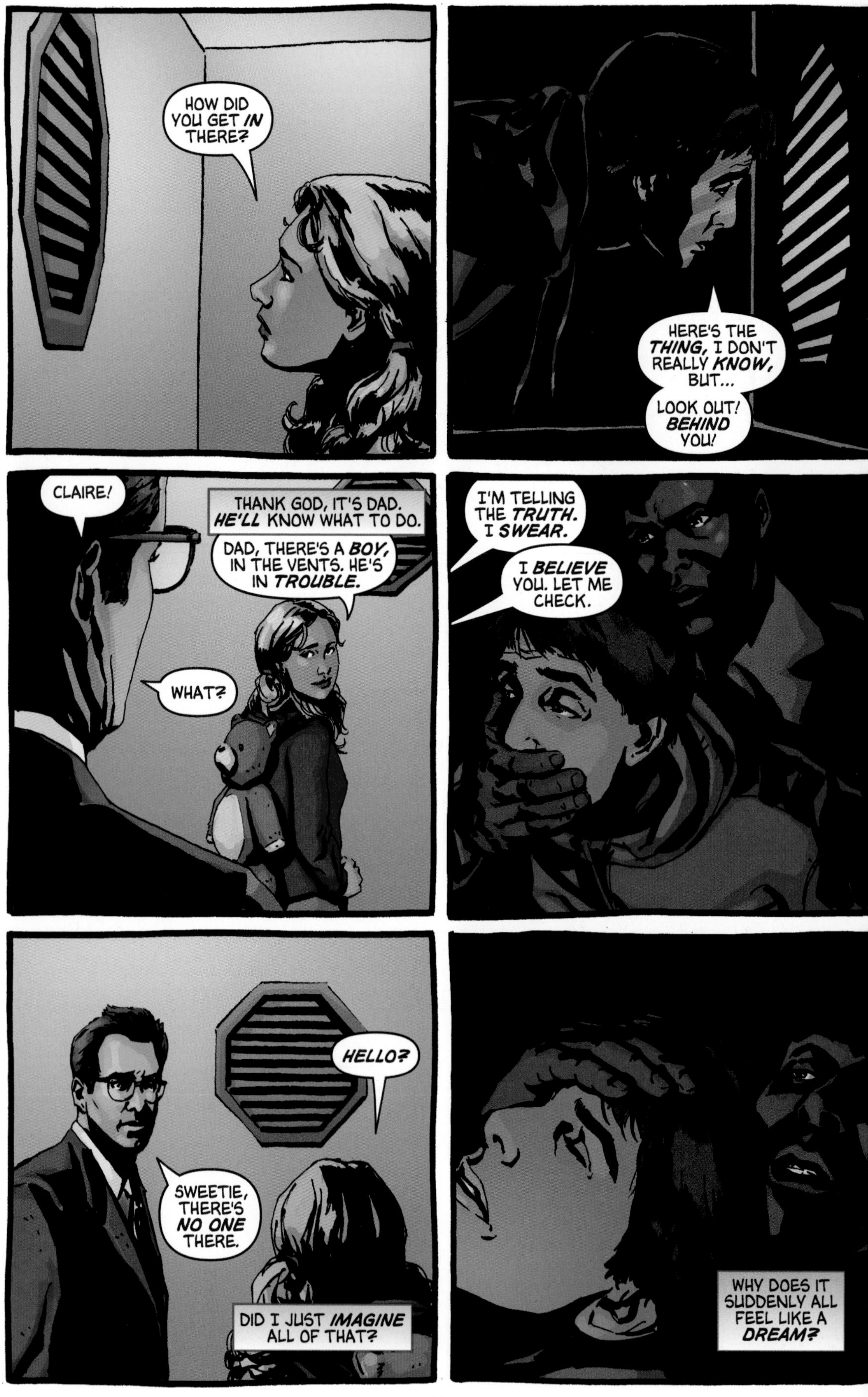
HOW DID YOU GET IN THERE?
HERE'S THE THING, I DON'T REALLY KNOW, BUT...
LOOK OUT! BEHIND YOU!
CLAIRE!
THANK GOD, IT'S DAD. HE'LL KNOW WHAT TO DO.
DAD, THERE'S A BOY, IN THE VENTS. HE'S IN TROUBLE.
WHAT?
I'M TELLING THE TRUTH. I SWEAR.
I BELIEVE YOU. LET ME CHECK.
HELLO?
SWEETIE, THERE'S NO ONE THERE.
DID I JUST IMAGINE ALL OF THAT?
WHY DOES IT SUDDENLY ALL FEEL LIKE A DREAM?

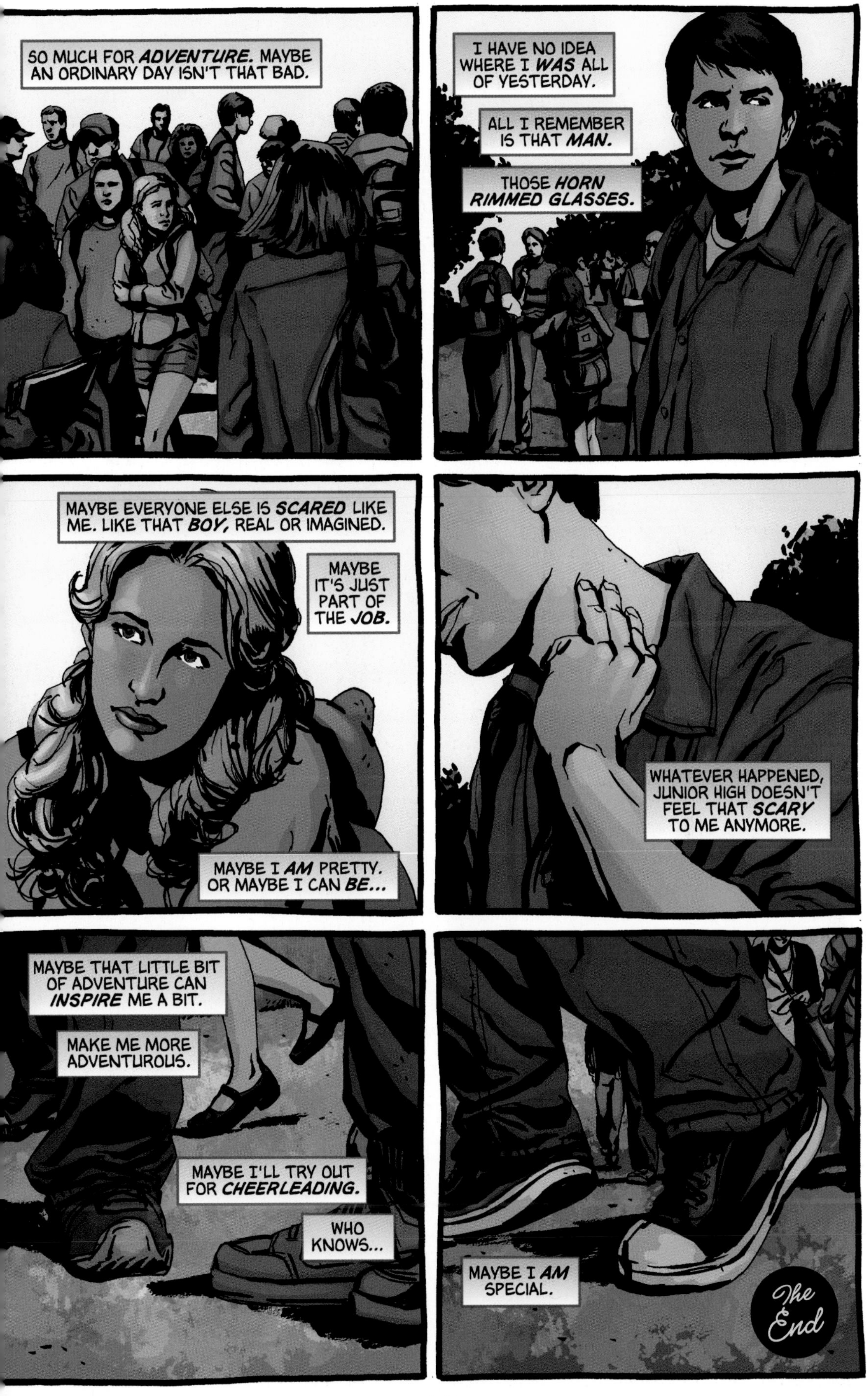
SO MUCH FOR ADVENTURE. MAYBE AN ORDINARY DAY ISN'T THAT BAD.
I HAVE NO IDEA WHERE I WAS ALL OF YESTERDAY.
ALL I REMEMBER IS THAT MAN.
THOSE HORN RIMMED GLASSES.
MAYBE EVERYONE ELSE IS SCARED LIKE ME. LIKE THAT BOY, REAL OR IMAGINED.
MAYBE IT'S JUST PART OF THE JOB.
MAYBE I AM PRETTY. OR MAYBE I CAN BE...
WHATEVER HAPPENED, JUNIOR HIGH DOESN'T FEEL THAT SCARY TO ME ANYMORE.
MAYBE THAT LITTLE BIT OF ADVENTURE CAN INSPIRE ME A BIT.
MAKE ME MORE ADVENTUROUS.
MAYBE I'LL TRY OUT FOR CHEERLEADING.
WHO KNOWS...
MAYBE I AM SPECIAL.
The End

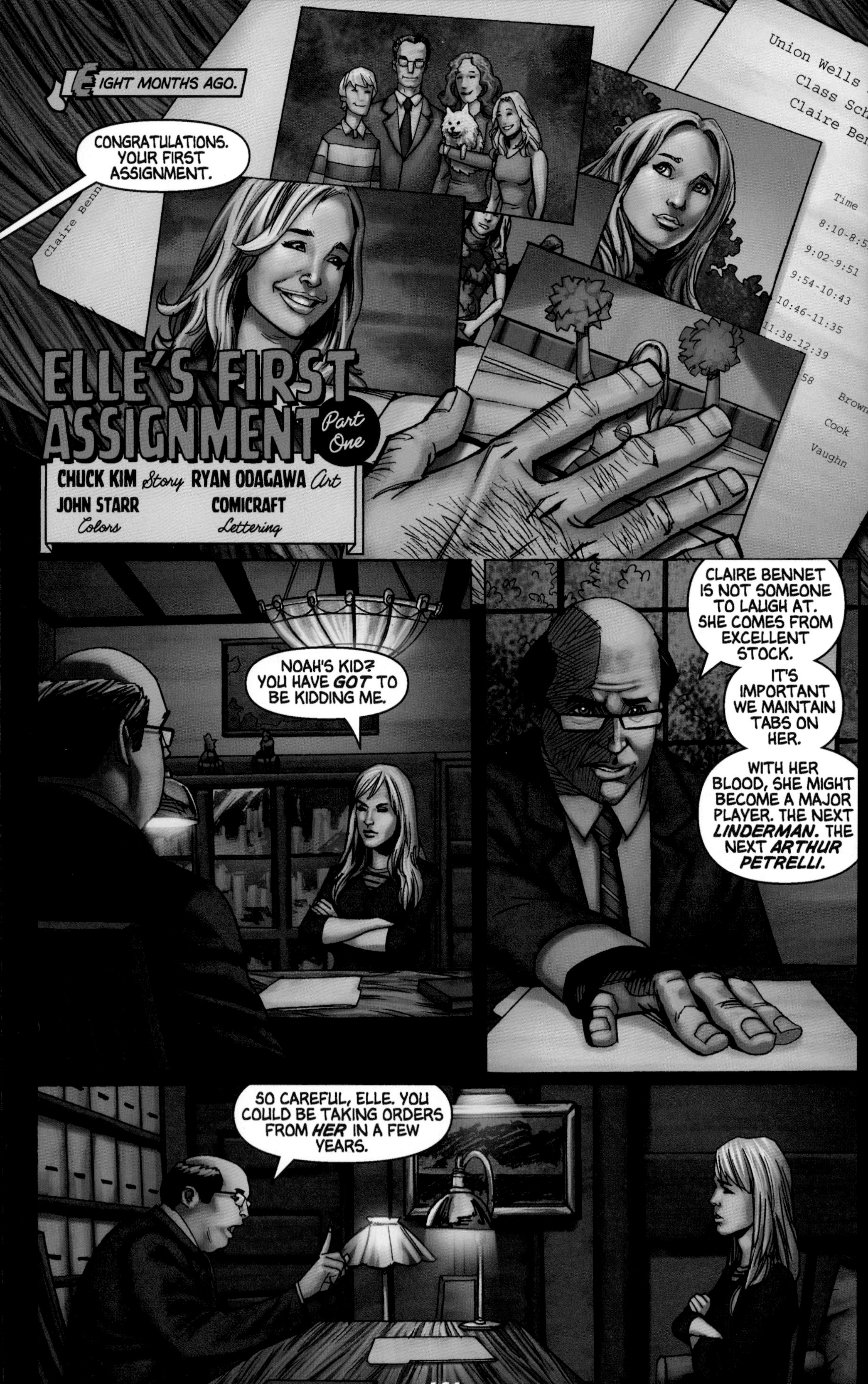
EIGHT MONTHS AGO.
CONGRATULATIONS. YOUR FIRST ASSIGNMENT.
Claire Benn
Union Wells
Class Sch
Claire Ben
Time
8:10-8:5
9:02-9:51
9:54-10:43
10:46-11:35
11:38-12:39
58
Brown
Cook
Vaughn
ELLE'S FIRST ASSIGNMENT Part One
CHUCK KIM Story RYAN ODAGAWA Art
JOHN STARR Colors
COMICRAFT Lettering
NOAH'S KID? YOU HAVE GOT TO BE KIDDING ME.
CLAIRE BENNET IS NOT SOMEONE TO LAUGH AT. SHE COMES FROM EXCELLENT STOCK.
IT'S IMPORTANT WE MAINTAIN TABS ON HER.
WITH HER BLOOD, SHE MIGHT BECOME A MAJOR PLAYER. THE NEXT LINDERMAN. THE NEXT ARTHUR PETRELLI.
SO CAREFUL, ELLE. YOU COULD BE TAKING ORDERS FROM HER IN A FEW YEARS.

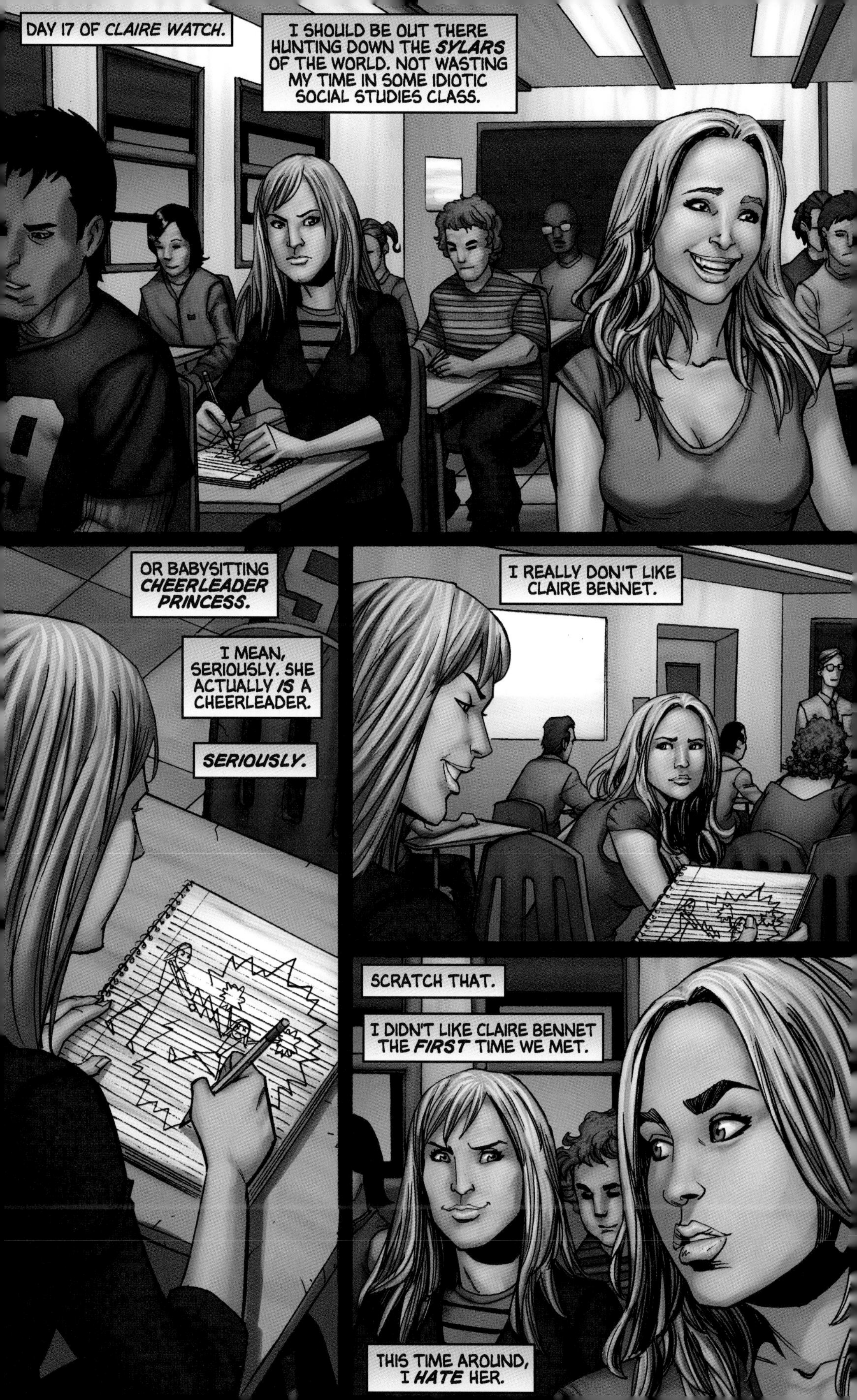
DAY 17 OF CLAIRE WATCH.
I SHOULD BE OUT THERE HUNTING DOWN THE SYLARS OF THE WORLD. NOT WASTING MY TIME IN SOME IDIOTIC SOCIAL STUDIES CLASS.
OR BABYSITTING CHEERLEADER PRINCESS.
I MEAN, SERIOUSLY. SHE ACTUALLY IS A CHEERLEADER.
SERIOUSLY.
I REALLY DON'T LIKE CLAIRE BENNET.
SCRATCH THAT.
I DIDN'T LIKE CLAIRE BENNET THE FIRST TIME WE MET.
THIS TIME AROUND, I HATE HER.

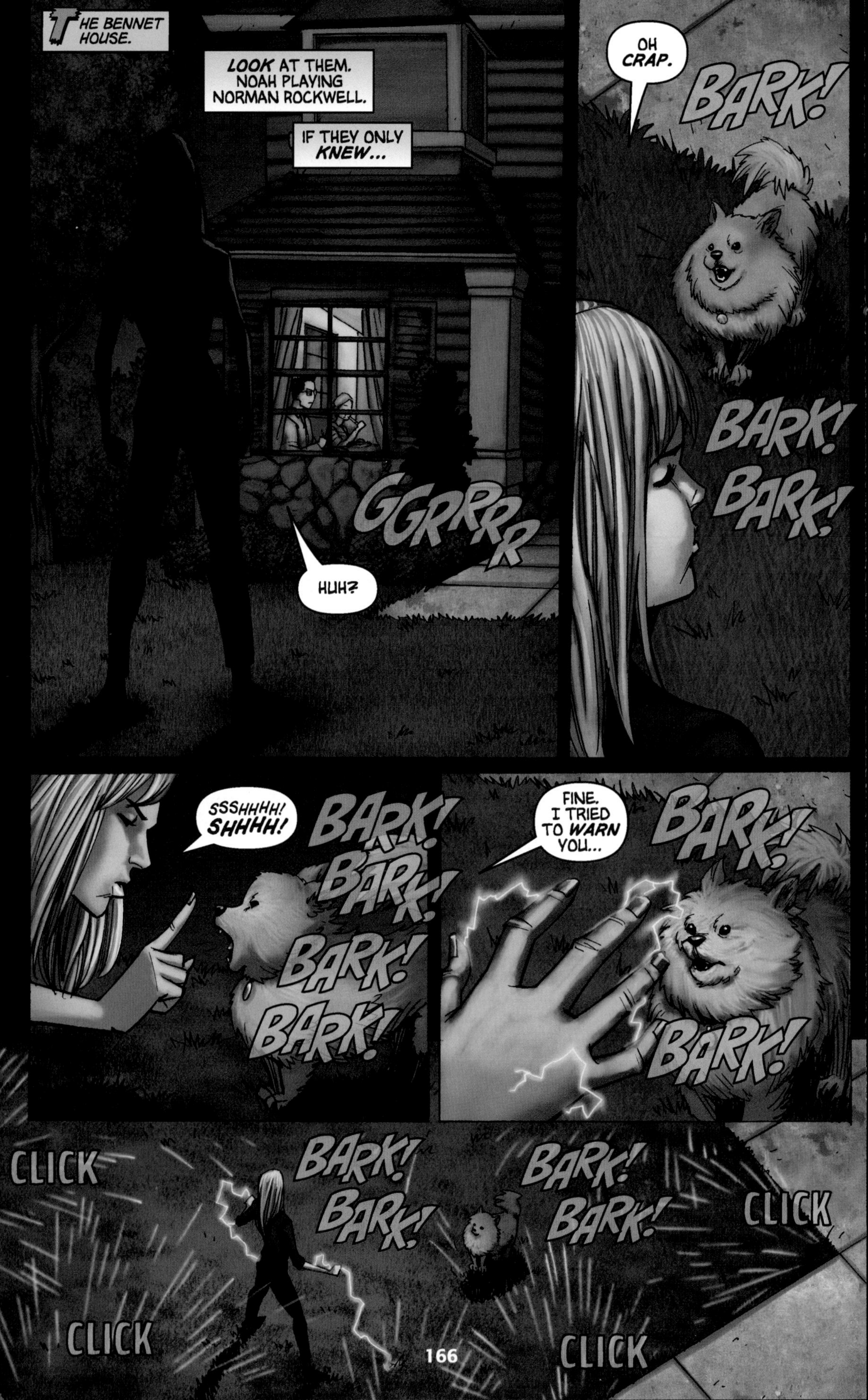
THE BENNET HOUSE.
LOOK AT THEM. NOAH PLAYING NORMAN ROCKWELL.
IF THEY ONLY KNEW...
GGRRRRR
HUH?
OH CRAP.
BARK!
BARK!
BARK!
SSSHHHH! SHHHH!
BARK! BARK! BARK! BARK!
FINE. I TRIED TO WARN YOU...
BARK!
BARK!
CLICK
BARK! BARK!
BARK! BARK!
CLICK
CLICK
CLICK

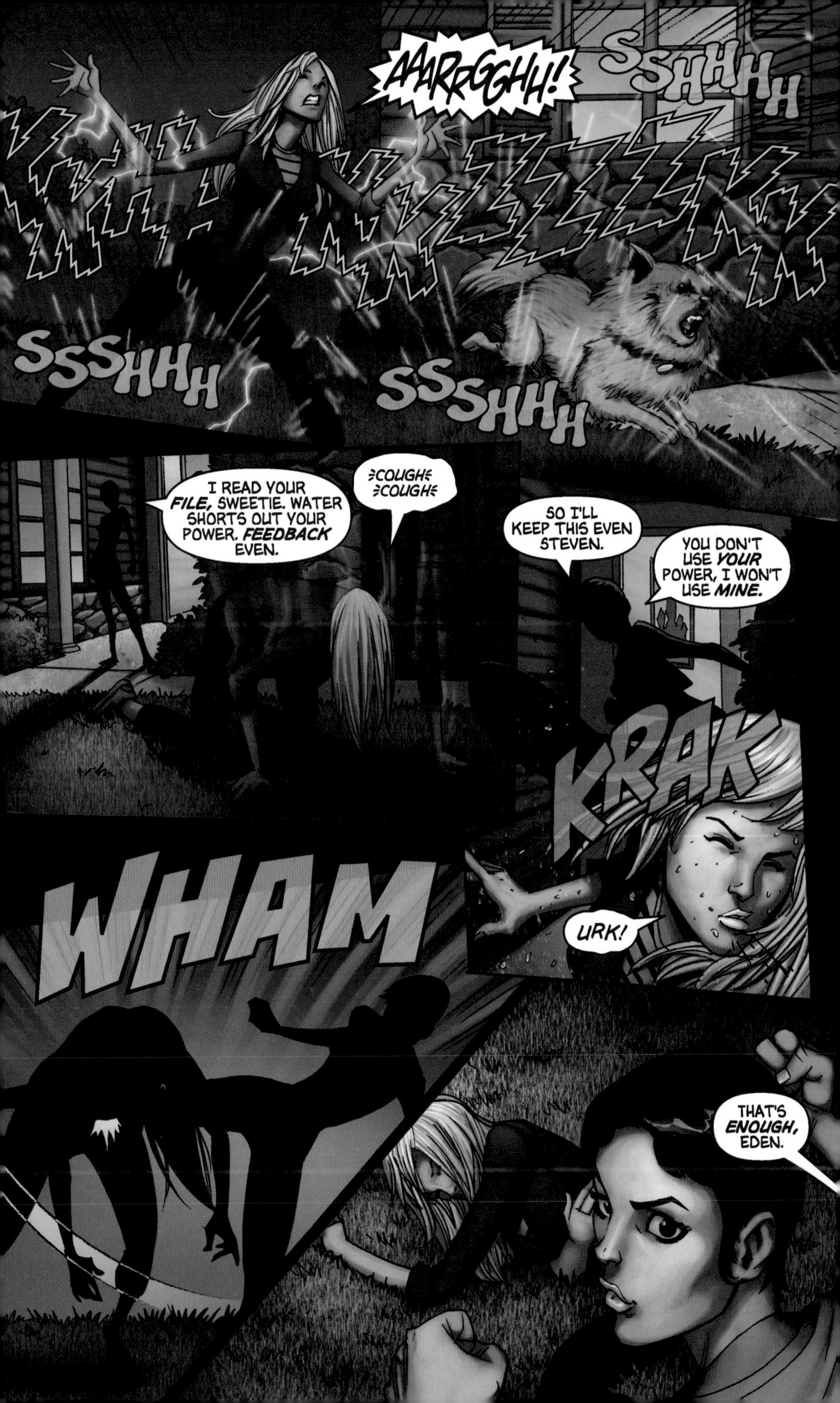

AAARRGGHH!
SSHHHH
SSSHHH
SSSHHH
I READ YOUR FILE, SWEETIE. WATER SHORTS OUT YOUR POWER. FEEDBACK EVEN.
COUGH COUGH
SO I'LL KEEP THIS EVEN STEVEN.
YOU DON'T USE YOUR POWER, I WON'T USE MINE.
KRAK
URK!
WHAM
THAT'S ENOUGH, EDEN.

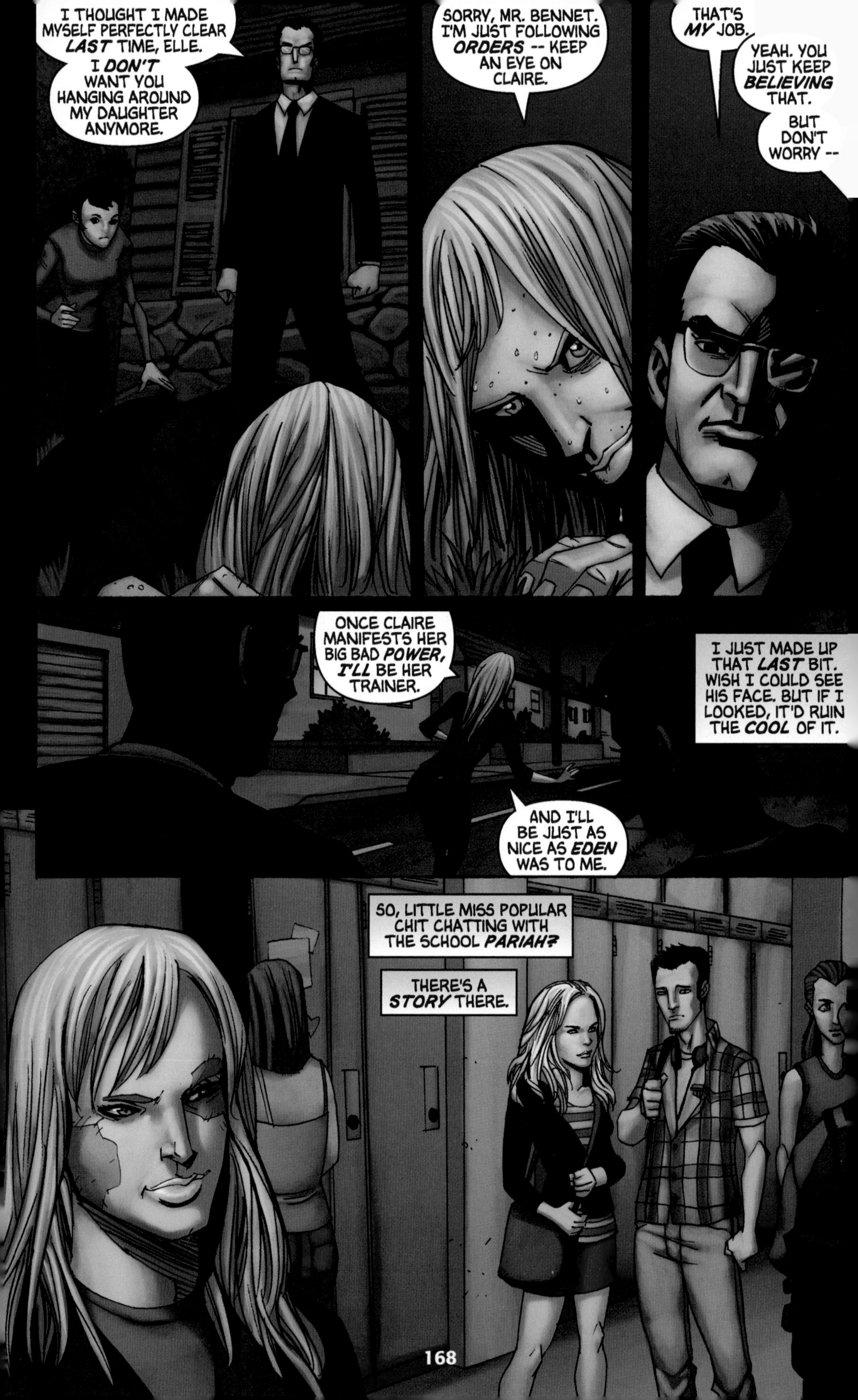
I THOUGHT I MADE MYSELF PERFECTLY CLEAR LAST TIME, ELLE.
I DON'T WANT YOU HANGING AROUND MY DAUGHTER ANYMORE.
SORRY, MR. BENNET. I'M JUST FOLLOWING ORDERS -- KEEP AN EYE ON CLAIRE.
THAT'S MY JOB.
YEAH. YOU JUST KEEP BELIEVING THAT.
BUT DON'T WORRY --
ONCE CLAIRE MANIFESTS HER BIG BAD POWER, I'LL BE HER TRAINER.
AND I'LL BE JUST AS NICE AS EDEN WAS TO ME.
I JUST MADE UP THAT LAST BIT. WISH I COULD SEE HIS FACE. BUT IF I LOOKED, IT'D RUIN THE COOL OF IT.
SO, LITTLE MISS POPULAR CHIT CHATTING WITH THE SCHOOL PARIAH?
THERE'S A STORY THERE.

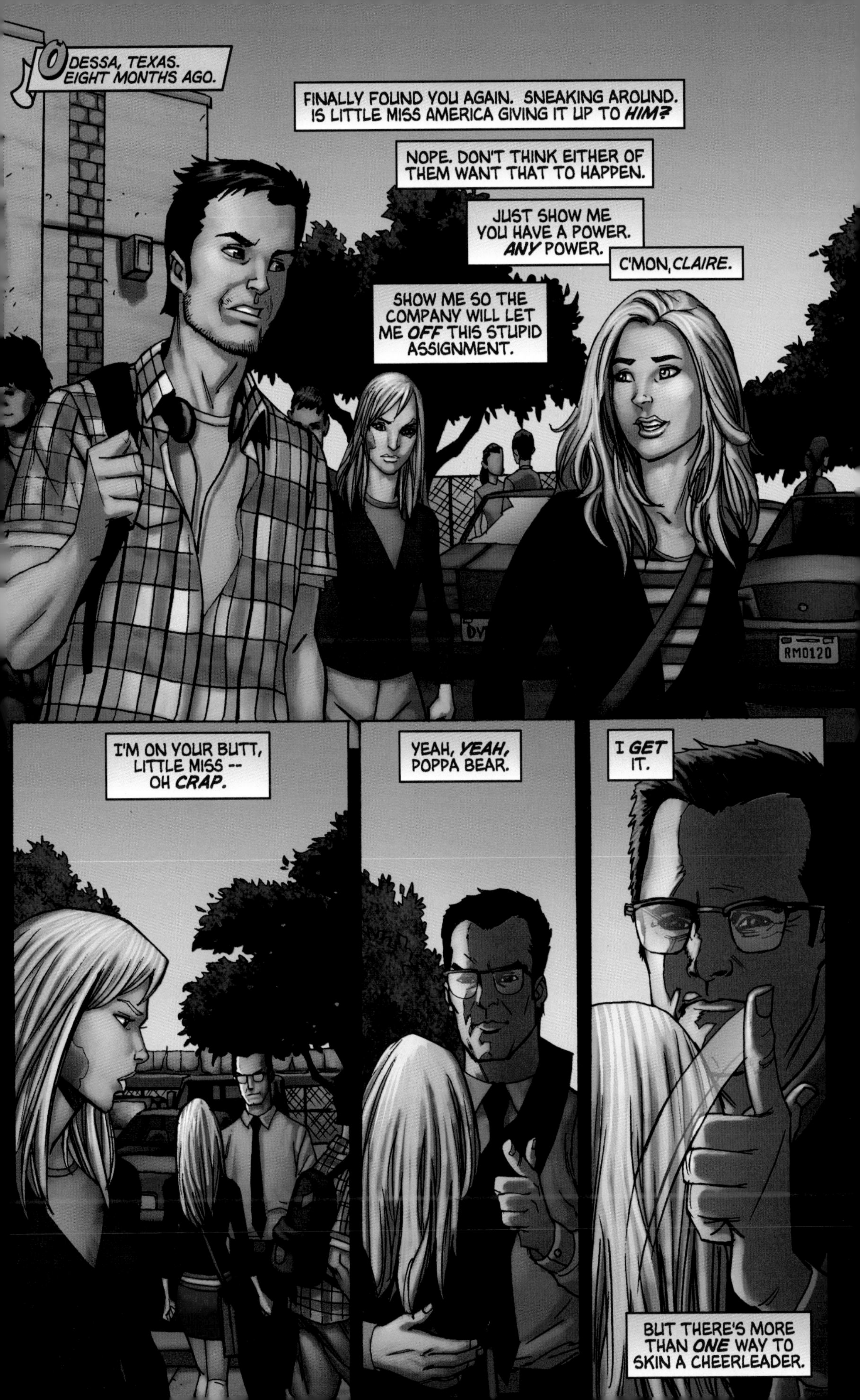
ODESSA, TEXAS.
EIGHT MONTHS AGO.
FINALLY FOUND YOU AGAIN. SNEAKING AROUND. IS LITTLE MISS AMERICA GIVING IT UP TO *HIM?*
NOPE. DON'T THINK EITHER OF THEM WANT THAT TO HAPPEN.
JUST SHOW ME YOU HAVE A POWER. *ANY* POWER.
C'MON, *CLAIRE.*
SHOW ME SO THE COMPANY WILL LET ME *OFF* THIS STUPID ASSIGNMENT.
RM0120
I'M ON YOUR BUTT, LITTLE MISS -- OH *CRAP.*
YEAH, *YEAH,* POPPA BEAR.
I *GET* IT.
BUT THERE'S MORE THAN *ONE* WAY TO SKIN A CHEERLEADER.

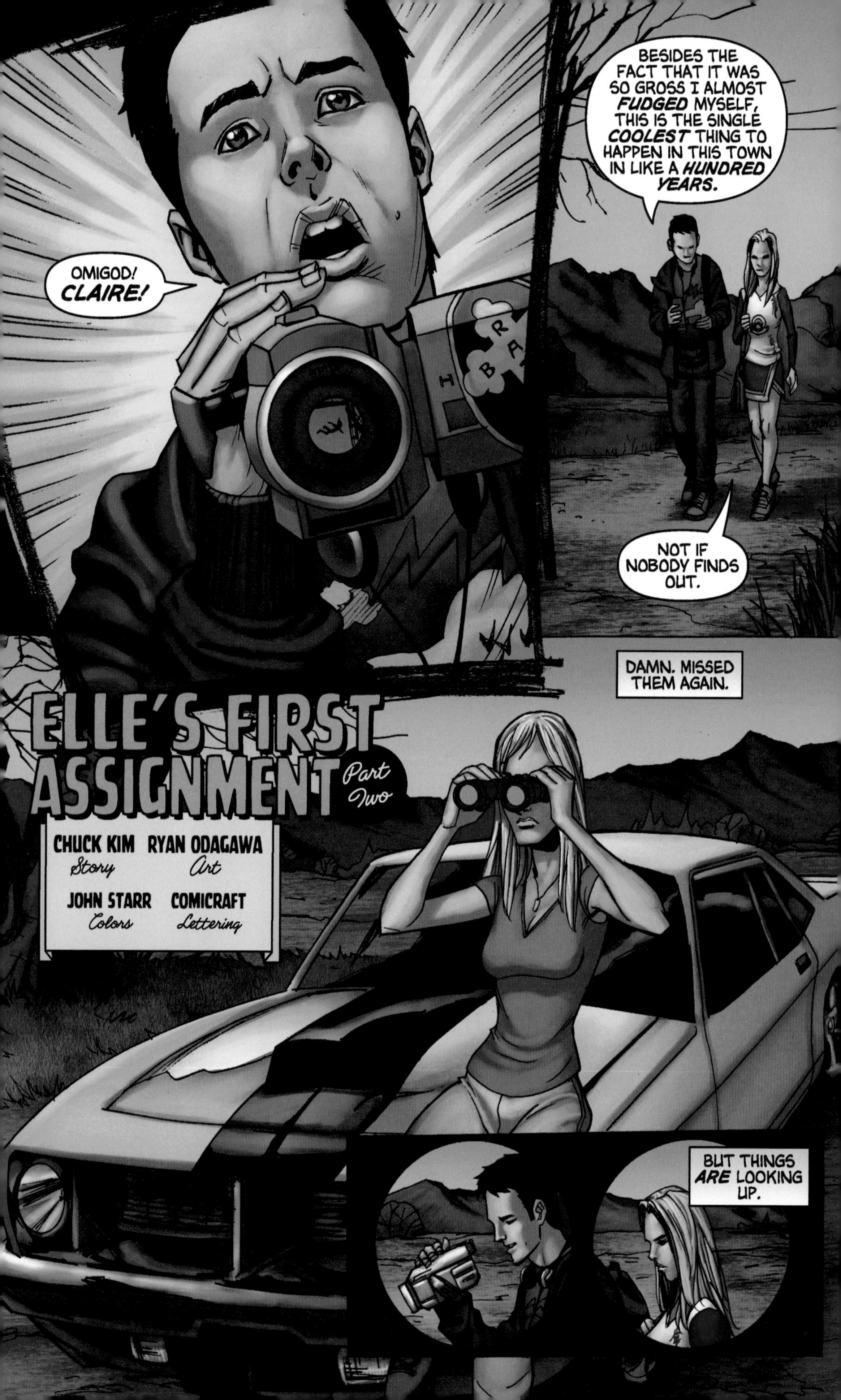
OMIGOD! CLAIRE!
BESIDES THE FACT THAT IT WAS SO GROSS I ALMOST FUDGED MYSELF, THIS IS THE SINGLE COOLEST THING TO HAPPEN IN THIS TOWN IN LIKE A HUNDRED YEARS.
NOT IF NOBODY FINDS OUT.
DAMN. MISSED THEM AGAIN.
ELLE'S FIRST ASSIGNMENT Part Two
CHUCK KIM Story
RYAN ODAGAWA Art
JOHN STARR Colors
COMICRAFT Lettering
BUT THINGS ARE LOOKING UP.

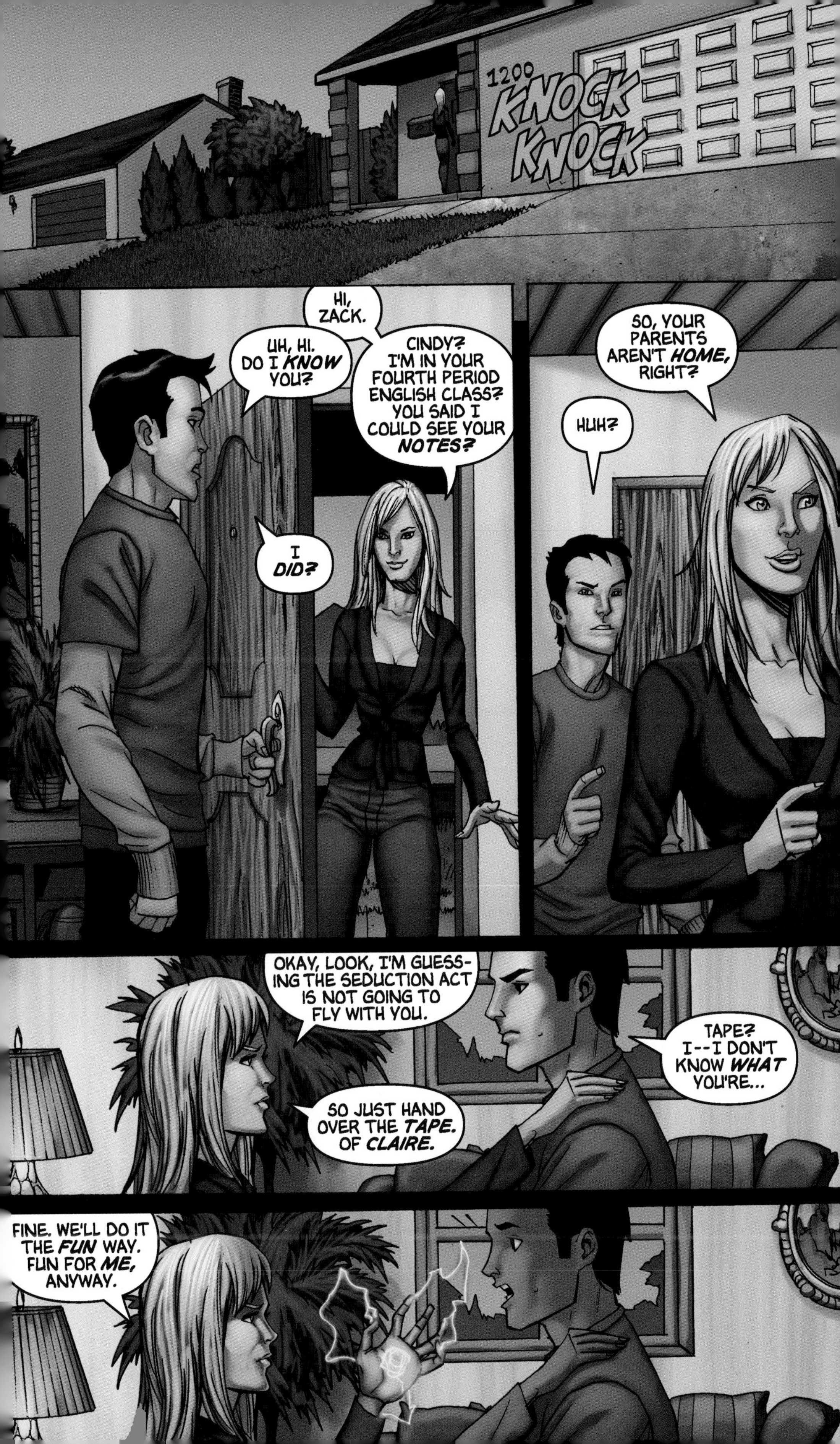
1200
KNOCK KNOCK
HI, ZACK.
UH, HI. DO I KNOW YOU?
CINDY? I'M IN YOUR FOURTH PERIOD ENGLISH CLASS? YOU SAID I COULD SEE YOUR NOTES?
I DID?
SO, YOUR PARENTS AREN'T HOME, RIGHT?
HUH?
OKAY, LOOK, I'M GUESS-ING THE SEDUCTION ACT IS NOT GOING TO FLY WITH YOU.
SO JUST HAND OVER THE TAPE. OF CLAIRE.
TAPE? I--I DON'T KNOW WHAT YOU'RE...
FINE. WE'LL DO IT THE FUN WAY. FUN FOR ME, ANYWAY.

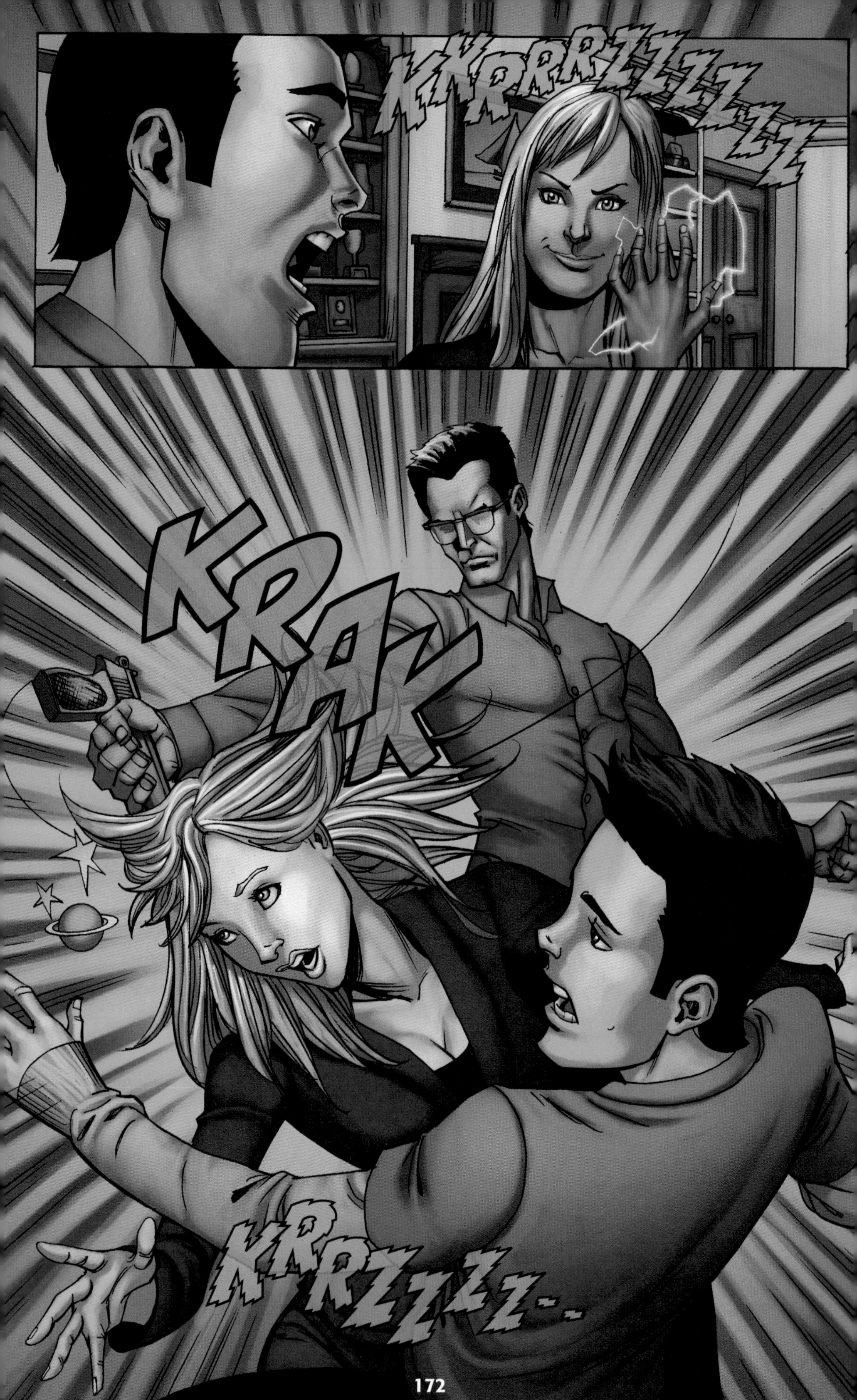
KKRRRZZZZZZZZ
KRAK
KRRZZZZZ--

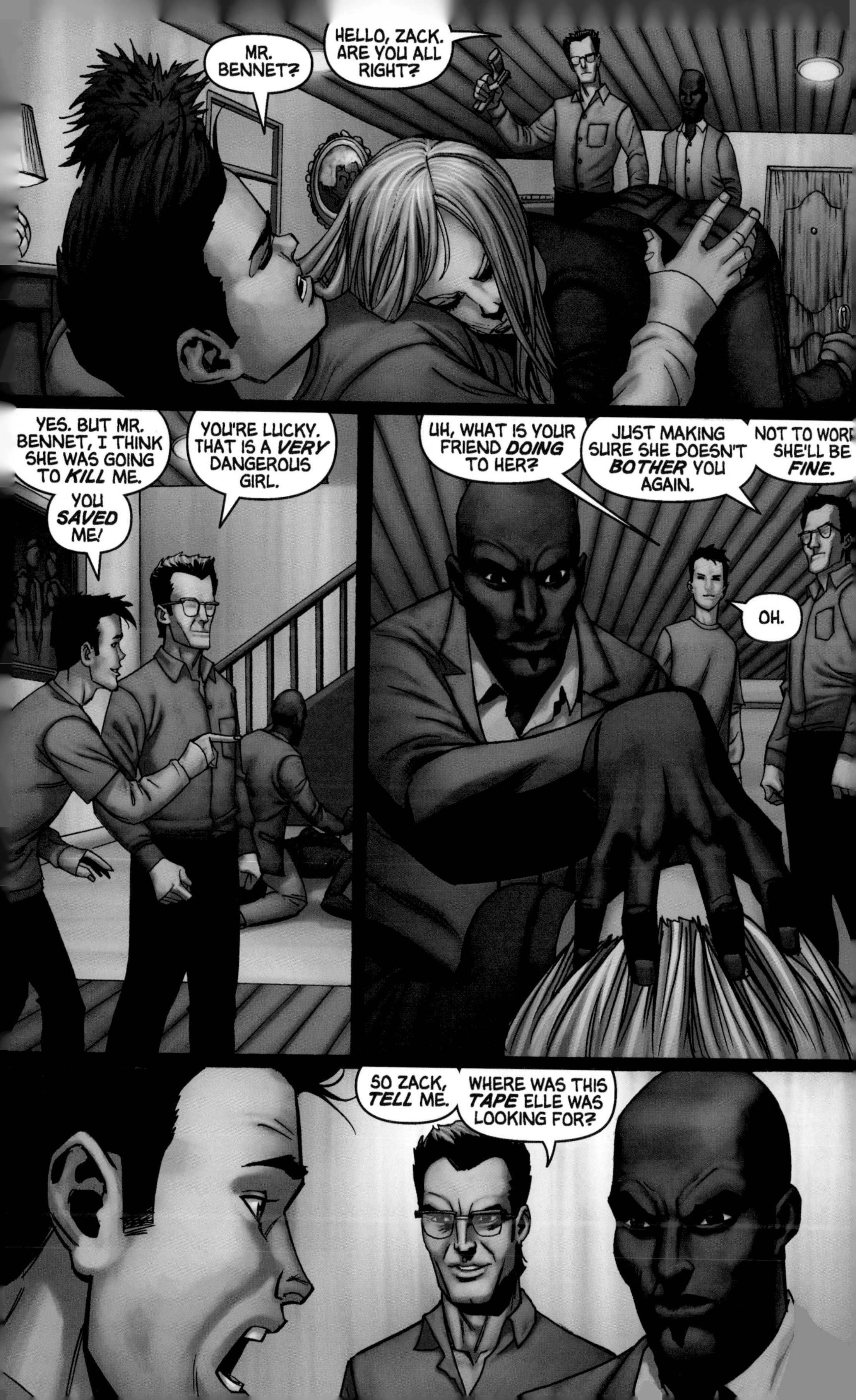

MR. BENNET?
HELLO, ZACK. ARE YOU ALL RIGHT?
YES. BUT MR. BENNET, I THINK SHE WAS GOING TO *KILL* ME.
YOU *SAVED* ME!
YOU'RE LUCKY. THAT IS A *VERY* DANGEROUS GIRL.
UH, WHAT IS YOUR FRIEND *DOING* TO HER?
JUST MAKING SURE SHE DOESN'T *BOTHER* YOU AGAIN.
SHE'LL BE *FINE.*
OH.
SO ZACK, *TELL* ME.
WHERE WAS THIS *TAPE* ELLE WAS LOOKING FOR?

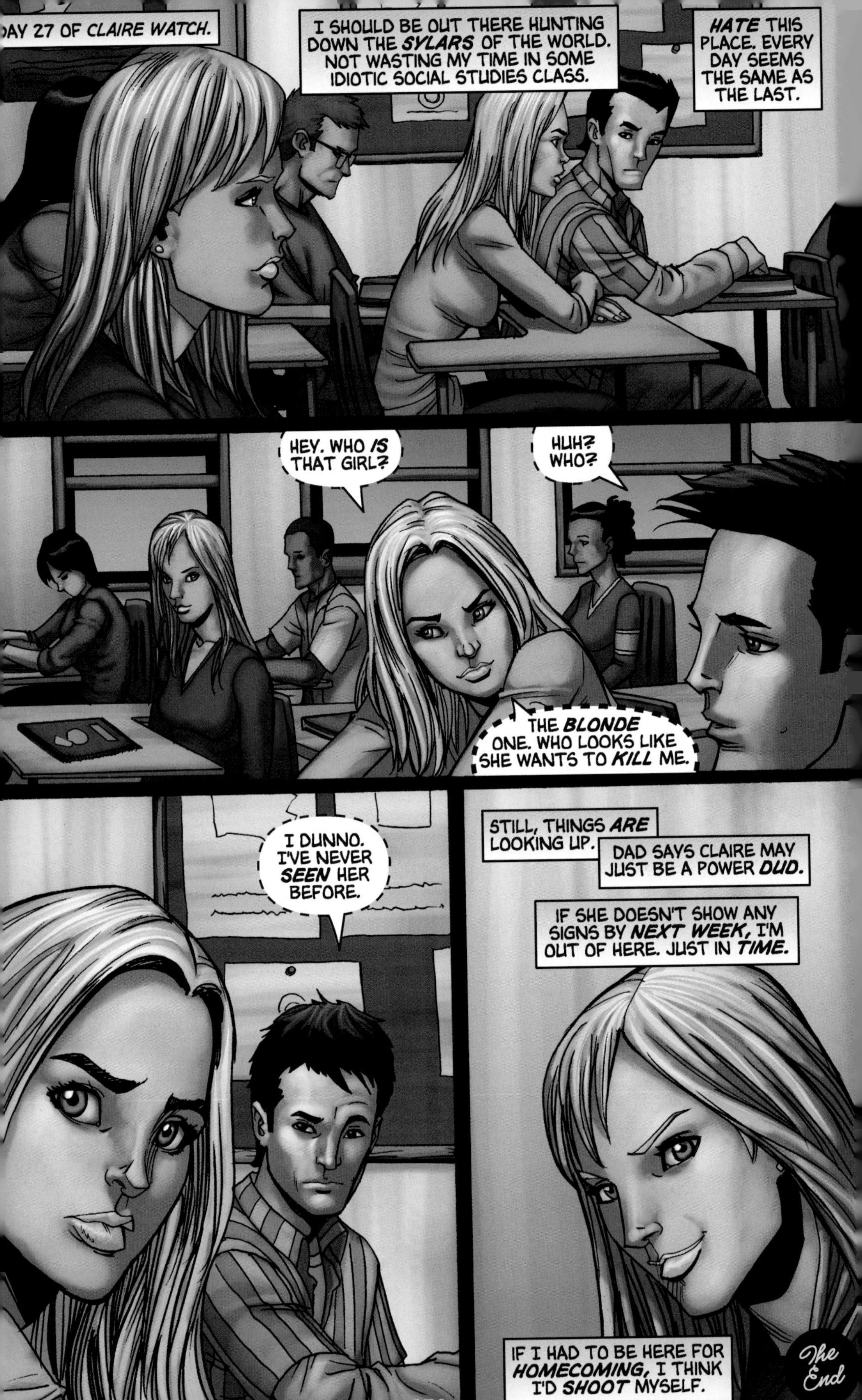
DAY 27 OF CLAIRE WATCH.
I SHOULD BE OUT THERE HUNTING DOWN THE SYLARS OF THE WORLD. NOT WASTING MY TIME IN SOME IDIOTIC SOCIAL STUDIES CLASS.
HATE THIS PLACE. EVERY DAY SEEMS THE SAME AS THE LAST.
HEY. WHO IS THAT GIRL?
HUH? WHO?
THE BLONDE ONE. WHO LOOKS LIKE SHE WANTS TO KILL ME.
I DUNNO. I'VE NEVER SEEN HER BEFORE.
STILL, THINGS ARE LOOKING UP.
DAD SAYS CLAIRE MAY JUST BE A POWER DUD.
IF SHE DOESN'T SHOW ANY SIGNS BY NEXT WEEK, I'M OUT OF HERE. JUST IN TIME.
IF I HAD TO BE HERE FOR HOMECOMING, I THINK I'D SHOOT MYSELF.
The End

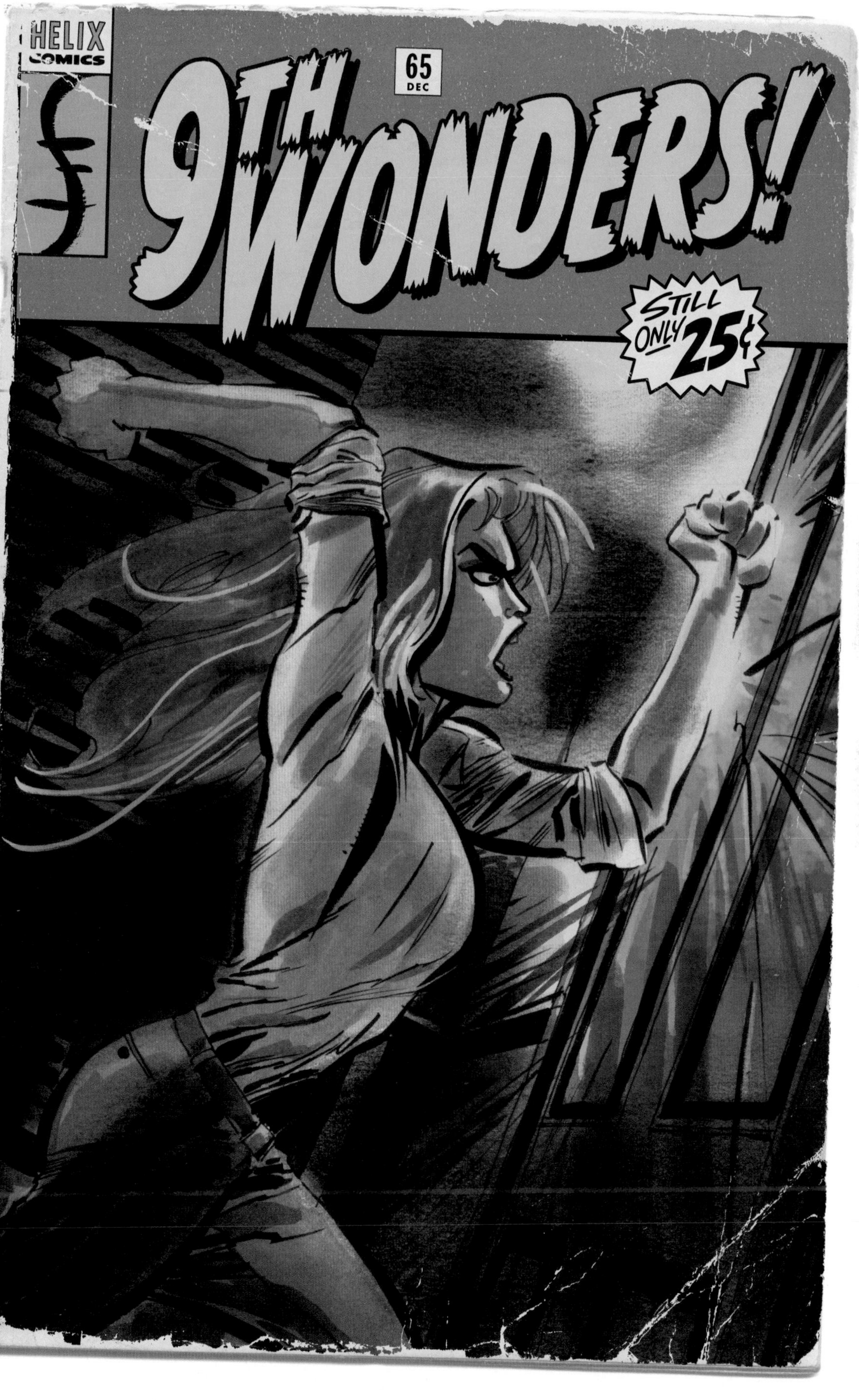
HELIX COMICS
65
DEC
9TH WONDERS!
STILL ONLY 25¢

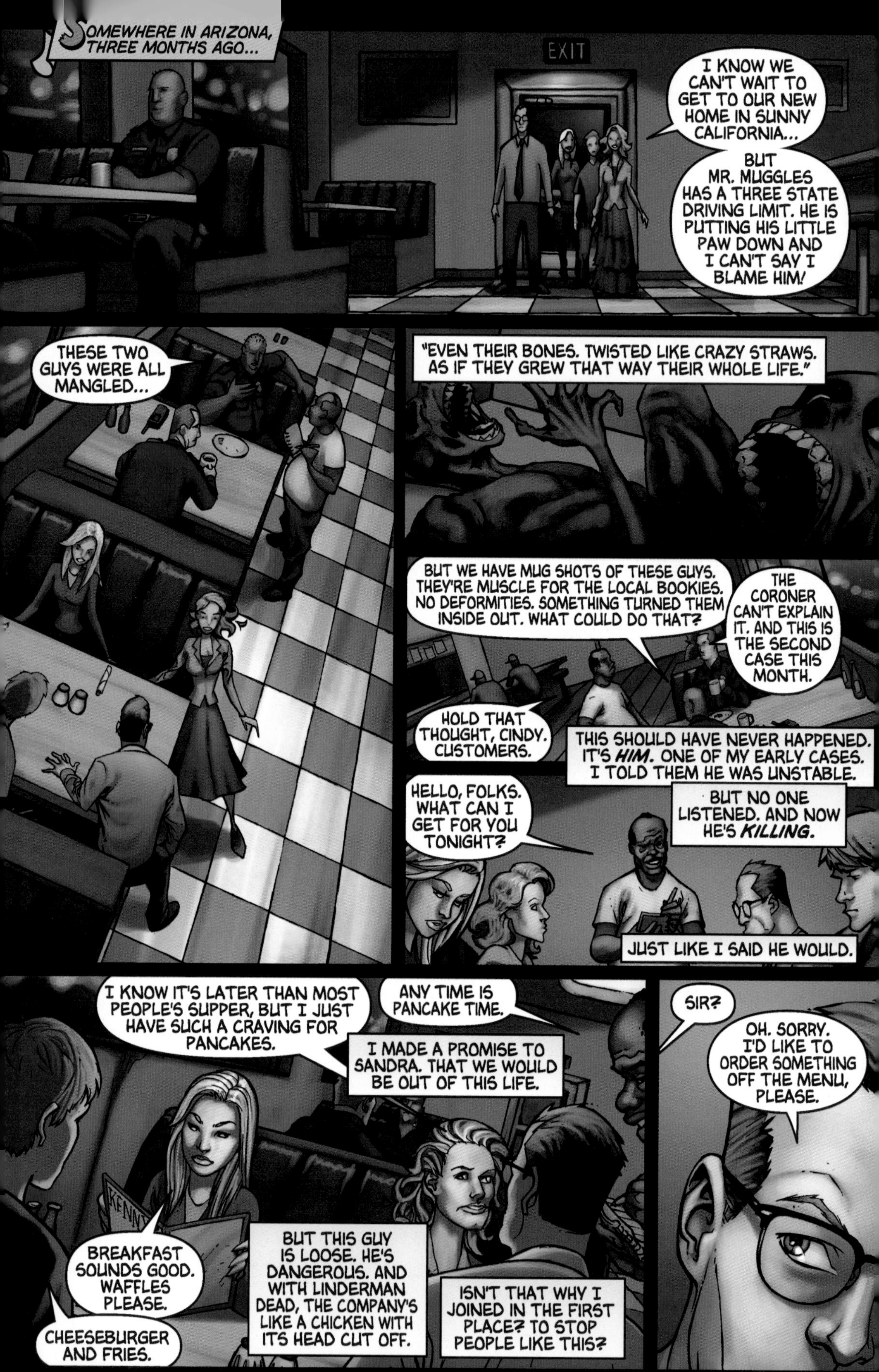
SOMEWHERE IN ARIZONA, THREE MONTHS AGO...
EXIT
I KNOW WE CAN'T WAIT TO GET TO OUR NEW HOME IN SUNNY CALIFORNIA...
BUT MR. MUGGLES HAS A THREE STATE DRIVING LIMIT. HE IS PUTTING HIS LITTLE PAW DOWN AND I CAN'T SAY I BLAME HIM!
THESE TWO GUYS WERE ALL MANGLED...
"EVEN THEIR BONES. TWISTED LIKE CRAZY STRAWS. AS IF THEY GREW THAT WAY THEIR WHOLE LIFE."
BUT WE HAVE MUG SHOTS OF THESE GUYS. THEY'RE MUSCLE FOR THE LOCAL BOOKIES. NO DEFORMITIES. SOMETHING TURNED THEM INSIDE OUT. WHAT COULD DO THAT?
THE CORONER CAN'T EXPLAIN IT. AND THIS IS THE SECOND CASE THIS MONTH.
HOLD THAT THOUGHT, CINDY. CUSTOMERS.
THIS SHOULD HAVE NEVER HAPPENED. IT'S HIM. ONE OF MY EARLY CASES. I TOLD THEM HE WAS UNSTABLE.
HELLO, FOLKS. WHAT CAN I GET FOR YOU TONIGHT?
BUT NO ONE LISTENED. AND NOW HE'S KILLING.
JUST LIKE I SAID HE WOULD.
I KNOW IT'S LATER THAN MOST PEOPLE'S SUPPER, BUT I JUST HAVE SUCH A CRAVING FOR PANCAKES.
ANY TIME IS PANCAKE TIME.
I MADE A PROMISE TO SANDRA. THAT WE WOULD BE OUT OF THIS LIFE.
SIR?
OH. SORRY. I'D LIKE TO ORDER SOMETHING OFF THE MENU, PLEASE.
BREAKFAST SOUNDS GOOD. WAFFLES PLEASE.
CHEESEBURGER AND FRIES.
BUT THIS GUY IS LOOSE. HE'S DANGEROUS. AND WITH LINDERMAN DEAD, THE COMPANY'S LIKE A CHICKEN WITH ITS HEAD CUT OFF.
ISN'T THAT WHY I JOINED IN THE FIRST PLACE? TO STOP PEOPLE LIKE THIS?

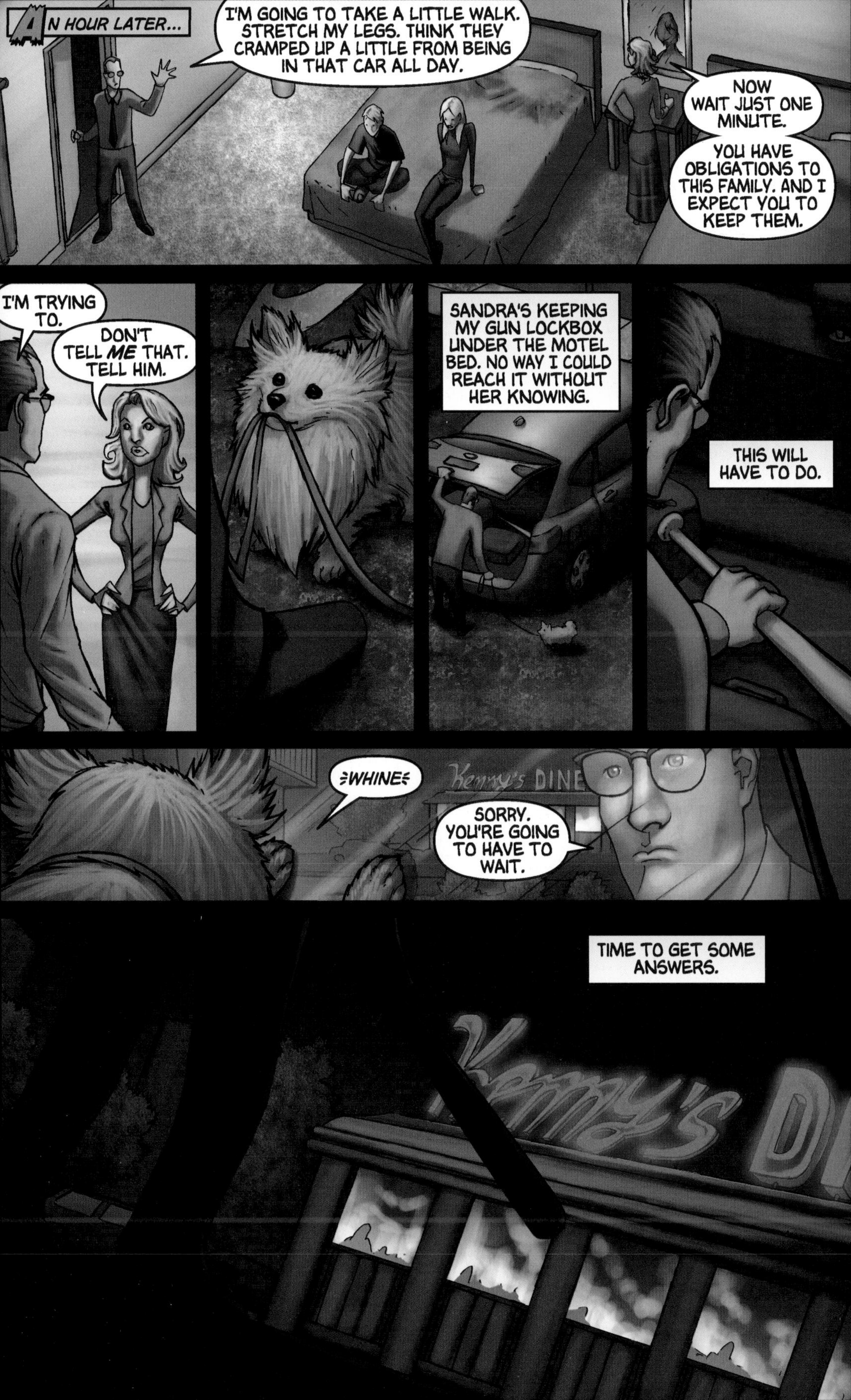
AN HOUR LATER...
I'M GOING TO TAKE A LITTLE WALK. STRETCH MY LEGS. THINK THEY CRAMPED UP A LITTLE FROM BEING IN THAT CAR ALL DAY.
NOW WAIT JUST ONE MINUTE.
YOU HAVE OBLIGATIONS TO THIS FAMILY. AND I EXPECT YOU TO KEEP THEM.
I'M TRYING TO.
DON'T TELL ME THAT. TELL HIM.
SANDRA'S KEEPING MY GUN LOCKBOX UNDER THE MOTEL BED. NO WAY I COULD REACH IT WITHOUT HER KNOWING.
THIS WILL HAVE TO DO.
WHINE
SORRY. YOU'RE GOING TO HAVE TO WAIT.
TIME TO GET SOME ANSWERS.

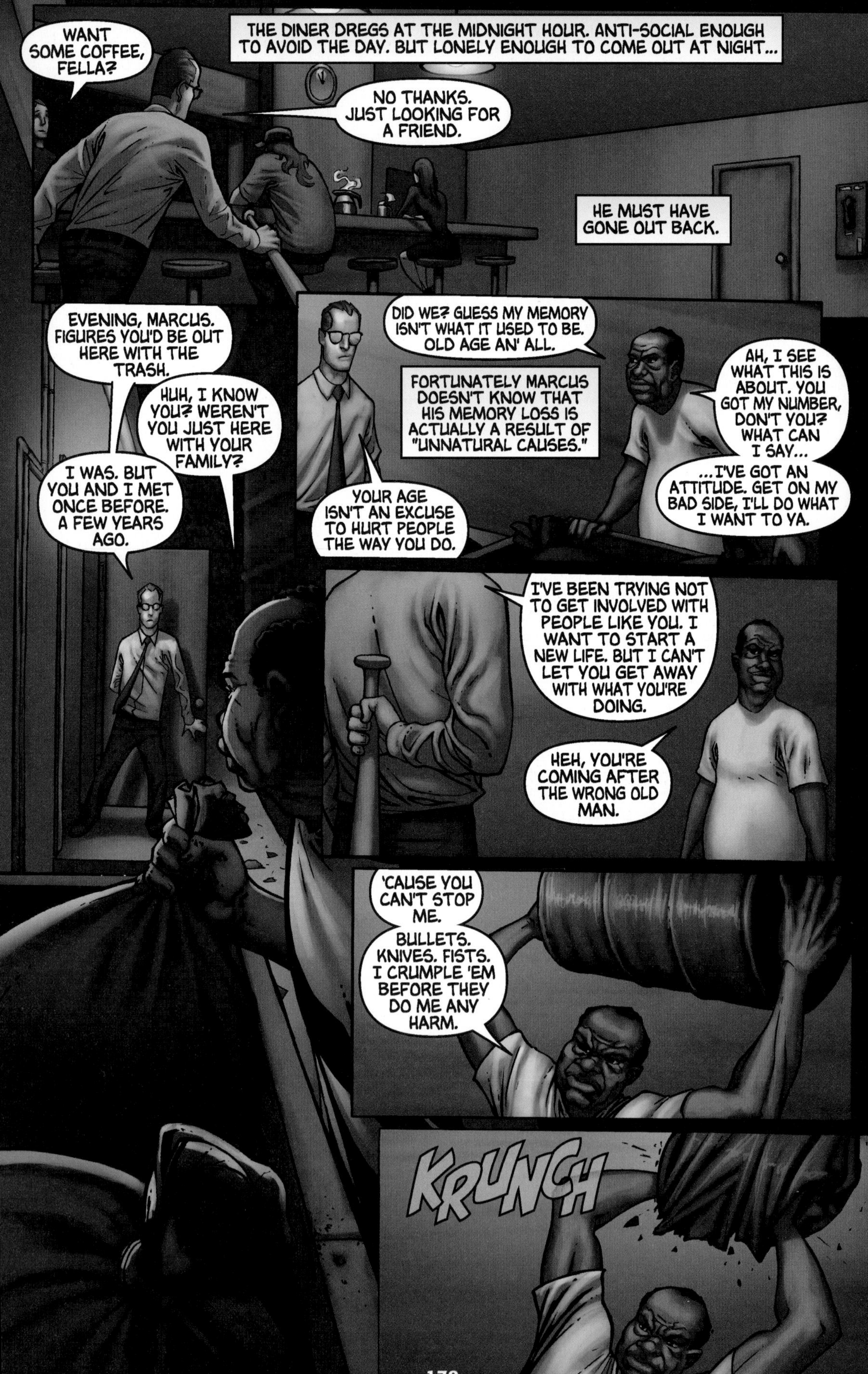
WANT SOME COFFEE, FELLA?
THE DINER DREGS AT THE MIDNIGHT HOUR. ANTI-SOCIAL ENOUGH TO AVOID THE DAY. BUT LONELY ENOUGH TO COME OUT AT NIGHT...
NO THANKS. JUST LOOKING FOR A FRIEND.
HE MUST HAVE GONE OUT BACK.
EVENING, MARCUS. FIGURES YOU'D BE OUT HERE WITH THE TRASH.
HUH, I KNOW YOU? WEREN'T YOU JUST HERE WITH YOUR FAMILY?
I WAS. BUT YOU AND I MET ONCE BEFORE. A FEW YEARS AGO.
DID WE? GUESS MY MEMORY ISN'T WHAT IT USED TO BE. OLD AGE AN' ALL.
FORTUNATELY MARCUS DOESN'T KNOW THAT HIS MEMORY LOSS IS ACTUALLY A RESULT OF "UNNATURAL CAUSES."
YOUR AGE ISN'T AN EXCUSE TO HURT PEOPLE THE WAY YOU DO.
AH, I SEE WHAT THIS IS ABOUT. YOU GOT MY NUMBER, DON'T YOU? WHAT CAN I SAY...
...I'VE GOT AN ATTITUDE. GET ON MY BAD SIDE, I'LL DO WHAT I WANT TO YA.
I'VE BEEN TRYING NOT TO GET INVOLVED WITH PEOPLE LIKE YOU. I WANT TO START A NEW LIFE. BUT I CAN'T LET YOU GET AWAY WITH WHAT YOU'RE DOING.
HEH, YOU'RE COMING AFTER THE WRONG OLD MAN.
'CAUSE YOU CAN'T STOP ME.
BULLETS. KNIVES. FISTS. I CRUMPLE 'EM BEFORE THEY DO ME ANY HARM.
KRUNCH

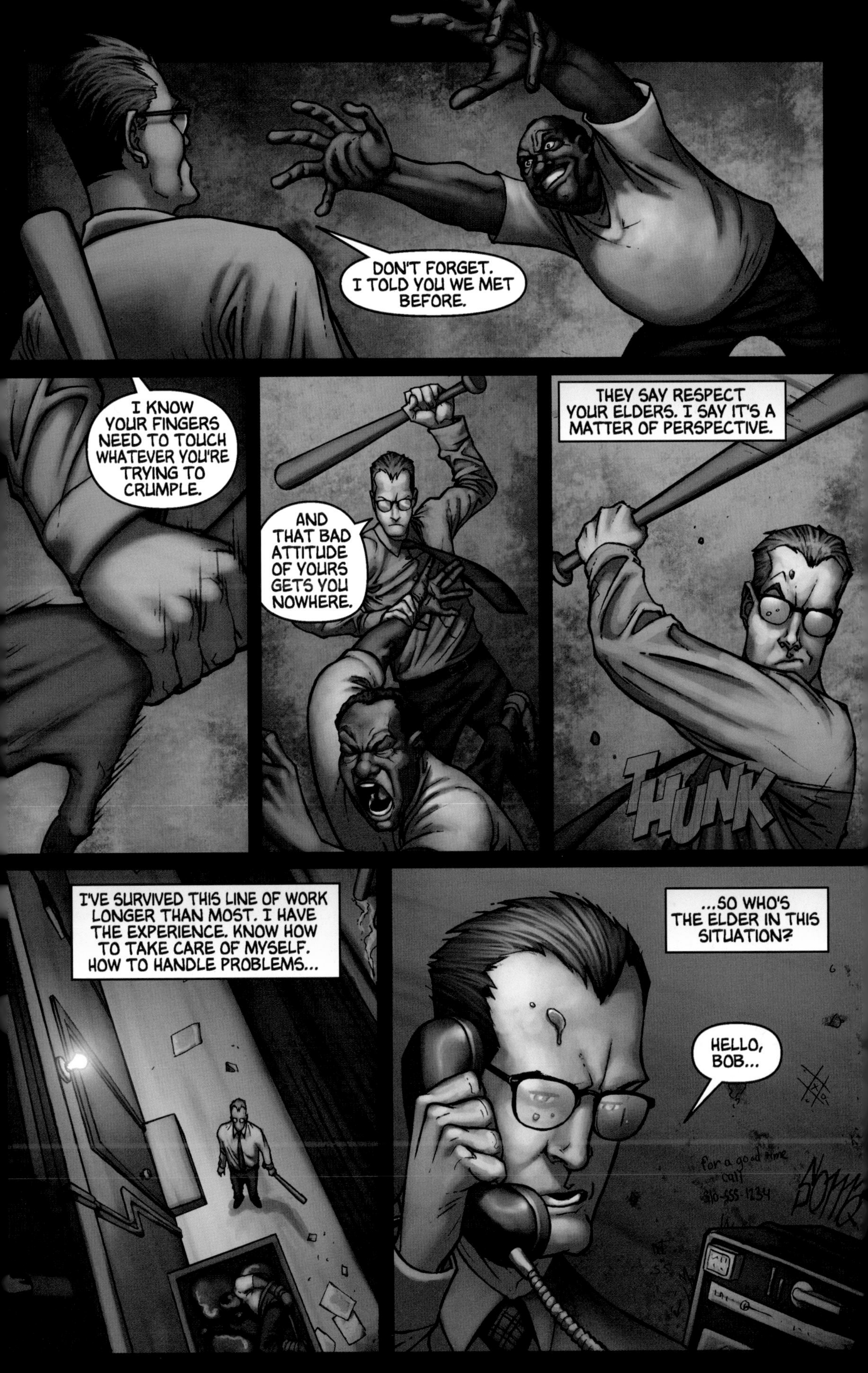
DON'T FORGET. I TOLD YOU WE MET BEFORE.
I KNOW YOUR FINGERS NEED TO TOUCH WHATEVER YOU'RE TRYING TO CRUMPLE.
AND THAT BAD ATTITUDE OF YOURS GETS YOU NOWHERE.
THEY SAY RESPECT YOUR ELDERS. I SAY IT'S A MATTER OF PERSPECTIVE.
THUNK
I'VE SURVIVED THIS LINE OF WORK LONGER THAN MOST. I HAVE THE EXPERIENCE. KNOW HOW TO TAKE CARE OF MYSELF. HOW TO HANDLE PROBLEMS...
...SO WHO'S THE ELDER IN THIS SITUATION?
HELLO, BOB...
For a good time call 310-555-1234

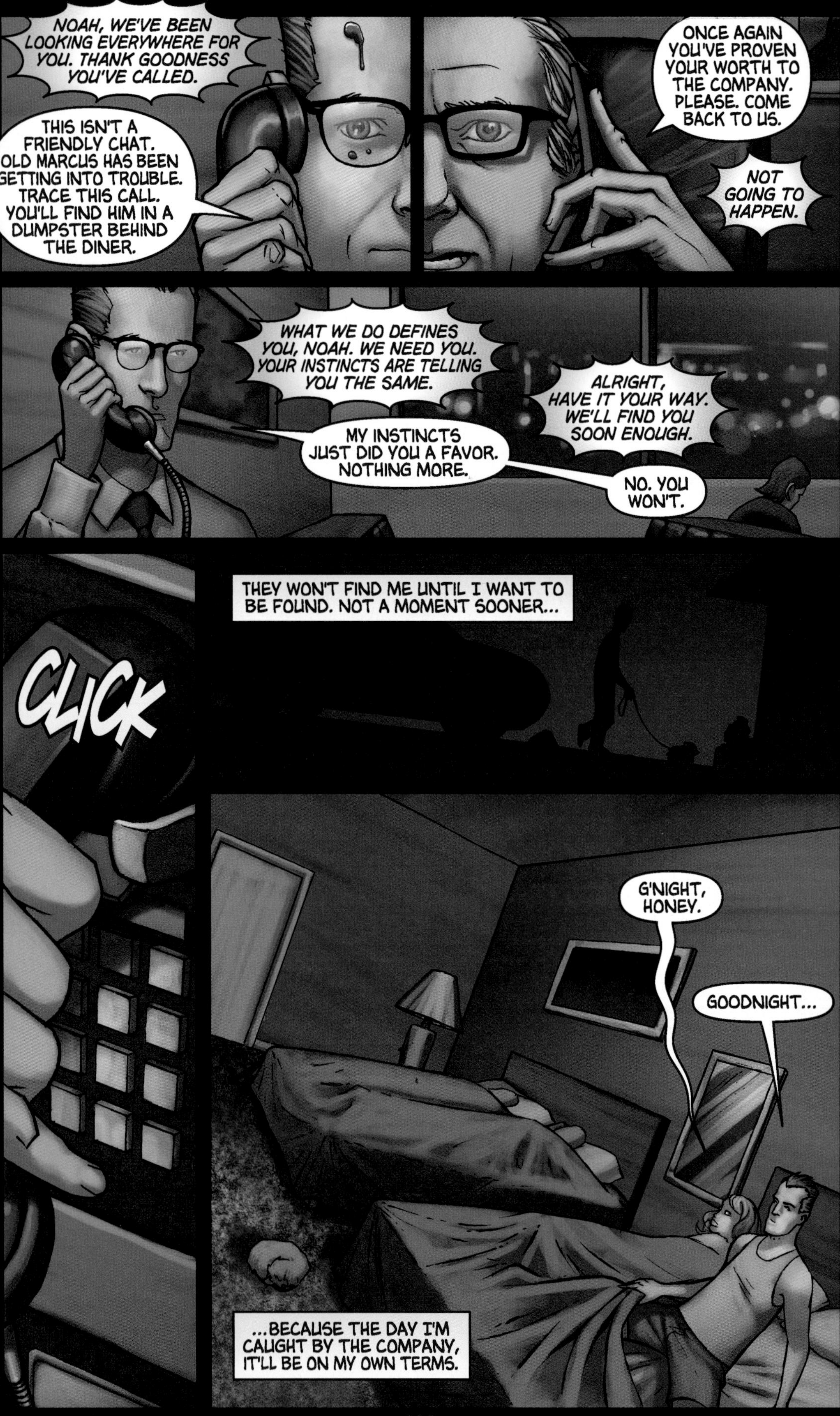
NOAH, WE'VE BEEN LOOKING EVERYWHERE FOR YOU. THANK GOODNESS YOU'VE CALLED.
THIS ISN'T A FRIENDLY CHAT. OLD MARCUS HAS BEEN GETTING INTO TROUBLE. TRACE THIS CALL. YOU'LL FIND HIM IN A DUMPSTER BEHIND THE DINER.
ONCE AGAIN YOU'VE PROVEN YOUR WORTH TO THE COMPANY. PLEASE. COME BACK TO US.
NOT GOING TO HAPPEN.
WHAT WE DO DEFINES YOU, NOAH. WE NEED YOU. YOUR INSTINCTS ARE TELLING YOU THE SAME.
MY INSTINCTS JUST DID YOU A FAVOR. NOTHING MORE.
ALRIGHT, HAVE IT YOUR WAY. WE'LL FIND YOU SOON ENOUGH.
NO. YOU WON'T.
CLICK
THEY WON'T FIND ME UNTIL I WANT TO BE FOUND. NOT A MOMENT SOONER...
G'NIGHT, HONEY.
GOODNIGHT...
...BECAUSE THE DAY I'M CAUGHT BY THE COMPANY, IT'LL BE ON MY OWN TERMS.

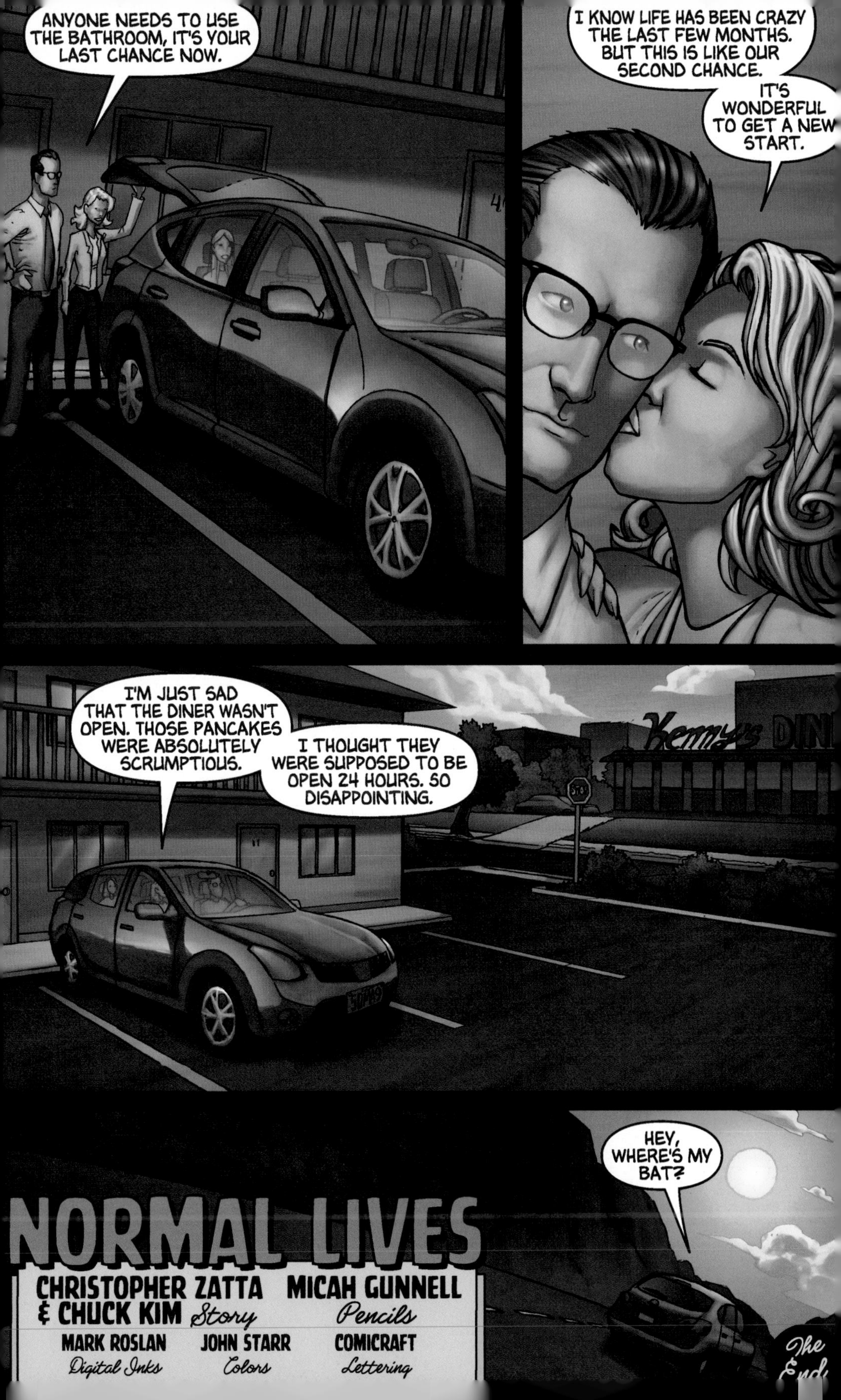
ANYONE NEEDS TO USE THE BATHROOM, IT'S YOUR LAST CHANCE NOW.
I KNOW LIFE HAS BEEN CRAZY THE LAST FEW MONTHS. BUT THIS IS LIKE OUR SECOND CHANCE.
IT'S WONDERFUL TO GET A NEW START.
I'M JUST SAD THAT THE DINER WASN'T OPEN. THOSE PANCAKES WERE ABSOLUTELY SCRUMPTIOUS.
I THOUGHT THEY WERE SUPPOSED TO BE OPEN 24 HOURS. SO DISAPPOINTING.
HEY, WHERE'S MY BAT?
NORMAL LIVES
CHRISTOPHER ZATTA & CHUCK KIM Story
MICAH GUNNELL Pencils
MARK ROSLAN Digital Inks
JOHN STARR Colors
COMICRAFT Lettering

KINGS AND QUEENS. WISE MEN AND LEADERS. PROPHETS AND WARRIORS. I'VE OUTLIVED THE GREATEST MEN AND WOMEN ON THE PLANET.

EVEN AMONG THOSE WHO COULD BEND STEEL WITH THEIR BARE HANDS. OR WIELD THE VERY ELEMENTS. I SURVIVED THEM ALL.

ALL EXCEPT *ONE.*

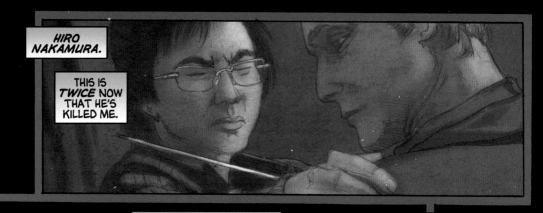

HIRO NAKAMURA.

THIS IS *TWICE* NOW THAT HE'S KILLED ME.

I'VE BEEN ON THIS EARTH FOR OVER FOUR CENTURIES.

BUT WHAT DO I HAVE TO *SHOW* FOR IT?

A FEW DOZEN *NAMES?* TAKEZO KENSEI? RICHARD SANDERS? ADAM MONROE?

WHAT GOOD IS *IMMORTALITY* WHEN YOU'RE *BURIED ALIVE?*

WHEN THE *LOVES* OF YOUR LIFE ARE ALL *DEAD AND GONE?*

The TEN BRIDES of TAKEZO KENSEI

CHUCK KIM
*Writer*

PETER STEIGERWALD
*Art & Colors*

COMICRAFT *Lettering*

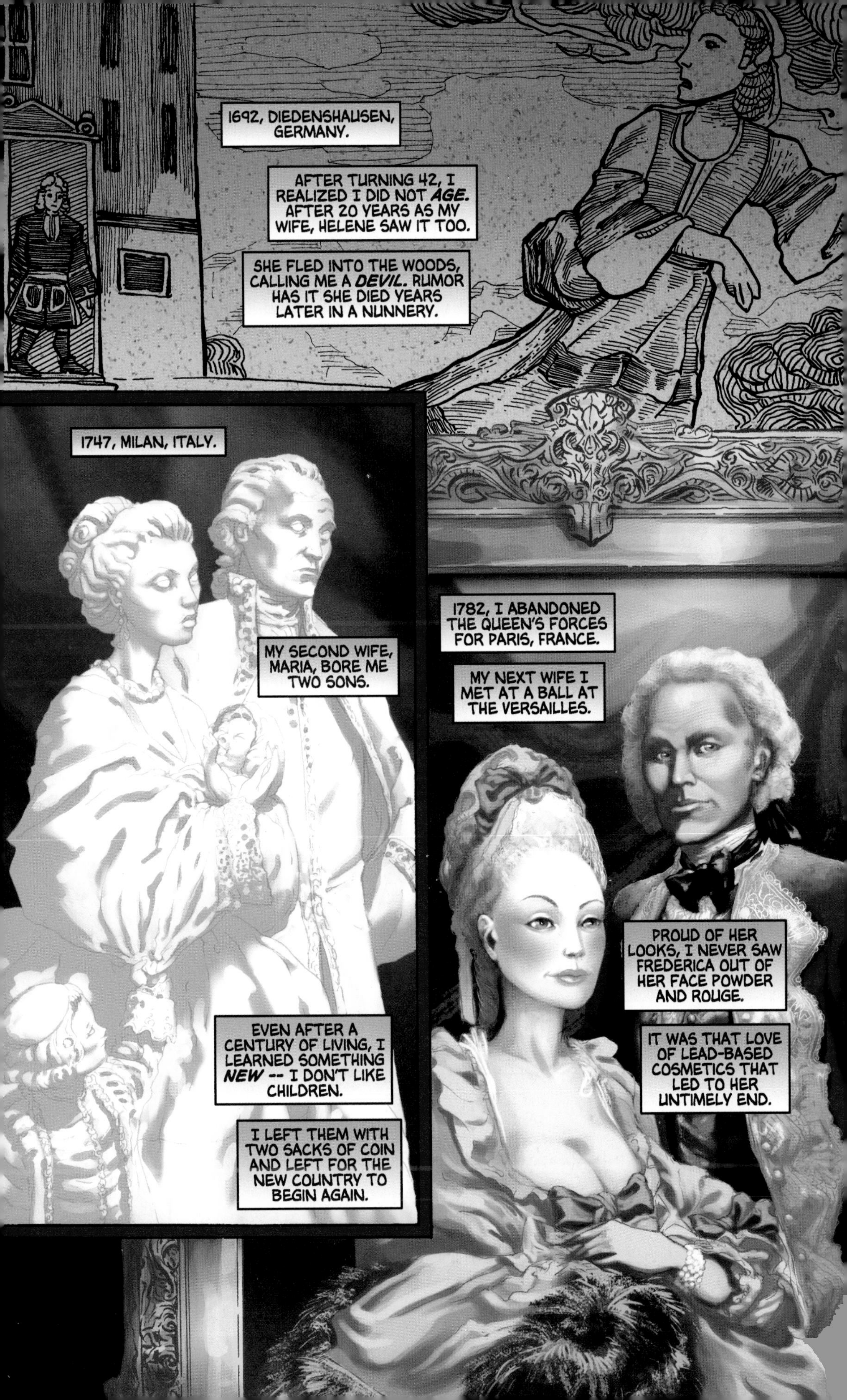

1692, DIEDENSHAUSEN, GERMANY.
AFTER TURNING 42, I REALIZED I DID NOT *AGE.* AFTER 20 YEARS AS MY WIFE, HELENE SAW IT TOO.
SHE FLED INTO THE WOODS, CALLING ME A *DEVIL.* RUMOR HAS IT SHE DIED YEARS LATER IN A NUNNERY.
1747, MILAN, ITALY.
MY SECOND WIFE, MARIA, BORE ME TWO SONS.
EVEN AFTER A CENTURY OF LIVING, I LEARNED SOMETHING *NEW* -- I DON'T LIKE CHILDREN.
I LEFT THEM WITH TWO SACKS OF COIN AND LEFT FOR THE NEW COUNTRY TO BEGIN AGAIN.
1782, I ABANDONED THE QUEEN'S FORCES FOR PARIS, FRANCE.
MY NEXT WIFE I MET AT A BALL AT THE VERSAILLES.
PROUD OF HER LOOKS, I NEVER SAW FREDERICA OUT OF HER FACE POWDER AND ROUGE.
IT WAS THAT LOVE OF LEAD-BASED COSMETICS THAT LED TO HER UNTIMELY END.

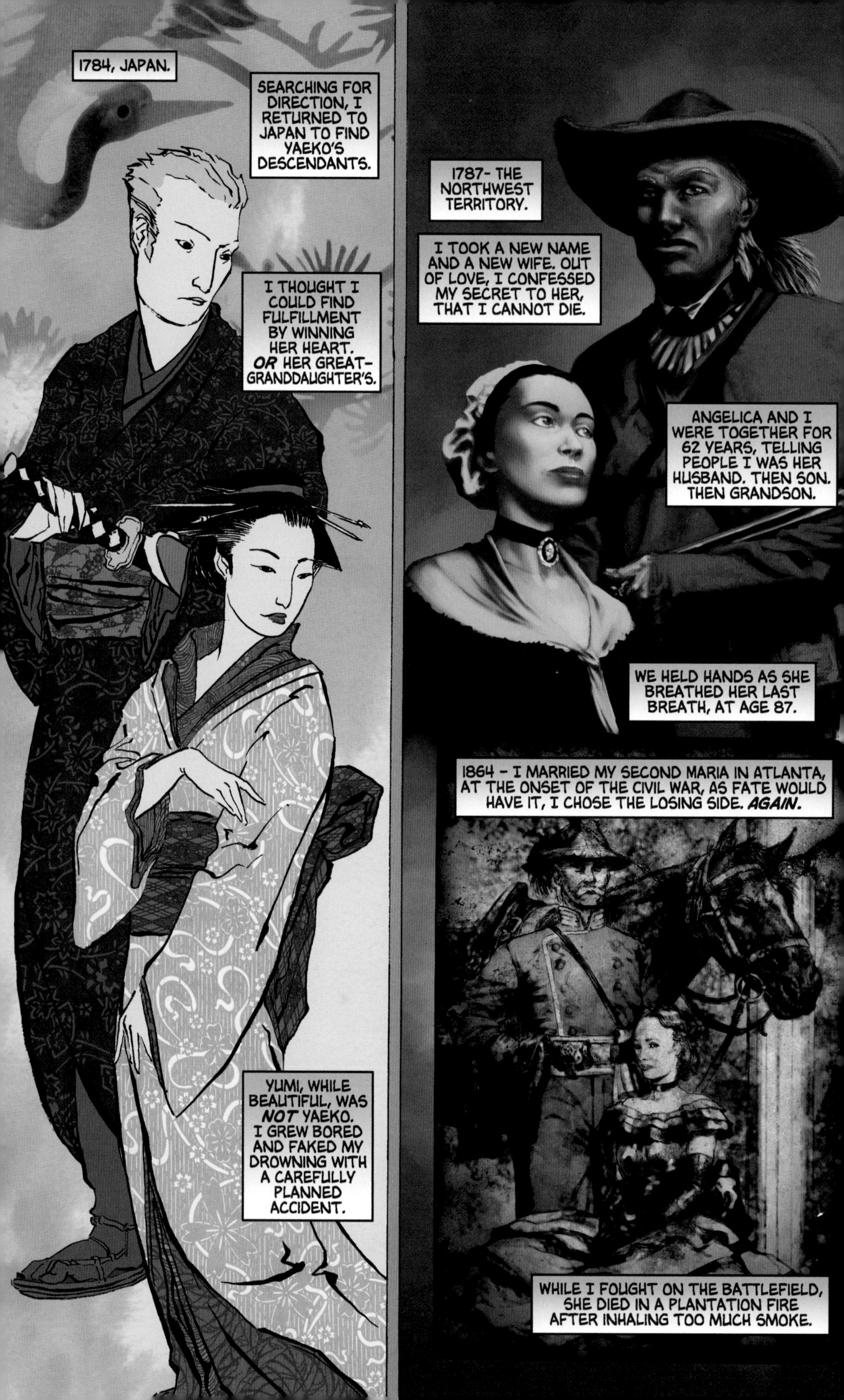
1784, JAPAN.
SEARCHING FOR DIRECTION, I RETURNED TO JAPAN TO FIND YAEKO'S DESCENDANTS.
I THOUGHT I COULD FIND FULFILLMENT BY WINNING HER HEART. **OR** HER GREAT-GRANDDAUGHTER'S.
YUMI, WHILE BEAUTIFUL, WAS **NOT** YAEKO. I GREW BORED AND FAKED MY DROWNING WITH A CAREFULLY PLANNED ACCIDENT.
1787- THE NORTHWEST TERRITORY.
I TOOK A NEW NAME AND A NEW WIFE. OUT OF LOVE, I CONFESSED MY SECRET TO HER, THAT I CANNOT DIE.
ANGELICA AND I WERE TOGETHER FOR 62 YEARS, TELLING PEOPLE I WAS HER HUSBAND. THEN SON. THEN GRANDSON.
WE HELD HANDS AS SHE BREATHED HER LAST BREATH, AT AGE 87.
1864 - I MARRIED MY SECOND MARIA IN ATLANTA, AT THE ONSET OF THE CIVIL WAR, AS FATE WOULD HAVE IT, I CHOSE THE LOSING SIDE. **AGAIN.**
WHILE I FOUGHT ON THE BATTLEFIELD, SHE DIED IN A PLANTATION FIRE AFTER INHALING TOO MUCH SMOKE.

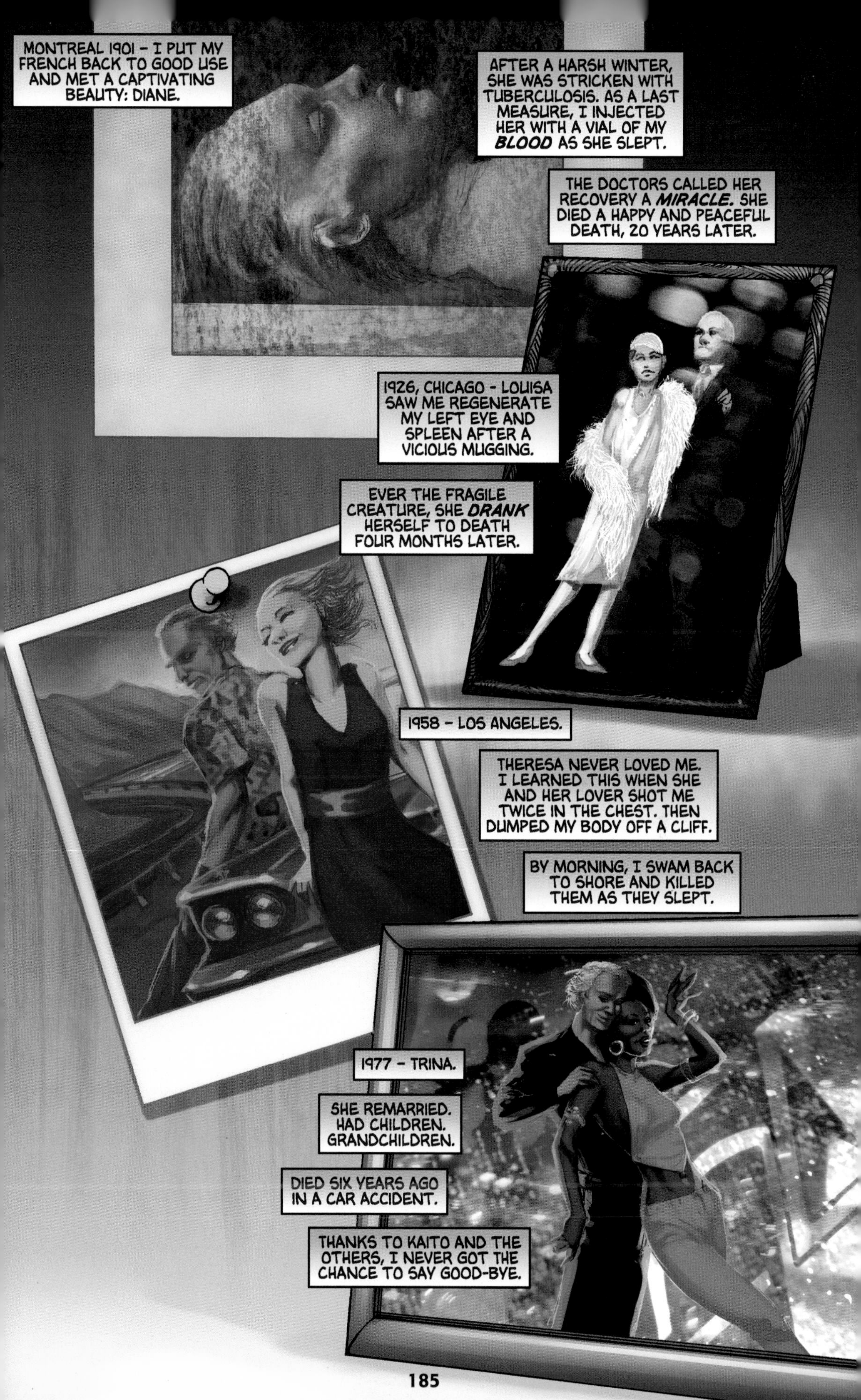
MONTREAL 1901 – I PUT MY FRENCH BACK TO GOOD USE AND MET A CAPTIVATING BEAUTY: DIANE.
AFTER A HARSH WINTER, SHE WAS STRICKEN WITH TUBERCULOSIS. AS A LAST MEASURE, I INJECTED HER WITH A VIAL OF MY *BLOOD* AS SHE SLEPT.
THE DOCTORS CALLED HER RECOVERY A *MIRACLE.* SHE DIED A HAPPY AND PEACEFUL DEATH, 20 YEARS LATER.
1926, CHICAGO – LOUISA SAW ME REGENERATE MY LEFT EYE AND SPLEEN AFTER A VICIOUS MUGGING.
EVER THE FRAGILE CREATURE, SHE *DRANK* HERSELF TO DEATH FOUR MONTHS LATER.
1958 – LOS ANGELES.
THERESA NEVER LOVED ME. I LEARNED THIS WHEN SHE AND HER LOVER SHOT ME TWICE IN THE CHEST. THEN DUMPED MY BODY OFF A CLIFF.
BY MORNING, I SWAM BACK TO SHORE AND KILLED THEM AS THEY SLEPT.
1977 – TRINA.
SHE REMARRIED. HAD CHILDREN. GRANDCHILDREN.
DIED SIX YEARS AGO IN A CAR ACCIDENT.
THANKS TO KAITO AND THE OTHERS, I NEVER GOT THE CHANCE TO SAY GOOD-BYE.

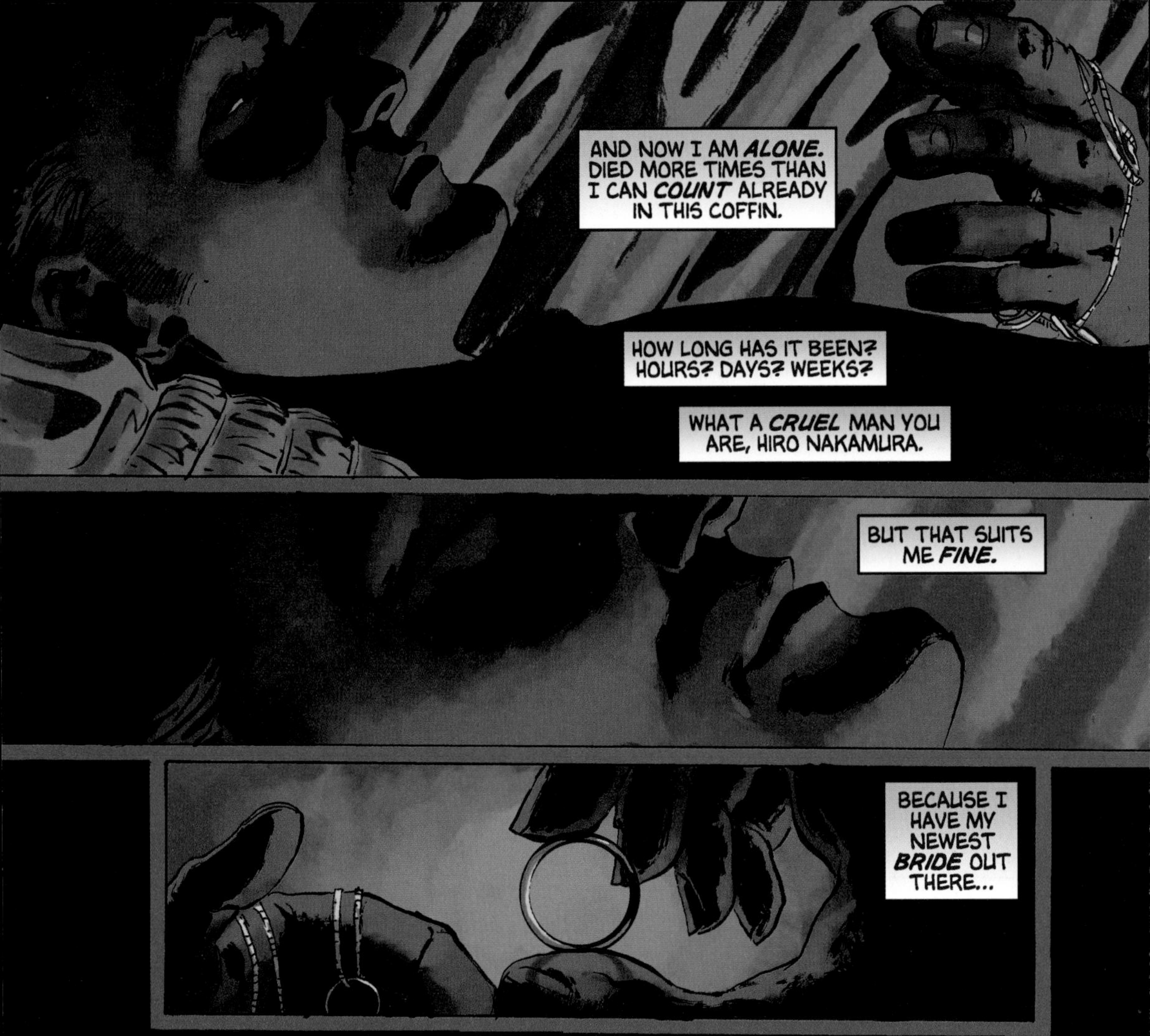
AND NOW I AM ALONE. DIED MORE TIMES THAN I CAN COUNT ALREADY IN THIS COFFIN.
HOW LONG HAS IT BEEN? HOURS? DAYS? WEEKS?
WHAT A CRUEL MAN YOU ARE, HIRO NAKAMURA.
BUT THAT SUITS ME FINE.
BECAUSE I HAVE MY NEWEST BRIDE OUT THERE...

...EARS AGO...

NAME'S *HAMPTON CONNOLLY.* SOME CALL ME "HAMP," BUT MOST CALL ME "GOOSE."

I WAS DRUCKER'S *PERSONAL PILOT.* I FLEW HIS COMPANY PLANES OVER THE MOUNTAINS *MANY* TIMES BEFORE...

...THIS WOULD BE MY *LAST.*

YOU *SURE* ABOUT THIS?

I GOT IT.

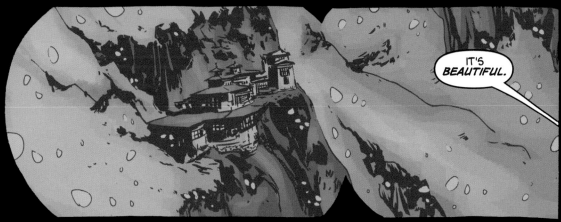

IT'S *BEAUTIFUL.*

GLAD YOU THINK SO. 'CAUSE WE'RE ABOUT TO *CRASH* THERE!

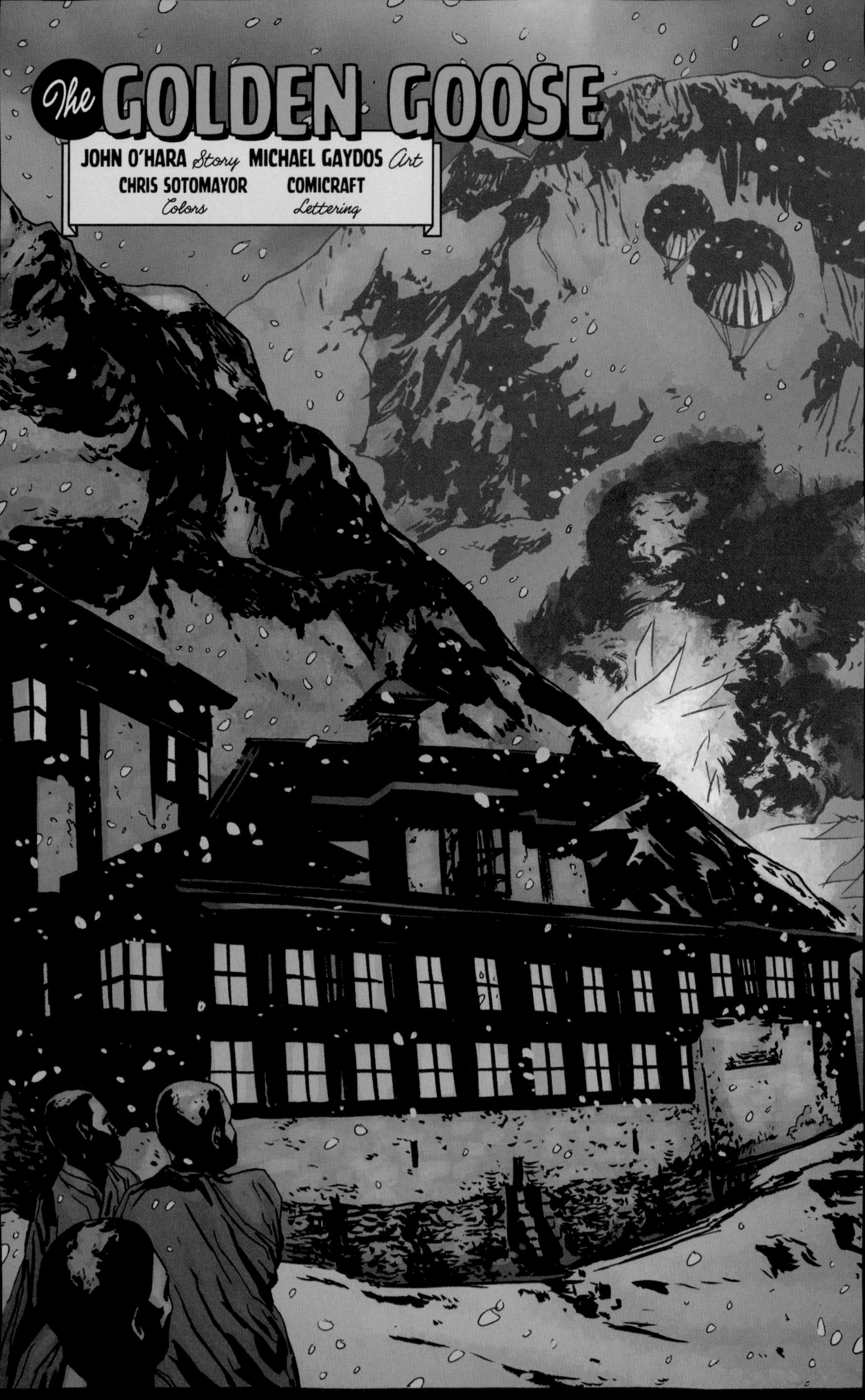
The GOLDEN GOOSE
JOHN O'HARA Story MICHAEL GAYDOS Art
CHRIS SOTOMAYOR Colors
COMICRAFT Lettering

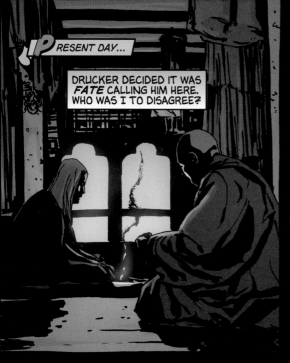

DRUCKER DECIDED IT WAS *FATE* CALLING HIM HERE. WHO WAS I TO DISAGREE?

PLUS, THE GIRLS WERE NICE AND I DIDN'T HAVE TO BE ANYWHERE. SO WE STAYED. FOR *FIFTEEN YEARS.*

I THOUGHT YOU HAD A *NO-COMPUTER* RULE HERE.

WHAT'S A RULE UNLESS YOU CAN *BREAK* IT.

*CLIK*

YOU'RE NOT *DRUCKER.*

AND I TAKE IT YOU'RE NOT MY *MASSEUSE.*

NO, I'M CERTAINLY *NOT.* WHERE IS HE?

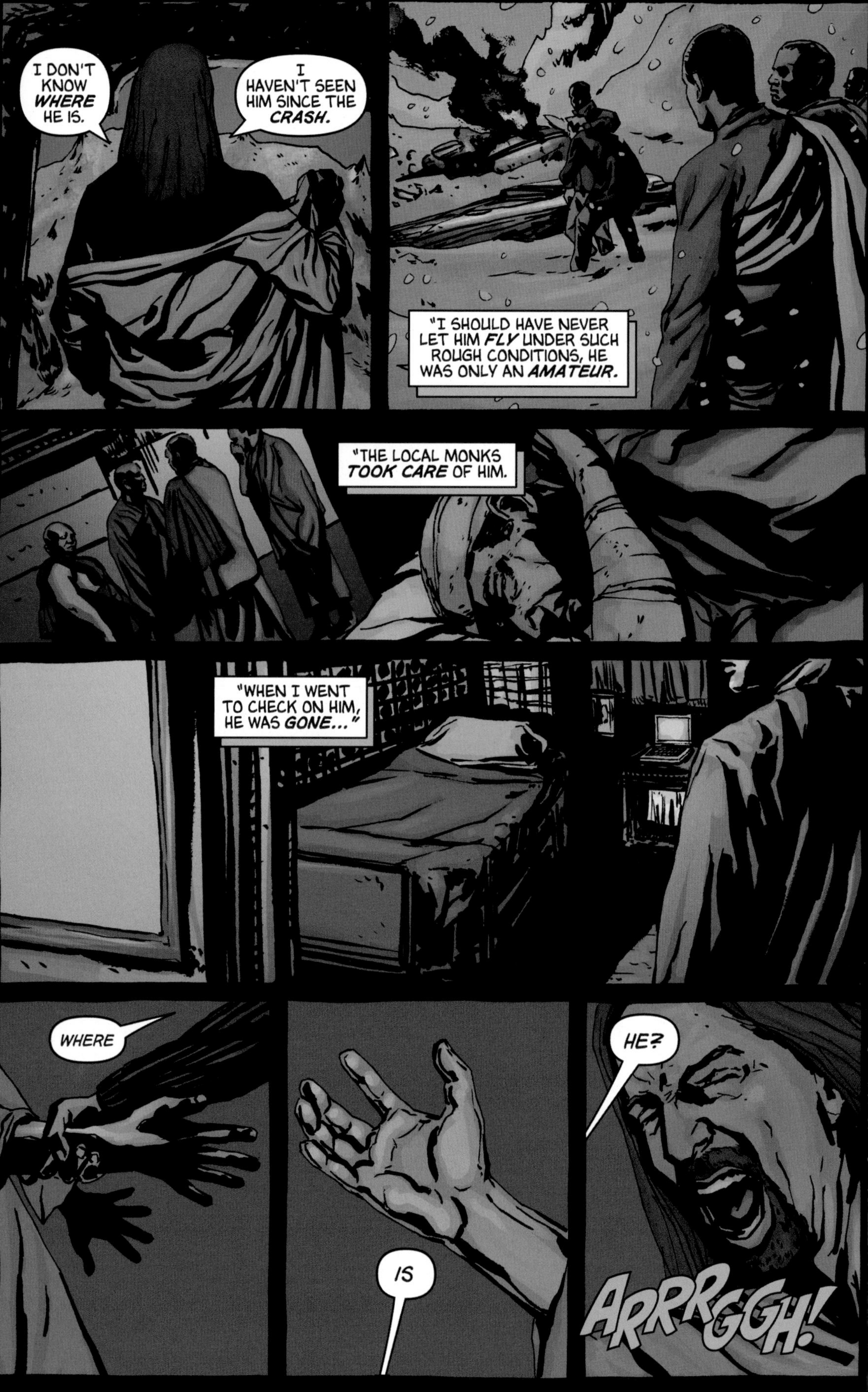
I DON'T KNOW WHERE HE IS.
I HAVEN'T SEEN HIM SINCE THE CRASH.
"I SHOULD HAVE NEVER LET HIM FLY UNDER SUCH ROUGH CONDITIONS, HE WAS ONLY AN AMATEUR.
"THE LOCAL MONKS TOOK CARE OF HIM.
"WHEN I WENT TO CHECK ON HIM, HE WAS GONE..."
WHERE
IS
HE?
ARRRGGH!

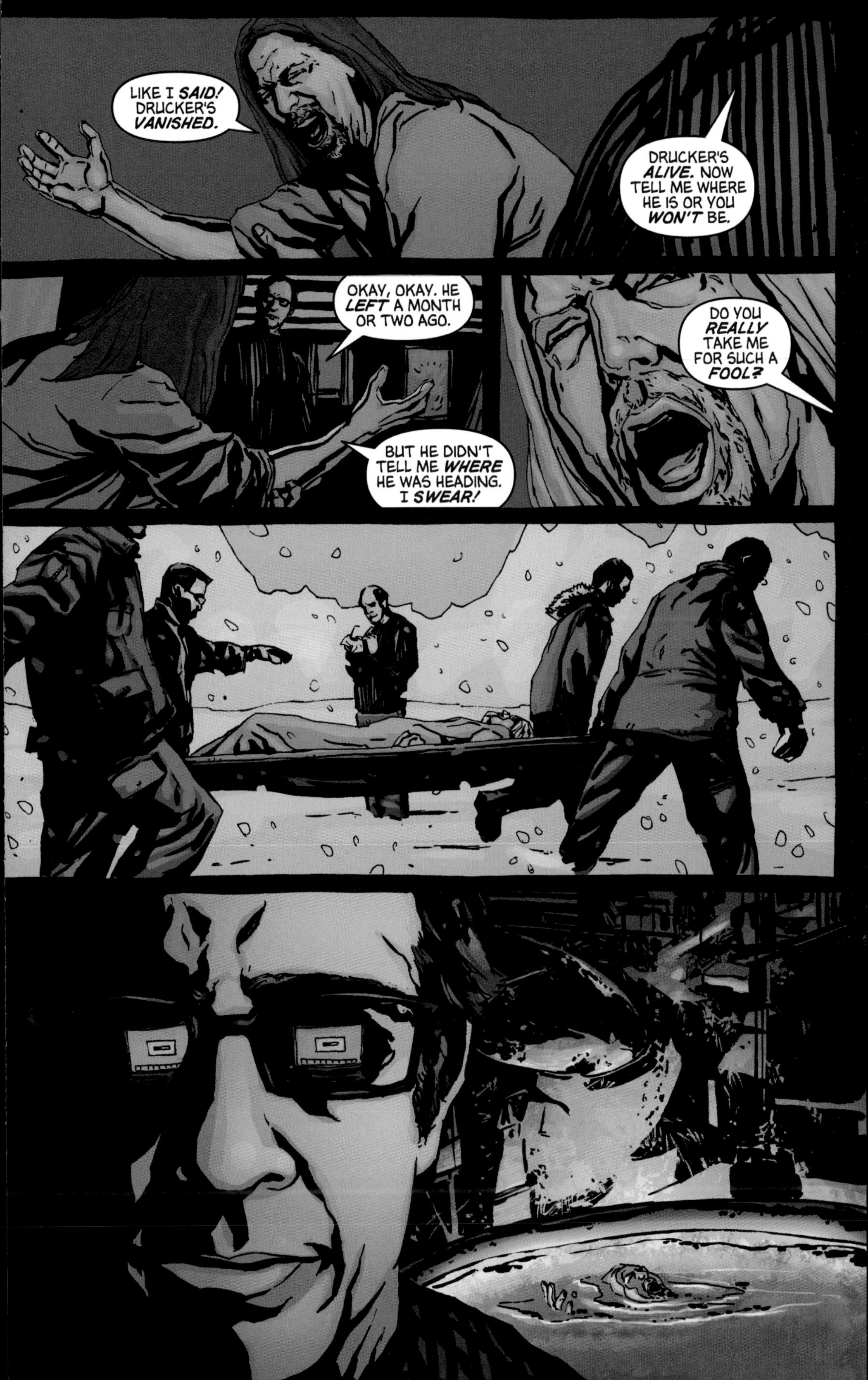
LIKE I SAID! DRUCKER'S VANISHED.
DRUCKER'S ALIVE. NOW TELL ME WHERE HE IS OR YOU WON'T BE.
OKAY, OKAY. HE LEFT A MONTH OR TWO AGO.
BUT HE DIDN'T TELL ME WHERE HE WAS HEADING. I SWEAR!
DO YOU REALLY TAKE ME FOR SUCH A FOOL?

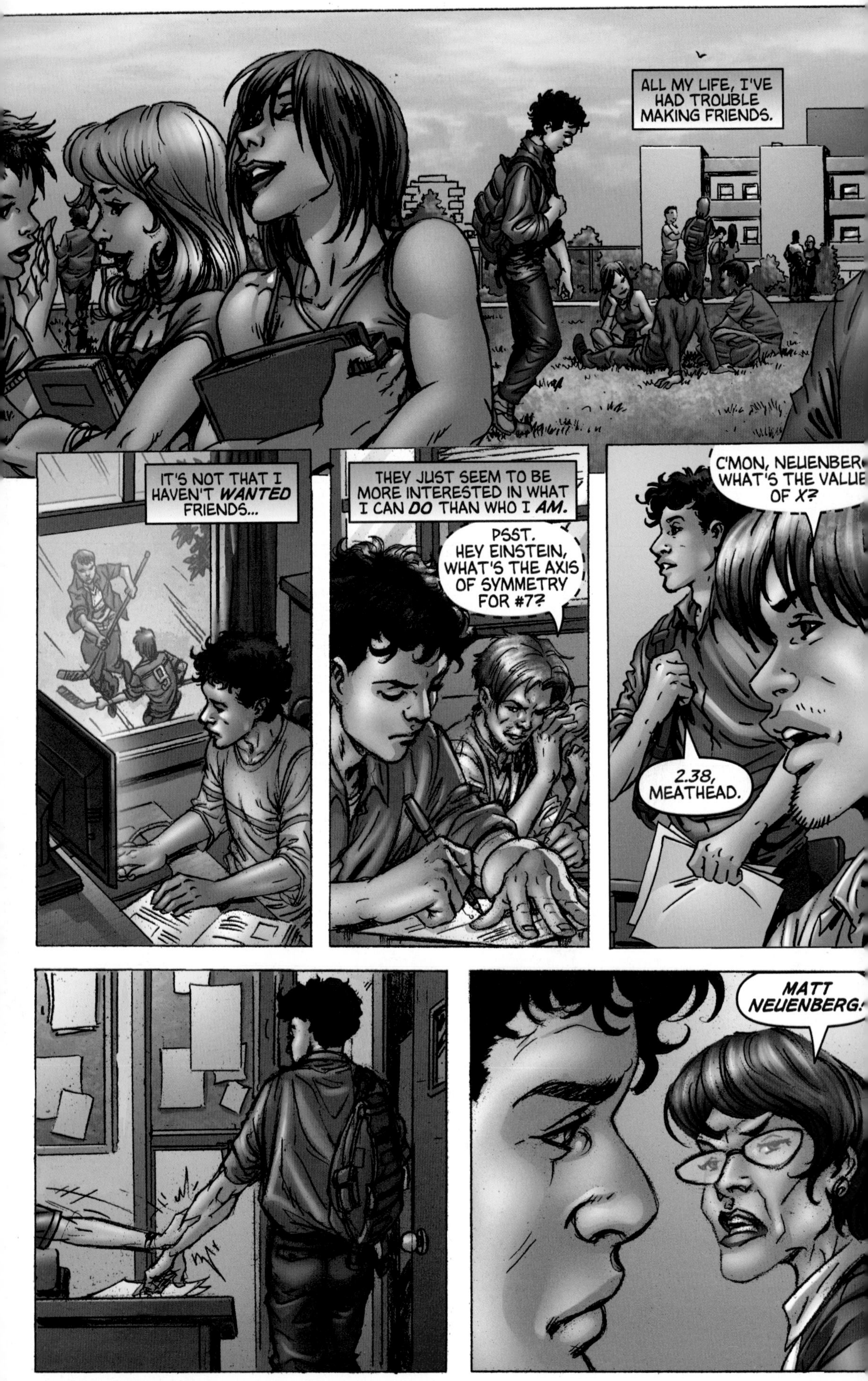
ALL MY LIFE, I'VE HAD TROUBLE MAKING FRIENDS.
IT'S NOT THAT I HAVEN'T WANTED FRIENDS...
THEY JUST SEEM TO BE MORE INTERESTED IN WHAT I CAN DO THAN WHO I AM.
PSST. HEY EINSTEIN, WHAT'S THE AXIS OF SYMMETRY FOR #7?
C'MON, NEUENBERG WHAT'S THE VALUE OF X?
2.38, MEATHEAD.
MATT NEUENBERG!

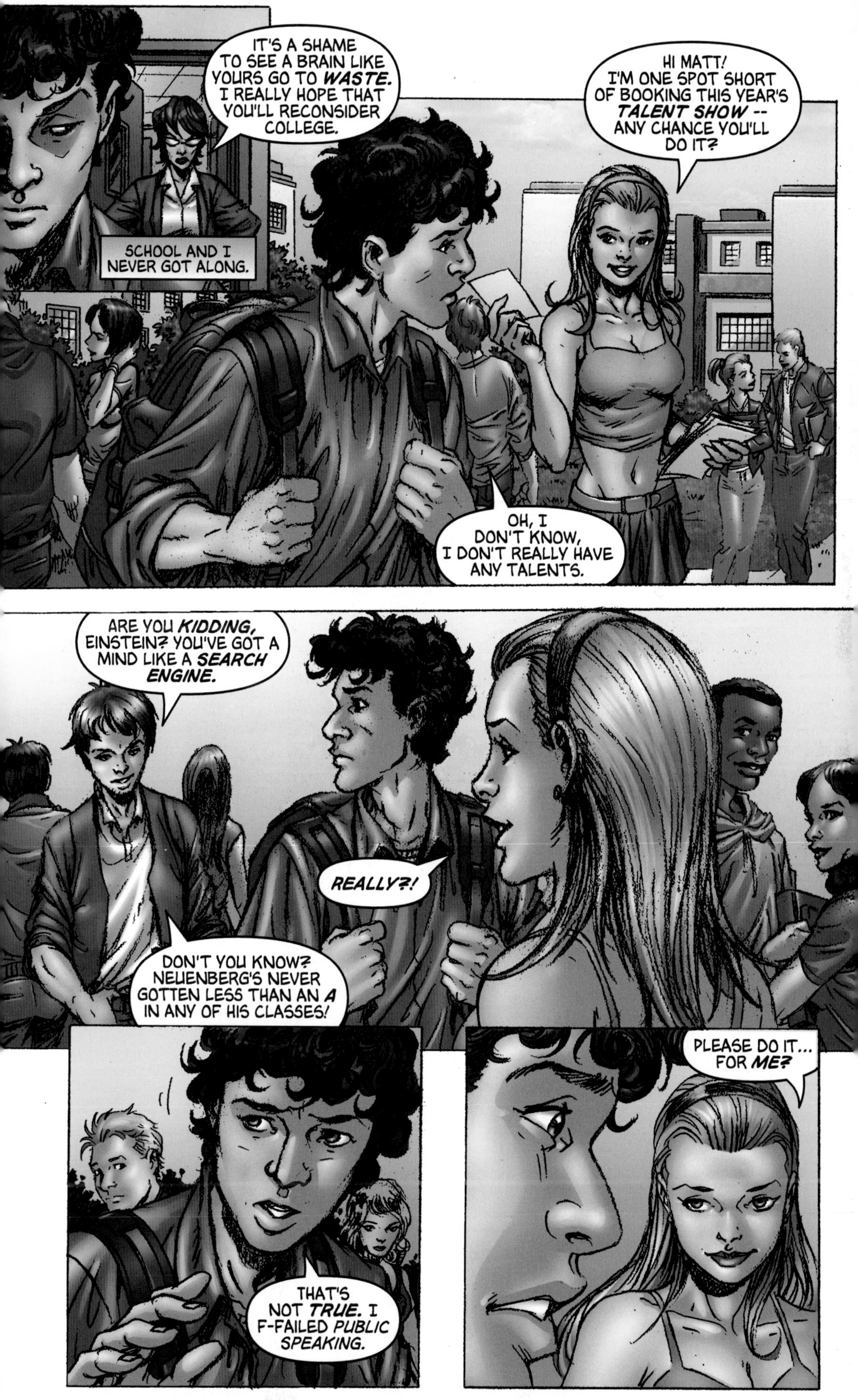
IT'S A SHAME TO SEE A BRAIN LIKE YOURS GO TO WASTE. I REALLY HOPE THAT YOU'LL RECONSIDER COLLEGE.
SCHOOL AND I NEVER GOT ALONG.
HI MATT! I'M ONE SPOT SHORT OF BOOKING THIS YEAR'S TALENT SHOW -- ANY CHANCE YOU'LL DO IT?
OH, I DON'T KNOW, I DON'T REALLY HAVE ANY TALENTS.
ARE YOU KIDDING, EINSTEIN? YOU'VE GOT A MIND LIKE A SEARCH ENGINE.
REALLY?!
DON'T YOU KNOW? NEUENBERG'S NEVER GOTTEN LESS THAN AN A IN ANY OF HIS CLASSES!
THAT'S NOT TRUE. I F-FAILED PUBLIC SPEAKING.
PLEASE DO IT... FOR ME?

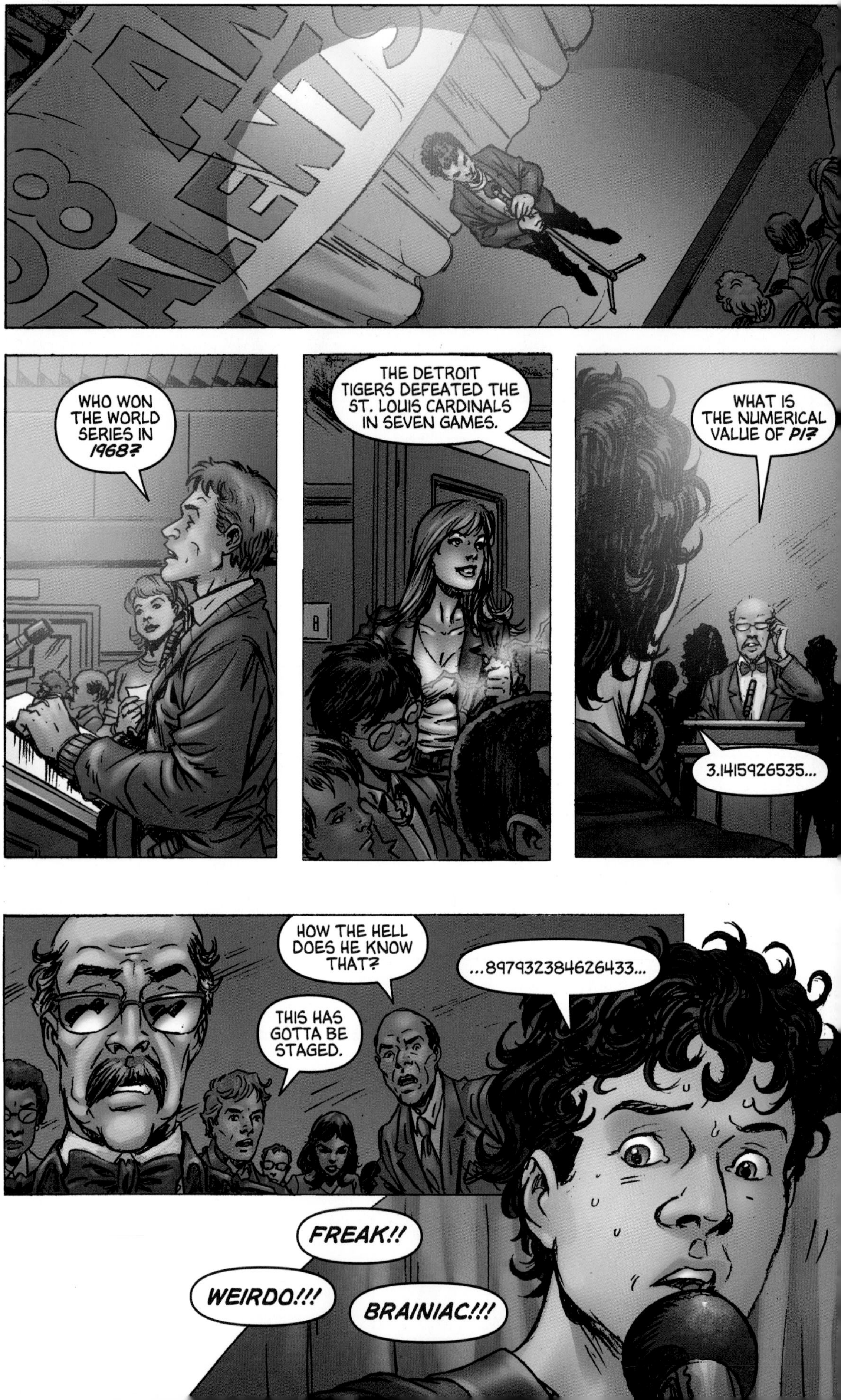
WHO WON THE WORLD SERIES IN 1968?
THE DETROIT TIGERS DEFEATED THE ST. LOUIS CARDINALS IN SEVEN GAMES.
WHAT IS THE NUMERICAL VALUE OF PI?
3.1415926535...
HOW THE HELL DOES HE KNOW THAT?
...897932384626433...
THIS HAS GOTTA BE STAGED.
FREAK!!
WEIRDO!!!
BRAINIAC!!!

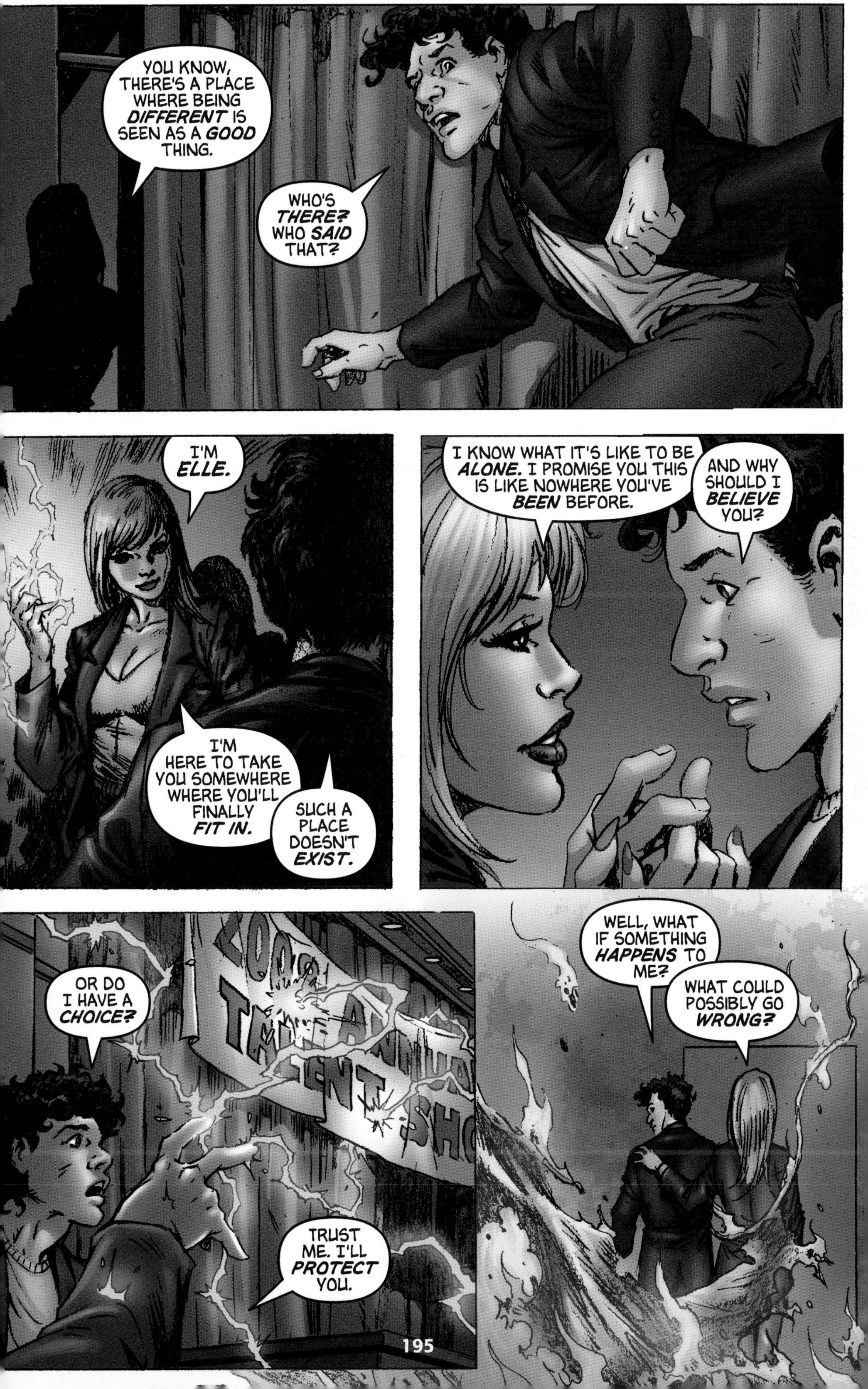
YOU KNOW, THERE'S A PLACE WHERE BEING DIFFERENT IS SEEN AS A GOOD THING.
WHO'S THERE? WHO SAID THAT?
I'M ELLE.
I'M HERE TO TAKE YOU SOMEWHERE WHERE YOU'LL FINALLY FIT IN.
SUCH A PLACE DOESN'T EXIST.
I KNOW WHAT IT'S LIKE TO BE ALONE. I PROMISE YOU THIS IS LIKE NOWHERE YOU'VE BEEN BEFORE.
AND WHY SHOULD I BELIEVE YOU?
OR DO I HAVE A CHOICE?
TRUST ME. I'LL PROTECT YOU.
WELL, WHAT IF SOMETHING HAPPENS TO ME?
WHAT COULD POSSIBLY GO WRONG?

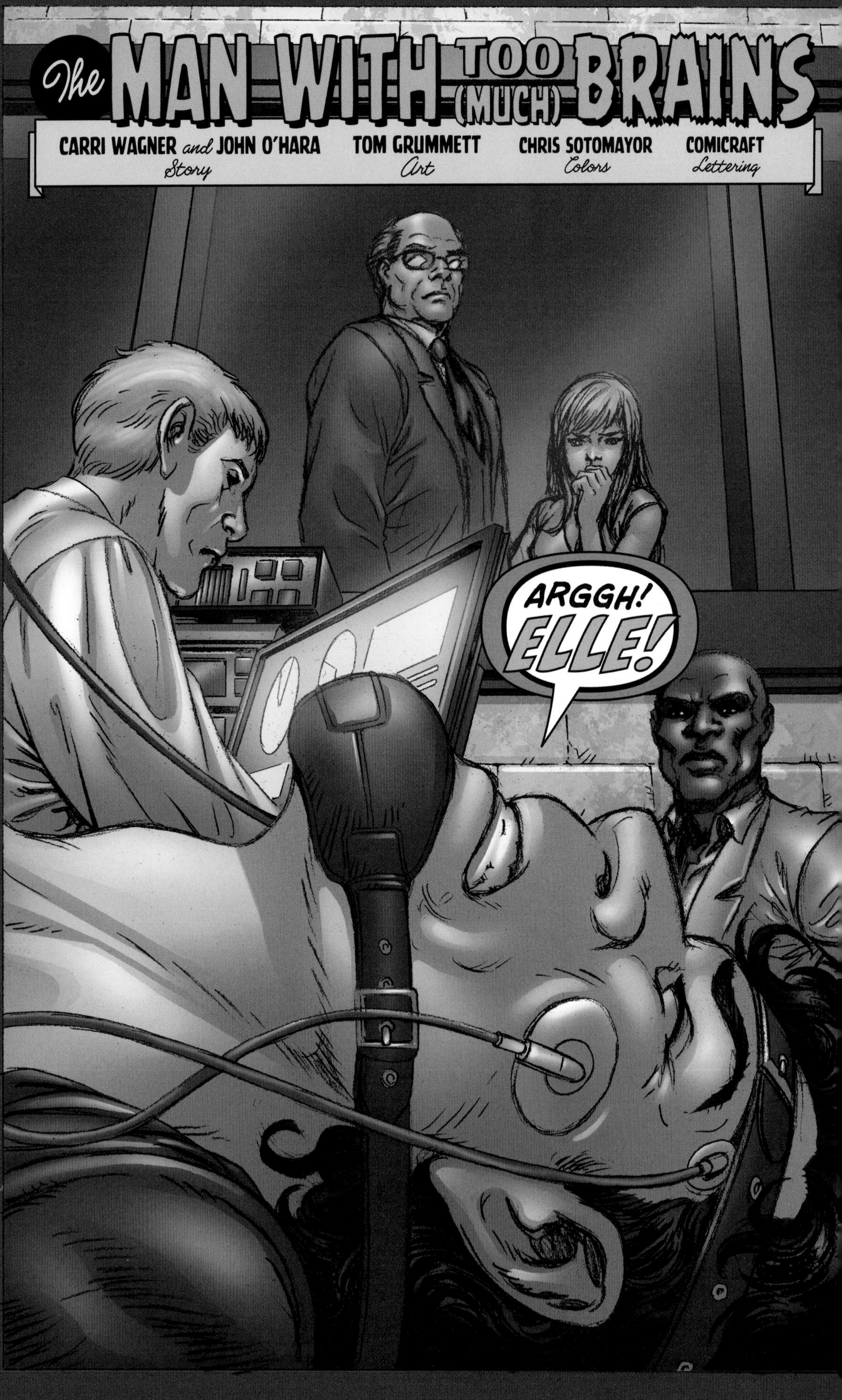
The MAN WITH TOO (MUCH) BRAINS
CARRI WAGNER and JOHN O'HARA Story
TOM GRUMMETT Art
CHRIS SOTOMAYOR Colors
COMICRAFT Lettering
ARGGH! ELLE!

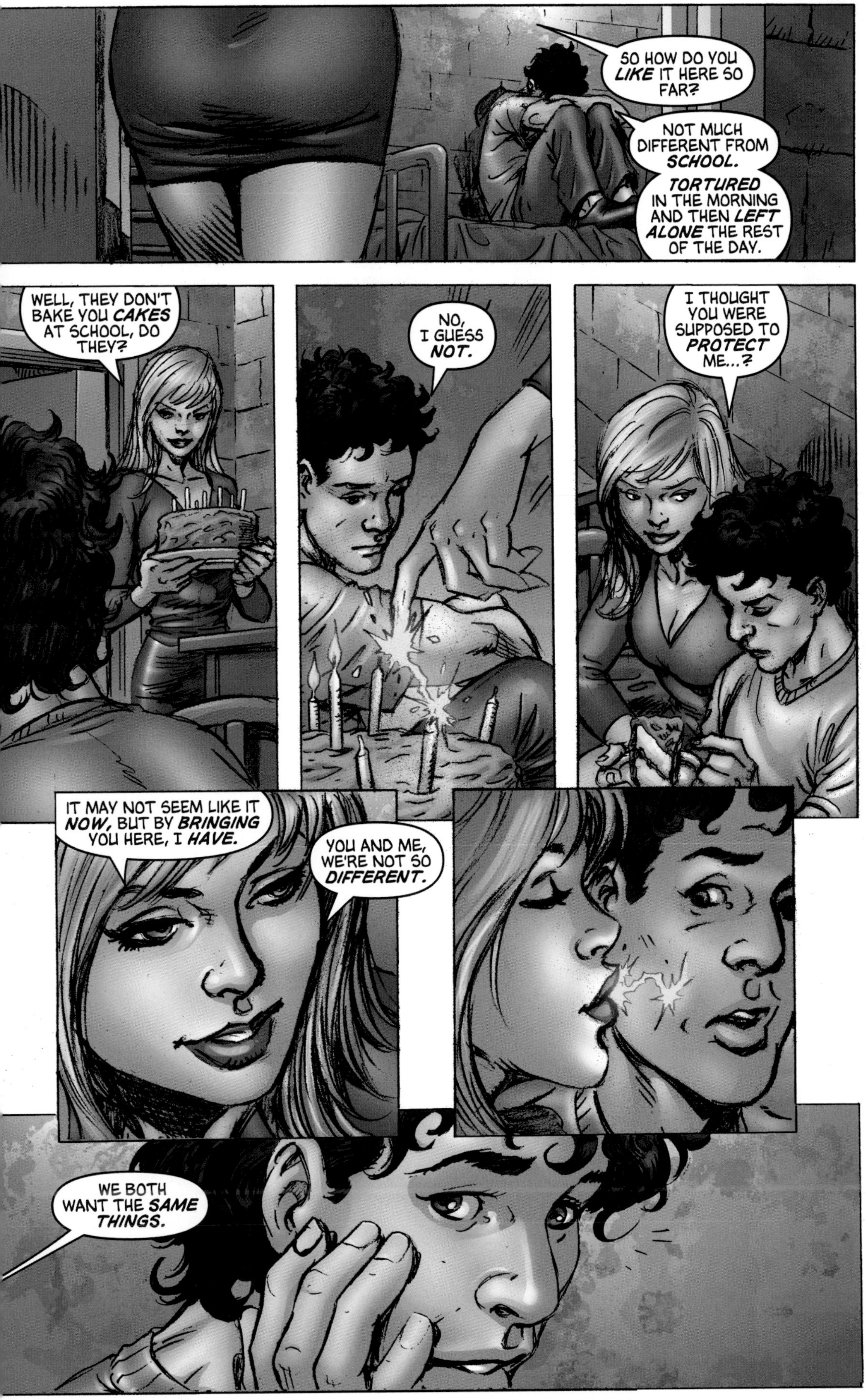
SO HOW DO YOU LIKE IT HERE SO FAR?
NOT MUCH DIFFERENT FROM SCHOOL.
TORTURED IN THE MORNING AND THEN LEFT ALONE THE REST OF THE DAY.
WELL, THEY DON'T BAKE YOU CAKES AT SCHOOL, DO THEY?
NO, I GUESS NOT.
I THOUGHT YOU WERE SUPPOSED TO PROTECT ME...?
IT MAY NOT SEEM LIKE IT NOW, BUT BY BRINGING YOU HERE, I HAVE.
YOU AND ME, WE'RE NOT SO DIFFERENT.
WE BOTH WANT THE SAME THINGS.

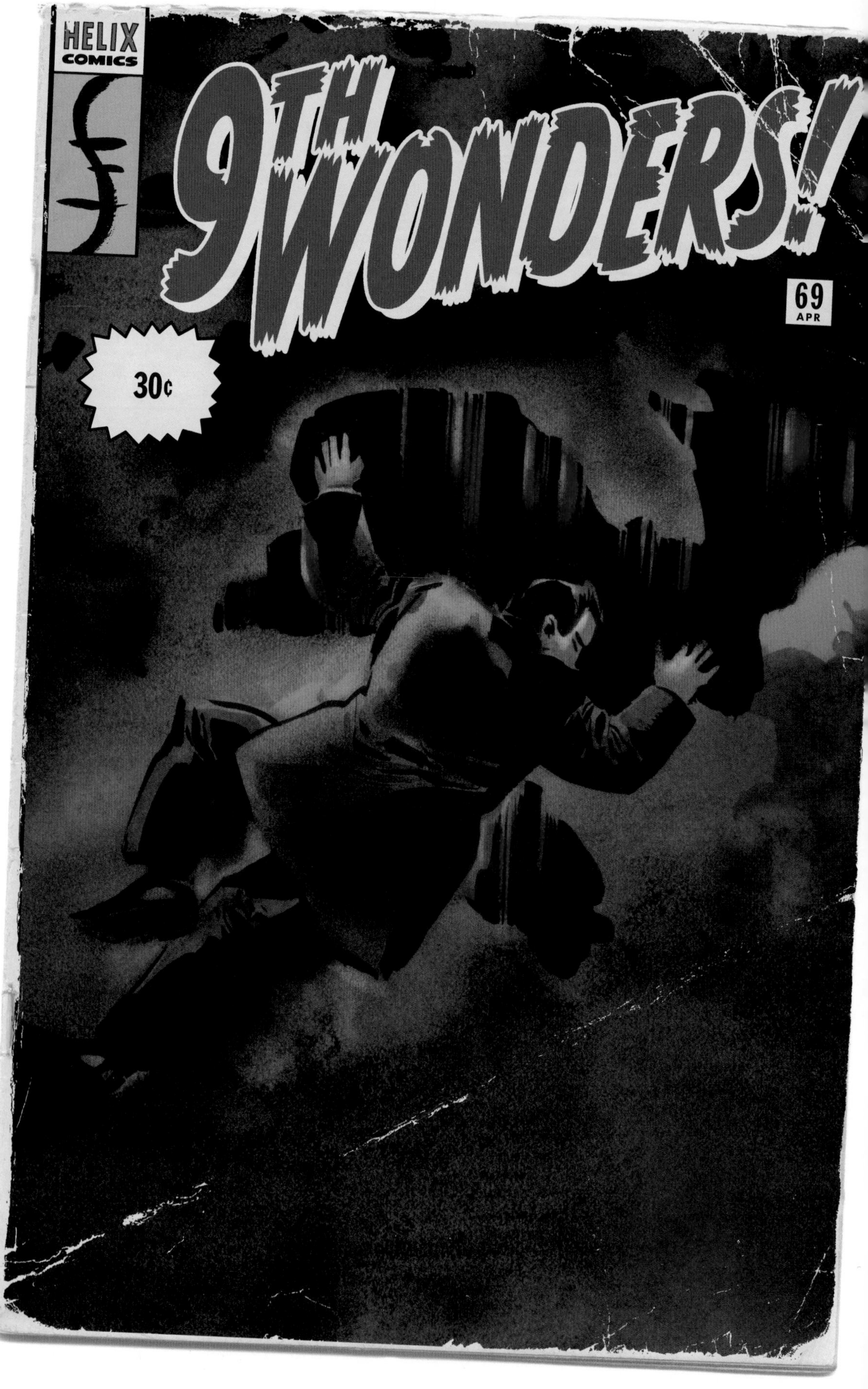
HELIX
COMICS
9TH WONDERS!
69
APR
30¢

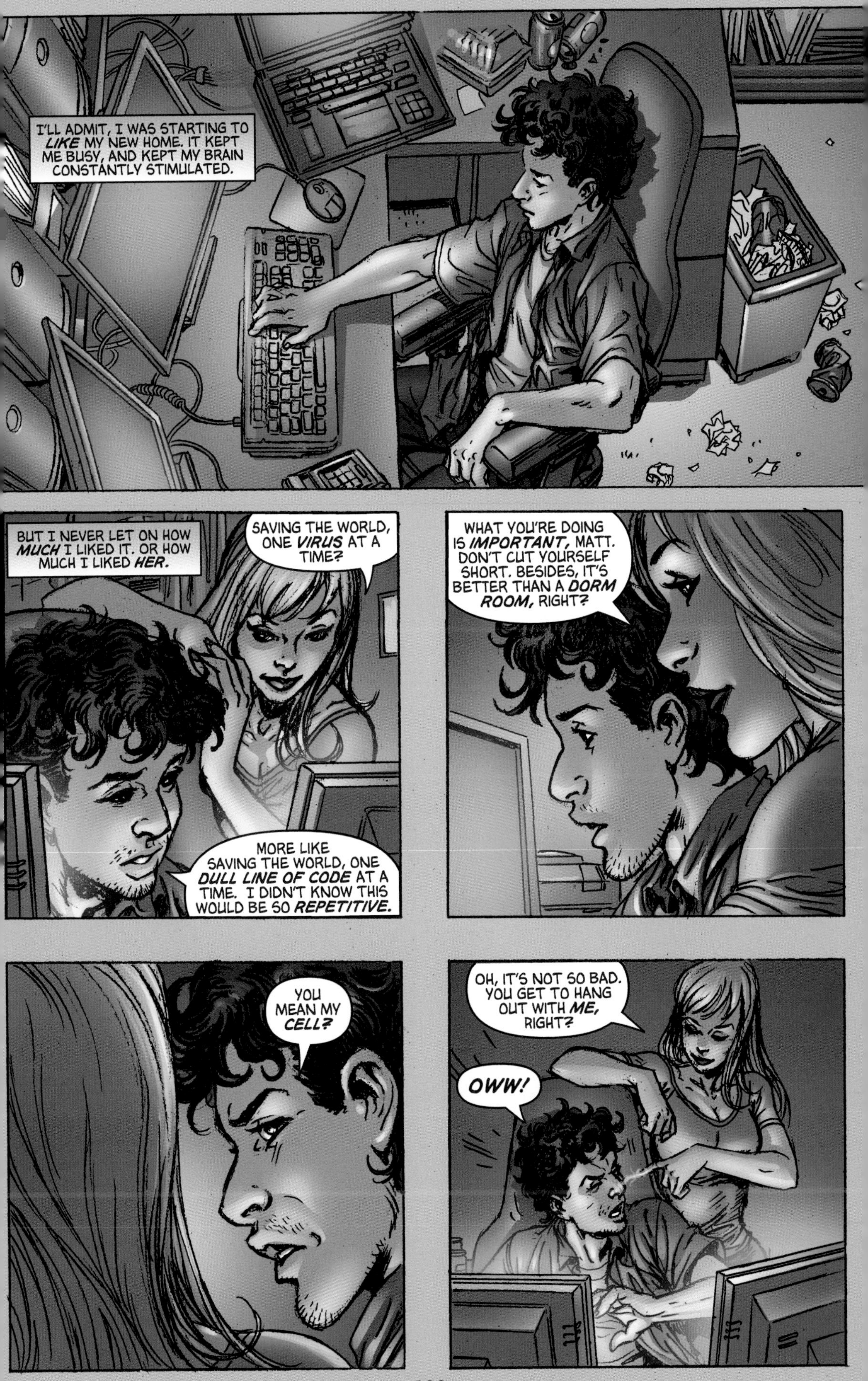
I'LL ADMIT, I WAS STARTING TO LIKE MY NEW HOME. IT KEPT ME BUSY, AND KEPT MY BRAIN CONSTANTLY STIMULATED.
BUT I NEVER LET ON HOW MUCH I LIKED IT. OR HOW MUCH I LIKED HER.
SAVING THE WORLD, ONE VIRUS AT A TIME?
MORE LIKE SAVING THE WORLD, ONE DULL LINE OF CODE AT A TIME. I DIDN'T KNOW THIS WOULD BE SO REPETITIVE.
WHAT YOU'RE DOING IS IMPORTANT, MATT. DON'T CUT YOURSELF SHORT. BESIDES, IT'S BETTER THAN A DORM ROOM, RIGHT?
YOU MEAN MY CELL?
OH, IT'S NOT SO BAD. YOU GET TO HANG OUT WITH ME, RIGHT?
OWW!

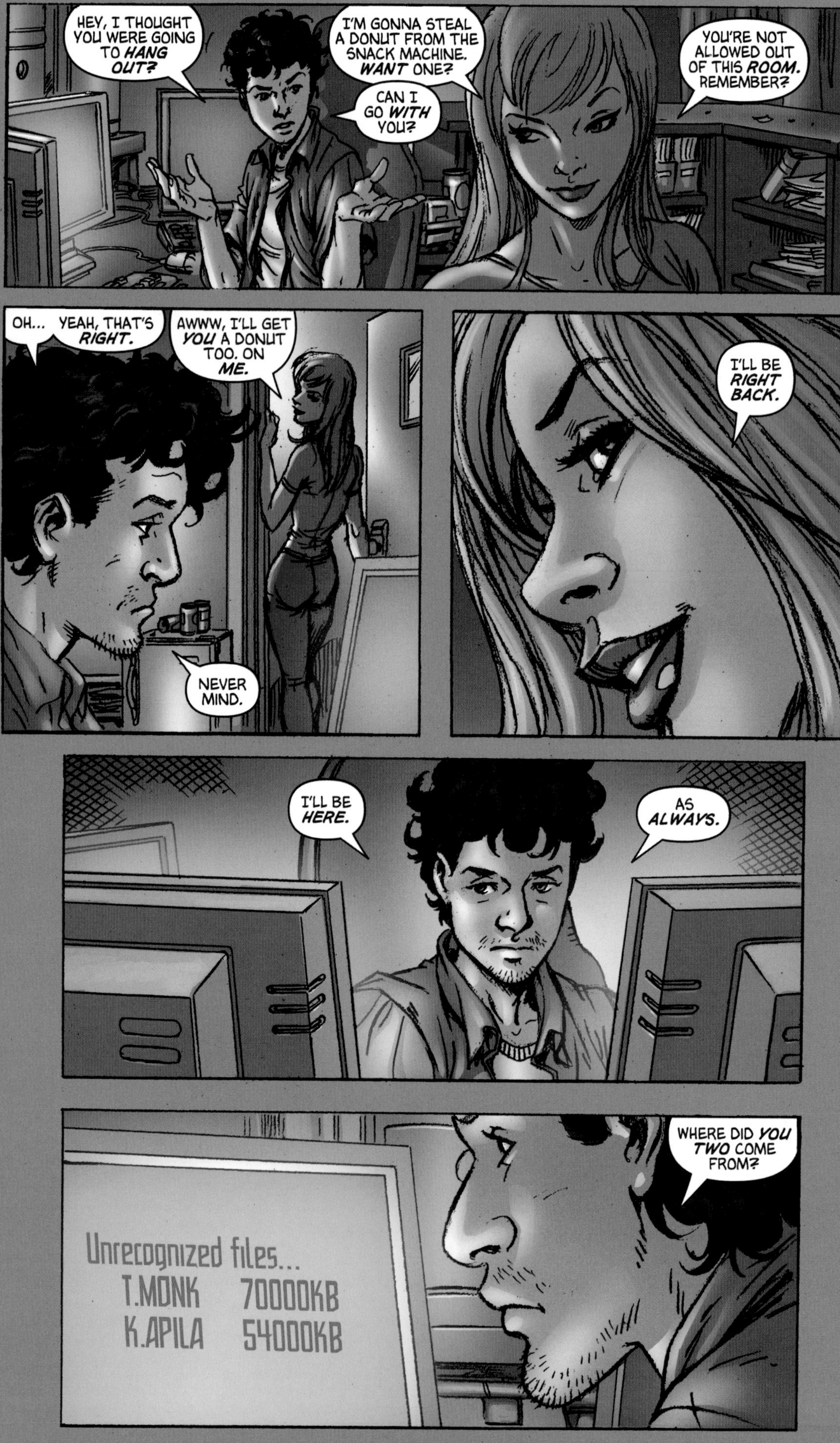
HEY, I THOUGHT YOU WERE GOING TO HANG OUT?
I'M GONNA STEAL A DONUT FROM THE SNACK MACHINE. WANT ONE?
CAN I GO WITH YOU?
YOU'RE NOT ALLOWED OUT OF THIS ROOM. REMEMBER?
OH... YEAH, THAT'S RIGHT.
AWWW, I'LL GET YOU A DONUT TOO. ON ME.
NEVER MIND.
I'LL BE RIGHT BACK.
I'LL BE HERE.
AS ALWAYS.
WHERE DID YOU TWO COME FROM?
Unrecognized files...
T.MONK 70000KB
K.APILA 54000KB

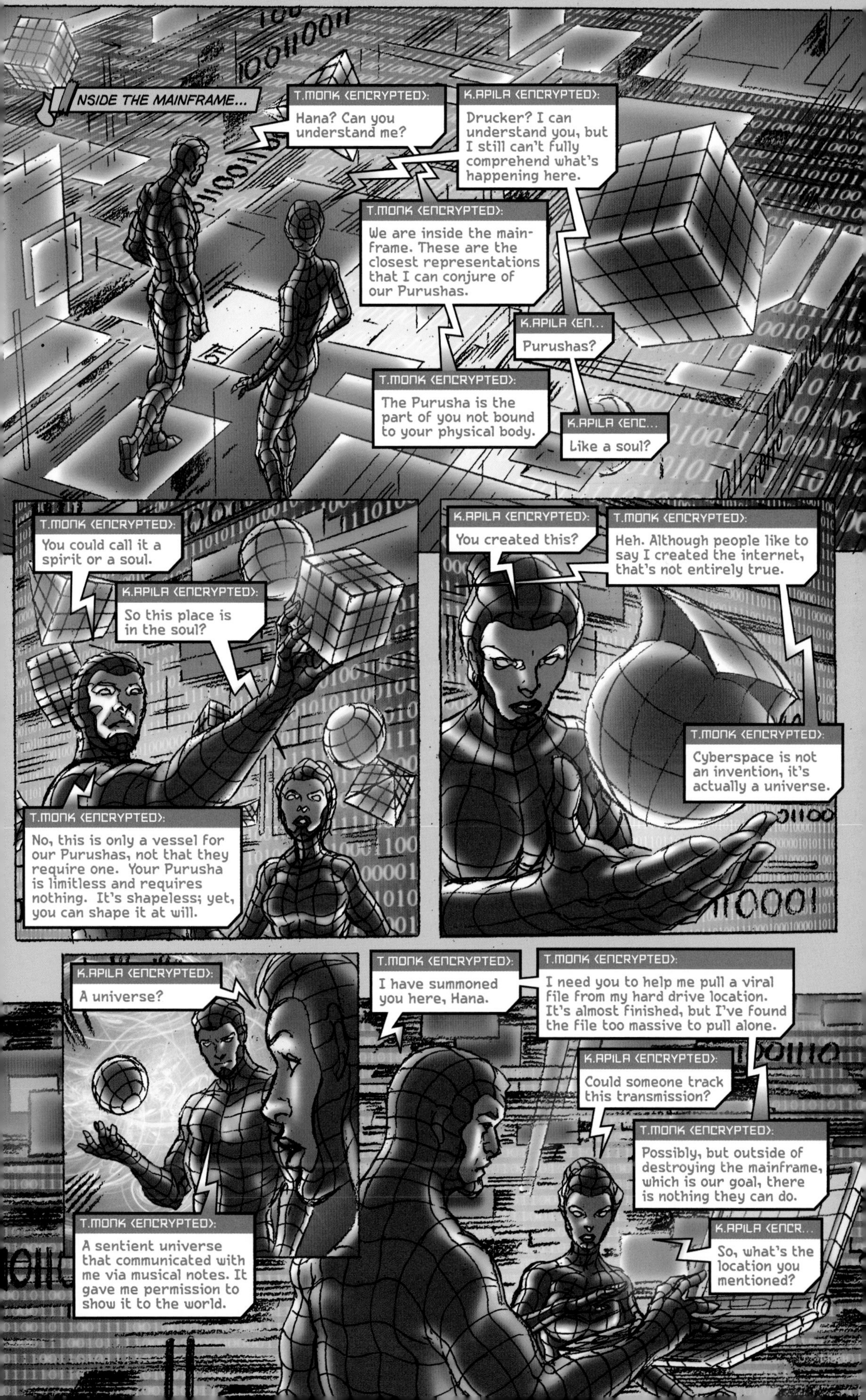
INSIDE THE MAINFRAME...
T.MONK <ENCRYPTED>:
Hana? Can you understand me?
K.APILA <ENCRYPTED>:
Drucker? I can understand you, but I still can't fully comprehend what's happening here.
T.MONK <ENCRYPTED>:
We are inside the main-frame. These are the closest representations that I can conjure of our Purushas.
K.APILA <EN...
Purushas?
T.MONK <ENCRYPTED>:
The Purusha is the part of you not bound to your physical body.
K.APILA <ENC...
Like a soul?
T.MONK <ENCRYPTED>:
You could call it a spirit or a soul.
K.APILA <ENCRYPTED>:
So this place is in the soul?
T.MONK <ENCRYPTED>:
No, this is only a vessel for our Purushas, not that they require one. Your Purusha is limitless and requires nothing. It's shapeless; yet, you can shape it at will.
K.APILA <ENCRYPTED>:
You created this?
T.MONK <ENCRYPTED>:
Heh. Although people like to say I created the internet, that's not entirely true.
T.MONK <ENCRYPTED>:
Cyberspace is not an invention, it's actually a universe.
K.APILA <ENCRYPTED>:
A universe?
T.MONK <ENCRYPTED>:
A sentient universe that communicated with me via musical notes. It gave me permission to show it to the world.
T.MONK <ENCRYPTED>:
I have summoned you here, Hana.
T.MONK <ENCRYPTED>:
I need you to help me pull a viral file from my hard drive location. It's almost finished, but I've found the file too massive to pull alone.
K.APILA <ENCRYPTED>:
Could someone track this transmission?
T.MONK <ENCRYPTED>:
Possibly, but outside of destroying the mainframe, which is our goal, there is nothing they can do.
K.APILA <ENCR...
So, what's the location you mentioned?

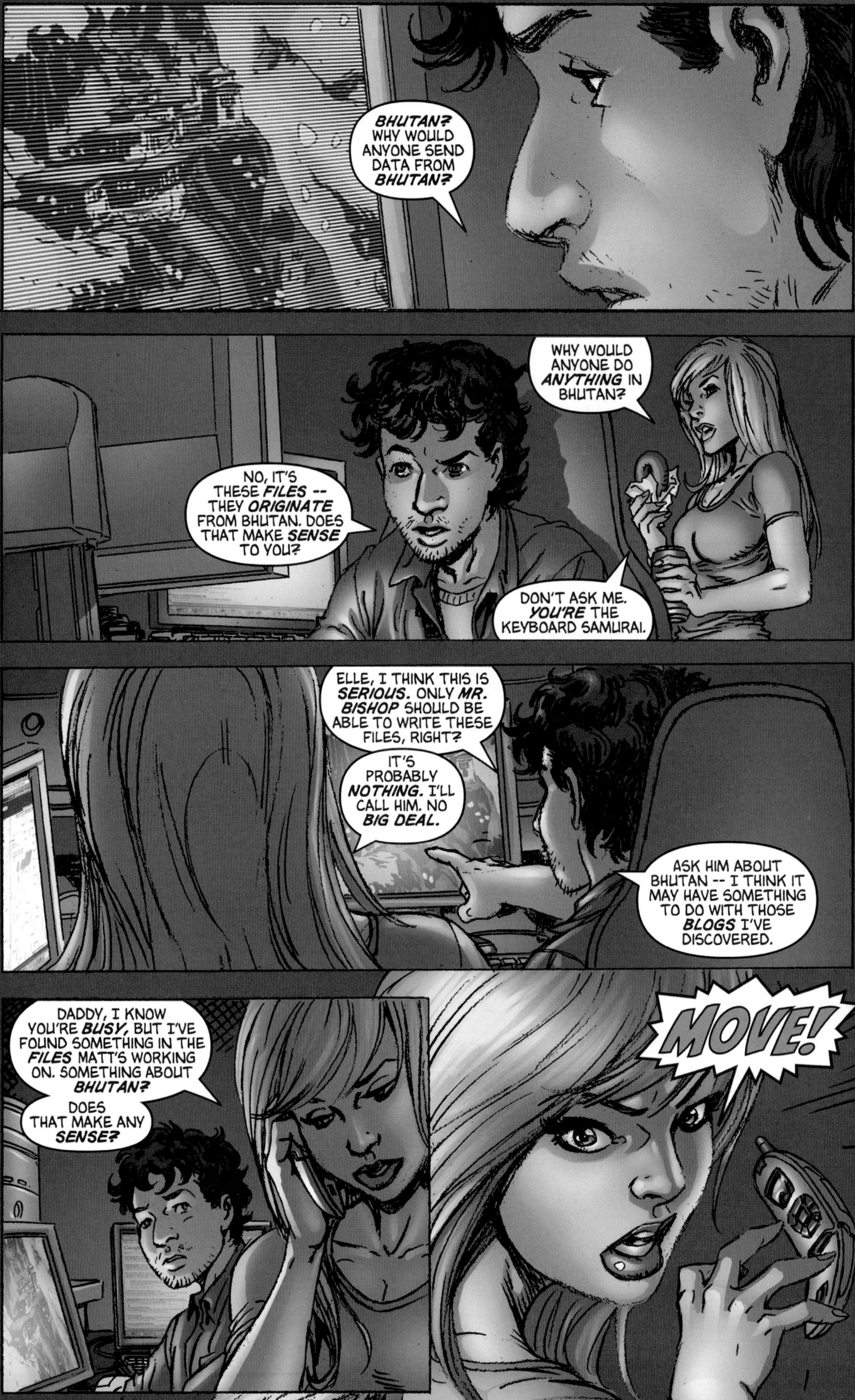
BHUTAN? WHY WOULD ANYONE SEND DATA FROM BHUTAN?
WHY WOULD ANYONE DO ANYTHING IN BHUTAN?
NO, IT'S THESE FILES -- THEY ORIGINATE FROM BHUTAN. DOES THAT MAKE SENSE TO YOU?
DON'T ASK ME. YOU'RE THE KEYBOARD SAMURAI.
ELLE, I THINK THIS IS SERIOUS. ONLY MR. BISHOP SHOULD BE ABLE TO WRITE THESE FILES, RIGHT?
IT'S PROBABLY NOTHING. I'LL CALL HIM. NO BIG DEAL.
ASK HIM ABOUT BHUTAN -- I THINK IT MAY HAVE SOMETHING TO DO WITH THOSE BLOGS I'VE DISCOVERED.
DADDY, I KNOW YOU'RE BUSY, BUT I'VE FOUND SOMETHING IN THE FILES MATT'S WORKING ON. SOMETHING ABOUT BHUTAN?
DOES THAT MAKE ANY SENSE?
MOVE!

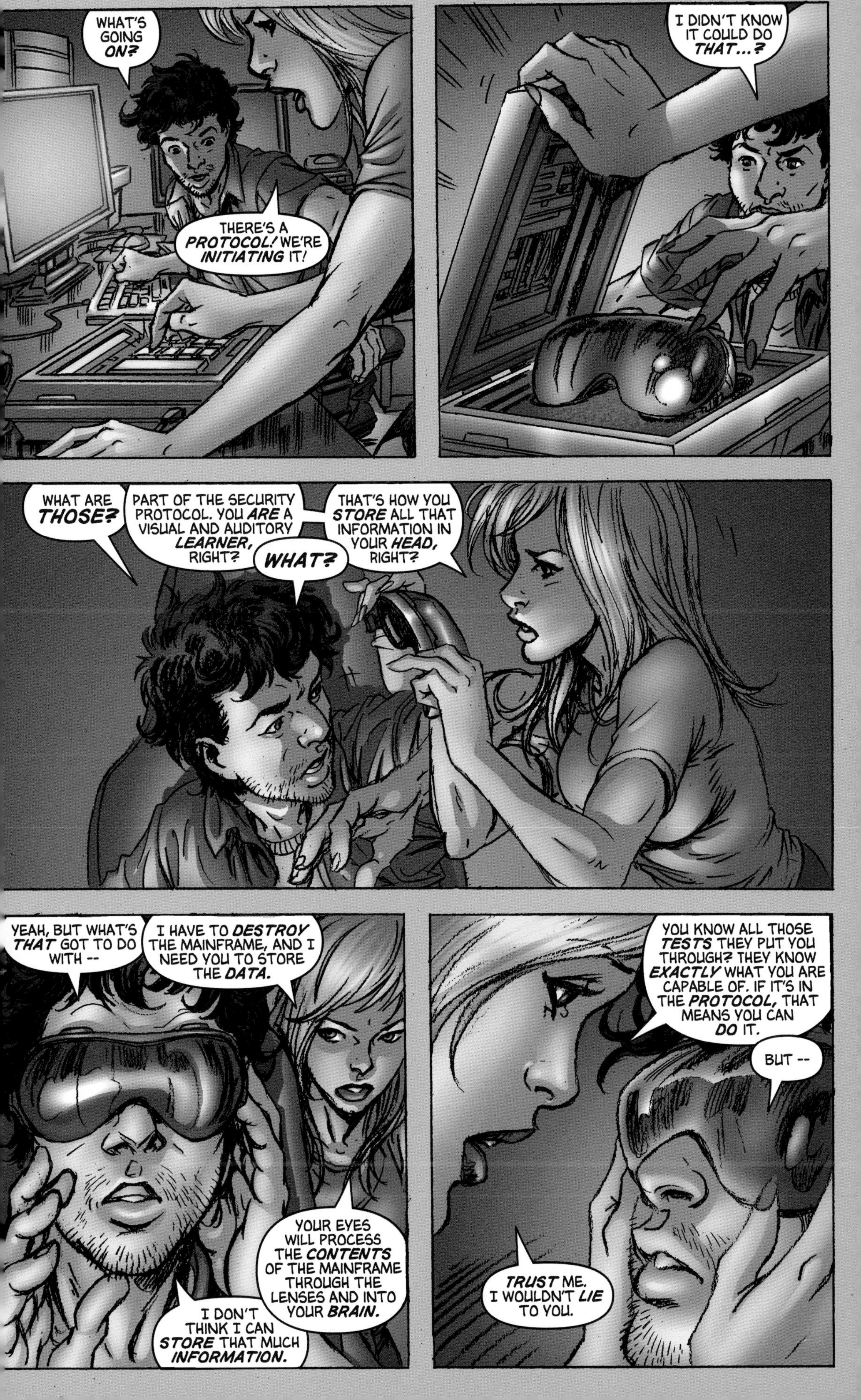
WHAT'S GOING ON?
THERE'S A PROTOCOL! WE'RE INITIATING IT!
I DIDN'T KNOW IT COULD DO THAT...?
WHAT ARE THOSE?
PART OF THE SECURITY PROTOCOL. YOU ARE A VISUAL AND AUDITORY LEARNER, RIGHT?
WHAT?
THAT'S HOW YOU STORE ALL THAT INFORMATION IN YOUR HEAD, RIGHT?
YEAH, BUT WHAT'S THAT GOT TO DO WITH --
I HAVE TO DESTROY THE MAINFRAME, AND I NEED YOU TO STORE THE DATA.
YOUR EYES WILL PROCESS THE CONTENTS OF THE MAINFRAME THROUGH THE LENSES AND INTO YOUR BRAIN.
I DON'T THINK I CAN STORE THAT MUCH INFORMATION.
YOU KNOW ALL THOSE TESTS THEY PUT YOU THROUGH? THEY KNOW EXACTLY WHAT YOU ARE CAPABLE OF. IF IT'S IN THE PROTOCOL, THAT MEANS YOU CAN DO IT.
BUT --
TRUST ME. I WOULDN'T LIE TO YOU.

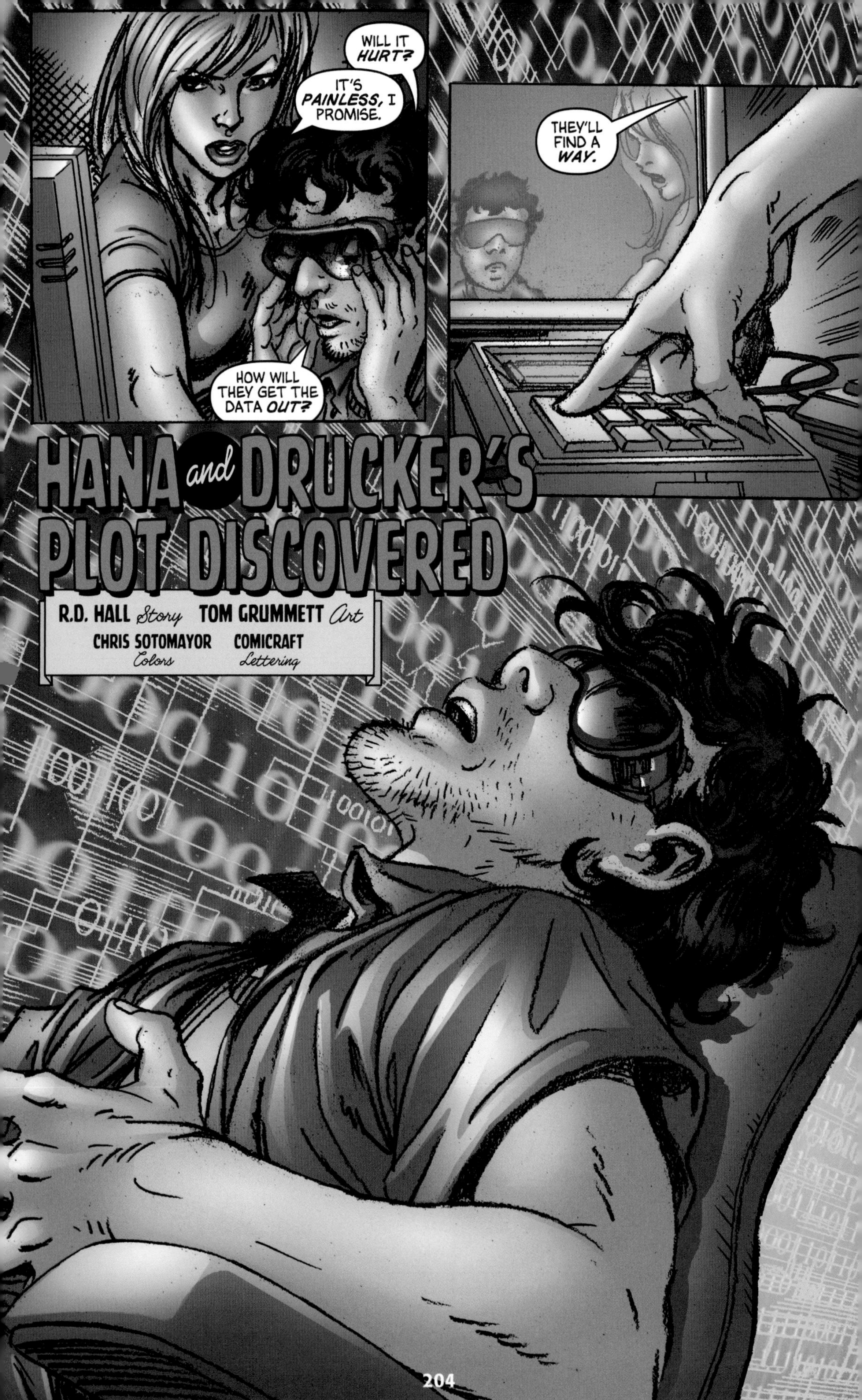
WILL IT HURT?
IT'S PAINLESS, I PROMISE.
HOW WILL THEY GET THE DATA OUT?
THEY'LL FIND A WAY.
HANA and DRUCKER'S PLOT DISCOVERED
R.D. HALL Story TOM GRUMMETT Art
CHRIS SOTOMAYOR Colors COMICRAFT Lettering

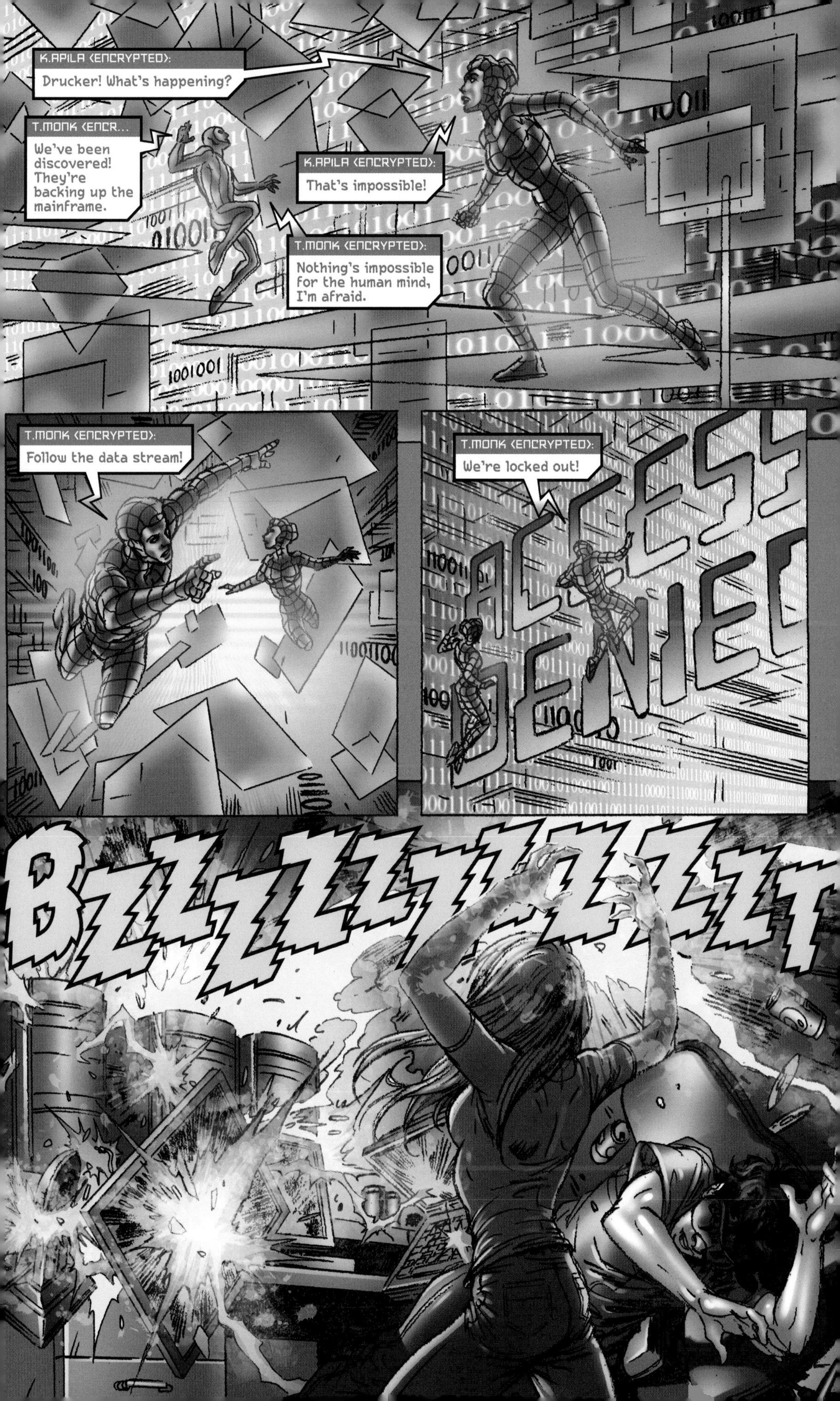
K.APILA <ENCRYPTED>:
Drucker! What's happening?
T.MONK <ENCR...
We've been discovered! They're backing up the mainframe.
K.APILA <ENCRYPTED>:
That's impossible!
T.MONK <ENCRYPTED>:
Nothing's impossible for the human mind, I'm afraid.
T.MONK <ENCRYPTED>:
Follow the data stream!
T.MONK <ENCRYPTED>:
We're locked out!
BZZZZZZZZZT

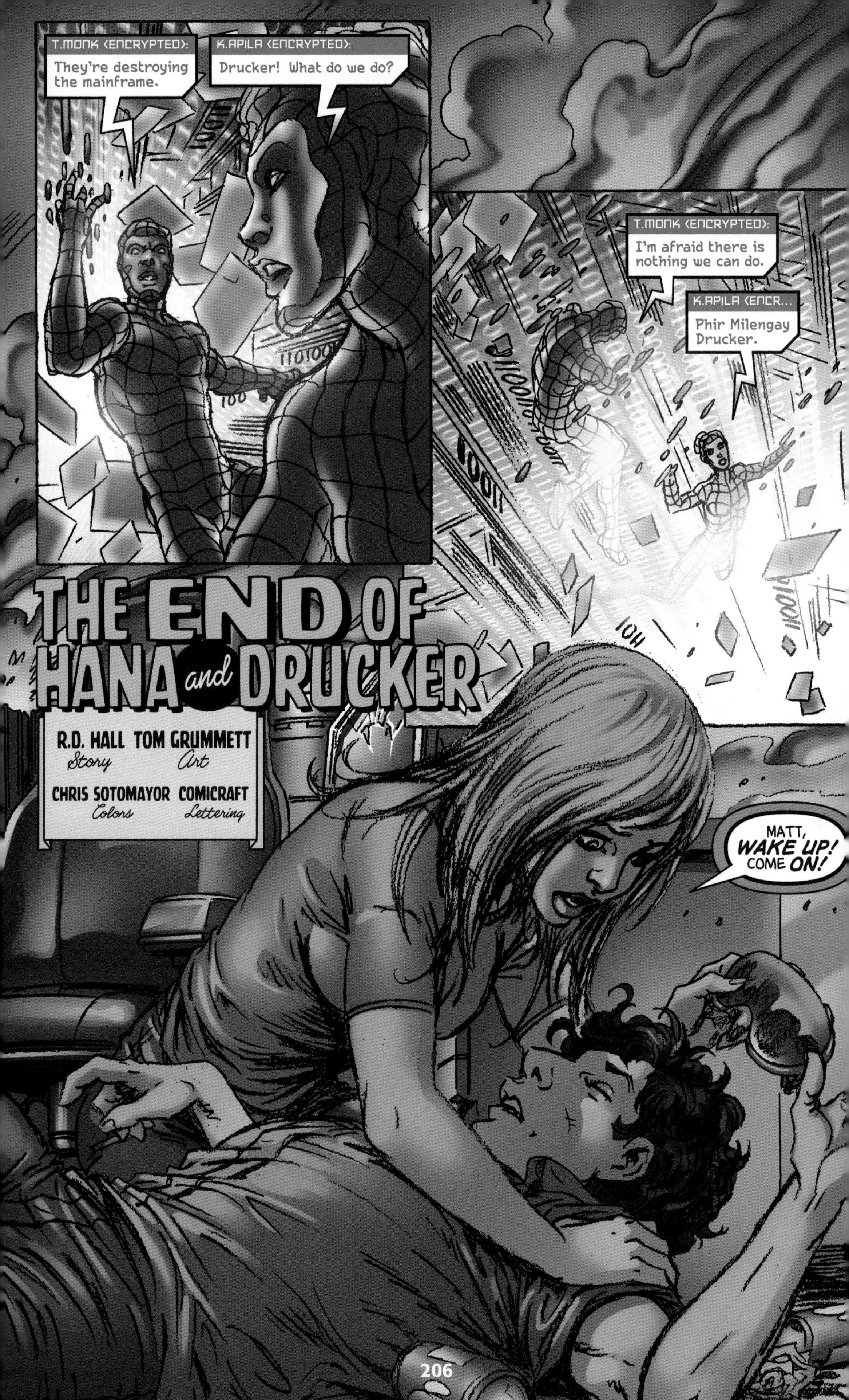

T.MONK <ENCRYPTED>:
They're destroying the mainframe.
K.APILA <ENCRYPTED>:
Drucker! What do we do?
T.MONK <ENCRYPTED>:
I'm afraid there is nothing we can do.
K.APILA <ENCR...
Phir Milengay Drucker.
THE END OF HANA and DRUCKER
R.D. HALL Story
TOM GRUMMETT Art
CHRIS SOTOMAYOR Colors
COMICRAFT Lettering
MATT, WAKE UP! COME ON!

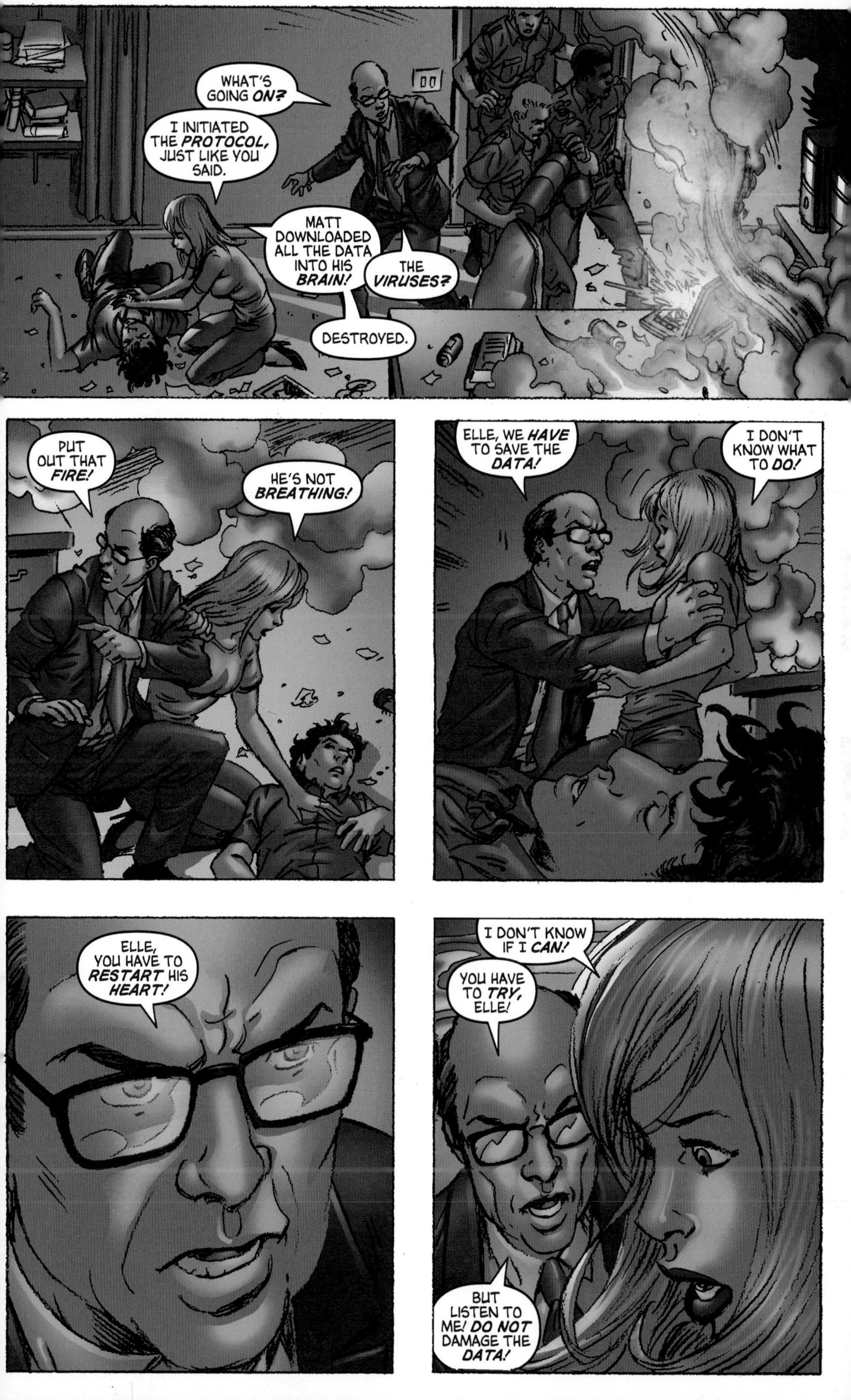
WHAT'S GOING ON?
I INITIATED THE PROTOCOL, JUST LIKE YOU SAID.
MATT DOWNLOADED ALL THE DATA INTO HIS BRAIN!
THE VIRUSES?
DESTROYED.
PUT OUT THAT FIRE!
HE'S NOT BREATHING!
ELLE, WE HAVE TO SAVE THE DATA!
I DON'T KNOW WHAT TO DO!
ELLE, YOU HAVE TO RESTART HIS HEART!
I DON'T KNOW IF I CAN!
YOU HAVE TO TRY, ELLE!
BUT LISTEN TO ME! DO NOT DAMAGE THE DATA!

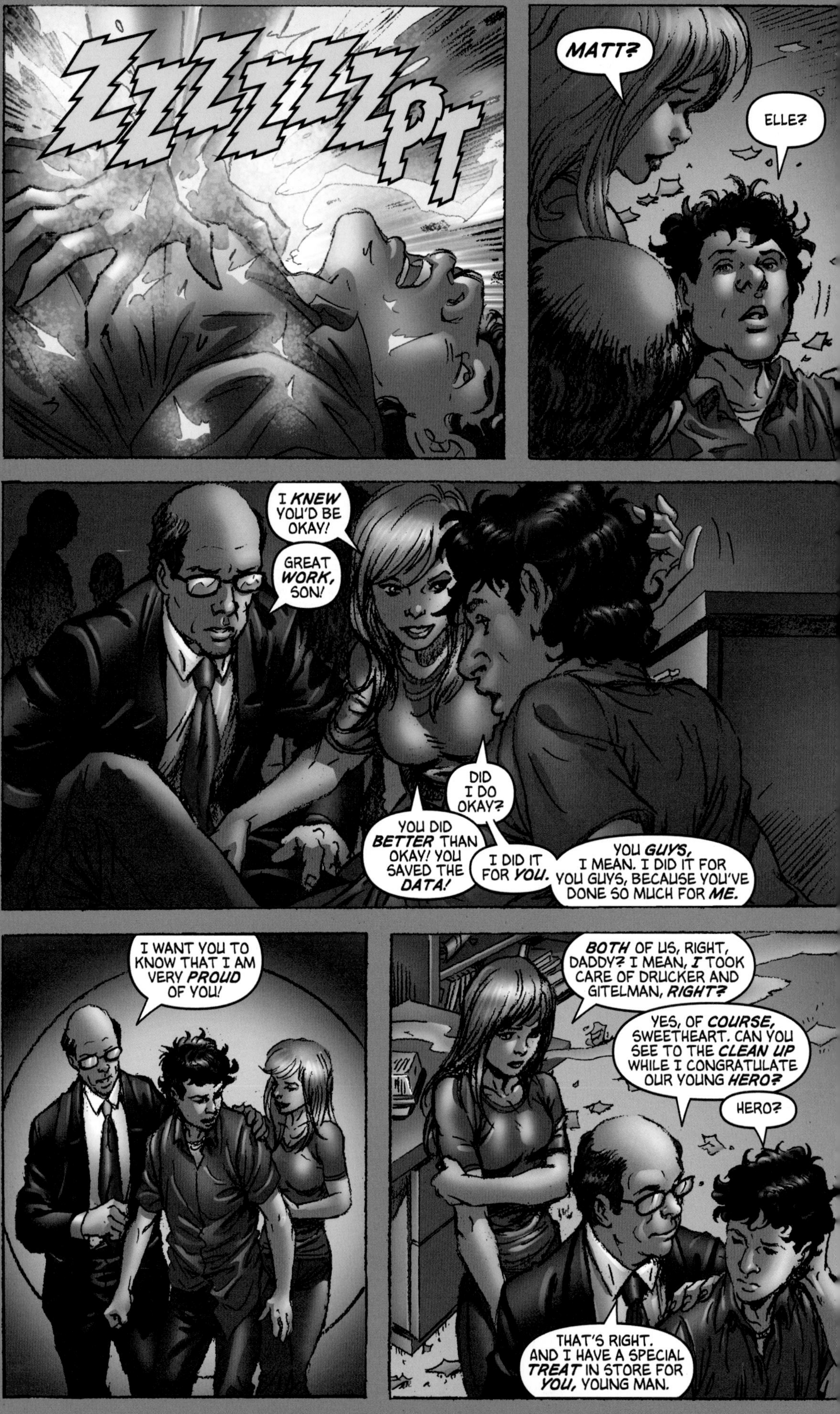
ZZZZZZZPT
MATT?
ELLE?
I KNEW YOU'D BE OKAY!
GREAT WORK, SON!
DID I DO OKAY?
YOU DID BETTER THAN OKAY! YOU SAVED THE DATA!
I DID IT FOR YOU.
YOU GUYS, I MEAN. I DID IT FOR YOU GUYS, BECAUSE YOU'VE DONE SO MUCH FOR ME.
I WANT YOU TO KNOW THAT I AM VERY PROUD OF YOU!
BOTH OF US, RIGHT, DADDY? I MEAN, I TOOK CARE OF DRUCKER AND GITELMAN, RIGHT?
YES, OF COURSE, SWEETHEART. CAN YOU SEE TO THE CLEAN UP WHILE I CONGRATULATE OUR YOUNG HERO?
HERO?
THAT'S RIGHT. AND I HAVE A SPECIAL TREAT IN STORE FOR YOU, YOUNG MAN.

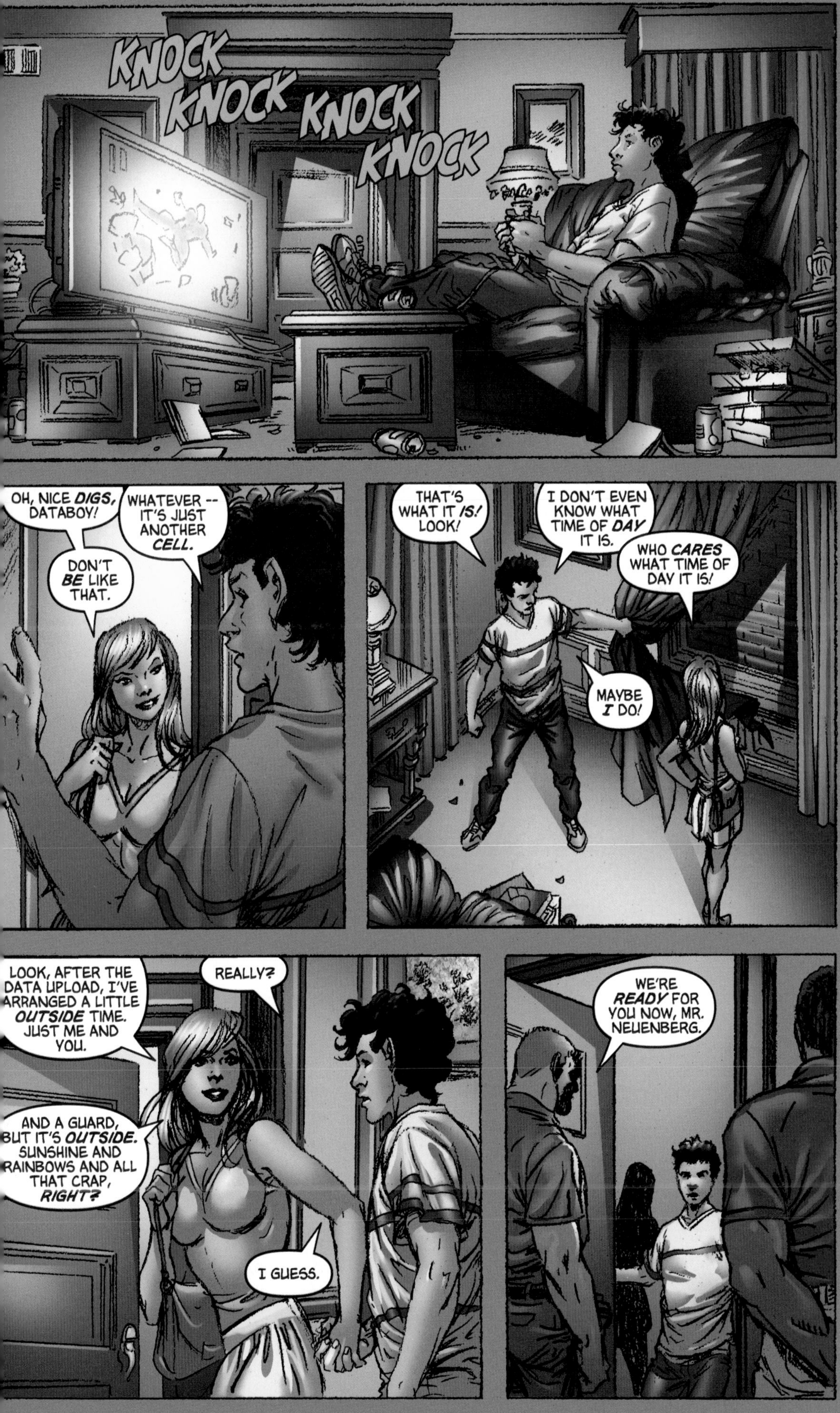
KNOCK KNOCK KNOCK KNOCK
OH, NICE DIGS, DATABOY!
WHATEVER -- IT'S JUST ANOTHER CELL.
DON'T BE LIKE THAT.
THAT'S WHAT IT IS! LOOK!
I DON'T EVEN KNOW WHAT TIME OF DAY IT IS.
WHO CARES WHAT TIME OF DAY IT IS!
MAYBE I DO!
LOOK, AFTER THE DATA UPLOAD, I'VE ARRANGED A LITTLE OUTSIDE TIME. JUST ME AND YOU.
REALLY?
AND A GUARD, BUT IT'S OUTSIDE. SUNSHINE AND RAINBOWS AND ALL THAT CRAP, RIGHT?
I GUESS.
WE'RE READY FOR YOU NOW, MR. NEUENBERG.

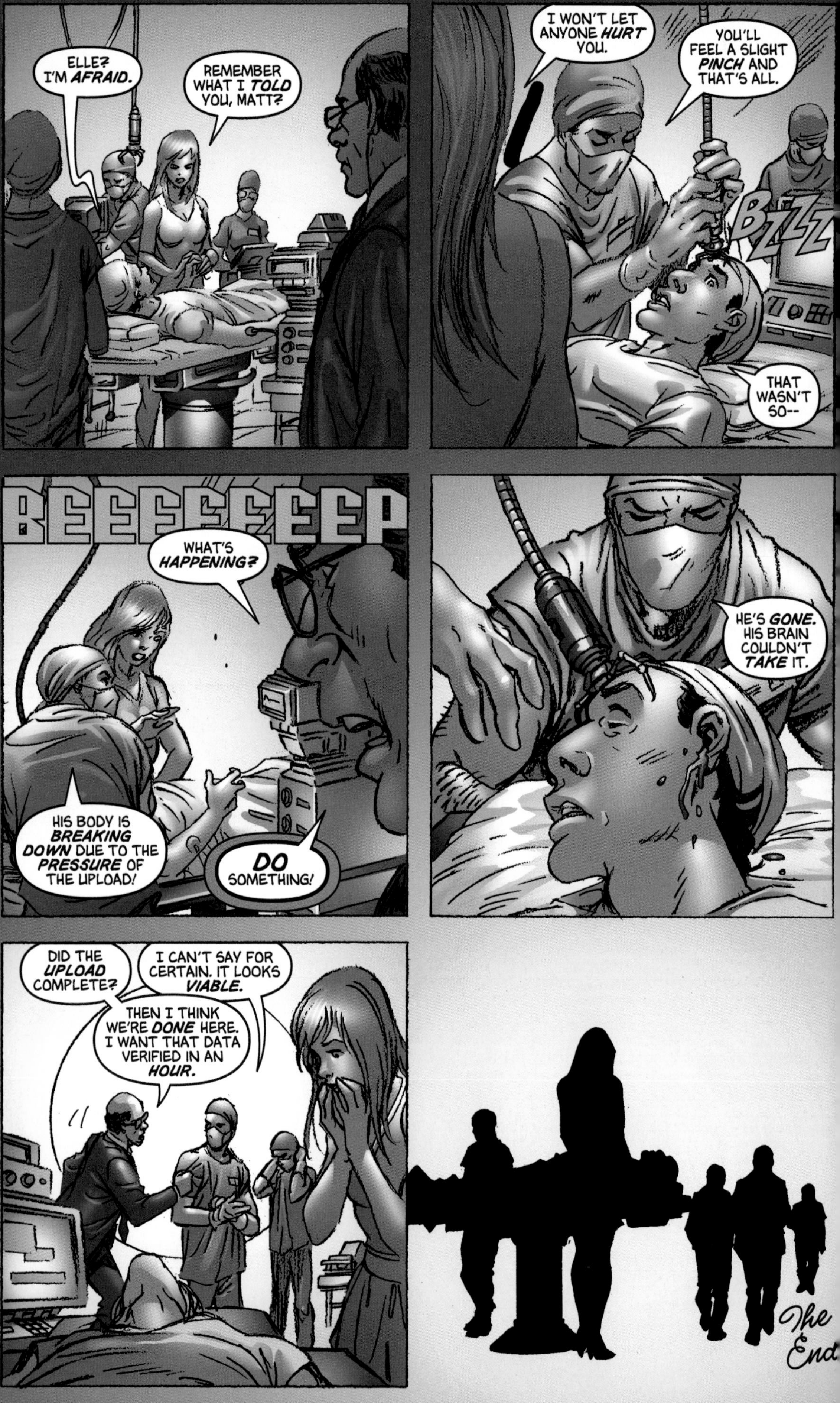
ELLE? I'M AFRAID.
REMEMBER WHAT I TOLD YOU, MATT?
I WON'T LET ANYONE HURT YOU.
YOU'LL FEEL A SLIGHT PINCH AND THAT'S ALL.
BZZT
THAT WASN'T SO--
BEEEEEEEP
WHAT'S HAPPENING?
HIS BODY IS BREAKING DOWN DUE TO THE PRESSURE OF THE UPLOAD!
DO SOMETHING!
HE'S GONE. HIS BRAIN COULDN'T TAKE IT.
DID THE UPLOAD COMPLETE?
I CAN'T SAY FOR CERTAIN. IT LOOKS VIABLE.
THEN I THINK WE'RE DONE HERE. I WANT THAT DATA VERIFIED IN AN HOUR.
The End

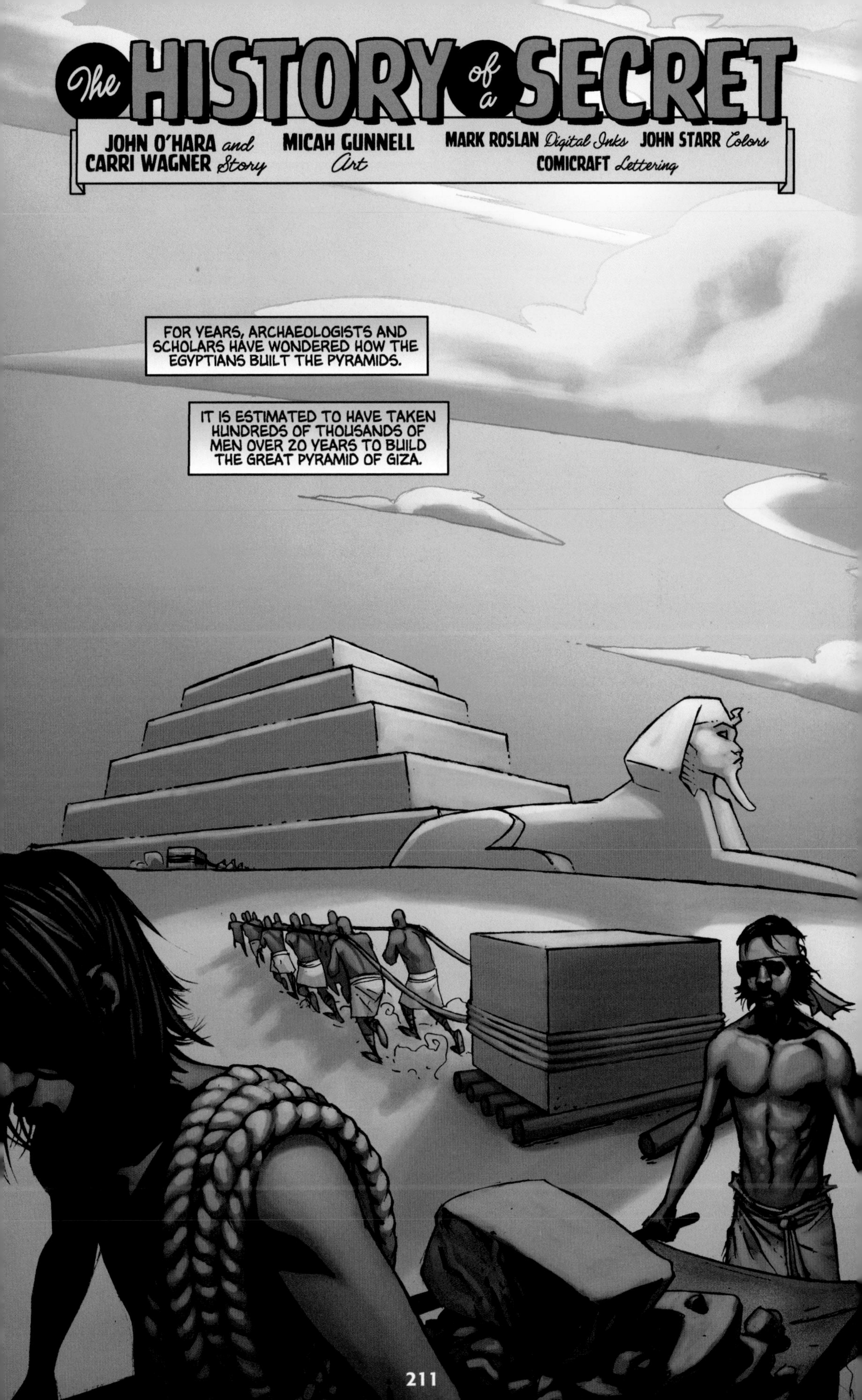
The HISTORY of a SECRET
JOHN O'HARA and CARRI WAGNER Story
MICAH GUNNELL Art
MARK ROSLAN Digital Inks JOHN STARR Colors
COMICRAFT Lettering
FOR YEARS, ARCHAEOLOGISTS AND SCHOLARS HAVE WONDERED HOW THE EGYPTIANS BUILT THE PYRAMIDS.
IT IS ESTIMATED TO HAVE TAKEN HUNDREDS OF THOUSANDS OF MEN OVER 20 YEARS TO BUILD THE GREAT PYRAMID OF GIZA.

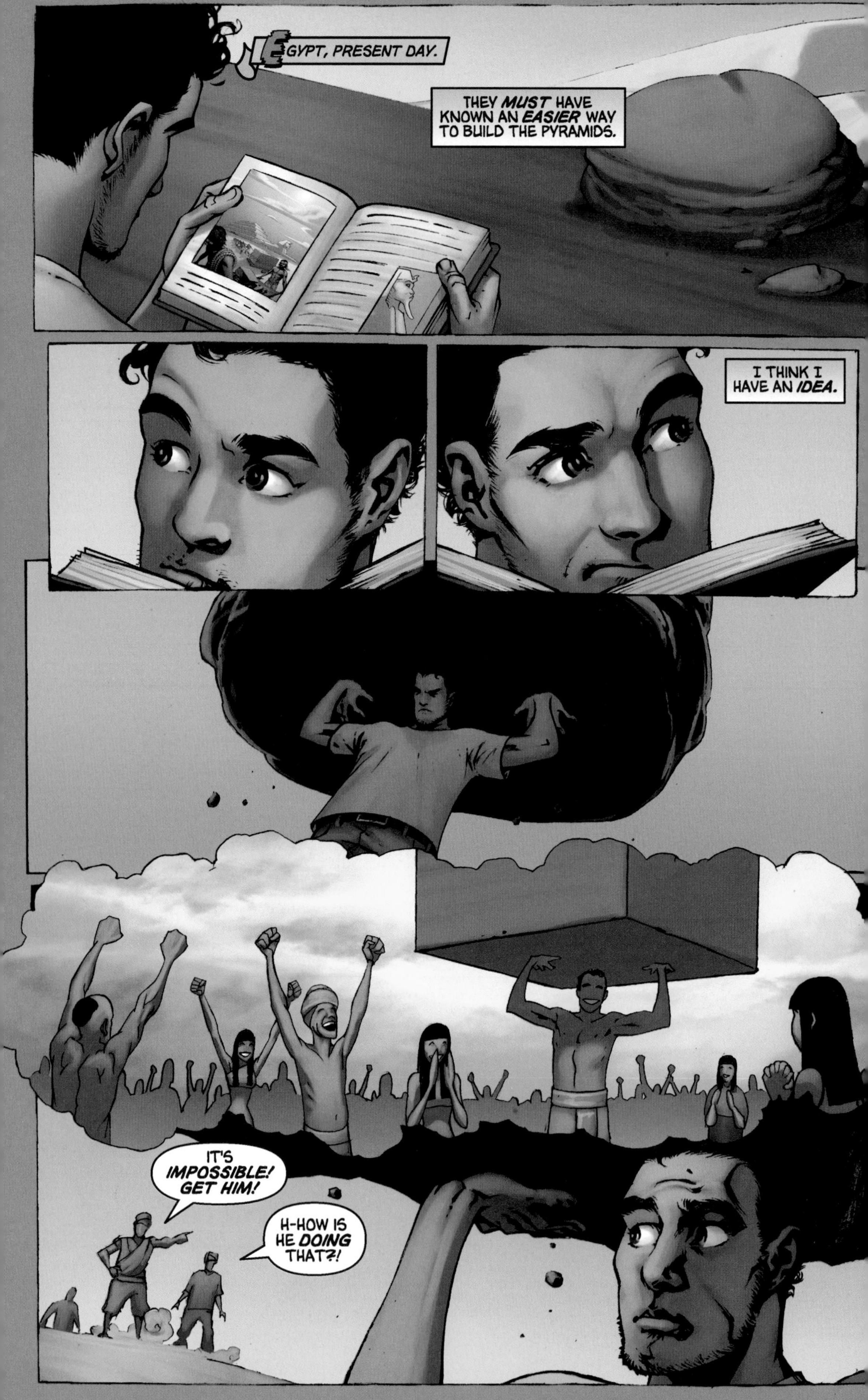
EGYPT, PRESENT DAY.
THEY MUST HAVE KNOWN AN EASIER WAY TO BUILD THE PYRAMIDS.
I THINK I HAVE AN IDEA.
IT'S IMPOSSIBLE! GET HIM!
H-HOW IS HE DOING THAT?!

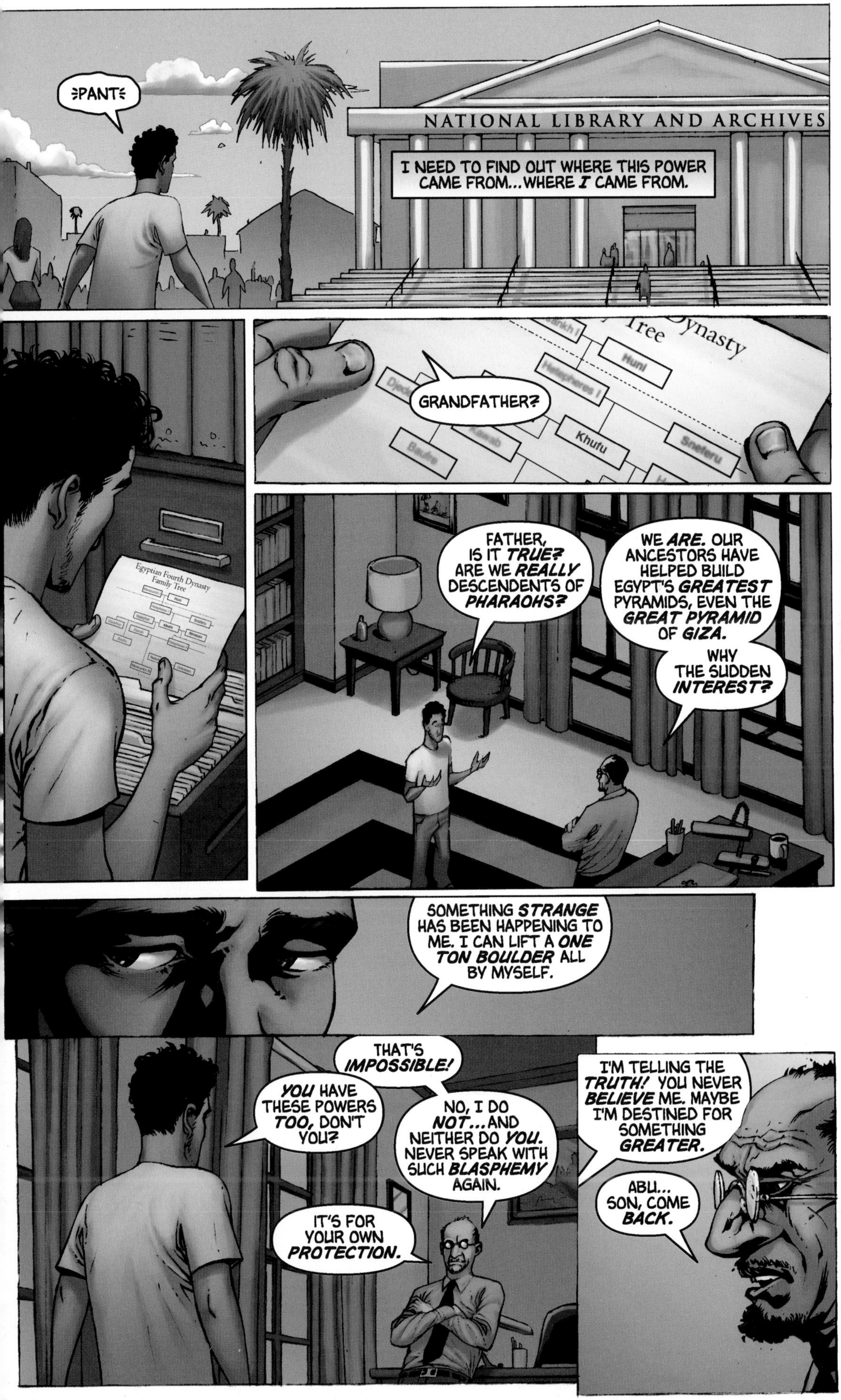

PANT
NATIONAL LIBRARY AND ARCHIVES
I NEED TO FIND OUT WHERE THIS POWER CAME FROM... WHERE I CAME FROM.
Egyptian Fourth Dynasty Family Tree
GRANDFATHER?
Huni
Khufu
Sneferu
FATHER, IS IT TRUE? ARE WE REALLY DESCENDENTS OF PHARAOHS?
WE ARE. OUR ANCESTORS HAVE HELPED BUILD EGYPT'S GREATEST PYRAMIDS, EVEN THE GREAT PYRAMID OF GIZA.
WHY THE SUDDEN INTEREST?
SOMETHING STRANGE HAS BEEN HAPPENING TO ME. I CAN LIFT A ONE TON BOULDER ALL BY MYSELF.
THAT'S IMPOSSIBLE!
YOU HAVE THESE POWERS TOO, DON'T YOU?
NO, I DO NOT... AND NEITHER DO YOU. NEVER SPEAK WITH SUCH BLASPHEMY AGAIN.
IT'S FOR YOUR OWN PROTECTION.
I'M TELLING THE TRUTH! YOU NEVER BELIEVE ME. MAYBE I'M DESTINED FOR SOMETHING GREATER.
ABU... SON, COME BACK.

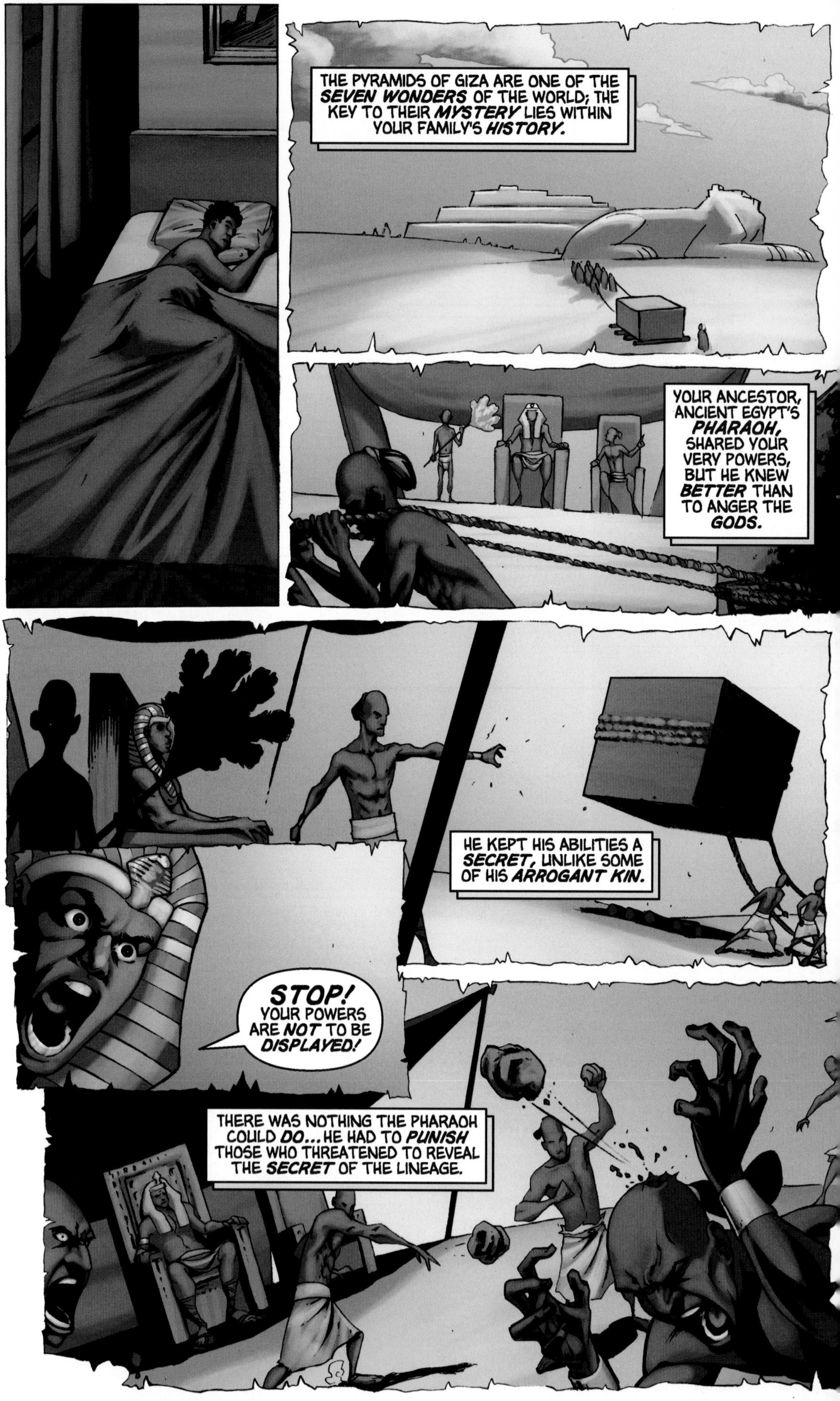
THE PYRAMIDS OF GIZA ARE ONE OF THE SEVEN WONDERS OF THE WORLD; THE KEY TO THEIR MYSTERY LIES WITHIN YOUR FAMILY'S HISTORY.
YOUR ANCESTOR, ANCIENT EGYPT'S PHARAOH, SHARED YOUR VERY POWERS, BUT HE KNEW BETTER THAN TO ANGER THE GODS.
HE KEPT HIS ABILITIES A SECRET, UNLIKE SOME OF HIS ARROGANT KIN.
STOP! YOUR POWERS ARE NOT TO BE DISPLAYED!
THERE WAS NOTHING THE PHARAOH COULD DO... HE HAD TO PUNISH THOSE WHO THREATENED TO REVEAL THE SECRET OF THE LINEAGE.

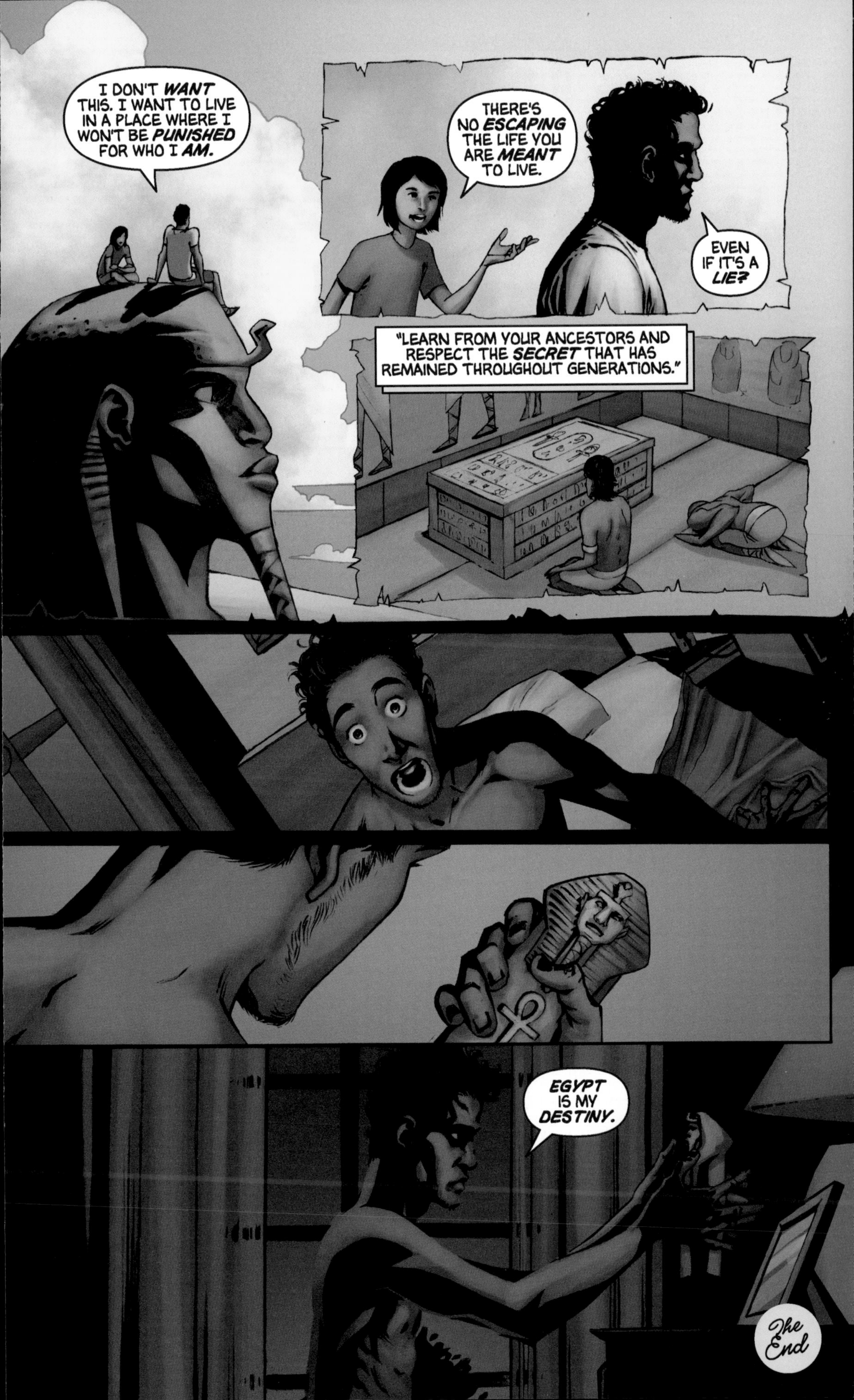
I DON'T WANT THIS. I WANT TO LIVE IN A PLACE WHERE I WON'T BE PUNISHED FOR WHO I AM.
THERE'S NO ESCAPING THE LIFE YOU ARE MEANT TO LIVE.
EVEN IF IT'S A LIE?
"LEARN FROM YOUR ANCESTORS AND RESPECT THE SECRET THAT HAS REMAINED THROUGHOUT GENERATIONS."
EGYPT IS MY DESTINY.
The End

# PAST EXPERIENCE

**J.T. KRUL** *Script* **JASON BADOWER** *Art*
**COMICRAFT** *Lettering*

TO CALL *IKEBANA* THE ACT OF ARRANGING FLOWERS WOULD BE TO LIKEN POETRY TO A GROCERY LIST.

IN TRUTH, IT IS AN EXPRESSION OF THE SOUL, A MEANS BY WHICH TO CONVEY THE WONDROUS BEAUTY AND SPIRITUAL ESSENCE OF NATURE.

THROUGH ITS DESIGN, ONE COULD SPEAK DIRECTLY TO THE HEART OF THE VIEWER WHO SAW IT.

BUT, NONE OF THAT MATTERED.

NOT TO MY FATHER. HE CARED NOTHING FOR THE BEAUTY IN THIS WORLD.

INSTEAD, HE LIVED IN THE PAST...RECOUNTING THE GLORY OF WARRIORS AND THEIR VICTORIES ON ANCIENT BATTLEFIELDS.

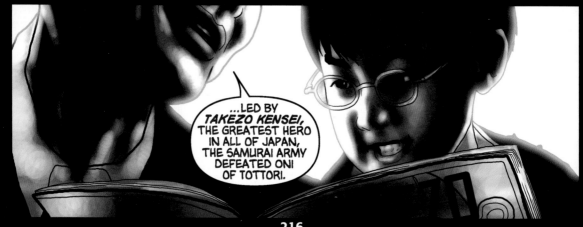

...LED BY *TAKEZO KENSEI*, THE GREATEST HERO IN ALL OF JAPAN, THE SAMURAI ARMY DEFEATED ONI OF TOTTORI.

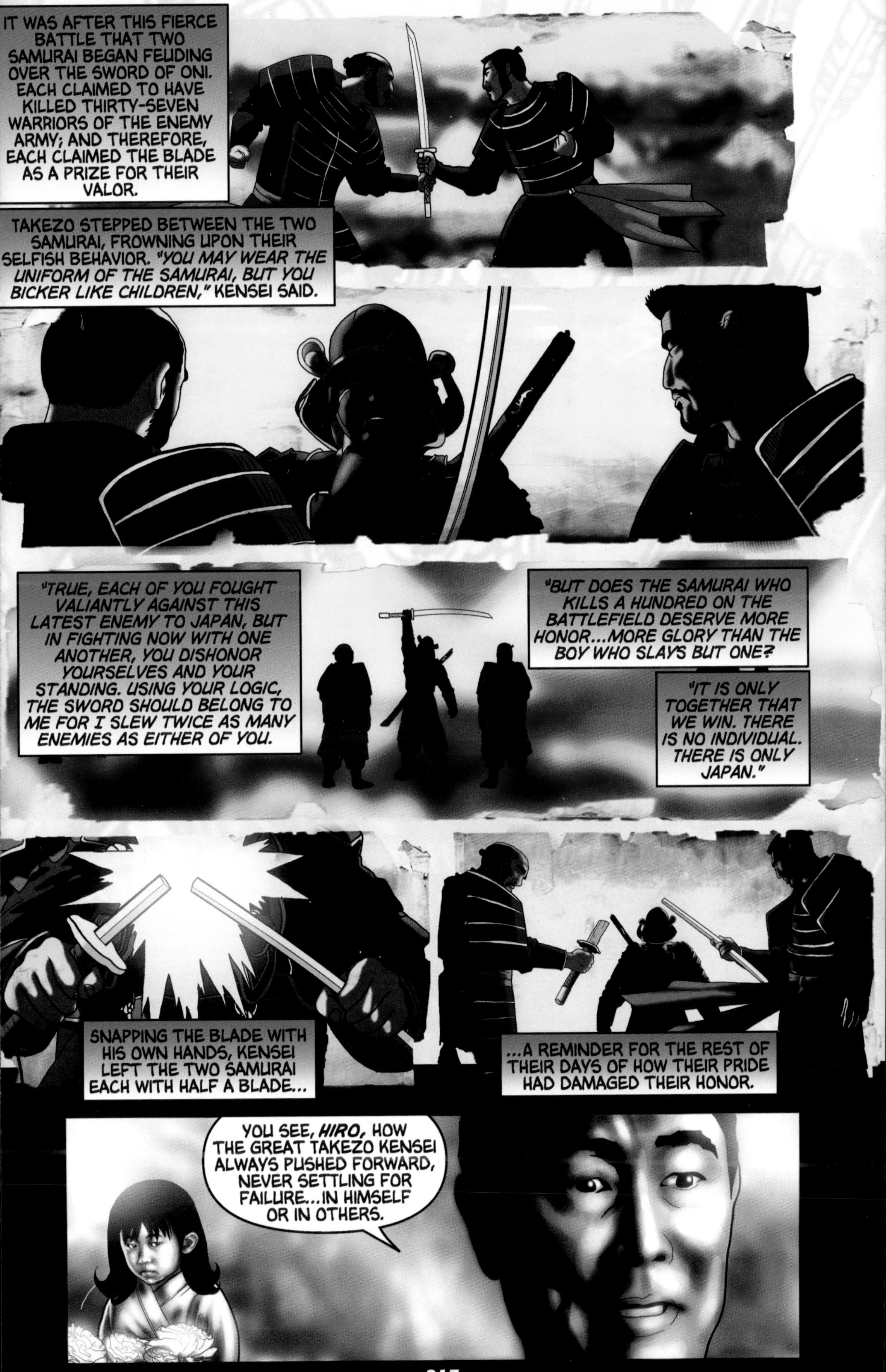

IT WAS AFTER THIS FIERCE BATTLE THAT TWO SAMURAI BEGAN FEUDING OVER THE SWORD OF ONI. EACH CLAIMED TO HAVE KILLED THIRTY-SEVEN WARRIORS OF THE ENEMY ARMY; AND THEREFORE, EACH CLAIMED THE BLADE AS A PRIZE FOR THEIR VALOR.
TAKEZO STEPPED BETWEEN THE TWO SAMURAI, FROWNING UPON THEIR SELFISH BEHAVIOR. "YOU MAY WEAR THE UNIFORM OF THE SAMURAI, BUT YOU BICKER LIKE CHILDREN," KENSEI SAID.
"TRUE, EACH OF YOU FOUGHT VALIANTLY AGAINST THIS LATEST ENEMY TO JAPAN, BUT IN FIGHTING NOW WITH ONE ANOTHER, YOU DISHONOR YOURSELVES AND YOUR STANDING. USING YOUR LOGIC, THE SWORD SHOULD BELONG TO ME FOR I SLEW TWICE AS MANY ENEMIES AS EITHER OF YOU.
"BUT DOES THE SAMURAI WHO KILLS A HUNDRED ON THE BATTLEFIELD DESERVE MORE HONOR...MORE GLORY THAN THE BOY WHO SLAYS BUT ONE?
"IT IS ONLY TOGETHER THAT WE WIN. THERE IS NO INDIVIDUAL. THERE IS ONLY JAPAN."
SNAPPING THE BLADE WITH HIS OWN HANDS, KENSEI LEFT THE TWO SAMURAI EACH WITH HALF A BLADE...
...A REMINDER FOR THE REST OF THEIR DAYS OF HOW THEIR PRIDE HAD DAMAGED THEIR HONOR.
YOU SEE, HIRO, HOW THE GREAT TAKEZO KENSEI ALWAYS PUSHED FORWARD, NEVER SETTLING FOR FAILURE...IN HIMSELF OR IN OTHERS.

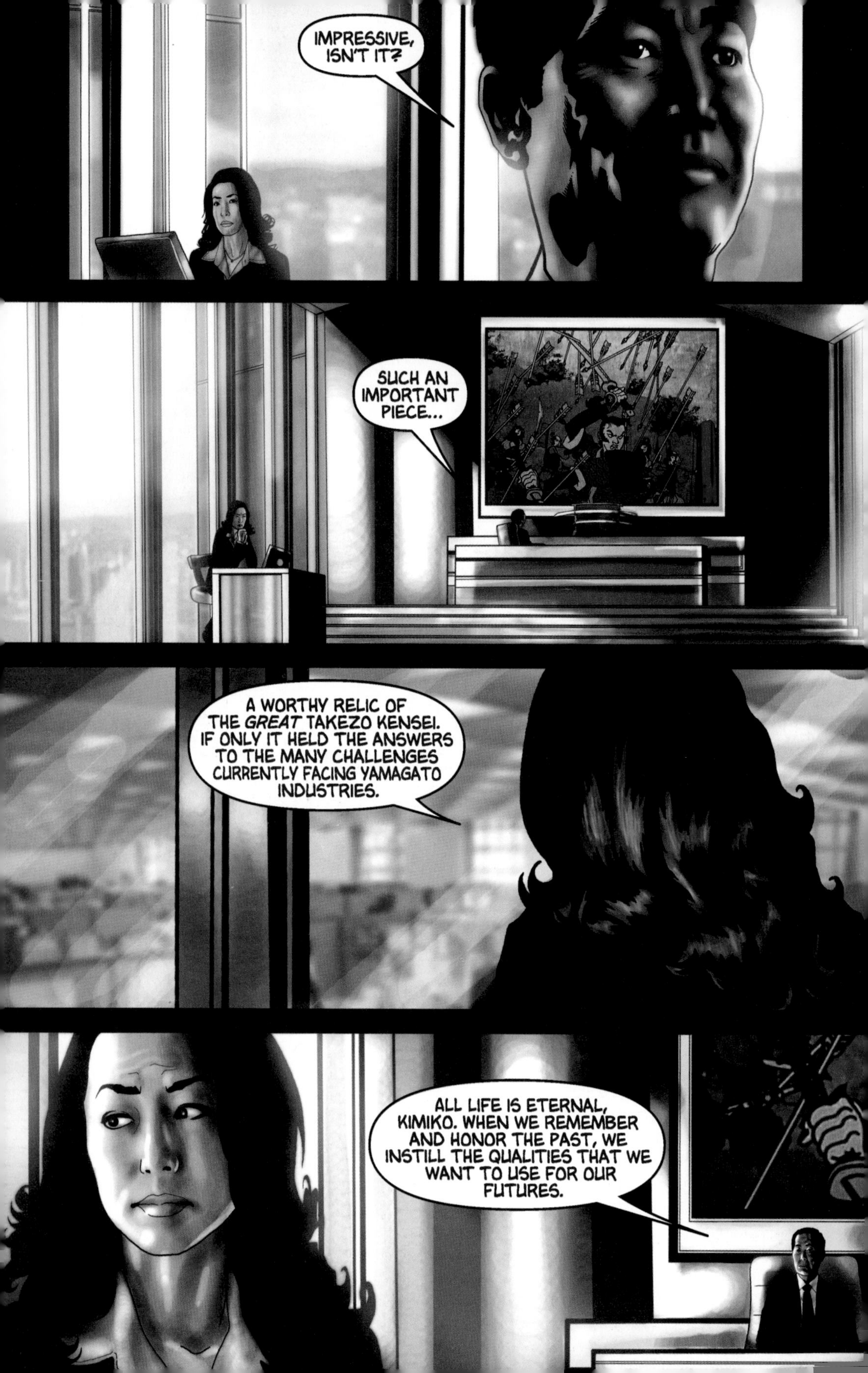
IMPRESSIVE, ISN'T IT?
SUCH AN IMPORTANT PIECE...
A WORTHY RELIC OF THE *GREAT* TAKEZO KENSEI. IF ONLY IT HELD THE ANSWERS TO THE MANY CHALLENGES CURRENTLY FACING YAMAGATO INDUSTRIES.
ALL LIFE IS ETERNAL, KIMIKO. WHEN WE REMEMBER AND HONOR THE PAST, WE INSTILL THE QUALITIES THAT WE WANT TO USE FOR OUR FUTURES.

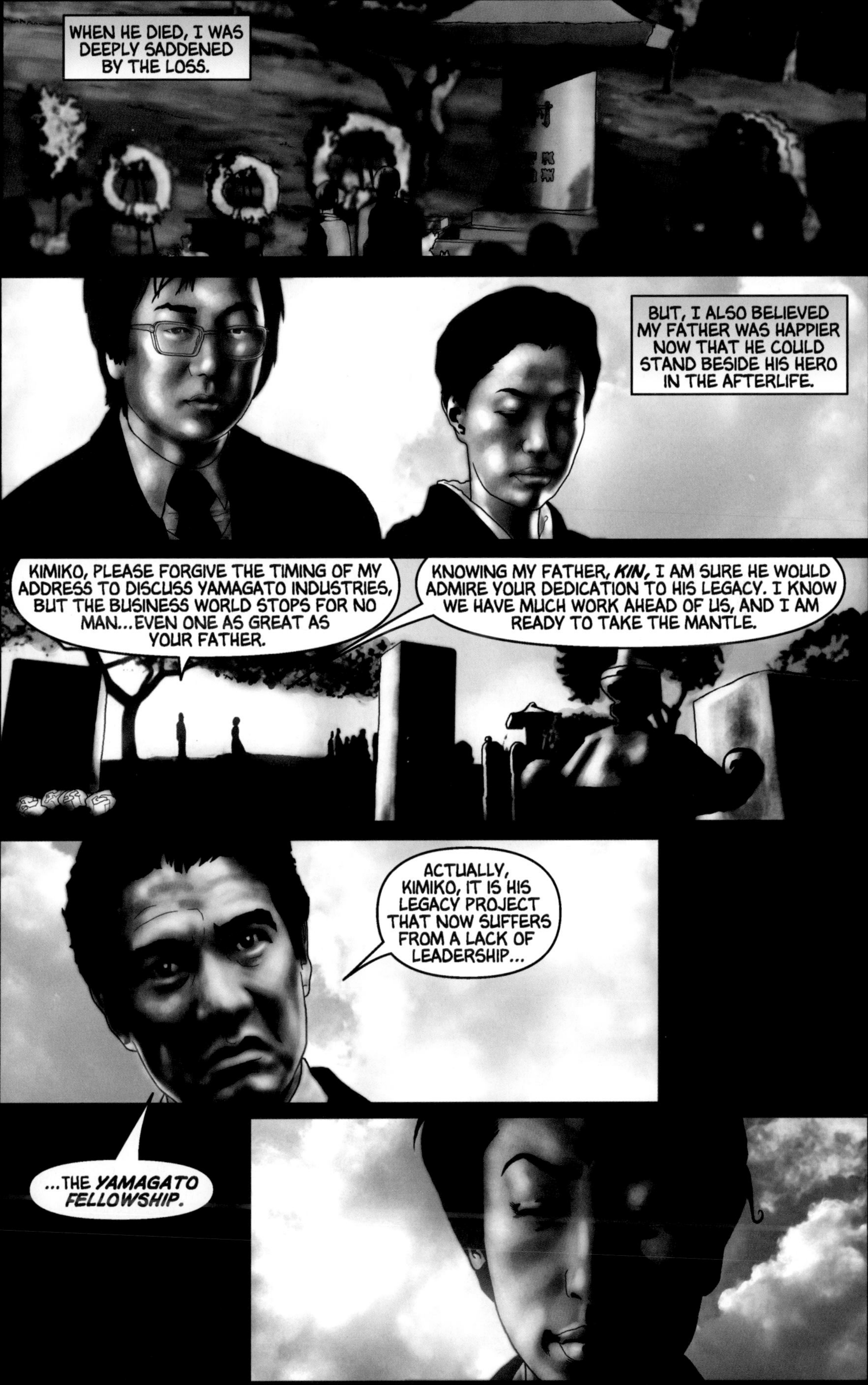
WHEN HE DIED, I WAS DEEPLY SADDENED BY THE LOSS.
BUT, I ALSO BELIEVED MY FATHER WAS HAPPIER NOW THAT HE COULD STAND BESIDE HIS HERO IN THE AFTERLIFE.
KIMIKO, PLEASE FORGIVE THE TIMING OF MY ADDRESS TO DISCUSS YAMAGATO INDUSTRIES, BUT THE BUSINESS WORLD STOPS FOR NO MAN...EVEN ONE AS GREAT AS YOUR FATHER.
KNOWING MY FATHER, *KIN,* I AM SURE HE WOULD ADMIRE YOUR DEDICATION TO HIS LEGACY. I KNOW WE HAVE MUCH WORK AHEAD OF US, AND I AM READY TO TAKE THE MANTLE.
ACTUALLY, KIMIKO, IT IS HIS LEGACY PROJECT THAT NOW SUFFERS FROM A LACK OF LEADERSHIP...
...THE *YAMAGATO FELLOWSHIP.*

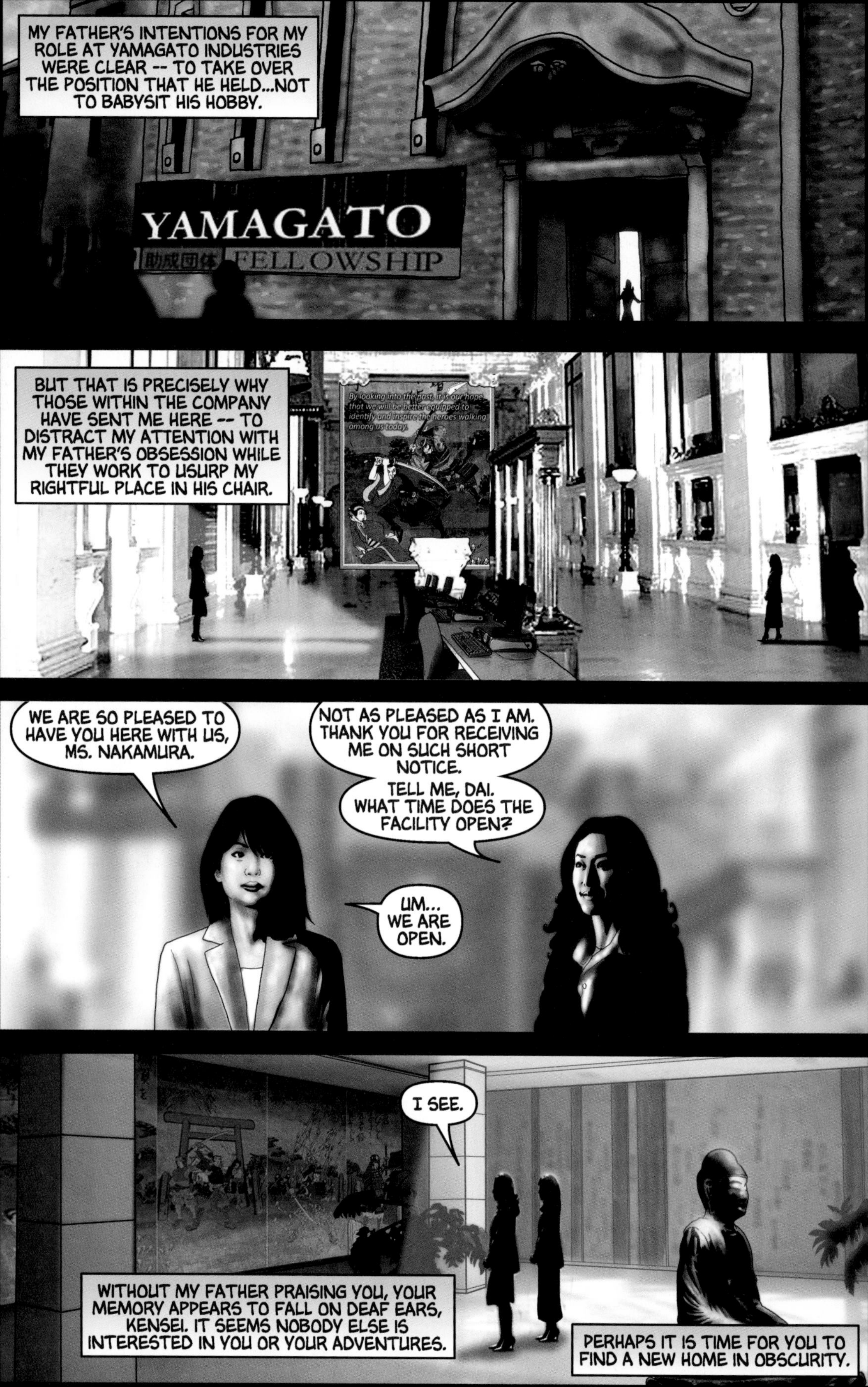
MY FATHER'S INTENTIONS FOR MY ROLE AT YAMAGATO INDUSTRIES WERE CLEAR -- TO TAKE OVER THE POSITION THAT HE HELD...NOT TO BABYSIT HIS HOBBY.
YAMAGATO
助成団体 FELLOWSHIP
BUT THAT IS PRECISELY WHY THOSE WITHIN THE COMPANY HAVE SENT ME HERE -- TO DISTRACT MY ATTENTION WITH MY FATHER'S OBSESSION WHILE THEY WORK TO USURP MY RIGHTFUL PLACE IN HIS CHAIR.
By looking into the past, it is our hope that we will be better equipped to identify and inspire the heroes walking among us today.
WE ARE SO PLEASED TO HAVE YOU HERE WITH US, MS. NAKAMURA.
NOT AS PLEASED AS I AM. THANK YOU FOR RECEIVING ME ON SUCH SHORT NOTICE.
TELL ME, DAI. WHAT TIME DOES THE FACILITY OPEN?
UM... WE ARE OPEN.
I SEE.
WITHOUT MY FATHER PRAISING YOU, YOUR MEMORY APPEARS TO FALL ON DEAF EARS, KENSEI. IT SEEMS NOBODY ELSE IS INTERESTED IN YOU OR YOUR ADVENTURES.
PERHAPS IT IS TIME FOR YOU TO FIND A NEW HOME IN OBSCURITY.

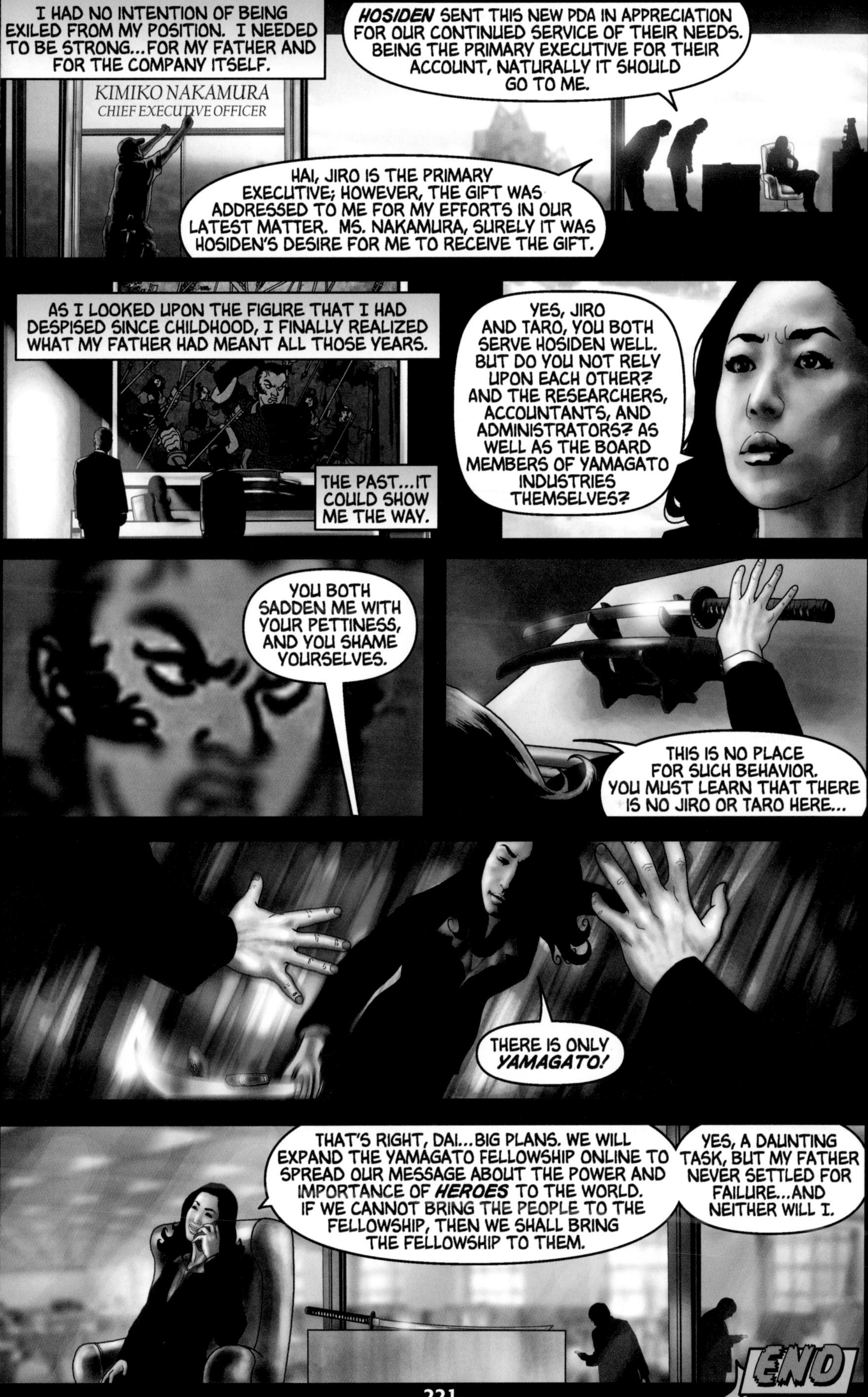
I HAD NO INTENTION OF BEING EXILED FROM MY POSITION. I NEEDED TO BE STRONG...FOR MY FATHER AND FOR THE COMPANY ITSELF.
HOSIDEN SENT THIS NEW PDA IN APPRECIATION FOR OUR CONTINUED SERVICE OF THEIR NEEDS. BEING THE PRIMARY EXECUTIVE FOR THEIR ACCOUNT, NATURALLY IT SHOULD GO TO ME.
KIMIKO NAKAMURA
CHIEF EXECUTIVE OFFICER
HAI, JIRO IS THE PRIMARY EXECUTIVE; HOWEVER, THE GIFT WAS ADDRESSED TO ME FOR MY EFFORTS IN OUR LATEST MATTER. MS. NAKAMURA, SURELY IT WAS HOSIDEN'S DESIRE FOR ME TO RECEIVE THE GIFT.
AS I LOOKED UPON THE FIGURE THAT I HAD DESPISED SINCE CHILDHOOD, I FINALLY REALIZED WHAT MY FATHER HAD MEANT ALL THOSE YEARS.
THE PAST...IT COULD SHOW ME THE WAY.
YES, JIRO AND TARO, YOU BOTH SERVE HOSIDEN WELL. BUT DO YOU NOT RELY UPON EACH OTHER? AND THE RESEARCHERS, ACCOUNTANTS, AND ADMINISTRATORS? AS WELL AS THE BOARD MEMBERS OF YAMAGATO INDUSTRIES THEMSELVES?
YOU BOTH SADDEN ME WITH YOUR PETTINESS, AND YOU SHAME YOURSELVES.
THIS IS NO PLACE FOR SUCH BEHAVIOR. YOU MUST LEARN THAT THERE IS NO JIRO OR TARO HERE...
THERE IS ONLY YAMAGATO!
THAT'S RIGHT, DAI...BIG PLANS. WE WILL EXPAND THE YAMAGATO FELLOWSHIP ONLINE TO SPREAD OUR MESSAGE ABOUT THE POWER AND IMPORTANCE OF HEROES TO THE WORLD. IF WE CANNOT BRING THE PEOPLE TO THE FELLOWSHIP, THEN WE SHALL BRING THE FELLOWSHIP TO THEM.
YES, A DAUNTING TASK, BUT MY FATHER NEVER SETTLED FOR FAILURE...AND NEITHER WILL I.
END

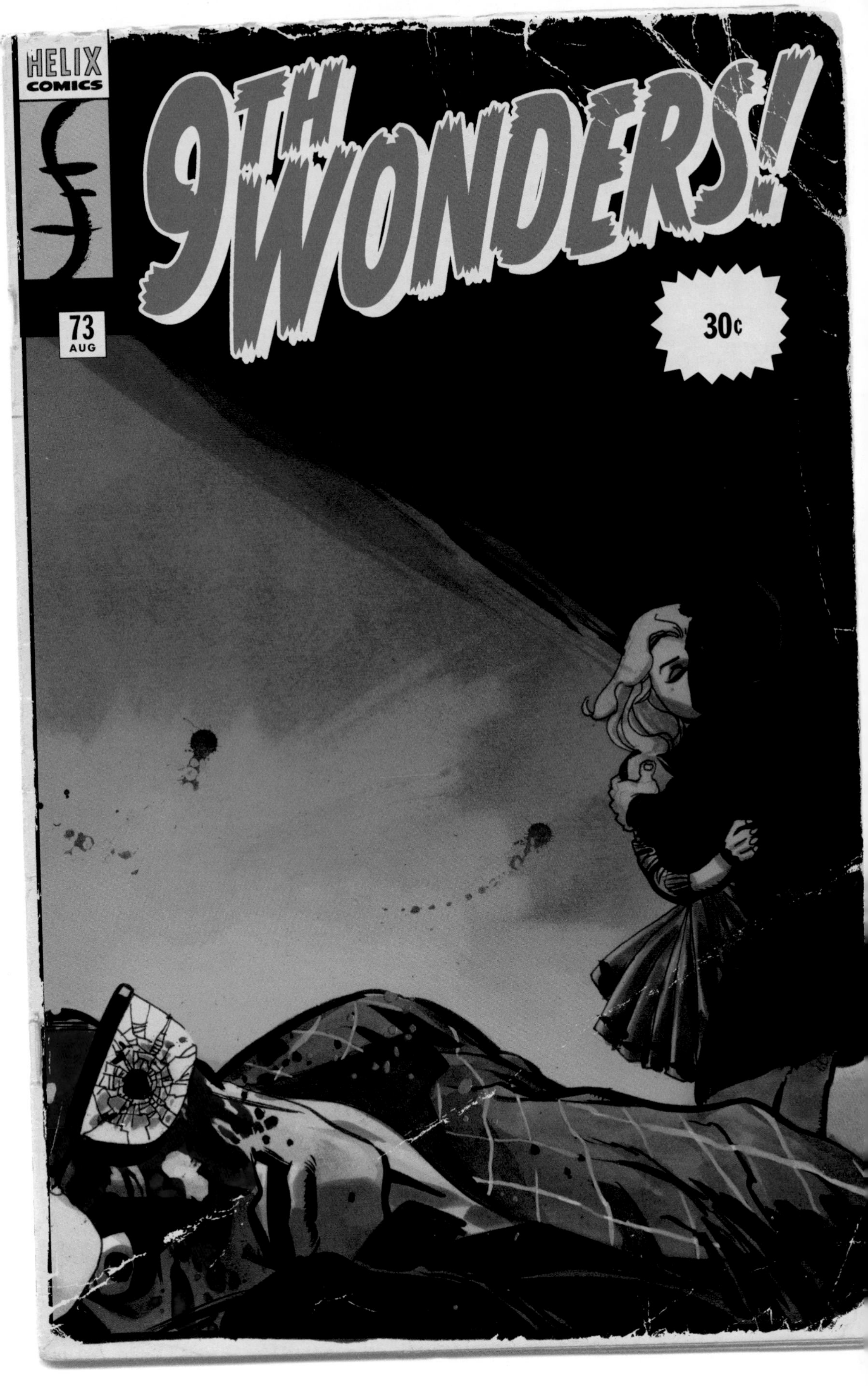
HELIX
COMICS
9TH WONDERS!
73
AUG
30¢

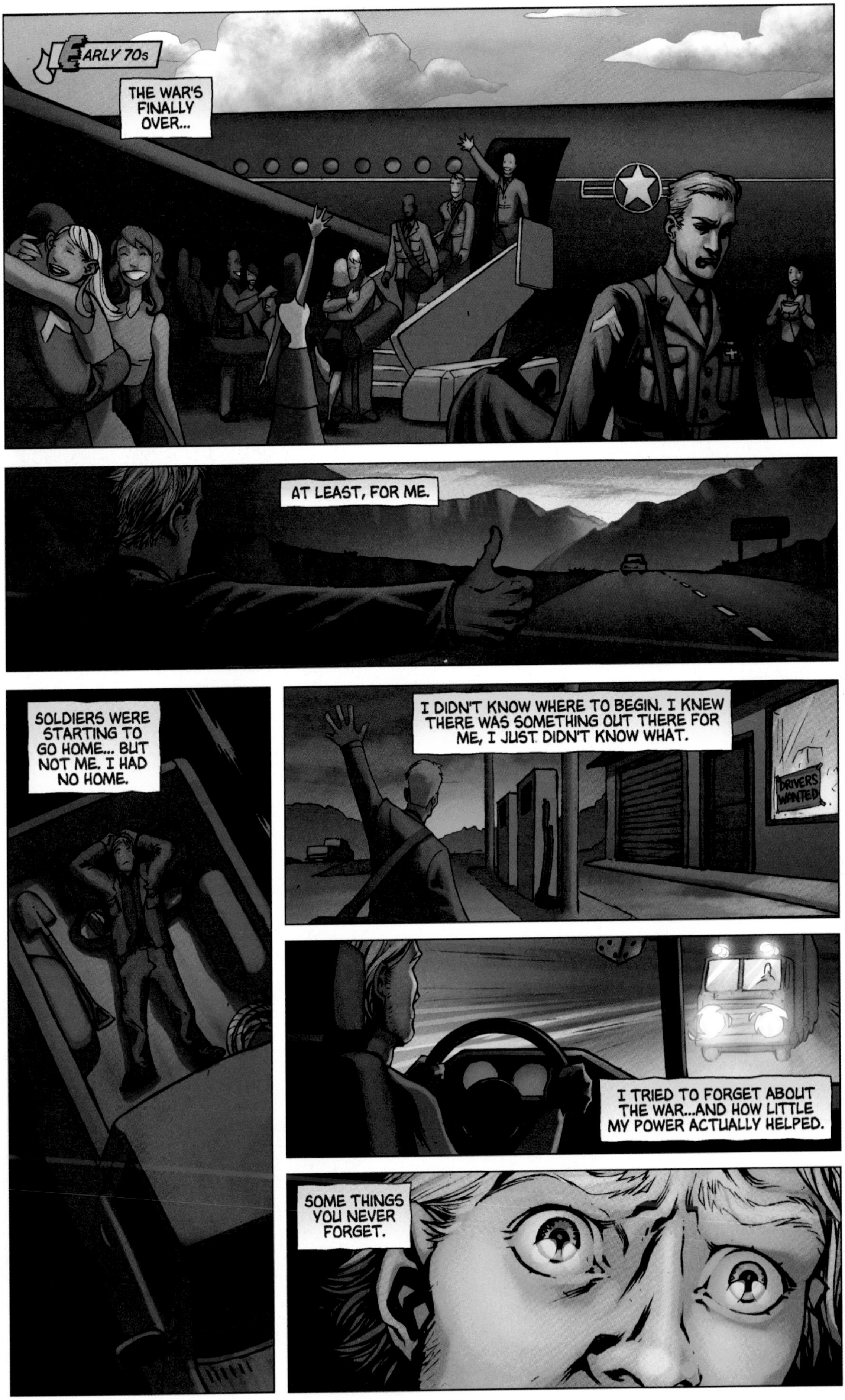
EARLY 70s
THE WAR'S FINALLY OVER...
AT LEAST, FOR ME.
SOLDIERS WERE STARTING TO GO HOME... BUT NOT ME. I HAD NO HOME.
I DIDN'T KNOW WHERE TO BEGIN. I KNEW THERE WAS SOMETHING OUT THERE FOR ME, I JUST DIDN'T KNOW WHAT.
DRIVERS WANTED
I TRIED TO FORGET ABOUT THE WAR...AND HOW LITTLE MY POWER ACTUALLY HELPED.
SOME THINGS YOU NEVER FORGET.

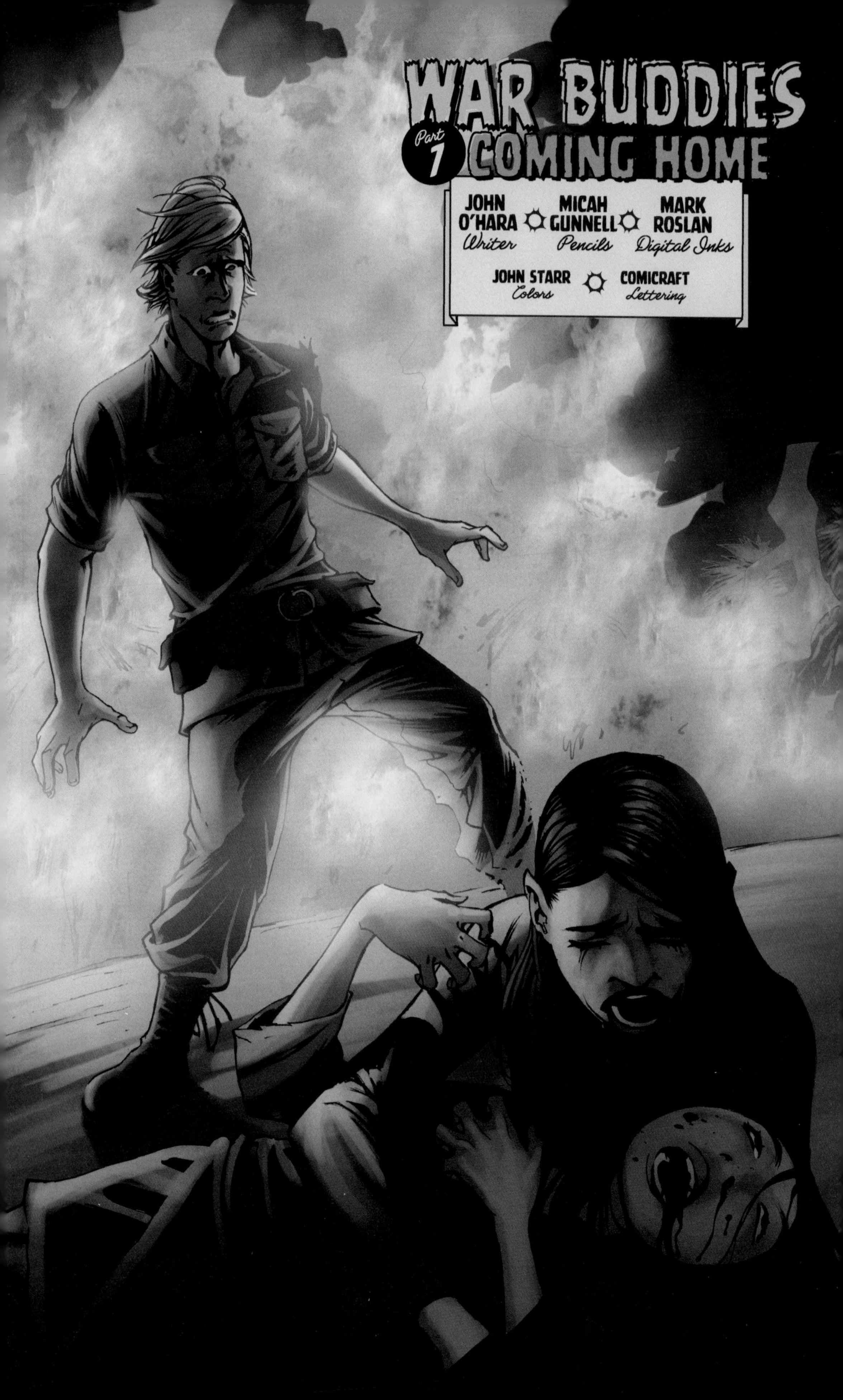

WAR BUDDIES
Part 1 COMING HOME
JOHN O'HARA Writer
MICAH GUNNELL Pencils
MARK ROSLAN Digital Inks
JOHN STARR Colors
COMICRAFT Lettering

I PICKED UP MORE THAN A FEW BAD HABITS.

YOU SHOULD REALLY EAT SOMETHING, DANIEL. CAN I HAVE THE KITCHEN WHIP SOMETHING UP FOR YOU?

SURE, WHY NOT?

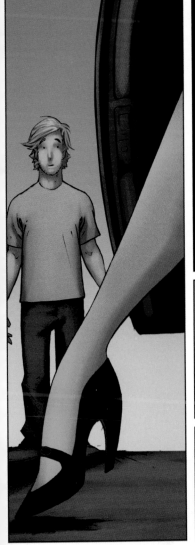

WHAT'S A BEAUTIFUL WOMAN LIKE YOU DOING ALL THE WAY OUT HERE?

STOP BY LATER AND I'LL TELL YOU.

Black Hawk Campgrounds. Site #09

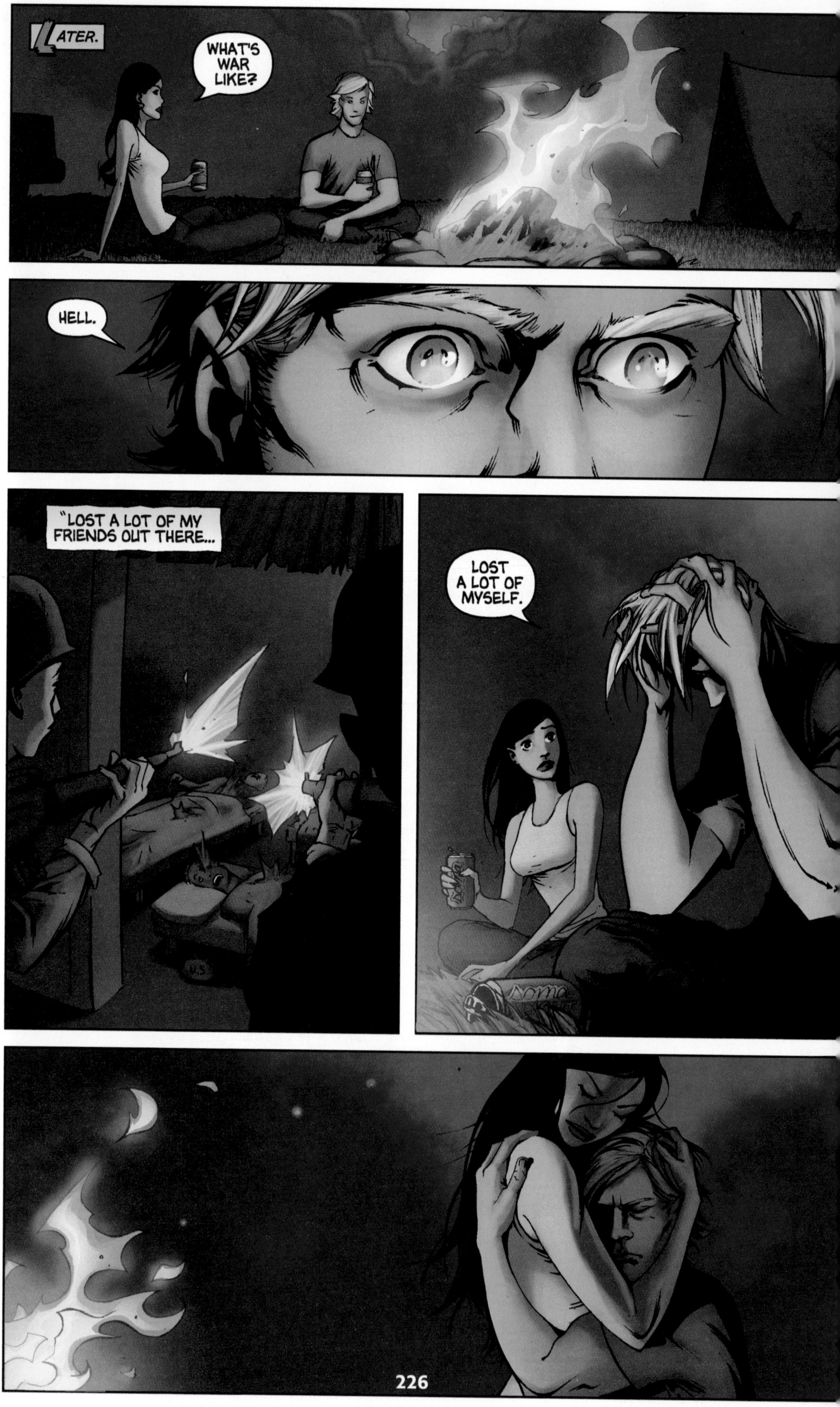
LATER.
WHAT'S WAR LIKE?
HELL.
"LOST A LOT OF MY FRIENDS OUT THERE...
LOST A LOT OF MYSELF.

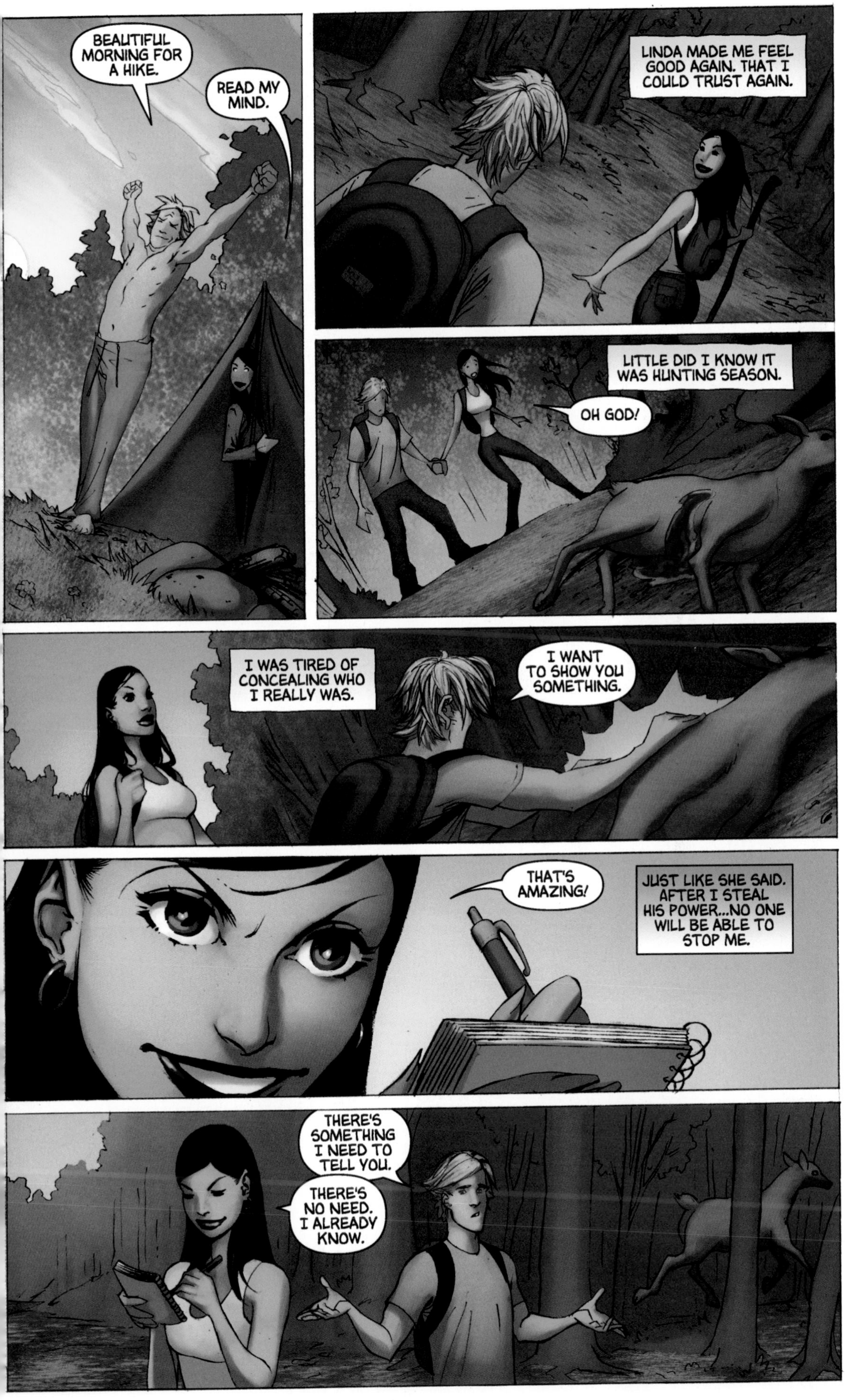
BEAUTIFUL MORNING FOR A HIKE.
READ MY MIND.
LINDA MADE ME FEEL GOOD AGAIN. THAT I COULD TRUST AGAIN.
LITTLE DID I KNOW IT WAS HUNTING SEASON.
OH GOD!
I WAS TIRED OF CONCEALING WHO I REALLY WAS.
I WANT TO SHOW YOU SOMETHING.
THAT'S AMAZING!
JUST LIKE SHE SAID. AFTER I STEAL HIS POWER...NO ONE WILL BE ABLE TO STOP ME.
THERE'S SOMETHING I NEED TO TELL YOU.
THERE'S NO NEED. I ALREADY KNOW.

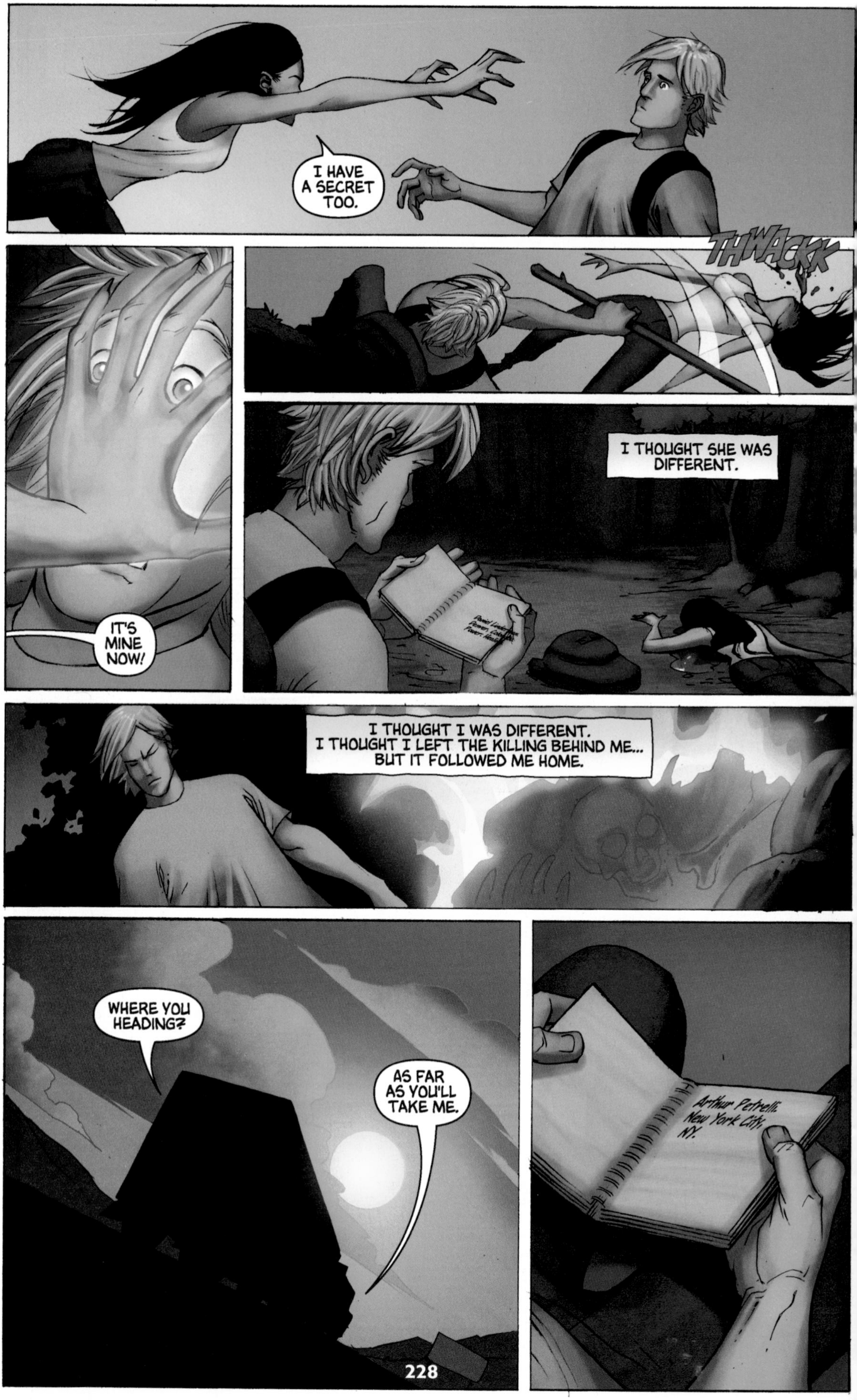
I HAVE A SECRET TOO.
IT'S MINE NOW!
THWACKK
I THOUGHT SHE WAS DIFFERENT.
I THOUGHT I WAS DIFFERENT.
I THOUGHT I LEFT THE KILLING BEHIND ME...
BUT IT FOLLOWED ME HOME.
WHERE YOU HEADING?
AS FAR AS YOU'LL TAKE ME.
Arthur Petrelli.
New York City,
NY.

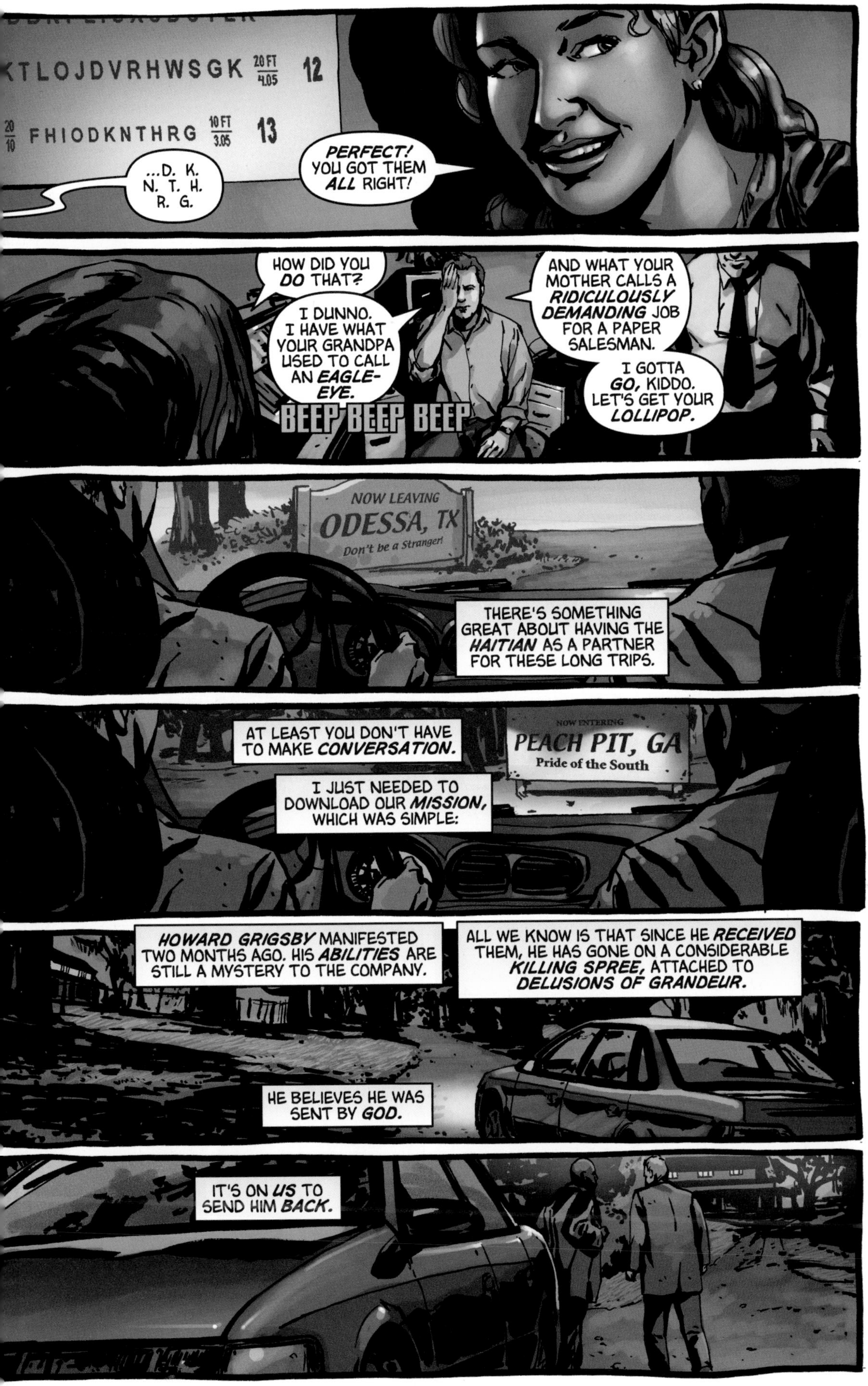
KTLOJDVRHWSGK 20 FT 4.05 12
20/10 FHIODKNTHRG 10 FT 3.05 13
...D. K. N. T. H. R. G.
PERFECT! YOU GOT THEM ALL RIGHT!
HOW DID YOU DO THAT?
I DUNNO. I HAVE WHAT YOUR GRANDPA USED TO CALL AN EAGLE-EYE.
BEEP BEEP BEEP
AND WHAT YOUR MOTHER CALLS A RIDICULOUSLY DEMANDING JOB FOR A PAPER SALESMAN.
I GOTTA GO, KIDDO. LET'S GET YOUR LOLLIPOP.
NOW LEAVING ODESSA, TX Don't be a Stranger!
THERE'S SOMETHING GREAT ABOUT HAVING THE HAITIAN AS A PARTNER FOR THESE LONG TRIPS.
AT LEAST YOU DON'T HAVE TO MAKE CONVERSATION.
NOW ENTERING PEACH PIT, GA Pride of the South
I JUST NEEDED TO DOWNLOAD OUR MISSION, WHICH WAS SIMPLE:
HOWARD GRIGSBY MANIFESTED TWO MONTHS AGO. HIS ABILITIES ARE STILL A MYSTERY TO THE COMPANY.
ALL WE KNOW IS THAT SINCE HE RECEIVED THEM, HE HAS GONE ON A CONSIDERABLE KILLING SPREE, ATTACHED TO DELUSIONS OF GRANDEUR.
HE BELIEVES HE WAS SENT BY GOD.
IT'S ON US TO SEND HIM BACK.

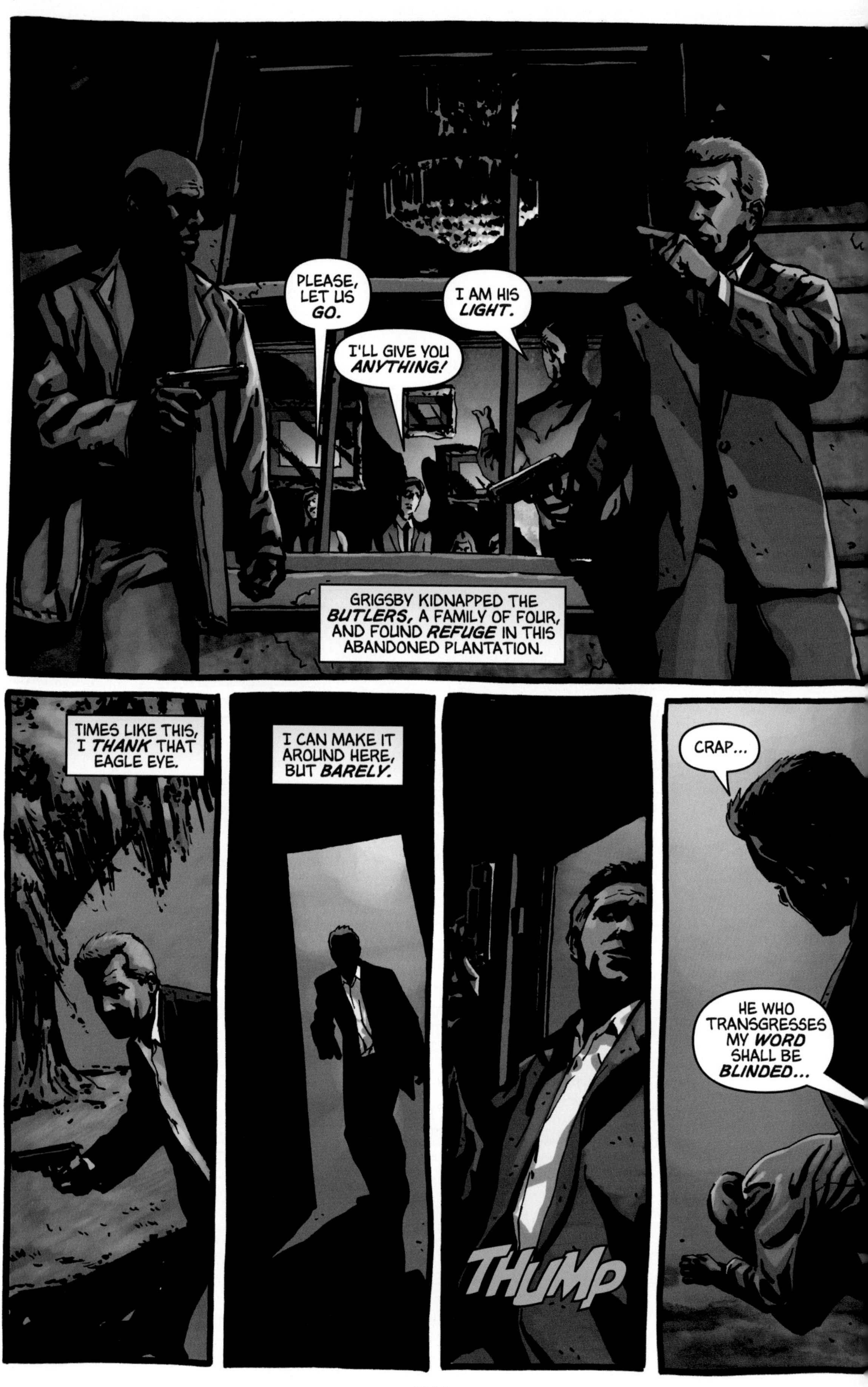
PLEASE, LET US GO.
I'LL GIVE YOU ANYTHING!
I AM HIS LIGHT.
GRIGSBY KIDNAPPED THE BUTLERS, A FAMILY OF FOUR, AND FOUND REFUGE IN THIS ABANDONED PLANTATION.
TIMES LIKE THIS, I THANK THAT EAGLE EYE.
I CAN MAKE IT AROUND HERE, BUT BARELY.
THUMP
CRAP...
HE WHO TRANSGRESSES MY WORD SHALL BE BLINDED...

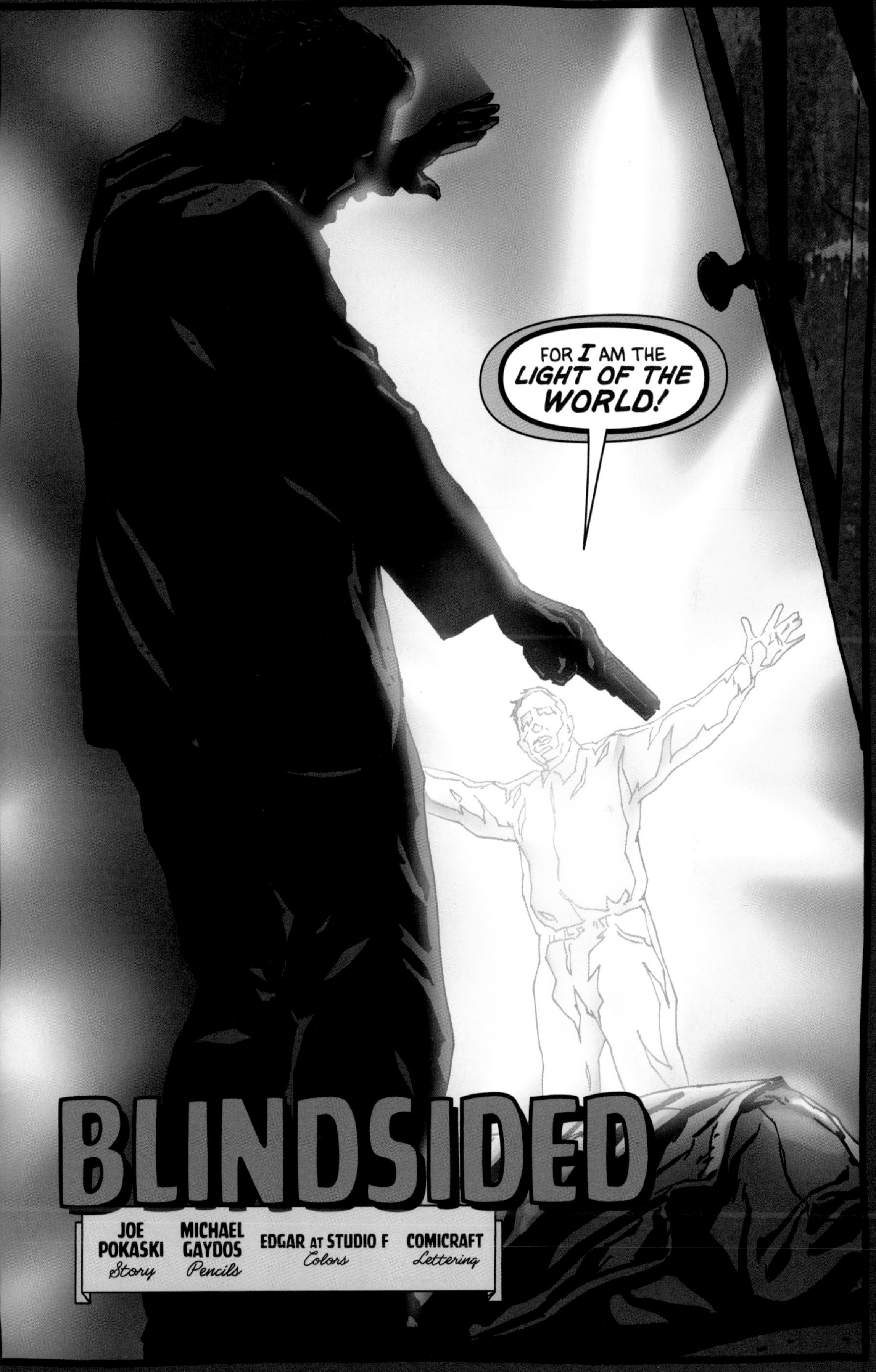
FOR I AM THE LIGHT OF THE WORLD!
BLINDSIDED
JOE POKASKI Story
MICHAEL GAYDOS Pencils
EDGAR AT STUDIO F Colors
COMICRAFT Lettering

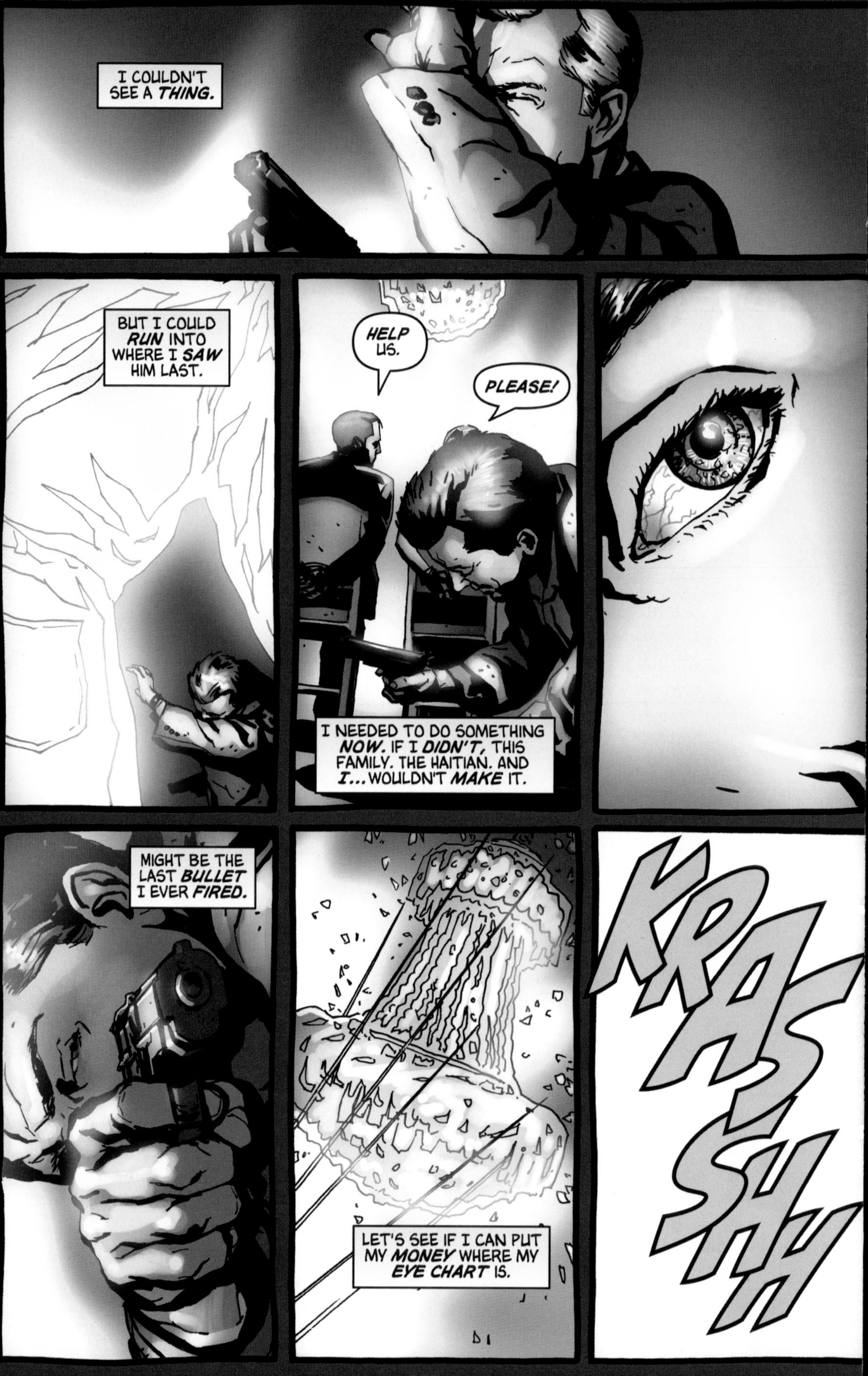
I COULDN'T SEE A *THING.*
BUT I COULD *RUN* INTO WHERE I *SAW* HIM LAST.
*HELP* US.
*PLEASE!*
I NEEDED TO DO SOMETHING *NOW.* IF I *DIDN'T,* THIS FAMILY. THE HAITIAN. AND *I...* WOULDN'T *MAKE* IT.
MIGHT BE THE LAST *BULLET* I EVER *FIRED.*
LET'S SEE IF I CAN PUT MY *MONEY* WHERE MY *EYE CHART* IS.
KRASHH

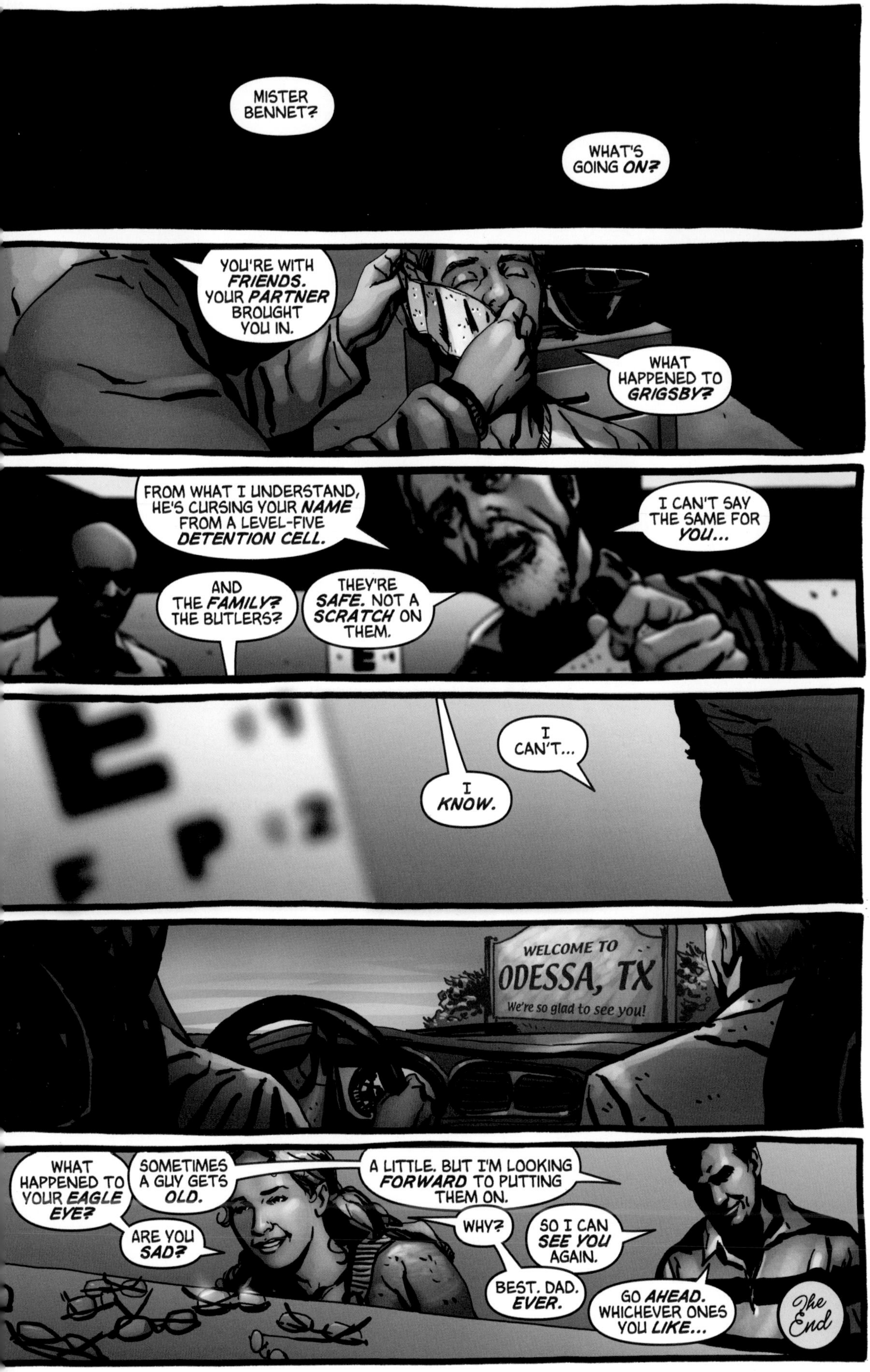
MISTER BENNET?
WHAT'S GOING ON?
YOU'RE WITH FRIENDS. YOUR PARTNER BROUGHT YOU IN.
WHAT HAPPENED TO GRIGSBY?
FROM WHAT I UNDERSTAND, HE'S CURSING YOUR NAME FROM A LEVEL-FIVE DETENTION CELL.
I CAN'T SAY THE SAME FOR YOU...
AND THE FAMILY? THE BUTLERS?
THEY'RE SAFE. NOT A SCRATCH ON THEM.
I CAN'T...
I KNOW.
WELCOME TO
ODESSA, TX
We're so glad to see you!
WHAT HAPPENED TO YOUR EAGLE EYE?
SOMETIMES A GUY GETS OLD.
ARE YOU SAD?
A LITTLE. BUT I'M LOOKING FORWARD TO PUTTING THEM ON.
WHY?
SO I CAN SEE YOU AGAIN.
BEST. DAD. EVER.
GO AHEAD. WHICHEVER ONES YOU LIKE...
The End

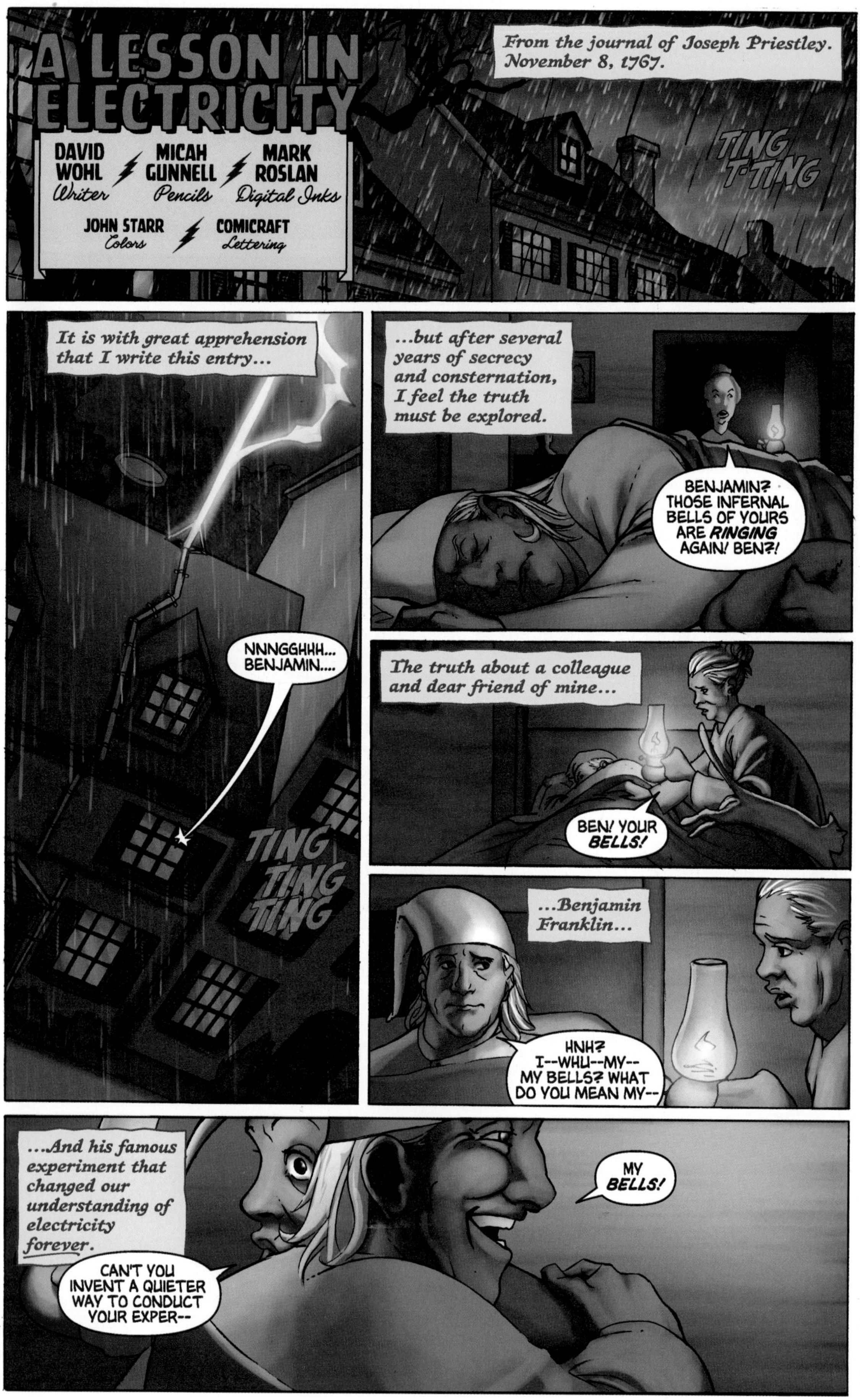
A LESSON IN ELECTRICITY
DAVID WOHL Writer
MICAH GUNNELL Pencils
MARK ROSLAN Digital Inks
JOHN STARR Colors
COMICRAFT Lettering
From the journal of Joseph Priestley. November 8, 1767.
TING T-TING
It is with great apprehension that I write this entry...
NNNGGHHH... BENJAMIN....
TING TING TING
...but after several years of secrecy and consternation, I feel the truth must be explored.
BENJAMIN? THOSE INFERNAL BELLS OF YOURS ARE RINGING AGAIN! BEN?!
The truth about a colleague and dear friend of mine...
BEN! YOUR BELLS!
...Benjamin Franklin...
HNH? I--WHU--MY-- MY BELLS? WHAT DO YOU MEAN MY--
...And his famous experiment that changed our understanding of electricity forever.
CAN'T YOU INVENT A QUIETER WAY TO CONDUCT YOUR EXPER--
MY BELLS!

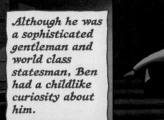

Although he was a sophisticated gentleman and world class statesman, Ben had a childlike curiosity about him.

FATHER? IS EVERYTHING ALL RIGHT?

THE BELLS ARE RINGING, WILL! ISN'T THAT *WONDERFUL?!*

He relished every small discovery, and, once he was interested, needed to thoroughly under~stand anything and everything about a myriad of topics...

...including, in this case, *lightning.*

Contrary to the conventional wisdom of the day, Mr. Franklin believed that lightning was, in fact, made of electricity~and that it could be <u>controlled.</u>

To prove it, he first attached a large strip of iron to his roof and connected it to a series of bells.

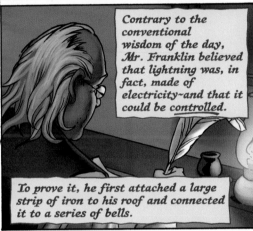

This, he surmised, would alert him when there was lightning in the area.

Armed with this knowledge, he was determined to find a way to "capture" the lightning...

...thus proving that the so~called "Law of Conservation of Charge" applied to lightning.

MOTHER WISHES TO KNOW IF SHE CAN EXPECT YOU FOR BREAKFAST THIS MORNING.

But to do so, he was going to need some <u>help.</u>

AH, WILLIAM. I'M GLAD YOU'RE HERE. THERE'S SOMETHING I NEED TO SPEAK WITH YOU ABOUT...

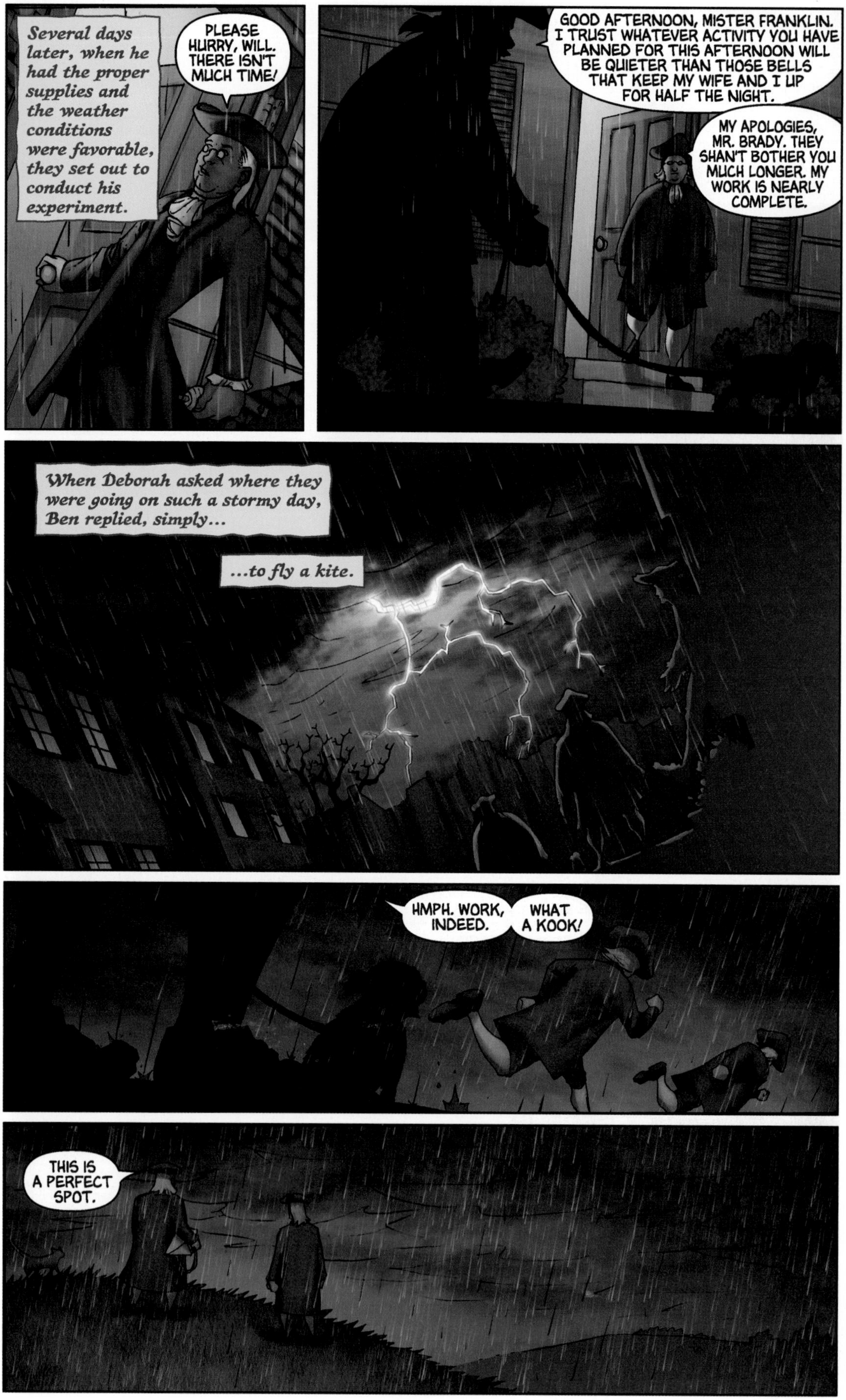

Several days later, when he had the proper supplies and the weather conditions were favorable, they set out to conduct his experiment.
PLEASE HURRY, WILL. THERE ISN'T MUCH TIME!
GOOD AFTERNOON, MISTER FRANKLIN. I TRUST WHATEVER ACTIVITY YOU HAVE PLANNED FOR THIS AFTERNOON WILL BE QUIETER THAN THOSE BELLS THAT KEEP MY WIFE AND I UP FOR HALF THE NIGHT.
MY APOLOGIES, MR. BRADY. THEY SHAN'T BOTHER YOU MUCH LONGER. MY WORK IS NEARLY COMPLETE.
When Deborah asked where they were going on such a stormy day, Ben replied, simply...
...to fly a kite.
HMPH. WORK, INDEED.
WHAT A KOOK!
THIS IS A PERFECT SPOT.

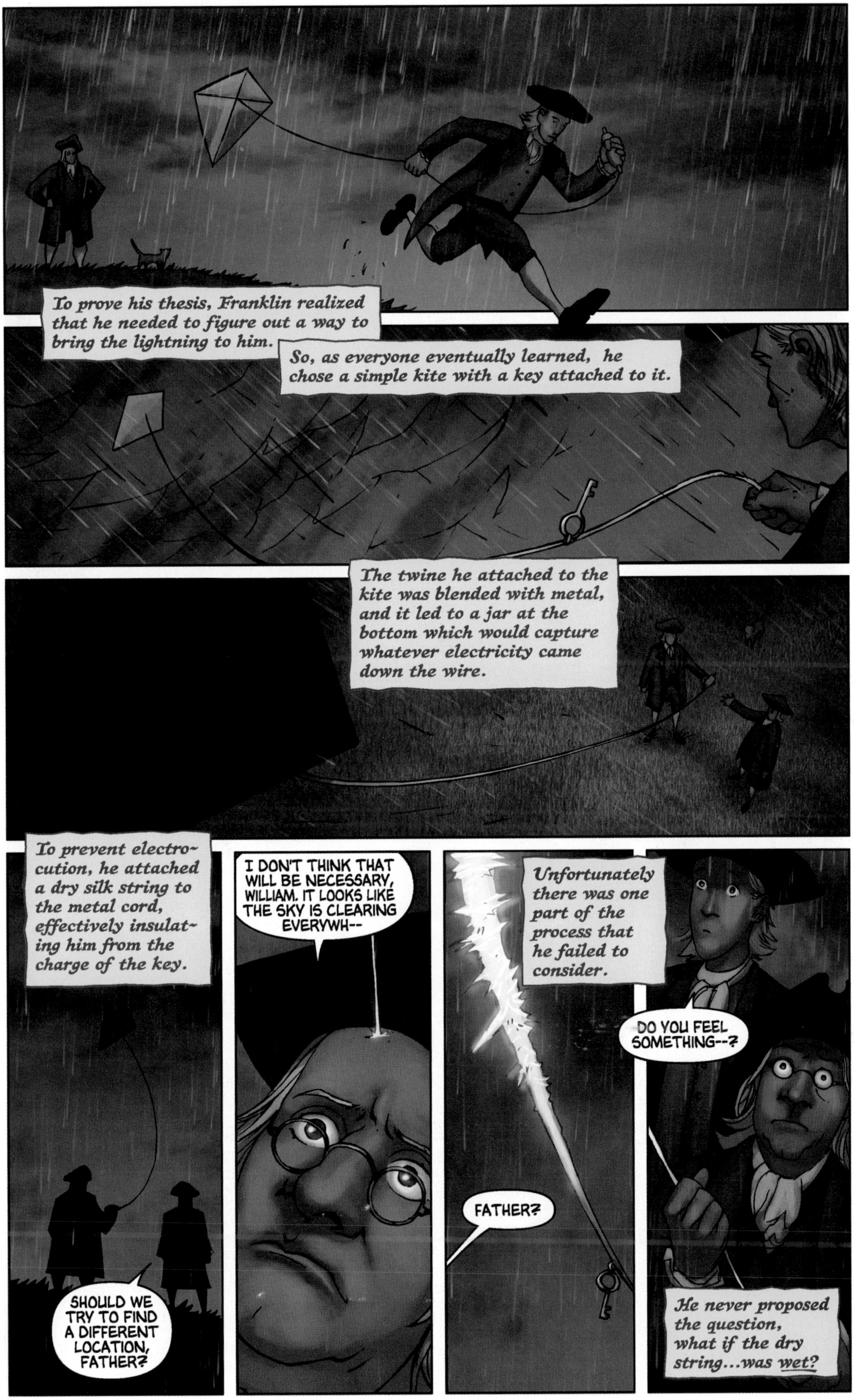
To prove his thesis, Franklin realized that he needed to figure out a way to bring the lightning to him.
So, as everyone eventually learned, he chose a simple kite with a key attached to it.
The twine he attached to the kite was blended with metal, and it led to a jar at the bottom which would capture whatever electricity came down the wire.
To prevent electrocution, he attached a dry silk string to the metal cord, effectively insulating him from the charge of the key.
SHOULD WE TRY TO FIND A DIFFERENT LOCATION, FATHER?
I DON'T THINK THAT WILL BE NECESSARY, WILLIAM. IT LOOKS LIKE THE SKY IS CLEARING EVERYWH--
Unfortunately there was one part of the process that he failed to consider.
FATHER?
DO YOU FEEL SOMETHING--?
He never proposed the question, what if the dry string...was wet?

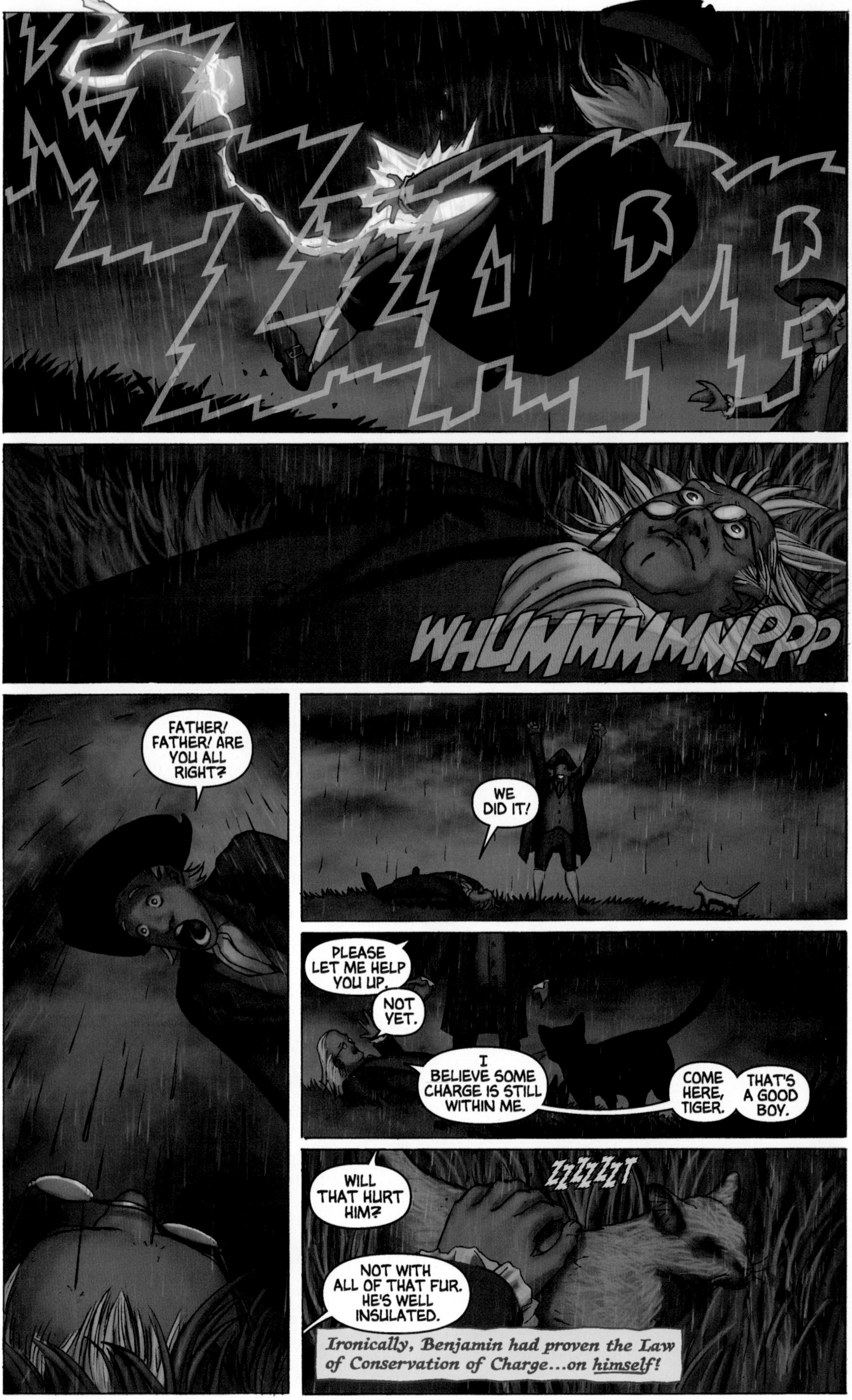
WHUMMMMMMPPP
FATHER! FATHER! ARE YOU ALL RIGHT?
WE DID IT!
PLEASE LET ME HELP YOU UP.
NOT YET.
I BELIEVE SOME CHARGE IS STILL WITHIN ME.
COME HERE, TIGER.
THAT'S A GOOD BOY.
ZZZZZZT
WILL THAT HURT HIM?
NOT WITH ALL OF THAT FUR. HE'S WELL INSULATED.
Ironically, Benjamin had proven the Law of Conservation of Charge...on himself!

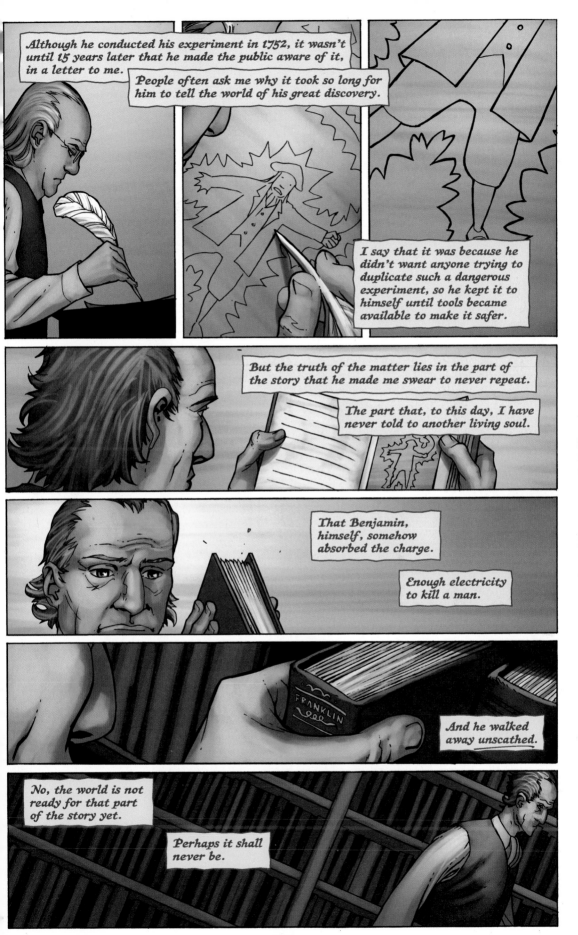

Although he conducted his experiment in 1752, it wasn't until 15 years later that he made the public aware of it, in a letter to me.

People often ask me why it took so long for him to tell the world of his great discovery.

I say that it was because he didn't want anyone trying to duplicate such a dangerous experiment, so he kept it to himself until tools became available to make it safer.

But the truth of the matter lies in the part of the story that he made me swear to never repeat.

The part that, to this day, I have never told to another living soul.

That Benjamin, himself, somehow absorbed the charge.

Enough electricity to kill a man.

And he walked away unscathed.

No, the world is not ready for that part of the story yet.

Perhaps it shall never be.

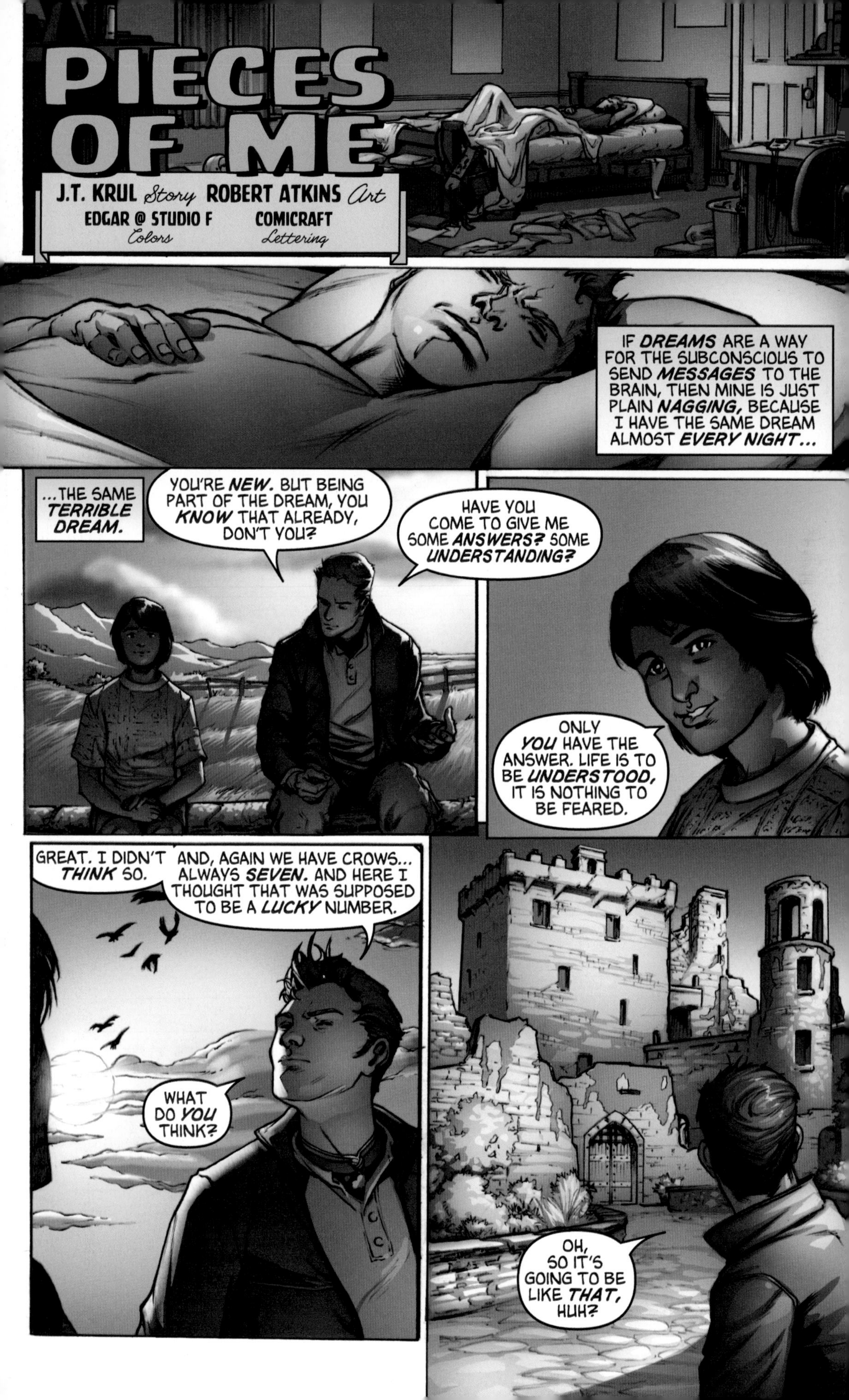
PIECES OF ME
J.T. KRUL Story ROBERT ATKINS Art
EDGAR @ STUDIO F Colors
COMICRAFT Lettering
IF DREAMS ARE A WAY FOR THE SUBCONSCIOUS TO SEND MESSAGES TO THE BRAIN, THEN MINE IS JUST PLAIN NAGGING, BECAUSE I HAVE THE SAME DREAM ALMOST EVERY NIGHT...
...THE SAME TERRIBLE DREAM.
YOU'RE NEW. BUT BEING PART OF THE DREAM, YOU KNOW THAT ALREADY, DON'T YOU?
HAVE YOU COME TO GIVE ME SOME ANSWERS? SOME UNDERSTANDING?
ONLY YOU HAVE THE ANSWER. LIFE IS TO BE UNDERSTOOD, IT IS NOTHING TO BE FEARED.
GREAT. I DIDN'T THINK SO.
AND, AGAIN WE HAVE CROWS... ALWAYS SEVEN. AND HERE I THOUGHT THAT WAS SUPPOSED TO BE A LUCKY NUMBER.
WHAT DO YOU THINK?
OH, SO IT'S GOING TO BE LIKE THAT, HUH?

Issued Date:
Nov 17, 200

Coto De Caza

Permit ID:
8-1083402

# G-PASS

## VALID FOR OVERNIGHT PARKING

Valid Through:

# Dec 02

Issued To:

**KEVIN FITZPATRICK**

Guest Of:

**2 VELA COURT**

# LIC#: **5RAD948**

Directions to Residence:

**PASS SANDY KNOLL ON RIGHT. TURN EITHER LEFT OR RIGHT AT NEXT STREET, VELA CT.**

Gate: South Bend

Time: 11:10:48

**PLACE ON DRIVER'S SIDE DASH**

## THE ISSUANCE OF THIS PASS IS CONTINGENT UPON THE FOLLOWING RESTRICTIONS AND REGULATIONS TO WHICH VISITOR AGREES AS A CONDITION OF ADMISSION:

1. This pass must be placed in the lower left side of the windshield and remain visible at all times.

2. Our speed limit is **25 MPH** unless otherwise posted. Coto de Caza is a family community - watch for children at play.

3. Motorists are required to observe all traffic and parking regulations and signs. Overnight parking on any street in Coto de Caza is prohibited unless prior authorization is obtained.

4. Fires and fireworks are not permitted.

5. Use of CZ Master Association facilities is permitted only when accompanied by a resident.

6. Pets must be leashed at all times.

7. Operator of vehicle possesses a valid driver's licence and agrees to present it upon request of any security officer of Coto de Caza.

8. Operator/Owner of vehicle has, at a minimum, general liability insurance required by law and agrees to show evidence of such coverage upon request of any security officer of Coto de Caza.

9. Permission to pass may be revoked at any time.

**Any violation of these restrictions will subject vehicle to towing at owner's expense under authority of CVC 22658 and/or 22658.2.**

# www.GateWorksGroup.com

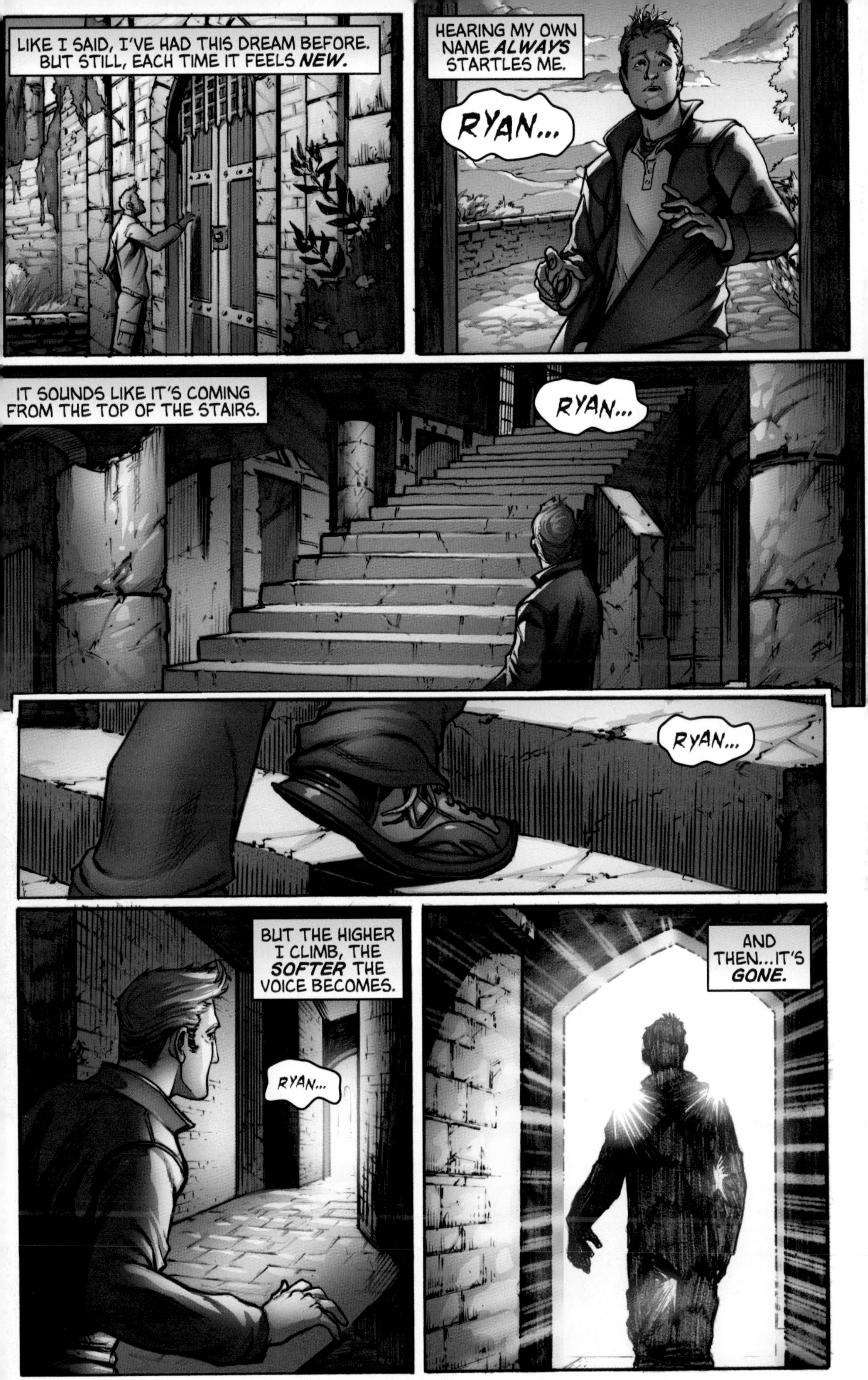
LIKE I SAID, I'VE HAD THIS DREAM BEFORE. BUT STILL, EACH TIME IT FEELS *NEW.*
HEARING MY OWN NAME *ALWAYS* STARTLES ME.
RYAN...
IT SOUNDS LIKE IT'S COMING FROM THE TOP OF THE STAIRS.
RYAN...
RYAN...
BUT THE HIGHER I CLIMB, THE *SOFTER* THE VOICE BECOMES.
RYAN...
AND THEN...IT'S *GONE.*

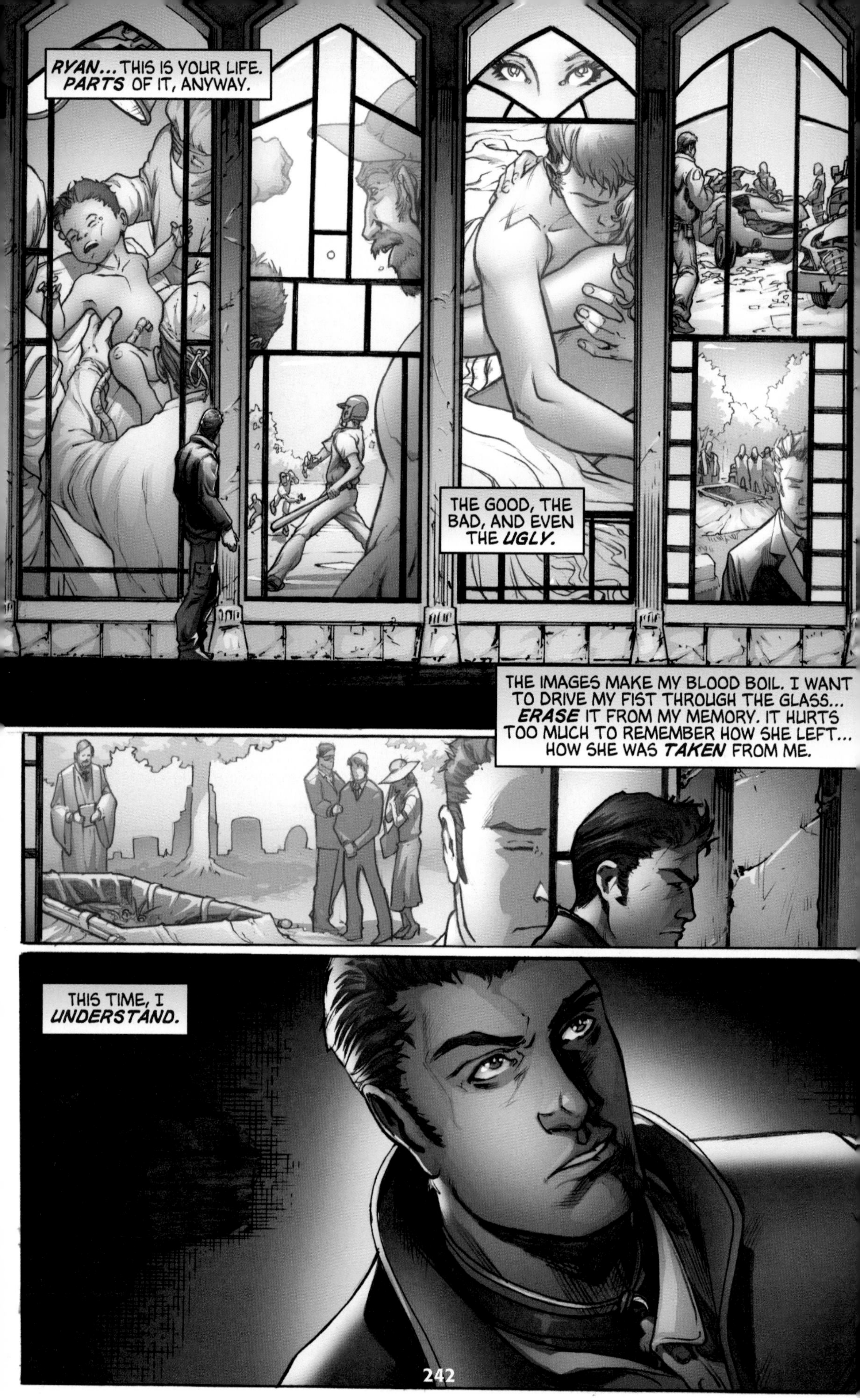
RYAN... THIS IS YOUR LIFE. PARTS OF IT, ANYWAY.
THE GOOD, THE BAD, AND EVEN THE UGLY.
THE IMAGES MAKE MY BLOOD BOIL. I WANT TO DRIVE MY FIST THROUGH THE GLASS... ERASE IT FROM MY MEMORY. IT HURTS TOO MUCH TO REMEMBER HOW SHE LEFT... HOW SHE WAS TAKEN FROM ME.
THIS TIME, I UNDERSTAND.

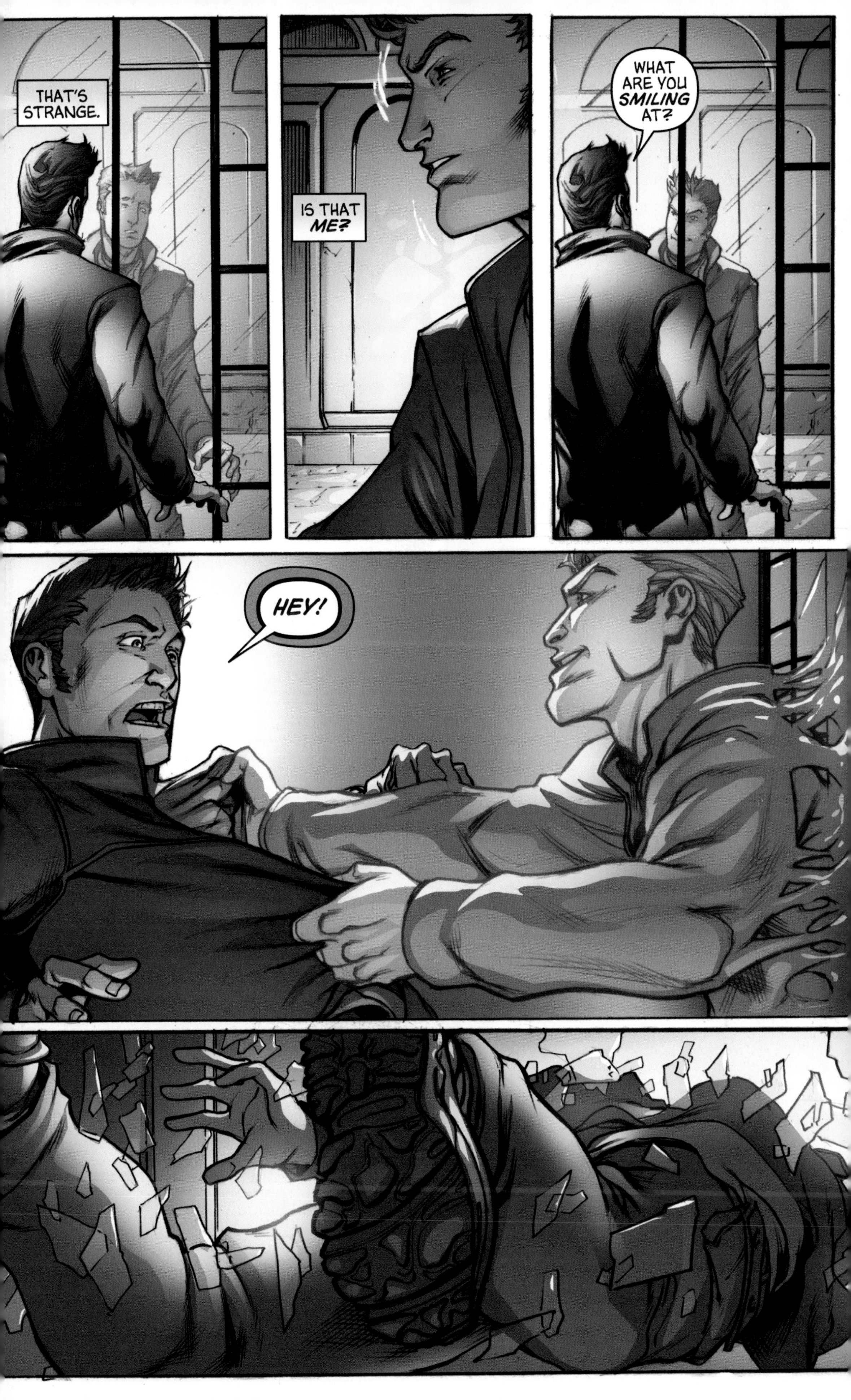
THAT'S STRANGE.
IS THAT ME?
WHAT ARE YOU SMILING AT?
HEY!

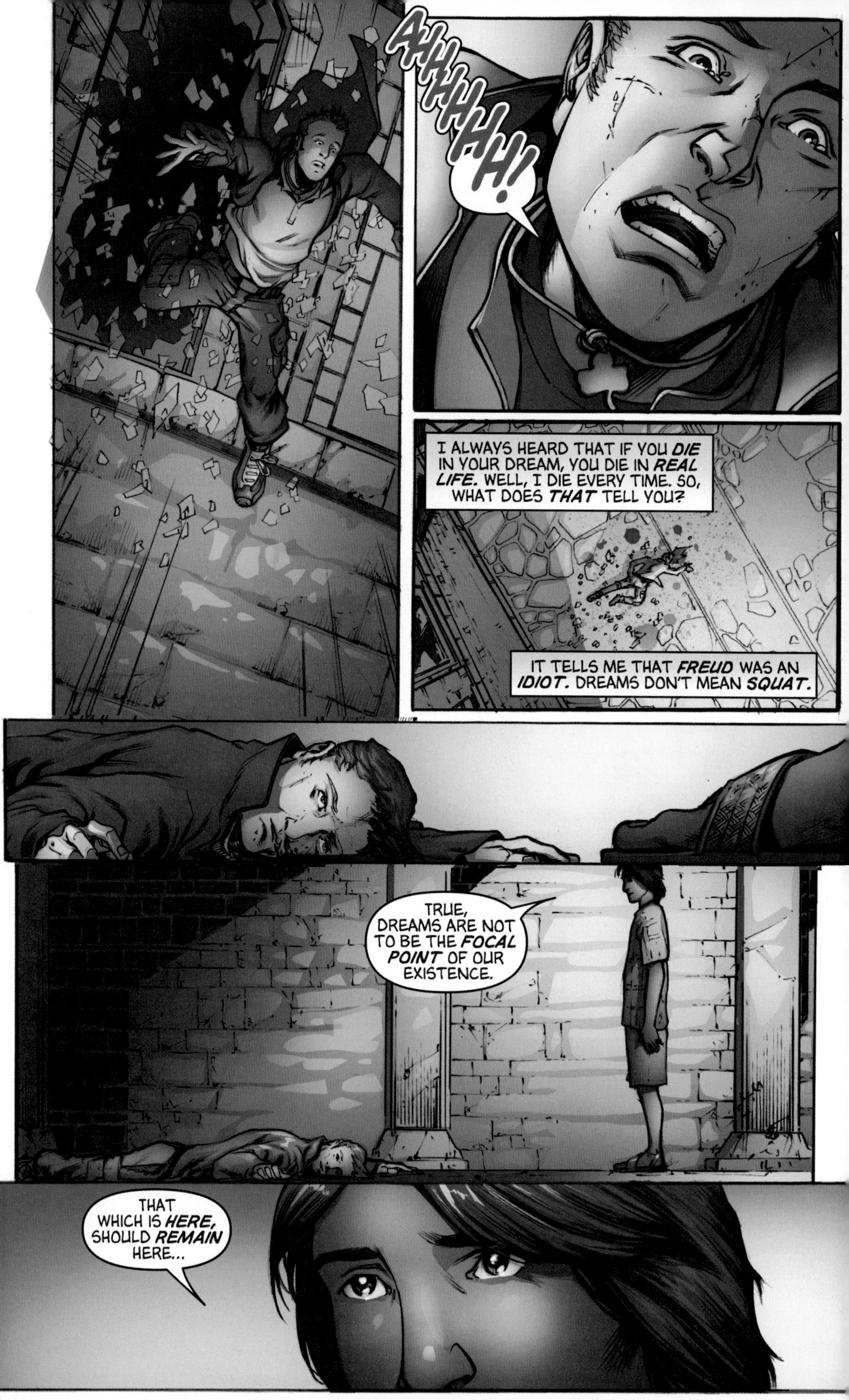
AHHHHH!
I ALWAYS HEARD THAT IF YOU DIE IN YOUR DREAM, YOU DIE IN REAL LIFE. WELL, I DIE EVERY TIME. SO, WHAT DOES THAT TELL YOU?
IT TELLS ME THAT FREUD WAS AN IDIOT. DREAMS DON'T MEAN SQUAT.
TRUE, DREAMS ARE NOT TO BE THE FOCAL POINT OF OUR EXISTENCE.
THAT WHICH IS HERE, SHOULD REMAIN HERE...

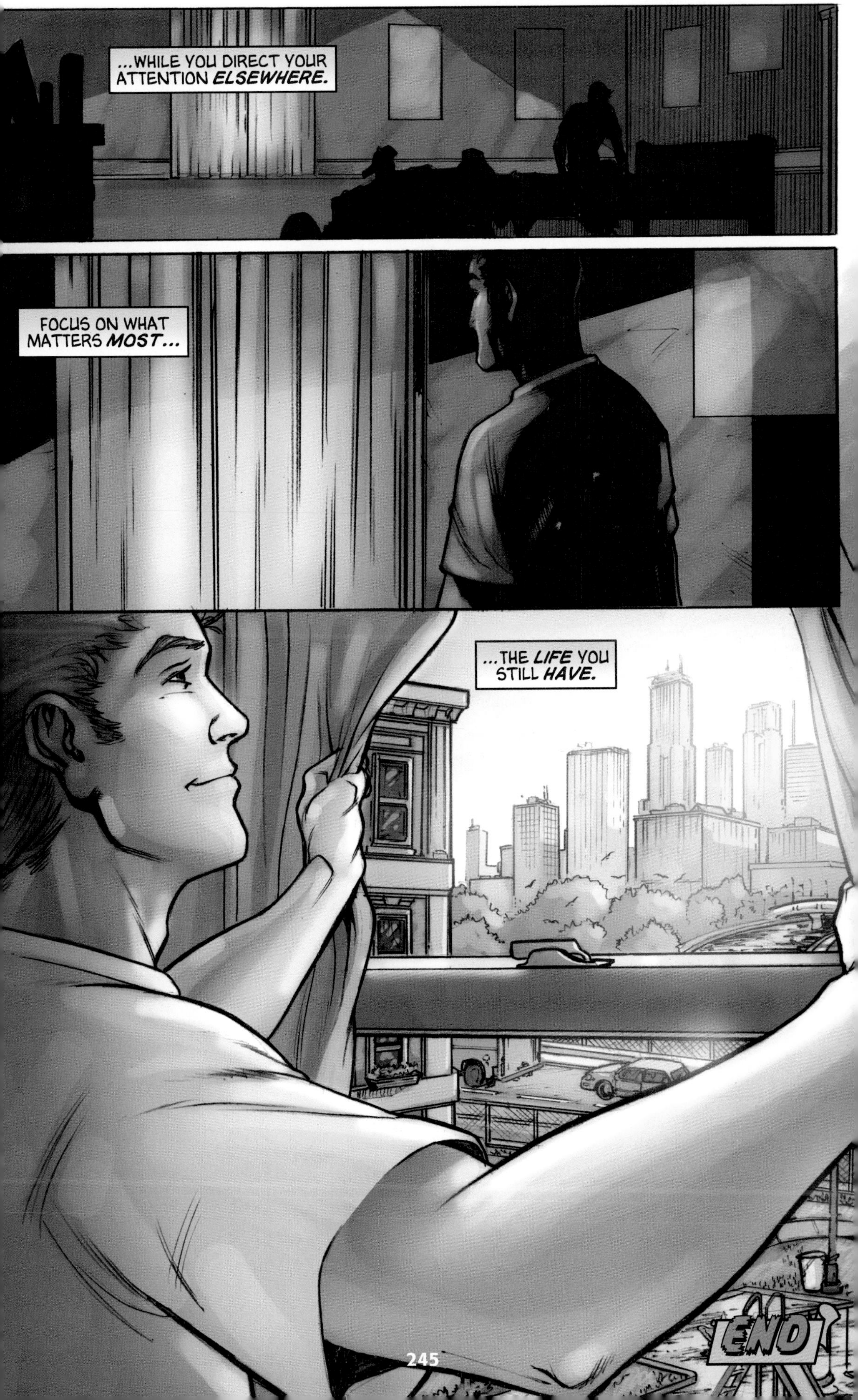
...WHILE YOU DIRECT YOUR ATTENTION *ELSEWHERE.*
FOCUS ON WHAT MATTERS *MOST...*
...THE *LIFE* YOU STILL *HAVE.*
END

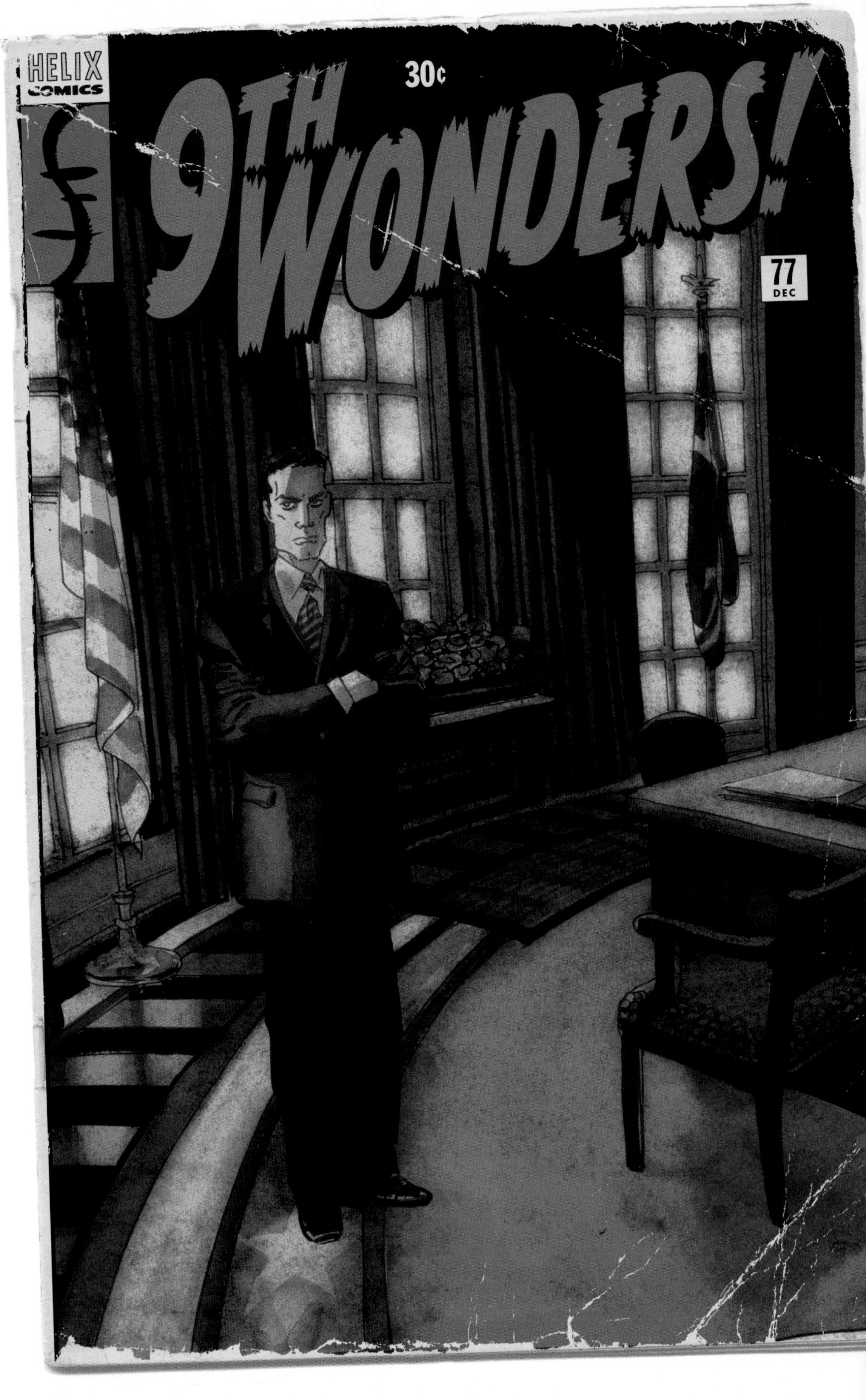
HELIX COMICS
30¢
9TH WONDERS!
77
DEC

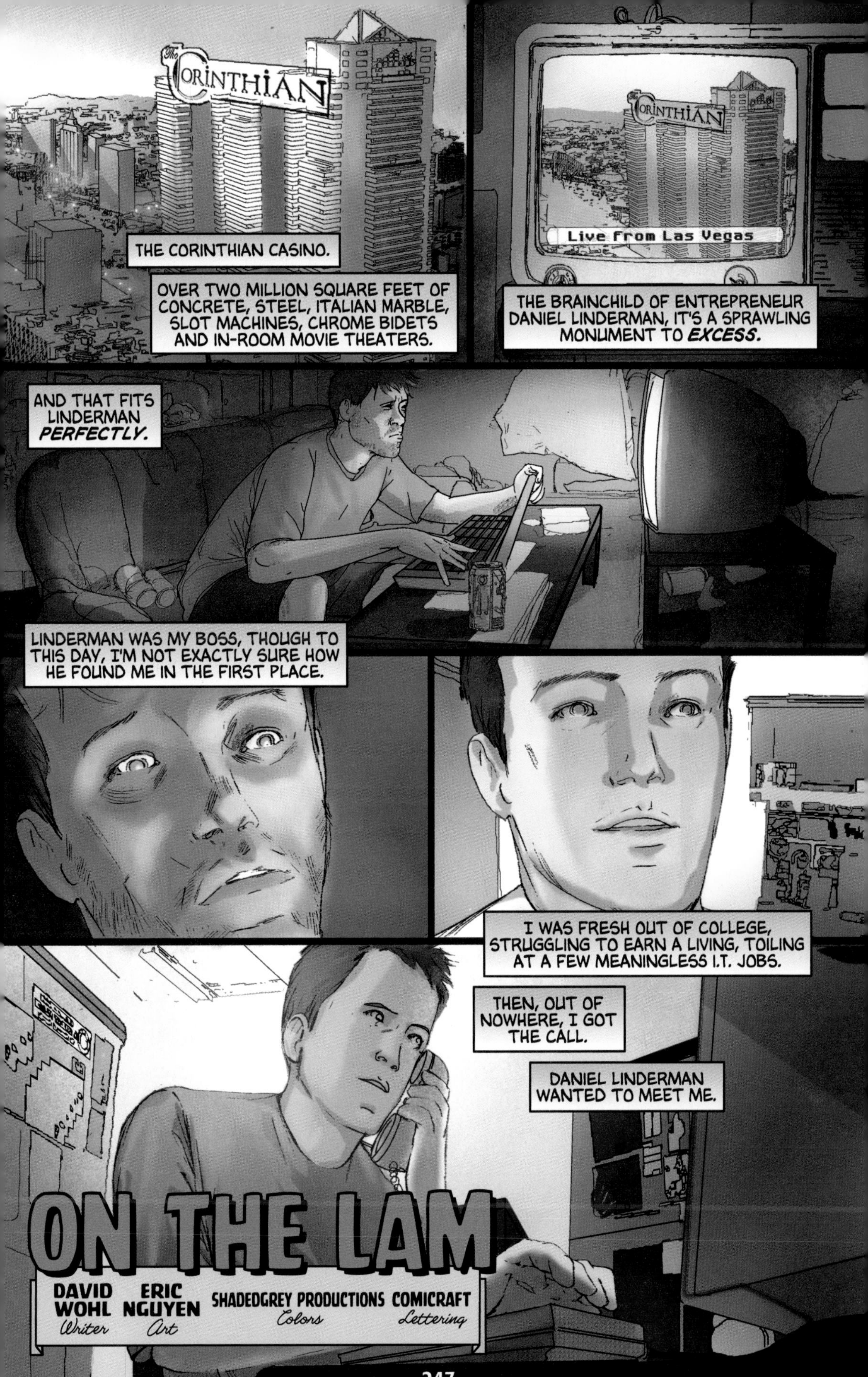
The CORINTHIAN
THE CORINTHIAN CASINO.
OVER TWO MILLION SQUARE FEET OF CONCRETE, STEEL, ITALIAN MARBLE, SLOT MACHINES, CHROME BIDETS AND IN-ROOM MOVIE THEATERS.
The CORINTHIAN
Live From Las Vegas
THE BRAINCHILD OF ENTREPRENEUR DANIEL LINDERMAN, IT'S A SPRAWLING MONUMENT TO *EXCESS.*
AND THAT FITS LINDERMAN *PERFECTLY.*
LINDERMAN WAS MY BOSS, THOUGH TO THIS DAY, I'M NOT EXACTLY SURE HOW HE FOUND ME IN THE FIRST PLACE.
I WAS FRESH OUT OF COLLEGE, STRUGGLING TO EARN A LIVING, TOILING AT A FEW MEANINGLESS I.T. JOBS.
THEN, OUT OF NOWHERE, I GOT THE CALL.
DANIEL LINDERMAN WANTED TO MEET ME.
ON THE LAM
DAVID WOHL Writer
ERIC NGUYEN Art
SHADEDGREY PRODUCTIONS Colors
COMICRAFT Lettering

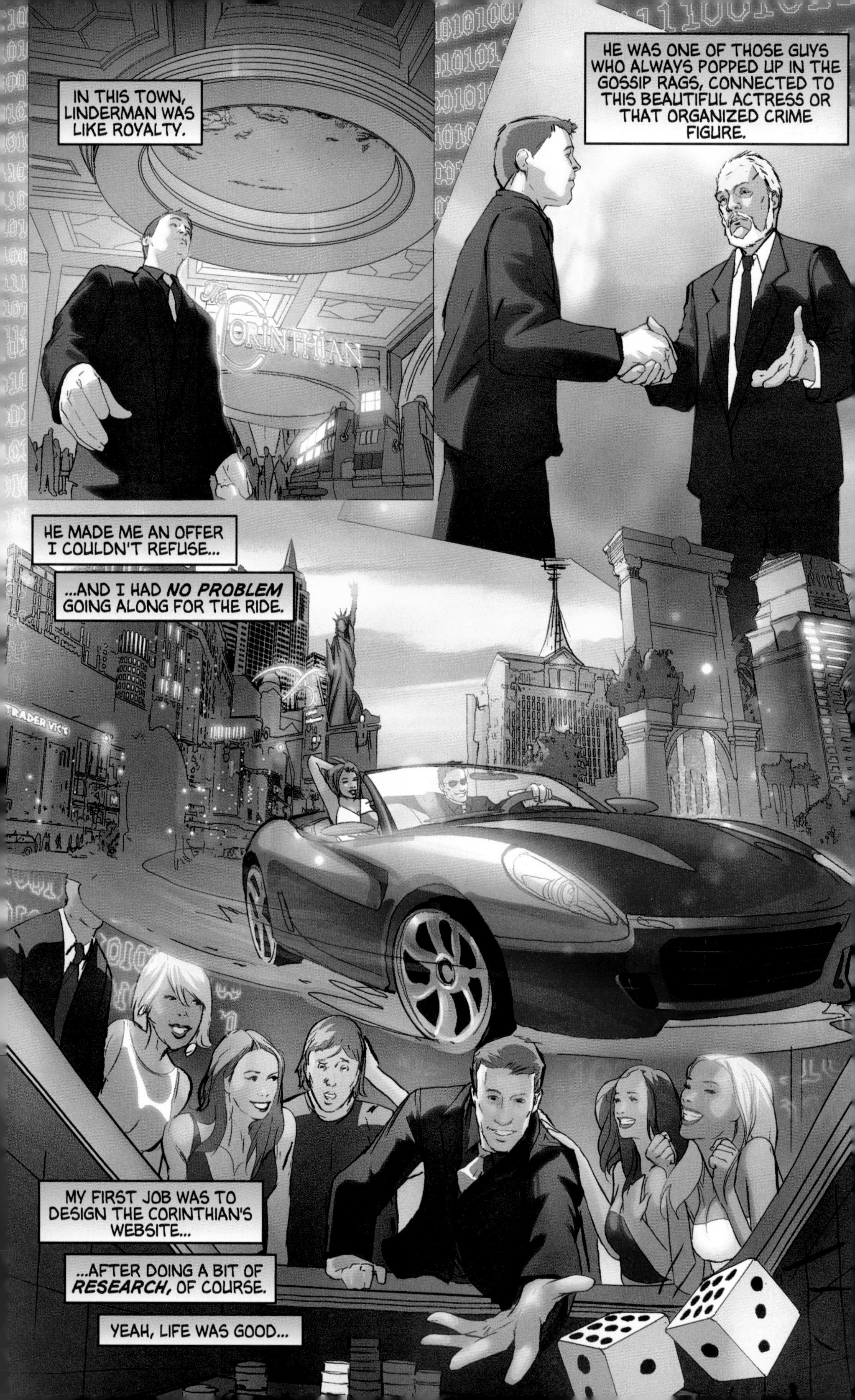

IN THIS TOWN, LINDERMAN WAS LIKE ROYALTY.
THE CORINTHIAN
HE WAS ONE OF THOSE GUYS WHO ALWAYS POPPED UP IN THE GOSSIP RAGS, CONNECTED TO THIS BEAUTIFUL ACTRESS OR THAT ORGANIZED CRIME FIGURE.
HE MADE ME AN OFFER I COULDN'T REFUSE...
...AND I HAD NO PROBLEM GOING ALONG FOR THE RIDE.
TRADER VIC'S
MY FIRST JOB WAS TO DESIGN THE CORINTHIAN'S WEBSITE...
...AFTER DOING A BIT OF RESEARCH, OF COURSE.
YEAH, LIFE WAS GOOD...

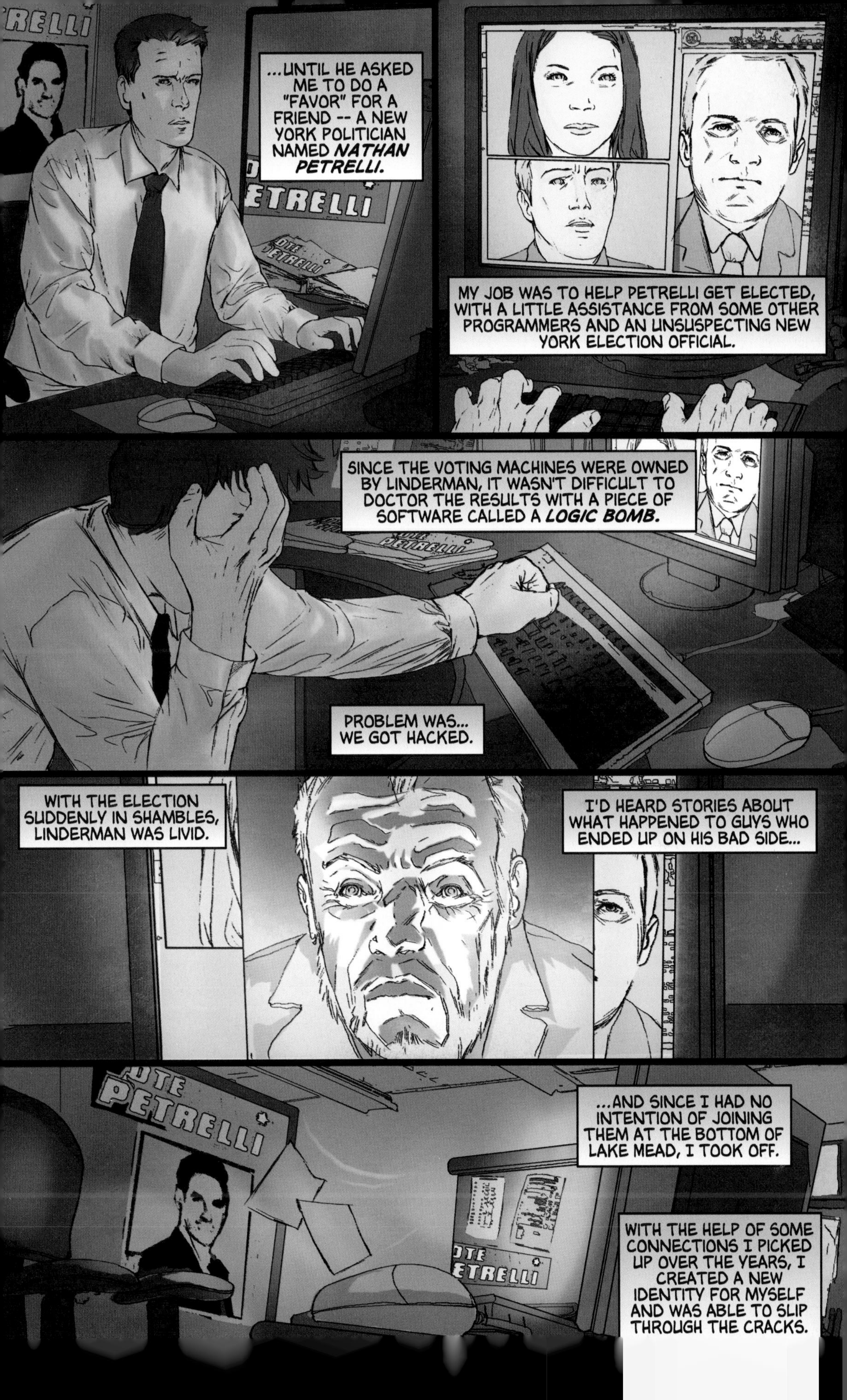

...UNTIL HE ASKED ME TO DO A "FAVOR" FOR A FRIEND -- A NEW YORK POLITICIAN NAMED ***NATHAN PETRELLI.***
MY JOB WAS TO HELP PETRELLI GET ELECTED, WITH A LITTLE ASSISTANCE FROM SOME OTHER PROGRAMMERS AND AN UNSUSPECTING NEW YORK ELECTION OFFICIAL.
SINCE THE VOTING MACHINES WERE OWNED BY LINDERMAN, IT WASN'T DIFFICULT TO DOCTOR THE RESULTS WITH A PIECE OF SOFTWARE CALLED A ***LOGIC BOMB.***
PROBLEM WAS... WE GOT HACKED.
WITH THE ELECTION SUDDENLY IN SHAMBLES, LINDERMAN WAS LIVID.
I'D HEARD STORIES ABOUT WHAT HAPPENED TO GUYS WHO ENDED UP ON HIS BAD SIDE...
...AND SINCE I HAD NO INTENTION OF JOINING THEM AT THE BOTTOM OF LAKE MEAD, I TOOK OFF.
WITH THE HELP OF SOME CONNECTIONS I PICKED UP OVER THE YEARS, I CREATED A NEW IDENTITY FOR MYSELF AND WAS ABLE TO SLIP THROUGH THE CRACKS.

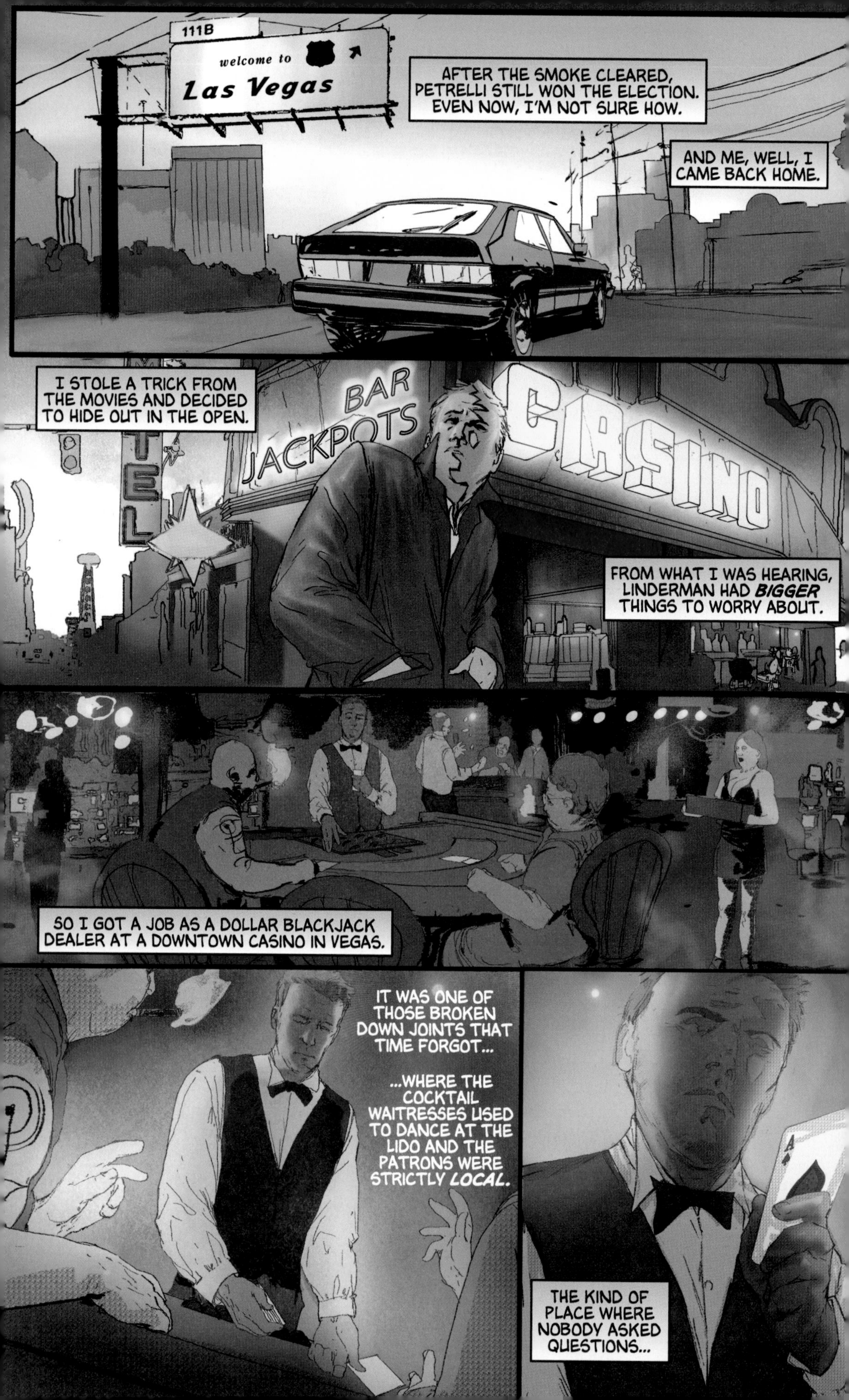
111B
welcome to
Las Vegas
AFTER THE SMOKE CLEARED, PETRELLI STILL WON THE ELECTION. EVEN NOW, I'M NOT SURE HOW.
AND ME, WELL, I CAME BACK HOME.
I STOLE A TRICK FROM THE MOVIES AND DECIDED TO HIDE OUT IN THE OPEN.
BAR
JACKPOTS
CASINO
FROM WHAT I WAS HEARING, LINDERMAN HAD *BIGGER* THINGS TO WORRY ABOUT.
SO I GOT A JOB AS A DOLLAR BLACKJACK DEALER AT A DOWNTOWN CASINO IN VEGAS.
IT WAS ONE OF THOSE BROKEN DOWN JOINTS THAT TIME FORGOT...
...WHERE THE COCKTAIL WAITRESSES USED TO DANCE AT THE LIDO AND THE PATRONS WERE STRICTLY *LOCAL*.
THE KIND OF PLACE WHERE NOBODY ASKED QUESTIONS...

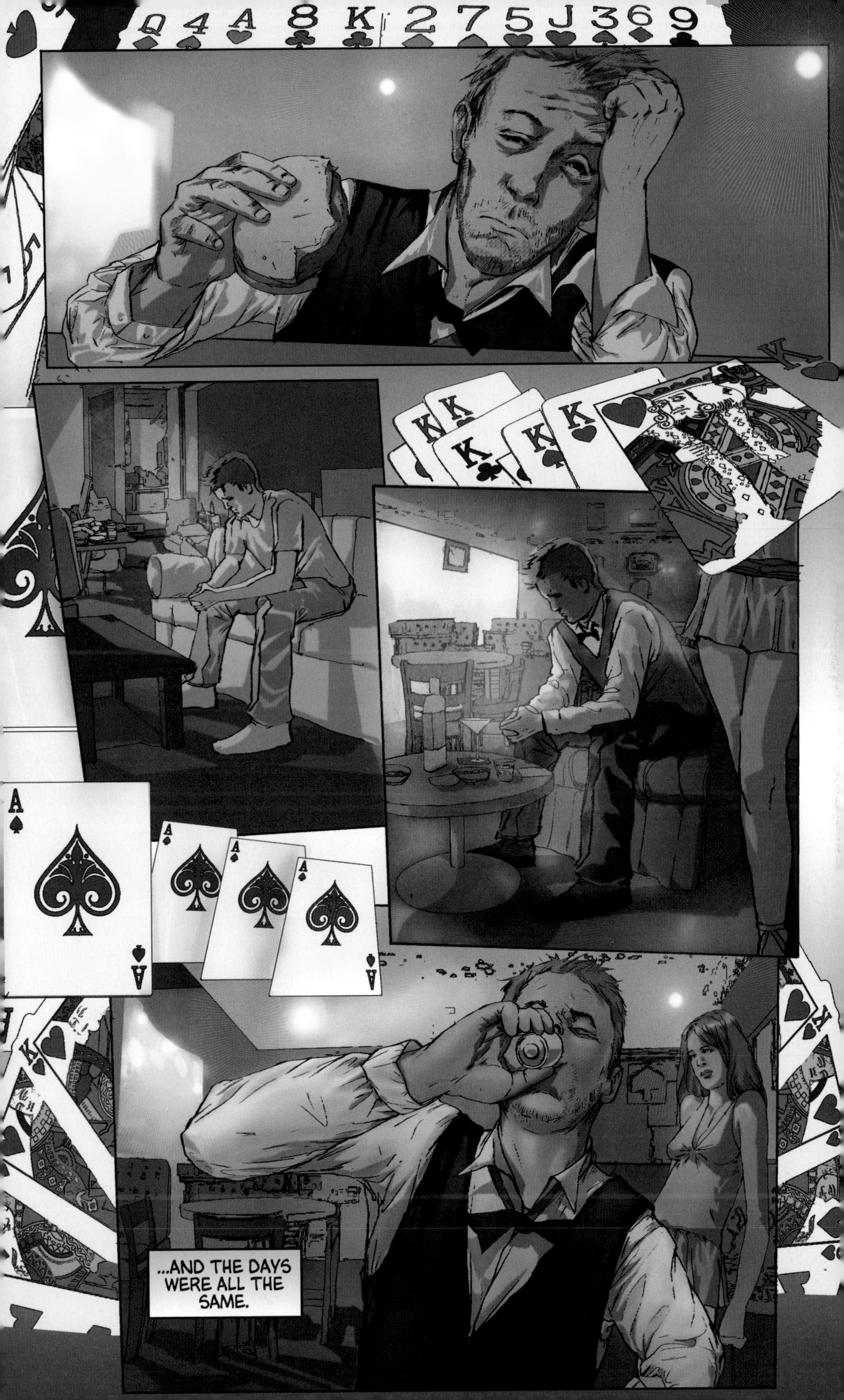
...AND THE DAYS WERE ALL THE SAME.

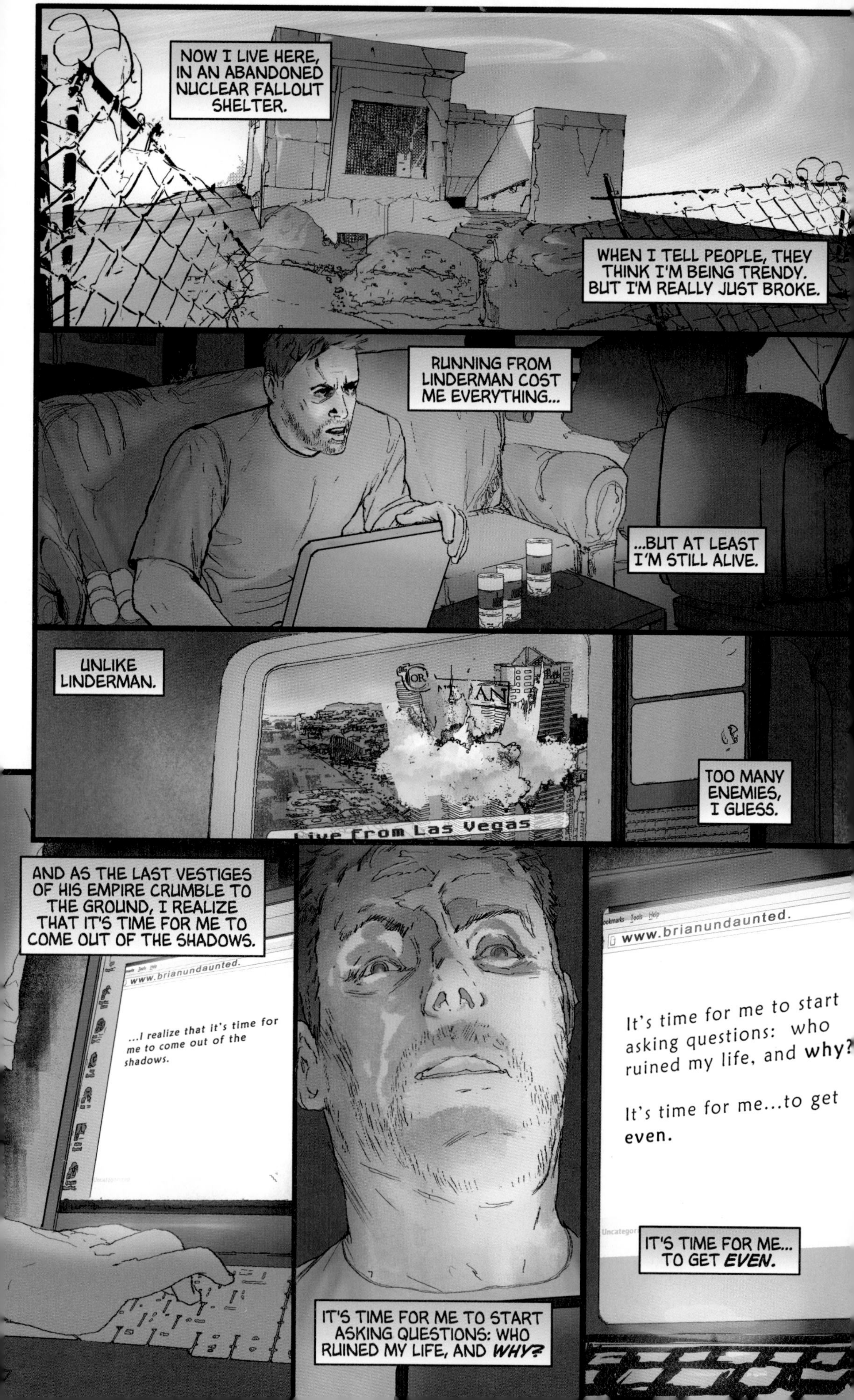
NOW I LIVE HERE, IN AN ABANDONED NUCLEAR FALLOUT SHELTER.
WHEN I TELL PEOPLE, THEY THINK I'M BEING TRENDY. BUT I'M REALLY JUST BROKE.
RUNNING FROM LINDERMAN COST ME EVERYTHING...
...BUT AT LEAST I'M STILL ALIVE.
UNLIKE LINDERMAN.
Live From Las Vegas
TOO MANY ENEMIES, I GUESS.
AND AS THE LAST VESTIGES OF HIS EMPIRE CRUMBLE TO THE GROUND, I REALIZE THAT IT'S TIME FOR ME TO COME OUT OF THE SHADOWS.
www.brianundaunted.
...I realize that it's time for me to come out of the shadows.
IT'S TIME FOR ME TO START ASKING QUESTIONS: WHO RUINED MY LIFE, AND *WHY?*
Tools Help
www.brianundaunted.
It's time for me to start asking questions: who ruined my life, and **why?**
It's time for me...to get **even.**
IT'S TIME FOR ME... TO GET *EVEN.*

**1972**

# BOUNTY HUNTER

| R.D. HALL | ROBERT ATKINS | EDGAR @ STUDIO F | COMICRAFT |
|-----------|---------------|------------------|-----------|
| *Writer* | *Art* | *Colors* | *Lettering* |

YOU'RE *OUTTA* HERE, TAVARA!

I DON'T GET IT, RONDO. WHAT'S UP WITH YOU?

YOU'RE A REAL LOOKER, AND YOU'RE PART BLOODHOUND WHEN IT COMES TO TRACKING DOWN MARKS, BUT I GOTTA--

THAT'S RIGHT, I DO MY JOB AND I DO IT WELL. I DON'T SEE THE *PROBLEM*.

IT'S THE ONES YOU DON'T FIND. THAT'S THE PROBLEM. *NO ONE* FINDS THEM. AT LEAST, NOT ALIVE ANYWAYS.

YOU GOT SOMETHING YOU WANT TO SAY TO ME, RONDO? BECAUSE IF YOU DO...

YOU CAN JUST SPIT IT OUT, RIGHT NOW!

LOOK, TAVARA, YOU'RE A GOOD KID. AND I'M NOT ACCUSING *YOU* OF ANYTHING. I JUST CAN'T HANDLE THIS KINDA HEAT FROM THE COPS RIGHT NOW. I'M SORRY.

THE COPS?

I'LL GET MY THINGS.

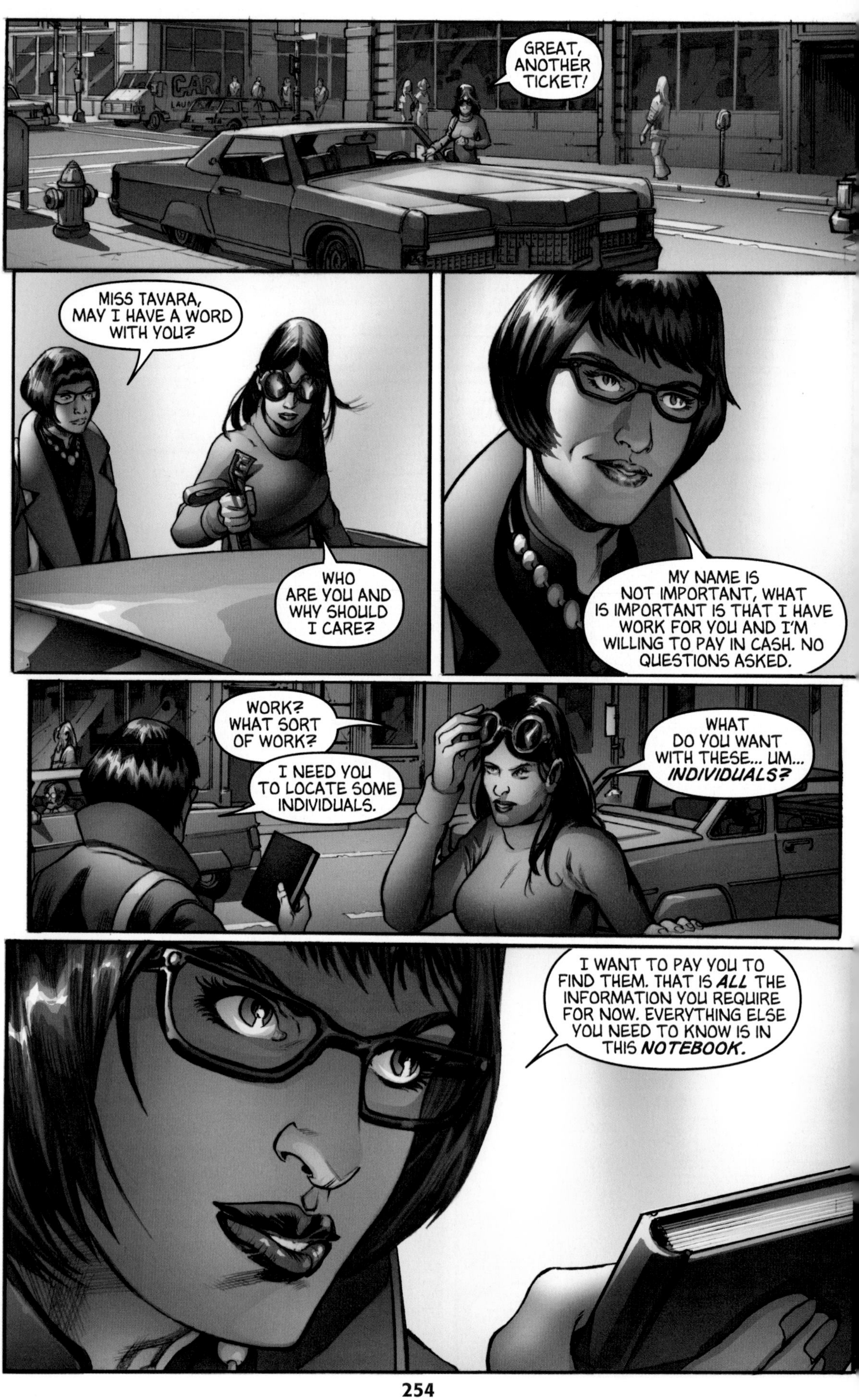
GREAT, ANOTHER TICKET!
MISS TAVARA, MAY I HAVE A WORD WITH YOU?
WHO ARE YOU AND WHY SHOULD I CARE?
MY NAME IS NOT IMPORTANT, WHAT IS IMPORTANT IS THAT I HAVE WORK FOR YOU AND I'M WILLING TO PAY IN CASH. NO QUESTIONS ASKED.
WORK? WHAT SORT OF WORK?
I NEED YOU TO LOCATE SOME INDIVIDUALS.
WHAT DO YOU WANT WITH THESE... UM... *INDIVIDUALS?*
I WANT TO PAY YOU TO FIND THEM. THAT IS *ALL* THE INFORMATION YOU REQUIRE FOR NOW. EVERYTHING ELSE YOU NEED TO KNOW IS IN THIS *NOTEBOOK.*

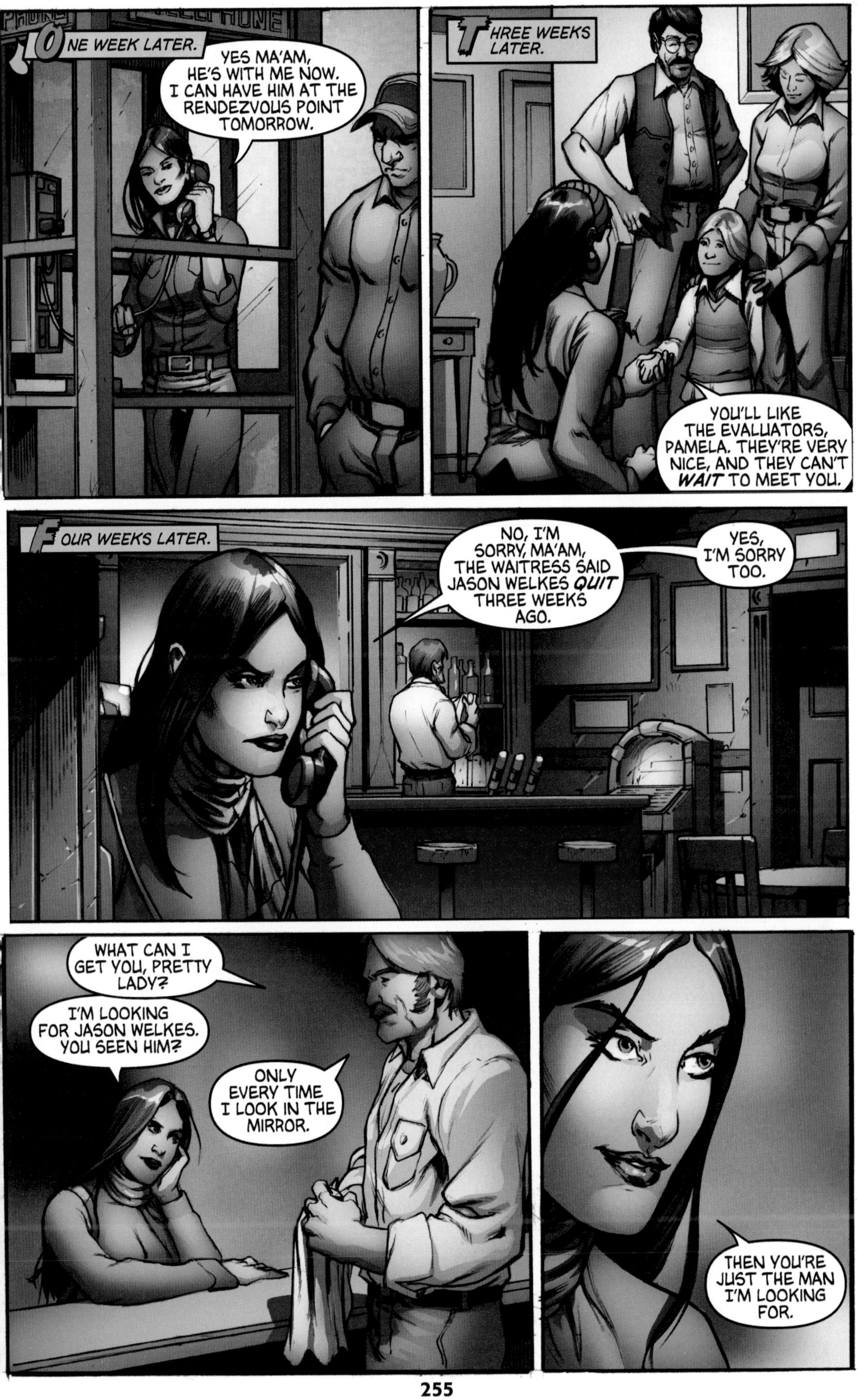
ONE WEEK LATER.
YES MA'AM, HE'S WITH ME NOW. I CAN HAVE HIM AT THE RENDEZVOUS POINT TOMORROW.
THREE WEEKS LATER.
YOU'LL LIKE THE EVALUATORS, PAMELA. THEY'RE VERY NICE, AND THEY CAN'T WAIT TO MEET YOU.
FOUR WEEKS LATER.
NO, I'M SORRY, MA'AM, THE WAITRESS SAID JASON WELKES QUIT THREE WEEKS AGO.
YES, I'M SORRY TOO.
WHAT CAN I GET YOU, PRETTY LADY?
I'M LOOKING FOR JASON WELKES. YOU SEEN HIM?
ONLY EVERY TIME I LOOK IN THE MIRROR.
THEN YOU'RE JUST THE MAN I'M LOOKING FOR.

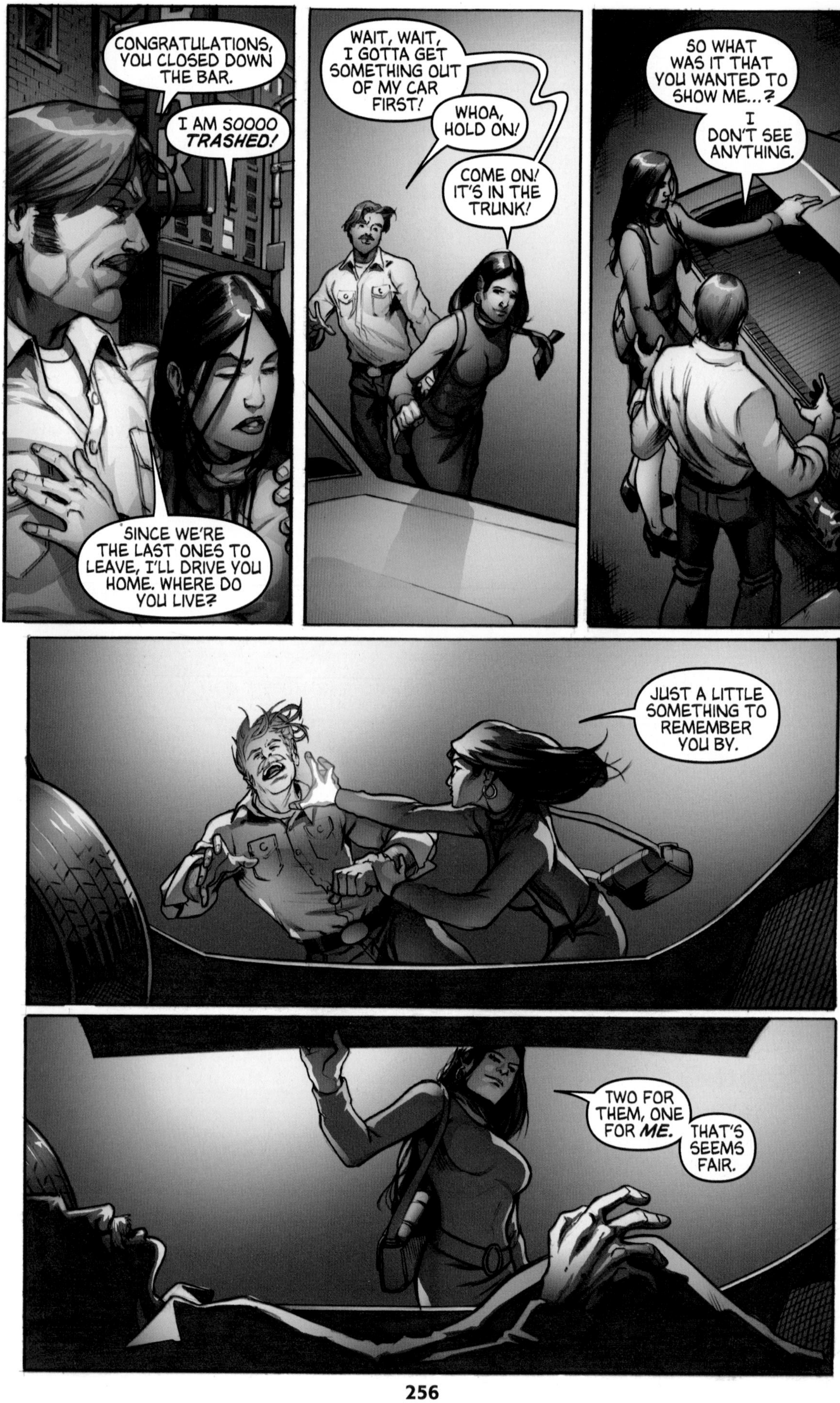
CONGRATULATIONS, YOU CLOSED DOWN THE BAR.
I AM SOOOO *TRASHED!*
SINCE WE'RE THE LAST ONES TO LEAVE, I'LL DRIVE YOU HOME. WHERE DO YOU LIVE?
WAIT, WAIT, I GOTTA GET SOMETHING OUT OF MY CAR FIRST!
WHOA, HOLD ON!
COME ON! IT'S IN THE TRUNK!
SO WHAT WAS IT THAT YOU WANTED TO SHOW ME...?
I DON'T SEE ANYTHING.
JUST A LITTLE SOMETHING TO REMEMBER YOU BY.
TWO FOR THEM, ONE FOR *ME.*
THAT'S SEEMS FAIR.

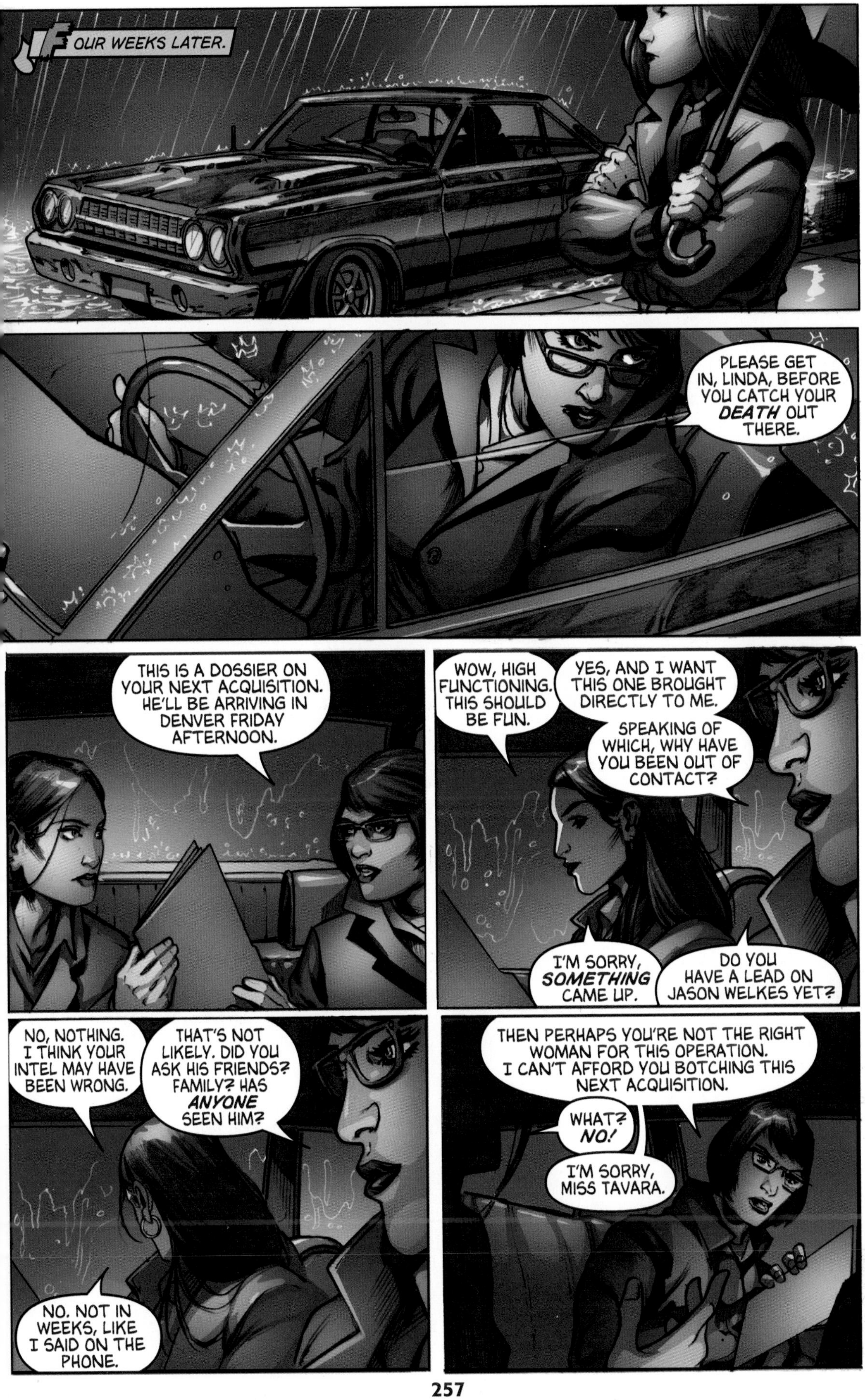
FOUR WEEKS LATER.
PLEASE GET IN, LINDA, BEFORE YOU CATCH YOUR DEATH OUT THERE.
THIS IS A DOSSIER ON YOUR NEXT ACQUISITION. HE'LL BE ARRIVING IN DENVER FRIDAY AFTERNOON.
WOW, HIGH FUNCTIONING. THIS SHOULD BE FUN.
YES, AND I WANT THIS ONE BROUGHT DIRECTLY TO ME.
SPEAKING OF WHICH, WHY HAVE YOU BEEN OUT OF CONTACT?
I'M SORRY, SOMETHING CAME UP.
DO YOU HAVE A LEAD ON JASON WELKES YET?
NO, NOTHING. I THINK YOUR INTEL MAY HAVE BEEN WRONG.
THAT'S NOT LIKELY. DID YOU ASK HIS FRIENDS? FAMILY? HAS ANYONE SEEN HIM?
NO. NOT IN WEEKS, LIKE I SAID ON THE PHONE.
THEN PERHAPS YOU'RE NOT THE RIGHT WOMAN FOR THIS OPERATION. I CAN'T AFFORD YOU BOTCHING THIS NEXT ACQUISITION.
WHAT? NO!
I'M SORRY, MISS TAVARA.

I *PANICKED*, I COULDN'T LET HER TAKE HIM AWAY FROM ME.

POWERS OR NOT, SHE HAD TO *DIE.*

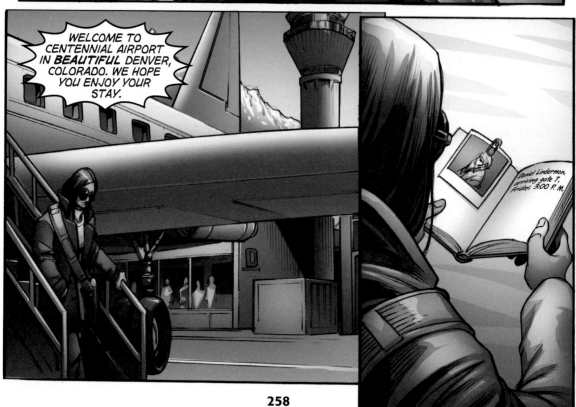

WELCOME TO CENTENNIAL AIRPORT IN *BEAUTIFUL* DENVER, COLORADO. WE HOPE YOU ENJOY YOUR STAY.

*Daniel Linderman, arriving gate 7, Friday, 3:00 P.M.*

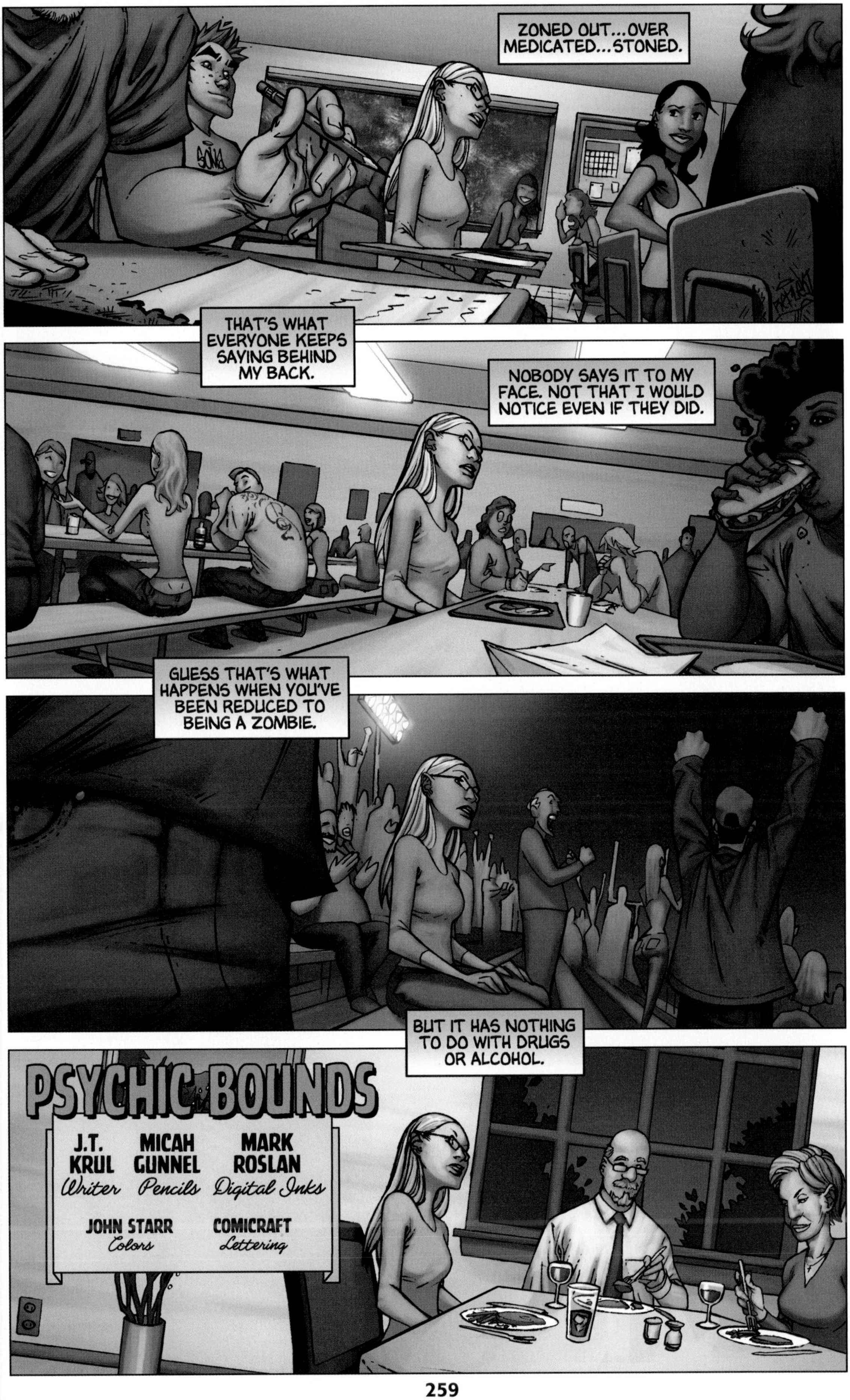
ZONED OUT...OVER MEDICATED...STONED.
THAT'S WHAT EVERYONE KEEPS SAYING BEHIND MY BACK.
NOBODY SAYS IT TO MY FACE. NOT THAT I WOULD NOTICE EVEN IF THEY DID.
GUESS THAT'S WHAT HAPPENS WHEN YOU'VE BEEN REDUCED TO BEING A ZOMBIE.
BUT IT HAS NOTHING TO DO WITH DRUGS OR ALCOHOL.
PSYCHIC BOUNDS
J.T. KRUL Writer
MICAH GUNNEL Pencils
MARK ROSLAN Digital Inks
JOHN STARR Colors
COMICRAFT Lettering

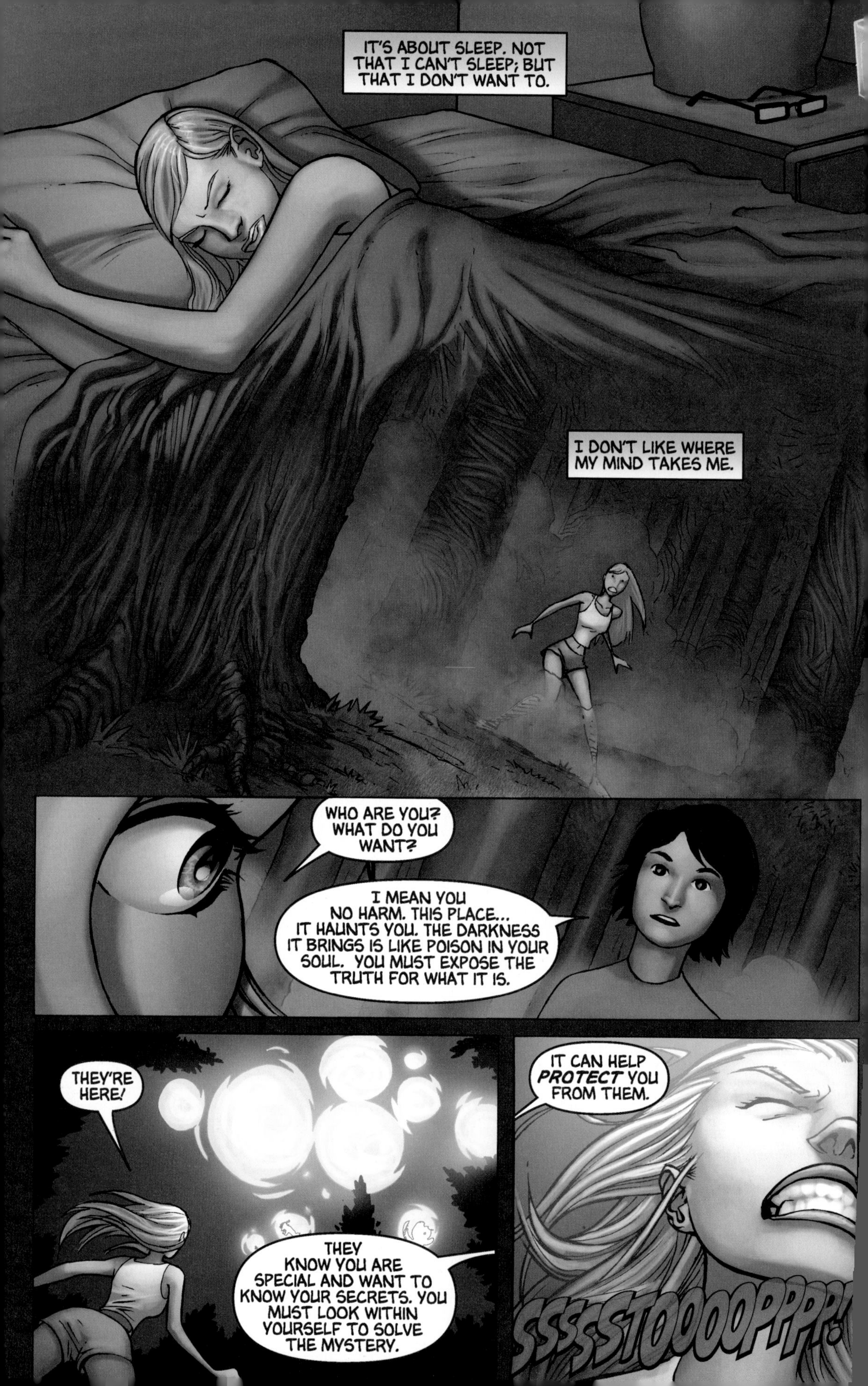
IT'S ABOUT SLEEP. NOT THAT I CAN'T SLEEP; BUT THAT I DON'T WANT TO.
I DON'T LIKE WHERE MY MIND TAKES ME.
WHO ARE YOU? WHAT DO YOU WANT?
I MEAN YOU NO HARM. THIS PLACE... IT HAUNTS YOU. THE DARKNESS IT BRINGS IS LIKE POISON IN YOUR SOUL. YOU MUST EXPOSE THE TRUTH FOR WHAT IT IS.
THEY'RE HERE!
THEY KNOW YOU ARE SPECIAL AND WANT TO KNOW YOUR SECRETS. YOU MUST LOOK WITHIN YOURSELF TO SOLVE THE MYSTERY.
IT CAN HELP *PROTECT* YOU FROM THEM.
SSSSSTOOOOPPPP!

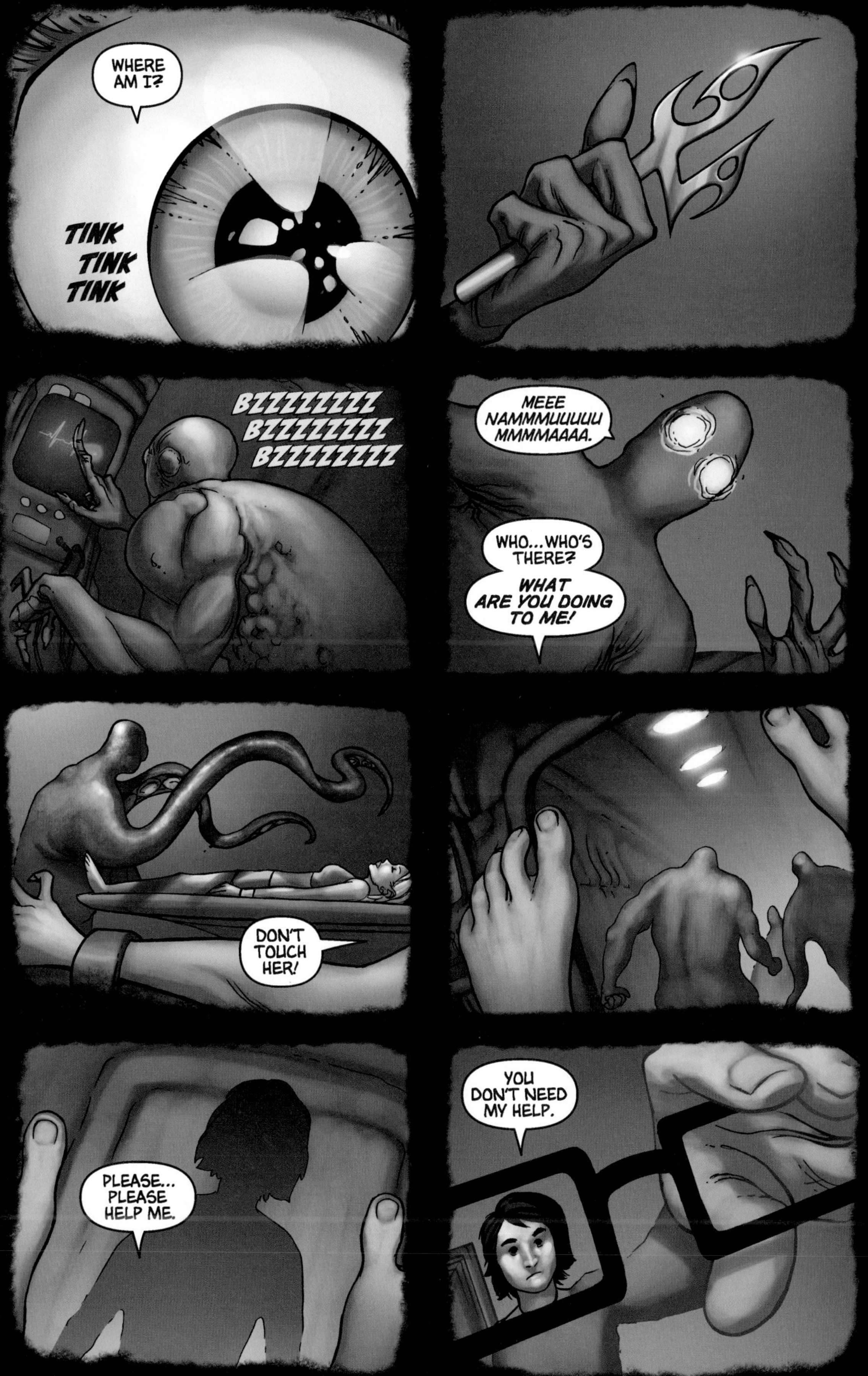
WHERE AM I?
TINK TINK TINK
BZZZZZZZZ BZZZZZZZZ BZZZZZZZZ
MEEE NAMMMUUUUU MMMMAAAA.
WHO...WHO'S THERE?
WHAT ARE YOU DOING TO ME!
DON'T TOUCH HER!
PLEASE... PLEASE HELP ME.
YOU DON'T NEED MY HELP.

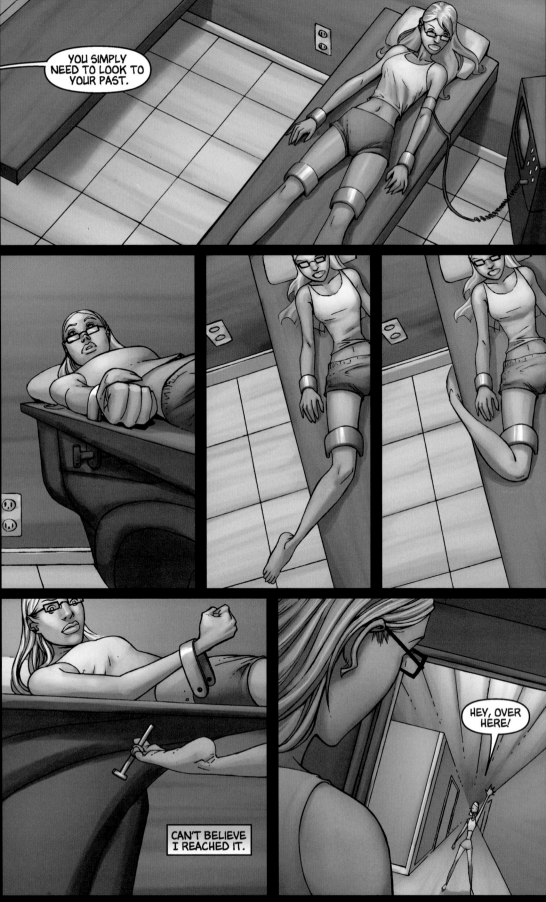

YOU SIMPLY NEED TO LOOK TO YOUR PAST.

CAN'T BELIEVE I REACHED IT.

HEY, OVER HERE!

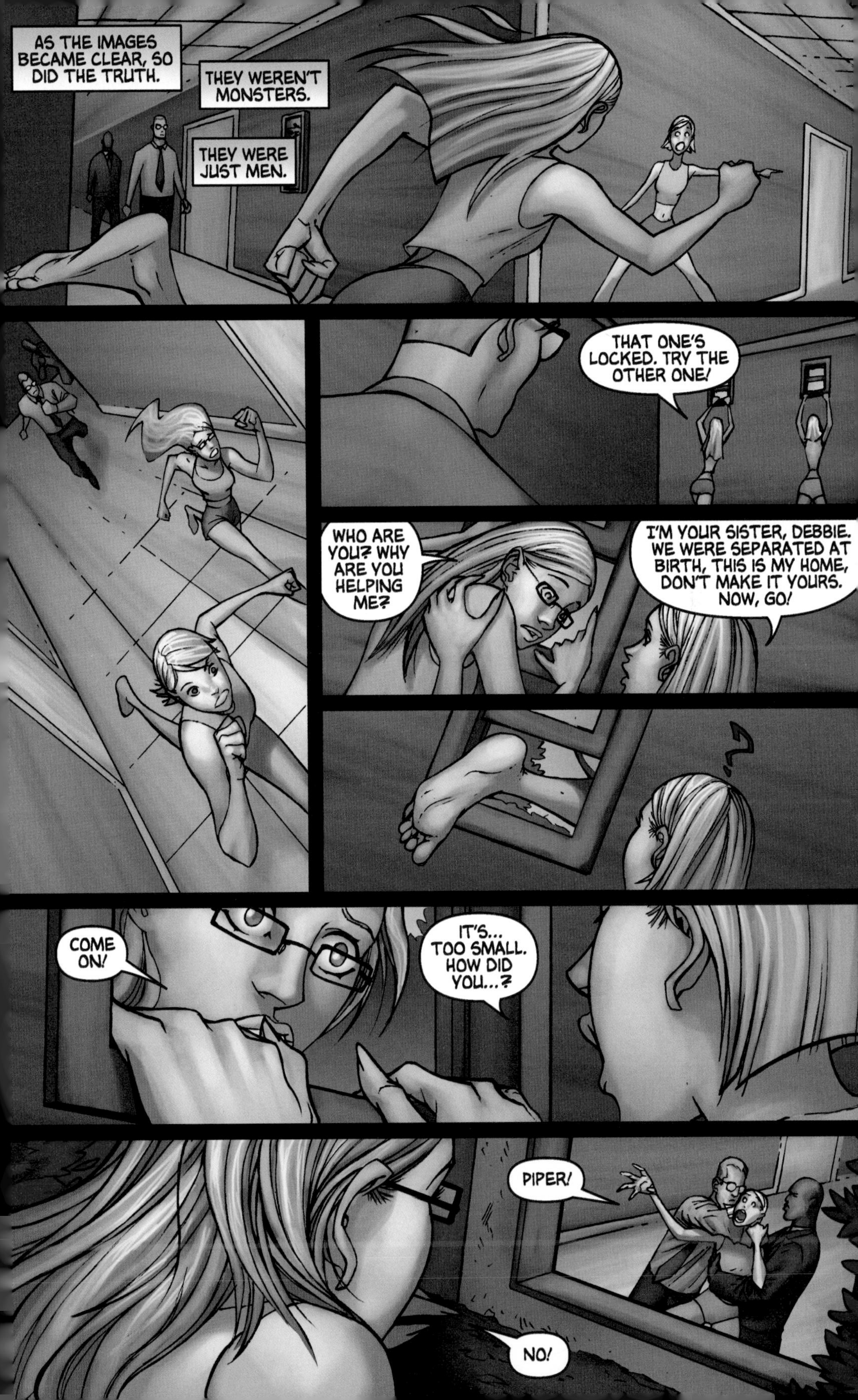
AS THE IMAGES BECAME CLEAR, SO DID THE TRUTH.
THEY WEREN'T MONSTERS.
THEY WERE JUST MEN.
THAT ONE'S LOCKED. TRY THE OTHER ONE!
WHO ARE YOU? WHY ARE YOU HELPING ME?
I'M YOUR SISTER, DEBBIE. WE WERE SEPARATED AT BIRTH. THIS IS MY HOME, DON'T MAKE IT YOURS. NOW, GO!
?
COME ON!
IT'S... TOO SMALL. HOW DID YOU...?
PIPER!
NO!

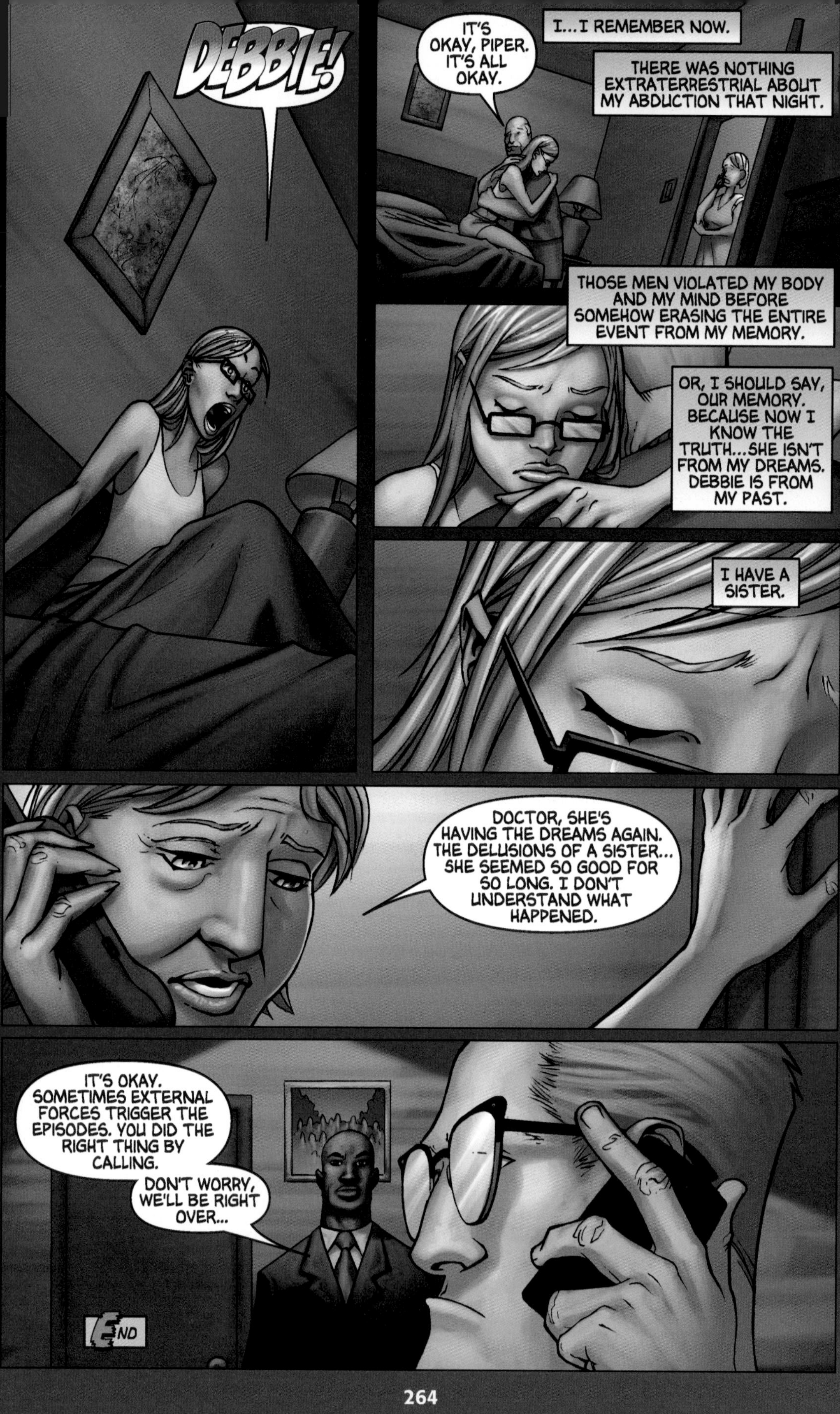
DEBBIE!
IT'S OKAY, PIPER. IT'S ALL OKAY.
I...I REMEMBER NOW.
THERE WAS NOTHING EXTRATERRESTRIAL ABOUT MY ABDUCTION THAT NIGHT.
THOSE MEN VIOLATED MY BODY AND MY MIND BEFORE SOMEHOW ERASING THE ENTIRE EVENT FROM MY MEMORY.
OR, I SHOULD SAY, OUR MEMORY. BECAUSE NOW I KNOW THE TRUTH...SHE ISN'T FROM MY DREAMS. DEBBIE IS FROM MY PAST.
I HAVE A SISTER.
DOCTOR, SHE'S HAVING THE DREAMS AGAIN. THE DELUSIONS OF A SISTER... SHE SEEMED SO GOOD FOR SO LONG. I DON'T UNDERSTAND WHAT HAPPENED.
IT'S OKAY. SOMETIMES EXTERNAL FORCES TRIGGER THE EPISODES. YOU DID THE RIGHT THING BY CALLING.
DON'T WORRY, WE'LL BE RIGHT OVER...
END

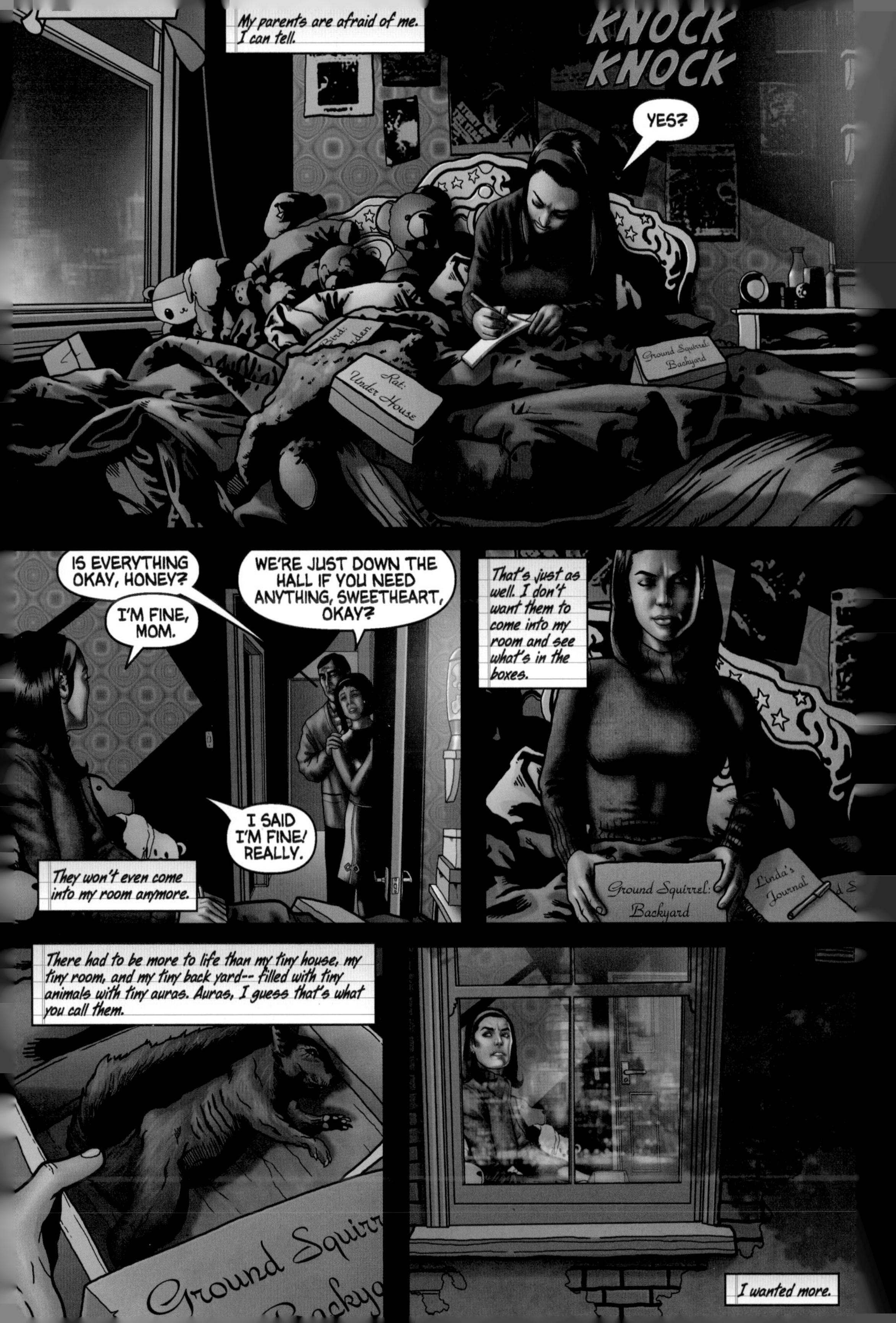
My parents are afraid of me. I can tell.
KNOCK KNOCK
YES?
Bird: Garden
Rat: Under House
Ground Squirrel: Backyard
IS EVERYTHING OKAY, HONEY?
I'M FINE, MOM.
WE'RE JUST DOWN THE HALL IF YOU NEED ANYTHING, SWEETHEART, OKAY?
I SAID I'M FINE! REALLY.
They won't even come into my room anymore.
That's just as well. I don't want them to come into my room and see what's in the boxes.
Ground Squirrel: Backyard
Linda's Journal
There had to be more to life than my tiny house, my tiny room, and my tiny back yard-- filled with tiny animals with tiny auras. Auras, I guess that's what you call them.
I wanted more.

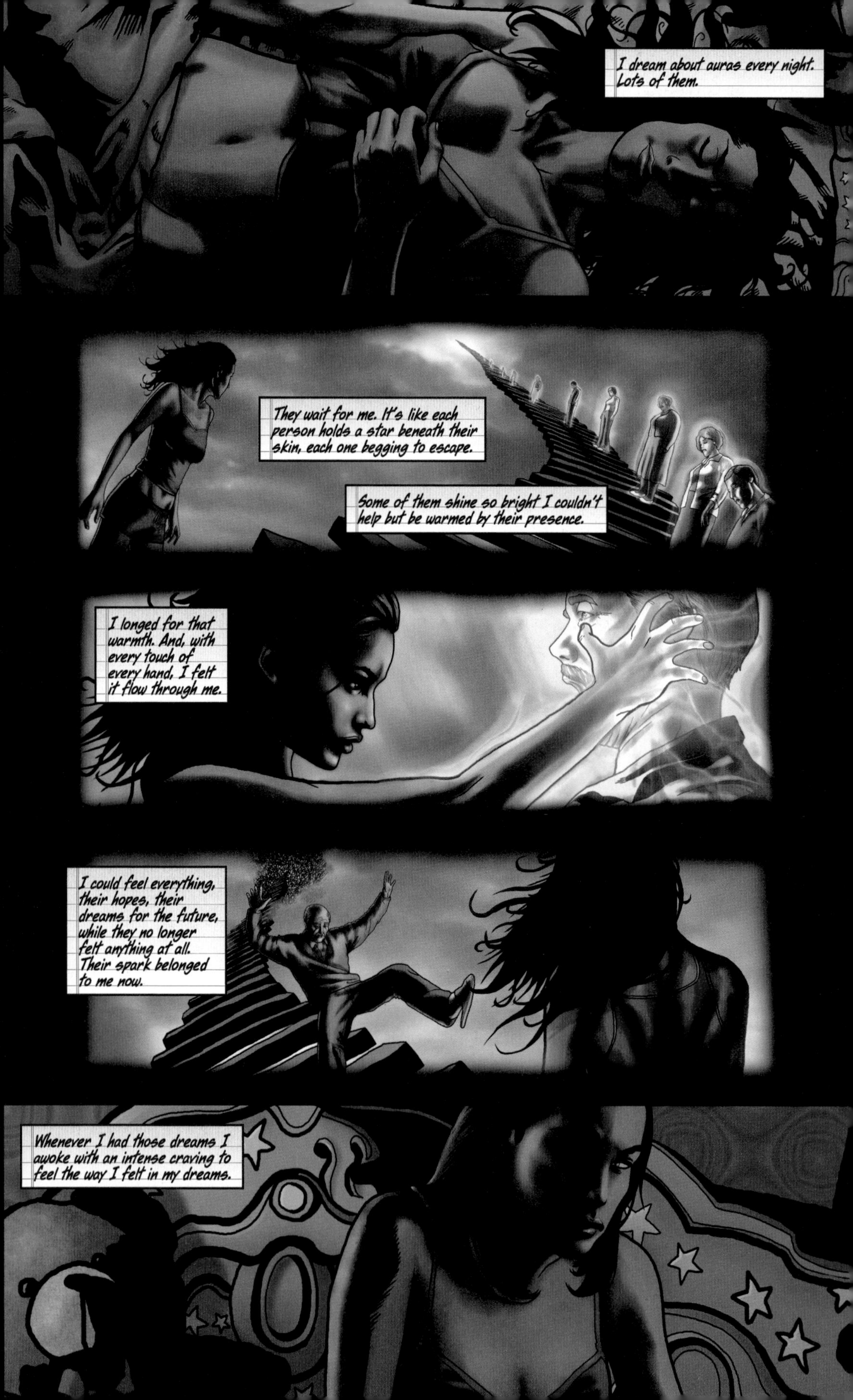
I dream about auras every night. Lots of them.
They wait for me. It's like each person holds a star beneath their skin, each one begging to escape.
Some of them shine so bright I couldn't help but be warmed by their presence.
I longed for that warmth. And, with every touch of every hand, I felt it flow through me.
I could feel everything, their hopes, their dreams for the future, while they no longer felt anything at all. Their spark belonged to me now.
Whenever I had those dreams I awoke with an intense craving to feel the way I felt in my dreams.

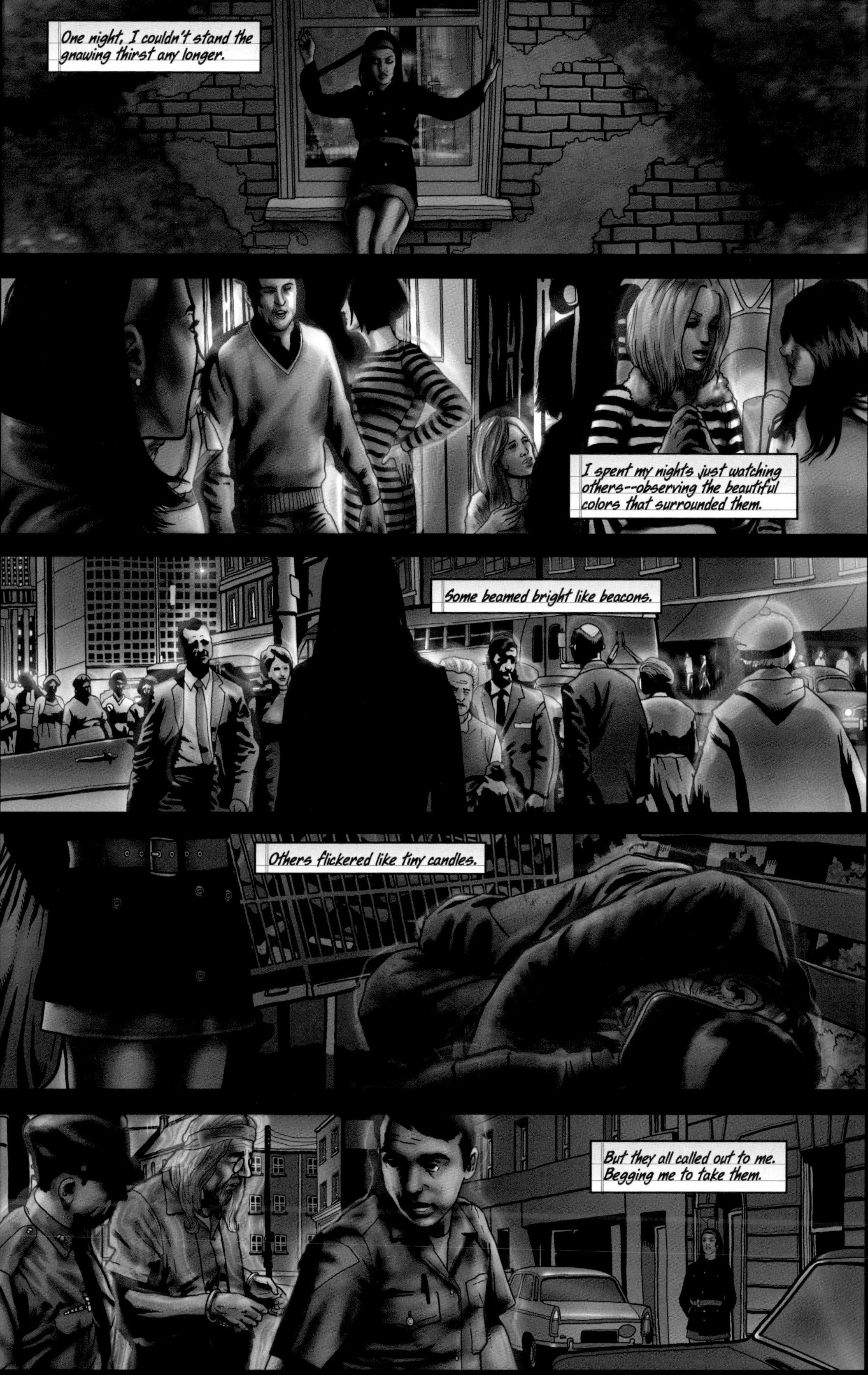
One night, I couldn't stand the gnawing thirst any longer.
I spent my nights just watching others--observing the beautiful colors that surrounded them.
Some beamed bright like beacons.
Others flickered like tiny candles.
But they all called out to me. Begging me to take them.

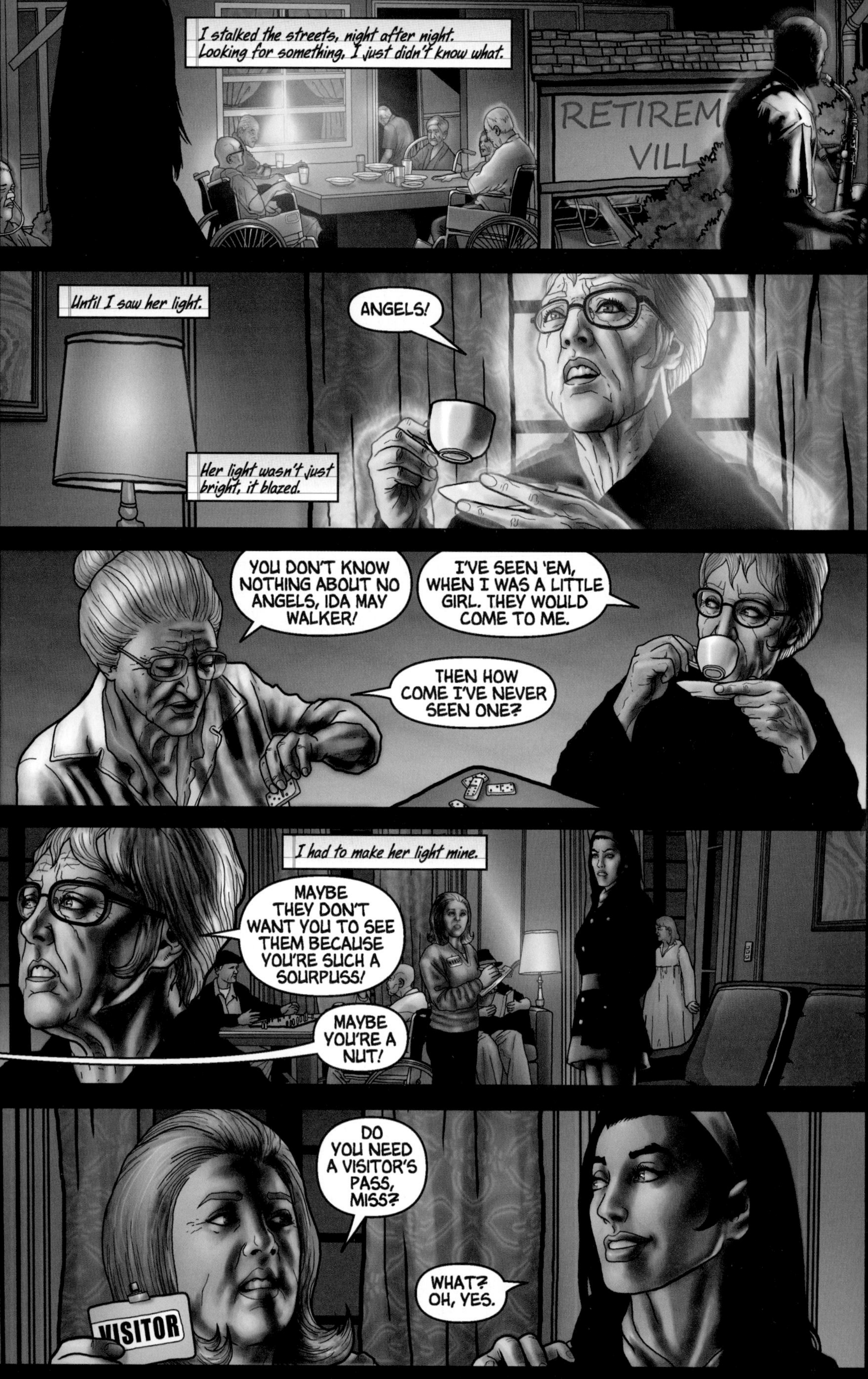
I stalked the streets, night after night. Looking for something, I just didn't know what.
RETIREM
VILL
Until I saw her light.
ANGELS!
Her light wasn't just bright, it blazed.
YOU DON'T KNOW NOTHING ABOUT NO ANGELS, IDA MAY WALKER!
I'VE SEEN 'EM, WHEN I WAS A LITTLE GIRL. THEY WOULD COME TO ME.
THEN HOW COME I'VE NEVER SEEN ONE?
I had to make her light mine.
MAYBE THEY DON'T WANT YOU TO SEE THEM BECAUSE YOU'RE SUCH A SOURPUSS!
MAYBE YOU'RE A NUT!
DO YOU NEED A VISITOR'S PASS, MISS?
VISITOR
WHAT? OH, YES.

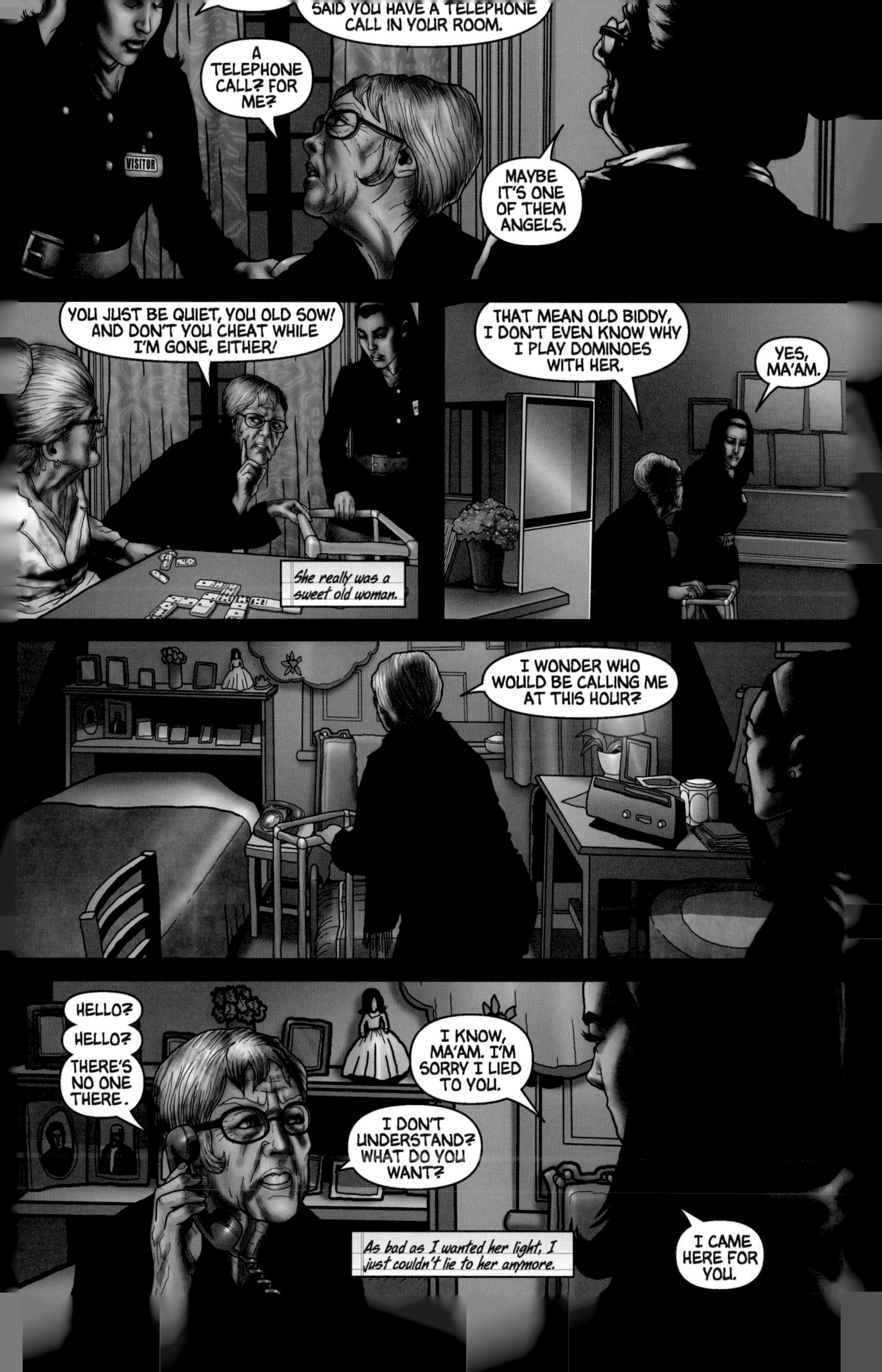
SAID YOU HAVE A TELEPHONE CALL IN YOUR ROOM.
VISITOR
A TELEPHONE CALL? FOR ME?
MAYBE IT'S ONE OF THEM ANGELS.
YOU JUST BE QUIET, YOU OLD SOW! AND DON'T YOU CHEAT WHILE I'M GONE, EITHER!
She really was a sweet old woman.
THAT MEAN OLD BIDDY, I DON'T EVEN KNOW WHY I PLAY DOMINOES WITH HER.
YES, MA'AM.
I WONDER WHO WOULD BE CALLING ME AT THIS HOUR?
HELLO?
HELLO?
THERE'S NO ONE THERE.
I KNOW, MA'AM. I'M SORRY I LIED TO YOU.
I DON'T UNDERSTAND? WHAT DO YOU WANT?
As bad as I wanted her light, I just couldn't lie to her anymore.
I CAME HERE FOR YOU.

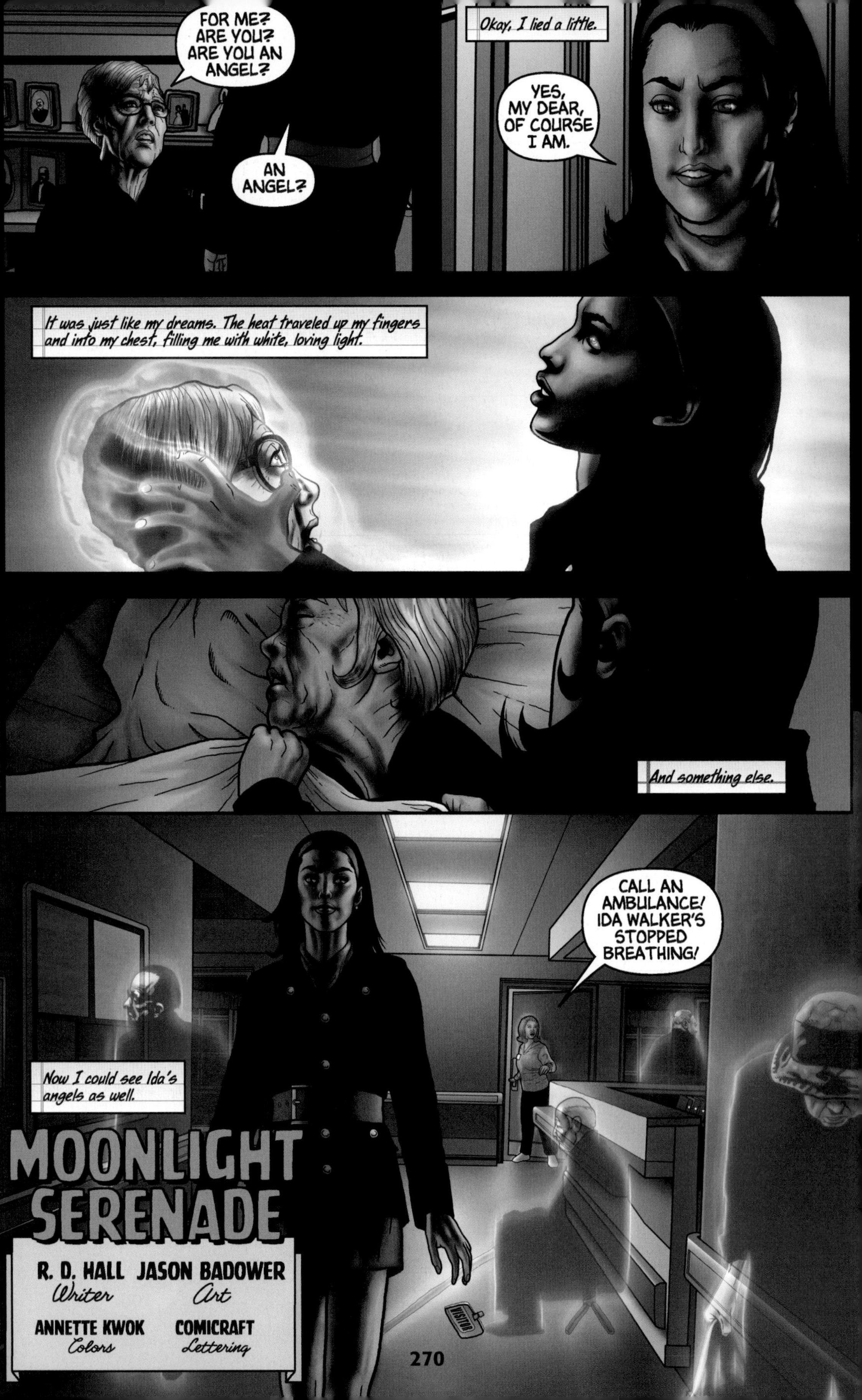
FOR ME? ARE YOU? ARE YOU AN ANGEL?
AN ANGEL?
Okay, I lied a little.
YES, MY DEAR, OF COURSE I AM.
It was just like my dreams. The heat traveled up my fingers and into my chest, filling me with white, loving light.
And something else.
CALL AN AMBULANCE! IDA WALKER'S STOPPED BREATHING!
Now I could see Ida's angels as well.
MOONLIGHT SERENADE
R. D. HALL Writer
JASON BADOWER Art
ANNETTE KWOK Colors
COMICRAFT Lettering
VISITOR

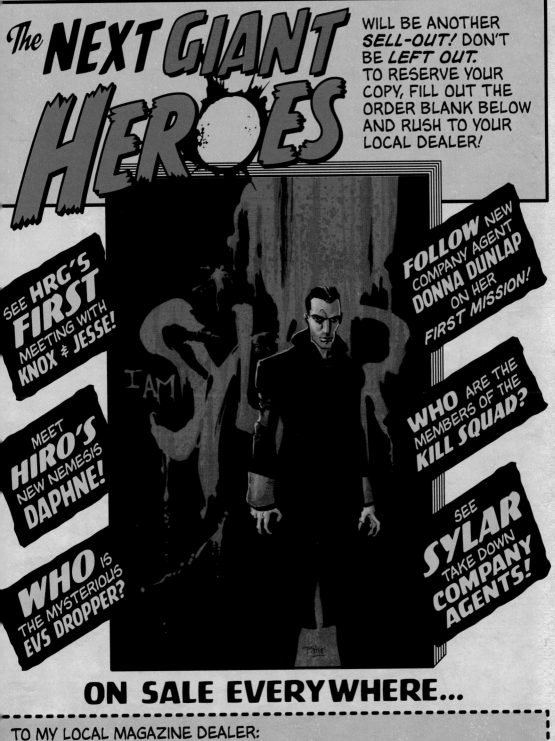

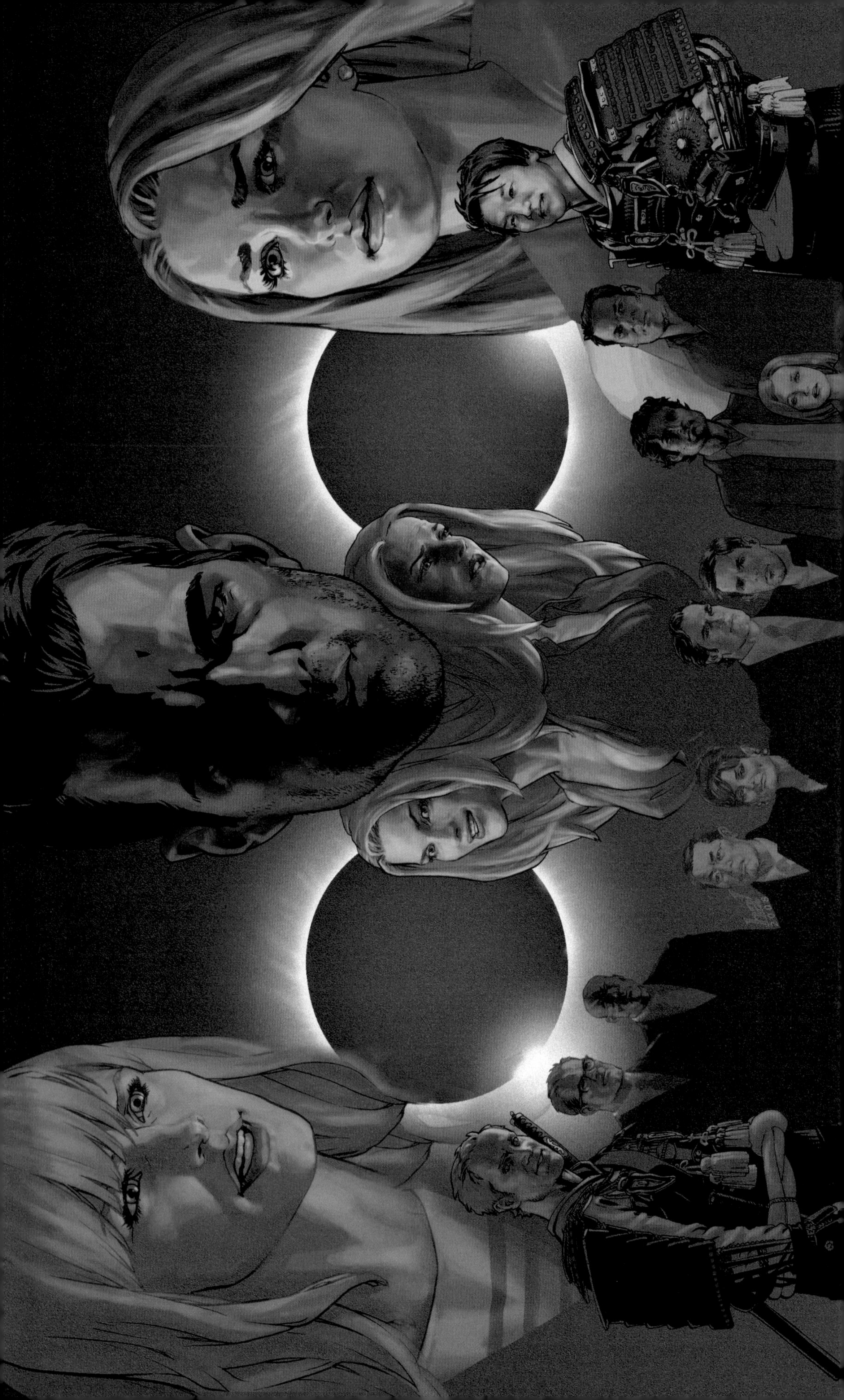